D1541164

ALBRIGHT COLLEGE
LIBRARY

READING, PENNSYLVANIA

PERSPECTIVES ON URBAN POLITICS

PERSPECTIVES ON URBAN POLITICS

edited by

JAY S. GOODMAN

Chairman
Department of Government
Wheaton College (Massachusetts)

Allyn and Bacon, Inc.
Boston

© Copyright 1970 by Allyn and Bacon, Inc., 470 Atlantic Avenue, Boston

All rights reserved. No part of this book may be reproduced in any form, or by any means, without permission in writing from the publisher.

Library of Congress Catalog Card Number: 72-97003

Printed in the United States of America

320.973
G653
P

123273

TABLE OF CONTENTS

PREFACE

One brings forth a reader on urban politics with uncertainty in the year 1970. Urban life in America is unsettled. A variety of once-cherished social alternatives may no longer be available to us. For those who are still hopeful that cities can provide settings of opportunity and justice for all Americans, black and white, an informed pessimism may be the best stance to take. At a far more pedantic level of vision, there is already a plethora of books about cities available. Why add one more?

My own responses to these problems are not complicated. Whatever conditions are, students and scholars have an obligation to learn all they can, whether their aim is knowledge for its own sake or as the basis for a strategy of social change. This reader presents a combination of up-to-date topical writings and thorough scholarly articles, organized along a set of dimensions designed to yield a comprehensive understanding for any reader. Not least, the micro-, people/problems, and macro-studies perspectives are arranged to stimulate the student's curiosity to learn more, to understand what is unknown, to try to find answers and knowledge which no one has today.

As editor, I am indebted to many persons. Professor Robert L. Lineberry of the University of Texas, Austin, offered many helpful comments and suggestions. Wheaton's faculty secretaries, Mrs. Helen Durant and Mrs. Nancy Shepardson, faithfully produced the permissions forms. Student assistants, Joan Tighe and Barbara Hausman, assembled many of the materials. Mr. Robert J. Patterson, Allyn and Bacon's Political Science Editor, was a source of always good advice and encouragement. Whatever errors of judgment that remain are mine.

Jay S. Goodman

PART I
THEORIES OF URBAN POLITICS

INTRODUCTION

Almost everyone, in today's America, can see why we need research into urban life. But some might ask: what is the point of "theory" about urban politics? Can we not learn whatever we want to know simply by looking at how things work? The answer has to be "no." Theory about urban life, in common with theory about other social phenomena from political participation to international politics, is necessary to order our observations and provide the conceptual framework without which there can be no meaningful research. Theories raise the questions which are truly relevant. They provide the intellectual bases from which any eventual problem-solving capacity will emerge.

The six theory pieces which comprise the first section of this reader are not "pure." Many contain examples, illustrations, and even limited tests of the concepts and hypotheses outlined in them. But they are uniformly concerned with providing, in a rigorous and scientific manner, a set of hypotheses about urban behavior. Taken together, they can be viewed as an illustration of the eclectic nature of thinking about urban America, and also of the fruitful avenues that such thinking has opened toward understanding our complicated urban scene.

Norton Long's classic, "The Local Community as an Ecology of Games," is an appropriate beginning for any student of city politics. At the heart of Long's imaginative article is the idea that local political behavior depends upon the "roles" of what amounts to a customary and relatively universal lineup of players. The idea of "role," of expected patterns of behavior which go with the position of banker or editor or "black power" leader, is familiar to sociologists, political scientists, even Broadway actors. Long was the first, however, to apply it to the local community and suggest some of the implications.

To use the concept of role is to emphasize the importance of "values" and routine patterns of behavior in urban politics as

3

opposed to, for example, ideology, the ideas about the proper activities of government which local activists may hold. The distinction is between relatively informal (implicit) and relatively formal (explicit) patterns and beliefs. Long postulates that the players in urban America occupy positions which carry with them rules about how they should behave; the location of all of these separate roles in a discrete local territory gives rise to a system of "games." Everyone, in today's language, does his "own thing." There is a banker's role, a politician's role, a protestor's role, and on down the list. The roles imply customs and expectations, and, in the urban area, Long interprets what happens as being analogous to gaming. People derive their values, strategies, and expectations from their roles, and even think to themselves in game-like terms about what they are doing—competing, keeping score, going to bat, winning or losing. From the role-game perspective, Long derives a series of propositions about city behavior in routine and non-routine situations, about sources of instability and stability.

It could be said that Robert C. Wood takes the group struggle as his starting point in explaining urban politics. In a selection from his book *1400 Governments,* he argues that the group "formally or informally organized," is the key unit in the regional urban decision-making process. Wood connects economic and political choices in the urban community, postulating that they are brought together through the budgetary processes of local governments. The products of governmental economic choices in an urban region are the public services provided at different levels and degrees. Wood offers a series of suggestive hypotheses about the interrelationships among groups, local governments, resources, and decisions.

Professor Robert Salisbury's approach to understanding urban politics is to focus on the shifting historical locations of power and initiative in city decision-making. He maintains that today's cities are witnessing a "new convergence of power," by which he means that a new coalition of groups has come to the ruling forefront. He postulates that the new coalition consists of the city's mayor, the major locally-based economic interests, and the city bureaucrats. Underlying this governing coalition is a base of voters who provide support and also inputs of demands. Salisbury emphasizes the importance of leadership in policy-making process. The man who gets things done, who ties it together in today's city—if indeed it can be tied together—is the modern mayor. Salisbury portrays the mayor as the man with enough support to get elected, enough brains to understand the complexity of the problems, and enough political clout to force the other elements of the coalition to work with him. An interesting question which flows from Salisbury's theory is this: if he is right about the central place of the mayor, then what are the policy implications of his theory for mayor cities as opposed to manager cities? Would it not follow from his ideas that mayor cities are more responsive to various demands? Or better able to get some kinds of things done?

The Agger, Goldrich, and Swanson selection, "Politics and the Scope of Government in the Community: Conceptual Considerations," calls attention to the importance of political ideology as a causal factor in urban behavior. From Plato to Marx to Guevara, theorists have argued that the ideas people hold shape how they act. But many, especially Americans, have tended to scoff at the thought that our local politics had anything to do with ideology. Probably the assumption that our local governments had nothing to do with abstract ideas about political life was a logical consequence of our experience with urban "machines," decidedly non-ideological operations in themselves. Yet the movement which attacked the machine, the urban "reform" movement, has been profoundly ideological from its beginnings in the 1800's to the present day. The urban reformers have had a well thought out rationale for their support of city manager government systems with non-partisan elections and rule by the "best man." So that upon reflection, anyone aware of urban governmental history should recognize the important part played by ideology.

Nonetheless, in political science and sociology, it remained for Agger, Goldrich, and Swanson, in their prize-winning book, *The Rulers and the Ruled,* from which the selection is drawn, to call attention to how the ideas held by local activists shape what occurs in local public life, and to operationalize this perspective in a systematic form. The authors picture local government as an arena wherein the action is a value conflict over expansion or contraction in the net scope of governmental activities. While a variety of considerations dominate the controversies over specific city decisions, the authors postulate that, at the heart of the matter, even group differences have an ideological basis. Local activists are, in their words, "articulate ideologists."

To help in understanding the role of ideology, the authors develop a typology of activists based upon two dimensions: conception of what the community consists of and conceptions of who shall properly rule. They categorize activists on these, and eventually the additional factors of cultural and socio-economic class, into eight types: the Orthodox Conservatives, Progressive Conservatives, Community Conservationists, Jeffersonian Conservatives, Radical Rightists, Liberals, Radical Leftists, and Supremacists.

The article by Ostrom, Tiebout, and Warren, "The Organization of Government in Metropolitan Areas: A Theoretical Inquiry," provides yet a different perspective on local government. The fundamental thesis of these authors is that a metropolitan area, rather than being an artificially created and maintained area of meaningless boundaries and authorities, is a natural "polycentric political system." Thus the piece could be said to be a "systems analysis" of the American metropolitan urban scene. Within the "polycentric system" there are many formally independent decision-making units which nonetheless interact with each other in a variety of relationships, some cooperative and some conflictual. Which it is depends upon choices made by the units themselves in response to their environments. The local governments which comprise the units are seen as analogous to individual consumers, or more accurately to firms, which act in a market-type situation. What is at stake are what economists call "public goods." What determines each unit's behavior is an assessment of the levels of public services and costs it is prepared to bear.

In a manner apparently analogous to the operation of a free market, the authors suggest that this system of free choices adds up to a "natural" system of political communication and adjustment which works. When there is conflict among local governments, arrangements may be worked out in secret by administrators or resolved in the courts. Through applying the concepts of economics to governmental behavior, the authors have managed to present an exceptionally provocative set of ideas about metropolitan politics.

Matthew Holden Jr.'s article, "The Governance of the Metropolis As a Problem in Diplomacy," is one of the most overlooked, yet most provocative, in the literature on cities. Part of his argument is that theory developed for the field of international relations is applicable to the study of urban politics. He postulates that the analogy is valid because American metropolitan politics, as in the case of international politics, takes place within an environment of independent corporate units. What one has are a set of diplomatic systems; the actors in metropolitan politics are governments, not individuals. They interact with the other actors because by ecological accident they find themselves sharing space and with overlapping interests. Holden argues that seeing urban governments in a framework of diplomatic systems is more fruitful than visualizing them as "political communities." To think of them as communities is to falsely attribute to local governments common symbolic value systems, common deliberative processes for arriving at decisions, and agreed-upon administrative procedures for executive decisions. In fact, local governments in America possess none of the "community" attributes *vis a vis each other* (whatever they may or may not possess within themselves in the way of local "nationalism").

Holden argues that if he is right about local governments in a metropolitan area being analogous to nation states in world politics then it follows that international relations theory will be useful in understanding local behavior. He thinks that four areas can be illuminated by such theory: the subject matter of local interactions; the power each of the local actors will have; whether relationships are likely to be permanent or transient; and what the procedures of interaction are likely to be. He draws upon the theory of Haas, Kaplan, and Deutch to illustrate his own thinking about local governments. From these intellectual bases, Holden offers a series of provocative conclusions, which are really hypotheses, about what the bases for interunit behavior are likely to be, and what environmental, personal, and political considerations underlie cooperation and conflict. If Holden is right, then two aspects of the common folklore about city problems become suspect. First, why should efforts at metropolitan government be any more successful than, for example, the United Nations at resolving problems? If the underlying interests of the local sovereignties diverge, what help will mechanisms alone be? Second, does it not follow that the argument that all suburbanites and urbanites need to do to resolve urban problems together is to understand each other better, is a myth?

Taken together, the six theory articles should give the reader many new ideas about local government—which is, after all, the aim of social science of this sort. The serious student wants to push beyond the headlines of the newspapers or even the still superficial analyses of the commentators to find out why things happen as they do. The theory articles in this reader are designed to provide some hypotheses. The subsequent two sections provide some tests.

1

THE LOCAL COMMUNITY
AS AN ECOLOGY OF GAMES*†

NORTON E. LONG

Abstract: The local community can be usefully conceptualized
as an ecology of games. In the territorial system a variety of games
goes on: banking, newspaper publishing, contracting, manufacturing, etc. The games give structures, goals, roles, strategies, tactics, and publics to the players. Players in each game make use of
players in the others for their particular purposes. A banker uses
the politician, the newspaperman, or the contractor in his game
and is, in turn, used by them in theirs. The interaction of the
games produces unintended but systemically functional results
for the ecology. An over-all top leadership and social game
provide a vague set of commonly shared values that promotes
co-operation in the system though it does not provide a
government.

The local community whether viewed as a polity, an economy,
or a society presents itself as an order in which expectations are
met and functions performed. In some cases, as in a new-company-
planned mining town, the order is the willed product of centralized
control, but for the most part the order is the product of a history
rather than the imposed effect ·of any central nervous system of
the community. For historic reasons we readily conceive the massive
task of feeding New York to be achieved through the unplanned,

*This paper is largely based on a year of field study in the Boston Metropolitan
area made possible by grants from the Stern Family Foundation and the
Social Science Research Council. The opinions and conclusion expressed
are those of the author alone.
†Reprinted from *The American Journal of Sociology, 64,* No. 3 (November
1958), 251-261. By permission of the University of Chicago Press and the
author.

9

historically developed co-operation of thousands of actors largely unconscious of their collaboration to this individually unsought end. The efficiency of this system is attested to by the extraordinary difficulties of the War Production Board and Service of Supply in accomplishing similar logistical objectives through an explicit system of orders and directives. Insofar as conscious rationality plays a role, it is a function of the parts rather than the whole. Particular structures working for their own ends within the whole may provide their members with goals, strategies, and roles that support rational action. The results of the interaction of the rational strivings after particular ends are in part collectively functional if unplanned. All this is the well-worn doctrine of Adam Smith, though one need accept no more of the doctrine of beneficence than that an unplanned economy can function.

While such a view is accepted for the economy, it is generally rejected for the polity. Without a sovereign, Leviathan is generally supposed to disintegrate and fall apart. Even if Locke's more hopeful view of the naturalness of the social order is taken, the polity seems more of a contrived artifact than the economy. Furthermore, there is both the hangover of Justinian sovereignty and the Greek view of ethical primacy to make political institutions seem different in kind and ultimately inclusive in purpose and for this reason to give them an over-all social directive end. To see political institutions as the same kind of thing as other institutions in society rather than as different, superior, and inclusive (both in the sense of being sovereign and ethically more significant) is a form of relativistic pluralism that is difficult to entertain. At the local level, however, it is easier to look at the municipal government, its departments, and the agencies of state and national government as so many institutions, resembling banks, newspapers, trade unions, chambers of commerce, churches, etc., occupying a territorial field and interacting with one another. This interaction can be conceptualized as a system without reducing the interacting institutions and individuals to membership in any single comprehensive group. It is psychologically tempting to envision the local territorial system as a group with a governing "they." This is certainly and existential possibility and one to be investigated. However, frequently, it seems likely, systems are confused with groups, and our primitive need to explain thunder with a theology or a demonology results in the hypostatizing of an angelic or demonic hierarchy. The executive committee of the bourgeoisie and the power elite make the world more comfortable for modern social scientists as the Olympians did for the ancients. At least the latter-day hypothesis, being terrestrial, is in principle researchable, though in practice its metaphysical statement may render it equally immune to mundane inquiry.

Observation of certain local communities makes it appear that inclusive over-all organization for many general purposes is weak or non-existent. Much of what occurs seems to just happen with accidental trends becoming cumulative over time and producing results intended by nobody. A great deal of the communities' activities consist of undirected co-operation of particular social structures, each seeking particular goals and, in doing so, meshing with others. While much of this might be explained in Adam Smith's terms, much of it could not be explained with a rational, atomistic model of calculating individuals. For certain purposes the individual is a useful way of looking at people; for many others the role-playing member of a particular group is more helpful. Here we deal with the essence of predictability in social affairs. If we know the game being played is baseball and that X is a third baseman, by knowing his position and the game being played we can tell more about X's activities on the field than we could if we examined X as a psychologist or a psychiatrist. If such were not the case, X would belong in the mental ward rather than in a ball park. The behavior of X is not some disembodied rationality but, rather, behavior within an organized group activity that has goals, norms, strategies, and roles that give the very field and grounds for rationality. Baseball structures the situation.

It is the contention of this paper that the structured group activities that coexist in a particular territorial system can be looked at as games. These games provide the players with a set of goals that give them a sense of success or failure. They provide the determinate roles and calculable strategies and tactics. In addition, they provide the players with an elite and general public that is in varying degrees able to tell the score. There is a good deal of evidence to be found in common parlance that many participants in contemporary group structures regard their occupations as at lease analogous to games. And, at least in the American culture, and not only since Eisenhower, the conception of being on a "team" has been fairly widespread.

Unfortunately, the effectiveness of the term "game" for the purposes of this paper is vitiated by, first, the general sense that games are trivial occupations and second, by the pre-emption of the term for the application of a calculus of probability to choice or decision in a determinate game situation. Far from regarding games as trivial, the writer's position would be that man is both a game-playing and a game-creating animal, that his capacity to create and play games and take them deadly seriously is of the essence, and that it is through games or activities analogous to game playing that he achieves a satisfactory sense of significance and a meaningful role.

While the calculability of the game situation is important, of equal or greater importance is the capacity of the game to provide a sense of purpose and a role. The organizations of society and polity produce satisfactions with both their products and their processes. The two are not unrelated but, while the production of the product may in the larger sense enable players and on-lookers to keep score, the satisfaction in the process is the satisfaction of playing the game and the sense in which any activity can be grasped as a game.

Looked at this way, in the territorial system there is a political game, a banking game, a contracting game, a newspaper game, a civic organization game, an ecclesiastical game, and many others. Within each game there is a well-established set of goals whose achievement indicates success or failure for the participants, a set of socialized roles making participant behavior highly predictable, a set of strategies and tactics handed down through experience and occasionally subject to improvement and change, an elite public whose approbation is appreciated, and, finally, a general public which has some appreciation for the standing of the players. Within the game the players can be rational in the varying degrees that the structure permits. At the very least, they know how to behave, and they know the score.

Individuals may play in a number of games, but, for the most part, their major preoccupation is with one, and their sense of major achievement is through success in one. Transfer from one game to another is, of course, possible, and the simultaneous playing of roles in two or more games is an important manner of linking separate games.

Sharing a common territorial field and collaborating for different and particular ends in the achievement of over-all social functions, the players in one game make use of the players in another and are, in turn, made use of by them. Thus the banker makes use of the newspaperman, the politician, the contractor, the ecclesiastic, the labor leader, the civic leader—all to further his success in the banking game—but, reciprocally, he is used to further the others' success in the newspaper, political, contracting, ecclesiastical, labor, and civic games. Each is a piece in the chess game of the other, sometimes a willing piece, but to the extent that the games are different, with a different end in view.

Thus a particular highway grid may be the result of a bureaucratic department of public works game in which are combined, though separate, a professional highway engineer game with its purposes and critical elite onlookers; a departmental bureaucracy; a set of contending politicians seeking to use the highways for political capital, patronage, and the like; a banking game concerned with bonds, taxes, and the effect of the highways on real estate; newspapermen interested in headlines, scoops, and the effect of highways on the papers' circulation; contractors eager to make money by building roads; ecclesiastics concerned with the effect of highways on their parishes and on the fortunes of the contractors who support their churchly ambitions; labor leaders interested in union contracts and their status as community influentials with a right to be consulted; and civic leaders who must justify the contributions of their bureaus of municipal research or chambers of commerce to the social activity. Each game is in play in the complicated pulling and hauling of siting and constructing the highway grid. A wide variety of purposes is subserved by the activity, and no single over-all directive authority controls it. However, the interrelation of the groups in constructing a highway has been developed over time, and there are general expectations as to the interaction. There are also generalized expectations as to how politicians, contractors, newspapermen, bankers, and the like will utilize the highway situation in playing their particular games. In fact, the knowledge that a banker will play like a banker and a newspaperman like a newspaperman is an important part of what makes the situation calculable and permits the players to estimate its possibilities for their own action in their particular game.

While it might seem that the engineers of the department of public works were the appropriate protagonists for the highway grid, as a general activity it presents opportunities and threats to a wide range of other players who see in the situation consequences and possibilities undreamed of by the engineers. Some general public expectation of the limits of the conduct of the players and of a desirable outcome does provide bounds to the scramble. This public expectation is, of course, made active through the interested solicitation of newspapers, politicians, civic leaders, and others who see in it material for accomplishing their particular purposes and whose structured roles in fact require the mobilization of broad publics. In a sense the group struggle that Arthur Bentley described in his *Process of Government* is a drama that local publics have been taught to view with a not uncritical taste. The instruction of this taste has been the vocation and business of some of the contending parties. The existence of some kind of over-all public puts general restraints on gamesmanship beyond the norms of the particular games. However, for the players these are to all intents as much a part of the "facts of life" of the game as the sun and the wind.

It is perhaps the existence of some kind of a general public, however rudimentary, that most clearly differentiates the local territorial system from a natural ecology. The five-acre woodlot in which the owls and the field mice, the oaks and the acorns, and other flora and fauna have evolved a balanced system has no public opinion, however rudimentary. The co-operation is an unconscious affair. For much of what goes on in the local territorial system co-operation is equally unconscious and perhaps, but for the occasional social scientist, unnoticed. This unconscious co-operation, however, like that of the five-acre woodlot, produces results. The ecology of games in the local territorial system accomplishes unplanned, but largely functional, results. The games and their players mesh in their particular pursuits to bring about over-all results; the territorial system is fed and ordered. Its inhabitants are rational within limited areas and, pursuing the ends of these areas, accomplish socially functional ends.

While the historical development of largely unconscious co-operation between the special games in the territorial system gets certain routine, over-all functions performed, the problem of novelty and breakdown must be dealt with. Here it would seem that, as in the natural ecology, random adjustment and piecemeal innovation are the normal methods of response. The need or cramp in the system presents itself to the players of the games as an opportunity for them to exploit or a menace to be overcome. Thus a transportation crisis in, for example, the threatened abandonment of commuter trains by a railroad will bring forth the players of a wide range of games who will see in the situation opportunity for gain or loss in the outcome. While over-all considerations will appear in the discussion, the frame of reference and the interpretation of the event will be largely determined by the game the interested parties are principally involved in. Thus a telephone executive who is president of the local chamber of commerce will be playing a civic association, general business game with concern for the principal dues-payers of the chamber but with a constant awareness of how his handling of this crisis will advance him in his particular league. The politicians, who might be expected to be protagonists of the general interest, may indeed be so, but the sphere of their activity and the glasses through which they see the problem will be determined in great part by the way they see the issue affecting their political game. The generality of this game is to a great extent that of the politician's calculus of votes and interests important to his and his side's success. To be sure, some of what Walter Lippmann has called "the public philosophy" affects both politicians and other game-players. This indicates the existence of roles and norms of a larger, vaguer game with a relevant audience that has some sense of cricket. This potentially mobilizable audience is not utterly without importance, but it provides no sure or adequate basis for support in the particular game that the politician or anyone else is playing. Instead of a set of norms to structure enduring role-playing, this audience provides a cross-pressure for momentary aberrancy from gamesmanship or constitutes just another hazard to be calculated in one's play.

In many cases the territorial system is impressive in the degree of intensity of its particular games, its banks, its newspapers, its downtown stores, its manufacturing companies, its contractors, its churches, its politicians, and its other differentiated, structured, goal-oriented activities. Games go on within the territory, occasionally extending beyond it, though centered in it. But, while the particular games show clarity of goals and intensity, few, if any, treat the territory as their proper object. The protagonists of things in particular are well organized and know what they are about; the protagonists of things in general are few, vague, and weak. Immense staff work will go into the development of a Lincoln Square project, but the twenty-two counties of metropolitan New York have few spokesmen for their over-all common interest and not enough staff work to give these spokesmen more substance than that required for a "do-gooding" newspaper editorial. The

Port of New York Authority exhibits a disciplined self-interest and a vigorous drive along the lines of its developed historic role. However, the attitude of the Port Authority toward the general problems of the metropolitan area is scarcely different than that of any private corporation. It confines its corporate good citizenship to the contribution of funds for surveys and studies and avoids acceptance of broader responsibility. In fact, spokesmen for the Port vigorously reject the need for any superior level of structured representation of metropolitan interests. The common interest, if such there be, is to be realized through institutional interactions rather than through the self-conscious rationality of a determinate group charged with its formulation and attainment. Apart from the newspaper editorial, the occasional politician, and a few civic leaders, the general business of the metropolitan area is scarcely anybody's business and, except for a few, those who concern themselves with the general problems are pursuing hobbies and causes rather than their own business.

The lack of over-all institutions in the territorial system and the weakness of those that exist insure that co-ordination is largely ecological rather than a matter of conscious rational contriving. In the metropolitan area in most cases there are no over-all economic or social institutions. People are playing particular games, and their playgrounds are less or more than the metropolitan area. But even in a city where the municipal corporation provides an apparent overall government, the appearance is deceptive. The politicians who hold the offices do not regard themselves as governors of the municipal territory, but largely as mediators or players in a particular game that makes use of the other inhabitants. Their roles, as they conceive them, do not approach those of the directors of a TVA developing a territory. The ideology of local government is a highly limited affair in which the office-holders respond to demands and mediate conflicts. They play politics, and politics is vastly different from government if the latter is conceived as the rational, responsible ordering of the community. In part, this is due to the general belief that little government is necessary or that government is a congery of services only different from others because it is paid for by taxes and provided for by civil servants. In part, the separation of economics from politics eviscerates the formal theory of government of most of the substance of social action. Intervention in the really important economic order is by way of piecemeal exception and in deviation from the supposed norm of the separation of politics and economics. This ideal of separation has blocked the development of a theory of significant government action and reduced the politician to the role or registerer of pressure rather than responsible governor of a local political economy. The politics of the community becomes a different affair from its government, and its government is so structured as to provide the effective actors in it neither a sense of general responsibility nor the roles calling for such behavior.

The community vaguely senses that there ought to be a government. This is evidenced in the nomination, by newspapers and others, of particular individuals as members of a top leadership, a "they" who are periodically called upon to solve community problems and meet community crises. Significantly, the "they" usually are made up of people holding private, not public, office. The pluralism of the society has separated political, ecclesiastical, economic, and social hierarchies from one another so that the ancient union of lords spiritual and temporal is disrupted. In consequence, there is a marked distinction between the status of the holders of political office and the status of the "they" of the newspapers and the power elite of a C. Wright Mills or a Floyd Hunter. The politicians have the formal governmental office that might give them responsible governing roles. However, their lack of status makes it both absurd and presumptuous that they should take themselves so seriously. Who are they to act as lords of creation? Public expectation neither empowers nor demands that they should assume any such confident pose as top community leaders. The latter position is reserved for a rather varying group (in some communities well defined and clear-cut, in others vague and amorphous) of holders, for the most part, of positions of private power, economic, social, and ecclesiastical. This group, regarded as the top leadership of the community, and analogous to the top management of a corporation, provides both a sense that there are gods in the heavens whose will, if they exercise it, will take care of the community's problems and a set of demons whose misrule accounts for the evil in the world. The "they" fill an office left vacant by the dethronement of absolutism and aristocracy. Unlike the politicians in that "they" are only partially visible and of untested powers, the top leadership provides a convenient rationale for explaining what goes on or does not go on in the community. It is comforting to think that the executive committee of the bourgoisie is exploiting the community or that the beneficient social and economic leaders are wearying themselves and their digestions with civic luncheons in order to bring parking to a congested city.

Usually the question is raised as to whether *de facto* there is a set of informal power-holders running things. A related question is whether community folklore holds that there is, that there should be, and what these informal power-holders should do. Certainly, most newspapermen and other professional "inside dopesters" hold that there is a "they." In fact, these people operate largely as court chroniclers of the doings of the "they." The "they," because they are "they," are newsworthy and fit into a ready-made theory of social causation that is vulgarized widely. However, the same newspaperman who could knowingly open his "bird book" and give you a run-down on the local "Who's Who" would probably with equal and blasphemous candor tell you that "they" were not doing a thing about the city and that "they" were greatly to be blamed for sitting around talking instead of getting things done. Thus, as with most primitive tribes, the idols are both worshipped and beaten, at least verbally. Public and reporters alike are relieved to believe both that there is a "they" to make civic life explicable and also to be held responsible for what occurs. This belief in part creates the role of top leadership and demands that it somehow be filled, it seems likely that there is a social-psychological table of organization of a community that must be filled in order to remove anxieties. Gordon Childe has remarked that man seems to need as much to adjust to an unseen, socially created, spiritual environment as to the matter-of-fact world of the senses.

The community needs to believe that there are spiritual fathers, bad or good, who can deal with the dark: in the Middle Ages the peasants combated a plague of locusts by a high Mass and a procession of the clergy who dammed the grasshoppers with bell, book, and candle. The Hopi Indians do a rain dance to overcome a drought. The harassed citizens of the American city mobilize their influentials at a civic luncheon to perform the equivalent and exorcise slums, smog, or unemployment. We smile at the medievals and the Hopi, but our own practices may be equally magical. It is interesting to ask under what circumstances one resorts to DDT and irrigation and why. To some extent it is clear that the ancient and modern practice of civic magic ritual is functional—functional in the same sense as the medicinal placebo. Much of human illness is benign; if the sufferer will bide his time, it

will pass. Much of civic ills also cure themselves if only people
can be kept from tearing each other apart in the stress of their
anxieties. The locusts and the drought will pass. They almost
always have.

While ritual activities are tranquilizing anxieties, the process of
experimentation and adaptation in the social ecology goes on. The
piecemeal responses of the players and the games to the challenges
presented by crises provide the social counterpart to the process
of evolution and natural selection. However, unlike the random
mutation of the animal kingdom, much of the behavior of the
players responding within the perspectives of their games is self-
conscious and rational, given their ends in view. It is from the
over-all perspective of the unintended contribution of their actions
to the forming of a new or the restoration of the old ecological
balance of the social system that their actions appear almost as
random and lacking in purposive plan as the adaptive behavior
of the natural ecology.

Within the general area of unplanned, unconscious social process,
technological areas emerge that are so structured as to promote rational, goal-oriented behavior and meaningful experience rather than
mere happenstance. In these areas group activity may result in
cumulative knowledge and self-corrective behavior. Thus problem-
solving in the field of public health and sanitation may be at a stage
far removed from the older dependence on piecemeal adjustment
and random functional innovation. In this sense there are areas
in which society, as Julian Huxley suggests in his *The Meaning
of Evolution,* has gone beyond evolution. However, these are as
yet isolated areas in a world still swayed by magic and, for the
most part, carried forward by the logic of unplanned, undirected
historical process.

It is not surprising that the members of the "top leadership"
of the territorial system should seem to be largely confined to
ritual and ceremonial roles. "Top leadership" is usually conceived
in terms of status position rather than specifiable roles in social
action. The role of a top leader is ill defined and to a large degree
unstructured. It is in most cases a secondary role derived from
a primary role as corporation executive, wealthy man, powerful
ecclesiastic, holder of high social position, and the like. The top-
leadership role is derivative from the other and is, in most cases,
a result rather than a cause of status. The primary job is bank
president, or president of Standard Oil; as such, one is naturally

picked, nominated, and recognized as a member of the top leadership. One seldom forgets that one's primary role, obligation, and source of rational conduct is in terms of one's business. In fact, while one is on the whole pleased at the recognition that membership in the top leadership implies—much as one's wife would be pleased to be included among the ten best-dressed women—he is somewhat concerned about just what the role requires in the expenditure of time and funds. Furthermore, one has a suspicion that he may not know how to dance and could make a fool of himself before known elite and unknown, more general, publics. All things considered, however, it is probably a good thing for the business, the contacts are important, and the recognition will be helpful back home, in both senses. In any event, if one's committee service or whatever concrete activity "top leadership" implies proves wearing or unsatisfactory, or if it interferes with business, one can always withdraw.

A fair gauge of the significance of top-leadership roles is the time put into them by the players and the institutionalized support represented by staff. Again and again the interviewer is told that the president of such-and-such an organization is doing a terrific job and literally knocking himself out for such-and-such a program. On investigation a "terrific job" turns out to be a few telephone calls and, possibly, three luncheons a month. The standard of "terrific job" obviously varies widely from what would be required in the business role.

In the matter of staffing, while the corporation, the church, and the government are often equipped in depth, the top-leadership job of port promotion may have little more than a secretary and an agile newspaperman equipped to ghost-write speeches for the boss. While there are cases where people in top-leadership positions make use of staff from their own businesses and from the legal mill with which they do business, this seems largely confined to those top-leadership undertakings that have a direct connection with their business. In general, top-leadership roles seem to involve minor investments of time, staff, and money by territorial elites. The absence of staff and the emphasis on publicity limit the capacity of top leadership for sustained rational action.

Where top leaderships have become well staffed, the process seems as much or more the result of external pressures than of its own volition. Of all the functions of top leadership, that of welfare is best staffed. Much of this is the result of the pressure of the professional social worker to organize a concentration of economic and social power sufficient to permit him to do a job. It is true, of course, that the price of organizing top leadership and making it manageable by the social workers facilitated a reverse control of themselves—a control of whose galling nature Hunter gives evidence. An amusing sidelight on the organization of the "executive committee of the bourgeoisie" is the case of the Cleveland Fifty Club. This club, supposedly, is made up of the fifty most important men in Cleveland. Most middling and even upper executives long for the prestige recognition that membership confers. Reputedly, the Fifty Club was organized by Brooks Emery, while he was director of the Cleveland Council on World Affairs, to facilitate the taxation of business to support that organization. The lead time required to get the august members of the Fifty Club together and their incohesiveness have severely limited its possibilities as a power elite. Members who have tried to turn it to such a purpose report fairly consistent failure.

The example of the Cleveland Fifty Club, while somewhat extreme, points to the need on the part of certain activities in the territorial system for a top leadership under whose auspices they can function. A wide variety of civic undertakings need to organize top prestige support both to finance and to legitimate their activities. The staff man of a bureau of municipal research or the Red Feather Agency cannot proceed on his own; he must have the legitimatizing sponsorship of top influentials. His task may be self-assigned, his perception of the problem and its solution may be his own but he cannot gain acceptance without mobilizing the influentials. For the success of his game he must assist in creating the game of top leadership. The staff man in the civic field is the typical protagonist of things in general—a kind of entrepreneur of ideas. He fulfils the same role in his area as the stock promoter of the twenties or the Zeckendorfs of urban redevelopment. Lacking both status and a confining organizational basis, he has a socially valuable mobility between the specialized games and hierarchies in the territorial system. His success in the negotiation of a port authority not only provides a plus for his taxpayers federation or his world trade council but may provide a secure and lucrative job for himself.

Civic staff men, ranging from chamber of commerce personnel to college professors and newspapermen, are in varying degrees interchangeable and provide an important network of communication.

The staff men in the civic agencies play similar roles to the Cohens and Corcorans in Washington. In each case a set of telephone numbers provides special information and an effective lower-echelon interaction. Consensus among interested professionals at the lower level can result in action programs from below that are bucked up to the prestige level of legitimitization. As the Cohens and Corcorans played perhaps the most general and inclusive game in the Washington bureaucracy, so their counterparts in the local territorial system are engaged in the most general action game in their area. Just as the Cohens and Corcorans had to mobilize an effective concentration of top brass to move a program into the action stage, so their counterparts have to mobilize concentrations of power sufficient for their purposes on the local scene.

In this connection it is interesting to note that foundation grants are being used to hire displaced New Deal bureaucrats and college professors in an attempt to organize the influentials of metropolitan areas into self-conscious governing groups. Professional chamber of commerce executives, immobilized by their orthodox ideology, are aghast to see their members study under the planners and heretics from the dogmas of free-enterprise fundamentalism. The attempt to transform the metropolitan appearance of disorder into a tidy territory is a built-in predisposition for the self-constituted staff of the embryonic top metropolitan management. The major disorder that has to be overcome before all others is the lack of order and organization among the "power elite." As in the case of the social workers, there is a thrust from below to organize a "power elite" as a necessary instrument to accomplish the purposes of civic staff men. This is in many ways nothing but a part of the general groping after a territorial government capable of dealing with a range of problems that the existing feudal disintegration of power cannot. The nomination of a top leadership by newspapers and public and the attempt to create such a leadership in fact by civic technicians are due to a recognition that there is a need for leadership with the status, capacity, and role to attend to the general problems of the territory and give substance to a public philosophy. This involves major changes in the script of the top-leadership game and the self-image of its participants. In fact, the insecurity and the situational limitations of their positions in corporations or other institutions that provide the primary roles for top leaders make it difficult to give more substance to what has been a secondary role. Many members of present top leaderships are genuinely reluctant, fearful, and even morally shocked at having their position become that of a recognized territorial government. While there is a general supposition that power is almost instinctively craved, there seems considerable evidence that at least in many of our territorial cultures responsibility is not. Machiavellian *virtu* is an even scarcer commodity among the merchant princes of the present than among their Renaissance predecessors. In addition, the educational systems of school and business do not provide top leaders with the inspiration or the know-how to do more than raise funds and man committees. Politics is frequently regarded with the same disgust as military service was by the ancient educated Chinese.

It is possible to translate a check pretty directly into effective power in a chamber of commerce or a welfare agency. However, to translate economic power into more general social or political power, there must be an organized purchasable structure. Where such structures exist, they may be controlled or, as in the case of *condottieri,* gangsters, and politicians, their hire may be uncertain, and the hired force retains its independence. Where businessmen are unwilling or unable to organize their own political machines, they must pay those who do. Sometimes the paymaster rules; at other times he bargains with equals or superiors.

A major protagonist of things in general in the territorial system is the newspaper. Along with the welfare worker, museum director, civic technician, etc., the newspaper has an interest in terms of its broad reading public in agitating general issues and projects. As the chronicler of the great, both in its general news columns and in its special features devoted to society and business, it provides an organizing medium for elites in the territory and provides them with most of their information about things in general and not a little of inside tidbits about how individual elite members are doing. In a sense, the newspaper is the prime mover in setting the territorial agenda. It has a great part in determining what most people will be talking about, what most people will think the facts are, and what most people will regard as the way problems are to be dealt with. While the conventions of how a newspaper is to be run, and the compelling force of some events limit the complete freedom of a paper to select what events and what people its public will attend to, it has great leeway. However, the newspaper is a business and a specialized game even when its reporters are idealists and its publisher rejoices in the title

123273

"Mr. Cleveland." The paper does not accept the responsibility of a governing role in its territory. It is a power but only a partially responsible one. The span of attention of its audience and the conventions of what constitute a story give it a crusading role at most for particular projects. Nonetheless, to a large extent it sets the civic agenda.

The story is told of the mayor of a large eastern metropolis who having visited the three capital cities of his constituents—Rome, Dublin, and Tel Aviv—had proceeded home via Paris and LeHarve. Since his staff had neglected to meet the boat before the press, he was badgered by reporters to say what he had learned on his trip. The unfortunate mayor could not say that he had been on a junket for a good time. Luckily, he remembered that in Paris they had been having an anti-noise campaign. Off the hook at last, he told the press that he thought this campaign was a good thing. This gave the newsmen something to write about. The mayor hoped this was the end of it. But a major paper felt in need of a crusade to sponsor and began to harass the mayor about the start of the local anti-noise campaign. Other newspapers took up the cry, and the mayor told his staff they were for it—there had to be an anti-noise campaign. In short order, businessmen's committees, psychiatrists, and college professors were mobilized to press forward on a broad front the suppression of needless noise. In vindication of administrative rationality it appeared that an anti-noise campaign was on a staff list of possibilities for the mayor's agenda but had been discarded by him as politically unfeasible.

The civic technicians and the newspapers have somewhat the same relationship as congressional committee staff and the press. Many members of congressional committee staffs complain bitterly that their professional consciences are seared by the insistent pressure to seek publicity. But they contend that their committee sponsors are only impressed with research that is newsworthy. Congressional committee members point out that committees that do not get publicity are likely to go out of business or funds. The civic agency head all to frequently communicates most effectively with his board through his success in getting newspaper publicity. Many a civic ghost writer has found his top leader converted to the cause by reading the ghosted speech he delivered at the civic luncheon reported with photographs and editorials in the press. This is even the case where the story appears in the top leader's own paper. The need of the reporters for news and of the civic technicians for publicity brings the participants of these two games together. As in the case of congressional committee, there is a tendency to equate accomplishment with publicity. For top influentials on civic boards the news clips are an important way of keeping score. This symbiotic relation of newsmen and civic staff helps explain the heavy emphasis on ritual luncheons, committees, and news releases. The nature of the newspapers' concern with a story about people and the working of marvels and miracles puts a heavy pressure for the kind of story that the press likes to carry. It is not surprising that civic staff men should begin to equate accomplishment with their score measured in newspaper victories or that they should succumb to the temptation to impress their sponsors with publicity, salting it to their taste by flattering newspaper tributes to the sponsors themselves. Despite the built-in incapacity of newspapers to exercise a serious governing responsibility in their territories, they are for the most part the only institutions with a long-term general territorial interest. In default of a territorial political party or other institution that accepts responsibility for the formulation of a general civic agenda the newspaper is the one game that by virtue of its public and its conventions partly fills the vacuum.

A final game that does in a significant way integrate all the games in the territorial system is the social game. Success in each of the games can in varying degrees be cashed in for social acceptance. The custodians of the symbols of top social standing provide goals that in a sense give all the individual games some common denominator of achievement. While the holders of top social prestige do not necessarily hold either top political or economic power, they do provide meaningful goals for the rest. One of the most serious criticisms of a Yankee aristocracy made by a Catholic bishop was that, in losing faith in their own social values, they were undermining the faith in the whole system of final clubs. It would be a cruel joke if, just as the hard-working upwardly mobile had worked their way to entrance, the progeny of the founders lost interest. The decay of the Union League Club in *By Love Possessed* is a tragedy for more than its members. A common game shared even by the excluded spectators gave a purpose that was functional in its time and must be replaced—hopefully, by a better one. A major motivation for seeking membership in and playing the top-leadership game is the value of the status it confers as a counter in the social game.

Neither the civic leadership game nor the social game makes the territorial ecology over into a structured government. They do, however, provide important ways of linking the individual games and make possible cooperative action on projects. Finally, the social game, in Ruth Benedict's sense, in a general way patterns the culture of the territorial ecology and gives all the players a set of vaguely shared aspirations and common goals.

2

THE POLITICAL ECONOMY
OF A METROPOLITAN AREA*

ROBERT C. WOOD

If the effects of governmental activities on Regional economic affairs now seem substantial—and destined to remain so—an important corollary follows from the fact. The *process* by which expenditures are authorized and programs carried out requires exploration before we can understand the functioning of the political economy. When we move from the private to the public sector we pass, in Harold Lasswell's words, from a set of interactions typically labeled "transactions" to one in which the concept of "decisions" is central. We could make no greater mistake than to suppose that the ways in which these political decisions are made parallel the behavior of firms and households.

One way to underscore the importance of process per se is to reflect on the difficulty of distinguishing between the public and private sectors in terms of the activities they carry out. Few public activities in the New York Region appear to be inherently "public" in the sense that the conduct of foreign affairs or the maintenance of national defense are public. The necessaries of modern urban life — for instance, water, electricity, gas, shelter — are supplied both by public agencies and private corporations. The responsibility for moving people and goods is shared by government and business. A large number of the Region's children are educated in private schools, and important relief activities are carried out by private charities. In some jurisdictions, the collec-

*Reprinted from *1400 Governments* (Cambridge: Harvard University Press, 1961) pp. 17-28. By permission of Regional Plan Association, Incorporated.

tion of refuse is a public responsibility; in many others, a private one. In some areas, public health officers provide treatment that elsewhere is provided only by the family doctor. Even the creation or enforcement of law is not an exclusive governmental prerogative; private police forces are found throughout the Region and private residential covenants often operate with more force than public legislation. So it is the distinction between the processes, not between the functions, which is critical to our analysis.

The central distinguishing feature of the governmental process is, of course, its monopoly on the lawful means of physical violence, its possession of power — not just on a parcel of private property, but everywhere in the political jurisdiction. This quality, in and of itself, sets the political economy apart, and endows it with a purpose quite separate from that of the private sector. Not only do governments have the means to compel compliance with their policies — in the provision of education, the acquisition of water reservoirs, the construction of highways — but the control over these means becomes a paramount objective of different groups within the Region's population struggling for influence and authority. Public programs are authorized for purposes other than the satisfaction of the material wants of all the residents or even of a majority. They are devices whereby political organizations survive. Taxes and public expenditures represent not just "costs" and "products" but "votes" and "influence." Political stability as much as economic prosperity is involved in the goals of a political economy.

Given this general characteristic of the governmental process, we should acknowledge three specific differences between the political economy and the private economy in the way resources are used and activities undertaken. First, in the political economy the basic unit of decision-making is not the individual producer or consumer; it is the group, formally or informally organized. Second, the mechanism through which resources are obtained and expenditures made is not the price mechanism of the marketplace, but the budgetary process. Finally, the "products" provided by government are public products; that is, theoretically they are always indivisible among persons, and practically, they are frequently so.

The significance of the group, not the individual, as the basic unit of governmental process is of course that resources are not allocated to the public sector by the invisible hand of thousands upon thousands of individual choices exercised constantly without explicit recognition of the preferences of the other participants in the marketplace. The allocation is, rather, the function of a relatively few persons presuming to speak for the voters in the name of the "public interest" and the "general will." The periodic limited expression of popular opinion in the voting booths and the occasional articulation of public preferences and expectations in opinion surveys are rarely interpreted as an aggregation of individual attitudes. Instead these expressions are analyzed in terms of ethnic blocks, silk-stocking districts, neighborhood attitudes, and common outlooks presumed to be held by persons of similar income, occupation, or racial types. And institutions — the church, the *New York Times,* the banks, business associations and labor — become significant as entities in themselves, exercising influence because they sway the preferences of citizens. Thus the aspirations of groups and leaders of groups, more than the opinions of the members themselves, become the critical elements in the process of determining what the political systems decide.

With the individual voter-consumer-citizen removed from the arena of decision-making, notions of marginal costs and prices, of income and wants, are replaced by the vaguer concept of the budget. The literature of public budgeting is replete with efforts to find a substitute for the price mechanism, to devise a common unit for comparing relative benefits among different services at the margin. In actuality, however, the process of allocating public moneys among competing needs still proceeds on a basis far removed from the price mechanism — on a system of preferences filtered through group representation.

So New York City's Board of Estimate calculates the outcries likely to arise from taxpayers' associations when the tax rate is increased, weighs such protests against the influence of recipients of public education or medical services, interjects a healthy dose of personal preferences, and, in a series of sustained and sometimes frenzied discussions, cuts or expands the estimates of professional budget-makers in the course of a few short days. Outside the City, even this institutional focal point for considering competing claims is lacking. Counties, towns, boroughs, cities, villages, special districts, existing side by side or overlying the same geographic territory, proceed in jurisdictional isolation to consider small segments of the Region's aggregate local expenditures and arrive at separate judgments of group needs and group influences. Political philosophy and estimates of political strength — operating through collective mechanisms — become the key factors in distributing the Region's public resources among different purposes.

Moreover, even if the individual had a mechanism by which he could make his preferences known, each and every citizen would not be satisfied. So long as a number of alternative courses of action were available, no "optimum" solution would result — even for the majority. Choices become too complicated for optimum solutions; what happens (as every politician knows) is a compromise. In the public sector, the individual citizen neither gets what he pays for nor pays a common price for what he gets. In the New York Region as elsewhere, he buys schools though he may have no children, roadways though he may not own an automobile, museums he may never visit, and hospitals he may not require. Nor does he pay for the services he receives on a basis equal to that of his fellows, but according to his presumed capacity to pay, crudely expressed in a politically constructed revenue system.

All this is justified of course in a concept of common purposes, a "public interest" or "the general welfare." But as real as the general welfare may be, the notion lacks the sharp distinction that exists between buyer and seller in the private economy, where each man knows his role in a transaction. In its place is the schizophrenic figure of the taxpayer, acutely conscious of what he pays to the government, but understandably suspicious of the "civilization" he receives in return. In the last analysis, his dissatisfaction with particular public products can be expressed in only a general way: a massive reversal in electoral behavior, a condemnation of those responsible for the general budget, or, more fundamentally, a revolt against the system.

Even public institutions expressly designed to "look and function" like private enterprises are understood best in terms of the calculus of power and the interplay of group influence. The great public corporations of the Region and the hundreds of special districts are established to provide particular services at the option of the individual. They depend on income derived from individual purchases of their services, and they are created with the explicit objectives of "keeping their programs out of politics." Yet the most businesslike of these agencies faces the reality that it exists only so long as influential political interests support, or at least tolerate, its existence. It suffers the indignities of living in a goldfish bowl in order to gain general, often inarticulate, support from the public at large and it faces always the danger of sporadic attacks by other envious agencies. And its officials, unlike those of a private corporation, expect with some confidence that dissolution will not result if, by some perilous circumstance, costs exceed revenue. Other sources of revenue will ultimately be found.

In explaining the behavior of the Region's political economy, then, we must do what some writers on municipal affairs have not done — abandon the assumptions of the Age of Reason. One cannot show how governments in fact behave by assuming the existence of the conscientious citizen rationally striving to do his duty, or the divisibility of public goods and services on a unit basis, or full knowledge on the part of each citizen of the character of his government's expenditures and receipts. The guidelines are in fact not very precise nor easily quantifiable.

So at rockbottom the significance of the Service State becomes this: as more and more resources pass from the private sector to the public sector, the process which determines their use changes from that of the marketplace to the uncertain world of politics.

SERVICE STATES AND SERVICE STATES

Decisions in the public sector, then, are made by groups that compromise to obtain benefits which are not equally enjoyed by all. The groups do not interact haphazardly, however, nor are their compromises accidental flashes of the moment. Instead, preferences are collected, budgets processed, and services allocated by systematic contacts and calculated agreements.

Participant groups engaging recurrently in these relations can be thought of as "systems." And "systems" making public decisions in the New York Metropolitan Region are diverse and countless. Some of them are internal in nature, existing within every group, institution, or political jurisdiction. So Wallace Sayre and Herbert Kaufman describe the municipality of New York City as a struggle among contestants in the population of the city, in its parties, and in its bureaucracy for prizes which government alone can offer. Other systems are largely external in character — the shifting alliances among the Region's elite groups which Norton Long has characterized as a series of games in which "the players in one game make use of the players in another, and are, in turn, made use of by them." Still other systems find expression in the battles waged between the City and the Port of New York Authority over respective responsibilities in port development, and in the jostling among the agencies concerned with the planning and construction of the Region's transportation network.

Systems can be informal in the sense that they involve groups and institutions which make no open declarations of political objectives but take part, for example, in the negotiations associated with a municipal bond issue or the acquisition of land destined to be a shopping center. But some systems are conducted by the most stylized rules and procedures, such as the procedures leading to zoning ordinances, or the procedures under which a municipality applies for a federal grant. And when the panorama of Regional politics and governments is unfolded, all sorts and kinds of systems come into view, each explicable in its own terms and each contributing to an explanation of the behavior of the Region's policy.

For our purposes, the two great systems we identified earlier are most relevant: the "local governments" and the "Regional enterprises." For any given program the Regional enterprises can be fairly quickly listed. In transportation, for example, the central actors are the Port of New York Authority, the Triborough Bridge and Tunnel Authority, the New York Transit Authority, the three state highway departments, and the U.S. Bureau of Public Roads.[1] But the "local government" system is a far more varied and complicated apparatus for decision-making.

At the center of the "local" system is New York City, which swallows up five counties.[2] To the east and north are the seven suburban counties of New York, including by Census count 801 governmental units within their borders, and the 55 local units of Fairfield County, Connecticut. To the west and south are the 606 local units of the nine New Jersey counties.

By legal standards the New York portion of the Region is undoubtedly the most complex. New York City encompasses the broadest array of legal responsibilities within a single formal structure. Though the five counties have judicial functions and the offices of

[1]Actually the Triborough and Transit Authorities are agencies of New York City, and their expenditures are often lumped into the municipal total; but they are semi-autonomous, highly specialized, and far-ranging in their effects, and therefore are best analyzed as "Regional enterprises" along with the bi-state Port of New York Authority.

[2]New York County (borough of Manhattan), Bronx County (borough of the Bronx), Queens County (borough of Queens), Kings County (borough of Brooklyn), and Richmond County (borough of Richmond), which is better known as Staten Island.

the five borough presidents supervise street paving and certain other activities, the municipality itself is the predominant government for local affairs, operating even the schools as a municipal department.

In New York State outside New York City, responsibilities for public functions are divided among counties, cities, towns, villages, school districts, and other special districts. Generally speaking the counties have major responsibilities with respect to tax assessment and collection, highways, courts, public works, welfare, and planning. In Westchester, Nassau, and most recently Suffolk, special county charters have streamlined the structure of the Board of Supervisors, established a county executive, and placed increasing responsibilities in the county rather than the smaller units. But where cities exist within county borders—for example, Yonkers and White Plains in Westchester County—almost every local function is likely to be carried out by the municipality. Towns have important duties in licensing, zoning, property records, parks and playgrounds, and streets. Depending on the circumstances, villages may assume town functions or concentrate on particular slices of town functions— for example, traffic control, recreation, some aspects of zoning and planning, and limited welfare activities. Special districts are primarily engaged in operating schools and in public utility and protection services—water, light, sewage, garbage, and fire-fighting, though they may also undertake recreational and parking activities.

But no hard and fast rules exist with respect to the divisions of functions among New York governments. To illustrate, the relations between town and village are individually tailored. Some towns have no villages at all; in others the boundary lines of town and village are coterminous; and in still others the town is simply a federation of villages which embrace the entire area of the town. Some counties abound with special districts of all shapes and sizes. Others assign the same services to the more general units of government.

In New Jersey, though the official names of local units are as numerous as in New York State, the allocation of duties is far more regular. With variations according to population size, the boroughs, villages, towns, townships, and cities to the west and south of Manhattan all carry out roughly the same array of public services. School districts are apt to be coterminous with municipal boundaries. Other special districts are scarcer than in New York State, averaging less than five a county. County governments are not as active. Multiplicity in New Jersey is a function of geography;

the territorial jurisdictions are much smaller, reaching their extreme in Bergen County where 246 square miles of land are divided among 70 units of government.

Fairfield County introduces still another pattern for the formal assignment of public responsibilities. Here, outside the city limits of the six largest municipalities, the New England heritage has established the town as the central instrument of government. The ₋Connecticut town is far more important than its New York counterpart. Its activities are usually more cohesively organized and are directed by a much smaller governing board. Its legal responsibilities extend even to public education—though the school committees in New England have a tradition of *de facto* if not legal independence. The number of special districts is proportionately far less than elsewhere in the Region, and the square mileage of single jurisdictions is greater.[3]

Besides variations in the way local governments are legally organized, differences in philosophies between the state governments separate the performance of New Jersey and New York local governments. New Jersey has been traditionally a "no new tax" state, one of the three in the nation with neither a personal income tax, a general sales tax, nor a gross receipts tax, and this attitude affects the character of its local public sector. Dedicated "to the goal of disproving the widely held belief that property taxes are more easily replaced than repaired," New Jersey proceeds—according to a state commission as recently as 1958—with "no clearly defined fiscal policy . . . no basic fiscal philosophy . . . the most regressive of all tax bases . . . and a mass of inequities that are almost unbelievable as the basis for the support of public services in a modern industrial state." New Jersey's tax pattern reflects a reliance upon local units of government to carry out major service activities. Its state grant-in-aid programs down to the present time have been relatively modest: it has shown a disinclination to experiment with new local governmental structures; and it has sanctioned public salaries and public services at considerably lower levels than in the neighboring states.

In contrast, New York State has displayed a far greater disposition toward innovation at the local level and toward buttressing local resources with state revenues. "Over the past several years," the

---

[3]But alas, Fairfield is not greater in the usefulness of its government statistics. The difficulty of obtaining comparable figures on expenditures has forced us to omit Fairfield from much of the analysis in this book.

State Fiscal Study Commission of 1955 observed, "New York has taken a number of significant steps to fortify local government finances against fluctuations in the economy." The state has abandoned almost entirely the practice of aiding municipalities by giving them a cut of specific taxes which rise and fall sharply, "and has evolved a system of grants geared partly to compensating for economic inequalities, partly to matching expenditures, and partly to counter cyclical protection." And, in the words of the New York State-New York City Fiscal Relations Committee, "the enveloping governmental relations" between state and localities "have changed and are changing." The national, state, and local governments "are participating simultaneously in several great functional fields." The committee "commends the twin concepts of interdependence and decentralization as the pillars of a new system of governmental relations." Thus, consistently, New York has established more comprehensive and more liberal grant programs to support local activities, and has shown a disposition to revamp county organizational structures within the Metropolitan Region and to establish new agencies and districts as special needs arise.

Still another kind of variety marks the local governments of New York Metropolitan Region — wide differences in the amounts of taxes and expenditures. In 1955, one municipality spent $4.30 per capita for current operations while another was spending $351.20. One jurisdiction was levying $24.60 per capita in local real property taxes; another, $376.89. The New York municipalities outside New York City spent considerably more than New Jersey municipalities, on the average. And the range of spending differences among the New York governments was much wider than the range among the New Jersey ones.

Finally, the different sub-areas of the Region exhibit its different political styles. In New York City, municipal elections are partisan in nature, with the preponderant Democratic majority often sharply limited in its actions by internal factional divisions and by the watchdog posture of the Liberal Party, which sometimes participates in Democratic affairs and sometimes joins forces with the Republican minority. In the City, too, important policy decisions are the responsibility of a highly organized and generally professional bureaucracy, possessing independent bases of political support in specific programs. At the center of the stage, mediating among party factions, pressure groups, and the main centers of bureaucratic power (such as the Park Commissioner and the Police Commissioner) is the Office of the Mayor. As a result of the 1938 City Charter and the interpretation of that instrument, notably by La Guardia, the Mayoralty and the Board of Estimate together represent a focus of power rarely found in American local government.

Outside the City, other styles abound. Impressionistically, one may identify a spirit of professionalism in public service, often associated with Westchester County. One may trace the atrophy of old-style machine organization, once dominant in Hudson County, where, as one observer has said, a transition is underway from "a one-party county with a rather rigid hierarchy and an undisputed leader" to a "two-party situation in which the nonorganization voter is becoming at least as important as the organization voter," "eash party has at least two important factions," and "a relative decline in the effectiveness of the ward and political clubs has occurred."

Alternatively, the style may be representative of courthouse cliques which survived the transformation of their jurisdiction from rural to suburban. The *Bergen Evening Record,* in analyzing Bergen problems, has characterized political activity in some of the small governments as "the vested interest in the status quo." Again, local political behavior may be a function of the different attitudes and objectives of old residents versus newcomers, or stay-at-homes against commuters. It may be characterized by the amateur dabbling in which part-time public officials assume local office in the same spirit in which they direct the Community Chest Drive. But by whatever indices are available — by party-strength, voter participation, sources of political leadership, or predominance of career employees — the Region offers an assortment of brands unparalleled in any other section of the nation.

Given such differences in formal powers, structure, area, taxing and spending levels, and political habits, it is not surprising that the local government system does not produce common policies and decisions for the Region as a whole. Nor is it surprising that municipalities apparently inhabited by the same type of people, in roughly the same stage of development, have adquired individual public sectors all their own. To some observers, the surprising thing is that conditions of political stability and economic development are maintained at all. For the local system is hundreds and hundreds of decision-centers, represented by individual governments. Each is bent on maintaining its autonomy and each fashions its own responses to the insistent public pressures that are generated as the nation's largest metropolitan area becomes even larger and rearranges itself on the landscape. Yet the responses to the pressures are not altogether arbitrary and individualistic. The responses are sometimes even predictable — once we identify the pressures.

3

URBAN POLITICS:
THE NEW CONVERGENCE OF POWER*†

ROBERT H. SALISBURY

Economically, culturally, and in many ways even politically, the United States has become a thoroughly urban nation.[1] One aspect of this urbanization is that scholars have increasingly paid attention to phenomena occurring in cities. Sociologists, political scientists, economists, geographers, and historians have all developed urban subfields of specialization; and in recent years the subfields have been infused with the great enthusiasm of virtual armies of researchers. When these efforts are combined with those of architects, planners, social workers, administrative managers, and all the other urbanists asking questions about life in the city, the resulting stack of data, reports, proposals, admonitions, and manifestos is truly staggering. Inevitably, perhaps, concern for the substance of city life gets mixed with concern for the methods of inquiry. Both, of course, are legitimate and important areas of concern, Each helps illuminate and is illuminated by the other. Specifically, the study of power structure—a basic issue for all political inquiry — has come to focus very largely on the city. In the process, both the substantive and methodological issues surrounding this generic political question — the question, as Dahl puts it,

* An earlier version of this paper was presented to the 59th Annual Meeting of the American Political Science Association, New York, September 5, 1963.
†Reprinted from *The Journal of Politics, 26*, No. 4 (November 1964), 775-797. By permission of *The Journal of Politics*.
[1]For a most comprehensive and thoughtful history of urban growth in America see Blake McKelvey, *The Urbanization of America* (New Brunswick, New Jersey: Rutgers University Press, 1963).

of Who Governs?—have been involved in virtually every discussion of urban affairs in recent years.[2]

Yet despite, or perhaps because of, this special ferment some important gaps on this question — who governs the city? — have remained. Many of these relate to the basic criticism to be made of almost all urban studies, the absence of comparative dimensions. Serious, theoretically sophisticated social and political analysis of urban data is relatively new on the scholarly scene, however. It is perhaps not so surprising therefore that so little genuine comparative work has been undertaken. One may be encouraged by the very recent emergence of a number of comparative studies.[3] Most of these, however, deal with relatively small communities. One who is interested in general patterns of big city politics must deal with a series of case studies, each study dealing with a single community. Each study then serves its author as the empirical foundation for a series of generalizations about politics (or society — the sociologists have been firmly in the tradition since the days of the Lynds). Some of these are brilliant. At best, however, they are sophisticated insights and theoretical conjectures built upon descriptions of a single case which, one hopes intuitively, may fit a larger number of cases.

The limitations of the data are compounded by variations in conceptual apparatus and/or data-gathering technique. One wishes that there were a clear basis for determining that Atlanta was or was not a pyramid-shaped monolith; that Springdale was "really" controlled by a caucus, and that New Haven actually conforms

---

[2]Robert A. Dahl's study of New Haven was a classic of political science almost before it was published. See *Who Governs?* (New Haven: Yale University Press, 1961). Dahl chose not to integrate his findings with those available concerning other communities, and in a number of respects one may argue that his conclusions are limited to the New Haven context. One cannot deny, however, that the larger question of how to approach the study of power has been given theoretically sophisticated stimulus from the work of Dahl and his associates. See Nelson W. Polsby, *Community Power and Political Theory* (New Haven: Yale University Press, 1963). For a convenient summary of many of the items in the large monographic literature on community power structure, see Charles Press, *Main Street Politics* (East Lansing: Michigan State University Institute for Community Development, 1962).

[3]Recent attempts to engage in genuinely comparative analysis include Oliver P. Williams and Charles Adrian, *Four Cities* (Philadelphia: University of Pennsylvania Press, 1963); Amos H. Hawley, "Community Power and Urban Renewal Success," American Journal of Sociology, VIII (1963), pp. 422-31; Leo F. Schnore and Robert R. Alford, "Forms of Government and Socio-economic Characteristics of Suburbs," *Administrative Science Quarterly, VIII* (1963), pp. 1-17.

to Dahl's analysis.[4] None of these three was studied in a manner which permits accurate comparisons with the other two (or twenty more which might be named), and hence no generalizations about either of two central points is possible. First, what is (are) the structure(s) of power in American cities? Second, what are the principal independent variables affecting the shape; scope and operation of these putative structures? It may turn out that each city is unique and no useful generalizations can be made using the city as the unit of analysis. Or the city may really be the most useful microcosm of the political system in which all essential processes, structures, and relationships can be found. The professional conclusion probably lies somewhere between. We will not know without systematic comparative study.

One major effort at synthesis of exciting materials about city, principally big city, politics is that of Edward C. Banfield and James Q. Wilson.[5] To a large extent they draw upon the same materials as this essay, and there are many areas of agreement. There are important differences, too, however, both in conclusions and approach. Thus Banfield and Wilson give only passing attention to the historical dimension of urban politics. I propose to examine the question of the structure of power and do so over time. By viewing the city historically a number of critical elements, particularly those which have changed, can be seen more clearly than if a more strictly contemporaneous study were made. My discussion focuses upon the big cities in the United States that experienced major growth prior to World War I. The pattern I shall describe may apply to other communities as well, but my model city in what follows is heterogeneous in ethnic and racial terms, contains considerable industry and a suburban ring, is experiencing core city decay, and is, in short, what those who write about urban problems generally have in mind when they refer to "the city."

Anyone who talks about urban structures of power must take a stand on two related questions: what is meant by power and how does one go about trying to establish its empirical dimensions. By "structure of power" I mean the set of relationships among community roles, durable over time, through which relationships scarce resources are allocated in a community. I am primarily concerned with those allocations which involve decisions by govern-

[4]See the categorization suggested by Peter Rossi, "Power and Community Structure," *Midwest Journal of Political Science*, IV (1960). p. 398.
[5]*City Politics* (Cambridge: Harvard University Press, 1963).

mental agencies. We should recognize, however, the shifting importance over time of public allocations to the total of allocations
made in the community, and remember, too, that public and private
actions are always mixed together, nowhere more than in the
city. I shall not give attention to the allocation of all those resources that might be deemed scarce, but only those that are of
substantial volume or scope. I recognize the difficulty of drawing
clear distinctions between "important" and "unimportant" decis-
sions, but there *is* a difference, and it is recognized by decision-
makers in a city. Thus the structure of power affecting a primary
fight over the nomination for recorder of deeds may bear no relationship to the structure within which the city's urban renewal program
is determined. In such a case it is only the latter that is of much
interest; the decisions involve much more substantial resource
allocations and the structure of power involved is therefore a
more important one.

In short, we shall examine the most crucial structures of policy-
relevant power in the large American city and attempt partly
to identify and partly to postulate a pattern of development that
seems warranted by the histories and present circumstances of
several such cities. In doing so we must necessarily make comparisons
among fragments of data drawn from sources that are widely
diverse in concept and method. The result must obviously fall
short of definitive status, but hoepfully it may at least provide
some stimulus to systematic comparative research in urban data.

II

Two systematic historical studies of urban power structure
are those of New Haven by Dahl and Cibola by Schulze.[6] Both
identify patterns of change that, despite considerable differences
between the communities, are roughly similar. Much of the other
published material on American urban history can be read as
confirming the general pattern.[7]

[6]Robert Schulze, "The Bifurcation of Power in a Satellite City," L. M.
Janowitz, ed., *Community Political Systems* (Gelncoe, Illinois: The Free Press
of Glencoe, Illinois, 1961), pp. 19-81.
[7]The volume of historical work dealing with American cities is immense in
weight but often disappointing when it comes to the questions of greatest
interest to political scientists. McKelvey's work is masterful both as a summary and as an introduction to the literature. *Op. cit., passim.*

Dahl finds that political office in New Haven was dominated first by the "patricians," then by the "entrepreneurs," and finally by the "ex-plebes." Patrician dominance rested upon oligarchic control of all of the major resources from which influence could be fashioned. "[S]ocial status, education, wealth, and political influence were united in the same hands."[8] The entrepreneur's prominence emerged as wealth and social standing were separated, and the new men of business displaced the patricians in controlling economic resources. The entrepreneurs, moreover, were popular as the crabbed patricians were not. But the increasing immigrant labor force led to changing standards of popularity, and by about 1900 "[P]opularity had been split off from both wealth and social standing. Popularity meant votes; votes meant office; office meant influence."[9] The resulting pattern Dahl refers to as one of "dispersed inequalities." Many actors possess politically relevant resources but none possesses enough to dominate a broad range of actions. Particular actors exercise influence over particular policy decisions depending on the resources relevant to that decision, and several types of coalitions may aggregate the influentials concerned with specific problems, but no continuous structure of influence is operative for the broad range of public decision.

Robert Schulze describes a similar historical pattern in Cibola except that Cibola, a much younger community, has no patrician era. Instead it experienced two stages, local capitalism and non-local or absentee capitalism. In the former stage, until 1900, the economic dominants were also the political dominants. They held public office as well as controlling local economic resources and their preeminent social standing reinforced their hegemony. After 1900 Cibola increasingly became an economic satellite and local economic resources came increasingly under the control of national firms. Local officials of these firms did not involve themselves in the active influence structure of the community, much less hold office. Rather, there developed a separate category of influentials, the public leaders, whose influence rested primarily upon such factors as popularity and commitment to the locality. Schulze describes this as a bifurcation of power, but it may not be amiss to suggest that Schulze's data permit the inference that Cibola is more polylithic—influence is widely dispersed and discontinuous —than the bifurcation image implies.

[8]Dahl, *op. cit.*, p. 24.
[9]*Ibid.*, p. 51.

Both Dahl and Schulze give support to the general view that roughly from the end of the Civil War until 1900 American cities were dominated by the merchantry. Where the community had long existed as a substantial population center, notably in the East, the entrepreneurs were likely, as Dahl describes, to have displaced the patricians. Where there hardly had been a city in the ante-bellum years, there were no patricians to displace, and the commercial elite, relatively open to talents and money, but an elite nonetheless, dominated all the major institutions of the community. Political offices were typically held for short terms with each important merchant expected to contribute some time to the marginal activity of public office-holding.

Although the economic elite of the mercantile city dominated political institutions as well, it is unlikely that much additional influence accrued to them as a result. Public authority did relatively little in this stage of urban development. Only gradually were such elemental functions as water supply and sewage disposal, street construction and maintenance, police and fire protection undertaken.[10] In many cases, too, the intitial phases of service were provided by a mixture of public and private effort that mirrored the mixture of public and private position held by influentials. Public improvements were undertaken not only to make life possible in the increasingly crowded and extended city, but also as "booster activities." "Let's put good old — on the map!" was an oft-repeated watchword of civic promotion. As McKelvey notes, chambers of commerce were formed to promote economic development in a number of post Civil War cities,[11] and the promotion of canals, railroads, exhibition halls, and—the classic booster gimmick—the World's Fair, all were part of the merchantry's effort to sell their particular community to the nation. Boosterism, even for the one-shot, short-run promotion, almost invariably involved a complex intermixture of public and private efforts and rested, therefore, on an elite which dominated both public and private office.

The gradual expansion of public services, however, had a significance for the structure of influence that booster gimmicks did not. Water and sewer systems, schools, streets, parks, police and fire were functions that required continuous operation by larger and larger corps of public employees. With the industrial growth

[10]See McKelvey, *op. cit.*, pp. 12-13.
[11]*Ibid.*, p. 43.

of the city, the object for which boosterism strove, more and more
people requiring near-geometric increases in services, came to
the city. Further, the new immigrants came to work in the new
industries. Whereas the mercantile city had been as nearly classless
as the frontier itself, the industrial city was the site of a differentiated class structure; differentiated by income and life chances,
by ethnic origins, by religion, and by political potential.

At the same time the industrial economic giant viewed the
city very differently from the merchant. He was far less dependent
on local sales or real estate values and thus less concerned with
growth itself. His was a contingent investment in the community—gradually in the several communities housing his several branches—and
his civil liability was therefore limited just as the corporate form
limited his legal liability. His participation in the allocation of
community resources, while potentially great, was infrequent
and discontinuous. He was concerned only to protect his relatively
narrowly defined corporate interests, not a generalized pattern
of influence.

The merchantry had been deeply committed to the city in an
economic and emotional way that was missing from the industrial
manager. In the industrial city the modes by which civic obligations
were discharged became more diverse and more specialized. Service
on special boards or committees for libraries or schools or parks
or slum dwellers was increasingly the way that the local notables—
and their wives!—made their community contributions. These
were likely to be structurally separated from the main body of
governmental institutions and something of a preserve for "the
best people" insulated from "politics." In addition, the slowly
growing concern for planning the City Beautiful and reforming
inefficient or corrupt government provided larger and larger amounts
of "program material" for the luncheon clubs and merchants'
association.[12] That occasionally reform campaigns would actually
elect a mayor or effect a change in governmental operation did
not cancel the fact that economic and social influence had been
separated from political influence, and that each now (ca. 1900)
rested on a different social base.

An autonomous political elite was, of course, a function of
expanded governmental activity and a growing working class

[12]The suggestion that civic reform issues provide "program material" and
sometimes little else is developed in Edward Banfield, *Political Influence* (New
York: The Free Press of Glencoe, 1961), pp. 298, ff.

population that altered the numerical balance of the city. As Dahl points out, not only were the political entrepreneurs now more popular than the economic entrepreneurs but the criteria of political popularity changed. Effective representation of the Booster spirit and promotion of industrial growth gave way to effective representation of the needs of the poor for elemental services and the promotion of the political organization itself. The boss and his machine we now recognize to have been functional for the newly industrial city; a growing army of public job-holders was recruited, a vast immigration was socialized and provided means of advancement in the urban society, welfare needs were at least minimally provided for, further extensions of public improvement programs were constructed, albeit expensively, and specific services were rendered to the economic elites as well. Railroad spurs, street car franchises, assessment adjustments, police protection of imported labor and a variety of other benefits could be conferred upon business by governmental agencies, even though the latter were no longer controlled by the businessmen themselves. Although businessmen were often appalled and sometimes intimidated by the "new men" of city politics, they rarely intervened or even protested against the system in any continuous way.

Surely a portion of the reason that the boss remained in power was that although government was far more formidable in this period than formerly, the major decisions allocating resources in the city were still made by private interests. Governmental functions were no doubt of crucial importance to the machine itself and to its followers, but, for the most part, they were of marginal importance to the private sector of the economy. It therefore made relatively little difference whether they were done well or not. This is the obverse of the point that economic notables tended to withdraw from civic involvement after about 1900. Not only did the changing city pretty well force them out of office; it was quite rational for them to tend their private gardens and only enter the political arena on behalf of specific policy questions with an immediate payoff to their specialized economic concerns.

What Schulze describes as the bifurcation of power between economic and political elites was thus a function of a changing industrial and social order in the city supported by the enlarged opportunities for political entrepreneurs in the growth of governmental activity. At the same time, the economic and social notables were fragmented by the split between absentee and local capital, the diffusion of energies in a myriad of specialized civic but largely nonpolitical enterprises, and finally by the exodus from the city's corporate limits of the middle class. The efforts of the Progressive WASPs to reform local government, to cleanse the stables of municipal corruption, were in the main doomed by the inexorable movements of people. The middle class moved to suburbia and put political popularity—the ability to get elected—permanently on a working class basis.

The final seal on the bifurcation was effected by the shift of the voting habits of the urban working class to overwhelming Democracy. From the beginning of the New Deal more and more of the large cities became safely Democratic. The metropolitan middle class maintained its Republican loyalties with respect to the national scene, but in local matters a modus vivendi on a business-like basis with the Democratic leadership—a matter of necessity for those with local interests at stake—was often achieved.

Yet the Democratic partisan hegemony provided a kind of cover by which middle class values could reappear in the public decisions of a working class city. By the end of the 1940's the machines were fading. The disciplined delivery of votes was rarely possible, at least on a city-wide basis, and the professionalization of the city bureaucracy was well along. Political office still went to those who mustered majorities from a predominantly working class city electorate but the circular pattern that characterized the era of "Politics for Profit"—votes gave power, power provided favors, favors provided votes—was increasingly broken. It is significant that a move toward "Good Government"—meaning rational policy making—came from within the political stratum itself in these years in Chicago, St. Louis, Pittsburgh, and New Orleans. This move coincided with a change in the agenda of urban resource allocation, and this change in turn has led to a change in the structure of influence.

III

I propose to designate the contemporary structure of urban power as the "new convergence." It is similar in many ways to what Dahl calls the executive-centered coalition. It is headed, and sometimes led, by the elected chief executive of the city, the mayor. Included in the coalition are two principal active groupings, locally oriented economic interests and the professional workers in technical city-related programs. Both these groupings are sources of initiative for programs that involve major allocations of resources, both public and private. Associated with the coalition, also, are whatever groups constitute the popular vote-base of the mayor's electoral success. Their association is more distant and permissive, however. Their power to direct specific policy choices is severely limited. In the following pages I shall examine each element in the coalition as well as some of the groups in the city that largely lack power. In all cases I am concerned with power that is relevant to key resource allocation decisions.

In the period roughly centered on the turn of the century business leadership was transformed from local to absentee capital, from merchantry to corporate managers. Accompanying this shift in economic organization was a shift in community political commitment and orientations, and this shift, in the direction of reduced interest, coincided with and reinforced the burgeoning autonomous political organization. Now, however, I am saying that business plays an important role in the structure of city affairs. The apparent contradiction points to some complexities in the notion of "business."

First, some kinds of business never experienced the nationalizing effects of industrial reorganization. These often remained intimately associated with politics throughout the era of the bosses. Real estate dealers, building supply firms, insurance agents, and corner confectioneries were always likely to have an iron or two in the political fire. They still do, but these interests are not part of the coalition we are examining. Their interests are small with respect to resource allocations, and they deal in channels that are peripheral to the main body of decisions. Their politics is a kind of eternal process which goes on in many different kinds of worlds without affecting them. Petty business and petty politics are thus hand-maidens but irrelevant to the larger issues of power.

The large international corporation continues to regard the local scene with the same investment calculus described earlier. In general, the branch plant will do only as much about the community as is required to develop and maintain an image of good corporate citizenship, and this is far less than is necessary for power or even concern about community resource allocation.[13] Occasionally, the needs of the firm may require it to intrude into the community

---

[13]See the provocative essay by Norton Long, "The Corporation and the Local Community," in Charles Press, ed., *The Polity* (Chicago: Rand McNally & Co., 1962), pp. 122-136.

political system, but such intrusions would be very much on an *ad hoc* basis. The same is likely to be true of large, nationally-oriented unions.[14] The exception occurs when the union or the firm has a large home office or plant in the city or has grown large from a base in a particular community. Then "good citizenship" may require more than charitable work and involve the company or union leadership in larger urban policy issues.

The most active business firms in the new convergence, however, are those with major investments in the community, which are dependent on the growth of a particular community, and which have come to recognize that all the major issues and decisions of the city affect their interests.[15] Furthermore, they all share a growing concern with that congeries of problems labeled "core city decay." They include the major banks, railroads, department stores, large real estate firms, and metropolitan newspapers. Functionally, the list is remarkably similar from city to city. Also similar is the fact that active concern with community affairs is relatively recent, largely post-World War II, and coincides with the perception of threat to tangible "downtown" economic values. Finally, the reentry of these groups into the active quest for power coincides with the weakening of the party-political dominance of the governmental arena. This permitted the numerically inferior business groups to assert their claims on a more continuous basis than formerly had been the case. In Chicago, where the machine did not weaken so much, the loop businessmen continued to operate a largely *ad hoc* basis.[16] Elsewhere, however, the downtown business interests articulated their concerns more forcefully and organized their community-centered energies more efficiently than ever before. Instead of boosterism, business-centered groups helped to trigger a variety of problem-solving programs such as redevelopment and traffic revision and provided continuing support for efforts at solving other problems such as delinquency and crime. Much of the lay leadership of public campaigns for bonds, for example; much of the stimulus to action itself; and much of the private portion of new investment necessary to redevelopment came from this newly organized group. It is important to recognize,

---

[14]See Banfield and Wilson, *op. cit.,* pp. 277-80.
[15]See *Ibid.,* Ch. 18.
[16]See Banfield, *Political Influence,* pp. 291, ff. Banfield himself emphasizes the tangible conflicts of interest which divide Chicago business interests. Even so, however, one may suspect that without the Daley machine Loop business interests would have developed more commonality of interests.

however, that, although the support and stimulus of downtown business was and is an essential element in the coalition that dominates decisions in the city, downtown business does not constitute a power elite. It does not run the city, or call the shots for its puppets.

The second element in the coalition—one would be tempted to call it the Civic Establishment except that the term may connote more tradition-based power than this coalition possesses—is composed of the technician, the professional, the expert. As Barry Karl has pointed out, the innovative function of the Progressive reform groups has largely been taken over by the professional.[17] The social worker has replaced Jane Addams. The social scientist in a Charles Merriam has replaced the amateur politician/reformer. Police administration, comprehensive budgeting and capital programming, systematic traffic control, land use planning, and renewal and rehabilitation have all become, in one degree or another, the domains of the expert. Technical criteria play a far greater role than before in determining choices, and the specification of alternatives is likewise largely a function of the technician who, often alone, knows what is possible.[18]

Perhaps the policy area most obviously dominated by the expert is that of public education. Teachers and school administrators not only set the agenda for action. They provide most of the arguments and evidence relevant to the choices that can be made and constitute the most active and powerful interests participating in the decision-making process. If non-professionals protest against certain policies—Negroes denouncing *de facto* segregation, for example—the professional educators cite technical educational criteria as a sufficient justification for their decisions and frequently carry the day.

The existence of professional skills relevant to city problems is, of course, a relatively new feature on the urban scene. Even now we are a long way from a technocracy, for the skills fall far short of the problems. Nevertheless, the growth of what broadly

[17]See *Executive Reorganization and Reform in the New Deal* (Cambridge: Harvard University Press, 1963), Ch. 1.
[18]Banfield and Wilson note that the city manager often acquires power by virtue of "his virtual monopoly of technical and other detailed information," *op. cit.,* p. 175. They pay little attention to the possibility that other technicians in the city bureaucracy may acquire power over limited segments of policy in the same manner. Banfield and Wilson do note that in many cities it is the bureaucracy which can initiate and implement change but do not concede increasing significance to this group. See pp. 218-23.

may be called applied social science has added a significant number of new people in new roles to the urban system, and these people help articulate and specify the problems and alternative courses of action for the other interests in the coalition. In this way the technician exercises power over resource allocation that is every bit as real as that of the economic interests or authority-wielders.

Let us turn to the peak of the loose coalition of interests that dominate today's urban scene, the mayor. He presides over the "new convergence," and, if the coalition is to succeed, he must lead it. More than anyone else he determines the direction of urban development; yet his sanctions are few, his base of support insecure. The mayor is both the most visible person in the community and, on questions of public policy, probably the most influential. Yet his is a classic example of the separation of influence and power.[19] Few big-city mayors have significant patronage resources. Even fewer use their appointments to give themselves direct leverage over policy. Although the mayor in a partisan city is necessarily elected through processes that involve the ward organizations, no big-city mayor, not even Daley, can be regarded as the creature of the machine. Rather the mayor is an individual who has 1) sufficient mass appeal and/or organizational support to win election, 2) enough awareness of the complexity of urban problems to rely heavily on a professional staff for advice and counsel, and 3) the ability to negotiate successfully with the economic notables in the city to mobilize both public and private resources in efforts to solve core city economic and social problems.

Successful electioneering in the city requires that the candidate be palatable to a lower income constituency, especially to Negroes. Where there remain vestiges of party organization with vote-delivering capabilities the successful candidate must have some appeal for them, too. An ethnic background or family association that evokes support from the delivery wards is often helpful. At the same time, however, the successful mayoral candidate is likely to appeal

[19]Banfield and Wilson suggest that as the mayor's machine-based power has declined his formal authority has increased, by virtue of reformers' efforts to achieve greater centralization. They recognize, of course, that the increased authority does not compensate for the loss of power. Moreover, in the contemporary city the scope of the perceived problems and needs is often so broad that the strongest political machine could have done little about it from its own resources. Providing investment capital to rebuild downtown or opening employment opportunities for Negroes must be negotiated in the broader community. The mayor is likely to be the chief negotiator and neither formal authority nor political clout is as effective as bargaining skills. *Ibid.*, p. 336, ff.

to that portion of the urban electorate which historically has been reformist or mugwumpish in orientation.[20] He personifies good government by his espousal of professionalism in local administration. Frequently his personal style, despite his name or political forbears, is thoroughly white-collar and middle class. He is relatively articulate on local television, and his campaigns are likely to stress his competence at communal problem-solving rather than the particular group benefits that may accrue following his election. Nor is this mere campaign talk. His administration concentrates on solving or alleviating particular problems rather than building memorials or dramatizing the city's commercial prospects. Again, this posture requires collaboration with those possessing the relevant resources, the experts and the businessmen.

Obviously, there are variations in the way the mayoral role is played. From city to city and mayor to mayor many differences may appear. The main lines of demarcation may be twofold, however. Some mayors, possessing the gifts of self-dramatization, may more fully personify the programs of the city than others. This has little effect on the content of the decisions but may have consequences in terms of support. Mayors may also differ in the degree to which they actively seek out problems and solutions. Banfield describes Daley waiting for things to come to a head; other mayors more actively seek either to forestall the problem entirely or to structure the whole process through which the issue develops. The latter distinction may be related to the structure of the city; the larger and more diverse the city, the less effectively can the mayor actively shape the problem-solving process.

Of what is mayoral influence composed? Much of it is contained in the office itself. Of all the roles in the community, none is so well situated with respect to the flow of information concerning the city's problems. This alone gives the occupant of the office a great advantage over other influentials. He knows more about more things than anyone else. Although his patronage power may be relatively slight, his budgetary authority is typically substantial. Insofar as he, by himself or in a board or commission, presents the budget to the council, he is determining much of the agenda for the discussion of public affairs, and no one else in the city can compete with him. Third, his ability to co-opt persons

---

[20]Lorin Peterson greatly overstates the case for connecting contemporary urban influentials with the mugwump tradition, but there is something in his argument. See *The Day of the Mugwump* (New York: Random House 1961).

into *ad hoc* committees is unmatched in the city. As the only official with formal authority to speak for the entire city, he can confer legitimacy on co-opted leaders as no one else can. Thus, if he chooses to, a shrewd mayor may have a good deal to say about who shall be regarded as leaders and who shall not. Negotiations on civil rights issues in a number of cities illustrate the point well. Finally, as noted earlier, the mayor is, or soon becomes, far better known in the community than anyone else, and is far better able to command and structure public attention.[21]

A considerable factor in the mayor's ability to structure public debate is his superior access to and influence over the press. City hall reporters not only cover his office closely but their view of city problems is very largely gained through their daily contacts with the official city fathers. The latter, in turn, are cordial and by being helpful can be reasonably assured that most of the news stories out of city hall will reflect mayoral interpretation. The newspapers as major businesses with their economic future tied to the local community and its elites are likely to favor editorially a mayor whose style embraces their interests. Thus, even though the editors may differ with some specific recommendation of the mayor, they give him general support, while through them the mayor communicates his conceptions of city problems and program. One result, of course, is to make it difficult for others to challenge successfully the incumbent mayor for re-election.[22] Thus despite the unstable character of the coalition's base—predominantly low income voters and downtown businessmen—the mayor, once elected, may serve a good many terms. No outsider can find a sufficiently sharp wedge of controversy to drive between the disparate elements or sufficient visibility to exploit whatever gaps develop.

Nevertheless, the mayor is influential only relative to other groups in the city. He is not powerful relative to the problems he tries to solve. The mayor cannot determine by fiat or, apparently,

[21]Scott Greer found that Mayor Tucker was the only person in the St. Louis community, city or suburbs, with any substantial visibility with respect to community-wide issues. *Metropolitics* (New York: John Wiley & Sons, 1963). pp. 106-7.

[22]Banfield and Wilson note that the city hall reporter "is likely to be in a symbiotic relationship with the politicians and bureaucrats whose activities he reports." *op., cit.,* p. 316. They do not conclude, however, that this relationship strengthens the elected leadership. Indeed, they imply the opposite. See, *e.g.* p. 325. This difference in judgment calls for more systematic empirical analysis than is presently available.

any other way that the economic resources of the city shall increase, that crime and poverty shall decline, that traffic shall move efficiently. He only has rather more directly to say about how the problems shall be approached than anyone else.

This discussion omits those cities which have adopted the council-manager form of government. In Kansas City or Cincinnati, for example, the aggregative and legitimating functions are less likely to be performed by the mayor who is seldom more than the ceremonial head of the city. The manager can rarely perform these functions either, since they are largely incompatible with his professional role. The result may be that the functions are not performed at all. On the other hand, the manager does possess some of the elements of leadership, especially information. As Banfield and Wilson note, the manager "sits at the center of things, where all communication lines converge. In the nature of the case, then, the councilmen must depend on him for their information. Whether he likes it or not, this gives him a large measure of control over them."[23]

IV

The "new convergence" we have described actively seeks out solutions to certain problems it regards as critical to the city's growth. This activist posture may be viewed as somewhat at variance with the approaches to decision-making described by Dahl and by Banfield. Dahl suggests that in New Haven the coalition led by Mayor Lee has actively sought to resolve certain major issues with Lee serving as the principal negotiator among the contending forces. But, says Dahl, Lee selected issues with a view towards their effect upon his chances for re-election. Permanently conditioning the mayor's strategy was the fact that "the mayor and his political opponents were constantly engaged in a battle for votes at the next election, which was always just around the corner."[24] So far as most large cities are concerned, this may greatly overstate the impact of the necessity for re-election on the specific choices made by the mayor and his allies. We shall try to suggest both the role of the electorate and some of the more immediate restraints upon mayoral choice-making in a moment.

[23]*Ibid.,* p. 175. Banfield and Wilson, however, do not make this point concerning the position of the mayor in non-manager cities.
[24]*Political Influence,* p. 214.

Banfield's analysis of Chicago leads to the conclusion that issues are raised primarily by large formal organizations, some of which are governmental and some of which are not.[25] As the maintenance or enhancement needs of the organization require governmental decisions they enter the political arena and usually seek the support of Mayor Daley. Daley himself, however, operates in primarily a reflexive fashion. Although he desires to "do big things," he must move slowly and cautiously, fearful of generating further controversies, and aware that the ponderous and intricate structure of power he heads can be disrupted and his influence capital used up if he moves too soon or too often. But Banfield selects issues that illustrate this argument. His cases fall far short of representing the range of major resource allocation decisions for Chicago. It may still be true, therefore, that Daley initiates or actively participates in the process involved in making other decisions. Certainly it seems that other big-city mayors do.[26]

I focused originally on the processes of allocating scarce resources. These processes may sometimes involve bitter conflict among rival interests. They may sometimes be solved, however, in a highly consensual way. Particularly is this likely to be the case when the technical experts play a large role in shaping the decision. Much of the time such major areas of public policy as expressway planning, zoning, and budget-making are determined in ways that evoke little complaint or dispute. The fact that no one in the city effectively objects to the decision makes the decision no less important in terms of resource allocation.

A closely related aspect of urban decision-making is that a great many decisions are made in a fashion that may best be described as habitual. The pressures on the time and attention of decision-makers are such that many decisions must continue to be made (or avoided) as they have been in the past. No continuing calculation can be made of the costs and benefits for each area of possible choice. Much is done routinely. Much is left undone in the same way. Control of the routine is largely in the hands of the technicians with the mayor in the best position to alter it at the margins.

[25]Ibid., p. 263. ff.

[26]In addition to Dahl's discussion of Mayor Lee's active role, one may cite as particularly pertinent the discussions of Philadelphia, Detroit, Nashville and Seattle reported in the appropriate volumes of Edward Banfield, ed., *City Politics Reports* (Cambridge: Joint Center for Urban Studies, mimeo). My own research in St. Louis, the initial foundation for much of the argument in this essay, certainly leads to this conclusion.

Some issues are forced "from the outside," of course. Things which city leaders would prefer not to have to deal with may be pressed in the fashion Banfield describes. Race relations issues generally come under this category. Almost every large city mayor has been compelled to take action, not because he or his coalition particularly wanted to, but because they were forced to by external pressure.

The recent demands of militant Negro groups have often been concentrated on city hall, however, even when the substance of the demands dealt with jobs in private employment. Negro leaders have correctly identified the mayor as the appropriate figure to convene local elites in order to negotiate agreements that will open job opportunities to Negroes. Militant Negroes have often greatly overestimated the power of the mayor to effect a satisfactory solution, however. For while he is in a stronger position than any other person or group or functioning organization, his resources and those of his allies may fall far short of the requirements.

Pressure from the constituency would not be the usual way for policy to be initiated, however. The bulk of the city's working agenda is made up of proposals drawn up by the city's own technicians to meet problems identified by them or their allies in the problem-oriented sectors of the community. The need for new revenue sources, for example, is perceived by the mayor and his staff long before public pressure is exerted, and it is the mayoral coalition which seeks a viable solution to the problem.

Not all mayors, not all corps of technicians, and not all downtown business groups are equal in ability to perceive problems, devise solutions, or negotiate settlements. One of the significant variables that distinguishes one city's political system from another is the energy and imagination of its newly convergent elites. In some cities solutions may be found that escape the leaders of another. It is probably true, however, that these differences have been narrowed somewhat by the collaboration among urban elites throughout the nation. The American Municipal Association and the U.S. Conference of Mayors provide organized communication networks that link the political executives. So does HHFA in its field. So do the various associations of urban technicians in their respective specialties. The metropolitan press facilitates a certain amount of interchange with respect to both problems and solutions in urban areas. Thus there has developed some degree of consensus as to what should be done and some uniformity in the structure of power by which action may be accomplished.

Cities vary with respect not only to energy and skill of leadership but in tangible resources, public and private that may be mobilized for reallocation. In Pittsburgh, for example, there was probably no available substitute for the Mellon cash. In St. Louis the scarcity or stodginess or both of local private capital has made the redevelopment task more difficult. These are variables involved in the power structure of a community. That there are also variations in the range and severity of the problems cities face is obvious and complicates further the task of comparative analysis.

V

I have suggested that a large portion of the content of urban public policy is provided directly by one or more of the three main elements of the governing coalition: the mayor, the technical experts, and the downtown business community. They identify the problems, they articulate the alternative actions that might be taken, and they themselves take most of the relevant actions. This structure of decision-making provides no immediate role for the community-at-large, the voters; and, although Dahl may overstate the significance of their role in limiting New Haven's executive-centered coalition, they do play a role in resource allocations, and so do the organized groups that represent segments of the electorate that are outside the dominant coalition.

Dahl's attribution of "weight" to the electorate seems to be based on the relatively intense partisan competition in New Haven, and it may be reinforced by the need to run every two years. But in many cities the direct competition for office is neither so sharp nor so frequent. The tenure in office of prominent mayors such as Tucker, Daley, or Wagner suggests that survival in office may not always require the close attention to voter desires that Dahl suggests. Particularly is this likely in a city where elections are partisan, for the safety of the Democratic ticket is not often in question in many of these cities. The primary may occasionally present peril to the incumbent, and in both partisan and non-partisan cities incumbents sometimes lose. But there is little evidence to show that mayors, or other elected executives for that matter, have any reliable way of perceiving voter needs very accurately or consciously building support for himself among them. The new mayor may say, with Richard Daley, that "good government is good politics," in part because he doesn't have the option to engage in any other kind.

Nevertheless, generalized constituency sentiment remains a factor that affects policy-making, albeit in a secondary, boundary-setting way. It works primarily in three ways. First, the technician as social scientist often takes into account the interest and needs of the public he hopes to serve when making his plans and recommendations. If he proposes an enlarged staff of case workers for the Welfare Department, he does so partly because in some sense he expects the public to benefit. It is rarely, however, because any public demand for the larger staff is expressed. Rather, the technician believed the proposal would be "good" for the constituents. Secondly, the electorate must make certain broad choices directly. Bond issues and tax rates must often be voted upon; other types of referenda must be approved; key policy-making officials must be elected. Very often this involves "selling the public" on the desirability of the proposal. They have not demanded it. They often have no strong predispositions one way or another except perhaps for a class-related bias on public expenditures in general. But this approval is required, and in anticipation of the limits of tolerance the key decision-makers must tailor their proposals. This is influence, of course, but of a general and largely negative kind. Thirdly, there is the active demand stemming directly from the constituents to which policy-makers respond, but which response would not have been made in the absence of the public demand. Some of these demands go counter to the policies espoused by the coalition; spot zoning, for example, or construction unions' demands on the building code. In some instances the coalition may have the power to block the demands; in other cases, not. Some demands, however, are more difficult to deal with because, if they arise, they cannot be blocked by the exercise of power, but at the same time they are so controversial that almost any solution is likely to damage the overall position of the leaders. As we have noted, many of the issues of race relations are in this category. The city fathers have not agitated these issues, but once raised they must be met.

As we assign "the public" to a largely secondary role, we must also relegate those officials most closely associated with immediate constituency relationships to a similarly secondary position. Councilmen or aldermen, ward leaders, and other local party leaders are likely to play only supportive or obstructive roles in the community's decision-making process. The demands for action do not come from or through them, they are not privy to the councils either of the notables or the experts. They may well play out their traditional roles of precinct or ward politicians, but, unlike the machine leader of yore, these roles are separated quite completely from those of policy-making. Even in Chicago, where the mayor's position in part depends on his vote-getting strength through the party organization, very little participation in policy-making filters down to the ward leaders. Similarly, William Green's rise to power in the party organization in Philadelphia had little effect on the content of public policy. It is essential to see that the difference between the policy-making leadership and the "politicians" is more than rhetorical. It carries a substantial impact on the content of policy.[27]

Even though neither the party professionals nor the electorate generally are active participants in the process of resource allocation, is not the top political leadership, specifically the mayor, constrained by his desire for re-election? In part, of course, the answer is yes. In partisan cities the mayor must be nominated and elected on the party ticket, and, particularly in the primary, this may involve getting party organization support. In a nonpartisan community too, the mayor must get enough votes to win. It does not follow, however, that there is much connection between what is needed to gain votes and the specific decisions made once in office. Dahl emphasizes the vote-getting popularity of Richard Lee's program in New Haven, especially of urban renewal. Yet that popularity was not really evident in advance of the decisions and was largely dissipated within a very few years. Doubtless Mayor Collins has increased his popularity in Boston by rationalizing and reducing the fiscal burden, but, if Levin is at all correct, his election was not a mandate for *any* particular decisions he has made.[28] The same, I think, could be argued for Dilworth, Tucker, and others of the "new mayors." Certainly the limits of public understanding and acceptance constitute restraints upon the decision-making system, but these are broad restraints, rarely specific in directing choices, and operating

---

[27]For an illustration, see Robert H. Salisbury, "St. Louis: Relationships among Interests, Parties and Governmental Structure," *Western Political Quarterly*, XIII (1960), pp. 498-507.

[28]See *The Alienated Voter* (New York: Holt, Rinehart and Winston, 1960).

largely as almost subconscious limits to the kinds of choices that may be made.[29]

VI

It may not be amiss to conclude this discussion by juxtaposing three quite different strands of thought concerning the urban scene. On the one hand, Dahl and his associates have generally denied the existence of a single structure of power in the city. We have argued, not contradicting Dahl but changing the emphasis, that on a substantial set of key issues such a structure may be discerned. Hunter *et al,* have stressed on essentially monolithic structure heavily weighted in behalf of the economic elites. We have stressed the central role of elected political leadership. Finally, such writers as Lewis Mumford and Jane Jacobs, less interested in the problems of power, have doubted the capacity of the urban community to serve man's essential needs at all. In a sense, we are suggesting that each may be partly correct, partly wrong. The coalition of interests headed by the mayor may indeed lack the resources, public and private, separately or combined, to solve the communal problems now dominating the civic agenda. This is the irony that lies behind the convergence of power elements in the modern city. Where once there seemed to be ample resources to keep what were regarded as the major problems of urban life within quite tolerable limits, now, with far more self-conscious collaboration of governmental and private economic power than ever before, and with those structures of power themselves larger and more extensive than ever, the capacity to cope with the recognized problems of the environment seems almost pathetically inadequate. Partly, this may be because the problems have changed in magnitude, and, partly, that we perceive their magnitude in more sophisticated fashion. In any case, it makes the notion of an elite with ample power to deal with the urban community, if ever it chooses to,

[29]Banfield and Wilson also discuss a shift in the contemporary city, at least in political style, from working class to middle class. They conclude that the new style politician, reflecting middle class values in a working class city, will be compelled to offer broad inducements to the electorate in the form of major civic accomplishments if he wishes reelection. *Op., cit.,* p. 329 ff. This argument, like Dahl's, seems to me to assume that the urban electorate "shops" more actively than I think it does. It also assumes that political leaders in the urban community are more acutely conscious of their reelection problems than I think they are.

seem a romance, a utopian dream. Like other municipal utopias—
Progressive-era reform or today's metropolitan reorganization—it
may be yearned for but largely unrealized.

4

POLITICS AND THE SCOPE OF
GOVERNMENT IN THE COMMUNITY:
conceptual considerations *

ROBERT E. AGGER, DANIEL GOLDRICH, and
BERT E. SWANSON

A political theorist must be concerned with government. Whether he is interested in understanding a whole political system or a specific political process, the basic reference point in his theory-building is a functional-institutional conception. He studies the causes and consequences of the functions of government in people's lives whether he believes that government is best studied in a formalistic, legal orientation, or in a view of man and his world that focuses on the informal and the customary. Politics, in its broadest sense, is that aspect of life in which certain people act to maintain or to shift the patterns of action of government officials. The patterns of politics constitute the political system. The political system is distinct from the social, economic, or religious systems of human groups, at least analytically.[1]

*Reprinted from *The Rulers and the Ruled* (New York, 1964). pp. 1-36. By permission of John Wiley & Sons, Inc., Publishers.
[1]The words "polity" and "political system" are used interchangeably in this book. *Polity* refers to a multitude of dimensions that characterize political relations of people in a community and to people viewed as members of a political community. The term *political system* suggests the interrelatedness and interactional character of at least some of these dimensions. Probably the modern classic in the conception, mapping, and discussion of the domain of political analysts is Harold D. Lasswell and Abraham Kaplan, *Power and Society: A Framework for Political Inquiry* (New Haven: Yale University Press, 1950). See also David Truman, "The Impact on Political Science of the Revolution in the Behavioral Sciences," *Research Frontiers in Politics and Government* (Washington: The Brookings Institution, 1955), pp. 202-231; David Easton, *The Political System* (New York: Alfred A. Knopf, 1953); and William C. Mitchell, *The American Polity* (New York: Free Press of Glencoe, 1962).

A community is a set of people living in a spatially bounded area that may or may not coincide with a legally bounded jurisdiction of government. Every community has a government. The agencies of that government may be part of the national government, as in unitary, centralized nation-states, or they may constitute municipalities and counties created by state governments, as in federal systems. In either case the community's government can be distinguished from other non-governmental agencies and institutions in the community. Modern local governments are open systems; they are affected by what takes place in other systems within the community, by what takes place in other communities, by what takes place in the national and state systems of which they are a part, and by what takes place in foreign countries. However, it is useful to think of them as having functions of their own that affect and are affected by citizens in their own communities.

Local government, as does all government, produces and distributes goods and services. It regulates the production, distribution, and consumption patterns of other institutions in the community. Within limits specified by its parent government, it possesses the ultimate sanction of all minimally effective governments—a monopoly on the right to use physical force to deprive those within its jurisdiction who violate the government's rules and regulations of their life, liberty or property. Government in four United States cities concerns us here.

This study is primarily concerned with how the people decide to shift or maintain the scope—the ways of functioning—of local government in respect to the economic, social, and welfare systems of communities. It is also meant to provide an understanding of political decisions concerning the organization of government itself: the structure of power and the type of regime, and how the rulers relate to each other and to the ruled in making decisions. The relations are of concern both at a moment in time and over a period of time. However, the community's political system includes more than political decisions, its power structure, and its regime.

Political history may be viewed as the continuous development of and transformation in the roles and functions of government in man's attempt to control his environment. The roles and functions of government change as changes occur in conditions of life, in the patterns of making a livelihood, living with other people, and sharing in the amenities of civilization. Human society is a set of analytically distinct yet overlapping activities and institutions. Government has authoritative supremacy, a monopoly of legitimate force. Because of this it stands at the pinnacle of economic, social, and other activities and institutions of society. How government operates in relation to these other human activities varies from era to era, from polity to polity, and, over a period of time, within polities. The state of technology, the nongovernmental organization of the processes of production, distribution, and consumption of goods and services, social status, knowledge, and the political doctrines to which people subscribe vary also. Whether and how government overlaps, controls, dominates, or is subordinate to other institutions of society, and also the conditions under which it does so, should not be decided by formal definitions. This should be investigated by comparative studies of politics such as the present volume.

At both the national and local levels government may be analyzed in terms of its effect upon the economy, social or intergroup relations, and the welfare of its citizens. The history of politics might be viewed as a dynamic movement between opposite poles: an active, interventionist government and a passive, laissez-faire government. For example, the New and Fair Deals expanded the scope of the national government; the Eisenhower administration contracted it; and the direction of the New Frontier is as yet uncertain. To understand these shifts the analyst ordinarily concerns himself with such questions as who controls government, who has most political influence with government officials, and how can the patterns of political power and their changes in the context of national and world economic and military policy conditions be explained.[2] The dynamics of local politics may be investigated similarly.

Of particular interest will be the ebb and flow of political conflict in four communities. Political conflict is sometimes thought to be brought about by aberrant behavior, a symptom that politics is unhealthy. Another view is that political conflcit is healthy and inevitable, and produces creative politics. Whichever view one takes, this analysis of the dynamics of political conflict in

[2]See Daniel Lerner and H. D. Lasswell, *The Policy Sciences* (Stanford: Stanford University Press, 1951).

the four communities will shed light on the nature of politics in the twentieth-century United States.[3]

A cursory study of political history suggests that political conflict is generally most apparent when demands are made for substantial expansion or contraction of the net scope of national or local government. Even when there are no demands for radical shifts in the net scope of government, conflicts may arise over the way government functions within a given domain and to whom it should respond. Although political power for power's sake may be a private motive, these desires are ordinarily presented as being for the improvement of public finance, social justice, or social welfare. Regardless of the way appeals for a redistribution of political power are phrased and of the motives of their makers, they are, in fact, appeals or demands for some sort of shift in the scope of government.

When political issues arise in a polity, the workings of politics become observable. Political conflict, however, may be relatively covert and not apparent to most people. The conflict may be potential rather than actual. Political consensus, agreement that the scope of the local government is appropriate or that a particular trend is desirable, may exist. This consensus may exist for a few interested people while many remain indifferent, or it may extend over a large proportion of the people in the polity. The conditions under which human needs give rise to conflicting political issues are of central interest in our analysis of community politics.

In all four communities conscious and purposeful decision-making regarding the scope of government was observed. Complete political consensus for extended periods of time was absent, but the communities differed in the extent to which there was open political conflict. A fundamental reason for the lack of complete consensus was the diversity of views about utopia in all four communities. Individuals' images of the good community and the good regime, of the proper power structure and the proper role of local government in community affairs, varied. The images of some were determined by immediate needs or problems needing amelioration or solution; others saw the proper scope of government as

[3]See Ralf Dahrendorf, *Class and Class Conflict in Industrial Societies* (Stanford: Stanford University Press, 1955). For a critical review of municipal government textbooks, see Lawrence J. R. Herson, "The Lost World of Municipal Government," *The American Political Science Review,* LI (June 1957), pp. 330-346.

being a long-range means of achieving the good life in the ideal community. Political ideoloy was found, somewhat unexpectedly, to be of major importance in the politics of all four communities.

Students of American politics have interpreted the importance of political ideology at the national level in various ways. Some have argued that ideological divisions have come to an end; others have said that these divisions have never been of much consequence in shaping political behavior in the United States. A minority of analysts have seen political ideology as an important factor not only in international politics but also in national and state politics. That political ideology has alwyas had or still does have important effects on American community politics is a proposition that is held by even fewer political analysts.[4]

Political ideology is viewed here as, in brief, a constellation of beliefs and preferences about the nature of the constituent elements in social or community life: Who should rule in this polity? What should the relationship of the government to private institutions be? Where is or should a person be located in the socio-economic-cultural orders of the society and polity? This conception of political ideology, which is discussed more fully later in this chapter, proved useful in understanding the workings of the political systems of the four research communities.

During periods of social, economic, and intellectual change, diverse political interests and divergent ideologies are likely to emerge from what was a more homogeneous set of values. All four communities have experienced currents of change in recent years, particularly since the Second World War. The forces of urbanization and industrialization and the currents and crosscurrents that shaped national politics in the first half of the twentieth century have affected the four communities and the two regions, the West and the South, in which they are located.[5]

[4]Among the important exceptions are: Herbert McCloskey, Paul J. Hoffman, and Rosemary O'Hara, "Issue Conflict and Consensus Among Party Leaders and Followers," *The American Political Science Review,* Vol. LIV, No. 2 (June 1960), pp. 406-427; Robert C. Stone, "Power and Values in Trans-community Relationships," *Current Trends in Comparative Community Studies* ed. by Bert E. Swanson, Public Monograph Series, No. 1 (Kansas City, Mo.: Community Studies, Inc., 1962), pp. 69-80).

[5]See Delbert Miller and William Form, *Industry, Labor and Community* (New York: Harper & Bros., 1960), Ch. XIV. For an analysis of the situation of a rural community in the context of these modern currents, see Arthur J. Vidich and Joseph Bensman, *Small Town in Mass Society* (Garden City, New York: Anchor Books, Doubleday & Co., Inc., 1958).

The political demands and decisions in the four cities were thus shaped by the larger national and international environment. The general conditions of life throughout the United States at the time of this study resulted in similarities in the potential for political conflict in the four communities. Regional and other special conditions including the particular historical development of the individual communities, also affected the potential issues. All these conditions that shaped political decision-making can be analyzed in relation to the perspectives and behavior of people in local politics. Thus this analysis is concerned with understanding the conditions—particularly the political conditions—under which potential conflict became actual conflict. It is concerned also with how the variations in the structure and functioning of the four political systems affected the outcomes of political decision-making, whether these outcomes were conflictive or not.

The scope of local government may be considered to affect human values. These values can be grouped under four categories that have psychological as well as social significance. The four categories refer to the institutionalized ways of organizing the production, distribution, and consumption of (1) wealth; (2) civic amenities; (3) social status, respect, affection, or prestige; and (4) governmental rights and obligations of citizenship.

Economic institutions in American communities involve those relationships primarily concerned with the production, distribution, and consumption of goods and services. Social institutions, such as the family, the friendship group, and the voluntary "social" association, more or less specialize in such areas as social status, respect, affection, or prestige. Institutional processes devoted to civic amenities and livability include housekeeping services, so-called public works and services, and preserving public order; planning and guiding development of the uses of land and buildings, including design and aesthetics; recreation, particularly out-of-doors; and health facilities, for example, chlorination and fluoridation of the water supply, and hospitalization. This category of "civic improvement" is a mixture of both public and private goods and services; whereas the areas of economic and social institutions tend to be generally thought of in America as private, even though government itself performs important economic and social functions.[6]

---

[6]For a fairly comprehensive theoretical analysis of five "major systems" in terms of which a community might be analyzed, see Irwin T. Sanders, *The Community* (New York: The Ronald Press Company, 1958).

The patterned sets of relationships that constitute the rights and obligations of citizenship are within the institution of government itself. For example, the jurisdiction and boundaries of local government determine who has the right to vote in local elections. Certain groups of citizens, such as Negroes, lower class people of any color, or union officials, may be ineligible, in fact if not in theory, to serve as elected or appointed officials. Citizens serving in government have rights and obligations relative to each other and to citizens at large.

The pattern of these relationships constitutes the organization of the particular institutional area. Local government has direct or indirect effects on other types of institutions at all times. Thus, demands or decisional processes involving shifts in the way government functions in reference to these relationships are classified into four categories: (1) Economic Reorganization, (2) Social Reorganization. (3) Civic Improvement Reorganization, and (4) Governmental Reorganization.

These categories are convenient, heuristic devices used for analytic purposes. Consequently, classifying a political decisional process under these frequently nondiscrete categories is not a simple matter. People have many values; they pursue social, economic, and civic livability and citizenship values simultaneously. Thus, the sentiments of those most active in promoting a shift in the functioning of local government are at the focus of attention. Even so, arbitrary classifications are sometimes necessary. For example, a decisional question about annexation of a fringe area may involve other considerations than governmental reorganization. Such a decision might effect levels of services and civic improvments, as well as social and economic relations between urban and rural citizens. A demand for school desegregation may be more a demand for social dignity or respect than for knowledge or income; but it may be both.

THE SCOPE OF GOVERNMENT: THE CORE OF POLITICS

It is useful at this point to present in summary form an analogue model of the political process on which the foregoing considerations have been based. This model will be elaborated on throughout the book. A government may be viewed at a moment in time as being more or less involved in people's lives. We may picture two opposite ideal states: one where there is no governmental functioning and one where governmental functioning is ever-present or total. In the one case private institutions meet all citizen needs; in the other a total—totalitarian—government is the sole value-producing, distributing, and consuming institution. The first would best characterize a pre-political society or community; the latter a postpolitical one. Both societies or communities would actually be apolitical. In order to evaluate the analysis that follows, it is essential to understand the rationale for the seeming paradox that these two opposites represent a single condition: the absence of politics.

As we have said, political history may be viewed as a series of large or small movements of government along a continuum of expansion and contraction. Governments may move in one or the other direction or they may alternate, making little net progress in either direction. The extremes of this continuum are situations in which (1) there is no government activity and consequently no governmental intervention in the other institutions of organized life, and (2) government is total. In the second case, government is so pervasive in the organized life of the community that its activities cannot be distinguished from nongovernmental activities. At either extreme, then, it would presumably be impossible, theoretically or empirically, to characterize a functionally distinct government.

There are thus two ways to attain such an apolitical condition. One is to reduce the functions of government; the other is to extend them. The former alternative is preferred by some people who are called reactionaries: they want to return to a previous era or to a state of nature where government is minimal.[7] Most "romantic" philosophical anarchists consider this the preferable path to a society without government. Point A in Figure 1 represents this condition as a result of the contraction of the scope of local government.

If life in "nature" is not considered brutish, nasty, and short, if it is considered idyllic instead, the society is pictured as being cohesive and organic, without conflicting social divisions. Philosophical reactionaries may advocate doing away with social antagonisms by returning to the imagined social harmony of earlier epochs.

Other philosophical anarchists prefer the second path: the extension of the scope of government to the point where its functioning

[7]A modern reactionary in this sense is Friedrich A. Hayek; see *The Road to Serfdom* (Chicago: University of Chicago Press, 1944).

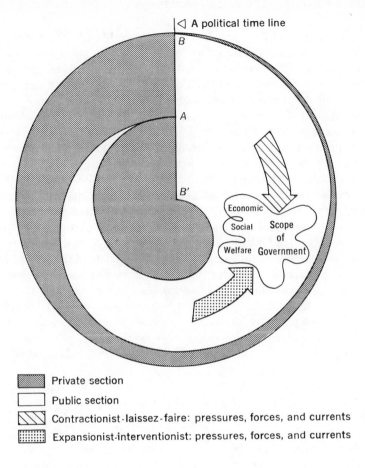

◁ A political time line

B

A

B′

Economic

Social   Scope
of
Welfare   Government

Private section
Public section
Contractionist-laissez-faire: pressures, forces, and currents
Expansionist-interventionist: pressures, forces, and currents

*FIGURE 1 Expansion-contraction continuum of the local scope
of government*

cannot be distinguished from "private" sectors of organized life.
Points B—B′ in Figure 1 represent the condition at the end
of this path. Marx advocated a political utopia without government,
to be achieved through a purposeful, planned extension of government's scope. He believed that the state or government with its
monopoly of force would "wither away" when the dictatorship
of the proletariat was established, rather than at some distant
time after the revolution. Some Marxists, particularly Engels,
have envisaged the withering away of government as an historical
stage that begins after the dictatorship destroys economically based
classes which are the reason government exists. Khrushchev blames

69

internal and external capitalist conspiracies for the failure of the Soviet government to begin to wither away. A more paradoxical but intellectually consistent view of Marxist thinking, in some ways more consistent than Engels', would propose that the increasing scope of government is an integral part of the withering-away process, and, is in being as soon as, if not before, the revolution.

At some undefined point in time, a distinctive or distinguishable government presumably could disappear if it had become inextricably mingled with the day-to-day living patterns of people.

The Marxist philosophical school sees man as historically locked in social conflict. Social antagonisms are expected to increase as history unfolds; it is only after a period of intensive economic, social, and political conflict among classes that the class struggle will end once and for all. The job of preparing for utopian social harmony can then be undertaken by the government of the proletariat. Engels has qualified Marx's view of the beginnings of organized life as being a condition of class struggle: he saw "primaeval communities" to be socially cohesive, cooperative, and harmonious.[8] The suggested model would be closer to Engels' than to Marx's view in that it indicates a return to a hypothetical earlier *agovernmental* condition by the juxtaposition or interpenetration of Points *A* and *B—B'* of Figure 1.

In order to understand national and international political movements in the nineteenth and twentieth centuries, this belief in the possibility of a withering-away of government by expanding or contracting its net scope is of critical importance. Whether either alternative can be realized is irrelevant for the student of politics. But the existence of these as conceptual possibilities shapes the model of politics for the analyst of community, national, and international politics. Although it would be virtually impossible to reach either extreme, pressures for or actual movements in one direction or the other are possible; these pressures constitute part of the basic forces of politics, local or otherwise, whether or not so intended.

The analogue model of politics may be pictured in the following way. Local government, or any government, is considered to be located in a public space. The boundaries of this public space

[8]Engles refers to the "natural simplicity," of such communities; he calls them "wonderful," "natural and spontaneous," and says they produce "splendid men and women." Frederick Engels, *The Origin of the Family, Private Property and the State* (Chicago: Charles H. Kerr & Co., Co-operative, 1902), pp. 117-119.

(curves *A—B* and *A—B'* on Figure 1 are represented by the extent to which government can actively function in the day-to-day lives of people. The activities of people may be viewed as a community space (the innermost and outermost circles). The private space is represented by the shaded portion of the total community space. In the public space are the currents, forces, or pressures directed toward moving government in the direction of expansion and intervention or that of contraction and laissez-faire, an increase or decrease in the scope of government. Movement in the former direction may result in a greater overlapping of the community space by the public space; movement in the latter direction may result in a relative decrease in the proportion of public community space. This ratio of public to private space is what we mean by the words "net scope" of government.

The mixed public and private character of activities in which purposeful government regulation is a manifest factor makes any set of curves for such a model of the real world difficult to construct. Further conceptualization and research are needed to make such models more useful and to establish the character of general and particular social-psychological distinctions between governmental and private institutions, as well as the conditions under which such conceptions undergo various kinds of reorganization. It may or may not be that, in social-psychological terms, as government extends its programs into formerly nongovernmental areas and apparently moves towards points *B—B'* people extend their activities and, hence, community space, so that the ratio of public to private space remains relatively constant.

The action units in this model are people; it is the demands of people that constitute the pressures for a shift in government's scope. It is through the actions of government officials that shifts in local government's scope finally occur. A demand that government act in a particular way may be made by any unit or group of units— any private citizen or government official—in the political system.

Every demand that government act in one way rather than another, or that it function in some way different from the way it has in the past, is a pressure for a shift in government's scope. For example, people may demand a higher level of welfare services. This constitutes a pressure on government to expand. If such demands are made at a time when the level of government services has been declining, it is, nevertheless, a demand for a move back toward the expansionist pole. Suppose a person suggests that his street be paved and the community paves it instead of someone else's. This is not an increase in the net scope of government; the total street paving resources of government are held constant. But for the man whose street is paved, there has seemed to be an increase in government's scope. The scope actually has been balanced by a decrease for those others whose streets were not paved. The petitioner was, in effect, demanding an increased scope of government for himself, but the decisional outcome balanced this demand by reducing someone else's scope of government. Thus, the total or net scope of local government may remain the same, as a result of two, sometimes simultaneous, movements. Such decisional outcomes are regarded as changes in the scope of government wherein there is an *internal* although no *net* shift in scope.

Suppose a question arose as to whether local government ought to build a civic center. Those urging that this be done would be demanding an increased scope of government, whether it was a matter of replacing an existing facility that was in poor condition or in a poor location, or one of extending government's recreational functions. If the most appropriate location became a decisional question, the proponents of one or another site would be demanding that government increase its scope to satisfy *their* needs. In effect they are saying that government will be serving them more fully by providing a convenient facility that will enable them to consume a greater amount of recreational resources than if the facility were located on some other site. If a proponent of one site asks that a civic center be built or moved there for aesthetic reasons or because it will take most people, but not himself, less time to reach the facility, his request is still a demand for an increased scope of government. Such a person would be urging government to expand its function to satisfy his aesthetic or altruistic need, needs as genuine as that for food.

Conflict may be generated by demands for an internal shift of government that would result in the deprivation of other citizens, or by demands that require a shift in the net scope of government. A demand for school desegregation is a case in point. Opposition to desegregation may be understood as opposition to the increased functioning of government to satisfy a multiplicity of needs of Negroes. Opponents of desegregation might cast the issue in terms of an undesirable increase in the net scope of government, or as a novel and unwarranted intervention of government in the social system. But since government has already exercised its authority to decide whose children should be educated, and how and where, these demands and counter-demands may be more appropriately viewed as involving a redistribution of government's need-satisfying functions, rather than a change in the ratio of public to private space. Only when there has been a change in the ratio of governmental to private satisfaction of human needs in the community has a net shift in scope occurred. If there is no such net shift, all other changes in the way government functions that result in the satisfaction of different needs of different people constitute internal shifts in the scope of local government.

What of demands to maintain the *status quo* rather than to expand or reduce the scope of government? Because of *status quo* demands, political decision-making obviously may result in maintaining rather than changing the scope of government. Politics was broadly defined earlier as that aspect of life wherein certain people act to maintain or to shift what now may be referred to as the scope of government. If all demands were directed to the maintenance of an extant scope of government, this would presumably reflect a fundamental consensus. In this unlikely situation, politics would be present but it would be a very special sort. Even in the absence of political decision-making, political demands can be made and political influence successfully exerted to maintain the scope of government. How long such a politics of consensus could endure in a modern, complex community is open to question.

The model of the political process encompasses demands for maintaining a given scope of government even though the demands may be outside a particular decision-making process; this may constitute an effective force for stasis in the body politic. Perhaps no broader definition of politics than that it is the web of political decision-making is required to study the conditions that may result in decisional questions leading to conflict or triggering other decisional processes. However, to understand what conditions produce variations among or within communities in the content of decision-making does require a broader definition. This definition includes action designed to increase or decrease general satisfaction with a current scope of government, even though no shifts in that scope have been or are currently being demanded. It is important that these definitions be clearly understood.

Some analysts of American politics view politics as the resolving of decisional issues or questions; others maintain that it encompasses the conditions that affect the raising of decisional issues and questions. Some analysts have maintained that American politics is characterized by a nearly unitary power structure wherein a relatively few like-minded men rule.[9] Others have countered by attempting to show that in the resolution of decisional controversies, the outcome is a function of compromise by numerous participants.[10] To some, the messages of the mass media and the propaganda of public relations specialists devoted to the glorification of the existing net scope of American government and the American way of life are the central facts of our politics. They presume that the exercise of political influence prevents demands for shifts in the scope of government and the appearance of radical alternatives. To others the influence of the media in particular decisional processes is relatively minor: they believe that the similarity in the various scopes of government that are subject to political decision-making results from the character of modern industrial society and is not due to the manipulation of political consensus by a top power elite.

For example, the "ruling elite model" of American national and community politics offered by such analysts as C. Wright Mills and Floyd Hunter has been criticized by Robert Dahl on the ground that it has not been put to the test of empirical research. Dahl admits that the influence of a ruling elite over ideas, attitudes, and opinions can create "a kind of false consensus" and proposes that this be tested in "a series of concrete cases where key decisions are made." Only in that way, he asserts, can it be determined whether one group initiates and vetoes, while others merely respond to the leaders. However, he does not consider that political influence might be exercised so skillfully by the few that they succeed in averting demands for other scopes of government or in preventing such preferences from being pursued or strengthened to the point of becoming issues in "key decisions."

We would propose studies of influence relations in which it

[9]C. Wright Mills, *The Power Elite* (New York: Oxford University Press, 1956); Floyd Hunter, *Community Power Structure* (Chapel Hill: University of North Carolina Press, 1953); Andrew Hacker, "Liberal Democracy and Social Control," *The American Political Science Review,* (Vol. LI, No. 4 (December 1957), pp. 1009-1025.
[10]Robert Dahl, "A Critique of the Ruling Elite Model," *The American Political Science Review,* Vol. LII, No. 2 (June 1958), pp. 463-469. See also David B. Truman, "The American System in Crisis," *Political Science Quarterly,* Vol. LXXIV, No. 4 (December 1959), pp. 481-497.

is recognized that the intentions of those attempting to influence others might be to prevent decisional questions from arising or to restrict the domain of decisional choices to a more or less acceptable few. The analyst should recognize that the absence of political decision-making or the existence of a political decision-making process with one particular set of options rather than another might well be the result of political action on the part of a "ruling elite." Since the possibility of such situations may result from a variety of causes, including unintentional political consequences of nonpolitical action, the problem of settling the question empirically is most complex. If we admit the possibility that political demands may be made to maintain a given scope of government and that the demands may not become part of a specific political decision-making process in the usual sense, the relative merits of pyramidal and pluralistic power structures become amenable to empirical tests.[11] Such issues are not likely to be resolved by empirical investigations unless and until a common definition of politics is agreed upon by those in dispute.

In the present study our interest extends to politics in the broad and general sense rather than in the specific, political decision-making one. Exactly what is meant by political decision-making processes is specified in the next chapter. But this is a limited and partial study, because the working definition of politics used in designing these comparative studies has been restricted to a political decision-making context. Actions intended to decrease general satisfaction with a current scope of government were ordinarily embedded in demands for relatively specific shifts in governmental functioning. Such action was accounted for when observations were made of one or another political decision-making process. Action intended to maintain or increase satisfactions with the scope of government, when successful, was not systematically studied because the research focus itself was concentrated upon actions that were part of actual decision making processes. When the significance of non-decision-making politics was realized, it was too late to extend the research focus appropriately.

In the real world of American community politics, government is far from either apolitical pole. Certain divisions of governmental and private institutional functioning were not at issue in making

[11]See Robert A. Dahl, *Who Governs?* (New Haven: Yale University Press, 1961), pp. 468-569. See also two forthcoming studies, Robert Presthus, *Men at the Top: A Study in Community Power* (Oxford, Spring 1964); and Aaron Wildavsky, *Leadership in a Smalltown* (Bedminister Press, 1964).

political decisions that involved questions of government's appropriate functions in a given domain. But in all four research communities there were net and internal shifts in the scope of government as well as conflicts over both. The direction of local government along the expansion-contraction continuum is, in part, the direct or indirect result of men's satisfaction or dissatisfaction with policies made in nongovernmental sectors of society. Systems of decision-making are necessary in the production and distribution of goods and services, status and dignity, and other values. Some men are more powerful decision-makers than others in such systems. Patterns of power relations emerge in private spheres of community life, in the private economic and social institutions. The ultimate sanctions possessed by private—nongovernmental—men of power stop short of force unless public order has broken down. Nevertheless, private men of power may command severe sanctions. For example, an employer can punish or reward by firing or hiring, or by cutting or raising income. Social leaders may use ostracism, rejection, ridicule, or approval to gain or maintain support for their policies. Leaders in different institutional areas may use a variety of sanctions affecting a multiplicity of men's values to enforce policy preferences.

It is when policies backed by such sanctions are considered to be made more appropriately by public government than by private institutions, or vice versa, that shifts in government's net scope may occur. Their direction and character, and whether or not they occur, may hinge on the perspectives of men who have control over governmental decisions. We shall now turn to groups of perspectives on the preferred net scope of government. These perspectives are referred to hereafter as political ideologies.

POLITICAL IDEOLOGIES

Political ideologies are present in national and local politics in the United States. Although they may range from integrated doctrines and eclectic views to inarticulate or even unconscious operating premises, they all affect preferences about the appropriate scope of government. Ideologists range from militant, articulate, doctrinaire proselytizers to passive, inarticulate, apathetic tolerants. Most citizens in the United States probably are closer to the latter pole.

It should be stressed that the components of the ideologies to be described do not always fit together as neatly as the following prototypes suggest; those who subscribe to them are not always conscious, articulate, doctrinaire, or militant in their subscription. Political ideologies are ways of perceiving and reacting to the political system. These perceptions and reactions in turn condition attitudes and behavior toward what the appropriate scope of government ought to be; they may determine, in large degree, a person's political action, or they may have little impact on political behavior, at least under "normal" conditions. They are ways of organizing one's concepts and precepts about politics, and, as is true of any cognitive-perceptual-evaluative structure, they may be shaped by a deeply rooted personality drive or by a surface attitude.

At the outset of this study, we fully expected to find a politics of personal or, at the most, particularistic group interests in the four communities. We did not expect to find an ideological politics, even to the limited extent to which it appeared to exist at the national level. When we perceived the importance of ideology as a factor "ordering" a series of variations in the politics of the four communities—within each community over a period of time and among the four communities at a given time—political ideology became a central analytic concept.[12]

A person may act on the basis of either personal or group interests. This distinction is simply a matter of whether the benefits contemplated are desired for the person himself or for a group of citizens with whom he identifies. The larger category may be a family, a voluntary social or economic association, a racial aggregate,

[12]That ideology is relatively unimportant for the citizens at large in the two-party national politics of the United States is documented in Angus Campbell *et al., The American Voter,* (New York: John Wiley & Sons, Inc., 1960), pp. 188-215; and in McCloskey *et at., op. cit.,* p. 406. The operational definition of ideologies in these two studies, unlike the present study, refers to policy or decisional preferences and to the traditional liberal-conservative distinctions. See also Philip E. Converse, "The Nature of Belief Systems in Mass Publics," in *Ideology and Discontent,* ed. by David E. Apter and Reinhard Bendix (New York: The Free Press of Glencoe, forthcoming, 1964). In Converse's important analysis, he documents the relatively greater ideological charter of "elite" than "mass" American Policy perspectives.

Several comments need to be made about such studies. First, in 1959 in selected communities in the West, identical measurements have revealed much stronger correlations between such policy matters as federal-government programs in social-welfare areas and the feeling that big business corporations should not have much to say about how the government is run than those for the Survey Research Center's national sample of 1956. Secondly, in one such study we have found a much greater degree of stability over a four-year period in such policy perspectives on the part of a random sample in

or an occupational category. A group interest, in this sense, may extend to the whole community or nation, to a regional collection of communities or nations, to a worldwide category of people who believe in democracy or in the class struggle, to a particular race, or to mankind as a whole.

Some analysts maintain that those in a particular economic, social, or ethnic category have by definition a group interest. If group interest is not seen in this way, the analytic questions become: to what extent does a potential group interest become an actual group interest, and to what extent do people with a group interest pursue that interest in politics?

In any event, an individual may have either a personal or a group interest, depending upon his psychological identifications and calculations; this interest may be related to and shaped by political ideology or it may have no ideological connection.[13]

By political ideology we mean a system of interrelated ideas about the polity that includes general answers to the following questions:

1. What sorts of general interests exist in a community, personal or group? If the latter, are the interests community-wide public interests or are they those of less inclusive sectors of the community?
2. Who ought to make the decisions about the proper scope of government and in whose interests?
3. What share of available socio-economic and cultural values is a person currently being allocated relative to others in a community?
4. What role should the government play in allocating values produced in the economy, in the society, and in the governmental institutions themselves?

one community than Converse has reported for a national sample, and an even greater degree of such stability for such items as attitudes towards a state sales tax. Thirdly, and most importantly, granting the greater ideological character of "elite" than "mass" political thinking in a variety of regards (and in no way do we in the following pages suggest that the masses of a community's citizens are "ideological," although we did not systematically assess the extent to which that may have been true in our communities), our use of the term "ideology" is in various ways quite different from that of the aforementioned studies. See also David W. Minar, "Ideology and Political Behavior," *Midwest Journal of Political Science,* Vol. V, No. 4 (November 1961), pp. 317-331.

[13]For a useful conception of political interests, see David B. Truman, *The Governmental Process* (New York: Alfred A. Knopf, 1951) and Harold Lasswell, *Politics: Who Gets What, When, and How* (New York: McGraw-Hill Book Company, Inc., 1936).

One may be inclined to view ideology as simply another type of political interest. Ideology, however, is broader and more general than political interest. Unlike mere political interest, it does not refer to the benefits and costs of *particular* policies, although it may refer to those of sets of policies. Furthermore, ideology takes into account the appropriate net scope of government, in general if not in particular. It is useful, therefore, to distinguish between these concepts. We prefer to make the distinction between ideology and interests rather than between ideological and non-ideological interests.[14]

Let us suppose that a decisional question has arisen in a community: Should the city government establish municipal parking lots in the downtown business district? Some individuals will have neither personal nor group interests in the matter; others will assess the political question according to their own personal or group interest. One person may decide that such a program would solve his personal parking problems; another may be equally in favor of the plan because he is one of a number of downtown businessmen who will benefit from it. He may then act in favor of that proposal without reference to his political ideology, assuming that he has an ideology or that it is important to him. Suppose, further, that a merchant has an ideology that puts the interests of merchants high on the list of those to be served by the government. If he invoked his ideology in assessing the parking lot proposal, he might find a convergence of his personal or group interest and his ideological doctrine. But if his ideology included the belief that government should not be extended into the economy and he saw municipal parking lots as an undesirable extension of government, his interest and ideology would come into conflict. Many people do not perceive a relationship between their ideology and a particular interest; others may find interests and ideology convergent and reinforcing; for still others the two may be divergent and conflicting.

The decisional preferences of most citizens in the four communities seemed to be more influenced by group and personal interests

[14]See Campbell *et al., op. cit.,* p. 192. They define ideology as "primarily political, although the scope of the structure is such that we expect an ideology to encompass content outside the political order as narrowly defined—social and economic relationships, and even matters of religion, education, and the like." See also McCloskey *et al., op. cit.,* p. 427. They properly point out that categorizing parties or politics as "ideological" depends on "how narrowly we define that term."

than by ideology. Some citizens were found to be apolitical—they did not see that local government affected personal or group interests to any great degree in either general or particular decisions. These people tended to be politically nonparticipant. Among those who did participate were people who had neither a nationally nor a community-oriented political ideology but did have personal or group interests; people who had a national ideology which they did not think had local relevance; and people whose political interests were more central and compelling than their ideologies. The proportion of citizens in any of the four communities whose ideologies were of equal or greater importance than their interests was very small. What, then, was the importance of ideology?

First of all, community politics was found to be largely group politics. Relatively enduring groups of people were found to be actively involved in the political decision-making of all four communities. Some of these groups followed or overlapped party or factional lines and some cut across them and were irrelevant to the local parties. They tended to be differentiated along ideological rather than interest lines.

These political groups were of special importance in community politics because they included those who were considered to be the leaders in decision-making by others in the community. The impulse to become a leader and obtain power appeared to be a manifestation of interest in proposed local government programs and of a desire to maintain or impose an ideology on the leaders of the community power structure. The latter desire was most intense in the key members of these political groups.

The key men were important because they had extraordinary political status and influence, at least within their own groups. Very small "inner cliques" were made up of articulate ideologists. These were the active spokesmen for the people who wanted interest-based decisional preferences filtered through the proper ideological sieve. They were the men who in their intimate subgroup operations constituted "a firmly established, authoritative, and continuing organizational center empowered to decide questions of doctrine and discipline."[15] McClosky et al. found this to be so, to a greater degree than many analysts suspected among the leaders of the two major national parties.

In every community some active participants in politics did stand outside the dominant ideologically bounded group or groups;

15McCloskey et al., op. cit.

some belonged to more than one of them. Yet much of the variation in the politics of the four communities is understandable only in the light of the variations within the ideological dimension.

Of special concern in this analysis is an examination of the conditions that produce varying degrees of citizen participation and conflict in political decision-making. Most American communities have complex economies and social structures. A potential exists in communities for the politicizing of group interests through existing voluntary associations or through new political organizations. With the organization of political interest groups, a community may experience extreme political group conflict or cooperation. Whether there is conflict or consensus along interest lines, citizen political participation can be either high or low. While these are all logical possibilities, what we actually find is that the informal political organization of ideologically differentiated groups is a necessary although insufficient condition for both extensive citizen participation in politics and intensive conflict in decision-making. Competitive ideological groups give rise to both situations, whereas the competition among groups lacking ideological interests is insufficient to produce "mass" participation of either a cohesive or conflicting character.

Ideologists indoctrinate others with their system of beliefs in order to enlist political participation as a means of achieving their ideological ends. When there is a competition of such political idea systems, each protagonist has to enlist more citizen support than if there were a consensus. Militant ideologists activate interests which become subject to the appeals of the protagonists. Political interests sometimes conflict with the ideological precepts even among the leaders of ideological groups. The extent to which this happens affects the strength of the group in political decision-making. The conditions under which conflict among leaders occurs are also an important subject for political analysis. Ideological groups also differ in the degree to which there is both potential and actual divergence and conflict between ideology and interest in the formation of decisional preferences.

In all four communities ideologists spent some of their time trying to bring together the ideology and the political interests of their members and citizens at large. A lesser degree of doctrinaire orthodoxy within political groups than otherwise might have been the case resulted. Neither this nor the fact that the ideologies had a quality of contingency when used to evaluate decisional options does away with the significance of ideology as an explanatory variable in the analysis that follows.

The five component variables of political ideologies are: (1) conception of the community, (2) preferences as to "who shall rule," (3) the sense of social (socio-economic) class, (4) the sense of cultural class or caste, and (5) attitudes toward the legitimate method of allocating values.

In Figure 2, a combination of the first two variables yields 18 possible cells when the conception of the community is treated as a threefold classification, and the answer to "who shall rule?" as a sixfold one. Only seven of these 18 cells were found to have empirical referents in the form of at least one actual political group in the leadership of at least one of the communities. One political group which aspired but failed to attain a leadership position in one community during the postwar period occupies an eighth cell.

The label "conservative" is found in four of these seven cells. Conservative ideologists feel that political leaders should be recruited from among the more affluent citizens. They differ from one another concerning the particular category of affluence from which they feel the political leadership should come—industrialists-financiers, proprietors-professionals, or the propertied generally; they differ also from ideologists—Community Conservationists, Liberals, Radical Leftists, and Supremacists—who consider as qualifying characteristics other dimensions than affluence or property. The Radical Right is treated at this point as a conservative ideology; it will be differentiated from the other ideology in the same cell, labeled Jeffersonian Conservatism, later. The Liberals and the Radical Leftists as well as businessmen-labor minorities, believe the political leadership should come from the disadvantaged sectors of the community. The Supremacists' requisite condition for leadership is the appropriate race.

Conservatives can also be internally distinguished by their conception of the community. Orthodox Conservatives view their communities as being composed of sections of people having different needs, values, or interests. The leaders should rule in the interests of their sectors and must expect that other sectors will advocate policies that need to be opposed.

Jeffersonian Conservatives, as well as Radical Rightists, view the community as being early Jeffersonian: the community is a collection of individuals and not a set of potentially or actually

Who shall rule?

Conception of community	Industrialists-financiers	Proprietors-professionals	Public officials-administrators	Propertied		Disadvantaged Businessmen and Minorities	Races
				Jeffersonian Conservatives	Radical Rightists		
Individuals	Orthodox Conservatives	Orthodox Conservatives		Jeffersonian Conservatives	Radical Rightists		
Interests and interest groups						Liberals	
Collectivity(ies)	Progressive Conservatives		Community Conservationists			Radical Leftists	Supremacists

*Perforated box indicates that the Radical Leftists did not actually attain political leadership positions in any of the four communities from the end of the Second World War to 1961 even though there was an aspiring group in one community, Metroville, for a short time during those years.

FIGURE 2 *Matrix of ideologies: two dimensions.*

83

conflicting interest groups. They distinguish two broad categories of individuals, the propertied and the propertyless, and, like Jefferson, are concerned with preserving the particular virtue that belongs to the propertied. They regard the propertyless as being not so much an interest group as a collection of individuals who have been lazy or who lack the personal capabilities that qualify men of property for a ruling voice in community affairs. The Jeffersonian Conservative strongly defends the rural community, where virtuous men may acquire property and live the good life; the big city is a place where alien philosophies of life and civic corruption deplorably, but inevitably, prevail.

Progressive Conservatives are fundamentally "collectivists" in outlook. They view the community as a collectivity—an organism with a common interest. The welfare of one person depends upon the welfare of others; they recognize that interdependency is the keystone of a naturally ordered community. Since they believe in rule by the industrialists and financiers, they view this rule as necessarily operating in the interest of the collectivity. This political leadership must be benevolent; the attitude of "what's good for the 'X' Corporation is good for the community" indicates an innate complement of self-interest and the common good.

Community Conservationists are also collectivists. They view the community as a complex of mutually interdependent parts where the individual good and the common good are naturally compatible, if not identical. They see the values of community life maximized when political leadership is exercised by men representing the public at large, rather than "special interests." They believe in a "public interest" that may differ from the short-sighted, limited interest of a portion of the community. Elected public officials and appointed professional public administrators must be the guardians, as well as the architects and builders, of this public interest.

Liberals believe that disadvantaged people or those who identify themselves with the disadvantaged should be the political leaders in communities which are complexes of interest groups. Organized labor is one of the major, fundamental interests of Liberalism. In addition, Liberals see racial minorities and even small businessmen as disadvantaged interests. Liberals want public officials to accord the needs of the disadvantaged the highest political status. These needs will be defined by the leaders of the disadvantaged. Community Conservationists want public officials to be accorded the highest political status by all interests, including the disadvantaged. The Radical Left's ideology advocates rule of the community by those disadvantaged under capitalism. Adherents of that ideology see the community as a collectivity in the Marxist sense and as having a single natural interest in the collective good of the proletariat. This single interest is to be implemented through the political leadership of the intelligentsia. The relatively large, disadvantaged proletariat would rule the community through the very small minority of progressive true believers who may work from the offices they hold in organizations of the disadvantaged, such as labor unions and racial groups.

Finally, the Supremacists believe that race should be the primary criterion for community rule. Race becomes the necessary and sufficient condition for participation as a political leader. Therefore, the appropriate racist sentiment tends to qualify any citizen for a position of political leadership. Supremacists can be either Whites or Negroes.[16]

The third component variable of these political ideologies is the "sense of social class." Social class not only adds depth to the picture of each ideology but also suggests bases for cooperation and conflict among different ideologies and among groups within one ideology. The sense of social class refers to people's self-images with regard to how much social status, respect, and affection they receive from others in the community. These feelings tend to be affected by the occupations people hold, their income or wealth, and their educational attainments. The sense of social class may be based on accurate perceptions of differential social status arising from admission to or exclusion from groups, associations, or organizations, although such admission or exclusion may be based on personal rather than socioeconomic characteristics.[17]

The political ideologies in the matrix in Figures 2 and 3 were set up to range from very high to low in the measurement of social class, reading from left to right. The Orthodox Conservatives and Progressive Conservatives believe that the industrialists-financiers should rule, because they are the most important, or

[16]It is common practice to capitalize the word "Negro" and not the word "white." We see no reason for unequal treatment in such a minor but symbolic matter and therefore capitalize both words.
[17]For discussions of social class in the United States, see Joseph A. Kahl, *The American Class Structure* (New York: Rinehart, 1957); and W. Lloyd Warner, M. Meeker, and K. Eells, *Social Class in America* (New York: Harper Torchbooks, 1960).

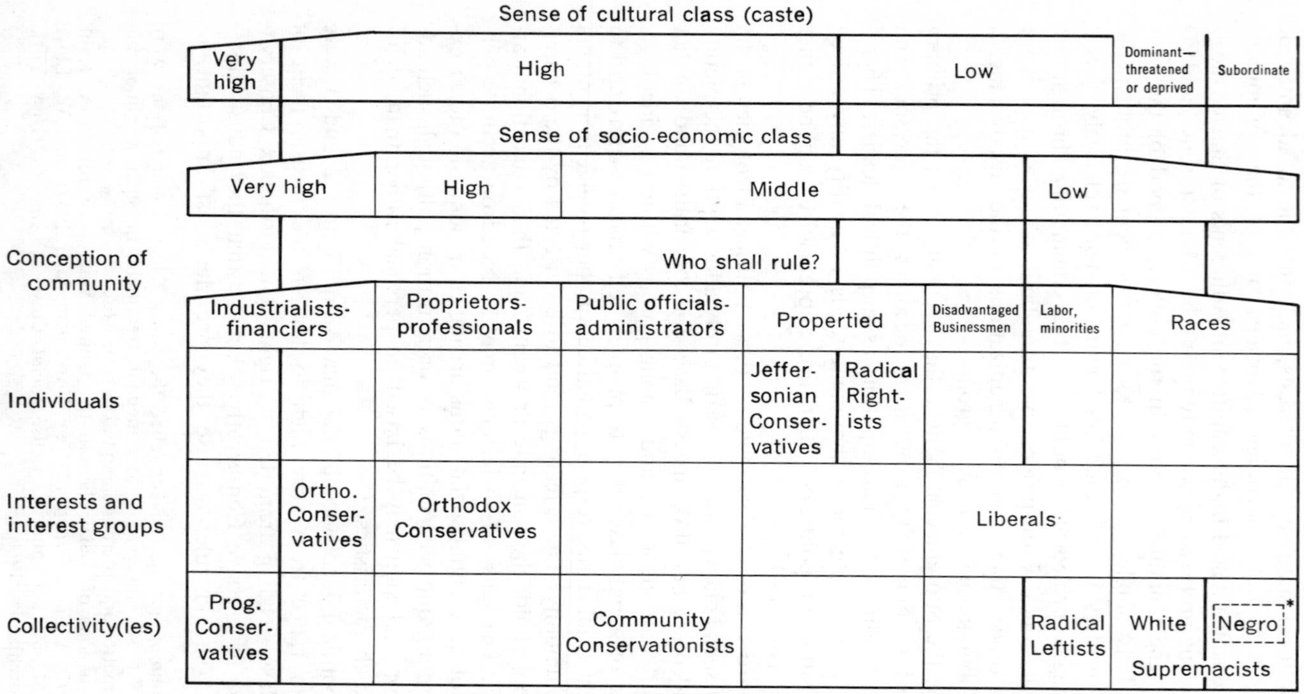

Sense of cultural class (caste)

	Very high	High			Low		Dominant—threatened or deprived	Subordinate

Sense of socio-economic class

Conception of community	Very high	High		Middle	Low	Low		
Who shall rule?	Industrialists-financiers	Proprietors-professionals	Public officials-administrators	Propertied	Disadvantaged Businessmen	Labor, minorities	Races	
Individuals	Ortho. Conservatives	Orthodox Conservatives		Jeffer-sonian Conser-vatives / Radical Right-ists				
Interests and interest groups					Liberals			
Collectivity(ies)	Prog. Conservatives	Community Conservationists				Radical Leftists	White Supremacists / Negro Supremacists*	

*The Perforated box enclosing Negro Supremacists indicates that there was no political group of this ideology aspiring to community leadership in any of the cities although there were individual Negro Supremacists in both southern cities.

FIGURE 3 Matrix of ideologies: four dimensions.

even superior, men in the community; they deserve their social and political status. The attainment of their high-income-producing occupational positions, whether by birth or through their own efforts, is seen as reason enough for the community to accord them the lion's share of respect or deference. Their wealth alone, apart from their manners or morality, leads naturally to places on boards of directors, or to the organization of country clubs which provide exclusive social settings for the development and maintenance of a sense of high social position.

The Orthodox Conservatives who believe that proprietorial-professional occupations should rule have a sense of high social class, as compared to groups they perceive as their protagonists in the community. They appear not to have quite the same feelings of social superiority as are evidenced by the aforementioned conservative ideologists. The Community Conservationists, the Jeffersonian Conservatives, and the Radical Rightists tend to perceive themselves as properly middle class; this is a matter of some pride and significance to them. Liberals include some people who feel they belong to the middle class and others who feel that they are members of the lower class. Blue-collar and Negro Liberals tend to think that they receive a disproportionately small share of social status. Liberal businessmen and professionals tend to think of themselves as belonging to the middle class. The Radical Leftists have the strongest sense of receiving few social—and economic—gratifications in the community; they feel such gratifications belong to them by right because of the nature of the world and its inevitable historical forces. To Supremacists social class is irrelevant and racial purity is all-important.

Another defining characteristic of ideologies is the sense of cultural class, or caste. This refers to the people's self-images and feelings concerning how much status or respect their values, beliefs, opinions, judgments, and ideas receive from others. Sense of cultural class may follow, to a greater or lesser degree, the sense of social class, but there are important differences in the two concepts.

The sense of cultural class may be very general and refer to a host of matters or phenomena: political values, political beliefs, political opinions, political judgments, and ideas about the polity—the political culture—as well as matters of manners, morals, money, and music. Just as we treat theoretically distinct senses of social and economic class as a single dimension, so too do we deal with these various "senses" as a single, composite, general sense of cultural class.[18]

The three sets of political ideologists characterized by a high sense of social class—both kinds of Orthodox Conservatives and of Progressive Conservatives—have a comparably high sense of cultural class (Figure 3). The Progressive Conservatives have an extremely high sense of cultural superiority which extends throughout most areas of life. Their sense of cultural class makes them the most aristocratic of any set of Conservatives. When born to the highest social and economic positions, they accept their roles as cultural leaders as a matter of course. They have unquestioned faith that the cultural trends and heritage they oversee are superior to any alternatives. On occasion, they may be influenced by such men of lower cultural class as their professional advisors; but they regard themselves as without peer in the realm of judgment. The two sets of Orthodox Conservatives appear—in our communities at least—less certain that their cultural superiority is infallible, particularly in such peripheral cultural areas as the arts and letters.

Both Community Conservationists and Jeffersonian Conservatives, who identify themselves with the middle social class, have a high sense of cultural class which is comparable to that of the Orthodox Conservatives. Although the Community Conservationists believe

[18]The observations and instruments for evaluating and estimating the specific and general senses of cultural class were not precise enough to detect theoretically significant discrepancies between the specific and general sense of cultural class. While the senses of cultural and social class may be highly correlated under many conditions, we suspect that they diverge significantly in relatively open social class systems. By the use of such terms as "status frustrations" and "the dispossessed," Seymour Martin Lipset and Daniel Bell imply some aspects of what we mean by a sense of cultural class. Once the latter is conceptualized as a distinct analytic variable (of a multidimensional character), it becomes possible to test the degree to which cultural-class position is due to what Lipset and Bell both suggest is the cause of distance and hostility between upper- and lower-cultural-class groups, namely, psychological anxiety or confidence related to position in and understanding of the modern technological, corporate socio-economic structure and international order. We would question a predominant stress on a differential distribution of needs for, and frustrations regarding, social status and would hypothesize more of a socialization in differentiated cultures as a central factor in the motivational complex of forces producing a stratified cultural-class system. Whatever the original cause of different belief systems, their existence provides for the maintenance or the development of cultural-class systems based thereon, related to social class only to the extent that cultural belief systems follow social-class lines. See *The Radical Right*, ed. by Daniel Bell (Garden City, N.Y.: Doubleday & Co., Inc., 1963), especially Chapters 1, 2, 13, and 14.

their wisdom is superior in civic and political affairs, in some areas they assume that one man's values are as good as another's. For example, Community Conservationists do not see business success as an indication of cultural superiority; they view its attainment as a function of unimportant or chance factors. Their upper-cultural-class feelings derive in part from their awareness that they are currently well-informed and highly educated and that they have the most modern, progressive view of what is good for the community. This is in contrast to the old-fashioned, regressive views of most of their articulate opponents, of professional politicians, and perhaps, of many of the citizens. This sense of high cultural class characterizes Community Conservationists whether they are Harvard intellectuals, city managers or planners, or leaders of the League of Woman Voters. Community Conservationists value professionally trained public administrators and stress public planning; they tend to hold in disrepute the professional politician and "dirty politics." They are the most recent of a long line of "reformers," but differ in at least one major aspect: earlier reformers tended to concentrate on eliminating particular evils so that the political system might return to a sort of laissez-faire operation in cooperation with private institutions. The Community Conservationist, in contrast, stresses the need for and the duty of government to provide long-range planning in the public interest by nonpolitical administrators. There is a socialist-like emphasis on community planning without the socialist objective of increased public ownership of the means of production.[19]

Jeffersonian Conservatives differ sharply from the Radical Rightists in respect to cultural class. The Jeffersonian Conservatives' sense of belonging to the upper cultural class appears to be based in part on their images of themselves as being men of some affluence when compared to the propertyless, and as being believers in eternal verities rather than in the misconceived modern notions of the good life to which eccentrics adhere. In sharp contrast, Radical Rightists sense that they belong to the cultural class which is lowest in regard to community affairs. They feel deprived—not necessarily of social status or access to prestigious social organizations—because they are treated by a frequently subversive

---

[19]Some of these aspects of Community Conservation are well expressed in Catherine C. Bauer Wurster, "Framework for an Urban Society," in *Goals for Americans, The Report of the President's Commission on National Goals* (New York: A Spectrum Book, Prentice-Hall, Inc., 1960), pp. 223-247.

community leadership as part of a "lunatic fringe," as people with destructive ideas.

Both Liberals and Radical Leftists have a sense of being members of a low cultural class. The Radical Leftists, much like the Radical Rightists, feel that they are treated unjustly. Moral indignation seems stronger on the part of the Radical Rightists than on that of the Radical Leftists; this may be because the Leftists' belief in historical necessity accords them security, and the Rightists fear that history is constantly moving in the wrong direction. The Radical Leftists resemble in a sense Progressive Conservatives in their elite outlook because the cultural class to which each group feels it belongs is extremely small. Radical Rightists, if elitists, are of a Populist variety. They feel that there are many people in this same low cultural class position who would become associated with the Radical Right if they recognized the truth of the Rightist diagnosis of, and prescription for, the current illness in the body politic.

The Liberals, somewhat split on the basis of their sense of social class—some identify with the middle and some with the lower class—are united in their sense of a common cultural-class plight. They may feel as deprived as either the Radical Right or the Radical Left by the disregard of their cultural standards, but they seem more confident that a change in their relative cultural class position is attainable in the relatively near future.

White and Negro Supremacists may now be treated as separate groups. The White Supremacists see themselves as the racial caste which is currently dominant. However, they feel threatened by an overturn in the "natural order" of caste-control relations. Negro Supremacists feel they are treated as inferior, subordinate people. They feel that their destiny, and that of dark-skinned peoples throughout the world, is to reverse the traditional master-serf relationship.

Two important aspects of political culture are beliefs about the good regime and the good power structure. Of these ten political ideologies—including both types of Orthodox Conservatives and both types of Supremacists—six have as their ideal type of regime a "developed democracy." The ideal regime of all Conservative, the Liberal, and the Community Conservationist ideologies is one wherein the citizens correctly believe that they have full access to the political decision-making process, including the ballot.

Radical Rightists feel that an oligarchy is the desirable regime for the foreseeable future. Such a regime exists when some categories of citizens are aware that they do not have access to the political decision-making process. Until utopia is reached, Radical Leftists prefer a situation called "guided democracy." Under this system citizens believe that they have full access to the political decision-making process, but are in error: should certain demands be made for shifts in the scope of government illegitimate sanctions would be effectively applied to those making the demands. Such a situation prevails where there is a widespread sense of democracy with perhaps some of its forms, but without the necessary conditions to give it substance. Supremacists favor oligarchy for the other race; they vary in their preferences for the good regime for the master race.

All four conservative ideologies prefer a type of power structure wherein power is in the hands of a relatively small proportion of the citizens and the political leadership agrees on one set of values for the general scope of government. Although Jeffersonian Conservatives believe that the relatively large propertied segment should participate in ruling, the actual political leadership will naturally be relatively small in size. Relatively large numbers of shiftless, propertyless people and some misguided people with property are disqualified from sharing in political power and leadership positions because of their attachment to an alternative political ideology. The Orthodox Conservatives think politics is necessary in the competition with other interests for scarce resources; they try to attain or preserve a consensual power structure, in which Orthodox Conservatism is the prevailing political ideology.

The ideal power structure of Community Conservationists, Liberals, and Radical Leftists is more of a mass and less of an elite distribution of political power. The Radical Leftists understand that such a distribution of political power is necessary if they are to move from their present powerless position, in what they consider oligarchies run by and for their enemies, to a position of power in a pseudo-democracy that is guided by them. Community Conservationists prefer to see the masses share in political power through extensive electoral participation in support of the Conservationists and their policies; Liberals envisage the development of a complex of more active political roles for the rank-and-file. Supremacists tend to support a consensual elite power structure as the only safe way of preserving the oligarchy and the dominance of their race.

The fifth factor among political ideologies is a principle of community organization, which, in its most extreme form, may be stated in this way: The good community is a natural product of governmental noninterference with private allocation of social, economic, or other resources according to the individual's ability to compete for them, tempered by mercy and charity. The Radical Rightists adhere to this principle in a most uncompromising fashion. In their political ideology, almost all governmental action is seen as a dangerous violation of this natural law principle. Jeffersonian Conservatives also tend to view the growth of government as unwarranted interference, but they view this somewhat less rigidly.

The major difference between the two is that the Radical Right is restorationist in outlook, whereas the outlook of Jeffersonian Conservatives is preservationist. Jeffersonian Conservatism may be strongest in small or rural communities where government is minimal, and the Radical Right tends to be strong in communities where government has grown larger. But Jeffersonian Conservatism places its greatest emphasis on preventing further increases in the net scope of government, whereas the Radical Right stresses the need to decrease the net scope of government. Jeffersonian Conservatives may accept shifts in the functioning of government if the shifts accord with their cultural values, but the Radical Rightist consistently views government as evil. One of the cultural aims of Jeffersonian Conservatism is a community undivided by political controversy. Since the Jeffersonian Conservative has a sense of upper cultural class status and a duty to preserve the community consensus, he is more likely than the Radical Rightist to accept a governmental program if resistance will result in extensive or intensive community conflict. This would be particularly true if the Jeffersonian Conservatives were the political leaders of the polity and able to control administrative decision-making for any governmental program. The Radical Rightist has the hostility that goes with believing oneself treated as a member of an inferior cultural class; he also feels, as a political-cultural value, the need for conflict and extreme forms of political warfare to reestablish the principle of community organization in its pure form and to establish the desired oligarchic type of policy.[20] Both the Radical Right and Jeffersonian Conservatism are hostile to a profession-

---

[20]Classifying people as Jeffersonian Conservatives and Radical Rightists, as with the classification of people as ideologists of any other kind, will some-

al, independent governmental bureaucracy; they see these professionals as men who are by their very occupations, dedicated to the subversion of this basic principle of community life.

Conservatives other than Jeffersonians tend to have the latter's rhetoric, but differ in their interpretations of what constitutes governmental interference with the private distribution of goods, services, and other values. Alexander Hamilton's advocacy of certain national governmental programs made him no less conservative than Calvin Coolidge's negative sentiments toward government. If governmental programs are seen to serve the interests of the rulers, they may be thought to strengthen rather than weaken the rule of private allocations of values. The result of this qualification is that Conservatives have a contingent or dependent outlook toward the appropriate scope of government.[21] Primary among these contingent factors is whether or not particular governmental programs hurt or help conservative socio-economic interests, and the extent to which their adversaries, the Liberals, are likely to use shifts or expansions in the scope of government for antibusiness ends. Since these liberal shifts have been a national trend, the conservative political ideology tends to be more in favor of the *status quo* and retrenchment than of expansion.[22]

Progressive Conservatives are less opposed to the use of government where private collectivities are unable or less able to act effectively. Since they view their rule as benevolent and in the interests of the entire community, they find it easier than do other conservative groups to accept government's role as one of the mechanisms for resource distribution along with the major private corporations and the voluntary civic and social organizations.

---

times result in the problem of marginal or borderline cases. Senator Barry Goldwater may be considered such a case.

[21]The late Senator Robert Taft's shift in position from an "anti" to a "pro" stance on such matters as public housing and urban redevelopment illustrates the contingent outlook on the part of Orthodox Conservatives, or, possibly, a movement toward national Progressive Conservatism. For a description of a variant of Orthodox Conservatism at the community level which permits "quasi-public action by private groups for public collective ends" while at the same time maintaining a minimal scope of (public) government, see Stone's description of what he calls "social free enterprise" in *op. cit.*

[22]A useful description of Conservative and Liberal ideology, as well as descriptions of the differences in attitudes toward various aspects of the scope of national government by Republican and Democratic party leaders, is to be found in McCloskey *et al., op. cit.* For a discussion of some of the ideological premises of businessmen, see Francis X. Sutton *et al., The American Business Creed* (Cambridge, Massachusetts: Harvard University Press, 1956).

This is particularly the case when Progressive Conservatives are in dominant political leadership positions. Thus, they also have a contingent position on the preferred scope of government. Progressive Conservatives sometimes see such programs as organized, large-scale charity in everyone's interest, and government as an efficient welfare-dispensing institution; they may approve of public welfare programs that are anathema not only to the Radical Right and Jeffersonian Conservatives but also to Orthodox Conservatives.

Community Conservationists tend to see government as the most important institution for producing in the good community values that are neither produced by private efforts nor actually inspired by private activities. Community Conservationists do not advocate as general principles either the circumscription of the private sectors of the community or a particular scope of government. Their cultural values are such that the programs of civic improvement and repair which they favor tend to make them advocates of vigorous, expansionist government. These programs include a stress on the improved distribution of knowledge through the public schools, cleanliness and beauty in architecture, planning and guided development of land use and of the size and character of the community's population, and a spirit of harmonious cooperation on the part of the citizenry. They value civic pride, a strong sense of public spirit, and an efficient, corruption-free, integrated city government. They believe "good government" is possible only where small, inefficient, multiple jurisdictions do not exist to obstruct nonpartisan, professional public administrators, officials, and civic-minded citizens in their work of building the good community. Since the property tax is still the primary fiscal base of local government, their relative unconcern with the costs and the tax requirements of their programs makes them particularly unacceptable to both Jeffersonian Conservatives and the Radical Rightists. Furthermore, the tax-conscious, property-oriented Rightists are considered members of an extremely inferior cultural class by Community Conservationists. Community Conservationists are not adverse to accepting federal funds for programs of civic improvement. When they do receive such funds they become the mortal enemies of the Radical Rightists who see socialism and the triumph of the Radical Left as the inevitable consequence of the extension of federal funds and planning controls into the local community.

Liberals agree, in general, with the principle that resources should be distributed according to the ability of individuals to compete in the distribution process. They believe that, with the passive or active cooperation of government, the affluent have unfair advantages that only counter-organization of the disadvantaged can overcome. They distrust local government officials whom they do not control for their traditional alliance with the business community; they also look with some hostility on nonbusiness-oriented Community Conservationists and their "modern" conception of good government. Liberals may advocate shifts in local government's scope either internally or in an expansionist direction. They may even advocate contraction in the scope of government if this seems a way to reduce the advantages of the affluent in the competition for scarce resources. Liberals tend to have a very pragmatic approach to the scope of government, particularly at the local level. Although their rhetoric often stresses expansion of local government, their pragmatism and their fear of government when their opponents have power give the Liberals' political ideology the same contingent character as that of the Conservative ideologies.

The Supremacists, both White and Negro, see the appropriate scope of local government in relation to the implementation of their interests in racial supremacy and a rigid caste system. Under some conditions, they see local government as their strongest force against enemies who advocate desegregation, either from without or from within the community. Under other conditions, they try to reduce the scope of local government to repair or prevent breaches in the wall between the races. Their attitude toward the scope of government is variable, therefore, rather than fixed and determinate.

The only political ideology that rejects this principle of community organization completely is that of the Radical Left. To the Leftist, the good community is one wherein government, during the pre-utopian period, distributes resources. Even here there is a quality of contingency about the Radical Leftists' position on the appropriate scope of government. Marxists may work with Liberals or with Conservatives to generate resentment and rebellion among the disadvantaged; the international communist movement often has used this strategy. The flexibility of the Radical Leftists' tactics and strategy, within the framework of fixed long-range goals, lends even to this political ideology a quality of contingency shared by all the aforementioned political ideologies except that of the Radical Right.

We may return to the earlier point that political ideology may range from a deeply rooted personality trait to a surface attitude. It appears that while any group of ideologists may be deeply committed to ideological precepts, Radical Rightists, Supremacists, and Radical Leftists—the Leftists are currently least important in numbers and political significance in community politics—are people whose ideologies seem to play a more central role in their lives than do the ideologies of other groups. These are "deviant" political ideologies—ideologies subscribed to by a relatively few people and in which the preferred type of regime differs markedly from that in most other American political ideologies. Furthermore, Radical Rightists express open hostility to, and engage in open warfare with, the cultural classes they consider their enemies; they use tactics that the latter believe are as radical and as undesirable as are the ends of that ideology. The term "radical" for both left and the right has three connotations. It signifies that these ideologies advocate relatively sharp shifts in the scope of government although such shifts would be in different directions. It also signifies that these ideologies envisage the best political regime as being quite different from the regime desired by other ideologists. Finally, consistent with their preferences for other that developed democratic regimes, the Radical Rightists and Leftists advocate "radical" political tactics such as slander, smears, and secret societies which other ideologists view with disdain.

We purposely refer to government rather than to "local" government in the foregoing section. This suggests what may have been apparent all along: the taxonomy constructed for these political ideologies is relevant for national as well as for local American politics. By a consistent substitution of the word "nation" for the work "community," the Progressive Conservatives have their analogue in the Eisenhower administration and the Community Conservationists in Kennedy's New Frontier.[23] These counterparts are not perfect equivalents, of course. Furthermore, some people adhere strongly to one ideology at one level and to another ideology at another.[24] This alone will explain some of the apparent paradoxes

[23]That differences between Progressive Conservatives and Community Conservationists, particularly at the national level, may be difficult to discern is evidenced by the fact that many of the objectives mentioned in *Goals for Americans* are held by Eisenhower Republicans and Kennedy Democrats, as well as by Stevenson Liberals.

[24]It may be of interest to note at this point that leaders of the three community-oriented Radical Right movements found in our research communities

of current American politics, both locally and nationally. But our basic point is that political ideology did not disappear at the national level with the end of the Depression or the end of the New or Fair Deal; nor has it been as absent from local politics as many observers seem to think.

Important dimensions of a community's power structure are the extent to which a political leadership is characterized by single or by multiple ideologies and the extent to which there is ideological convergence or divergence. From the foregoing descriptions, it would seem that some political ideologies diverge substantially from others. If their proponents attained political leadership positions, the extent of the divergence would seem to be clearly established. However, this is problematical; such factors as the strength of the leaders' ideological commitment affect the degree of divergence. This chapter closes with the suggestion that the great ignorance about political ideology in the United States at the community, state, and national levels of government and politics should be reduced by additional research. Except for two follow-up sample surveys in one community, which was revisited several years after the first sample survey for the purpose of testing specific hypotheses, little systematic, comparative information is available on the political ideologies of the citizens at large in our four communities. Even fewer data are available at this time on the genesis and development of ideological orientation.[25] We have included this discussion of ideology in our analysis because we do have some comparative data on its nature and functions, particularly at the political leadership level of the power structure in our four communities, despite the many facets left unexplored.[26]

---

belonged to and received literature from nationally organized Radical Right groups.

[25]James S. Coleman stresses the importance in a large class of conflicts of "a few active oppositionists" who are "sometimes motivated by the hope of power, but often they are ideologically committed to a 'cause'." *Community Conflict* (Glencoe, Illinois: The Free Press, 1957), p. 8.

[26]For a useful discussion on how to study the importance of ideas in political systems, and an explanation of Max Weber's general comparative research design and logic of inquiry, see Talcott Parsons, *Essays in Sociological Theory Pure and Applied* (Glencoe, Illinois: The Free Press, 1949), pp. 151-165.

5

THE ORGANIZATION OF GOVERNMENT IN METROPOLITAN AREAS: A THEORETICAL INQUIRY*

VINCENT OSTROM, CHARLES M. TIEBOUT AND ROBERT WARREN†

Allusions to the "problem of metropolitan government" are often made in characterizing the difficulties supposed to arise because a metropolitan region is a legal non-entity. From this point of view, the people of a metropolitan region have no general instrumentality of government available to deal directly with the range of problems which they share in common. Rather there is a multiplicity of federal and state governmental agencies, counties, cities and special districts that govern within a metropolitan region.

This view assumes that the multiplicity of political units in a metropolitan area is essentially a pathological phenomenon. The diagnosis asserts that there are too many governments and not enough government. The symptoms are described as "duplication of functions" and "overlapping jurisdictions." Autonomous units of government, acting in their own behalf, are considered incapable of resolving the diverse problems of the wider metropolitan community. The political topography of the metropolis is called a "crazy-

*Reprinted from *The American Political Science Review, LV*, No. 4 (December 1961), 831-842. By permission of the *The American Political Science Review* and the authors.
†Ostrom and Warren wish to acknowledge the early support of their work by the Bureau of Governmental Research at U.C.L.A. Background for discussion of the final section on "conflict and conflict resolution" was derived from research supported by the Water Resources Center of the University of California, help which Ostrom wishes to acknowledge.

quilt pattern" and its organization is said to be an "organized chaos." The prescription is reorganization into larger units—to provide "a general metropolitan framework" for gathering up the various functions of government. A political system with a single dominant center for making decisions is viewed as the ideal model for the organization of metropolitan government. "Gargantua" is one name for it.[1]

The assumption that each unit of local government acts independently without regard for other public interests in the metropolitan community has only a limited validity. The traditional pattern of government in a metropolitan area with its multiplicity of political jurisdictions may more appropriately be conceived as a "polycentric political system."[2] "Polycentric" connotes many centers of decision-making which are formally independent of each other. Whether they actually function independently, or instead constitute an interdependent system of relations, is an empirical question in particular cases. To the extent that they take each other into account in competitive relationships, enter into various contractual and cooperative undertakings or have recourse to central mechanisms to resolve conflicts, the various political jurisdictions in a metropolitan area may function in a coherent manner with consistent and predictable patterns of interacting behavior. To the extent that this is so, they may be said to function as a "system."

The study of government in metropolitan areas conceived as a polycentric political system should precede any judgment that it is pathological. Both the structure and the behavior of the system need analysis before any reasonable estimate can be made of its performance in dealing with the various public problems arising

---

[1]The term is taken from Robert C. Wood, The New Metropolis: Green Belts, Grass Roots vs. Gargantua," this Review, Vol. 52 (March, 1958), pp. 108-122. Wood defines gargantua as "the invention of a single metropolitan government or at least the establishment of a regional superstructure which points in that direction." We do not argue the case for big units vs. small units as Wood does in his discussion of gargantua vs. grass roots. Rather, we argue that various scales of organization may be appropriate for different public services in a metropolitan area.

[2]We use this term for want of a better one. An alternative term might be "multinucleated political system." We do not use "pluralism" because it has been preempted as a broader term referring to society generally and not to a political system in particular.

Polycentric political systems are not limited to the field of metropolitan government. The concept is equally applicable to regional administration of water resources, regional administration of international affairs, and to a variety of other situations.

in a metropolitan community. Better analysis of how a metropolitan area is governed can lead in turn to more appropriate measures of reorganization and reform.[3]

This paper is an initial effort to explore some of the potentialities of a polycentric political system in providing for the government of metropolitan areas. We view the "business" of governments in metropolitan areas as providing "public goods and services." The first section of the paper will examine the special character of these public goods and services.

We shall then turn to an analysis of the problems of scale in constituting the public organizations which provide them. This discussion seems relevant to an analysis of any political structure in a metropolitan area, and equally applicable to gargantua or to a polycentric political system. A brief reference will then be made to the problems of public organization in gargantua. Finally, patterns of organization in a polycentric political system will be analyzed with particular regard to the experience of the Los Angeles metropolitan area.

THE NATURE OF PUBLIC GOODS AND SERVICES

The conditions which give rise to public rather than private provision of certain goods and services are examined in this section. Three views of these conditions can usefully be distinguished: (1) public goods arising from efforts to control indirect consequences, externalities or spillover effects; (2) public goods provided because some goods and services cannot be packaged; and (3) public goods consisting of the maintenance of preferred states of community affairs.

The Control of Indirect Consequences as Public Goods.

The basic criterion traditionally offered for distinguishing between public and private affairs was formulated some years ago by John

---

[3]By analogy, the formal units of government in a metropolitan area might be viewed as organizations similar to individual firms in an industry. Individual firms may constitute the basic legal entities in an industry, but their conduct in relation to one another may be conceived as having a particular structure and behavior as an industry. Collaboration among the separate units of local government may be such that their activities supplement or complement

Dewey: ". . . the line between private and public is to be drawn on the basis of the extent and scope of the consequences of acts which are so important as to need control whether by inhibition or by promotion."[4] The indirect consequences of a transaction, which affect others than those directly concerned can also be described as "externalities" or "spillover effects." Those indirectly affected are viewed as being external to the immediate transaction. Some externalities are of a favorable or beneficial nature; others are adverse or detrimental.

Favorable externalities can frequently be recaptured by the economic unit that creates them. The builder of a large supermarket, for example, may create externalities for the location of a nearby drugstore. If the builder of the supermarket also controls the adjacent land, he can capture the externalities accruing to the drugstore through higher rents or by common ownership of the two enterprises. From the builder's point of view he has "internalized"[5] the externalities.[6]

Where favorable externalities cannot be internalized by private parties, a sufficient mechanism to proceed may be lacking and public agencies may be called upon to provide a good or service. A privately owned park, even with an admission charge, may not be able to cover costs. If the externalities in the form of the dollar value of a better neighborhood could be captured, such a park might be profitable.

Unfavorable spillovers or externalities are another matter. The management of a refinery which belches out smoke has little incentive to install costly equipment to eliminate the smoke. Control or internalization of dis-economies usually falls upon public agencies.

---

each other, as in the automobile industry's patent pool. Competition among them may produce desirable self-regulating tendencies similar in effect to the "invisible hand" of the market. Collaboration and competition among governmental units may also, of course, have detrimental effects, and require some form of central decision-making to consider the interests of the area as a whole. For a comprehensive review of the theory of industrial organization see Joe S. Bain, *Industrial Organization* (New York, 1959).

[4]John Dewey, *The Public and Its Problems* (New York, 1927), p. 15.

[5]John V. Krutilla and Otto Eckstein, *Multiple Purpose River Development: Studies in Applied Economic Analysis* (Baltimore: The Johns Hopkins Press, 1958), p. 69 ff. Krutilla and Eckstein develop the concept of "internalizing" external economies as a criterion for determining scale of a management unit in the administration of water resources.

[6]In practice, shopping centers may also give favorable rents to large supermarkets as "traffic generators." This recognizes the externalities they create.

A function of government, then, is to internalize the externalities—positive and negative—for those goods which the producers and consumers are unable or unwilling to internalize for themselves, and this process of internalization is identified with the "public goods."

Not all public goods are of the same scale. Scale implies both the geographic domain and the intensity or weight of the externality. A playground creates externalities which are neighborhoodwide in scope, while national defense activities benefit a whole nation—and affect many outside it. Thus, for each public good there corresponds some "public." As John Dewey has formulated the definition, the public consists of all those who are affected by the indirect consequences of transactions to such an extent that it is deemed necessary to have those consequences systematically provided for.[7] The concept of the public is important to later considerations in determining the criteria of scale appropriate to public organizations.

Packageability.

Public goods and services and, in turn, the functions of governments in metropolitan areas can be distinguished from private goods by a criterion commonly used by economists. A private good must be "packageable", *i.e.,* susceptible of being differentiated as a commodity or service before it can be readily purchased and sold in the private market. Those who do not pay for a private good can then be excluded from enjoying its benefits. This notion is formulated by economists as the exclusion principle."[8] In contrast with Dewey's formulation of the nature of public goods, the exclusion principle focuses attention on the practicability of denying benefits. National defense, for example, will not be provided by private firms because, among other reasons, the citizen who did not pay would still enjoy the benefits. Furthermore, if citizens understate their preferences for defense—as by failing to build bomb shelters—on the assumption that it will be paid for by others, the result will be an inadequate provision for defense.

Most municipal public goods such as fire and police protection, or the abatement of air pollution, are not easily packageable, either;

[7]John Dewey, *op. cit.,* pp. 15-16.
[8]Richard Musgrave, *The Theory of Public Finance* (New York, 1959), esp. ch. 1.

they cannot be sold only to those individuals who are willing to pay.[9] This suggests two problems for public organization.

First, private goods, because they are easily packageable, are readily subject to measurement and quantification. Public goods, by contrast, are generally not so measureable. If more police are added to the force, output will presumably increase. But how much, is a question without an exact answer. Moreover, when factors of production can be quantified in measurable units of output, the production process can be subject to more rigorous controls. A more rational pricing policy is also possible. With quantifiable data about both input and output, any production process can be analyzed and the performance of different modes of production can be compared for their efficiency. Rational control over the production and provision of public goods and services therefore depends, among other things, upon the development of effective standards of measurement; this gets into the allocation of joint costs as well as of joint benefits.

A second, closely related, problem arises in the assessment of costs upon persons who can benefit without paying directly for the good. Only public agencies with their taxing powers can seek to apportion the costs of public goods among the various beneficiaries. The scale criterion of political representation discussed below, takes account of how this difference between private and public goods affects the organization of public agencies.

Public Goods as the Maintenance of Preferred States of Community Affairs.

The exclusion principle provides a criterion for distinguishing most public goods from private, but it does not, as commonly stated, clarify or specify the conditions which determine the patterns of organization in the public service economy. However, by viewing public goods as "the maintenance of preferred states of community affairs," we may introduce a modified concept of packageability, one that is amenable to some measurement and quantification, and that therefore may be more helpful in clarifying criteria for the organization of public services in metropolitan areas. The modification consists in extending the exclusion principle from an individual consumer to all the inhabitants of an area within designated boundaries.

[9]Charles M. Tiebout, "A Pure Theory of Social Expenditures," *Journal of Political Economy,* Vol. 64 (October, 1956), pp. 416-24.

The concept can be illustrated on a small scale in the operation of a household heating system which uses conveniently measurable units of inputs. However, the household temperature it maintains is a joint benefit to the family and a marginal change in family size will have no material effect upon the costs of maintaining this public good for the family. Yet since the family good derived from it is effectively confined to the household, outsiders are excluded and there are no substantial spillover effects or externalities for them. The family good is not a public good in the larger community. So household heating is treated as a private good in most communities. Similarly, a public good on a neighborhood or community scale can be viewed as "packaged" within appropriate boundaries so that others outside the boundaries may be excluded from its use. In this way, in some communities adjacent to New York City, for example, the use of parks and beaches is restricted to local residents whose taxes presumably support these recreation facilities.

Wherever this is practicable, the analogy of a household as a "package" for an atmosphere with controlled temperature may be generalized and applied to the maintenance of a desired state of affairs within particular local government boundaries. Just as the temperature and cost of heating can be measured, so it may be possible to develop direct or closely approximate measures both of a given state of community affairs resulting from the production of many public goods and services and also of the costs of furnishing them. An air pollution abatement program, for example, may be measured by an index of quantities of various pollutants found in air samples. Given costs of abatement, some preferred tolerance levels may then be specified.

Similarly, any community has a "fire loss potential," defined as the losses to be expected if no provision for fire protection is made. The difference between this potential and the actual fire losses is then the output or "production" of the fire protection service, and the net fire loss can be termed the "state of affairs" in that community with respect to fire losses. Fire protection, of course, does not eliminate but only reduces fire losses. Any effort at complete elimination would probably be so expensive that the costs would greatly exceed the benefits. The "preferred" state of affairs is some optimal level of performance where benefits exceed costs. The provision of a community fire department as a public good can thus be viewed as the maintenance of a preferred state of affairs in fire protection for the community, and the benefits can ordinarily be confined to its residents.

Police protection can be regarded in the same way. The traffic patrol, for example, operates to optimize the flow of traffic while reducing the losses to property and injury to persons. Even if perfect control were possible, the costs would be so great that the preferred state of affaris in police protection would be something less.

It must be acknowledged, however, that in the case of police protection and many other public services, in contrast, say, with garbage collection or air pollution abatement, the performance level or net payoff is much more difficult to measure and to quantify. Proximate measures such as the gross number of arrests for different types of offenses per month or per 10,000 population annually have little meaning unless considered in relation to various conditions existing in the community. Decision-makers consequently may be forced, for want of better measurements, to assume that the preferred state of affairs is defined as a balance between the demands for public services and the complaints from taxpayers.

While the output of a public good may not be packaged, this does not, of course, mean that its material inputs cannot be. The preferred state of affairs produced by mosquito spraying is enjoyed by the whole community, while spraying supplies and equipment are readily packageable. Mosquito spraying, that is to say, can be produced by a private vendor under contract to a public agency.

This illustrates an important point, that the *production* of goods and services needs to be distinguished from their *provision* at public expense. Government provision need not involve public production—indeed, at some stage in the sequence from raw materials to finished products virtually every public good, not already a natural resource, is of private origin. So, a public agency by contractual arrangements with private firms—or with other public agencies—can provide the local community with public services without going into the business of producing them itself.

When the desired performance level of the net payoff can be specified by a measurable index, an element of rigor can be introduced to assure substantial production controls in providing a public good, even where the production itself is the function of a separate agency or entrepreneur. The producer can be held accountable for maintaining affairs within certain tolerances, and the agency responsible for providing the service can ascertain the adequacy of performance. Advances in the measurement and quantification of performance levels in the public service economy will consequently permit much greater flexibility in the patterns of organization for the production and provision of public goods and services.

If Dewey's definition is extended to include "events" generally rather than being limited to "acts" or to "transactions" among actors, his formulation is consistent with the conception of public goods as the maintenance of preferred states of affairs.[10] Public control seeks to internalize those events, viewed as consequences which impinge directly and indirectly upon diverse elements in a community, in such a way that adverse consequences will be inhibited and favorable consequences will be promoted.

In the final analysis, distinctions between private and public goods cannot be as sharply made in the world of human experience as this analysis might imply. In part, the technical character of specific goods influences the degree of differentiation or isolability that characterizes their distribution and utilization. Vegetables and landscapes cannot be handled in the same way. Many private goods have spillover effects such that other members of the community bear some portion of the benefits and losses, whatever the degree of public regulation. In every large community most people philosophically accept some of the costs of bigness—air pollution, traffic congestion, noise, and a variety on inconveniences—on the assumption that these are inevitable concomitants of the benefits that derive from living in a metropolis.

SCALE PROBLEMS IN PUBLIC ORGANIZATION

Viewing the boundaries of a local unit of government as the "package" in which its public goods are provided,[11] so that those outside the boundaries are excluded from their use, we may say that where a public good is adequately packaged within appropriate boundaries, it has been successfully internalized. Where externalities spill over upon neighboring communities, the public good has not been fully internalized.

In designing the appropriate "package" for the production and provision of public goods, several criteria should be considered.

[10]Op. cit., pp. 4-5. Dewey's use of the terms "acts" and "transactions" implies that only social behavior is contemplated in public action. But physical events, e.g., floods, may also become objects of public control.
[11]See the discussion of "district boundaries and the incidence of benefits" in Stephen C. Smith, "Problems in the Use of the Public District for Ground Water Management," Land Economics, Vol. 32 (August, 1956), pp. 259-269.

Among these are control, efficiency, political representation and self-determination. Needless to say, they are sometimes in conflict.

The Criterion of Control.

The first standard applicable to the scale of public organization for the production of public services requires that the boundary conditions[12] of a political jurisdiction include the relevant set of events to be controlled. Events are not uniformly distributed in space; rather, they occur as sets under conditions such that boundaries can be defined with more or less precision. Rivers flow in watershed basins, for example. Patterns of social interaction are also differentially distributed in space, and boundaries can generally be defined for them too. In other words, all phenomena can be described in relation to specifiable boundary conditions and the criterion of control requires that these be taken into account in determining the scale of a public organization. Otherwise the public agency is disabled in regulating a set of events in order to realize some preferred state of affairs. If the boundaries cannot be suitably adjusted, the likely result is a transfer to the governmental function to a unit scaled to meet the criterion of control more adequately.

Pasadena, for example, is subject to severe smog attacks, but the city's boundary conditions do not cover an area sufficient to assure effective control of the appropriate meteorological and social space that would include the essential variables constituting the "smogisphere" of Southern California. None of the separate cities of southern California, in fact, can encompass the problem. Instead, county air pollution control districts were organized for the Los Angeles metropolitan community. The failure even of these counties to meet adequately the criterion of effective control has led the California state government to assume an increasingly important role in smog control.

The Criterion of Efficiency.

The most efficient solution would require the modification of boundary conditions so as to assure a producer of public goods and services the most favorable economy of scale, as well as effective

[12]The boundary conditions of a local unit of government are not limited to the legally determined physical boundaries but should include reference to extra-territorial powers, joint powers, etc.

control. Two streams with different hydrologic characteristics, for example, might be effectively controlled separately; but, by being managed together, the potentialities of one may complement the other. This has certainly been the case in Los Angeles' joint management of the Owens River and the Los Angeles River by making one the tributary of the other through the 300-mile Los Angeles Aqueduct, skirting the Sierras. Joint management permits a greater joint payoff in recreational facilities and water and power production.

Other factors such as technological developments and the skill or proficiency of a labor force can bear upon efficiency as a criterion of the scale of organization needed. If machinery for painting center stripes on city streets can only be efficiently used on a large scale, special arrangements may be required to enable several small cities to act jointly in providing such a service. The same may be true in the utilization of uncommon and expensive professional skills; and it accounts for the fact that mental institutions and prisons are apt to be state rather than municipal undertakings.

The Criterion of Political Representation.

Another criterion for the scale of public organization requires the inclusion of the appropriate political interests within its decision-making arrangements. The direct participants in a transaction are apt to negotiate only their own interests, leaving the indirect consequences or spillover effects to impinge upon others. Third-party interests may be ignored. Public organizations seek to take account of third-party effects by internalizing the various interests in rendering public decisions and in controlling public affairs. Specification of the boundary or scale conditions of any political jurisdiction is important in determining the set of interests which are to be internalized within the organization.

In considering the political design of a public organization three elements of scale require consideration. The *scale of formal organization* indicates the size of the governmental unit which provides a public good. The *public,* as noted above, consists of those who are affected by its provision. The *political community* can be defined as those who are actually taken into account in deciding whether and how to provide it. Those who are affected by such a decision may be different from those who influence its making. An ideal solution, assuming criteria of responsibility and accountability consonant with democratic theory, would require that these three boundaries be coterminous. Where in fact the boundary conditions differ, scale problems arise.

If both the direct and indirect beneficiaries of a public transaction are included within the domain of a public organization, the means are in principle available for assessment of the cost of public control upon the beneficiaries. Except where a re-distribution of income is sought as a matter of public policy, an efficient allocation of economic resources is assured by the capacity to charge the costs of providing public goods and services to the beneficiaries.[13]

The public implicated in different sets of transactions varies with each set: the relevant public for one set is confined to a neighborhood, while for another the relevant public may be most of the population of the globe. Between these two extremes are a vast number of potential scales of public organizations. Given certain levels of information, technology, communication, and certain patterns of identification, a scheme might be imagined which had an appropriate scale of public organization for each different public good. As these conditions and circumstances change, the scale of the public for any set of transactions should be altered correspondingly. If it is not, what then?

Where the political community does not contain the whole public, some interests may be disregarded. A city, for instance, may decide to discharge its sewage below its boundaries, and the affected public there may have no voice in the decision. On the other hand, where the political community contains the whole public and, in addition, people unaffected by a transaction, the unaffected are given a voice when none may be desired. Capricious actions can result. The total political community in a city of three million population may not be an appropriate decision-making mechanism in planning a local playground.

Nevertheless, the statement that a government is "too large (or too small) to deal with a problem" often overlooks the possibility that the scale of the public and political community need not coincide with that of the formal boundaries of a public organization. Informal arrangements between public organizations may create a political community large enough to deal with any particular public's problem. Similarly, a public organization may also be

---

[13]This factor might be separately characterized as a criterion of equitable distribution of costs and benefits, but we have chosen to consider it here in the context of political representation.

able to constitute political communities within its boundaries to deal with problems which affect only a subset of the population. It would be a mistake to conclude that public organizations are of an inappropriate size until the informal mechanisms, which might permit larger or smaller political communities, are investigated.

Seen in relation to the political community, the scale of formal public organizations merely specifies the formal boundaries. Since the feasible number of governmental units is limited when compared to the number of public goods to be provided, a one-to-one mapping of the public, the political community and the formal public organization is impracticable. Moreover, the relevant public changes. Even if, at one time, formal public organizations, political communities and the publics were coterminous, over time they would become dislocated. As a result, public organizations may (1) reconstitute themselves, (2) voluntarily cooperate, or, failing cooperation, (3) turn to other levels of government in a quest for an appropriate fit among the interests affecting and affected by public transactions.

The Criterion of Local Self-Determination.

The criteria of effective control, of efficiency and of the inclusion of appropriate political interests, can be formulated on general theoretical grounds, but their application in any political system depends upon the particular institutions empowered to decide questions of scale. The conditions attending the organization of local governments in the United States usually require that these criteria be controlled by the decisions of the citizenry in the local community, i.e., subordinated to considerations of self-determination.

The patterns of local self-determination manifest in incorporation proceedings usually require a petition of local citizens to institute incorporation proceedings and an affirmative vote of the local electorate to approve. Commitments to local consent and local control may also involve substantial home rule in determining which interests of the community its local officials will attend to and how these officials will be organized and held responsible for their discharge of public functions.

Local self-government of municipal affairs assumes that public goods can be successfully internalized. The purely "municipal" affairs of a local jurisdiction, presumably, do not create problems for other political communities. Where internalization is not possible and where control, consequently, cannot be maintained, the local unit of government becomes another "interest" group in quest of public goods or potential public goods that spill over upon others beyond its borders.

The choice of local public services implicit in any system of self-government presumes that substantial variety will exist in patterns of public organization and in the public goods provided among the different local communities in a metropolis. Patterns of local autonomy and home rule constitute substantial commitments to a polycentric system.

PUBLIC ORGANIZATION IN GARGANTUA

Since all patterns of organization are less than perfectly efficient, responsive or representative, some consideration should be given to the problem of organizing for different types of public services in gargantua, in contrast to the problems in a polycentric political system. This brief discussion will only touch on theoretical considerations involved in organizing diverse public services in the big system.

Gargantua unquestionably provides an appropriate scale of organization for many huge public services. The provision of harbor and airport facilities, mass transit, sanitary facilities and imported water supplies may be most appropriately organized in gargantua. By definition, gargantua should be best able to deal with metropolitan-wide problems at the metropolitan level.

However, gargantua with its dominant center of decision-making, is apt to become a victim of the complexity of its own hierarchical or bureaucratic structure. Its complex channels of communication may make its administration unresponsive to many of the more localized public interests in the community. The costs of maintaining control in gargantua's public service may be so great that its production of public goods becomes grossly inefficient.

Gargantua, as a result, may become insensitive and clumsy in meeting the demands of local citizens for the public goods required in their daily life. Two to three years may be required to secure street or sidewalk improvements, for example, even where local residents bear the cost of the improvement. Modifications in traffic control at the local intersection may take an unconscionable amount of time. Some decision-makers will be more successful in pursuing their interests than others. The lack of effective organization for these others may result in policies with highly predictable biases. Bureaucratic unresponsiveness in gargantua may produce frustration and cynicism on the part of the local citizen who finds no point of access for remedying local problems of a public character. Municipal reform may become simply a matter of "throwing the rascals out." The citizen may not have access to sufficient information to render an informed judgment at the polls. Lack of effective communication in the large public organization may indeed lead to the eclipse of the public and to the blight of the community.

The problem of gargantua, then, is to recognize the variety of smaller sets of publics that may exist within its boundaries. Many of the interests of smaller publics might be properly negotiated within the confines of a smaller political community without requiring the attention of centralized decision-makers concerned with the big system. This task of recognizing the smaller publics is a problem of "field" or "area" organization. The persistence of bureaucratic unresponsiveness in the big system, however, indicates it is not easily resolved. Large-scale, metropolitan-wide organization is unquestionably appropriate for a limited number of public services, but it is not the most appropriate scale of organization for the provision of all public services required in a metropolis.

PUBLIC ORGANIZATION IN A POLYCENTRIC
POLITICAL SYSTEM

No *a priori* judgment can be made about the adequacy of a polycentric system of government as against the single jurisdiction. The multiplicity of interests in various public goods sought by people in a metropolitan region can only be handled in the context of many different levels of organization. The polycentric system is confronted with the problem of realizing the needs of wider community interests or publics beyond the functional or territorial bounds of each of the formal entities within the broader metropolitan region. The single jurisdiction, in turn, confronts the problem of recognizing and organizing the various subsidiary sets of interests within the big system. It is doubtful that sub-optimization in gargantua is any easier to accomplish than supra-optimization in a polycentric political system.

The performance of a polycentric political system can only be understood and evaluated by reference to the patterns of cooperation, competition and conflict that may exist among its various units. Cooperative arrangements pose no difficulty when joint activities produce a greater return to all parties concerned, if the appropriate set of public interests are adequately represented among the negotiators. A contractual arrangement will suffice. As a result, this discussion of the behavior of a polycentric political system will focus upon the more difficult problems of competition, of conflict and its resolution. If a polycentric political system can resolve conflict and maintain competition within appropriate bounds it can be a viable arrangement for dealing with a variety of public problems in a metropolitan area.

Competition.[14]

Where the provision of public goods and services has been successfully internalized within a public jurisdiction, there are no substantial spill-over effects, by definition. In such circumstances there need be no detrimental consequences from competition in the municipal services economy. Patterns of competition among producers of public services in a metropolitan area, just as among firms in the market, may produce substantial benefits by inducing self-regulating tendencies with pressure for the more efficient solution in the operation of the whole system.

Variety in service levels among various independent local government agencies within a larger metropolitan community may give rise to a quasi-market choice for local residents in permitting them to select the particular community in the metropolitan area that most closely approximates the public service levels they desire. Public service agencies then may be forced to compete over the service levels offered in relation to the taxes charged. Such competition, however, would only be appropriate for those public goods which are adequately internalized within the boundaries of a given political jurisdiction.

Conditions amenable to competition normally exist among local units of government where a number of units are located in close proximity to each other and where information about

[14]This analysis is confined to competition between units of government and makes no reference to competitive forces within a unit of government. Competition among pressure groups, factions and political parties is a fundamental feature of the democratic political process, but is not within the primary focus of this paper and its concern with the polycentric system.

each other's performance is publicly available. Information can lead to comparison and comparison can lead to pressure for performances to approximate the operations of the more efficient units. Where more than one public jurisdiction is capable of rendering service in a single area, further competitive tendencies may develop. Contractual arrangements among public jurisdictions for the provision of specific public services have long provided a competitive alternative to each jurisdiction which might otherwise produce its own services.

The separation of the *provision* of public goods and services from their *production* opens up the greatest possibility of redefining economic functions in a public service economy. Public control can be maintained in relation to performance criteria in the provision of services, while allowing an increasing amount of competition to develop among the agencies that produce them.

With the incorporation of the City of Lakewood in 1954, Los Angeles County, for example, expanded its system of contracting for the production of municipal services to a point approaching quasi-market conditions. Newly incorporated cities, operating under the so-called Lakewood Plan, contract with the county or other appropriate agencies to produce the general range of municipal services needed in the local community.

Each city contracts for municipal services for the city as a whole. Services beyond the general level of performance by county administration in unincorporated areas are subject to negotiation for most service functions. Each city also has the option of producing municipal services for itself. Private contractors too have undertaken such services as street sweeping, engineering, street maintenance and repair, and related public works. Some contracts have been negotiated with neighboring cities. As the number of vendors increases, competition brings pressures toward greater responsiveness and efficiency.

By separating the production from the provision of public goods it may be possible to differentiate, unitize and measure the production while continuing to provide undifferentiated public goods to the citizen-consumer. Thus Los Angeles County has, under the Lakewood Plan, unitized the production of police services into packages, each consisting of a police-car-on-continuous-patrol with associated auxiliary services. A price is placed on this police-car-on-continuous-patrol package, and a municipality may contract for police service on that basis. Within the local community, police service is still provided as a public good for the community as a whole.

Problems of scale arising from possible conflicts between criteria of production and criteria of political representation may be effectively solved in this way. Efficient scales of organization for the production of different public goods may be quite independent of the scales required to recognize appropriate publics for their consumption of public goods and services. But competition among vendors may allow the most efficient organization to be utilized in the production, while an entirely different community of interest and scale of organization controls the provision of services in a local community.

The separation of production from provision may also have the consequence of turning local governments into the equivalents of associations of consumers. While Sidney and Beatrice Webb viewed local governments as associations of consumers, the dominance of production criteria in American municipal administration has largely led to the subordination of consumer interests.[15] However, cities organized to provide the local citizenry with public services produced by other agencies may be expected to give stronger representation to consumer interests. Among the so-called Lakewood Plan cities in Los Angeles County, for example, the local chief administrative officer has increasingly become a spokesman or bargainer for local consumer interests.

In this role, the chief administrative officer is similar to a buyer in a large corporation. Recognizing that the greater the number of vendors of public services, the greater the competition, the local chief administrative officer may seek to expand the number of his potential suppliers. As competition increases, vendors become more sensitive to the consumer demands he negotiates.

The production of public goods under the contract system in Los Angeles County has also placed considerable pressure upon the county administration to become more responsive to demands of the public service clientele organized through their local cities. Important changes in operating procedures and organizational arrangements have been introduced into the county's administration of police protection, fire protection, library services, street maintenance, building inspection and engineering services in order to increase efficiency and responsiveness.

[15]Sidney and Beatrice Webb, *English Local Government: Statutory Authorities for Special Purposes* (London: Longmans, Green and Co., 1922), p. 437 ff.

Under these circumstances, a polycentric political system can be viable in supplying a variety of public goods with many different scales of organization and in providing optimal arrangements for the production and consumption of public goods. With the development of quasi-market conditions in production, much of the flexibility and responsiveness of market organization can be realized in the public service economy.

Several difficulties in the regulation of a competitive public service economy can be anticipated. Economic pricing and cost allocation are dependent upon the development of effective measurement of municipal services. Since the preferred states of affairs in a community cannot be converted to a single scale of values, such as dollar profits in a private enterprise, it may be more difficult to sustain an objective competitive relationship in a public service economy. Although costs of contract services from different vendors of a public good may be the same, objective standards for determining the value of the benefits are needed, and may be hard to come by; otherwise the latitude of discretion available to the negotiators may limit the competitive vitality of the system and shift the competition to side-payoffs.

Without careful control of cost allocations and pricing arrangements, funds from noncompetitive welfare functions might be used to subsidize the more competitive service areas. In Los Angeles County, close scrutiny of cost accounting practices and pricing policies by the grand jury has helped to prevent funds from being so transferred.

Any long-term reliance upon quasi-market mechanisms in the production of public goods and services no doubt will require more of such careful scrutiny, control and regulation than has been applied toward maintaining the competitive structure of the private market economy. The measurement of cost and output performance may become an essential public function of the state in the administration of metropolitan affairs if continued reliance is placed primarily upon a polycentric system in the government of metropolitan areas.

Reliance upon outside vendors to produce public services may also reduce the degree of local political control exercised. The employee is subject to the control of the vendor and not directly to the control of the municipality. In contrast to the more immediate lines of responsibility and communication between local municipal employees, and city officials, reliance upon vendors to provide municipal services may also restrict the quality and quantity of information about community affairs that are provided to the city's decision-makers. This constraint on information might reduce the degree of their control over public affairs.

This discussion merely indicates some of the considerations to be examined in an analysis of the effects of competitive arrangements in providing public services. As long as the particular contracting agencies encompass the appropriate sets of public interests no absolute impediment to their use need exist. With appropriate public control, competitive arrangements may afford great flexibility in taking advantage of some of the economies of scale for the production of public services in a metropolitan area, while, at the same time, allowing substantial diversity in their provision for the more immediate communities, based upon political responsibility within local patterns of community identification.

Conflict and Conflict Resolution.

More difficult problems for a polycentric political system are created when the provision of public goods cannot be confined to the boundaries of the existing units of government. These situations involving serious spill-over effects are apt to provoke conflict between the various units in the system. Arrangements must be available for the resolution of such conflicts if a polycentric political system is to solve its problems. Otherwise, competition and conflict are apt to become acute.

No community, on its own initiative, has much incentive to assume the full costs of controlling adverse consequences which are shared by a wider public. The competitive disadvantage of enforcing pollution abatement regulations, for example, against individuals and firms within a single community, when competitors in neighboring communities are not required to bear such costs, leads each community to excuse its failure to act by the failure of other similarly situated communities to act. In a polycentric system this is especially serious where many of the public "goods" involve the costly abatement of public nuisances.

Concerted action by various units of government in a metropolitan area is easier to organize when costs and benefits are fairly uniformly distributed throughout the area. By way of example, this has been done under contractual agreements for mutual aid to assure the mobilization of greater fire-fighting capability in case of serious conflagrations. The random and unpredictable nature of such fires causes them to be treated as a uniform risk that might occur to any community in the larger metropolitan area.

Similar considerations apply to efforts to control mosquito infestations or air pollution. Leagues of cities, chambers of commerce and other civic associations have frequently become the agencies for negotiating legislative proposals for the creation of mosquito abatement districts, air pollution control districts and the like.

More difficult problems for the polycentric political system arise when the benefits and the costs are not uniformly distributed. Communities may differ in their perception of the benefits they receive from the provision of a common public good. In turn, a community may be unwilling to "pay its fair share" for providing that good simply because its demands for provisions are less than in neighboring communities. These situations call for effective governmental mechanisms which can internalize the problem. If necessary, sanctions must be available for the enforcement of decisions.

The conflicting claims of municipal water supply systems pumping water from the same underground basins in Southern California, for example, have uniformly been resolved by recourse to legal actions in the state courts. The courts have thereby become the primary authorities for resolving conflicts among water supply agencies in Southern California; and their decisions have come to provide many of the basic policies of water administration in the Southern California metropolitan region. The state's judiciary has played a comparable role in conflicts among other local government agencies in such diverse fields as public health, incorporation and annexation proceedings, law enforcement, and urban planning.

The heavy reliance upon courts for the resolution of conflicts among local units of government unquestionably reflects an effort to minimize the risks of external control by a superior decision-maker. Court decisions are taken on a case-by-case basis. The adversaries usually define the issues and consequently limit the areas of judicial discretion. This method also minimizes the degree of control exercised following a judgment. California courts, in particular, have accepted the basic doctrines of home rule and are thus favorably disposed to the interests of local units of government in dealing with problems of municipal affairs.

The example of municipal water administration may be pursued further to illustrate other decision-making arrangements and their

consequences which bear upon the resolution of conflict in a polycentric political system.[16]

While litigation may be an appropriate means of resolving conflicts over a given supply of water, local water administrators in
Southern California have long recognized that law suits never produced any additional water. Organization for the importation of
new water supplies was recognized as the only means for solving
the long-term problem.

Los Angeles built the first major aqueduct to import water into
the area on its own initiative. This water supply was used to
force adjoining areas to annex or consolidate to the City of Los
Angeles if they wished to gain access to the new supply. The condition for the provision of water required adjoining areas to sacrifice their identities as separate political communities. To get at
one public good they were forced to give up other public goods.
This provoked sufficient opposition to block any new developments
which were not based upon consent and cooperation. The mechanisms for the resolution of subsequent conflicts were required to take
on new forms.

The importation of Colorado River water was later undertaken
by a coalition of communities in Southern California formed through
the agency of the southern section of the League of California
Cities. The League afforded a neutral ground for the negotiation
of the common interests of the City of Los Angeles and the other
cities in the metropolitan area which shared common water problems. After satisfactory arrangements had been negotiated, including
provision for the formation of a new metropolitan water district and
endorsement of the Boulder Canyon project, a Boulder Dam Association was formed to realize these objectives. In due course a new
agency, the Metropolitan Water District of Southern California,
was formed; and the Colorado River aqueduct was constructed and
put into operation by this new district.

More recently, the Southern California Water Coordinating Conference, meeting under the auspices of the Los Angeles Chamber
of Commerce, has been the agency for negotiating regional interests in the development of the California Water Program. The
Metropolitan Water District was not able to represent areas in
Southern California which did not belong to that district; and the
rise of a variety of special municipal water districts precluded the

[16]For further detail see: Vincent Ostrom, *Water and Politics* (Los Angeles,
Haynes Foundation, 1953), esp. chs. 3, 6 and 7.

League of California Cities, which represents cities only, from again serving as the agency for the negotiation of metropolitan interests in municipal water supply.

These illustrations suggest that a variety of informal arrangements may be available for negotiating basic policies among local government agencies in a metropolitan area. Such arrangements are vital in negotiating common interests among them. The larger public is taken into account in an informally constituted political community. These arrangements work effectively only so long as a substantial unanimity can be reached, for formal implementation of such decisions must be ratified by each of the appropriate official agencies, including the state government when changes in state law or administrative policies are involved.

Higher levels of government may also be invoked in seeking the resolution of conflict among local governments in metropolitan areas. Again recourse is sought to a more inclusive political community. Under these circumstances, conflict tends to centralize decision-making and control. The danger is that the more inclusive political community will not give appropriate recognition to the particular public interests at issue and tend to inject a variety of other interests into settlements of local controversies.

Appeal to central authorities runs the risk of placing greater control over local metropolitan affairs in agencies such as the state legislature, while at the same time reducing the capability of local governments for dealing with their problems in the local context. Sensitivity over the maintenance of local control may produce great pressure for the subordination of differences while conflicting parties seek a common position approximating unanimity. A substantial investment in informal negotiating and decision-making arrangements can be justified from the perspective of the local authorities if such arrangements can prevent the loss of local autonomy to higher levels of government.

Ironically but logically, this effort to avoid recourse to conflict and the consequent centralization of decision-making tends also to reduce the local autonomy or degree of independence exercised by the local governing boards. Pressure for agreement on a common approach to some metropolitan problem limits the choices available to any particular local government. However, this range of choice may still be greater than that which would result from a settlement by a central authority. Negotiation among independent agencies allows the use of a veto against any unacceptable position. Agreement must be negotiated within the limits of the various veto positions if the alternative of recourse to an external authority at a higher level of political jurisdiction is to be avoided.

To minimize the costs of conflict to their power positions, administrators of local government agencies in metropolitan areas have tended to develop an extensive system of communication about each other's experience and to negotiate standards of performance applicable to various types of public services. Professional administrative standards may, thus, operate to constrain the variety of experience in local government agencies. Information about areas of difference and of potential conflict tend to be repressed under these circumstances. The negotiations about common problems through informal agencies are apt to be conducted in secrecy, and careful control may be developed over sensitive information.

These pressures to avoid the costs of conflict and seek agreement about metropolitan problems reflect the importance to local governments of resolving general public problems by negotiation at the local level in a metropolitan community. To the extent that these pressures are effective, the patterns of local government in a metropolitan area can only be understood by attention to the variety of formal and informal arrangements that may exist for settling area-wide problems.

Contrary to the frequent assertion about the lack of a "metropolitan framework" for dealing with metropolitan problems, most metropolitan areas have a very rich and intricate "framework" for negotiating, adjudicating and deciding questions that affect their diverse public interests. Much more careful attention needs to be given to the study of this framework.

6

THE GOVERNANCE OF THE METROPOLIS AS A PROBLEM IN DIPLOMACY[*][†]

MATTHEW HOLDEN, JR.

This paper results from an effort to make explicit the theoretical and research consequences of the insight which compares metro-politics and international politics.[1] It undertakes three specific tasks in this connection: (1) to indicate the relationships in terms of which these two political realms may be analytically compara-ble; (2) to define some gross categories for the collection of data; and (3) to indicate some elements of international relations theory which may provide slightly better clues than we should otherwise have for the interpretation of these data, chiefly in rela-tion to the goal of consensus formation through intergovernmental consultation.

[*]Reprinted from *The Journal of Politics, V. 26,* No. 3 (August 1964) pp. 627-647. By permission of *The Journal of Politics.*

[†]An earlier version of this paper was read at the American Political Science Association, September 1962, Washington, D.C. It is part of a larger study of American, British, and Canadian metropolitics now in preparation under the working title: *Diplomacy, Community, and Metropolitics.* Chadwick F. Alger, Robert J. Alperin, Scott A. Greer, Aaron Wildavsky, and Robert C. Wood have made particularly helpful criticisms of earlier editions.

[1]*Cf.,* William T. R. Fox, as cited by Victor Jones, "The Organization of a Metropolitan Region," *University of Pennsylvania Law Review,* CV (1958), 538-539. Also, Richard C. Snyder and James A. Robinson, *National and In-ternational Decision-Making: A Report to the Committee on Research for Peace,* (New York: Institute for International Order, 1960), p. 32; and, Ross Stagner, "Attitude Change and the Reduction of International Tensions," Paper Read at the University of Texas, June 23, 1961, Ditto.

METROPOLITICS AND INTERNATIONAL POLITICS:
THE CONCEPT OF DIPLOMATIC SYSTEMS

The basic contention is that metropolitics and international politics are analogous in that each occurs not within *political communities* but within *diplomatic systems.*

1. Diplomatic systems are social systems consisting of corporate units bound within an "ecological community."[2] These corporate units are the *primary*[3] actors in the system.

For present purposes, we may restrict attention to those diplomatic systems in which formal governments are the key actors.[4] Objective interdependence, which is the test of "ecological community," can hardly be denied either in international relations or in metropolitics. Actions by unit A may have predictable effects in units B, C, and D. Simply to illustrate this point, a decision to build the Aswan High Dam was taken as a matter of Egyptian national economic planning, but it has manifold ramifications for six other countries in the Great Lakes–Nile System: Congo Republic, Ethiopia, Kenya, Sudan, Tanganyika, and Uganda. In much the same way, an inner city slum clearance may have important effects—through population displacements—upon a suburb or group of suburbs several miles away.

2. Diplomatic systems are not political communities in that they lack a sufficiently thorough *symbol* system, an adequate *deliberative* process for arriving at system decisions, and an adequate *administrative* process for assuring reasonably effective execution of such decisions as might be reached.

In the metropolitan case, the countries, school districts, special authorities, cities and other corporate actors each seek to maintain their own "interest." To this end, each mobilizes available resources of many kinds: money, lawyers, retaliatory legislation, "civic

[2]On the concept of "ecological community," See, Amos H. Hawley, *Human Ecology, A Theory of Community Structure* (New York: Ronald Press Company, 1953).

[3]Other kinds of actors—corporations, trade unions, universities, even individuals—may play important roles, but the usual expectation is governments will predominate. *Cf.,* Arnold Wolfers, "The Actors in International Politics," in William T. R. Fox (ed.), *Theoretical Aspects of International Relations.* (Notre Dame, Indiana: University of Notre Dame Press, (1959), pp. 83-106.

[4]For example, the AFL-CIO is another type of diplomatic system in which jurisdiction relates to occupation rather than territory.

pride," and public relations. It is this pattern which *is* "the metropolitan problem," *i.e.,* the inability to produce "rational" metropolitan decisions.

3. Diplomatic communication is governed by a ritual which proscribes non-governmental initiatives toward the resolution of substantive issues in which governments are partisans.

Under the ritual, issues are raised and formulated by the highest political officials of the corporate units or those specialized functionaries ("ambassadors") who carry and interpret messages between units. Since issues are thus put in *inter-corporate* form, nongovernmental actors are deprived of opportunity to break up and redirect the terms of a given dispute. This happens in two ways.

(a) *There is the latent stigma of moral impropriety which may be activated* at the discretion of the official decision-makers.[5]

Thus, in a dispute between units "A" and "B", the citizen or member of either who independently proposes an alternative may find himself accused of wanting to "sell out to the other side."

(b) *Since the ritual leaves initiatives in the hands of the official decision-makers, it also segregates non-gavernmental actors from the information necessary to enable these non-governmental actors to influence decision-makers directly with any real efficiency.* Thus, the chances that like-minded non-governmental actors in different units—disagreeing with their corporate spokesmen[6]— can mount successful internal pressure or a successful inter-unit coalition against the wishes of their corporate spokesmen is reduced virtually to a nullity.

---

[5]The Ford "peace ship," Mr. Henry Wallace's difficulties in 1946-47, and Mr. Cyrus Eaton's difficulties in the present era are all illustrative. The episode of the "Tractors-for-Freedom Committee" illustrate that the freedom to invoke, or let lie, the stigma of moral impropriety is in the hands of official decision-makers. In the latter case, the non-governmental actors were but a thin veil for action which the United States Government wished pursued but which it did not wish officially to undertake. The Logan Act. is the *legal* embodiment of the moral restraint which is involved.

[6]It should also be pointed out that the "like-mindedness" of dissenting unofficials, separate from any immediate decisions which they have to make, may be of very low salience. "In 1933, the students of the Oxford Union, under the inspiration of a Mr. Joad, passed their ever-shameful resolution, 'That this House refuses to fight for King and Country' . . . Little did the foolish boys who passed the resolution dream that they were destined quite soon to conquer or to fall gloriously in the ensuing war, and prove themselves the finest generation ever bred in Britain. Less excuse can be found for their elders, who had no chance of self-repudiation in action." Winston S. Churchill, *The Gathering Storm.* (Boston: Houghton Mifflin Company, 1948), p. 85.

The burden of the characterization above, when applied to metropolitics, denies that "the metropolitan problem" is one of structural irrationality in an existent community. Rather, it asserts, it is an inherent feature of the social system. If this is so, predictions as to the possibilities of integration must be based upon knowledge of specific kinds of data about the system *and* upon theories which would specify (in terms of these data) whether the system were subject to alteration and in what manner.

FOUR DESCRIPTIVE CATEGORIES

If this conception of the comparability of metropolitan and international action is accepted, what are the aspects of concrete activity which we may wish to observe? At least four topic-areas may provide convenient foci for this purpose: (a) the subject-matter of interaction, (b) "power" of the actors, (c) permanence of transience of relationships, and (d) procedures of interaction.

SUBJECT-MATTERS OF INTERACTION

The probable subject-matters of interaction may be predicted upon a "requisites" approach.[7] What must local governments in metropolitan areas undertake? Among the things which they must undertake, what are those which are likely to bring them into official contact with other local governments? Among the things which are likely to bring them into official contact, what are those which are most likely to bring them into conflict? Whatever else may be the case, one set of answers lies in the necessity for local governments to *exert control and direction over the physical environment*. Many activities may relate directly to physical environment—air pollution control, water supply, sanitation, fire prevention, land use planning. However, not all such activity is likely to produce important intergovernmental action, at least in the short run. While inner city slum clearance may very well have impacts which a demographer or a land economist might predict, the *indirectness*

[7]See, Marion J. Levy, Jr., *The Structure of Society,* (Princeton: Princeton University Press, 1952).

of such impacts insulates decision-makers from any "need" to calculate them or, often, even to perceive them. If, however, action by unit A portends external impacts which are both: (a) immediately significant (from the viewpoints of units, B, C, D, etc.) and (b) likely to persist, then inter-governmental contact becomes extremely likely. Moreover, *contact is likely to be acrimonious if it concerns resources which local decision-makers perceive as crucial and over which they are in actuality (or believe themselves to be) little able to control.*

From this perspective, *the* basic reality is probably the transportation system[8]—the ways of permitting people and goods to move—and roads are the basic reality of transportation.[9] While decision-makers may long be insulated from many matters which, by some objective criterion, do have important inter-governmental aspects, transportation is a function in which the external impacts are almost immediately perceptible.[10] It is thus that, in the modern period, freeway planning in metropolitan areas becomes one of the commonest points of dispute. It involves matters—control over space—in which there is a comprehensible and official presumption that "benefit" for some actors in the system means "deprivation" for others.

RELATIVE STATUS OF ACTOR-GOVERNMENTS

If we may identify some matters where conflict is inherent, the next question becomes: what is the distribution of "power," and what difference would an unequal distribution make? That the answers are not quick and easy may be illustrated in three cases where the central city is "dominant" with respect to a critical resource which suburbs require, namely water. These cases are Cleveland, Columbus, Ohio, and Milwaukee.

[8]Cf., Scott A. Greer, "Traffic, Transportation, and the Problems of the Metropolis," in Robert K. Merton and Robert A. Nisbet (eds.), *Contemporary Social Problems,* (New York: Harcourt, Brace and World, Inc., 1961), pp. 605-650; also, Delos F. Wilcox, *The American City: A Problem in Democracy.* (New York: Macmillan, 1904), pp. 28-29.

[9]However, see the argument which Robert C. Wood makes for rapid transit in his essay, "A Division of Powers in Metropolitan Areas," in Arthur Maass (ed.) *Area and Power: A Theory of Local Government.* (Glencoe: The Free Press, 1959), pp. 67-69.

[10]*Cf.,* Myres S. McDougal and William T. Burke, "Crisis in the Law of the Sea: Community Perspectives versus National Egoism," *Yale Law Journal* LXVII (1958), 539-589.

Cleveland is a monopolistic supplier. About 95% of all water consumed in the metropolitan area comes through its system. Suburban officials have little practical alternative to the Cleveland supply since they characteristically regard the dollar cost of establishing their own plants as prohibitive. Nonetheless, the central city has not tried to use the water controls as an instrument of power.[11] On the contrary the exactions have been secured by the suburbs who have been permitted to achieve service for themselves at particularly favorable conditions.[12] Columbus, on the other hand adopted a highly aggressive policy between 1953 and 1959 and used its position as chief supplier to force large portions of the surrounding area to annex to the city proper.

One initial hypothesis might be that the difference arises from Cleveland's infinitely greater freedom to expand the water system by virtue of access to Lake Erie, while Columbus—though not in an arid region—depends on the small Scioto River which means that suburban demands put particularly heavy burdens upon it. The Milwaukee experience, however, seems to negate such an hypothesis. Like Cleveland, Milwaukee is a Great Lakes city which lives in a condition of acquatic plenty. Nonetheless, it has long adopted the position that annexation is the price which suburbs desirous of central city services ought to be willing to pay. In this connection, it has maintained a sort of "foreign office" in its Annexation Department and has sought to use water control as a lever to induce suburban governments to be "cooperative" in the matter.[13]

This is a trio thrown up by chance. If one surveyed, instead, a systematically chosen sample what would one find? What are the outer limits beyond which the more powerful units do not

---

[11]However, recent signs of growing Negro political power have raised suburban worries that a Negro-controlled Administration might seek to exact open occupancy as the return for water service. This prospect is also taken seriously by some of the Negro politicians and the matter lay very much at the background of the 1959 metropolitan government campaign. See Matthew Holden, Jr., *Decision-Making on a Metropolitan Government Proposition: Cuyahoga County, Ohio. 1958-59* (Unpublished Ph.D. Dissertation, Political Science, Northwestern University, 1961), p. 156, n.2.

[12]As the condition for an easement to a sewage treatment plant, which for topographical reasons had to be located in Cuyahoga Heights, the Village of Cuyahoga Heights was given (in 1917) the right to free service in perpetuity.

[13]For a succinct exposition of one dispute in the Milwaukee area, see, David D. Gladfelter, "Water for Wauwatosa," in Richard T. Frost (ed.), *Cases in State and Local Government.* (Englewood Cliffs, New Jersey: Prentice-Hall, Inc., 1961), pp. 282-291.

even *try* to exert pressure upon the weaker units (as Cleveland has very seldom tried)? What action is characteristic of the smaller units? Does it make a difference whether the ingredients of "power" are legal status, money, control of a physical resource, location, or "prestige"? Does it make a difference if there are two or more "powerful" units in the same system as, for example, Minneapolis and St. Paul?

PERMANENCE AND TRANSIENCE

The third set of necessary data relate the permanence or transience of conflict or of co-operation.

Does a conflict leave a heritage of suspicion long after the overt issue is "settled"? Is there a tendency toward long-term conflict in the sense that Russia and Turkey are said to be "traditional" antagonists? What appears to have existed was a tendency toward long-term suspicion based on past conflict but bearing no relationship to any current policy. I label it the "phenomenon of historical persistence." In the Cleveland metropolitan government campaign, and the study which preceded it, some surburban officials often expressed the fear that metropolitan government was a "backdoor" device to bring them under Cleveland's "domination."[14] Under the circumstances, these expressions seemed patently spurious. Once one got fairly deeply into the *history* of metropolitan proposals, however, one began to see these expressions as related to policies which had not been seriously advocated for a quarter century.

PROCEDURES OF INTERACTION

The fundamental framework in a given metropolis may be regarded as set by the three factors suggested above: *subject-matters* of interaction, the *relative status* or *"power"* of the actors, and the *permanence or transience* of past experience. At any particular time, these will set the outer limits beyond which manipulation is not feasible. Within these limits, however, manipulation is a

[14]On "past experience" factors and the relevance of learning theory, of Harold Guetzkow, "Isolation and Collaboration: A Partial Theory of Inter-Nation Relations," *Journal of Conflict Resolution, I* (1957), 51-52.

function of the procedures of interaction or methods of doing business deliberately. The three sub-aspects which seem open to inquiry are: (1) frequency and instrumentalities of interaction, (2) scope of interaction, and (3) forms of ultimate conflict.

1. Frequency and Instrumentalities.

How *often* do local governments deal with each other and what are the communication channels? How many mayors have known each other since grade school? How many have exchanged private phone numbers? How many have never spoken to each other? The answers to these questions will indicate how far face-to-face contact is institutionalized.

One suspects that the web of contact between the political officials at the top is thin and tenuous. If this is so, then the decision-makers really will be dependent on what one may call "the ambassadorial structure"—the cluster of adviser-messengers whom the decision-makers may (or may not) trust.[15] Though we may know only in part, and prophesy for the rest, it seems highly probable that the "ambassadorial structure" consistently contains at least three elements: the civic entrepreneurs, the municipal bureaucrats, and the municipal lawyers.

"Civic entrepreneurs" are defined as those actors who specialize in the formulation of issues in the rhetoric of "the public interest."[16] The relevant municipal bureaucrats are those more-or-less permanent senior officials of the government departments and an impressionistic judgment would be that most inter-governmental contact takes place at this level (finance director-to-finance director or health officer-to-health officer and so on). The third element is the cluster of legal advisers. The lawyers may be expected to play particularly important roles for two reasons. In the first place, they give more than merely legal advice but sit in on discussions of program content, procedure, public relations, personnel and "political" matters. In the second place, their professional bonds give them enormously greater occasion for socially defensible contact with their opposite numbers. (All that they need do is

[15]George H. Deming predicts "the day will come when every municipality of consequence will employ an individual whose major concern is inter-community relationships." See his, "Metro and the Little Places," *National Civic Review*, L (1961), 305.

[16]For Cleveland, the structure of civic entrepreneurship is discussed at greater length in Holden, *Decision-Making*, pp. 57-66.

go to the Bar Association for lunch.) If none of these channels is effective for communication, then decision-makers will be reduced to "flying blind" with significant increase in the prospects for collision.

2. *Scope.*

Scope refers to the *proportion* of the governments in the metropolis which may be involved in any particular relationship. In 1958, the City of Cleveland increased certain sewage treatment rates to suburban municipalities. Around this single issue, there emerged a coalition (twelve suburban municipalities plus the County) which sued the City to prevent this price rise. This was a bilateral confrontation dealing with one issue although there were tentative indications that Cleveland might expand the bargaining range. Thus, a few months later one Cleveland Official told a suburban counterpart: "If you expect the (metropolitan) Charter to pass, you had better drop that law suit." However, there was no clear indication that he was speaking for the Administration and the matter was later resolved in a judicial proceeding.

Does any particular conflict (or type of conflict) tend to involve most of the governments in the area or only relatively few of them? Do situations characteristically involve single issues or are many issues linked somehow and is there something comparable to "escalation"? Is conflict more easily resolved when the number of participants (or issues) is small—or does this make any difference at all?

3. *The Nature of "Ultimate Conflict."*

Exactly what activity is one referring to if one says that local governments get into "fights" and what is the ultimate form of conflict? Granted that conflict is restricted by "higher governments" which will—at *some* point—intervene, by the fact that "satisfaction" of fewer municipal "needs" is dependent on external relations, and by participation in a common culture, there are still the points at which functional analogues to war do come into play. One such analogue is the use of litigation to achieve *victories,* rather than negotiation to achieve settlements,[17] one process functionally analogous to warfare.

[17]Here one follows the useful distinction advanced by Edward C. Banfield where "struggling" is defined as the situation where each "contender (or coali-

The role of litigation may be clarified if we consider two common-sense (and somewhat contradictory) notions in our language about recourse to the law.[18] "The rule of law" has an urbane tone, implying a widespread recognition of the "the law" in maintaining social peace and common values while "litigious" conjures up visions of some spite suit from the cases of Mr. Tutt.

It is the idea of litigiousness which points to the sense in which inter-governmental litigation serves as a functional equivalent of warfare.[19] Governments sometimes "struggle" rather than "bargain" and the law is their weapon.[20]

The second analogue is official complicity which confers a quasi-public character upon private violence. This is a rarer phenomenon although it exists along the border streets of racially segregated neighborhoods within individual cities.[21] Imagine, then, a legal boundary which divided the same neighborhoods into distinct municipal corporations.[22]

Would one be justified in predicting that tensions would diminish and private depredations cease now that the conventional boundary had become legal? If tension and conflict continued, would one be justified in predicting that the relevant municipal authorities

---

tion) seeks to acquire enough power to dictate a settlement" as against the situation where the "bargainer . . . expects to give up something in order to get something." See his "Note on Conceptual Scheme" in, Martin Meyerson and Edward C. Banfield, *Politics, Planning, and the Public Interest: The Case of Public Housing in Chicago.* (Glencoe: The Free Press, 1953), p. 307.

[18] I discuss the broader problem of (a) the motives of litigants, (b) the affective states of litigants vis-a-vis each other, and (c) the litigants' evaluation of the moral legitimacy of the adjudicative tribunal in an unpublished paper, "Litigation and the Political Order," *Western Political Quarterly,* Vol. 16, No. 4 (December 1963), pp. 771-781.

[19] *Cf.,* Jerome Frank, *Courts on Trial: Myth and Reality in American Justice.* (Princeton: Princeton University Press, 1950), pp. 5-13, 80-107.

[20] *Cf.,* Gladfeller, *op. cit,;* litigation and violence are joined in the history of the Los Angeles water system as reported in, Vincent Ostrom, *Water and Politics: A Study of Water Policies and Administration in the Development of Los Angeles,* (Los Angeles: Haynes Foundation, 1953).

[21] On racial violence see, Allen D. Grimshaw, "Lawlessness and Violence in America and Their Special Manifestations in Changing Negro-White Relationships," XLIV (1959), 52-72.

[22] This is almost exactly what was at stake in *Gomillion v. Lightfoot,* 364 U.S. 339 (1960); A datachment of territory from Inkster, Michigan (a Detroit suburb) to form a new municipality (Dearborn Heights) was recently under litigation in the state courts with substantially the same problem being alleged by one group of litigants. *Inkster v. Supervisors,* 363 Mich 165 (1961); *Thomasina Taylor, et. al. v. Township of Dearborn* (Circuit Court, Wayne County, No. 612 284, July 31, 1962); and "Dearborn Township Plan to Annex Ruled OK." *Detroit Free Press,* August 6, 1962, p. 8C.

would be zealous to "uphold the law?" Indeed not! Obviously, of course, the degree of social integration in the larger system is variable, thus limiting the extent of deviation which may be possible for local officials,[23] but the possibilities are very considerable and are not limited to the ethnic conflict[24] by any means.[25]

INTERNATIONAL RELATIONS THEORY AND THE PROBLEM OF CONSENSUS FORMATION

Whether the approach sketched above permits us to know anything we would not otherwise know is its critical test. One element of such a test is to put the problem in terms of *strategies* of integration and to ask whether international relations theories give any insight into the soundness of such strategies. Recent disenchantment with attempts to create full-scale metropolitan governments has been given new impetus to the strategy of consensus formation through inter-governmental bodies such as the Supervisors' Inter-County Committee (Detroit) and the New York Metropolitan Regional Council. In effect, the strategy predicts the development of procedural consensus which can be turned into substantive agreement.[27] Samuel Humes refers to these consultative bodies as "new and novel means of meeting the problems of overcoming the geographical fragmentation of our urban regions" and "fore-runners of *what may become one of the most significant contributions*

[23]Alleged nonfeasance by local law officers in some Philadelphia suburbs was an important part of consolidationist propaganda in 1854. See, Eli Kirk Price, *The History of the Consolidation of the City of Philadelphia*. (Philadelphia: J. B. Lippincott and Co., 1873), pp. 14, 53, 61, 110-120, 135.
[24]Nor is *this* primarily an American phenomenon. In most of the "developing nations," urbanization means the creation of multi-ethnic metropolises in which substantially the same process is involved.
[25]Assume that America had survived a thermo-nuclear war and that military dictatorship had not come into existence (or at least did not concern itself with the place of our interest). If this place of our interest, Luxuriant Heights managed to guarantee food to its population from a community emergency supply, but Deprivation Valley, whose people before the cataclysm were either too poor or too anomic to establish an emergency center was without food: (a) What would one expect the residents of Deprivation Valley to do? (b) How welcome would one expect them to be in Luxuriant Heights?
[27]There is an admirable summary of these developments by Samuel Humes, *Comparison of Voluntary Metropolitan Regional Organization,* Paper prepared for 1961 American Municipal Congress Workshop on "Voluntary Metropolitan Regional Organizations," August 24, 1961.

to public administration in the latter half of the twentieth century."[28] (Emphasis additional.—.MH)

For the social scientist the pertinent question is *will* this procedural consensus be achieved and, if so, will it be a political currency convertible into substantive policy? Let us assume a consulting political scientist were called upon to advise on these points. What professional knowledge would he require in order to give his advice *more than common sense validity?*[29] Could he justify prediction that a dismal repetition of history threatened or that a glorious transformation impended—except by the "feeling in his bones"? For these purposes, at least three international relations approaches may offer testable propositions applicable to the metropolitan system. These are found in the works of Ernst B. Haas, Morton A. Kaplan, and Karl W. Deutsch.[30]

In a short study of the Council of Europe, Haas defines consensus substantively: ". . . agreement on a clearly stated program of action endorsed by a clear majority of the members."[31] Recognizing that impediments to such substantive consensus may exist, Haas also forecasts the interim development of procedural consensus. Members would come to be sensitive to the rights and prerogatives of themselves and their fellow-members in the Council. From his reading of the role of parties in the history of federalism, he undertakes to measure the importance of parties in consensus formation in, the Council, anticipating greater cohesion first around the essentially federalist parties and, then, in reaction around their opposition. Two findings seem particularly pertinent for metropolitics.

> First, consensus formation was obstructed by a search for unanimity.
> The issues were blurred, in a partisan sense, by the striving for unanimity in an area where almost everybody's values

[28]In my opinion, this overstates their originality whatever the practical outcomes. For predecessor effects see, Paul Studenski, *The Government of Metropolitan Areas in the United States.* (New York: National Municipal League, 1930), pp. 43-54.

[29]Perhaps I ought to say that I am not opposed to common sense. I even try to use it. But we cannot claim that our common sense is better than other people's. We do not claim that our *professional knowledge* is better. At least it is supposed to help us separate common sense from common nonsense.

[30]The treatment of these three major contributions is necessarily cursory in this paper but it may serve to indicate the kinds of relevance which I think international relations literature may have.

[31]See, Ernst B. Haas, *Consensus Formation in the Council of Europe.* (Berkeley: University of California Press, 1960), p. 3.

converged from the outset. The pattern of agreement, in short, is real enough; but it conforms to the practice of polite diplomatic negotiations among governments not seriously divided over the merits of the issues at stake. It refers to the ways of doing things and not to the things themselves.[32]

The outcome in the Council of Europe is said to have been in marked contrast to the "old Common Assembly of the Coal and Steel Community and its successor, the European Parliamentary Assembly, (which) witnessed a decided growth of international party unity at the expense of the solidarity of national delegation."[33] One important variable, argues Haas, is task orientation. The Common Assembly and the European Parliamentary Assembly had specific tasks defined for them in their treaties, which in turn (gave) rise to definite programs of action to which transnational party action was relevant." The Council of Europe, with no defined sphere of action and no means of implementation, was left searching for something to do.

Such a conclusion is contrary to common-sense expectation and, accordingly provokes disbelief. Thus Amitai Etzioni writes:

> While Haas's argument on this point is potent and convincing, it should be pointed out that one could make a strong case *if the findings were reversed.* One would suggest that it is easier to reach consensus on vague ideas than on concrete policies where execution directly affects interests—policies which involve control over an international executive.[34]

Etzioni's point, which is precisely the same as that of those who see consultation as the high road to metropolitan consensus, might be stated in the hypothesis that: *the development of consensus requires the avoidance of controversy.*[35] But the findings are *not* reversed and, coupled with the relatively trivial outcomes of non-controversial approaches to metropolitan action in the past,[36] suggest an apparently paradoxical hypothesis, to wit: *the development of consensus requires a sufficient level of controversy over "real" issues that the multiplicity of contending groups will be forced to choose between policy "A" and policy "not—A."* If the institution has tasks to perform which are *material* to most

[32]*Ibid.*, p. 70.
[34]*Ibid.*, p. 59.
[34]See review by Etzioni in *American Journal of Sociology*, Vol. 66, No. 5., (March 1961), p. 534.
[35]Walter C. Kaufman describes this as "The frictionless theory of making fire with sticks," Personal Communication.
[36]Studenski, *op. cit.*

participants, and within this framework some disparate participants are given a good reason to seek a new goal which can be achieved within the institution, other disparate participants will, *in reaction,* form an "opposition," *thus strengthening the decision-making capacity of the institution itself.*

The second finding with important metropolitan implications is that *overlapping memberships* among various European institutions had very low spillover effect. Many persons were members, for example, of both the Council of Europe and the Coal and Steel Assembly, they did not behave similarly in the two bodies. If this may be extended, it casts very grave doubt upon the supposition that "cooperation" in one sphere—e.g. regional planning—necessarily augurs a general receptivity to metropolitan action, even on the part of the elite personnel who take part directly in the metropolitan bodies.

Morton A. Kaplan's attempt to unite systems analysis and process analysis[37] is the second international relations source to be considered here. Kaplan locates the specific manifestations of integrative and disintegrative processes which are to be found in the connections of role functions (jobs) and personality systems (individual persons) in specific decision-making organizations. Although somewhat prickly and abstruse, Kaplan's method of analysis clearly recognizes that *people* (indeed, persons!) are the carriers of political culture; it asks, in effect: "by what mechanism do those people who are politically active internalize new values and then translate those new values into policy?"[38] This recognition of the connection between personality and role performance, between belief and performance in the political culture, converts the fundamental assumption of the "consensus-through-consultation" strategy into a more nearly operational question.

Let us now consider, with their metropolitan implications, two hypotheses which may be fruitful for analysis of this strategy of consensus-formation.

Hypothesis A.[39] Multiple role functions operate on personality systems in such a fashion that the personality systems perceive the objectives and values of the decision-making units linked

[37]Morton A. Kaplan, *System and Process in International Politics.* (New York: John Wiley and Sons, Inc., 1957).
[38]For relevant observations on this point see *ibid.,* p. 128, n.l.; also, Robert B. Mowat, *The Concept of Europe* (London: Macmillan and Company, Ltd., 1930), p. 315.
[39]The full series (nine hypothesis) with ancillary argumentation is pre-

by the multiple role functions as more similar than they would if they entered into only single role functions.

This hypothesis emphasizes *role* inputs as variables which may perform step-level[40] functions in the process of integration by modifying the characteristic responses of individual decision-makers. Thus, the political official whose job requires him to participate in two bodies will see more similarities between these bodies than the political official whose job requires him to participate in only one of the same two bodies. Two sub-hypotheses elaborate the point:

(1) to the extent that one of the decision-making units is persuasive in structure, the personalities linked to the decision-making roles in that unit tend to accommodate the objectives and values of the decision-making units; (2) to the extent that one of the decision-making units is chain-of-command in structure, the personality linked to the chain-of-command role tends to assimilate the values of both decision making units to the values of the unit in which he performs chain-of-command decision-making functions.[41]

Under the sub-hypotheses, therefore, city councilmen would be *more* likely to absorb the values of the consultative body than would mayors. On this hypotheses, one who wanted to make the system would seek to make available places for as many members of councils as possible.

Hypothesis B (slightly paraphrased): Insulation inhibits those processes of accommodation and assimilation which are necessary for integration of a decision-making unit.

A strategy of consensus formation seeks to transform the consultative bodies themselves into decision-making units. By Hypothesis B, insulation would be a barrier which the strategy would have to be devised to penetrate. Kaplan presents six sub-hypotheses which make explicit some of the ways in which such insulation might occur. Three of these may have immediate relevance in the practical politics of the metropolis.

Sub-hypothesis 1: Command decision role functions insulate the chain-of-command decision maker from (1) the opinions of

---

sented in Kaplan's book *op. cit.,* at pp. 104-112. These hypotheses might, of course, apply to other types of organizations.

[40] A step-level function ". . . alters the characteristic behavior of a system." *Ibid.,* p. 5.

[41] Kaplan, *op. cit.,* p. 106.

his consulted but non-decision-making colleagues, (2) his role functions in persuasive units which includes as an element the unit in which he exercises chain-of-command role functions.

An elected "strong mayor" is a chain-of-command decision-maker within his own government. By the sub-hypothesis such a mayor would place relatively little emphasis on his role as a participant in the consultative organ and some bureaucratic adviser —a legal counsel, a highway engineer or a fiscal officer—would probably "represent" him in its deliberations. But the binding quality of any commitment which such a representative might make would be problematical. When a crucial issue is at hand, the exposed eminence on which the mayor stands would tend to make him once more the "solitary" executive.

Suppose the consultative body's judgment is that, *on metropolitan criteria,* the best route for a new freeway is directly through an area the electorate of which is politically indispensable to the mayor. No matter how much his adviser may have internalized the criteria of the consultative organ and press them upon the mayor, his tendency will be to obfuscate them at minimum and, more likely, to repudiate them.[42]

Sub-hypotheses 2: Delegating and rewarding decision-making units insulates against non-delegating and non-rewarding units.

If the municipal political system is the primary source of rewards, the current emphasis on the purely consultative nature of the metropolitan bodies *might actually inhibit integration.* The most desired rewards are allocated to those playing the roles "mayor," "councilman," or "law director." Consequently, the metropolitan liaison post would tend to become a secondary assignment of about as much importance as those "additional duties" given second lieutenants or, if an independent role, a "left-over" position for an actor who could not be wholly ignored but who could not enforce a claim to a better position.[43] Participation in the metropolitan institution, with commitment to defend that institution and *its*

[42]This is analogous to the President's problem: shall a foreign policy decision mainly reflect (a) his personal views? (b) his party interest? (c) interest in the Anglo-American alliance? (d) interest in the UN per se? etc.?

[43]See, Haas, *Consensus Formation,* pp. 67-68, reports that European parliamentarians find their participation in consultative bodies does them little good from the career point of view. If one feeds this back to international organizational analysis, study of the processes of assigning people to United Nations duty might be instructive. From this viewpoint, the attempts of Ambassadors

role, would be attractive only if it offered *equally good or better* rewards than the municipal system *which cannot be true in a purely consultative body.*

> *Sub-hypothesis 3:* Frequent changes of decision-makers in multiple decision-making roles have insulating effects upon the personality systems of the role holders.[44]

That "birds of passage" are likely to be less motivated forming firm attachments and *to have less opportunity* to form firm attachments seems indubitable. Given the hazards of the professional politician's existence one would expect this to lead to considerable turnover in the metropolitan consultative bodies. Since development of consensus—particularly in the procedural realm—requires that many discrete acts should congeal into a "tradition," and this implies a *corps* of *people* who understand *each other and the tradition,*[45] turnover would constitute an impediment to the strength of the consultative bodies.

Of the three sources here noted, the most comprehensive approach to metropolitics might be derived from the studies of North Atlantic integration and disintegration undertaken by Karl W. Deutsch and associates.[46] The general problem is how "security" communities—areas in which the prospect of war is negated—[47] are brought into being. The principal aspects of this work which appear

---

Lodge and Stevenson to enhance their impact on U.S. foreign policy decision-making might have a greater than idiosyncratic significance. Would Foreign Service types who had not played major independent roles in U.S. national politics be equally insistent? Or: how many Asian delegates are at the United Nations as a form of political exile?

[44]*Cf.,* Hypothesis A and the discussion thereof, above.

[45]This is an important behavioral ingredient in seniority systems—whether in Congress or political science departments.

[46]See, Deutsch, *et al., Political Community and the North Atlantic Area: International Organization in the Light of Historical Experience.* (Princeton, Princeton University Press, 1957). This volume summarizes eight historical cases: (a) formation of the United States in 1789, its disruption in 1861, and the post Civil War reunion, (b) the union of England and Scotland, (c) the British-Irish rupture of 1921. (d) the unification of Germany. (e) the unification of Italy, (f) the development and deterioration of the Austro-Hungarian Empire, (g) the Norwegian-Swedish union (1814) and separation (1905), and (h) the integration of Switzerland. The theoretical analysis was mainly Deutsch's work although the historical reconstructions were undertaken by several other scholars.

[47]The four key concepts are:

Security-community: "a group of people which has become integrated."
Integration: "attainment, within a territory, of a 'sense of community' and of institutions and practices strong enough and widespread enough to assure

potentially fruitful for the strategy of metropolitan consensus formation come from Deutsch's discussion of the three "background
conditions" for pluralistic security-communities."[48]

1. The Main Politically Relevant Values of the Participating Units Must Be Compatible.

Presumably, no one would disagree with such a proposition
but the critical point is that values must not be mere generalities
but practical criteria for decision-making. However metropolitan
actors may accept "free enterprise," the "right of a man to live
his own life," or "the equality of man," these values are not meaningful for their decisions until they become as explicit as: is it
legitimate to use the city building inspector to harass a contractor
who sells to Negroes (if land use is one of the matters which they
wish to decide)? or is it legitimate to let contracts to those who
are your partisan allies (if they are engaged in capital improvements)?

2. Participating Units Must Have the Capability of Responsive Practical Action.

"Decision-makers must be able to receive messages from other
political units, to give these messages from other political units
adequate weight in the making of their own decisions, to perceive
the needs of the population and elites of these other units, and
to respond to them quickly and adequately in terms of political
or economic action."[49] Capability means, in other words, "power"
to act (in the bare sense of economic strength, administrative
efficiency, etc.) and the ability to communicate. It is questionable
that metropolitan local governments often have the resources
to satisfy their potential partners.

More important, the communication system is so primitive
that there often appears to be mutual ignorance of needs, demands,

---

for a 'long' time dependable expectations of 'peaceful change' among its population."
Sense of Community, belief on the part of individuals in a group that
they have come to agreement on at least this one point—that common social
problems must and can be resolved by processes of 'peaceful change.'
Peaceful Change: resolution of social problems, normally by institutionalized
procedures without resort to large-scale physical force *Ibid.,* p. 5.
[48]"Pluralistic" security-communities are those in which there is integration
but no common government. "Amalgamated" security-communities are those
in which there *are* common governments. *Ibid.,* pp. 6-7.
[49]*Ibid.,* p. 40.

and opportunities for negotiation. For example, when the Cleveland metropolitan charter proposal was being considered in 1959, the Mayor of Cleveland and the suburban mayors were each significantly and explicitly interested in the outcome.[50] Each side tended to formulate its interest in ways difficult to reconcile with the interests of the other. These formulations took place neither in face-to-face contact of the adversaries nor through explicitly *autho-rized* intermediaries but simply through statements on the public record.

When an observer suggested to one suburban mayor that there might be room for serious private discussion with the Cleveland mayor he agreed, but asked: "how do we get together with him?" Then, somewhat uncertainly: "maybe we ought to call him up." In the end, they never achieved any authorized communication with the Mayor of Cleveland, the Mayor's inability to establish communication would seem to imply that the "ambassadorial" structure was to fragile to provide a basis for rapprochment[51] either because: (a) the adviser-messengers were not trusted by their principals or (b) could not deal candidly with each other.[52] The fact that they could not even get together for a necessarily con-fidential talk was the source of one "incapability" to respond meaningfully.[53]

3.   The Potential Partners Must Be Able to Predict Each Other's Behavior Within An Atmosphere of Trust.

The matter of trust raises the problem of the *permanence or transience* of prior relationships amongst participants on a metro-politan area. One would normally expect that, unless some solvent had been operative, officials representing units which had been in conflict would tend to be suspicious and those representing units which had been cooperative would tend to be open to persua-

---

[50]The suburban officials were "represented" by a committee of the Associ-ation of Mayors and City Managers. Most members of the committee could not have conceived of calling him on the telephone. The one committee mem-ber who *could* do so was marginal to the decisions of the committee.

[51]*Cf.,* Kaplan, *op. cit.,* p. 128, n.l.

[52]*Cf.,* Philip E. Moseley, *The Kremlin and World Politics: Studies in So-viet Policy and Action,* (New York: Vintage Books, 1960), pp. 4-8.

[53]This is not to imply that the ability to talk is sufficient. It is merely necessary. Once positions are reciprocally understood, it may still be neces-sary to say "I understand you but I can't do anything for you. It costs too much money," or "It will cost me votes," or "I just don't agree."

sion.[54] Of course one may find that it is not so. However, on the expectation that it is the case, one would further expect that the new series of consultative bodies will have relatively rough going until an atmosphere of trust can be established.

REVIEW AND CONCLUSION

Three main lines of argument have been advanced.

A. The basic contention of the paper is that metropolitics and international politics can be studied significantly within a common frame of reference on the ground that each is predominantly conducted within diplomatic systems. Diplomatic systems are defined in terms of three major characteristics.

1. They constitute ecological communities but, on the whole, not political communities.
2. The primary actors are governmental.
3. The communication structure is dominated by a mythology which makes governments the only "legitimate" actors and, thus, inhibits the activity of potential non-governmental actors.

The second main contention of the paper is that metropolitics, viewed in these terms, may usefully be studied through analysis of four factors: (1) the subject-matters of interaction between governments, (2) the "power" of the actor-governments, (3) the permanence or transience of effective relationships between actor-governments, and (4) the procedures of inter-governmental relations, particularly:

a. The scope of any particular organization or conflict,
b. The frequency and instrumentalities of contact, and,

---

[54]In this connection, one would raise the question whether Deutsch may not understate the importance of the "arrival of a new generation in politics." In my Cleveland study, at least, the emergence of a new generation was of crucial importance since it meant that dominant decision-making roles—among potential competitive factors and parties—were occupied by personnel who had less sensitivity to the issues which had divided their predecessors and were, therefore, more able to re-examine *de novo* and on "the facts" issues which their predecessors had taken as articles of faith. This does not mean that they were more "reasonable" but that the specific issues about which they might be divided had not quite so clearly crystallized and ossified. Holden, *Decision-Making,* pp. 276-277.

   c. The nature of "ultimate conflict." "Ultimate conflict" in
metropolitics is said to take one of two forms (or some
combination of them), to wit:
   (1) litigation, and,
   (2) official complicity in private violence.

The third contention of the paper is that the usefulness of this
approach may be tested by applying international relations theory
to the evaluation of strategies of metropolitan consensus formation
through inter-governmental consultation, three sources of international relations theory are considered: the models developed by
Ernst B. Hass, Morton A. Kaplan, and Karl W. Deutsch. Greater
theoretical sophistication or a better acquaintance with the data
might lead to substantial revision. However, with a generous helping
of *ceteris paribus,* the following judgments are offered:

1. The most important feature of the Haas model is the *task
orientation.* If it is desired to give a metropolitan consultative body its best chance of taking root, then it will be
necessary to give it practical tasks of a magnitude that
important actors can expect benefits from its operations.

2. The emphasis on *role and personality* inputs gives the
Kaplan model a greater concern with the attitudes and
responses of the individual decision-makers who will undertake roles. Thus, the Kaplan model is concerned with the
internalization of values by individuals rather than the
pragmatic adaptations of blocs. However, these are convergent because—in terms of the Kaplan model—the
*assignment of trivial goals to the unit will tend to insulate
the individual decision-makers from the unit.* (This model
also contains implications about the method of choice and
tenure of participants.)

3. The Deutsch model deals with background conditions for
the success of the consultative approach. Whether any or
all the conditions exist, in any particular case, could be
ascertained by putting together the data required under the
four gross categories indicated in Part II. Given the
existence of a consultative body, the dynamic process of
establishing its position would depend, at least in part, on
considerations raised in the other two models. Particularly
is this so with respect to mutual trust. If trust is to increase,
it must rest upon performance in matters of moment. This
means that (1) the organization must operate long enough
for the roleholders to develop confidence in each other's
willingness to accept "rules of the game" and (2) it must

"produce desirable results" with respect to substantive goals
for at least some participants.

This metropolitan consultative bodies actually in existence appear to be based on a strategy of risk nought. But the criteria derived from these models all suggest the folk wisdom that risk nought implies gain nought. In this sense, they are fully congruent with the basic tradition of political theory that politics is choice—but to choose well implies that one must accept risk of choosing badly.

PART II
MICRO-STUDIES—
PEOPLE, PROBLEMS, and POLITICS

INTRODUCTION

In this section the aim is to give the reader some of the flavor of urban politics. The focus shifts sharply from proposition generating theory to specific studies of people, problems, and politics, separately or in the usual combinations of the urban scene. The narrow range of the focus leads to the title "micro-studies." What is covered is in all instances something less than a "whole" of urban politics. Some articles cover some issues for some cities, but not all issues for all cities or even some issues for all cities. Several of the most interesting pieces in this section deal with the politics of a few cities in terms of elections for mayors or ethnic voting. The reader should gain from this section not so much the sense of data tested against the theories which preceded, as a sense of what the issues and politics of cities are like in very concrete cases. This section aims to provide impressions and insight as a precursor to the systematic testing of the comparative articles of the final third section.

The first three articles, "Views on Urban Problems" by Berk, Boesel, Eidson, and Groves, "Police in the Ghetto" by Groves, and "Teachers in Urban Public Schools" by Boesel, are all taken from a remarkable volume called *Supplemental Studies for the National Advisory Commission on Civil Disorders. The Supplemental Studies* were research surveys done by leading social scientists for the same commission which produced the "Riot Commission Report" — the National Advisory Commission on Civil Disorders, sometimes called the Kerner Commission — in March 1968. The articles reprinted here, and completed by July 1968, were intended to provide the Committee with greater information in some of the areas raised by the original report. Thus, for example, the three pieces which begin this section are all based on a special survey of occupational groups in fifteen cities.

The fifteen cities studied were classified into those which had riots during the hot summer of 1967 (riot), those which had no riots in 1967 but had seen disorders previously (medium-riot), and those which had experienced no disorders at all by the time of the study (non-riot). There were five cities in each category and 150 interviews were conducted in each city. Groups interviewed included police, merchants, social workers, teachers, political workers, and major employers.

"Views on Urban Problems," gives a composite picture of the most important urban problems as seen by the six groups listed above. Why choose this perspective? In part, because the authors felt these groups had professional reasons to know what was going on, and thus a more accurate view of what was really happening than a random sample of residents might possess. More important, "because they are in the front lines of the delivery systems of urban services, these perspectives are an index of the stance and spirit in which such services are rendered."

In this first article the authors were probing for insights into two differing views: differences which might show up among the three sets of cities (riot, medium-riot, non-riot); and differences among the six groups of people (police, merchants, social workers, teachers, political workers, and major employers). They found, interestingly, that there were fewer differences among the sets of cities than there were among the occupational groups in perceptions of what the problems were. Almost everyone was more aware of "problems" than of "improvements" in urban life.

The data should be looked at carefully by the reader; each may find different items of significance in it. One intriguing finding is surely that non-riot cities were more likely to be rated as having political leaders who were imaginative. They were also perceived as more likely to provide access to the average citizen.

The second article in the sequence, Eugene W. Groves' "Police in the Ghetto" reports on the fifteen city survey interviews with policemen only, providing the police-eye view, as it were. The findings confirm the general impression that today's police, especially those who serve in the ghettos, perceive themselves as a beleaguered and unloved group. The author found that police were most dissatisfied with their external relations; only moderately unhappy with their immediate working conditions; and happy with each other. The reader should note carefully the findings about police perceptions of Negroes and of young people. Groves seems to feel that the police's own reports on how they have to go about doing their day-to-day work reveals a great deal about the sources of ghetto tension.

David Boesel's "Teachers in Urban Public Schools" offers the specific views of still another front-line and often beleagured city occupational group. The teachers are markedly more conscious of the social problems of the ghettos than are the police, not surprisingly. Yet, perhaps significantly, their view of the human situation is much more optimistic. The teachers seem to respect their schools and have a high regard for the parents of the slum children they teach; their attitudes towards the students are, however, ambivalent. Black teachers appeared to have better relationships with their pupils. In all, this brief article contains a fascinating array of attitudes and insights into what the educational world looks like from a very particular city perspective.

The Abel Wolman article, "The Metabolism of Cities: Water and Air," reprinted from a 1965 issue of *Scientific American* devoted entirely to cities, shifts the focus from a people perspective to a technical one. His piece is a good description of the general problems of water supply, sewage, and air pollution facing American cities. Anyone who has lived in a big city and tasted the often sour water or noticed the certainly occasionally smarting "smog," will not be inclined to underrate the importance of these environmental issues for our urban life.

Some of Wolman's findings are less pessimistic than the nightly newscasts: the number of Americans served by waterworks is rising well in line with population, and intelligent water conservation programs should make shortages in cities unnecessary well beyond the year 2000. On the other hand, the sewage disposal problem is not being handled as well by cities, in part perhaps it is a more difficult service to get taxpayers to approve than the provision of drinking water. The most acute urban sewerage difficulty is the discharge of untreated wastes into nearby lakes and rivers, a process which has already severely damaged, for example, Chicago's Lake Michigan and Cleveland's Lake Erie shores. Air pollution, the author implies, is a more difficult public problem for cities to control because of the number of people involved in any alteration of a major source of such pollution, namely private automobiles. The Wolman article serves as a good reminder that not all urban problems are social; many are environmental.

"Profiles of Disorder: Detroit," is a description of the Detroit riot of July 1967, taken directly from the original "Report" of the President's National Advisory Commission on Civil Disorders. It is more than a portrayal of a specific and destructive outburst in a major city; it is a good case study of the kinds of conditions and events that formed the background of the long-to-be-remembered violent summer. The Detroit riot of 1967 was not the first such event in that northern city; chronically tense race relations were characteristic of the community which had seen a disasterous race riot in 1943. As "Profiles of Disorder: Detroit" documents, the 1967 riot followed a long and specific cycle of decline in the 12th Street neighborhood.

The neighborhood had seen the exodus of its white population, deteriorating police-community relations, and the development of a crime rate double that of the city at large. Black residents of the community were known to be highly discontented. After a police raid was followed by early outbursts of looting, the situation slowly became worse. After five days the toll stood at 43 dead, hundreds injured, over 7000 arrested, and property damage of over $50 million. Anyone reading the Riot Commission's Report must be struck with how poorly and inappropriately many major public officials and agencies—from President Lyndon B. Johnson to the Michigan National Guard—responded to the disaster. Only the federal troops, with their restraint, and black troops who could establish rapport with the ghetto residents, could point to truly constructive behavior. The Detroit riot was one of eight major, 32 serious, and 123 minor disorders in the first nine months of 1967. "Profiles of Disorder: Detroit" is a story of civic frustration and destruction. The next article, "The San Francisco Community Renewal Program: A Summary" by Louis K. Loewenstein and Cyril C. Hermann, is a story of civic determination and construction. The "Summary" is a document produced by the authors as consultants to the City of San Francisco. It is really two things at once: an analysis of the difficulties of the urban environment and a set of strategies — a blueprint if you like — on how to change the environment through public policy. The "Summary" is what is commonly called a "systems analysis," and as such is also an example of the widespread effort to transform analytical techniques utilized in defense and aerospace industries to urban problems.

The program itself was based on a computer model of residential housing markets. Two complete computer analyses of San Francisco's future housing situation were tried out or "simulated" on the computer. In the first instance, the intent was to project housing trends in San Francisco in the absence of concerted civic action; in the second run, the aim was to project likely outcomes if the city acted in accordance with the recommendations of the Community Renewal Program. That program divided the entire city into five types of areas, with a different prescription for city housing efforts in each type. The reader is urged to note the "mix" of strategies recommended and also the predicted results, because it is analyses such as these that are the beginning of what might be expected to be a future social science called "urbanology." Does the reader find promise in this approach?

"Leadership in a Large Manager City: the Case of Kansas City" by Stanley T. Gabis provides detailed insights into some of the issues and personalities in a changing city operating under the council-manager system of government. In the last section of this reader a number of propositions about this form of government receive generalized, comparative testing; the inclusion of the article on Kansas City was intended to give the reader some illustration of the types of people and problems rising to the surface in one "case." Gabis describes how, contrary to the "ideology" of council-manager government, the Kansas City system was actually put into effect and dominated by a traditional political boss for the first fifteen years of its existence. He then portrays the shift from boss-domination to control by a civic-oriented "good government" association, the temporary "regression" into partisan politics, and the shift back again to a good government coalition. The reader should ask himself: what seems to be at stake in the struggle for control in Kansas City? What is the form that "politics" has taken behind the council-manager system? And what roles have various managers played?

The next article is also concerned with executive politics in big cities. "The Making of the Negro Mayors — 1967" by Hadden, Massotti, and Thiessen raises some issues of great contemporary relevance — the chances of black political leaders in electoral politics. The cases they consider, the successful elections of Richard Hatcher in Gary and Carl Stokes in Cleveland, were the first two of their kind. Yet the conditions under which these two won their initial elections were quite different. Cleveland was a city with a predominantly white population, yet undergoing considerable shifts in population. Its political environment required that Stokes pass two complicated hurdles. First, he had to win a Democratic primary against an incumbent mayor; then he had to defeat an attractive Republican in a general election in which race played a subtle but pervasive role. In Gary the racial issue was on the surface at all times, although the sequence of primary-general election challenges was quite similar.

The authors place these landmark elections in a definite historical-political context: a kind of test for America of whether black people could rely upon electoral politics to achieve their ends, as other groups in America had in the past. Despite the victories, the authors felt that the outcomes were ambiguous in this larger sense, in part because there was such great evidence of the effects of prejudice in each election. Both Stokes and Hatcher won because they received a small minority of white votes on top of great turnout and solidarity in their respective black communities. But, as liberal Democrats, if race were not an issue, they could have expected overwhelming election. Further, the problems of their cities could hardly be expected to vanish, as indeed they have not. The subsequent efforts of each to govern their communities received widespread publicity. With the passage of time and the continuing evolution of the "black power" movement, how does one look back upon these elections?

The reasons for the support given to the idea of "black power" in black communities becomes clear upon reading the next selection, "Black Powerlessness in Chicago," by Harold M. Baron. His thesis is straightforward: "Negroes remain second-class citizens partly because of the discrimination of individual whites, but mainly because of the way whites control the major institutions of our society." Baron proceeds to analyze the extent of black participation at the policy-making levels in a series of public and private institutions in Chicago. What he finds is chronic underrepresentation of black people at the decision-making level. Although they represent 20% of the metropolitan Chicago population, for example, blacks held only 5% of the 1088 government positions in the area at the time of the research. Interestingly, blacks stood a better chance of being represented through the electoral process than through a variety of appointment systems.

Nonetheless, government was a more open arena than private organizations. Although businesses were least open to black executives, it should be noted that the powerful Chicago area universities were hardly much better. Unions turned out to be the most ópen private organizations, an interesting finding in the light of frequent academic and governmental critiques of the labor movement. Baron's findings lead him to a rather clear set of conclusions about strategies which the black community should follow in the future. Does the reader agree?.

Banfield's and Wilson's "Public-Regardingness as a Value Premise in Voting Behavior," continues the focus on group behavior in city politics. The primary concern is with broad patterns of sub-cultural values, put forth as an hypothesized conflict between those who participate on the basis of a "public-interest" or "general welfare" in city politics and those who pursue private, self or family, interests in the same arena. The basis of the cleavage is seen to be ethnic or income group membership. In fact, the authors are virtually enunciating a theory of city political behavior based upon differing value systems of different ethnic groups. The test of the idea is an analysis of voting on referenda in Chicago and Cleveland.

The authors find an interesting voting alliance of upper and lower income groups. The primary "private-regarding" groups turn out to be Poles and Czechs. The reader should consider the questions raised by this article carefully, because the Banfield and Wilson hypothesis is tested systematically in several of the articles in the last section of the reader.

7

VIEWS ON URBAN PROBLEMS*

PETER H. ROSSI, RICHARD A. BERK, DAVID P. BOESEL, BETTYE K. EIDSON, AND W. EUGENE GROVES

Even the slightest attention to the mass media provides one with the impression that our cities are facing a set of crises common to all. Our cities' problems are in the headlines of daily newspapers, fill the pages of both popular and "serious" magazines, provide the materials for television and radio specials, and even now are raw timber for major planks in the platforms of political parties in this presidential year.

Between the objective existence of a social problem and its recognition in popular attention may intervene a time lag of years, the length of which seems dependent on how serious the problem is and how many of the public are directly affected. For example, there can be little doubt that air pollution has been with us for some decades, but it took the stinging smogs of Los Angeles and the tragedies of Danamora, Pennsylvania to bring about widespread public concern. Similarly high unemployment rates among urban Negroes have been with us for some time, but it was not until the drama of the War on Poverty that the plight of the urban poor became a widely recognized social problem.

The widespread perception that a social problem exists depends largely on two elements: first, the objective nature of the problem determines whether it is one which strikes directly at large numbers of individuals or one which is confined to relatively few. For example, those who are unemployed and whose friends and relatives

*Reprinted from *Supplemental Studies for the National Advisory Commission on Civil Disorders* (Washington, U.S. Government Printing Office, 1968), pp. 81-86.

are unemployed know something is wrong, but if the unemployment is not widespread its direct apprehension may be limited mainly to those directly affected. Secondly, a major role must be given to public officials, civic leaders and the media of communications. The major actors in the public arena help to define a problem, draw attention to it, and, by transforming a social problem into an issue, bring the public decision-making machinery into play.

The men and women we have interviewed in this study have a perspective on urban social problems which is more extensive than that of the general public, and yet they are not in a position to transform an objective condition into a widely recognized social problem. In short, because their occupations bring them into contact with the city (and particularly with residents of Negro ghettos) in an intensive way, their direct knowledge of the existence of social problems can be expected to be greater and more intimate. But, because they are located on the lower echelons of public agencies, run smaller businesses, or are middle management in large-scale business enterprises, their access to the media of communications is hardly greater than that of the average resident.

Their perspectives on the problems of their cities are therefore of some special interest because they are in some ways in a better position to know what is going on than many other residents of the city. At the same time, their perspectives are interesting in another sense. Because they are in the front lines of the delivery systems of urban services, these perspectives are an index of the stance and spirit in which such services are rendered. Hence, as we examine in this chapter how our respondents view their communities, our interest in their responses is from two perspectives: first, their views can be considered to be more informed than that of the ordinary resident; secondly, their views also tell us something about the postures rank and file members of central community institutions take towards their clients, customers, and employees.

Each interview started with a question asking the respondent to cite what he thought to be the "two or three major problems facing your city?" The array of answers given is shown in Table 1.

Note that there are no surprises in Table 1. The problems cited are those which are widely recognized to be seriously affecting most of our major cities. No new, as yet widely unrecognized, problems were cited. What may be of some interest is the relative emphasis given to one rather than another problem. Respondents gave

TABLE 1

Major Problems Facing City

(Q 1 — Core)

(in percent)

		Proportion citing problem
I.	Physical aspects	49.3
	Housing and urban renewal	39.1
	Traffic and street lighting	7.8
	Other: Pollution, sanitation, etc.	2.4
II.	Social and economic aspects	152.9
	Poverty and unemployment	37.9
	Provision of quality education	25.2
	Racial tensions	23.3
	Crime and juvenile delinquency	21.9
	Welfare and recreation	11.4
	Integration	10.3
	Riots and civil disorders	9.9
	Business conditions	6.5
	Other: Moral decay, disrespect for law and order, family disorganization	6.5
III.	Political aspects	30.8
	Taxes	9.2
	Inadequate leadership	7.2
	Police	4.9
	Community apathy	4.6
	Law enforcement and courts	3.8
	Other: Corruption, etc.	1.1
	100 percent equals	(1953)

NOTE: Since respondents could cite up to three problems, percentages add up to considerably more than 100%.

prominent place both to problems of housing and poverty, each being cited by almost four out of five persons interviewed. Education, racial tensions, and crime and juvenile delinquency were next in order of mention, each being cited by between one in five and one in four.

Far down on the list (in terms of frequency of mention) were problems of integration, highway and traffic control, and taxes,

each being mentioned by about one in ten. Also included among
this group of problems was the category "riots and civil disorders,"
mentioned by ten percent of the respondents. Considering that
one third of the cities studied had experienced very serious disorders in the summer previous to interviewing, and that three
of the cities were about to experience serious levels of disorder
shortly after the interviewing was over, riots and civil disorders
did not achieve a very high level of salience.

TABLE 2
Major Problems Facing City as Cited by Five
Occupational Groups
(Q 1 — Core)
(in percent)

Problem cited	Occupational Group					
	Police	Edu-cators	Social workers	Political workers	Mer-chants	Em-ployers
Housing and urban renewal	36	55	57	55	29	38
Traffic and lighting	7	3	5	2	5	18
Other physical	2	2	8	4	2	4
	45	57	70	61	37	60
Poverty, unemployment ...	29	45	58	64	27	36
Quality education	17	44	28	32	16	28
Racial tensions	24	33	19	11	21	24
Crime and delinquency	36	8	10	17	35	11
Welfare and recreation ...	10	12	17	16	8	11
Integration	10	19	12	18	6	8
Riots and civil disorders ...	14	6	7	5	10	12
Business conditions	1	6	8	3	7	12
Other social problems	13	14	4	7	8	9
	154	187	163	173	138	151
Taxes	10	4	5	4	8	17
Inadequate leadership	5	7	12	14	5	7
Police	4	3	1	7	10	3
Community apathy	8	5	4	4	2	3
Law and courts	9	0	0	1	8	1
Other political	0	2	2	2	3	1
	36	21	24	32	36	42
100 percent equals	(437)	(273)	(264)	(103)	(442)	(434)

Given the full array of cited problems, our respondents are focussing on underlying long-range problems rather than immediate symptoms. Or at least such an interpretation is in line with the relative emphasis put upon riots and civil disorders as compared with housing and poverty.

Each occupation studied provides a slightly different perspective, as the results in Table 2 indicate. Crime and juvenile delinquency appear particularly important to both police and merchants, who cite this problem more frequently than any other groups and more frequently than any other problem. As one might anticipate, poverty and unemployment is important to social workers, but, less expectably, also to political workers: more than half of each group cite poverty and unemployment as a major problem. Educators (almost half) are concerned about the quality of education, and education receives relatively high levels of mentions from political workers and employers as well.

Educators, social workers, and political workers are particularly likely to cite housing problems, with the merchants least likely to do so (with about half the mentions of the former groups).

Among the lesser problems, taxes appear especially salient to the employers and the policemen. Riots and civil disorder are important to the police, merchants, and employers. Political leadership appears more important to the social workers and the political workers.

Another important way to view the perceptions of major problems is to divide the respondents according to whether they live in a city which experienced severe riots in 1967, mild riots in 1967 (or riots prior to 1967), and those which had no riots up to 1968. This categorization is shown in Table 3.

The most outstanding characteristic of Table 3 is that there are fewer differences among groups of cities than there were among the occupational groups. The major problems are cited with about equal frequency by the respondents in each city type. Only some of the minor themes show systematic variation from city type to city type. For example, crime and juvenile delinquency is cited more and more frequently as one considers riot cities, medium-riot, and non-riot cities with the proportion being more than twice as high in the latter type as compared with the first type (30% as compared with 14%). Similarly, racial tensions and political problems are cited with greater frequency in riot as compared with non-riot cities.

TABLE 3
Major Problems as Cited in Riot and Non-riot Cities
(Q 1 — Core)
(in percent)

Problems cited	City type		
	Riot	Medium riot	Non-riot
Housing and urban renewal	39	39	39
Traffic and street lighting	6	9	8
Other physical problems	1	4	1
Total	46	52	48
Poverty, unemployment	34	36	42
Quality education	27	25	23
Racial tensions	27	23	19
Crime and delinquency	14	21	30
Welfare and recreation	9	8	11
Integration	8	12	11
Riots and civil disorders	13	9	8
Business conditions	5	7	8
Other social problems	9	8	9
Total	146	149	161
Taxes	11	8	8
Adequate leadership	10	7	9
Police	4	6	4
Community apathy	18	6	4
Law and courts	1	3	3
Other political problems	1	1	2
Total	45	31	30

"Riot" cities include: Newark, Detroit, Milwaukee, Cincinnati, and Boston.
"Medium Riot" cities: Brooklyn, N.Y. (Bedford Stuyvesant), Cleveland, Chicago, San Francisco, Philadelphia.
"Non-Riot" Cities: Washington, D.C., Baltimore, Gary, Pittsburgh, St. Louis.

By and large, the cities in our sample have much the same problems, as seen through the eyes of our respondents.[1] Poor

[1]As we shall see further on in this chapter, there are significant differences among individual cities which are obscured by grouping them as we have in Table 3. Since our purpose here is to see what particularly differentiates those which have had severe riots from those which have not, individual city variation within types of cities is not particularly important or illuminating.

housing, poverty and unemployment, the provision of quality
education are major problems all over.

Perhaps the major differences among types of cities lies in what
has been accomplished in meeting these major problems. In order
to tap this aspect, we asked each respondent to cite the "major
improvements" over the "last few years." The results are shown
in Table 4 for the three types of cities and for all cities combined.

TABLE 4

Major Improvements Cited in City Types

(Q 2 — Core)

(in percent)

Improvements cited	Type of city			
	Riot	Medium riot	Non-riot	All cities combined
No improvements	15	18	12	15
Worsening of conditions	4	6	4	4
	19	24	16	19
Housing and urban renewal ...	38	36	25	33
Highways and lighting	13	12	12	12
Other physical improvements	1	2	3	2
	52	50	40	47
Poverty and unemployment ...	24	20	25	23
Education	14	15	17	15
Welfare and recreation	12	7	12	11
Racial tensions	4	5	5	5
Integration	2	4	10	6
Crime and delinquency	1	2	3	2
Business conditions	3	1	3	2
Riots and civil disorders	1	0	1	1
Other social problems	0	0	1	0
	57	54	77	65
Inadequate leadership	7	8	13	10
Community apathy	5	6	4	5
Police	1	4	3	1
Taxes	0	1	1	1
Laws and courts	1	1	0	1
	14	20	21	18

The improvements perceived tend to be in the same areas in which there are problems. Although about one in five respondents claim either that no improvements have been made or even that a worsening of conditions has occurred, the remainder of the replies indicate that improvements have been made in housing, meeting the problems of poverty and unemployment, and in education, welfare, and recreation. Note that the citations of improvements are lower than the citation of problems. Our respondents tended to cite more problems than improvements, and the levels of improvements are uniformly lower than the levels of problems. An extreme example is shown by crime and juvenile delinquency, cited by twenty-two percent of the respondents as a problem with only two percent claiming improvements have been made. Another extreme example is racial tensions, where the proportion citing this as a problem were twenty-three percent and those who see improvement were only five percent.

The differences among types of cities are not very striking or systematic. Thus respondents from riot cities claim that the housing situation has improved more frequently than those in non-riot cities. However, non-riot city respondents were considerably more likely to claim improvements in social and economic respects and in the political life of the cities involved.[2]

We turn now to another measure of urban problems as seen by the respondents. Rather than let each person interviewed bring up the two or three problems most salient to him, these measures came from a series of identical questions asking about ten common problems, obtaining ratings of how serious each problem was in his city. The advantage of this measure lies in its uniform coverage of a series of topics.

The results for the sample as a whole are shown in Table 5. The ten topics are arranged roughly in the order of decreasing perceived seriousness, from top to bottom. Thus we see that seven out of ten respondents rated the control of crime as a very serious problem, at the one extreme, with only one out of five rating corruption of public officials as serious, at the other extreme.

Note that the rank order of problems resulting from this procedure is quite different from that considered in the earlier parts of this

[2]Differences among occupational groups will not be shown here mainly because the patterning of differences tends to parallel the patterning of problems. Thus social workers tend to see improvements in unemployment and poverty, educators improvements in education, and political workers improvements in political leadership.

TABLE 5
Seriousness of Selected Problems Faced by City
(Q 3 — Core)
(in percent)

Problem	Proportion rating problem as				
	Very serious	Some-what serious	Slightly serious	Not at all	Don't know and no answer
Control of crime	71	23	4	2	0
Preventing violence and other civil disorder	55	24	13	6	2
Race relations	52	28	13	6	1
Providing quality education	45	22	14	16	3
Finding tax funds for municipal services	42	25	15	12	6
Unemployment	36	27	18	17	2
Air pollution	33	29	22	12	4
Lack of recreation facilities	31	24	21	21	3
Traffic and highways	27	28	25	20	0
Corruption of public officials	19	17	20	33	11

chapter. For example, control of crime ranked very far behind housing, unemployment, and race relations in Table 1, while in Table 5 it is regarded as a very serious problem by more respondents than any other problem rated. It is difficult to interpret these differences without detailed analysis, but the variation is consistent with the idea that the control of crime is considered very serious in its own terms but not as critical a problem as unemployment. Thus it becomes more important to make progress on clearing up unemployment even if it is less of a serious problem *as unemployment* (i.e. unemployment rates could be much higher) because employment is more of a critical area than crime control.[3] Similar statements could be made about the other problems rated in Table 5. Note that the problems rated as very serious by half or more of the respondents consist of crime control, the prevention of violence and civil disorders, and race relations.

Considerable variations can be found among the six occupational groups in the kinds of urban problems which they view as very

[3]Some degree of confidence in the meaning of these ratings can be gleaned from looking at individual city differences for problems in which it is known that the cities differ in an objective sense. Thus, the seriousness of air pollution is highest in Gary, Indiana and least in San Francisco, a reflection of objective circumstances easily seen by persons who have visited both places.

serious, as is shown in Table 6. Educators, social workers and political party workers have given higher ratings of seriousness to most of the problems than police, merchants, and employers. More than half of the latter groups have given ratings of very

TABLE 6
Seriousness of Selected Urban Problems in Five
Occupations
(Q 3 — Core)
(in percent)

Problem	Proportion rating problem very serious among					
	Police	Educa-tors	Social Workers	Political Workers	Mer-chants	Em-ployers
Crime	74	66	61	67	83	64
Preventing dis-order	50	58	53	52	65	50
Race relations	45	65	62	57	49	46
Education	34	54	62	68	43	35
Tax funds	43	55	40	47	33	41
Unemployment	25	53	62	58	30	21
Air pollution	34	40	34	38	31	26
Recreation	25	37	43	66	37	11
Traffic	28	22	22	36	25	31
Corruption	14	19	22	28	29	9

serious to only two problems, control of crime and preventing disorder, while the educators, social workers, and political workers, have given percentages of very serious ratings of over fifty percent to those problems and in addition to race relations, education, and unemployment.

Looked at from another view point, the police, merchants and employers seem to consider only crime and civil disorders very serious while the educators, social workers, and political workers also express concern over unemployment, race relations, and education. In part this pattern may represent the fact that social workers, educators, and political party workers are closer to individual members of the ghetto in roles where social problems have a considerably easier time to show themselves.

Table 7 shows variations among city types. Clear patternings show up only with respect to two problem areas, race relations and civil disorders. Respondents from riot cities are much more likely to consider both problems very serious as compared to non-

riot cities, with the medium riot cities standing somewhere in
between the extremes.

The regular pattern of differences with respect to these two
problems—race relations and civil disorders—that appears in

TABLE 7
Seriousness of Urban Problems by City Types
(Q 3 — Core)
(in percent)

Problem	Proportion rating problem very serious in		
	Riot cities	Medium riot	Non-riot cities
Control of crime	74	68	70
Preventing violence and other civil disorders	65	58	44
Race relations	60	58	38
Providing quality education	44	50	41
Finding tax funds	44	37	44
Unemployment	32	43	33
Air pollution	23	40	34
Lack of recreation facilities	32	29	32
Traffic and highways	22	28	29
Corruption of public officials	18	19	20

Table 7 raises in a more dramatic form a question of interpretation
which has been present in prevous tables and which will remain
open throughout the present report. The problem is whether or
not the patterning discerned is an antecedent of rioting or a consequence. Thus it is plausible that in cities where the relations between the races had deteriorated far enough that our respondents
were much aware of difficulties and rated them as serious are
likely to be cities in which riots were to occur. It is equally plausible
that in cities which had riots respondents would be especially aware
that race relations were tense and strained. Similarly it seems equally
plausible that the occurrence of riots leads to a higher rating of the
seriousness of riots as to entertain the converse. Indeed, a stronger
case can probably be made for the former interpretation as against
the latter.

This problem of interpretation will come up with particular
force whenever we deal with areas of attitude and opinion which
are closely related to relations between the races and with civil
disorders. Areas which are more remote from the riots themselves

—e.g. unemployment rates, air pollution, etc.—are less open to equivocal interpretation, but as we shall see, the differences among types of cities (as in Table 7) that ordinarily appear will be in areas closely related to the civil disorders themselves. Indeed, in Table 7 the only set of strong systematic inter-city differences are the two identified earlier. Other problems either show no strong differences or patterns which are not easily related to whether or not riots occurred in the cities studied.

One of the leading ideas behind the design of this study was that the quality of public leadership had much to do with the outbreak of civil disorders in that city and the course of events which led to a potential disorder becoming large or remaining small. We hypothesized that a city whose civic and political leaders were in communication with Negro organizations, and who were regarded by the citizenry as responsive and sensitive to citizen needs, was less likely to have had a riot and less likely to experience a severe disorder when a riot occurred.

As part of a test of this hypothesis we made up a series of statements designed to measure how our special occupational groups characterized the officials and workers in local city government. These statements (shown in Table 8) were read to each respondent, who was then asked to indicate how true that statement was as applied to local government in his city. The responses are shown in Table 8.

Note that our respondents were neither overwhelmingly enthusiastic about their local governments nor condemnatory. For example, only one out of four denied that local political leaders were imaginative, but only a little more than one out of ten thought that the statement was "completely true." Most respondents were willing to concede that local leaders were to some extent imaginative and innovative. Similarly with other statements: few saw their public officials as completely accessible (last statement in Table 8) and few saw them as completely inaccessible.

The only statement which seemed to attract denials from respondents concerned whether the city was lagging behind other communities in adopting new ideas. A little more than half of the respondents denied that this was the case.

In short, the portrait of the composite city described by our respondents is one in which there is some degree of imaginative leadership provided by public officials, in which city employees are neither held back in their zeal by their superiors nor hold

TABLE 8
Perceived Political "Styles"
(Q 27 — Core)
(in percent)

Statement	Com-pletely true	Mostly true	Some-what true	Not true	DK & NA
"The political leaders of our city are imaginative and are always coming up with new ideas on how to meet the city's problems"	12	25	39	23	1
"This is a city which has always been the last to try new ideas like urban renewal, educational reforms and so on"	10	12	23	53	2
"One of the good things about this city is the tremendous amount of cooperation various agencies give to each other"	10	19	33	30	8
"The rank and file city employee tries his best to do his job but he gets little support from his superiors" ...	6	12	30	37	15
"No matter how imaginative our city officials may be, the rank and file public employees just plug away doing the same things anyhow"	8	15	30	35	12
"The average citizen can always find someone in the city government who is willing to help him solve his problem"	14	23	32	27	4

their superiors back by bureaucratic foot dragging, and in which the average citizen has neither complete access nor is denied access.[4]

[4]Differences existed among the five occupations, although for the sake of not cluttering up this report with too many tables, we have omitted presentation of these findings. Some general statements may be made however: social workers, educators and political party workers tended to be close together in their ratings of local government, with policemen, merchants, and employers being similar to each other. The latter tended to hold a more charitable view of local government, with the social workers, educators, and political party workers being more critical.

Comparing types of cities, as in Table 9, some weak patterns emerge in the direction of confirming the expectations described above. Non-riot cities are more likely to be rated as having political leaders who are imaginative, less likely to be considered cities lagging in innovativeness, and somewhat more likely to provide access to the average citizen.

TABLE 9

Political Styles and City Types

(Q 27 — Core)

(in percent)

Statement[2]	Proportion Rating Statement as "True"[1]		
	Riot cities	Medium riot	Non-riot cities
Political leaders are imaginative	66	78	79
City last to try new ideas	53	42	40
Cooperation among city agencies	60	58	67
Rank and file tries his best	48	50	49
Rank and file plugs away	51	56	54
Average citizen can find someone to listen...	67	68	72

[1]Combining "Completely true," Mostly true," and "Somewhat true."
[2]See Table 8 for complete test of statement.

Providing a summary measure of how our respondents saw their cities are the answers to a question asking "how well" they thought their city was doing in comparison with other cities of the same size. Their answers are tabulated in Table 10. In the top half of that table are shown the array of responses given by the occupational groups and the totals for the combined sample. In the bottom half of the table are shown answers given by respondents in different types of cities.

A little less than a third of the respondents saw their cities as doing better than average, a little more than half saw their cities as perfectly ordinary average cities, and the remaining dissidents (sixteen percent) thought their cities were doing less well than average.

Differences among occupational groups show employers and policemen as the most charitable toward their communities, with educators and political workers the least charitable, leaving social workers and merchants in the unusual situation of presenting a similar array of answers.

TABLE 10

Ratings of How Well City is Doing by Occupational
Groups and Type of City
(Q 4 — Core)
(in percent)

Ratings	Police	Educa-tors	Social workers	Politi-cal workers	Mer-chants	Em-ployers	Com-bined total
I. Ratings by occu-pational groups							
Much better than average ...	36	23	23	19	24	35	28
About average	48	54	61	54	53	52	53
Less than aver-age	14	20	15	23	17	11	16
DK & NA	2	3	1	4	6	2	3

	Riot cities	Medium riot	Nonriot cities
II. Ratings by type of city			
Much better than average	21	30	33
About average	54	53	52
Less than average	22	14	12
DK & NA	3	3	3

More interesting are the differences by city types. Respondents
in riot cities were the most critical of their cities, while those in
the non-riot cities produced higher proportions rating their communities as being above average. Again, we are plagued by ambiguities
of interpretation: perhaps cities which have experienced serious
riots in 1967 are *ipso facto* to be considered as performing less
than average. However, because this question is not very directly
related in content to the areas of civil disorders and race relations,
we have a better argument for considering that cities whose "front-
line" personnel have a sense of belonging to a community which
is doing better than the average are cities in which riots were less
likely to occur.

8

POLICE IN THE GHETTO *

W. EUGENE GROVES

If the policeman's lot has always been a hard one it is especially difficult in this historical period. Police have borne the brunt of criticism from many quarters. In the wake of the several hundred riots, near-riots, and serious civil disorders, the police have been criticized on the one hand for alleged brutality, hostility, and insensitivity; and on the other hand for their inability to contain mass violence and to bring it rapidly under control. Some of our most important civil rights are in the hands of the uniformed men of our local police forces; it is scarcely surprising that, in the struggle Negroes are waging for parity in this respect, the police should come under strong criticism.

Not only is the policeman both the guardian of and possible infringer upon individual civil rights, he is also the around-the-clock representative of authority in the ghetto. It is the policeman who is on duty twenty-four hours a day and who represents the go-between to get medical treatment, who settles marital spats, and who watches to see that you do not break regulations, make too much noise or hang out on street corners. The friction between police and the ghetto has raised enough heat to make this relationship of particular importance in understanding why civil disorders have appeared.

The purpose of this chapter is to look at the police in finer detail than was possible in the earlier chapters of this report. The police were questioned using a specially designed questionnaire,

*Reprinted from *Supplemental Studies for the National Advisory Commission on Civil Disorder* (Washington: U.S. Government Printing Office, 1968), pp. 103-114.

aimed at getting a statistical portrait of what the policeman's job is like in the ghetto and what his views are concerning ghetto residents.

THE SAMPLE

Interviews with 437 policemen distributed across eleven of the fifteen cities were included in the preliminary analysis. Forty respondents in each city were selected from those precincts which contain the 1960 census tracts with the highest percentage Negro in the city. In all cities, precincts that had over fifty percent Negro residents were sampled. All those interviewed worked primarily in the Negro neighborhoods within the precincts. Five of the forty policemen occupied positions higher than patrolmen (e.g., sergeants, lieutenants); and one fourth were Negroes (one supervisor and nine patrolmen) in each city.

Unfortunately, access to the policemen in some cities proved to be difficult. Even when the leadership of the department officially cooperated, seldom was it possible to draw a probability sample of policemen in the precincts sampled. Our final sample expresses the biases of police captains and other officials who often chose men to be interviewed. While we cannot determine the bias that has entered, it is reasonable to assume that the selectivity operated in favor of the images police departments consciously wish to project to the public.

The entire sample of fifteen cities has not yet been completed because of official non-cooperation in several departments. This item of information, in itself, might be considered indicative of the general accessibility and openness to criticism and suggestions in police departments. Milwaukee has been particularly adament against permitting any access, while Boston, and Chicago have been quite difficult. Most other cities gave some measure of cooperation, though often somewhat grudgingly. Few actively encouraged the study.[1]

THE POLICEMAN'S JOB

The task of a policeman, to paraphrase the Report of the National Advisory Commission on Civil Disorder, is to protect persons

---

[1]Further reports from this study will contain interviews with police in all cities, save Boston and Milwaukee. In both those cities, police officials ordered their men not to cooperate with our interviewers.

and property in a manner that embodies the predominant moral values of the community he is serving. This role is one of the most difficult in the society. Furthermore, the conscientious policeman in the predominantly Negro areas of our central cities faces perhaps, the greatest difficulties of all. At present the total efforts of the police departments neither effectively control crime in the ghetto nor achieve legitimacy in the eyes of many residents of the community. The policemen interviewed clearly reflected this situation. Seventy-three percent said they worked in neighborhoods where the crime rate was higher than average for the city. Almost forty-five percent listed their neighborhoods among the highest in the city in its crime rate. At the same time a majority of the respondents felt that a lack of support from the public, from the courts, from other officials and agencies were among the major problems in doing their job in the neighborhood to which they were assigned.

The police interviewed were asked to name the two or three major problems they faced. Forty-eight percent of the responses (Table 1) dealt with the lack of external support for the policeman. Answers to other questions confirm this assessment. Forty-two percent of the policemen considered non-cooperation from residents

TABLE 1

What Policemen See As The Major Problems
Facing Them in Doing Their Job in
Negro Neighborhoods
(Q 1 — Police)
(100 Percent =622)

	Percentage of all responses given [1]
Lack of external support — public, courts, officials, and other agencies	48
Internal departmental problems in doing the job — facilities, supervision, policies	21
Crime, violence, riots, etc.	16
Racial problems — hostility, agitation	9
Living conditions of residents — unemployment, housing, schools, government services, etc.	6

[1]Each of the 437 respondents could give several answers, the first three of which were coded and used in this analysis. Individuals gave an average of 1.4 answers.

a very serious problem; and sixty-four percent thought lack of support from the laws and courts was very serious (Table 17). Likewise, almost fifty-nine percent of the policemen thought that most of the residents in the precinct where they worked either regarded policemen as enemies or were indifferent towards them (Table 5). As both Table 5 and 17 illustrate, Negro policemen are less likely to perceive the ghetto as hostile and non-supportive.

Police work in these neighborhoods was viewed by the majority both as harder (sixty-one percent) and more hazardous (sixty-two percent) than elsewhere in the same city (Table 2). However

TABLE 2
Comparative Ratings of Assignments in Ghetto
Precincts and Overall Satisfaction
(Q 2-3 Police)

	Percent
A. Harder or easier than other assignments?	
Harder	61
About the same	30
Easier	6
Don't know and no answer	3
B. Is work safer or more hazardous than in other assignments?	
Safer	6
No difference	36
More hazardous	62
Don't know and no answer	2
C. Would you prefer working here or some other assignment?	
Prefer present assignment	47
Prefer another assignment	26
Does not matter	26
Don't know and no answer	1
D. How satisfied are you with police work?	
Very satisfied	36
Somewhat satisfied	36
Somewhat dissatisfied	21
Very dissatisfied	6
Don't know and no answer	1

great the difficulties and hazards of the job, the police did not express a comparable overall dissatisfaction with the job of a policeman. Seventy-three percent seemed at least somewhat satisfied with being a policeman, and only twenty-six percent preferred another assignment somewhere else in the city. There was no striking difference between Negroes and whites in these assessments.

The respondents were asked if they were very satisfied, somewhat satisfied, somewhat dissatisfied, or very dissatisfied with eight aspects of their work. The largest number complained about poor pay and lack of respect from citizens (Table 3). The policemen's assessment of the eight job aspects might best be summarized as indicating that these men are the most dissatisfied with the external

TABLE 3

The Policeman's Satisfactions and
Dissatisfactions With His Job
(Q 33 — Police)

	Dissatisfied		Satisfied		Don't know	100	No answer
	Very	Some-what	Very	Some-what			
	Per-cent	Per-cent	Per cent	Per-cent	Per cent		
The respect you get from citizens	22	32	10	33	1	(434)	3
Pay	28	26	9	36	0	(435)	2
Physical danger you often face	17	32	11	28	11	(431)	6
Resources and facilities for your job	22	27	19	31	0	(436)	1
Working conditions	13	34	11	42	0	(436)	1
Flexibility in doing your job	15	22	24	38	1	(435)	2
Other policemen with whom you work	2	12	52	33	1	(436)	1
Your supervisor	3	10	51	33	1	(432)	5

rewards, only moderately dissatisfied with the immediate conditions under which they usually work, and quite satisfied with their colleagues. Such a pattern is consistent with the observation of James Q. Wilson[2] that, when there is little public respect for policemen, they tend to develop subcultural identification or "codes" in order to achieve self-respect independent of civilian attitudes.

INTERNAL RESOURCES

As Table 1 shows, the second most frequent spontaneous complaint voiced by the policemen was of the lack of internal support for their work: manpower, facilities, supervision, etc.

[2]"Police Morale, Reform, and Citizen Respect: The Chicago Case," David J. Bordua, Ed., *The Police: Six Sociological Essays* (New York, Wiley, 1967), p. 138.

Twenty-one percent of the police citations of major problems were of this type. Within this category of problems, the most frequently mentioned single item was manpower. Ten percent of the policemen listed this as one of three major problems facing them.[3]

Even though the policemen felt disliked by so many citizens, and operated with inadequate facilities and support, very few mentioned low morale as a problem they faced. Only three respondents volunteered a comment about pay or morale as major problems they faced in doing their jobs. A few more, six percent (Table 2), reported that they were "very dissatisfied" with a policeman's job. Apparently, high morale has been maintained, at least among most of the respondents, in spite of many perceived difficulties and negative sanctions.

Another aspect of the policeman's resources is the training given him to cope with the problems he faces daily. While our information does not enable us to assess the effectiveness of comprehensiveness of police training for these difficult assignments, we can report that eighty-five percent of our respondents have had special training in riot control and prevention, and seventy-eight percent have had some training in human relations, psychology, counseling, etc. Very few policemen reported lack of training as a major problem they faced in doing their job (only seven respondents spontaneously referred to this).

When we consider some of the findings shown later on in this chapter, our respondents' feelings of satisfaction with their training can easily be brought into question.

EXTERNAL RELATIONS OF POLICE DEPARTMENTS

Ghetto critics of the police often charge them with being essentially "occupation" forces rather than "community protectors": agents of external, often alien, norms and interests rather than agents of social control for the community in which they are assigned. Undoubtedly much of this charge rests on exaggeration of actions and attitudes of both sides; however, it is important that we search for indications of such large scale group conflict as opposed to

[3]When asked in another context whether the control of crime and the enforcement of the law is hampered by shortage of men, cars, facilities, etc., eighty-nine percent considered this to be a problem; sixty-one percent thought it "very serious."

isolated individual defiance of legal norms. In addition, we shall examine how the police tend to explain or justify actions that are deemed by many to be provocatively and punitively directed against a large class of people—those with black skins and little money.

From their own reporting (Table 3), fifty-four percent of the policemen queried were disatisfied with the respect they receive from citizens. In fact (Table 4), thirty percent suggested that

TABLE 4
Respect Accorded to Police by Average
Resident of Precinct
(Q 5 — Police)

	Percent
"How much respect does the average resident of this precinct have for the police?"	
A great deal of respect	12
Some respect	44
Neither respect nor contempt	11
Some contempt	20
A great deal of contempt	10
Don't know and no answer	3

the average citizen in their patrol precincts held the police in some degree of contempt. The police were asked several questions about whether residents considered the police as enemies, assuming this to be a good indication of the degree to which the policemen feel like aliens in the community. Nineteen percent suggested that most people in the precinct in general look on the police as enemies (Table 5). While thirty-seven percent reported the people they protect as regarding police on their side, the largest portion (forty percent) perceived the residents as indifferent.

When asked about the attitudes of Negroes, a higher proportion of policemen (twenty percent) felt they were viewed as enemies. Indeed, the policemen's perceptions of hostility were primarily reserved for the Negroes. Only one percent of the respondents thought most whites considered them enemies, and seventy-two percent thought whites considered them on their side.

The policemen apparently feel much more a part of the "white community" than of the "Negro community" at least in regard to their official activities within their patrol precinct. What hos-

TABLE 5

The Policeman's View of Whether the Residents
Consider Police as Enemies, Friends or
are Indifferent

	Regard police—					
	As on their side	As enemies	Indifferent	Don't know	100 percent	No answer
	Percent	Percent	Percent	Percent		
Residents in general	37	19	40	3	(432)	5
Most old persons in the neighborhood	94	1	5	0	(437)	—
Most storekeepers	83	0	14	0	(436)	1
Most teachers	83	1	13	2	(435)	2
Most whites	72	1	25	2	(437)	—
Most Negroes	34	29	35	2	(434)	3
Most young adults	16	39	44	1	(437)	—
Most adolescents	16	51	32	1	(436)	1

The policeman's view of whether or not the residents consider the police
as enemies, by race of respondent
(Percentage responding that most regard police as enemies)

	White[1] (N = 335)	Negro[1] (N = 101)
The residents in general	21	11
Most old persons in the neighborhood	1	0
Most storekeepers	0	0
Most teachers	2	0
Most whites	1	2
Most Negroes	30	22
Most young adults	43	27
Most adolescents	52	46

[1]One respondent was neither white nor Negro, or was miscoded.

tility is perceived by the police seems not to be a manifestation
of racial antagonism against individual policemen. Negro policemen
report the same pattern of perceived hostility that the whites report,
although a consistently smaller percentage of the Negro police
regard any one group of people (except whites) as antagonists
(Table 5).

Perhaps more important to observe than the relatively low
respect and cooperation between police and Negroes in general

is the marked distance between police and the young generation. At a time in which juvenile crime is rapidly on the increase and complaints are loudly voiced about the lawlessness of ghetto youth, the police seem to be least in touch with the people. While it is beyond the scope of this report to analyze whether the generation and perhaps racial gaps between police and Negro youth are more an antecedent or consequent of a reported increase in antisocial and criminal behavior among that group, we can quite clearly see that police think themselves disliked more by the young than by any other segment of the population. Fifty-one percent of the policemen believe that most adolescents view them as enemies, and thirty-nine percent think most young adults share that hostility. In contrast, the elderly, the storekeepers, and the teachers are perceived as friends or at least friendly.

What lies behind this perception of hostility? The Commission's report[4] cited several surveys of the opinions of Negroes and whites about such things as police brutality and police respect, indicating that in the last two or three years a sizeable fraction of urban Negroes believe that there has been police brutality, while considerably fewer whites believe that police use unnecessary force. Although a survey of the opinion of residents would be the most appropriate measure of their view of police actions, we had to rely upon the police themselves as informants, asking how frequently they had heard certain complaints from the citizens. Six types of actions were listed and the respondents asked how frequently they had heard them—often, sometimes, seldom, or never—as complaints about the police.

As we can see from Table 6, policemen think that residents frequently see them as brutal, annoying and inconsiderate. They sometimes hear complaints about corruption and general hostility, but seldom are charged with being too lenient. In fact, only sixteen percent of the policemen "often" hear complaints that they are not tough enough, while thirty-one percent never hear these charges. In the view of the policemen themselves the residents complain frequently about the actions of the police but there is no wide-spread demand for a crackdown on "crime."

What truth is there to many of these complaints? What actions and attitudes of policemen might stimulate such complaints? A closer examination of the common practices of the police might indicate possible situations and types of police-resident contact

[4]Chapter 11, Section I.

TABLE 6
Complaints Policemen Hear About Their
Actions
(Q 26 — Police)
(in percent)

	Often or sometimes	Seldom or never	Don't know
Policemen are physically brutal to people on the streets	75	25	0
They give too many tickets and do not help the residents	64	35	1
They do not understand the problems of the residents	64	36	0
They are corrupt and take bribes from those with money	52	48	1
Policemen are generally hostile to the residents	52	48	0
Policemen do not adequately prevent crime because they are not tough enough	42	57	1

that would be most likely to generate hostile feelings. Six types of activity were listed, and each respondent was asked to tell whether he was frequently, sometimes, seldom or never called upon to do each (Table 7).

Although we cannot compare these types of activity with ones considered more supportive by those possibly affected by the actions, some conclusions are reasonable. It is clear that police quite frequently intervene in domestic quarrels and break up loitering groups. This often places them in delicate situations where they

TABLE 7
What Policemen are Called Upon to Do
(Q 9 — Police)

	Fre-quently	Never	100 percent	No answer
	Percent	Percent		
Intervene in domestic quarrels	94	0		(2)
Breakup loitering groups	63	1		(2)
Interrogate suspected drug users	35	6		(4)
Stop and frisk suspicious people	34	11		(2)
Search on suspicion but without a warrant	24	16		(4)
Search with a warrant	20	7		(4)

interfere with groups of people who may consider their own behaviour normal and legitimate, and at the least not a proper subject of forceful interference. The tension that may be created by indelicate actions in these circumstances is hardly helped by the frequent practice of placing the least skilled policemen in the higher crime areas.

The other activities that policemen report frequently engaging in seldom can be expected to endear them to the residents. About a third are frequently stopping people to question or frisk them, implying thereby that the person stopped is suspected of some crime or potential crime. Almost a fourth report frequently searching without a warrant, further indicating to a great number of residents that they do not merit the justification of due cause to a court.[5] More than a third frequently interrogate suspected drug users. Since the use of the less habituating drugs is considered less onerous by ghetto norms than by white middle-class standards, such interrogation is easily interpreted as the imposition of alien and unjustified standards of conduct upon a powerless people. The police, then, are constantly interferring with many of the day-to-day activities of a significant portion of the residents of the neighborhood. It is quite understandable how this imposition—whether justified or not—could generate a considerable level of hostility.

Some degree of hostility can be expected to be generated by the regular surveillance activity of the police. Those who were innocent of any intended or actual wrong doing are likely to dislike being stopped and frisked. Indeed, the probability of a person who is stopped and frisked by the police being innocent is much larger than the probability of being caught in some illegal activity. The President's Commission on Law Enforcement and the Administration of Justice reported that in some high crime areas only ten percent of those stopped and frisked were found to be carrying a gun, and another ten percent were found to be carrying knives. The policemen in our sample claim a higher success rate, as the evidence in Table 8 indicates. The median number of persons found to be "carrying something that might lead to crime" when stopped and frisked is 5.1, according to our policemen. Furthermore, the police also claim that a median of 3.5 individuals were found to be wanted criminals or to have committed some illegal act.

We think it would be safe to assume that the policemen are claiming more positive results from the stop-and-frisk procedure

[5]From the way in which the question was worded we are uncertain whether respondents referred to searching premises, searching persons, or both.

than is actually the case. In any event, the majority of persons stopped are innocent of any wrongdoing. If the rate of stopping and frisking in the Negro community is very high, then it would not take long for the police to antagonize a large number of residents.[6] Interestingly, there were no differences between Negro and white policemen in the reported median frequency with which suspicions were verified in frisks.

TABLE 8

Proportion of Positive Finds in Stopping and
Frisking

(Q 10 — Police)

Out of every 10 persons stopped	Carrying something that might lead to crime (e.g. gun, knife)	Actually turned out to be criminals you are looking for
None ....percent...	3	5
One ....do......	13	22
Two ....do......	10	13
Three ....do......	10	10
Four ....do......	7	10
Five ....do......	12	16
Six ....do......	8	3
Seven ....do......	12	6
Eight ....do......	11	7
Nine ....do......	10	5
Ten ....do......	3	3
100 percent equals	(366)	(344)
Median number[1]	5.1	3.5
Number responding otherwise		
Desk job	18	17
Illegal to frisk	24	26
Don't know, no answer	29	50

[1]Calculated assuming that responses "five," for example, are evenly distributed between 4.5 and 5.5.

The general tenor with which the policeman reported their dealings with people in the neighborhood seemed to be a hardened Hobbesian pessimisim in only a small fraction of the respondents.

[6]It may also be the case that those policemen who do a great deal of stopping and frisking may have lower overall "take rates," even though they may apprehend more criminals in total. Hence a policy which would increase the amount of stopping and frisking bears the risk of antagonizing very large proportion of the non-criminal even though it would significantly increase the number of criminals or alleged criminals who are apprehended.

In dealing with suspects only ten percent suggested that the policemen should "deal aggressively and authoritatively from the start so that the suspect knows who is in control," while eighty-nine percent agreed that they should "deal firmly from the start, but be polite until a hostile move is made by the suspect." Similarly, only eight percent felt that most people they deal with on the job respond primarily to power and force. A full forty percent thought that people respond in the end primarily to reason and respect, with few responding only to power and force. The rest (fifty-two percent) thought there were some of both kinds of people (Q 13 Police). In total, sixty percent felt that some sizable proportion of people responded only to power and force, providing some justification for its frequent use.

The typical interaction between policemen and suspect, when people are questioned and frisked, is not congenial. Only nine percent of the policemen report that people they stop are usually fully cooperative (Table 9). More than eighty percent admit that the usual reaction is at least a dislike of being frisked. Forty-one percent of the policemen report that they usually have to use threats or force to get the suspect to respond adequately. Eleven percent find that their suspects usually physically resist their efforts to question and frisk. Such responses from suspects would be expected from hardened criminals. But in a situation on which a majority of those stopped are neither carrying weapons nor are criminals, and in which thirty-four percent of the policemen frequently stop and frisk people, it is clear that considerable hos-

TABLE 9

Response of Suspects When They Are Stopped and Frisked

(Q 12 — Police)

Response	Race of policemen		
	White	Negro	All police
Cooperative ....percent...	10	8	9
Cooperative, but don't like being frisked ....do......	36	48	39
Respond finally under threats and pressure ....do......	30	29	30
Physically resist ....do......	13	5	11
Don't know, don't frisk, no answer ....do......	11	10	11
100 percent equals	(335)	(101)	(437)

tility is generated among many others than those directly engaged in criminal behavior. Table 9 illustrates that hostility is generated in stopping and frisking by police of both races. However, citizens are perceived as slightly more cooperative by Negro policemen.

Some critics have suggested that it is easy for a policeman to get away with brutal treatment of Negroes. But, whether or not police actions are more aggressive in the Negro ghetto than elsewhere, the police seem to worry more about the restraints placed upon them there. When asked whether they worried about getting into trouble because of their mistakes or because of citizens complaints, a sizable porportion (thirty-nine percent) expressed more anxiety about such constraint in their Negro precincts than in other sections of the city. Most saw no difference. Only six percent indicated that they need be less cautious in the Negro precinct to which they currently were assigned. Interestingly, this pattern holds for Negroes as well as whites (see Table 10). The complaints

TABLE 10
How Much Policemen Worry About Mistakes
and Complaints
(Q 15 — Police)

Worry about mistakes, complaints from public	White	Negro	All
Worry more here than elsewhere in city........................percent...	40	35	39
Worry more in most other precincts ....do......	5	11	6
Makes no difference ....do......	53	52	54
Don't know, no answer ......do......	2	2	1
100 percent equals	(335)	(101)	(437)

that bring the threat of discipline apparently do not arise primarily from racial antagonisms alone. As suggested earlier, the conflict stems more from the overall nature of the police relationship to the Negro community.

The relationship between police and the Negro residents is partially characterized as extensive "anti-crime" activity by the police and many outraged complaints, sometimes leading to collective expressions, by the residents. The desire by city and police leadership for some measure of caution is understandable. The policemen on the beat, defining the precincts as high crime areas, frequently frisk people, break up loitering groups, and intervene in domestic quarrels. The residents complain about many of these activities and resent the manner in which they are carried out. Complaints of police brutality are frequently heard by the police themselves. Seventy-five percent said they "often" or "sometimes" heard them (Table 6). Few policemen (four percent), however, listed complaints of police brutality as major problems in doing their jobs (Q 1 — Police).

Both Negro and white policemen often hear these complaints from citizens, but only the Negroes consider black-skinned people to be ill-treated by police, public officials, and the general public. Table 11 indicates that a majority of Negro police felt that Negroes are treated worse than others by police and public officials; only

TABLE 11
Police Attitudes Towards Treatment of
Negroes by Police and Public Officials
(Q 6 — Core)

Treatment of Negroes	Race of police	As well off	Less well off	Better off	Don't know, no answer	100 per-cent
		Per-cent	Per-cent	Per-cent	Per-cent	
Treatment by police ....White...		78	5	17	1	(335)
	Negro...	36	57	6	1	(101)
Treatment by public ....White...		59	5	34	2	(335)
officials.	Negro...	39	54	5	2	(101)

five percent of the white police believed this. Similarly, as shown in Table 12, sixty-two percent of the white policemen felt that Negroes are treated equally or better than any other part of the population, while only eight percent of the Negroes agreed. The pervasive feeling among white policemen that Negroes are treated equally, or even better, than whites may indicate that many feel that the Negro community has more power and privilege than it deserves, including the power to wield some restraint upon police.

In summary, the complaints from ghetto residents are not considered major obstacles by most police. If a policeman feels more anxiety about these complaints in some precincts than in others, he is likely to perceive more pressure in Negro areas. Furthermore, as the preceding considerations suggest, and as later discussions will indicate, it is clear that the white policeman finds less justice in these constraints than does the Negro.

TABLE 12
Policeman's View of How Negroes are Treated
in His City
(Q 5 — Core)
(Percentage of respondents agreeing with statement)

	White	Negro	Total
Treated better than any other part of the population	20	2	16
Treated equally	42	6	33
Treated as other people of the same income	26	24	26
Treated worse than other people of the same income	8	38	14
Treated worse than any other part of the population	2	26	7
Don't know or no answer	2	5	3

Note: 100 percent equals: white – 335; Negro – 101; total – 437.

ATTITUDES TOWARDS THE COMMUNITY

What do the policemen think of the people in the neighborhoods where they patrol? Some earlier studies have indicated that a large fraction of white policemen working in Negro neighborhoods exhibit prejudice toward Negroes. Albert Reiss reported to the National Advisory Commission on Civil Disorders that three out of four of the white policemen in predominantly Negro neighborhoods in one city studied exhibited some prejudicial attitudes.[7] As noted earlier, not many of the police, especially white, were sympathetic to Negro causes: fifty-nine percent claimed that the Negroes were moving "much too fast" or "too fast" in gaining what they feel to be equality. Seventy-three percent of the whites and twelve percent of the Negroes felt this way. Forty-nine percent of the whites expressed some chagrin about Negroes socializing with whites, and fifty-six percent were at least "slightly disturbed" with Negroes moving into white residential areas. Very few, including the Negro policemen, expressed any active support of Negro causes. Five percent of all the respondents had been active in a civil rights group during the previous two years (four percent of the whites and seven percent of the Negroes).

[7]Chapter 11, Section 1.

The images an individual holds of traits and attitudes of a group have often been used as an index of prejudice. At least, the policeman's stereotypes of the residents with whom he is working can be expected to influence the manner in which he deals with them. In assessing six characteristics, police were quite mixed. (Table 13). On each characteristic a sizable fraction thought highly of the residents, but a large fraction held low opinions. Comparing positive to negative assessments, both Negro and white policemen rated the residents best on "honesty." Negroes thought somewhat better of the residents than did whites, on the average.

POLICE ASCRIPTION OF RESPONSIBILITY
FOR THE COMMUNITY PROBLEMS

Many factors influence the collective behavior of a community, particularly the characteristics of the people themselves, the relationship they have with organizers and representatives of many outside agencies, their relationship to various government agencies— welfare, police, educational system, etc., and the economic exchange relationships they have with those who control economic resources. The National Advisory Commission on Civil Disorders, in assessing the basic causes of rioting, stressed the centuries of neglect and discrimination on the part of the white community toward their Negro neighbors. The Commission concluded that agitators and militants were not basically responsible for the outbreaks of violence; even less responsible was the general nature of the Negro community. Rather, the lack of adequate private and governmental response to the problems of unemployment, housing, deficient education and, most basically, the pervasive discrimination against Negroes in American life were seen as the root causes of the disturbances.

The policeman, who is the most visible agent of the society in maintaining law and order, sees the causes of rioting and civil disturbances quite differently. It is reasonable to expect that his viewpoint will reflect the enforcement actions and strategy which he daily uses in an attempt to minimize violence and disorder. The viewpoint he expresses appears to be one of short-run criminal control, rather than one of long-term eradication of the causes of discontent. While individual policemen differed considerably

TABLE 13
Attitudes Toward Residents of the Precinct
(Q 8 — Police)
(in percent)

Attribute (stated positively)	Very positive assessment		Very negative assessment		Partially true		Don't know, no answer		Total	
	White	Negro	White	Negro	White	Negro	White	Negro	White	Negro
They are often friendly to outsiders	22	40	32	21	42	37	4	3	100	101
They look after their health very well	22	28	28	16	42	52	8	4	100	100
They are industrious people	16	26	28	12	53	60	2	2	99	100
They care very much for law and order	33	48	22	14	44	38	2	1	101	101
They are respectable, religious people	19	28	18	3	59	67	4	2	100	100
They are honest people	32	50	10	4	56	46	1	0	99	100
Average on six items	24	37	23	12	49	50	—	—	100	

Note: N(White) = 335; N(Negro) = 101.

in their ascription of responsibility for the problems they face, most tended to see disorders as a result essentially of a lawless, negligent, belligerent, and criminal uprising of some elements of the Negro community.

All respondents were asked what they considered the major causes of the 1967 civil disturbances. Fifty-six percent of the reasons given (Table 14, categories one, forty-four percent; three, eight percent; and seven, four percent) ascribed the causes to the lawlessness, anger, disorder and agitation in the Negro community. The remaining forty-four percent of the reasons given ascribed at least some responsibility to the total society and by implication to the white community.

But, if we probe deeper, the policeman's emphasis becomes clearer. For example, the profile of responses for policemen who reported their city having a major civil disturbance in Summer, 1967, was somewhat different than that for policemen reporting no serious disturbance that Summer. Where there had been a

TABLE 14
Reasons Given for Civil Disturbances
(Q 15 and 18 — Core)
(in percent)

Reasons	Reporting riot in 1967 in city (N = 289)	Reporting no serious disturbance in city in 1967 (N = 141)	All police responding (N = 430)
(1) Causes attributed to faults of the Negro community — disrespect for law, crime agitation, unrest, broken families, etc.	49	33	44
(2) Causes attributed to failure system to meet problems — unemployment, housing, poverty, welfare, schools, indifference, leadership	22	38	27
(3) Negro anger, frustration, and unfulfilled aspirations	7	8	8
(4) General white and official discrimination and provocation	7	5	6
(5) Contagion — media, rumors, etc.	5	4	5
(6) Lack of interracial communication	3	8	5
(7) Lack of adequate enforcement and control by authorities	3	5	4
(8) Specific person or event	4	0	2
Total responses, 100 percent equals	(542)	(274)	(816)

serious disturbance, forty nine percent of the reasons given cited agitation and criminal elements—basic Negro lawlessness—while twenty-two percent of the causes given ascribed some responsibility to the failure of the system and the white community. In cities where policemen reported no serious disturbance that summer the frequency of reasons listed was reversed. Thirty-five percent of the responses blamed the criminal and lawless elements, while thirty-eight percent blamed the system in part.

Whether this difference is due primarily to the impact of the riots and subsequent rationalizations for police actions or whether it existed prior to the riots and might have, in part, been responsible for whether or not there was a riot cannot be known from our limited information in those interviews. However, in our judgment such a difference in police assignment of causes is primarily a result of having recently experienced a riot. Those cities in which policemen emphasized social-economic causes seemed just as likely to have a riot in 1968 as did the other cities.

Quite significant racial differences appear, as Table 15 illustrates. Twice as many whites basically blame the Negro community as blame the socioeconomic system. The reverse is true for the Negro policemen. In addition, approximately three times as many Negroes as whites place the emphasis upon lack of interracial communication.

TABLE 15
Reasons Given for Civil Disturbances
(Q 15 and 18 — Core)

	(Total for all police)[1]		
	White (N = 329)	Negro (N = 100)	Both (N = 429)
Causes attributed to faults of Negro community — disrespect for law, agitation, crime, unrest broken families, etc.	50	24	44
Causes attributed to failure of system to meet problems — unemployment, poverty, bad housing, poor schools, poor leadership from city, etc.	21	44	27
Lack of interracial communication	3	9	5
All other reasons	25	23	25

[1]Seven of the 437 interviewers did not give answers to these questions; the eighth was neither white nor Negro.
Note: 100 percent equals: White 609; Negro 206; both 815.

When police were more directly questioned about the causes of riots, they strongly supported the agitation, criminal element explanations as opposed to police brutality or white neglect (Table 16). Seventy-eight percent and sixty-nine percent, respectively, saw militant agitation and criminal elements as either the main reason or a major reason for the recent civil disturbances. Only nine percent and thirty percent, respectively, subscribed to the police brutality and unresponsiveness explanations. Table 16 also

TABLE 16

How Negro and White Policemen Differ in
Attributing Causes to the Riots
(Q 67-72 — Core)
(Percent agreeing that cause listed is main reason
or largely true)

	White (N = 335)	Negro (N = 101)	All Police (N = 437)
Local authorities not paying sufficient attention to complaints	24	52	30
Result of criminal element in Negro ghetto ...	74	52	69
Result of militant agitation	84	55	78
Deliberate political actions	28	23	27
Police brutality	4	25	9
Negroes basically violent and disrespectful ...	33	11	28

shows that Negro police subscribe much less than whites to the militant and criminal explanations, and much more than whites to the police brutality and unresponsiveness explanations.

While very few of the policemen considered inadequate laws or lenient courts as direct causes of riots (two percent volunteered this explanation), they quite strongly resented the restraint placed upon them by the courts and the laws. In a question asking for their major problems as policemen, fifteen percent volunteered complaints about courts and judges being too lenient. This was second only to the forty percent who gave "lack of public support" as one of the major problems they face in doing their jobs. In another question (Table 17) more of the policemen considered laws and courts to hamper their jobs than any of the other three problems.

Table 17 illustrates again how the races differ. Laws and courts were most frequently perceived as an obstacle by whites, but only third most frequently by Negroes. In contrast, Negroes

TABLE 17

Seriousness of Four Problems in the Policeman's
Job

(Q 16 — Police)

(Percent of policemen who consider problem
"Very serious" and "Not at all serious")

(N (White) = 335; N (Negro) = 101)

Problem	Very serious			Not serious		
	White	Negro	Total	White	Negro	Total
Noncooperation of residents	44	32	42	10	18	12
Laws and court decisions hamper investigations and convictions	68	50	64	5	17	8
Inadequate resources: Men, cars, facilities, etc.	61	60	61	12	10	11
Other agencies lack adequate resources	40	57	44	13	6	12

felt most hampered by inadequate resources for themselves and
by the inadequate resources of other agencies in the city. The
white police were least concerned about the supportive functions
of the other agencies in dealing with community problems.

The policeman is under conflicting pressures and expectations.
As Reiss[8] and Bordua point out, enforcement of the laws is
separated from the outcome of an arrest. The policeman is under
professional and public pressure to catch criminals and to keep
public order, but the final conviction and sentencing of an offender
is out of his hands, as are judgments of police brutality. It is
therefore expected that the average policeman should resent occasional
court rejection of his decisions, and frequent court scrutiny of
his actions. Likewise, we might add to this conflicting expectation
another—that enforcement is separated from prevention. Prevention
of many of the situations a policeman handles rests in hands other
than his own—city officials, poverty workers, employers, teachers,
et al. He has at his disposal only the resources of persuasion and
force. With this he must handle the results of the inadequacies
of all other segments of the system.

The policeman's perception of other people who work on social
problems in his neighborhood is varied. We asked whether the

[8]Environment and Organization: A Perspective on the Police," in David
Bordua, op. cit.

efforts of four types of agencies, organizations, or individuals made his job easier or more difficult (Table 18). Consistent with their assessment of the causes of riots, the policemen rated the more militant organizations as most deleterious to law enforcement. For every one policeman who considered the civil rights and poverty organizations helpful in the long run, eight thought they were deleterious. On the other hand those workers most directly associated with the same work as the police consider themselves doing — the gang workers — are considered beneficial to the policeman's work by five policemen for every one who thinks them harmful. Policemen are much more evenly split on the benefit of poverty and welfare workers, though the poverty workers are perceived slightly more helpful. A large fraction of the respondents considered poverty and welfare workers as irrelevant to the policeman's job of law enforcement.

The Negro policemen have a greater appreciation for the functions of the various organizations (Table 18). The percentage of Negro police who consider all of the four types of agencies to be beneficial is approximately twice that of the white police. Consistently fewer Negroes than whites consider the agencies deleterious. In all cases, however, the Negro and white policemen agree in the way most think about each type of organization. A larger fraction of both races think that civil rights groups make life more difficult, while the others make it easier.

POLICE PARTICIPATION IN THE COMMUNITY

The policeman's task consists primarily of the immediate enforcement of rules of law and order, and hence he is concerned with establishing a criminal-non-criminal dichotomy in his encounters with citizens. McNamara[10] observed in his study of New York police that such dichotomous stereotypes can often interfere with the policeman's ability to skillfully handle a variety of situations and different types of people in a sensitive manner. This ability partly requires an understanding of the community in which the policeman works. Such an understanding, in turn, would seem to require extensive and frequent informal and non-hostile communi-

[10]John H. McNamara, "Uncertainties in Police Work: The Relevance of Police Recruits' Background and Training," David Bordua, *op. cit.*

TABLE 18

How the Work of Other Agencies Affects the
Policeman's Job

(Q 14 — Police)

(N (White) = 335- N (Negro) = 101)

(In percent)

Agency	Easier			More Difficult			No Difference			Don't Know			Total
	White	Negro	Total	White	Negro	Total	White	Negro	Total	White	Negro	Total	
Gang workers	46	71	52	13	5	11	31	18	28	10	6	9	100 100 100
Poverty program workers (Head-start, VISTA, CAA, etc.)	36	61	42	23	4	19	34	31	33	6	4	6	99 100 100
Welfare workers	29	36	30	20	13	18	46	46	46	5	6	6	100 101 100
SNCC, CORE, NAACP, and Poverty Rights groups[1]	6	16	8	75	39	68	10	22	13	8	22	12	99 99 100

[1]Five percent of the whites and sixteen percent of the Negroes indicated that NAACP makes their job easier, while other groups make it more difficult.

cation with all major segments of the population with which the policeman is dealing. Not only would this communication increase the policeman's information about the neighborhood and the activities of its residents—thus minimizing mistakes and increasing surveillance of possible criminals—but such communication would tend to increase the policeman's perception and understanding of the resident's problems and concerns and activities, enabling him to avoid insensitivity in treatment of subjects. In short, in seeking the community cooperation and effectively creating a legal order, the policeman could perform best—if this argument is valid—if he is personally familiar with the adult and youth leaders, the community agency volunteers, the possible trouble-makers, et al.

Our respondents, however, seem strikingly isolated from the neighborhoods in which they patrol. As noted earlier fifty-one percent of the police thought adolescents, and thirty-nine percent thought young adults, regarded police as enemies. In contrast, ninty-four percent of the police perceived storekeepers as regarding police as friends. Whether isolation has caused the hostility or hostility the isolation is beyond our scope to determine. However, it is clear that police communicate very little with the youth and a lot with the merchants. Thirty-one percent of the police do not know a single important teenage or youth leader in the neighborhood well enough to speak to him when they see him (Table 19), Fifty-nine percent know five or fewer this well. On the other hand over fifty-five percent of the policemen report that they know more than twenty-five shop owners, managers and clerks well enough to speak with them whenever they see them. Where the most communication is occurring between the police and citizens in the neighborhood is reasonably clear. Such a pattern illustrates the grounds on which policemen are often perceived as a force of occupation, stationed in the ghetto to protect the property of the white merchant.

Table 19 shows the policeman's priorities in the community. He makes it his business to be aware of the "continual trouble-makers" and the merchants. But the community adult and youth leadership, as well as people working on eradicating the social and economic conditions that contribute to crime, are apparently considered largely irrelevant to the policeman's work of law enforcement. One would not usually expect the average patrolman to know very many organizers of crime well enough to exchange

TABLE 19
Extent of Personal Acquaintance With
People in the Precinct
(Q 23 — Police)
Question: ". . . In your precinct, for example, about
how many people among (name group) do you know
well enough to speak with whenever you see them?"
(N = 437)

Group	None	Five or fewer	Six or more	Don't know	100 per-cent	No an-swer
	Per-cent	Per-cent	Per-cent	Per-cent		
Shop owners, managers, clerks	3	9	89	1	(435)	2
Residents in general	5	12	86	1	(433)	4
Continual trouble makers	6	14	84	2	(436)	1
Important adult leaders	15	49	54	2	(436)	1
People from various government and private agencies who work in the neighborhood, e.g. welfare, religious, utilities	19	49	49	1	(436)	1
Organizers of unlawful activities like crime syndicates, numbers rackets, drug pushers	31	57	40	3	(434)	3
Important teenage and youth leaders	31	59	38	2	(433)	4

Note: (Answers were recorded in seven categories, which were collapsed to
form the third category above. The second response category listed above is
cumulative, including the first category.)

greeting on occasional meetings. But he knows as many of these
as he does of teenage and youth leaders. Yet the policeman regards
juveniles as presenting a particularly pressing problem. We should
note that comparison and conclusions from the information on
Table 19 must be made with caution, since there are quite different
numbers of people in the neighborhood in each category considered.
Thus, there are probably many more merchants than important
youth leaders in any precinct. Secondly, we must note that thirteen
percent of the respondents (about equal percentages for Negro
and white) have desk jobs. While this would not necessarily mean
that they would not be acquainted with anyone in the community,
it would be expected to reduce the number of residents with whom
they frequently communicate. However, what we are particularly
emphasizing is the large percentage of policemen who know just

a very small number, or even none, of the teenage and youth leaders and the people from other agencies.

Table 20 compares by race of respondent his contact with people in the neighborhood. With one exception (continual trouble-makers) the white police are more isolated—as measured by the percent who have no acquaintance at all—than the Negro police.

TABLE 20

Extent of No Personal Acquaintance With
Police in the Patrol Neighborhood
(Q 23 — Police)
(Percentage of respondents admitting knowing none
well enough to casually speak with)

	White (N = 335)	Negro (N = 101)
Shop owners, managers, clerks, etc.	3	1
Residents in general	5	4
Continual troublemakers	5	6
Important adult leaders	18	7
People from various government and private agencies	22	12
Organizers of crime, et al	31	30
Important teenage and youth leaders	35	18

One of the reasons that Negro policemen have more contact with the neighborhood in which they patrol, and have a greater sympathetic understanding of its problems, is that they are much more likely to informally participate in the community than are their white colleagues. Table 21 lists four measures of community participation. The general level of participation is rather low. Eighty-three percent of the respondents do not live where they work; and seventy-six percent do not have relatives in the neighborhood. Only twelve percent have friends there they see "a lot" off duty. On these three measures the Negro policeman understandably rate considerably higher. But for both races, the number who have friends in the neighborhood whom they see "a lot" is smaller than the percentage of policemen who live in that neighborhood.

Even if a policeman does not live in the neighborhood, he can engender community cooperation by attending meetings of various organizations. While thirty percent reported attending meetings

TABLE 21
Neighborhood Participation by Policemen
(Q 29-32 — Police)
(Percentage who responded affirmatively)

	White (N = 335)	Negro (N = 101)	Total (N = 437)
Live in same area as work	11	37	17
Any relatives live where you work ...	13	56	24
See friends from neighborhood socially "a lot"	6	30	12
Attend meetings in neighborhood "often" or "sometimes"	16	37	21

at least occasionally only seven percent attend "often." But police-men in general, as would be expected of lower-middle-class occupa-tional groups, are not frequent participants in groups and organized activity outside the job. Sixteen percent do not belong to any organization, and fifty-six percent belong either to one or none. (Q 6—BKGD). Their informal contact with their own residential community, aside from the neighborhood in which they work, is not very high.

Another set of questions has frequently been raised about the police department's relationship to the community. These deal with training in human relations for the individual officers, and with departmental policies that may be interpreted as discriminatory. Seventy-eight percent of the sample reported some training in human relations, psychology, counseling, law, etc. We have no way to assess the nature, extent, and effectiveness of this training.

The outward symbol of integration is a mixed patrol. Eighty-four percent of those who are on patrol report that they have patrolled with an officer of the opposite color. However, only thirty-six percent of those on a beat report travelling interracially more than "once in a while." The more subtle form discrimination might take is in hiring and promotion. Recently, of course, most cities have been encouraging Negroes to join the force, particularly placing them in the Negro community. When asked how likely it would be that a man of another race would take one's place if he were to change his present job, seventy-one percent reported that it would be either "very likely." or "somewhat likely." Only six percent said it would be not at all likely. While this gives no indication of promotion and assignment practices—since most of the respondents were patrolmen (eighty-three percent)—it does signify that very little effective discrimination in hiring or in general assignment to a Negro neighborhood is perceived by those presently employed.

SUMMARY

The nature of the police relationship to the community is of critical importance in maintaining order and in protecting persons and property. We have found that in the predominantly Negro areas of several large cities, many of the police perceive the residents as basically hostile, especially the youth and adolescents. A lack of public support—from citizens, from courts, and from laws — is the policeman's major complaint. But some of the public criticism can be traced to the activities in which he engages day by day, and perhaps to the tone in which he enforces the "law" in the Negro neighborhoods, Most frequently he is "called upon" to intervene in domestic quarrels and break up loitering groups. He stops and frisks two or three times as many people as are carrying dangerous weapons or are actual criminals, and almost half of these don't wish to cooperate with the policeman's efforts. Most police, however, report that a sizeable proportion of people they deal with respond to reason and respect in the end.

The broader relationship between the officers and the community with which they deal is one of low participation, and often unfavorable attitudes toward the residents, especially among the white policemen. Those segments of the population which the police perceive as most hostile, they are least in touch with on a day-to-day basis. Thirty-one percent admit not knowing a single important youth leader well enough to casually greet him when they see each other. Few police participate in community organizations or have friends they regularly see in the neighborhood. Seventeen percent actually live in the neighborhood in which they work.

There are no obvious signs of discrimination by race in most of these police departments, at least by report of the interviews. However, many differences appear between races in the way individuals view community problems. White policemen see riots as stemming primarily from agitation and criminal elements in the ghetto, seeing their job as one of short term criminal control. Negro policemen, however, tend to see disturbances as caused by more underlying social and economic conditions. The white policemen typically feel that Negroes are treated as well or better than anyone else. Quite to the contrary, the Negro policeman sees his people as mistreated and not moving too fast to achieve equality. Few policemen of either race, however, have recently participated in any civil rights groups. Most of the overall difference between the Negro and white respondents can most likely be attributed to their race, and related community ties and associations. However, the fact that fifty percent of the Negro policemen interviewed had at least some college education, while only thirty-two percent of the whites had some college, might contribute somewhat to the broader and more sympathetic outlook and analysis of the Negro policeman.

Generally speaking, the policemen are dissatisfied with the external rewards for their job, about half-way satisfied with the immediate conditions under which they work, and very happy with their colleagues. Such in-group solidarity, while maintaining morale in the department, might well tend to remove them even further from an already unsupportive, and even threatening world in which they work. Such isolation most likely exacerbates the already marked hostility that exists in many areas between the "residents" and the "enforcers."

9

TEACHERS IN URBAN
PUBLIC SCHOOLS*

DAVID BOESEL

The quality of education available to any group of citizens is thought to be a critical determinant of the chances its members will have to acquire the benefits of society. It is evident that the education Negroes are receiving is inferior to that afforded white people, and it follows for this reason alone, leaving aside the others, that they are at a competitive disadvantage. Therefore, education has been a battleground for the civil rights movement. The main emphasis has been on efforts to integrate the schools, although there is some evidence of a shift toward efforts to assure the best possible education within the ghetto.

Over the past few years the ghetto schools have become increasingly volatile. Negro high school students in New Haven, Philadelphia, Washington, Cincinnati, and dozens of other cities have begun to protest, sometimes violently, against the policies of their schools and the practices of their teachers. Their demands for better education, and for education more on their own terms, are beginning to be stated with clarity and coherence.

We wanted to find out how flexible and responsive our school system is at the line of contact between the institution itself and the Negro community. To this end we have interviewed two hundred ·and seventy-three teachers and supervisory personnel (principals and assistant principals, amounting to one fifth of the total)[1] in our

*Reprinted from *Supplemental Studies for the National Advisory Commission on Civil Disorder* (Washington: U.S. Government Printing Office, 1968), pp. 133-138.

[1]The terms "educators" and "teachers" will be used interchangeably in this chapter, referring to both the teachers and the supervisory personnel.

sample cities. The educators surveyed were chosen equally from elementary schools and junior high and high schools. Forty-five percent of the teachers were men, and fifty-five percent were women. Half were Negro, the other half white. Contrary to a widespread impression of teachers in ghetto schools, their formal credentials were impressive. All were college graduates, and a substantial majority (seventy percent) had had some professional or graduate training. Half of them had had special training for work with "culturally deprived" youngsters. Almost all of them (ninety percent) considered themselves committed professionals, having chosen teaching as a permanent career. The average teacher had been in this field about ten years.

As a group the educators were quite well-to-do, having a median family income of around $13,000. Since the median salary for teachers is not that high, two other factors help to explain this income level. First, many of them undoubtedly are in double-income families, and second, the supervisory personnel probably pulled up the average.

Only about one-tenth of the educators considered themselves Republicans. The rest were split about evenly between Democrats and independents, though the independents voted Democratic as often as not. Their policital and social views, especially on the question of race, can best be characterized as liberal, as both their racial composition and their party affiliation would lead us to expect. They were much more inclined than the average respondent to say that Negroes were subject to racial discrimination (seventy as opposed to forty-two percent). They saw Negroes making less progress in the past five years: only eleven percent said that Negroes are "a lot better off" now, while the average response was twenty-seven percent. And they were twice as likely to say that Negroes were moving too slowly in their drive for equality (fifty-one percent as opposed to twenty-seven percent).

On the whole, the teachers said they were happy with their present positions. A solid majority indicated that they were either "very satisfied" or "somewhat satisfied" with their jobs in eight out of nine ways (Table 1). In fact, reminiscent of the old paradox that the whole is greater than the sum of its parts, they declared themselves more satisfied with their "position in general" than with any of its aspects. They liked their colleagues next best, and the flexibility permitted them in the classroom, after that. The one aspect capable of drawing only a weak endorsement was "the com-

TABLE 1

Teachers' Job Satisfaction Ranked
By Total (+) Percent
(Q 19 — Ed)

	Satisfied			Dissatisfied			Don't know and no answer
	Very	Some-what	Total (+)	Some-what	Very	Total (—)	
The position in general	61.5	26.7	88.2	9.5	1.8	11.3	—
Colleagues	46.2	39.6	85.8	12.1	2.2	14.3	—
The flexibility permitted in the classroom	58.2	26.4	84.6	9.9	2.6	12.5	1.5
Supervisors	54.2	27.1	81.3	13.6	4.0	17.6	.7
The pupils	36.6	43.2	79.8	16.1	2.6	18.7	.7
The salary	34.1	41.0	75.1	18.7	6.2	24.9	—
Working conditions in general	26.0	37.7	63.7	26.0	10.3	36.3	—
The teaching load	32.2	29.7	61.9	22.7	12.8	35.5	2.2
The community	17.6	39.9	57.5	28.7	11.0	39.2	2.2

munity," which got a fifty-eight percent positive response from the teachers.

Since the teachers said that they liked their current jobs, it is not surprising that about two thirds of them indicated their intention to stay in their present schools as long as they continued teaching. But it does not seem likely that the respondents would fulfill their stated intentions. Half of the teachers had been in their schools for four years or less.[2] In fact, the largest proportion of teachers (seventeen percent) had been there only one year, and the proportion dropped dramatically after five years (Table 2). This suggests that teachers in ghetto schools do not stay there indefinitely, however satisfied they may be.

TABLE 2
Length of Time at Present School
(Q 15 — Ed)

Number of years:		Percentage of educators
1		17
2		11
3		13
4		10
5		12
6		6
7		4
8		3
9		4
10		5

We have seen in Chapter 2 that there is a tendency for members of each occupational group to see their own field as a major problem area more than others do. The teachers are no exceptions. Asked to name the two or three major problems facing their cities, they mentioned education and poverty with about the same frequency (sixteen percent and seventeen percent of the references respectively), naming education more often than did any other group. Only housing was mentioned more frequently by the educators (twenty-one percent); in all other categories the references were less than seven percent.

Not only did the teachers think that their field posed a major problem for their cities, they also thought that education in the

[2]This would be an improvement over the leaving rate which Clark found in Harlem in 1963. In that case almost half the teachers had held their posts for three years or less. (Clark, K. B., *Dark Ghetto,* Harper, New York, 1965, p. 138.)

ghetto posed a special problem. Fifty-eight percent believed that Negroes were less well off than whites in getting an education, while only thirty-eight percent thought that they were as well off.

What is wrong with the educational process, then? More specifically, since the respondents teach in the ghetto, what is wrong with education in the ghetto? The problem is not with the schools, according to the teachers—at least, not with their schools. A solid majority rated their own schools average, above average, or superior in seven out of eight categories (Table 3). The quality of the teaching staff, so rated by eighty-four percent of the respondents, was rivalled only by the quality of the textbooks (again eighty-four percent). The one doubtful area, the educators said, was the adequacy of the physical plant, which seemed to be just barely competitive; forty-four percent considered their own school below average or inferior in this respect.

TABLE 3

Adequacy of Respondent's School
As Compared to Other Schools in City
(Q 12 — Ed)
(in percent)

	Superior	Above average	Average	Below average	Inferior	Don't know
Overall quality	8	19	50	15	6	1
Adequacy of physical plant	9	17	29	25	18	0
Adequacy of supplies	10	26	46	11	5	0
Textbooks	12	22	50	11	4	1
Quality of teaching staff	7	36	41	11	2	2
Extracurricular activities	5	25	36	22	8	1
Counseling and guidance	8	27	38	15	9	1
Library for students	10	30	37	14	7	1

If the schools are not the source of the difficulty — and the teachers said they are not — where do we look next? It is often suggested that the lack of parental concern for education is at the root of the problem. But the teachers did not think so (Table 4). On the whole they felt that the parents were a positive force; they said they communicated easily with parents (eighty-one per-

TABLE 4
Educator's Perceptions of Parents
(Q 6, 8, 9, 10 — Ed)

Percentage

A. Concern of Parents for Education:
      Negro parents are generally more concerned than whites ...   21
      Less concerned than whites   20
      Both have about the same concern   56
      Don't know and no answer   4
B. Difficulty in Communicating with Parents:
      Very little difficulty   81
      Some difficulty   17
      A great deal of difficulty   1
      Don't know and no answer   2
C. Treatment of Teachers by Parents:
      Mostly respect   85
      Mostly indifference   13
      Mostly hostility or contempt   2
      Don't know and no answer   0
D. Parents' View of Teachers:
      Mainly on their side   83
      Mostly as Adversaries   10
      Don't know and no answer   7

cent), that they had the respect of the parents (eighty-five percent), and that the parents generally thought of the teachers as being "on their side" in the educational effort (eighty-three percent). Most of the teachers (seventy-seven percent) thought that Negro parents were as concerned as white parents, or more concerned, with their children's education. Indeed, they considered parental concern the greatest strength of the local community in helping the school achieve its educational objectives. (In an open-ended question, references to parental concern accounted for thirty-five percent of the strong points mentioned. Good school programs were mentioned with the second most frequency — twenty percent.)

When it came to their pupils, the teachers were not so sure (Table 5). On the one hand, they strongly rejected the stereotype of ghetto schools as places where education was forfeited to the sheer need for order: eighty-five percent said it was not true that pupils in their school were uneducable and that teachers could do little more than maintain discipline (though the fourteen percent who saw some truth in the statement are unlikely to enhance the ends of education). On the other hand, the teachers as a group could not agree that their students were as educable as they should be. There was little consensus among them on whether their pupils

TABLE 5
Perceptions of Students
(Q 4 — Ed)
(in percent)

Ratings of statements about pupils	Mainly true	Partially true	Not true	Don't know and no answer
Pupils are uneducable and teachers can do little more than maintain discipline	1	14	85	0
Pupils can be taught only by teachers with great skill	33	41	25	1
Pupils are interested but their preparation is poor	26	57	17	0
These are ordinary pupils with average interest and ability	28	41	31	0
Almost any teacher can be successful if she puts her mind to it	43	24	31	1
Pupils are above average in ability but only interested in some things ...	4	29	65	2
Pupils are above average in ability and cooperate with teachers	8	33	59	0

were "about average" in interest and ability: twenty-eight percent thought that they were, by and large; forty-one percent thought it only partially true that they were; and thirty-one percent thought it not true. But the teachers had less difficulty agreeing that their students were not "above average in ability and . . . generally co-operative with teachers." (Mainly true, eight percent; partially true, thirty-three percent; not true, fifty-nine percent.)

The prevailing attitude of the teachers toward their students was ambivalence. They neither endorsed nor rejected the assertion that "pupils come into school with an interest in learning, but their preparation is so poor they are hard to help." (Mainly true, twenty-six percent; partially true, fifty-seven percent; not true; fourteen percent.) There was little consensus on the proposition that "pupils can be taught only by the most skillful of teachers who can arouse their interest." (Mainly true, thirty-three percent; partially true, forty-one percent; not true, twenty-five percent.) And while they all agreed (ninety-nine percent) that they got along well with all or most of their students, a significant minority, (thirty-one percent), in response to another question, said that students regarded their teachers either indifferently or as adversaries.

In light of the difficulties of finding a coherent stance in relation
to their pupils, it was not surprising that the teachers should also
have had some difficulty finding an appropriate educational approach
to them. The educators again failed to agree or disagree with the
proposition that "pupils can be taught only by the most skillful
of teachers who can arouse their interest." (Mainly true, thirty-
three percent; partially true, forty-one percent; not true, twenty-
five percent.) In response to another question, "is your school
teaching pupils what they are interested in . . . or are most pupils
interested in other things?" Fifty-four percent of the teachers
thought that the school was teaching what interested the students,
but forty-three percent thought the students were interested in
other things.

It is instructive to discover what that forty-three percent thought
the students were interested in. Significantly, serious matters were
mentioned most frequently as the object of student interest. Twenty-
three percent of the references indicated that the students were
concerned with larger social problems; another twenty-three percent
that they were concerned with their own futures; and seventeen percent dealt with practical, day-to-day matters of a serious nature —
relations with parents, making money, etc. The first of these seems
to be of particular relevance today in light of the evident militancy
and race-consciousness among Negro students in the public schools.
However, a substantial minority of the references (thirty-seven
percent) indicated that students were interested in a variety of
leisure activities—joking, horsing around, casual sex, and so on.

Having said that something is wrong with education in the
ghettos, the educators have, on the whole, rejected the notion
that the problem lies in the quality of the schools or of the teaching staff; nor do they accept the idea that lack of parental concern
is the root of the problem. They do think, however, that the students
are not up to par. Why not? The educators, as a group, are adherents
of the "cultural deprivation" thesis, which finds the reason for
bad education primarily in the student's environment rather than
in the schools. The local community, they believe, is not doing
its job, is not giving the students the basic support and direction
they need to get a good education. Asked to name the major problems
facing their schools, the teachers most frequently mentioned community apathy (twenty-seven percent). The second most-mentioned
problem, a derivation of the first, was the lack of preparation
and motivation in the students (twelve percent).

In another question fifty-six percent of the educators agreed to some extent with the proposition that "many communities provide such a terrible environment for the pupils that education doesn't do much good in the end." (An important twenty-five percent, however, disagreed strongly with the statement.) And a solid majority (eighty-one percent agreed wholly or partly with the more moderate proposition that "most parents try to help their children get a good education, but far too many other influences distract the pupils." (Table 6.)

In the educators' view, then, the community—the ghetto—constitutes an all-important negative force in the background which undercuts and disrupts educational efforts. This is a problem which lies beyond their capacities. Conceivably they could improve the schools, a step which they do not think is required; but they cannot transform the ghetto.

Nor do they have much confidence in the ability of the city's leadership to remedy the situation. Eighty-two percent in some degree rejected the statement that "the political leaders of our city are imaginative and are always coming up with new ideas on how to meet the city's problems." (The average response was sixty-two percent.) This view of the political elite is related to the sense of alienation evident in their rejection (seventy-four percent) of the assertion that "the average citizen can always find someone in the city government who is willing to help him solve his problem." (The average response was fifty-nine percent.)

While the main thrust of the responses to this survey of teachers leads to a certain futility, one also finds a more encouraging "minority opinion" which suggests that it is possible for educators themselves to do something to improve education in the ghetto. Without cross-tabulations, not available at this writing, we do not know that this opinion reflects the views of a definite group; we have to work mainly with the views themselves. But a breakdown by race supports the notion that such a group does exist. It indicates that Negro teachers are more likely than white teachers to think that efforts within the schools can be productive. A comparison of responses by race helps to highlight key features of the "minority opinion."

To begin with, Negro teachers were somewhat less sanguine about the adequacy of their schools than were white teachers, as is seen in the fact that they were less willing to give them "above average" or "superior" ratings (Table 7). In assessing

TABLE 6
Educators' Evaluation of the Community
In Its Relation to the Schools
(Q 13 — Ed)
(in percent)

	Strongly agree	Slightly agree	Total (+)	Slightly disagree	Strongly disagree	Total (—)	Don't know
Many communities provide such a terrible environment for the pupils that education doesn't do much good in the end	22.3	33.7	56.0	17.2	24.9	42.2	1.5
Most parents try to help their children get a good education but far too many other influences distract the pupils	38.8	41.8	80.6	10.3	7.0	17.3	1.8

the overall quality of their schools, for example, thirty percent of the whites, but only twenty-two percent of the Negroes, gave such ratings. In another important area, quality of the teaching staff, forty-six percent of the whites said their schools were "above average" or "superior," as compared with thirty-nine percent of the Negroes. Differences of this order are reflected in most of the other categories. The disparity between Negro and white opinion here is not large, but, except for the item on "extra-curricular activities," it is consistent. It does not mean that Negro teachers regarded their schools as inferior, only that they were somewhat less convinced of their adequacy than were the white teachers.

TABLE 7

Adequacy of Respondent's School,
As Compared to Other Schools in City,
By Race

(Q 12 — Ed)

(Percentage of each race who call their school
"above average" or superior")

	White	Negro
Overall quality	30	22
Adequacy of physical plant	28	24
Adequacy of supplies	44	27
Textbooks	38	29
Quality of teaching staff	46	39
Extracurricular activities	28	31
Counseling and guidance	42	28
Library	48	33

The tendency of the Negro educators to be more critical of their schools than white teachers did not lead them to be less critical of the local community. Both saw the ghetto environment as a major obstacle to education; both mentioned community apathy as a major problem, in each case to the same degree: twenty-seven percent of the references. But the Negro educators were less likely than the whites to consider the students damaged by the environment. Again, the disagreement is not great — in most cases the majority on each side agreed — but again it is fairly consistent. Table 8 shows the responses of Negro and white teachers to questions dealing with their students' abilities. In response to the first question, thirty-four percent of the Negroes said that

TABLE 8
Teachers' Assessments of Students' Abilities
by Race of Respondent
(Q 4 — Ed)
(in percent)

	White	Negro
These are ordinary pupils with just about average interest in schooling and with average ability.		
Mainly true	20	34
Partly true	40	43
Not true	39	23
Don't know and no answer	1	...
The pupils are above average in ability and interest and are generally co-operative with teachers.		
Mainly true	4	11
Partly true	26	38
Not true	67	49
Don't know and no answer	3	2

their pupils were about average in interest and ability, whereas only twenty percent of the whites said so. In the second, thirty-seven percent of the Negroes said it was partly true that "the pupils are above average in ability and interest, and are generally co-operative with teachers"; the corresponding figure for the white teachers was twenty-six percent.

Negro teachers also seemed to have a better relationship with their pupils. Fifty-two percent of them said that they got along well with all their students, while only thirty-nine percent of the white respondents said so. Again, asked if most of the pupils regarded their teachers as friends, adversaries, or if most were indifferent, seventy-one percent of the Negro teachers said that the students considered the teachers friends, as compared to sixty-one percent of the white teachers.

While the Negro educators were not overenthusiastic about their students, they regarded them more positively and saw in them more potential, than did white teachers. The difference between these assessments increases in their implications for action. Half of the Negro teachers (fifty-two percent), but only a third (thirty-six percent) of the white teachers agreed to the proposition that "almost any teacher can teach these pupils successfully if he or she puts his mind to it and works hard at it."

Just as the Negro teachers saw more constructive potential than did the whites in the relation between students and teachers, so they also saw more in the relation between community and school. In two questions the teachers were asked, in somewhat different ways, whether they thought it would be a good idea for the community to have more control of the schools. Table 9 presents the statements, together with the responses by race. When the proposition was first posed, the white teachers rejected it fifty-eight percent to thirty-eight percent. But a bare majority of Negro teachers (fifty-three percent) endorsed it to some extent. (The two "agree" categories are combined here, as are the two "disagree" categories.) The second time the question was posed both Negro and white teachers endorsed it in some degree, but the Negroes were more solidly behind it (seventy-six percent) than the whites (sixty-seven percent).

·Setting the racial distinction aside for a moment, it is interesting that both groups were more favorable to the second statement of the proposition than to the first. The difference between these responses to two adjacent questions which are the same in their essentials requires some interpretation. To begin with, the first question, which drew a rather negative response, mentions only the community's being given more voice in running the school.

TABLE 9

Teachers' Assessment of Community-Control
Proposals by Race
(in percent)

	White	Negro
If the average community was given more voice in running the school, it would better meet the needs of the pupils.		
Agree	38	53
Disagree	58	45
Don't know and no answer	4	2
Some schools are trying to give the parents and other community residents more control over running the school in their neighborhoods, even sometimes letting parents come into the classroom to help with the teaching and other work as sub-professionals.		
Agree	67	76
Disagree	30	22
Don't know and no answer	3	2

and it is placed in context with three other questions posed as negative statements about the community. Given the educators' opinions of "the community," particularly when understood in its less personal aspects as "environment" or "background," it is plausible to assume that the educators would be adverse to seeing its influence in the schools increased.

In the second question, on the one hand, the community is personalized ("parents and other community residents"), and the parents, whom the teachers regard as a positive force, are mentioned twice. Moreover, the statement indicated specifically the kinds of things the parents might be doing in the school and points to the possibility of their helping the teachers. With the question presented this way, the positive response seems more understandable.

There may be a connection between the inclination to see a constructive potential in the relation between community and school on the one hand, and the ability to see the community in personal terms, on the other. The Negro teachers, who were more favorable to the community-participation statements, also had more extensive contact with the community. While a majority of both groups lived outside the school area, a much larger proportion of the Negroes than of whites lived in the area (twenty-seven percent as opposed to four percent). Sixty-six percent of the Negro teachers said they had visited students' homes; one third of these (thirty-three percent) said quite a few homes." The comparable figures for whites were forty-nine percent, and one seventh (fourteen percent).

In sum, the educators from our fifteen cities see education in the ghetto not as a blackboard jungle, but as a hard task of motivating students of poor preparation and inadequate community backing in achieving up to their potentials. Theirs is a view of the problems of education in the ghetto which relies heavily on the "cultural deprivation" theory. They saw their schools as adequate, their own preparation as good, but their success as teachers hampered by the material they have to work with. However, a minority of the educators, among whom Negroes are disproportionately represented, put more responsibility for the difficulties of ghetto education on the schools, and suggested that changes must take place there.

10

THE METABOLISM OF CITIES*

ABEL WOLMAN

The metabolic requirements of a city can be defined as all the materials and commodities needed to sustain the city's inhabitants at home, at work and at play. Over a period of time these requirements include even the construction materials needed to build and rebuild the city itself. The metabolic cycle is not completed until the wastes and residues of daily life have been removed and disposed of with a minimum of nuisance and hazard. As man has come to appreciate that the earth is a closed ecological system, casual methods that once appeared satisfactory for the disposal of wastes no longer seem acceptable. He has the daily evidence of his eyes and nose to tell him that his planet cannot assimilate without limit the untreated wastes of his civilization.

No one article could describe the complete metabolism of the modern city. Moreover, many of the metabolic inputs such as food, fuel, clothing, durable goods, construction materials and electric energy present no special problem. Their supply is handled routinely, in part through local initiative and in part through large organizations (public or private) that operate about as effectively in one city as another. I shall be concerned therefore with three metabolic problems that have become more acute as cities have grown larger and whose solution rests almost entirely in the hands of the local administrator. Although he can call on many outside sources for advice, he must ultimately provide solutions fashioned

*Reprinted with permission. Copyright © 1965 by Scientific American, Inc. All rights reserved.

to the unique needs of his own community. These three problems are the provision of an adequate water supply, the effective disposal of sewage and the control of air pollution.

That these three problems vary widely from city to city and that they are being managed with widely varying degrees of success is obvious to anyone who reads a daily newspaper. It is ironic, for example, that New York City, which houses the nation's (if not the world's) greatest concentration of managerial talent, should be running short of water while billions of gallons of fresh water flow past it to the sea. It is not easy for people living in arid countries, or even for those living in the southwestern part of the U.S., to have much sympathy with New York's plight.

This summer, while New Yorkers were watching their emptying reservoirs and hoping for rain, Californians were busy building an aqueduct that would carry water some 440 miles from the Sacramento River, near Sacramento, to Los Angeles and other cities in the southern part of the state. And thanks to earlier examples of foresight, people in southern California were watering their lawns and filling their swimming pools without restriction, while in New York and New Jersey lawns were dying and pools stood empty. In the water-rich Middle Atlantic states water shortages are largely the result of delayed action and failures of management—sometimes exacerbated by political jockeying.

If American cities have had such unequal success in supplying their citizens with water, it is hardly surprising that some should have an even less satisfactory record in controlling water and air pollution, areas in which the incentives for providing remedies are much weaker than hose that motivate the supplying of water. To make matters worse, pollutants of water and air often do not respect state boundaries. For example, the wastes of five states—Michigan, Indiana, Ohio, Pennsylvania and New York—have contributed to the accelerated pollution of Lake Erie. "The lake," according to the U.S. Public Health Service, "has deteriorated in quality at a rate many times greater than its normal aging process." The fourth-largest and shallowest of the five Great Lakes, Lake Erie is the main water supply for 10 million U.S. citizens as well as for the huge industrial complex that extends for 300 miles along the lake's southern shore from Detroit to Buffalo. The combination of treated and partially treated municipal sewage and industrial wastes that enters Lake Erie directly, and also reaches it indirectly through a network of rivers, has disrupted the normal cycle of aquatic life, has led to the closing of a number of beaches

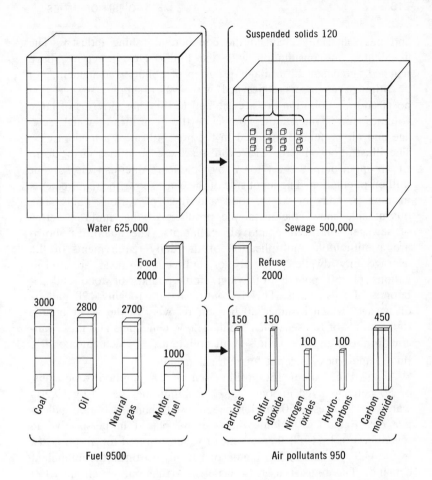

Suspended solids 120

Water 625,000

Sewage 500,000

Food 2000

Refuse 2000

3000 Coal

2800 Oil

2700 Natural gas

1000 Motor fuel

Fuel 9500

150 Particles

150 Sulfur dioxide

100 Nitrogen oxides

100 Hydro-carbons

450 Carbon monoxide

Air pollutants 950

METABOLISM OF A CITY involves countless input-output transactions. This chart concentrates on three inputs common to all cities, namely water, food and fuel, and three outputs, sewage, solid refuse and air pollutants. Each item is shown in tons per day for a hypothetical U.S. city with a population of one million. Water, which enters the city silently and unseen, overshadows all other inputs in volume. More than .6 ton (150 gallons) must be supplied to each inhabitant every day. After about 20 percent of the water has been diverted to lawns and other unrecoverable uses, it returns, contaminated, to the city's sewers. The city's most pervasive nuisance, air pollution, is accounted for chiefly by the combustion of fuels. (If refuse is burned in incinerators, it can also contribute heavily, but that contribution is not included here.) Most of the particle emission (soot and fly ash) is produced by coal burned in electric power plants, and in well-designed plants more than 90 percent of the particles can be removed from the stack gases. For this hypothetical city one may assume that 135 of the 150 tons of particles produced by all fuel consumers are removed before they reach the atmosphere. All other emissions, however, pollute the atmosphere in the volumes shown. Sulfur dioxide is based on use of domestic fuels of average sulfur content.

and has materially changed the commercial fishing industry. The five states, in consultation with the Public Health Service, have reached agreement on a major program of pollution abatement.

Although engineers concerned with water supply, sewage disposal and air pollution are accustomed to thinking in terms of large volumes, few laymen quite appreciate the quantities of water, sewage and air pollutants involved in the metabolism of a modern city. The illustration on page 215 expresses these quantities in the form of an input-output chart for a hypothetical American city of one million population. The input side of the chart shows the requirements in tons per day of water, food and fuels of various kinds. The output side shows the metabolic products of that input in terms of sewage, solid refuse and air pollutants. The quantities shown are a millionfold multiplication of the daily requirements of the average city dweller. Directly or indirectly he uses about 150 gallons (1,250 pounds) of water, four pounds of food and 19 pounds of fossil fuels. This is converted into roughly 120 gallons of sewage (which assumes 80 percent recovery of the water input), four pounds of refuse (which includes food containers and miscellaneous rubbish) and 1.9 pounds of air pollutants, of which automobiles, buses, and trucks account for more that half.

As of 1963 about 150 million out of 189 million Americans, or 80 percent, lived in some 22,000 communities served by 19,200 waterworks. These 150 million people used about 23 billion gallons per day (b.g.d.), a volume that can be placed in perspective in several ways. In 1960 the amount of water required for all purposes in the U.S. was about 320 b.g.d., or roughly 15 times the municipal demand. The biggest user of water is irrigation, which in 1960 took about 140 b.g.d. Steam electric utilities used about 98 b.g.d. and industry about 60 b.g.d. Since 1960 the total U.S. water demand has risen from about 320 b.g.d. to an estimated 370 b.g.d., of which municipalities take about 25 b.g.d. *(See illustration on opposite page.)*

Thus municipalities rank as the smallest of the four principal users of water. Although it is true that water provided for human consumption must sometimes meet standards of quality that need not be met by water used in agriculture or industry, nevertheless throughout most of the U.S. farms, factories and cities frequently draw water from a common supply.

For the country as a whole the supply of available water is, enormous: about 1,200 b.g.d. This is the surface runoff that remains from an average daily rainfall of some 4,200 b.g.d. About 40

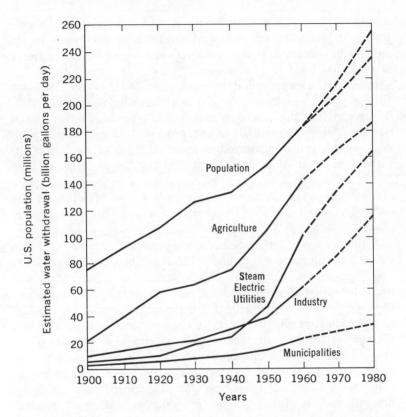

U.S. WATER REQUIREMENTS will be 53 percent greater in 1980 than in 1960, according to the most recent estimates of the Department of Commerce. Virtually all water used by agriculture is for irrigation; nearly 60 percent of all irrigated land in the U.S. is in five Western states (California, Texas, Colorado, Idaho and Arizona) where water tends to be scarcest. Steam power plants need water in hugh amounts simply to condense steam. In 1960 municipalities used about 22 billion gallons per day (b.g.d.), which represented only about 7 percent of the total water withdrawal of about 320 b.g.d. The important distinction between water "withdrawal" and "consumptive use" is shown in the illustration on page 219.

percent of the total precipitation is utilized where it falls, providing water to support vegetation of economic value: forests, farm crops and pasturelands. Another 30 percent evaporates directly from the soil or returns to the atmosphere after passing through vegetation that has no particular economic value except insofar as it may prevent erosion of the land.

It is obvious that one cannot expect to capture and put to use every drop of the 1,200 b.g.d. flowing to the sea. The amount that can be captured depends on what people are willing to pay for water. One recent estimate places the economically available supply at somewhat less than half the total, or 560 b.g.d. In my opinion this estimate is too conservative; I would suggest a figure at least 700 b.g.d.

Even this volume would be inadequate by the year 2000—if all the water withdrawn for use were actually consumed. This, however, is not the case now and will not be then; only a small fraction of the water withdrawn is consumed. In 1960 "consumptive use," as it is called, amounted to about 90 b.g.d. of the 320 b.g.d. withdrawn. Most of the remaining 230 b.g.d. was returned after use to the source from which it was taken, or to some other body of water (in some instances the ocean). A small fraction of the used water was piped into the ground to help maintain local water tables.

Estimates by a Senate Select Committee a few years ago projected a consumptive use of about 120 b.g.d. in 1980 and of nearly 160 b.g.d. in the year 2000, when total demand may reach 900 b.g.d. It will be apparent in the illustration on the next page where these projections are plotted, that agriculture accounts for the biggest consumptive use of water. It is conservatively estimated that 60 percent of the water employed for irrigation is lost to the atmosphere as the result of evaporation directly from the soil or indirectly by transpiration through the leaves of growing plants. (The amount of water incorporated into plant tissue is insignificant; roughly 1,000 gallons of water is needed to produce about 10 cents' worth of crop.) In contrast, from 80 to 98 percent of the water withdrawn by municipalities, industry and electric utilities is available for reuse. It is for this reason that the projected withdrawal rate of 900 b.g.d. in the year 2000 should not prove difficult to meet, whether the economically available supply is 560 b.g.d. or 700 b.g.d. Of the 900 b.g.d. that may be required in A.D. 2000 to meet human, industrial and agricultural needs, approximately 740 b.g.d. should be available for reuse.

These estimates, moreover, are pessimistic in that they make only minor allowances for reductions in industrial or agricultural demands as a result of technological changes and in that they provide for no significant increase in the cost of water to hasten such changes. Thus we must reasonably conclude that for many years beyond A.D. 2000 total water shortages for the U.S. as a whole are highly improbable.

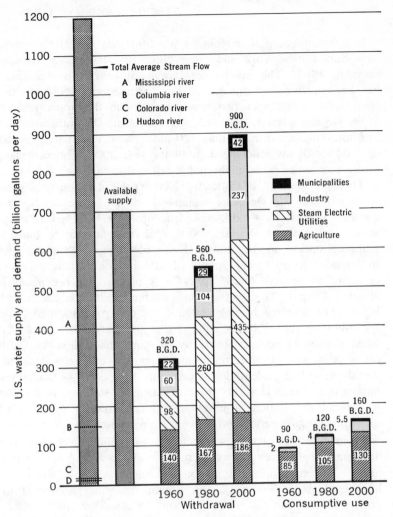

U.S. WATER SUPPLY consists of the approximately 1,200 b.g.d. that flows to the sea through the nation's waterways. This is the streamflow that results from an average precipitation volume of some 4,200 b.g.d. About 70 percent of all precipitation returns to the atmosphere without ever reaching the sea. The average flow of four important rivers is marked on the streamflow column. The author estimates that about 700 b.g.d. of the total streamflow can be made available for use at a cost acceptable to consumers. The estimates of water withdrawal and consumptive use for 1980 and 2000 are (with slight rounding) those published a few years ago by a Senate Select Committee. The 1980 estimate is 13 percent higher than that of the Department of Commerce shown in the illustration on page 217. "Consumptive use" represents the amount of water withdrawn that subsequently becomes unavailable for reuse. Except for irrigation, consumptive use of water is and will remain negligible. Thus a 700 b.g.d. supply should easily meet a 900 b.g.d. demand.

If water is going to remain so plentiful into the 21st century, why should New York and other cities find themselves running short in 1965? The immediate answer, of course, is that there has been a five-year drought in the northeastern U.S. With the completion in 1955 of two new reservoirs in the upper reaches of the Delaware River, and with extension of the Delaware aqueduct to a total distance of more than 120 miles, New York City believed it could satisfy its water needs until the year 2000. This confident forecast reckoned without the unprecedented drought.

There is no point in criticizing New York's decision to depend so heavily on the Delaware watershed for its future needs. The question is what New York should do now. As long ago as 1950, in an earlier water shortage, New York was advised to build a pumping station on the Hudson River 65 miles north of the city to provide an emergency supply of 100 million gallons per day, or more as needed. (New York City's normal water demand is about 1.2 b.g.d. The average flow of the Hudson is around 11 b.g.d.) The State of New York gave the city permission to build the pumping station but stipulated that the station be dismantled when the emergency was over. By the time the station was built (at a point somewhat farther south than the one recommended) the drought had ended; the station was torn down without ever having been used. This July the city asked the state for permission to rebuild the station, a job that will take several months, but as of mid-August permission had not been granted.

Meanwhile there has been much talk of building atomic-energy desalination plants as the long-term solution to New York's water needs. The economic justification for such proposals has never been explained. New York now obtains its water, delivered by gravity flow to the city, for only about 15 cents per 1,000 gallons (and many consumers are charged only 12 cents). The lowest predicted cost for desalination, assuming a plant with a capacity of 250 million or more gallons per day, is a highly optimistic 30 to 50 cents per 1,000 gallons. Since a desalination plant would be at sea level, its entire output would have to be pumped; storage and conveyance together would add about 20 cents per 1,000 gallons to the basic production cost. Recent studies in our department at Johns Hopkins University have shown that if desalinated water could be produced and delivered for as little as 50 cents per 1,000 gallons, it would still be cheaper to obtain fresh water from a supply 600 miles away. (The calculations assume a water demand of 100 million gallons per day.) In other words, it would be much cheaper for New York City to pipe water 270 miles from the St. Lawrence River, assuming that Canada gave its consent, than to build a desalination plant at the edge of town. New York City does not have to go even as far as the St. Lawrence. It has large untapped reserves in the Hudson River and in the upper watershed of the Susquehanna, no more than 150 miles away, that could meet the city's needs well beyond the year 2000.

Few cities in the U.S. have the range of alternatives open to New York. The great majority of inland cities draw their water supplies from the nearest lake or river. Of the more than 150 million Americans now served by public water supplies, nearly 100 million, or 60 percent, are reusing water from sources that have already been used at least once for domestic sewage and industrial waste disposal. This "used" water has of course been purified, either naturally or artificially, before it reaches the consumer. Only about 25 percent of the 25 b.g.d. now used by municipalities is obtained from aquifers, or underground sources. Such aquifers supply about 65 b.g.d. of the nation's estimated 1965 requirement of 370 b.g.d. Most of the 65 b.g.d. is merely a subterranean portion of the 1,200 b.g.d. of the precipitation flowing steadily to the sea. It is estimated, however, that from five to 10 b.g.d. is water "mined" from aquifers that have been filled over the centuries. Most of this mining is done in West Texas, New Mexico, Arizona, and California.

The fact that more than 150 million Americans can be provided with safe drinking water by municipal waterworks, regardless of their source of supply, attests the effectiveness of modern water-treatment methods. Basically, the treatment consists of filtration and chlorination. The use of chlorine to kill bacteria in municipal water supplies was introduced in 1908. It is fortunate that such a cheap and readily available substance is so effective. A typical requirement is about one part of chlorine to a million parts of water (one p.p.m.). The amount of chlorine needed to kill bacteria and also to "kill" the taste of dissolved organic substances — many of which are introduced naturally when rainwater comes in contact with decaying vegetation—is adjusted by monitoring the amount of free chlorine present in the water five to 10 minutes after treatment. This residual chlorine is usually held to about .2 p.p.m. In cases where unusually large amounts of organic compounds are present in the water causing the public to complain of a bad taste, experience has shown that the palatability of the water can often be improved simply by adding more chlorine. Contrary

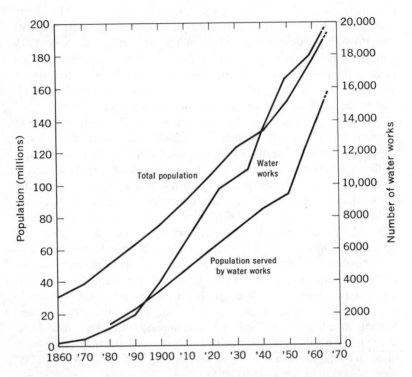

GROWTH OF MUNICIPAL WATER SUPPLIES accelerated after 1880, when less than a fourth of the U.S. population was served by waterworks. By 1939 the number served by waterworks exceeded 60 percent and by 1963 the figure had reached nearly 80 percent.

to a widely held impression, free chlorine itself has little taste; the "bad" taste usually attributed to chlorine is due chiefly to organic compounds that have been too lightly chlorinated. When they are more heavily chlorinated, the bad taste usually disappears.

Throughout history impure water has been a leading cause of fatal disease in man; such waterborne diseases as typhoid fever and dysentery were still common in the U.S. less than a century ago. In 1900 the U.S. death rate from typhoid fever was 35.8 per 100,000 people. If such a rate persisted today, the deaths from typhoid would far exceed those from automobile accidents. By 1936 the rate had been reduced to 2.5 per 100,000, and today the disease is almost unknown in the U.S.

In underdeveloped nations, where many cities are still without

222

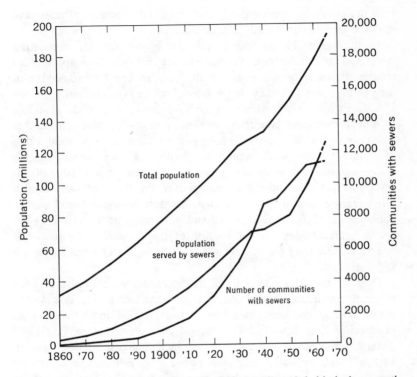

GROWTH OF SEWERAGE FACILITIES has lagged behind the growth of community water supplies, chiefly because people are reluctant to pay taxes for what long seemed a nonessential service. Nevertheless, 63 percent of the population was served by sewers in 1962.

adequate water supplies, waterborne diseases are among the leading causes of death and debility. In Central and South America more than a third of 75 million people living in towns or cities with a population of more than 2,000 are without water service. Similarly, in India about a third of the urban population of 80 million are without an adequate water supply.

No general prescription can be offered for bringing clean water to the vast urban populations that still lack it. I have found in my own experience, however, that the inhabitants of communities both large and small can do much more to help themselves than is customarily recognized. If the small towns and villages of India and elsewhere wait for their central governments to install public water supplies, most of them will wait indefinitely. It is surprising how much can be accomplished with local labor and local materials, and the benefits in health are incalculable.

In the larger cities, where self-help is not feasible, municipal water systems can be built and made to pay their way if an appropriate charge is made for water and if the systems can be financed with long-term loans, as they have been financed traditionally in the U.S. Such loans, however, have only recently been made available to underdeveloped countries. A few years ago, when loans for waterworks had to be paid off in six to 12 years, the total value of external bank loans made to South American countries for water supply and sewerage projects was less than $100,000 in a six-year period. Under the leadership of the Pan-American Health Organization and the U.S. Agency for International Development bankers were encouraged to extend the repayment period to 28 or 30 years. Today the total value of bank loans made to South American countries for waterworks and sewage systems has surpassed $660 million.

Outside the U.S., as within it, adequate water resources are generally available. The problem is to treat water as a commodity whose cost to the user must bear a fair relation to the cost of its production and delivery. The total U.S. investment in municipal waterworks is about $17.5 billion (replacement cost would approach $50 billion), or about half the nation's investment in telephone service. More significant than investment is the cost of service to the consumer. The average American family pays about $3 a month for water, which it cannot live without, compared with about $7.30 for telephone service. One might also note that the average household expenditure for alcoholic beverages is more than $15 a month. It should be clear that Americans can afford to pay for all the water they need.

The question of fair payment and allocation of costs is even more central to the problem of controlling water pollution than to the problem of providing water. Whereas 150 million Americans were served by waterworks in 1963, only about 120 million were served by sewers (see illustration on page 223). Thus the wastes of nearly 70 million Americans, who live chiefly in the smaller towns and suburbs, were still being piped into backyard cesspools and septic tanks. When these devices are properly designed and the receiving soils are not overloaded, they create no particular sanitation hazard. Unfortunately, in too many suburban areas neither of these criteria is met.

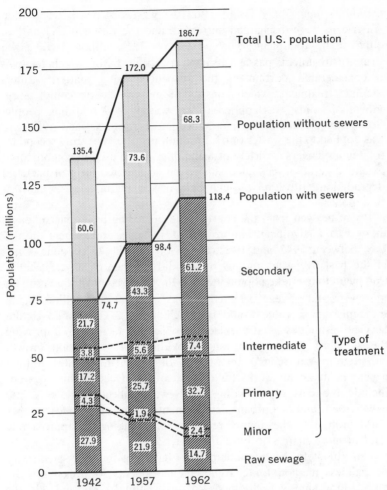

RACE BETWEEN SEWERS AND POPULATION GROWTH is depicted in this chart. Between 1942 and 1957 population outstripped the increase in sewerage service. Between 1957 and 1962 sewerage service grew slightly faster than population. People without sewers do not necessarily contribute to the water pollution problem if they use effective septic tanks and cesspools. The principal pollution is caused by communities — and by industries — that discharge wastes into waterways with little treatment or no treatment at all. Data for this chart and the two preceding ones were supplied by the U.S. Public Health Service.

The principal pollution hazard arises where sewage collected by a sewerage system is discharged into a lake or river without adequate treatment or without any treatment at all *(see illus-*

tration on page 225). As of 1962 the wastes of nearly 15 million Americans were discharged untreated, and the wastes of 2.4 million only minor treatment. The wastes of 32.7 million were given primary treatment: passage through a settling basin, which removes a considerable portion of the suspended solid matter. Intermediate treatment, which consists of a more nearly complete removal of solids, was applied to the wastes of 7.4 million people. Secondary treatment, the most adequate form of sewage treatment, was applied to the wastes of 61.2 million people. The term "secondary treatment" covers a variety of techniques, often used in combination: extended aeration, activated sludge (an accelerated form of bacterial degradation), filtration through beds of various materials, stabilization ponds.

It can be seen from the chart of the preceding page that although there was a significant improvement in sewage treatment in the U.S. between 1942 and 1962, a big job remains to be done. Only in the past five years of this period did the rate of sewer installation begin to overtake population growth. The present U.S. investment in sewers and sewage-treatment works is about $12 billion (again the replacement value would be much higher). The Public Health Service estimates that replacing obsolete facilities, improving the standard of treatment and providing for population growth will require an annual investment of more than $800 million a year in treatment works for the rest of the decade. This does not include the cost of extending the sewage-collection systems into new urban and suburban developments. This may add another $800 million to the annual requirements, making an approximate total of more than $1.6 billion a year.

Unfortunately, some municipalities have not found a satisfactory or painless method for charging their residents for this vital service. Many simply float bonds to meet capital costs and add the cost to the individual's bill for property taxes. In Baltimore (where the tax bill is completely itemized) it was decided some years ago that sewerage costs should not be included in the citizen's *ad valorem* taxes but should be made part of his water bill. In the Baltimore system the charge for sewerage service is half the water service charge. A good many other cities charge for sewerage service on a similar basis.

Cities, of course, account for only a part, and probably not the major part, of the pollution that affects the nation's waterways.

Industrial pollution is a ubiquitous problem. Industrial pollutants are far more varied than those in ordinary sewage, and their removal often calls for specialized measures. Even in states where adequate pollution-control laws are on the books, there are technological, economic and practical obstacles to seeing that the laws are observed. The Federal Water Pollution Control acts of 1954 and 1962, which enlarged the role of the Public Health Service in determining the pollution of interstate waterways, have sometimes been helpful in strengthening the hand of local law-enforcement agencies.

My final topic—air pollution—is much harder to discuss in quantitative terms than water pollution, which it otherwise resembles in many ways. It is never going to be possible to provide a collection system for air pollution emissions, almost all of which result from combustion processes. Every house, every apartment, every automobile, truck, bus, factory and power plant is vented directly into the open air and presumably will have to remain so.

There are perhaps only three general approaches to controlling the amount of pollutants entering the atmosphere. One is to switch from a fuel that produces undesirable combustion products to one that produces fewer such products. Thus fuel oil produces less soot and fly ash than bituminous coal, and natural gas produces less than either. The second expedient is to employ a new technology. For example, atomic power plants produce none of the particulate and gaseous emissions that result from the burning of fossil fuels. One must then decide, however, whether the radioactive by-products that are released into the environment—either in the short run or the long—by an atomic power station are more or less hazardous than the fossil-fuel by-products they replaced. The third recourse is to remove the undesired components from the vented gases. Fly ash, for example, can be largely removed by suitable devices where coal or oil is used in large volume, as in a power plant, but cannot readily be removed from the flue gases of thousands of residences. The problem of dealing with many small offending units also arises in trying to reduce the unburned hydrocarbons and carbon monoxide emitted by millions of automobiles.

At this point it is worth asking: Why should air pollution be considered objectionable? Many people enjoy the smell of the pollutants released by a steak sizzling on a charcoal grill or by dry leaves burning in the fall. The cigarette smoker obviously enjoys the smoke he draws into his lungs. In other words, a pollutant per se need not necessarily be regarded as a nuisance. If by accident or design the exhaust gases emitted by a diesel bus had a fragrant aroma, (or worse yet, led to physiological addiction), not many people would complain about traffic fumes.

The criteria of what constitutes an objectionable air pollutant must, therefore, be subjectively defined, unless, of course, one can demonstrate that a particular pollutant is a hazard to health. In the absence of a demonstrated health hazard the city dweller would probably list his complaints somewhat as follows: he objects to soot and dirt, he does not want his eyes to burn and water, he dislikes traffic fumes and he wishes he could see the clear blue sky more often.

Many conferences have been held and many papers written on the possible association of air pollution with disease. As might be expected, firm evidence of harmfulness is difficult to obtain. The extensive epidemiological data collected in the U.S. on smoking and human health suggest that in general, place of residence has a minor influence on the incidence of lung cancer compared with the smoking habit itself. British statistics, however, can be interpreted to show that at times there is something harmful in the British air. In any event, it will be difficult to demonstrate conclusively—no matter how much one may believe it to be so—that air pollution is associated with long-term deterioration of the human organism. Eric J. Cassell of the Cornell University Medical College recently summarized the situation as follows: "I do not think that it is wrong to say that we do not even know what disease or diseases are caused by everyday pollution of our urban air . . . We have a cause, but no disease to go with it."

Two diseases frequently mentioned as possibly associated with air pollution are chronic bronchitis and pulmonary emphysema. In Britain some investigators have found strong associations between chronic bronchitis and the level of air pollution, as measured by such indexes as fuel use, sulfur dioxide in the air and sootfall. In California the death rate from emphysema increased fourfold in the seven-year period from 1950-1957. This increase may indicate nothing more than the fact that older people go to California to retire, but there is objective evidence that emphysematous patients in Los Angeles showed improved lung function when allowed to breathe carefully filtered air for 48 hours.

In response to mounting public concern, and the urging of President Johnson, Congress two years ago passed the Clean Air

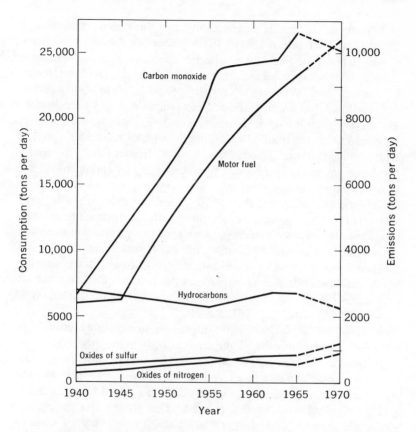

LOS ANGELES AIR POLLUTION is tied closely to the steep rise in automobile use in Los Angeles County. This chart compares gasoline consumption with the computed output from all sources of carbon monoxide, hydrocarbons, oxides of nitrogen and oxides of sulfur. Motor vehicles produce only small amounts of the last two substances and their output has been controlled chiefly by curbs on the emission of pollutants by industry. Carbon monoxide and hydrocarbon emissions should decline when cars start carrying exhaust-control systems.

Act, which states in its preamble that "Federal financial assistance and leadership is essential for the development of cooperative Federal, state, regional and local programs designed to prevent and control air pollution." The regulatory abatement procedures authorized in the act are similar to those found in the most recent Water Pollution Control Act. When an interstate pollution problem is identified, the Public Health Service is empowered, as a first step, to call a conference of state and local agencies. The second step is to call a public hearing, and the third step, if needed, is to bring a court action against the offenders.

The Clean Air Act takes special cognizance of air pollution caused by motor vehicles; it requires the Secretary of Health, Education, and Welfare to report periodically to Congress on progress made on control devices. He is also invited to recommend any new legislation he feels is warranted. Eventually the secretary may help to decide if all new U.S. motor vehicles should be equipped with exhaust-control systems, such as "afterburners," to reduce the large amounts of unburned hydrocarbons and carbon monoxide that are now released.

California studies in the 1950's showed that exhaust gases accounted for 65 percent of all the unburned hydrocarbons then produced by motor vehicles. Another 15 percent represented evaporation from the fuel tank and carburetor, and 20 percent escaped from the vent of the crankcase. As a first step in reducing these emissions California began in 1961 to require the use of crankcase blowby devices, which became standard on all U.S. cars beginning with the 1963 models.

A new California law will require exhaust-control systems on all 1966 automobiles and light trucks sold in the state. The law is intended to reduce by 70 or 80 percent the amount of hydrocarbons now present in exhaust gases and to reduce the carbon monoxide by 60 percent. All the carbon monoxide is generated by combustion and is now released in the exhaust. The steady rise in carbon monoxide vented into the atmosphere of Los Angeles County is plotted in the illustration on the preceding page.

No one questions that an affluent society can afford to spend its money without a strict accounting of benefits received. Any reasonable expenditure that promises to improve the quality of life in the modern city should be welcomed. It is not obvious, however, that, an American city except Los Angeles will be significantly benefited by the installation of exhaust-control systems in motor vehicles. The cost of these systems will not be trivial. At an estimated $40 to $50 per car, such systems would add more than $300 million to the sales price of new cars in an eight-million-car year—and this does not include the annual cost of their inspection and maintenance. If one objective of reducing the air pollution caused by automobiles is to increase the life expectancy of the city dweller, or simply to make his life more pleasant, it can be argued that $300 million a year could be spent more usefully in other directions.

In most large cities, for example, the electric utilities consume up to half of all fuel burned. Most utilities have made reasonable efforts to reduce the emission of soot and fly ash; virtually all new power plants, and many old ones, are now equipped with devices capable of removing a large fraction of such emissions. Utilities, however, are still under pressure, both from the public and from supervising agencies, to use the cheapest fuels available. This means that in New York and other eastern-seaboard cities the utilities burn large volumes of residual fuel oil imported from abroad, which happens to contain between 2.5 and 3 percent of sulfur, compared with only about 1.7 percent for domestic fuel oil. When the oil is burned, sulfur dioxide is released. Recent studies show that the level of sulfur dioxide in New York City air is almost twice that found in other large cities.

Sulfur dioxide is difficult to remove from stack gases, but it is estimated that for about $1 a barrel most of the sulfur could be removed from the oil before it is burned. For the volume of oil burned by the Consolidated Edison Company in New York City the added cost would come to about $15 million annually. If the cost were divided among Consolidated Edison's three million customers, the average electric bill would be increased about $5 per year. One would like to know how this expenditure would compare in improving the quality of New York City's air with New York's pro rata share of the more than $300-million-a-year investment that would be required by the installation of exhaust-control systems in motor vehicles. That share would be on the order of $8 million a year. Perhaps New Yorkers should insist on both investments. But these are only two of many options, all of them expensive. It is the responsibility of the city administrator and the public health officer to make choices and assign priorities, even while admitting that air pollution is never beneficial.

One must also recall that when large-scale changes are contemplated, the whole spectrum of society is involved. Rarely do all forces march forward in step, particularly where public policy and scientific verity are not crystal clear. Competitive forces delay correctives until public opinion rises in wrath and pushes for action on an *ad hoc* and intuitive basis.

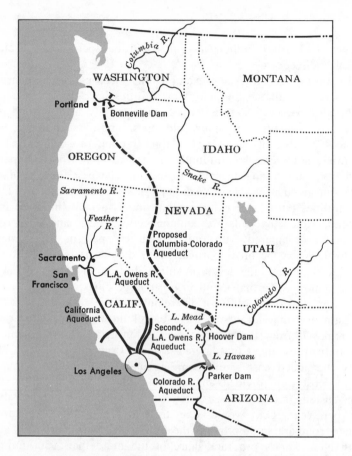

DISTANT TRANSPORTATION OF WATER has been practiced in the
West for many years. Los Angeles now has three major sources of supply
to meet its daily demand of 470 million gallons. About 15 percent comes
through the 300-mile Colorado aqueduct, completed in 1941, about 21
percent is pumped from local wells and the remainder, 64 percent, comes
from Owens Valley, 340 miles to the north. An enlargement of the Owens
Valley supply system is nearly completed. Meanwhile the state is building
a new 444-mile aqueduct that will deliver water from the Sacramento
River to southern California. Proposals are now being made to move water
from the Columbia River, which accounts for more than 12 percent of total
U.S. streamflow, to the arid Southwest. The water might be taken from
below Bonneville Dam and diverted some 800 miles to Lake Mead on
the Colorado River, following the general route shown (*broken line*).

Let me sum up by observing that in the case of water supply
the accomplishments of the U.S. have been extraordinarily good,
not only in the prevention of waterborne and water-associated

diseases but also in providing water generously for comfortable living in most places at most times. The prospect for the future is likewise good. The realities are that we are not running out of water and that are capable of managing our water resources intelligently.

In the area of water and air pollution our successes are only partial. Rapid urbanization and industrialization have intensified the problems of controlling both. At the same time one must concede that there is much stronger scientific justification for mounting vigorous programs to abate water pollution than to abate air pollution. Nevertheless, public pressure on behalf of the latter is increasing, and as has happened so often in the past, we may find acton running ahead of knowledge. This is not necessarily to be deplored.

My own view coincides with that recently expressed by P. B. Medawar of University College, London at a symposium on the interaction of man and his environment. "We are not yet qualified," he said, "to prescribe for the medical welfare of our grandchildren . . . I should say that present skills are sufficient for present ills."

11

PROFILES OF DISORDER: DETROIT*

On Saturday evening, July 22, the Detroit Police Department raided five "blind pigs." The blind pigs had had their origin in prohibition days, and survived as private social clubs. Often, they were after-hours drinking and gambling spots.

The fifth blind pig on the raid list, the United Community and Civic League at the corner of 12th Street and Clairmount, had been raided twice before. Once 10 persons had been picked up; another time, 28. A Detroit vice squad officer had tried but failed to get in shortly after 10 o'clock Saturday night. He succeeded, on his second attempt, at 3:45 Sunday morning.

The Tactical Mobile Unit, the Police Department's crowd control squad, had been dismissed at 3 a.m. Since Sunday morning traditionally is the least troublesome time for police in Detroit—and all over the country—only 193 officers were patroling the streets. Of these, 44 were in the 10th precinct where the blind pig was located.

Police expected to find two dozen patrons in the blind pig. That night, however, it was the scene of a party for several servicemen, two of whom were back from Vietnam. Instead of two dozen patrons, police found 82. Some voiced resentment at the police intrusion.

An hour went by before all 82 could be transported from the scene. The weather was humid and warm—the temperature that

*Reprinted from *The Report of the National Advisory Commission on Civil Disorders* (Washington: U.S. Government Printing Office, 1968), pp. 47-61.

day was to rise to 86 — and despite the late hour, many people were still on the street. In short order, a crowd of about 200 gathered.

In November of 1965, George Edwards, Judge of the United States Court of Appeals for the Sixth Circuit, and Commissioner of the Detroit Police Department from 1961 to 1963, had written in the *Michigan Law Review*:

> It is clear that in 1965 no one will make excuses for any city's inability to foresee the possibility of racial trouble. * * * Although local police forces generally regard themselves as public servants with the responsibility of maintaining law and order, they tend to minimize this attitude when they are patrolling areas that are heavily populated with Negro citizens. There, they tend to view each person on the streets as potential criminal or enemy, and all too often that attitude is reciprocated. Indeed, hostility between the Negro communities in our large cities and the police departments, is the major problem in law enforcement in this decade. It has been a major cause of all recent race riots.

At the time of Detroit's 1943 race riot, Judge Edwards told Commission investigators, there was "open warfare between the Detroit Negroes and the Detroit Police Department." As late as 1961, he had thought that "Detroit was the leading candidate in the United States for a race riot."

There was a long history of conflict between the police department and citizens. During the labor battles of the 1930's, union members had come to view the Detroit Police Department as a strike-breaking force. The 1943 riot, in which 34 persons died, was the bloodiest in the United States in a span of two decades.

Judge Edwards and his successor, Commissioner Ray Girardin, attempted to restructure the image of the department. A Citizens Complaint Bureau was set up to facilitate the filing of complaints by citizens against officers. In practice, however, this Bureau appeared to work little better than less enlightened and more cumbersome procedures in other cities.

On 12th Street, with its high incidence of vice and crime, the issue of police brutality was a recurrent theme. A month earlier, the killing of a prostitute had been determined by police investigators to be the work of a pimp. According to rumors in the community, the crime had been committed by a vice squad officer.

At about the same time, the killing of Danny Thomas, a 27-year-old Negro Army veteran, by a gang of white youths had inflamed the community. The city's major newspapers played down the story in hope that the murder would not become a cause for increased tensions. The intent backfired. A banner story in the *Michigan Chronicle,* the city's Negro newspaper, began: "As James Meredith marched again Sunday to prove a Negro could walk in Mississippi without fear, a young woman who saw her husband killed by a white gang, shouting: 'Niggers keep out of Rouge Park,' lost her baby.

"Relatives were upset that the full story of the murder was not being told, apparently in an effort to prevent the incident from sparking a riot."

Some Negroes believed that the daily newspapers' treatment of the story was further evidence of the double standard: playing up crimes by Negroes, playing down crimes committed against Negroes.

Although police arrested one suspect for murder, Negroes questioned why the entire gang was not held. What, they asked, would have been the result if a white man had been killed by a gang of Negroes? What if Negroes had made the kind of advances toward a white woman that the white men were rumored to have made toward Mrs. Thomas?

The Thomas family lived only four or five blocks from the raided blind pig.

A few minutes after 5 a.m., just after the last of those arrested had been hauled away, an empty bottle smashed into the rear window of a police car. A little basket was thrown through the window of a store. Rumors circulated of excess force used by the police during the raid. A youth, whom police nicknamed "Mr. Greensleeves" because of the color of his shirt was shouting: "We're going to have a riot!" and exhorting the crowd to vandalism.

At 5:20 a.m., Commissioner Girardin was notified. He immediately called Mayor Jerome Cavanagh. Seventeen officers from other areas were ordered into the 10th Precinct. By 6 a.m., police strength had grown to 369 men. Of these, however, only 43 were committed to the immediate riot area. By that time, the number of persons on 12th Street was growing into the thousands and widespread window-smashing and looting had begun.

On either side of 12th Street were neat, middle-class districts. Along 12th Street itself, however, crowded apartment houses created a density of more than 21,000 persons per square mile, almost double the city average.

The movement of people when the slums of "Black Bottom" had been cleared for urban renewal had changed 12th Street from an integrated community into an almost totally black one, in which only a number of merchants remained white. Only 18 percent of the residents were homeowners. Twenty-five percent of the housing was considered so substandard as to require clearance. Another 19 percent had major deficiencies.

The crime rate was almost double that of the city as a whole. A Detroit police officer told Commission investigators that prostitution was so widespread that officers made arrests only when soliciting became blatant. The proportion of broken families was more than twice that in the rest of the city.

By 7:50 a.m., when a 17-man police commando unit attempted to make the first sweep, an estimated 3,000 persons were on 12th Street. They offered no resistance. As the sweep moved down the street, they gave way to one side, and then flowed back behind it.

A shoe store manager said he waited vainly for police for 2 hours as the store was being looted. At 8:25 a.m., someone in the crowd yelled, "The cops are coming!" The first flames of the riot billowed from the store. Firemen who responded were not harassed. The flames were extinguished.

By midmorning, 1,122 men—approximately a fourth of the police department—had reported for duty. Of these, 540 were in or near the six-block riot area. One hundred eight officers were attempting to establish a cordon. There was, however, no interference with looters, and police were refraining from the use of force.

Commissioner Girardin said: "If we had started shooting in there *** not one of our policemen would have come out alive. I am convinced it would have turned into a race riot in the conventional sense."

According to witnesses, police at some roadblocks made little effort to stop people from going in and out of the area. Bantering took place between police officers and the populace, some still in pajamas. To some observers, there seemed at this point to be an atmosphere of apathy. On the one hand, the police failed to interfere with the looting. On the other, a number of older, more stable residents, who had seen the street deteriorate from a prosperous commercial thoroughfare to one ridden by vice, remained aloof.

Because officials feared that the 12th Street disturbance might be a diversion, many officers were sent to guard key installations in other sections of the city. Belle Isle, the recreation area in the Detroit River that had been the scene of the 1943 riot, was sealed off.

In an effort to avoid attracting people to the scene, some broadcasters cooperated by not reporting the riot, and an effort was made to downplay the extent of the disorder. The facade of "business as usual" necessitated the detailing of numerous police officers to protect the 50,000 spectators that were expected at that afternoon's New York Yankees-Detroit Tigers baseball game.

Early in the morning, a task force of community workers went into the area to dispel rumors and act as counterrioters. Such a task force had been singularly successful at the time of the incident in the Kercheval district in the summer of 1966, when scores of people had gathered at the site of an arrest. Kercheval, however, has a more stable population, fewer stores, less population density, and the city's most effective police-community relations program.

The 12th Street area, on the other hand, had been determined, in a 1966 survey conducted by Dr. Ernest Harburg of the Psychology Department of the University of Michigan, to be a community of high stress and tension. An overwhelming majority of the residents indicated dissatisfaction with their environment.

Of the interviewed, 93 percent said they wanted to move out of the neighborhood; 73 percent felt that the streets were not safe; 91 percent believed that a person was likely to be robbed or beaten at night; 58 percent knew of a fight within the last 12 months in which a weapon had been employed; 32 percent stated that they themselves owned a weapon; 57 percent were worried about fires.

A significant proportion believed municipal services to be inferior: 36 percent were dissatisfied with the schools; 43 percent with the city's contribution to the neighborhood; 77 percent with the recreational facilities; 78 percent believed police did not respond promptly when they were summoned for help.

U.S. Representative John Conyers, Jr., a Negro, was notified about the disturbance at his home, a few blocks from 12th Street, at 8:30 a.m. Together with other community leaders, including Hubert G. Locke, a Negro and assistant to the commissioner of police, he began to drive around the area. In the side streets, he asked people to stay in their homes. On 12th Street, he asked them to disperse. It was, by his own account, a futile task.

Numerous eyewitnesses interviewed by Commission investigators tell of the carefree mood with which people ran in and out of stores, looting and laughing and joking with the police officers. Stores with "Soul Brother" signs appeared no more immune than others. Looters paid no attention to residents who shouted at them and called their action senseless. An epidemic of excitement had swept over the persons on the street.

Congressman Conyers noticed a woman with a baby in her arms; she was raging, cursing "whitey" for no apparent reason.

Shortly before noon, Congressman Conyers climbed atop a car in the middle of 12th Street to address the people. As he began to speak, he was confronted by a man in his fifties whom he had once, as a lawyer, represented in court. The man had been active in civil rights. He believed himself to have been persecuted as a result, and it was Conyers' opinion that he may have been wrongfully jailed. Extremely bitter, the man was inciting the crowd and challenging Conyers: "Why are you defending the cops and the establishment? You're just as bad as they are!"

A police officer in the riot area told Commission investigators that neither he nor his fellow officers were instructed as to what they were supposed to be doing. Witnesses tell of officers standing behind sawhorses as an area was being looted—and still standing there much later, when the mob had moved elsewhere. A squad from the commando unit, wearing helmets with face-covering visors and carrying bayonet-tipped carbines, blockaded a street several blocks from the scene of the riot. Their appearance drew residents into the street. Some began to harangue them and to question why they were in an area where there was no trouble. Representative Conyers convinced the police department to remove the commandos.

By that time, a rumor was threading through the crowd that a man had been bayoneted by the police. Influenced by such stories, the crowd became belligerent. At approximately 1 p.m., stonings accelerated. Numerous officers reported injuries from rocks, bottles, and other objects thrown at them. Smoke billowed upward from four fires, the first since the one at the shoe store early in the morning. When firemen answered the alarms, they became the target for rocks and bottles.

At 2 p.m., Mayor Cavanagh met with community and political leaders at police headquarters. Until then there had been hope that, as the people blew off steam, the riot would dissipate. Now the opinion was nearly unanimous that additional forces would be needed.

A request was made for state police aid. By 3 p.m., 360 officers were assembling at the armory. At that moment looting was spreading from the 12th Street area to other main' thoroughfares.

There was no lack of the disaffected to help spread it. Although not yet as hard-pressed as Newark, Detroit was, like Newark, losing population. Its prosperous middle-class whites were moving to the suburbs and being replaced by unskilled Negro migrants. Between 1960 and 1967, the Negro population rose from just under 30 percent to an estimated 40 percent of the total.

In a decade, the school system had gained 50,000 to 60,000 children. Fifty-one percent of the elementary school classes were overcrowded. Simply to achieve the statewide average, the system needed 1,650 more teachers and 1,000 additional classrooms. The combined cost would be $63 million.

Of 300,000 school children, 171,000, or 57 percent were Negro. According to the Detroit superintendent of schools, 25 different school districts surrounding the city spent up to $500 more per pupil per year than Detroit. In the inner city schools, more than half the pupils who entered high school became dropouts.

The strong union structure had created excellent conditions for most working men, but had left others, such as civil service and Government workers, comparatively disadvantaged and dissatisfied. In June, the "Blue Flu" had struck the city as police officers, forbidden to strike, had staged a sick-out. In September the teachers were to go on strike. The starting wage for a plumber's helper was almost equal to the salary of a police officer or teacher.

Some unions, traditionally closed to Negroes, zealously guarded training opportunities. In January, 1967, the school system notified six apprenticed trades it would not open any new apprenticed classes unless a large number of Negroes were included. By fall, some of the programs were still closed.

High school diplomas from inner-city schools were regarded by personnel directors as less than valid. In July, unemployment was at a 5-year peak. In the 12th Street area, it was estimated to be between 12 and 15 percent for Negro men and 30 percent or higher for those under 25.

The more education a Negro had, the greater disparity between his income and that of a white at the same level of education. The income of white and Negroes with a seventh-grade education was about equal. The median income of whites with a high school diploma was $1,600 more per year than that of Negroes. White college graduates made $2,600 more. In fact, so far as income was concerned, it made very little difference to a Negro man whether he had attended school for 8 years or for 12. In the fall of 1967, a study conducted at one inner-city high school, Northwestern, showed that, although 50 percent of the dropouts had found work, 90 percent of the 1967 graduating class was unemployed.

Mayor Cavanagh had appointed many Negroes to key positions in his administration, but in elective offices the Negro population was still underrepresented. Of nine councilmen, one was a Negro. Of seven school board members, two were Negroes.

Although Federal programs had brought nearly $360 million to the city between 1962 and 1967, the money appeared to have had little impact at the grassroots. Urban renewal, for which $38 million had been allocated, was opposed by many residents of the poverty area.

Because of its financial straits, the city was unable to produce on promises to correct such conditions as poor garbage collection and bad street lighting, which brought constant complaints from Negro residents.

On 12th Street, Carl Perry, the Negro proprietor of a drugstore and photography studio, was dispensing ice cream, sodas, and candy to the youngsters streaming in and out of his store. For safekeeping, he had brought the photography equipment from his studio, in the next block, to the drugstore. The youths milling about repeatedly assured him that, although the market next door had been ransacked, his place of business was in no danger.

In midafternoon, the market was set afire. Soon after, the drug store went up in flames.

State Representative James Del Rio, a Negro, was camping out in front of a building he owned when two small boys, neither more than 10 years old, approached. One prepared to throw a brick through a window. Del Rio stopped him: "That building belongs to me," he said.

"I'm glad you told me, baby, because I was just about to bust you in!" the youngster replied.

Some evidence that criminal elements were organizing spontaneously to take advantage of the riot began to manifest itself. A number of cars were noted to be returning again and again, their occupants methodically looting stores. Months later, goods stolen during the riot were still being peddled.

A spirit of carefree nihilism was taking hold. To riot and to destroy appeared more and more to become ends in themselves. Late Sunday afternoon, it appeared to one observer that the young people were "dancing amidst the flames."

A Negro plainclothes officer was standing at an intersection when a man threw a Molotov cocktail into a business establishment at the corner. In the heat of the afternoon, fanned by the 20 to 25 m.p.h. winds of both Sunday and Monday, the fire reached the home next door within minutes. As residents uselessly sprayed the flames with garden hoses, the fire jumped from roof to roof of adjacent two- and three-story buildings. Within the hour, the entire block was in flames. The ninth house in the burning row belonged to the arsonist who had thrown the Molotov cocktail.

In some areas, residents organized rifle squads to protect fire-fighters. Elsewhere, especially as the wind-whipped flames began to overwhelm the Detroit Fire Department and more and more residences burned, the firemen were subjected to curses and rock-throwing.

Because of a lack of funds, on a per capita basis, the department is one of the smallest in the Nation. In comparison to Newark, where approximately 1,000 firemen patrol an area of 16 square miles with a population of 400,000, Detroit's 1,700 firemen must cover a city of 140 square miles with a population of 1.6 million. Because the department had no mutual aid agreement with surrounding communities, it could not quickly call in reinforcements from outlying areas, and it was almost 9 p.m. before the first arrived. At one point, out of a total of 92 pieces of Detroit firefighting equipment and 56 brought in from surrounding communities, only four engine companies were available to guard areas of the city outside of the riot perimeter.

As the afternoon progressed, the fire department's radio carried repeated messages of apprehension and orders of caution:

> There is no police protection here at all; there isn't a police-man in the area. * * * If you have trouble at all, pull out! * * * We're being stoned at the scene. It's going good. We need help! * * * Protect yourselves! Proceed away from the scene. * * * Engine 42 over at Linwood and Gladstone. They

are throwing bottles at us so we are getting out of the area.
* * * All companies without police protection—all companies
without police protection—orders are to withdraw, do not try
to put out the fires. I repeat—all companies without police
protection orders are to withdraw, do not try to put out the
fires!

It was 4:30 p.m. when the firemen, some of them exhausted
by the heat, abandoned an area of approximately 100 square
blocks on either side of 12th Street to await protection from police
and National Guardsmen.

During the course of the riot, firemen were to withdraw 283
times.

Fire Chief Charles J. Quinlan estimated that at least two-thirds
of the buildings were destroyed by spreading fires rather than
fires set at the scene. Of the 683 structures involved, approximately
one-third were residential, and in few, if any, of these was the
fire set originally.

Governor George Romney flew over the area between 8:30
and 9 p.m. "It looked like the city had been bombed on the west
side and there was an area two-and-a-half miles by three-and-
a-half miles with major fires, with entire blocks in flames," he
told the Commission.

In the midst of chaos, there were some unexpected individual
responses.

Twenty-four-year-old E.G., a Negro born in Savannah, Georgia,
had come to Detroit in 1965 to attend Wayne State University.
Rebellion had been building in him for a long time because,

You just had to bow down to the white man. * * * When the
insurance man would come by he would always call out to
my mother by her first name and we were expected to smile
and greet him happily. * * * Man, I know he would never have
thought of me or my father going to his home and calling
his wife by her first name. Then I once saw a white man slap-
ping a young pregnant Negro woman on the street with such
force that she just spun around and fell. I'll never forget that.

When a friend called to tell him about the riot on 12th Street,
E. G. went there expecting "a true revolt" but was disappointed as
soon as he saw the looting begin: "I wanted to see the people rise up
to revolt. When I saw the first person coming out of the store with
things in his arms, I really got sick to my stomach and wanted to go
home. Rebellion against the white suppressors is one thing, but one
measly pair of shoes or some food completely ruins the whole concept."

E. G. was standing in a crowd, watching firemen when Fire Chief Alvin Wall called out for help from the spectators. E. G. responded. His reasoning was: "No matter what color someone is, whether they are green or pink or blue, I'd help them if they were in trouble. That's all there is to it."

He worked with the firemen for four days, the only Negro in an all-white crew. Elsewhere, at scattered locations, a half dozen other Negro youths pitched in to help the firemen.

At 4:20 P.M. Mayor Cavanagh requested that the National Guard be brought into Detroit. Although a major portion of the Guard was in its summer encampment 200 miles away, several hundred troops were conducting their regular weekend drill in the city. That circumstance obviated many problems. The first troops were on the streets by 7:00 P.M.

At 7:45 P.M. the mayor issued a proclamation instituting a 9:00 P.M. to 5:00 A.M. curfew. At 9:07 P.M. the first sniper fire was reported. Following his aerial survey of the city, Governor Romney, at or shortly before midnight, proclaimed that "a state of public emergency exists" in the cities of Detroit, Highland Park, and Hamtramck.

At 4:45 P.M. a 68-year-old white shoe repairman, George Messerlian, had seen looters carrying clothes from a cleaning establishment next to his shop. Armed with a saber, he had rushed into the street, flailing away at the looters. One Negro youth was nicked on the shoulder. Another, who had not been on the scene, inquired as to what had happened. After he had been told, he allegedly replied: "I'll get the old man for you!"

Going up to Messerlian, who had fallen or been knocked to the ground, the youth began to beat him with a club. Two other Negro youths dragged the attacker away from the old man. It was too late. Messerlian died four days later in the hospital.

At 9:15 P.M. a 16-year-old Negro boy, superficially wounded while looting, became the first reported gunshot victim.

At midnight Sharon George, a 23-year-old white woman, together with her two brothers, was a passenger in a car being driven by her husband. After having dropped off two Negro friends, they were returning home on one of Detroit's main avenues when they were slowed by a milling throng in the street. A shot fired from close range struck the car. The bullet splintered in Mrs. George's body. She died less than two hours later.

An hour before midnight a 45-year-old-white man, Walter Grzanka together with three white companions, went into the street. Shortly thereafter a market was broken into. Inside the show window a Negro man began filling bags with groceries and handing them to confederates outside the store. Grzanka twice went over to the store, accepted bags, and placed them down beside his companions across the street. On the third occasion he entered the market. When he emerged, the market owner, driving by in his car, shot and killed him.

In Grzanka's pockets police found seven cigars, four packages of pipe tobacco, and nine pairs of shoelaces.

Before dawn four other looters were shot, one of them accidentally while struggling with a police officer. A Negro youth and a National Guardsman were injured by gunshots of undetermined origin. A private guard shot himself while pulling his revolver from his pocket. In the basement of the 13th Precinct Police Station a cue ball, thrown by an unknown assailant, cracked against the head of a sergeant.

At about midnight three white youths, armed with a shotgun, had gone to the roof of their apartment building, located in an all-white block, in order, they said, to protect the building from fire. At 2:45 A.M. a patrol car, carrying police officers and National Guardsmen, received a report of "snipers on the roof." As the patrol car arrived, the manager of the building went to the roof to tell the youths they had better come down.

The law enforcement personnel surrounded the building, some going to the front, others to the rear. As the manager, together with the three youths, descended the fire escape in the rear, a National Guardsman, believing he heard shots from the front, fired. His shot killed 23-year-old Clifton Pryor.

Early in the morning a young white fireman and a 49-year-old Negro homeowner were killed by fallen power lines.

By 2:00 A.M. Monday, Detroit police had been augmented by 800 State Police officers and 1,200 National Guardsmen. An additional 8,000 Guardsmen were on the way. Nevertheless, Governor Romney and Mayor Cavanagh decided to ask for federal assistance. At 2:15 A.M. the mayor called Vice President Hubert Humphrey, and was referred to Attorney General Ramsey Clark. A short time thereafter telephone contact was established between Governor Romney and the attorney general.[1]

[1] A little over two hours earlier, at 11:55 P.M. Mayor Cavanagh had informed the U.S. Attorney General that a "dangerous situation existed in the city." Details are set forth in the Final Report of Cyrus R. Vance, covering the Detroit Riots, released on September 12, 1967.

There is some difference of opinion about what occurred next. According to the attorney general's office, the governor was advised of the seriousness of the request and told that the applicable federal statute required that, before federal troops could be brought into the city, he would have to state that the situation had deteriorated to the point that local and state forces could no longer maintain law and order. According to the governor, he was under the impression that he was being asked to declare that a "state of insurrection" existed in the city.

The governor was unwilling to make such a declaration, contending that, if he did, insurance policies would not cover the loss incurred as a result of the riot. He and the mayor decided to re-evaluate the need for federal troops.

Contact between Detroit and Washington was maintained throughout the early morning hours. At 9:00 A.M., as the disorder still showed no sign of abating, the governor and the mayor decided to make a renewed request for federal troops.

Shortly before noon the President of the United States authorized the sending of a task force of paratroopers to Selfridge Air Force Base, near the city. A few minutes past 3:00 P.M., Lt. General John L. Throckmorton, commander of Task Force Detroit, met Cyrus Vance, former Deputy Secretary of Defense, at the air base. Approximately an hour later the first federal troops arrived at the air base.

After meeting with state and municipal officials, Mr. Vance, General Throckmorton, Governor Romney, and Mayor Cavanagh, made a tour of the city, which lasted until 7:15 P.M. During this tour Mr. Vance and General Throckmorton independently came to the conclusion that—since they had seen no looting or sniping, since the fires appeared to be coming under control, and since a substantial number of National Guardsmen had not yet been committed—injection of federal troops would be premature.

As the riot alternately waxed and waned, one area of the ghetto remained insulated. On the northeast side the residents of some 150 square blocks inhabited by 21,000 persons had, in 1966, banded together in the Positive Neighborhood Action Committee (PNAC). With professional help from the Institute of Urban Dynamics, they had organized block clubs and made plans for the improvement of the neighborhood. In order to meet the need for recreational facilities, which the city was not providing, they had raised $3,000 to purchase empty lots for playgrounds. Although opposed to urban renewal, they had agreed to co-sponsor with the Archdiocese of Detroit a housing project to be controlled jointly by the archdiocese and PNAC.

When the riot broke out, the residents, through the block clubs, were able to organize quickly. Youngsters, agreeing to stay in the neighborhood, participated in detouring traffic. While many persons reportedly sympathized with the idea of a rebellion against the "system," only two small fires were set—one in an empty building.

During the daylight hours Monday, nine more persons were killed by gunshots elsewhere in the city, and many others were seriously or critically injured. Twenty-three-year old Nathaniel Edmonds, a Negro, was sitting in his back yard when a young white man stopped his car, got out, and began an argument with him. A few minutes later, declaring that he was "going to paint his picture on him with a shotgun," the white man allegedly shotgunned Edmonds to death.

Mrs. Nannie Pack and Mrs. Mattie Thomas were sitting on the porch of Mrs. Pack's house when police began chasing looters from a nearby market. During the chase officers fired three shots from their shotguns. The discharge from one of these accidentally struck the two women. Both were still in the hospital weeks later.

Included among those critically injured when they were accidentally trapped in the line of fire were an 8-year-old Negro girl and a 14-year-old white boy.

As darkness settled Monday, the number of incidents reported to police began to rise again. Although many turned out to be false, several involved injuries to police officers, National Guardsmen, and civilians by gunshots of undetermined origin.

Watching the upward trend of reported incidents, Mr. Vance and General Throckmorton became convinced Federal troops should be used, and President Johnson was so advised. At 11:20 P.M. the President signed a proclamation federalizing the Michigan National Guard and authorizing the use of the paratroopers.

At this time there were nearly 5,000 Guardsmen in the city, but fatigue, lack of training, and the haste with which they had had to be deployed reduced their effectiveness. Some of the Guardsmen traveled 200 miles and then were on duty for 30 hours straight. Some had never received riot training and were given on-the-spot instructions on mob control—only to discover that there were no mobs, and that the situation they faced on the darkened streets was one for which they were unprepared.

Commanders committed men as they became available, often

in small groups. In the resulting confusion, some units were lost in the city. Two Guardsmen assigned to an intersection on Monday were discovered still there on Friday.

Lessons learned by the California National Guard two years earlier in Watts regarding the danger of overreaction and the necessity of great restraint in using weapons had not, apparently, been passed on to the Michigan National Guard. The young troopers could not be expected to know what a danger they were creating by the lack of fire discipline, not only to the civilian population but to themselves.

A Detroit newspaper reporter who spent a night riding in a command jeep told a Commission investigator of machine guns being fired accidentally, street lights being shot out by rifle fire, and buildings being placed under siege on the sketchiest reports of sniping. Troopers would fire, and immediately from the distance there would be answering fire, sometimes consisting of tracer bullets.

In one instance, the newsman related, a report was received on the jeep radio that an Army bus was pinned down by sniper fire at an intersection. National Guardsmen and police, arriving from various directions, jumped out and began asking each other: "Where's the sniper fire coming from?" As one Guardsman pointed to a building, everyone rushed about, taking cover. A soldier, alighting from a jeep, accidentally pulled the trigger on his rifle. As the shot reverberated through the darkness an officer yelled: "What's going on?" "I don't know," came the answer. "Sniper, I guess."

Without any clear authorization or direction someone opened fire upon the suspected building. A tank rolled up and sprayed the building with .50 caliber tracer bullets. Law enforcement officers rushed into the surrounded building and discovered it empty. "They must be firing one shot and running," was the verdict.

The reporter interviewed the men who had gotten off the bus and were crouched around it. When he asked them about the sniping incident he was told that someone had heard a shot. He asked "Did the bullet hit the bus?" The answer was: "Well, we don't know."

Bracketing the hour of midnight Monday, heavy firing, injuring many persons and killing several, occurred in the southeastern sector, which was to be taken over by the paratroopers at 4:00 A.M. Tuesday, and which was, at this time, considered to be the most active riot area in the city.

Employed as a private guard, 55-year-old Julius L. Dorsey, a Negro, was standing in front of a market when accosted by two Negro men and a woman. They demanded he permit them to loot the market. He ignored their demands. They began to berate him. He asked a neighbor to call the police. As the argument grew more heated, Dorsey fired three shots from his pistol into the air.

The police radio reported: "Looters, they have rifles." A patrol car driven by a police officer and carrying three National Guardsmen arrived. As the looters fled, the law enforcement personnel opened fire. When the firing ceased, one person lay dead.

He was Julius L. Dorsey.

In two areas—one consisting of a triangle formed by Mack, Gratiot, and E. Grand Boulevard, the other surrounding Southeastern High School—firing began shortly after 10:00 P.M. and continued for several hours.

In the first of the areas, a 22-year-old Negro complained that he had been shot at by snipers. Later, a half dozen civilians and one National Guardsman were wounded by shots of undetermined origin.

Henry Denson, a passenger in a car, was shot and killed when the vehicle's driver, either by accident or intent, failed to heed a warning to halt at a National Guard roadblock.

Similar incidents occurred in the vicinity of Southeastern High School, one of the National Guard staging areas. As early as 10:20 P.M. the area was reported to be under sniper fire. Around midnight there were two incidents, the sequence of which remains in doubt.

Shortly before midnight Ronald Powell, who lived three blocks east of the high school and whose wife was, momentarily, expecting a baby, asked the four friends with whom he had been spending the evening to take him home. He, together with Edward Blackshear, Charles Glover, and John Leroy climbed into Charles Dunson's station wagon for the short drive. Some of the five may have been drinking, but none was intoxicated.

To the north of the high school they were halted at a National Guard roadblock, and told they would have to detour around the school and fire station at Mac, and St. Jean Streets because of the firing that had been occurring. Following orders, they took a circuitous route and approached Powell's home from the south.

On Lycaste Street, between Charlevoix and Goethe, they saw a jeep sitting at the curb. Believing it to be another roadblock, they slowed down. Simultaneously a shot rang out. A National Guardsman fell, hit in the ankle.

Other National Guardsmen at the scene thought the shot had come from the station wagon. Shot after shot was directed against the vehicle, at least 17 of them finding their mark. All five occupants were injured, John Leroy fatally.

At approximately the same time firemen, police, and National Guardsmen at the corner of Mack and St. Jean Streets, two and one-half blocks away, again came under fire from what they believed were rooftop snipers to the southeast, the direction of Charlevoix and Lycaste. The police and Guardsmen responded with a hail of fire.

When the shooting ceased, Carl Smith, a young firefighter, lay dead. An autopsy determined that the shot had been fired at street level, and, according to police, probably had come from the southeast.

At 4:00 A.M. when paratroopers, under the command of Col. A. R. Bolling, arrived at the high school, the area was so dark and still that the colonel thought, at first, that he had come to the wrong place. Investigating, he discovered National Guard troops, claiming they were pinned down by sniper fire, crouched behind the walls of the darkened building.

The colonel immediately ordered all the lights in the building turned on and his troops to show themselves as conspicuously as possible. In the apartment house across the street nearly every window had been shot out, and the walls were pockmarked with bullet holes. The colonel went into the building and began talking to the residents, many of whom had spent the night huddled on the floor. He reassured them no more shots would be fired.

According to Lt. Gen. Throckmorton and Colonel Bolling, the city, at this time, was saturated with fear. The National Guardsmen were afraid, the residents were afraid, and the police were afraid. Numerous persons, the majority of them Negroes, were being injured by gunshots of undetermined origin. The general and his staff felt that the major task of the troops was to reduce the fear and restore an air of normalcy.

In order to accomplish this, every effort was made to establish contact and rapport between the troops and the residents. Troopers—20 percent of whom were Negro—began helping to clean up the streets, collect garbage, and trace persons who had disappeared in the confusion. Residents in the neighborhoods responded with soup and sandwiches for the troops. In areas where the National Guard tried to establish rapport with the citizens, there was a similar response.

Within hours after the arrival of the paratroops the area occupied by them was the quietest in the city, bearing out General Throckmorton's view that the key to quelling a disorder is to saturate an area with "calm, determined, and hardened professional soldiers." Loaded weapons, he believes, are unnecessary. Troopers had strict orders not to fire unless they could see the specific person at whom they were aiming. Mass fire was forbidden.

During five days in the city, 2,700 Army troops expended only 201 rounds of ammunition, almost all during the first few hours, after which even stricter fire discipline was enforced. (In contrast, New Jersey National Guardsmen and State police expended 13,326 rounds of ammunition in three days in Newark.) Hundreds of reports of sniper fire—most of them false—continued to pour into police headquarters; the Army logged only 10. No paratrooper was injured by a gunshot. Only one person was hit by a shot fired by a trooper. He was a young Negro who was killed when he ran into the line of fire as a trooper, aiding police in a raid on an apartment, aimed at a person believed to be a sniper.

General Throckmorton ordered the weapons of all military personnel unloaded, but either the order failed to reach many National Guardsmen, or else it was disobeyed.

Even as the general was requesting the city to relight the streets, Guardsmen continued shooting out the lights, and there are reports of dozens of shots being fired to dispatch one light. At one such location, as Guardsmen were shooting out the street lights, a radio newscaster reported himself to be pinned down by "sniper fire."

On the same day that the general was attempting to restore normalcy by ordering street barricades taken down, Guardsmen on one street were not only, in broad daylight, ordering people off the street, but off their porches and away from the windows. Two persons who failed to respond to the order quickly enough were shot, one of them fatally.

The general himself reported an incident of a Guardsman "firing across the bow" of an automobile that was approaching a roadblock.

As in Los Angeles two years earlier, roadblocks that were ill-lighted and ill-defined—often consisting of no more than a trash barrel or similar object with Guardsmen standing nearby—proved a continuous hazard to motorists. At one such roadblock, National

Guard Sergeant Larry Post, standing in the street, was caught in a sudden cross fire as his fellow Guardsmen opened up on a vehicle. He was the only soldier killed in the riot.

With persons of every description arming themselves, and guns being fired accidentally or on the vaguest pretext all over the city, it became more and more impossible to tell who was shooting at whom. Some firemen began carrying guns. One accidentally shot and wounded a fellow fireman. Another injured himself.

The chaos of a riot, and the difficulties faced by police officers, are demonstrated by an incident that occurred at 2:00 A.M. Tuesday.

A unit of 12 officers received a call to guard firemen from snipers. When they arrived at the corner of Vicksburg and Linwood in the 12th Street area, the intersection was well-lighted by the flames completely enveloping one building. Sniper fire was directed at the officers from an alley to the north, and gun flashes were observed in two buildings.

As the officers advanced on the two buildings, Patrolman Johnie Hamilton fired several rounds from his machinegun. Thereupon, the officers were suddenly subjected to fire from a new direction, the east. Hamilton, struck by four bullets, fell, critically injured, in the intersection. As two officers ran to his aid, they too were hit.

By this time other units of the Detroit Police Department, state police, and National Guard had arrived on the scene, and the area was covered with a hail of gunfire.

In the confusion the snipers who had initiated the shooting escaped.

At 9:15 p.m., Tuesday, July 25, 38-year-old Jack Sydnor, a Negro, came home drunk. Taking out his pistol, he fired one shot into an alley. A few minutes later, the police arrived. As his common-law wife took refuge in a closet, Sydnor waited, gun in hand, while the police forced open the door. Patrolman Roger Poike, the first to enter, was shot by Sydnor. Although critically injured, the officer managed to get off six shots in return. Police within the building and on the street then poured a hail of fire into the apartment. When the shooting ceased, Sydnor's body, riddled by the gunfire, was found lying on the ground outside a window.

Nearby, a state police officer and a Negro youth were struck and seriously injured by stray bullets. As in other cases where the origin of the shots were not immediately determinable, police reported them as "shot by sniper."

Reports of "heavy sniper fire" poured into police headquarters from the two blocks surrounding the apartment house where the battle with Jack Sydnor had taken place. National Guard troops with two tanks were dispatched to help flush out the snipers.

Shots continued to be heard throughout the neighborhood. At approximately midnight—there are discrepancies as to the precise time—a machinegunner on a tank, startled by several shots, asked the assistant gunner where the shots were coming from. The assistant gunner pointed toward a flash in the window of an apartment house from which there had been earlier reports of sniping.

The machinegunner opened fire. As the slugs ripped through the window and walls of the apartment, they nearly severed the arm of 21-year-old Valerie Hood. Her 4-year-old niece, Tonya Blanding, toppled dead, a .50-caliber bullet hole in her chest.

A few seconds earlier, 19-year-old Bill Hood, standing in the window, had lighted a cigarette.

Down the street, a bystander was critically injured by a stray bullet. Simultaneously, the John C. Lodge Freeway, two blocks away, was reported to be under sniper fire. Tanks and National Guard troops were sent to investigate. At the Harlan House Motel, 10 blocks from where Tonya Blanding had died a short time earlier, Mrs. Helen Hall, a 51-year-old white businesswoman, opened the drapes of the fourth floor hall window. Calling out to other guests, she exclaimed: "Look at the tanks!"

She died seconds later as bullets began to slam into the building. As the firing ceased, a 19-year-old Marine, carrying a Springfield rifle, burst into the building. When, accidentally, he pushed the rifle barrel through a window, firing commenced anew. A police investigation showed that the Marine, who had just decided to "help out" the law enforcement personnel, was not involved in the death of Mrs. Hall.

R.R., a white 27-year-old coin dealer, was the owner of an expensive, three-story house on L Street, an integrated middle-class neighborhood. In May of 1966, he and his wife and child had moved to New York and had rented the house to two young men. After several months, he had begun to have problems with his tenants. On one occasion, he reported to his attorney that he had been threatened by them.

In March of 1967, R.R. instituted eviction proceedings. These were still pending when the riot broke out. Concerned about the house, R.R. decided to fly to Detroit. When he arrived at the house, on Wednesday, July 26, he discovered the tenants were not at home.

He then called his attorney, who advised him to take physical possession of the house and, for legal purposes, to take witnesses along.

Together with his 17-year-old brother and another white youth, R.R. went to the house, entered, and began changing the locks on the doors. For protection they brought a .22 caliber rifle, which R.R.'s brother took into the cellar and fired into a pillow in order to test it.

Shortly after 8:00 P.M., R.R. called his attorney to advise him that the tenants had returned, and he had refused to admit them. Thereupon, R.R. alleged, the tenants had threatened to obtain the help of the National Guard. The attorney relates that he was not particularly concerned. He told R.R. that if the National Guard did appear he should have the officer in charge call him (the attorney).

At approximately the same time the National Guard claims it received information to the effect that several men had evicted the legal occupants of the house, and intended to start sniping after dark.

A National Guard column was dispatched to the scene. Shortly after 9:00 P.M., in the half-light of dusk, the column of approximately 30 men surrounded the house. A tank took position on a lawn across the street. The captain commanding the column placed in front of the house an explosive device similar to a firecracker. After setting this off in order to draw the attention of the occupants to the presence of the column, he called for them to come out of the house. No attempt was made to verify the truth or falsehood of the allegations regarding snipers.

When the captain received no reply from the house, he began counting to 10. As he was counting, he said, he heard a shot, the origin of which he could not determine. A few seconds later he heard another shot and saw a "fire streak" coming from an upstairs window. He thereupon gave the order to fire.

According to the three young men, they were on the second floor of the house and completely bewildered by the barrage of fire that was unleashed against it. As hundreds of bullets crashed through the first and second-story windows and ricocheted off the walls, they dashed to the third floor. Protected by a large chimney, they huddled in a closet until, during a lull in the firing, they were able to wave an item of clothing out of the window as a sign of surrender. They were arrested as snipers.

The firing from rifles and machine guns had been so intense that in a period of a few minutes it inflicted an estimated $10,000 worth of damage. One of a pair of stone columns was shot nearly in half.

Jailed at the 10th Precinct Station sometime Wednesday night R.R. and his two companions were taken from their cell to an "alley court," police slang for an unlawful attempt to make prisoners confess. A police officer, who has resigned from the force, allegedly administered such a severe beating to R.R. that the bruises still were visible two weeks later.

R.R.'s 17-year-old brother had his skull cracked open, and was thrown back into the cell. He was taken to a hospital only when other arrestees complained that he was bleeding to death.

At the preliminary hearing 12 days later the prosecution presented only one witness, the National Guard captain who had given the order to fire. The police officer who had signed the original complaint was not asked to take the stand. The charges against all three of the young men were dismissed.

Nevertheless, the morning after the original incident, a major metropolitan newspaper in another section of the country composed the following banner story from wire service reports:

DETROIT, July 27 (Thursday)—Two National Guard tanks ripped a sniper's haven with machine guns Wednesday night and flushed out three shaggy-haired white youths. Snipers attacked a guard command post and Detroit's racial riot set a modern record for bloodshed. The death toll soared to 36, topping the Watts bloodbath of 1966 in which 35 died and making Detroit's insurrection the most deadly racial riot in modern U.S. history.

In the attack on the sniper's nest, the Guardsmen poured hundreds of rounds of .50 caliber machine gun fire into the home, which authorities said housed arms and ammunition used by West Side sniper squads.

Guardsmen recovered guns and ammunition. A reporter with the troopers said the house, a neat brick home in a neighborhood of $20,000 to $50,000 homes, was torn apart by the machine gun and rifle fire.

Sniper fire crackled from the home as the Guard unit approached. It was one of the first verified reports of sniping by whites. . . .

A pile of loot taken from riot-ruined stores was recovered from the sniper's haven, located ten blocks from the heart of the 200-square block riot zone.

Guardsmen said the house had been identified as a storehouse of arms and ammunition for snipers. Its arsenal was regarded as an indication that the sniping—or at least some of it— was organized.

As hundreds of arrestees were brought into the 10th Precinct Station, officers took it upon themselves to carry on investigations and to attempt to extract confessions. Dozens of charges of police brutality emanated from the station as prisoners were brought in uninjured, but later had to be taken to the hospital.

In the absence of the precinct commander, who had transferred his headquarters to the riot command post at a nearby hospital, discipline vanished. Prisoners who requested that they be permitted to notify someone of their arrest were almost invariably told that: "The telephones are out of order." Congressman Conyers and State Representative Del Rio, who went to the station hoping to coordinate with the police the establishing of a community patrol, were so upset by what they saw that they changed their minds and gave up on the project.

A young woman, brought into the station, was told to strip. After she had done so, and while an officer took pictures with a Polaroid camera, another officer came up to her and began fondling her. The negative of one of the pictures, fished out of a waste basket, subsequently was turned over to the mayor's office.

Citing the sniper danger, officers throughout the department had taken off their bright metal badges. They also had taped over the license plates and the numbers of the police cars. Identification of individual officers became virtually impossible.

On a number of occasions officers fired at fleeing looters, then made little attempt to determine whether their shots had hit anyone. Later some of the persons were discovered dead or injured in the street.

In one such case police and National Guardsmen were interrogating a youth suspected of arson when, according to officers, he attempted to escape. As he vaulted over the hood of an automobile, an officer fired his shotgun. The youth disappeared on the other side of the car. Without making an investigation, the officers and Guardsmen returned to their car and drove off.

When nearby residents called police, another squad car arrived to pick up the body. Despite the fact that an autopsy disclosed the youth had been killed by five shotgun pellets, only a cursory investigation was made, and the death was attributed to "sniper fire." No police officer at the scene during the shooting filed a report.

Not until a Detroit newspaper editor presented to the police the statements of several witnesses claiming that the youth had been shot by police after he had been told to run did the department launch an investigation. Not until three weeks after the shooting did an officer come forward to identify himself as the one who had fired the fatal shot.

Citing conflicts in the testimony of the score of witnesses, the Detroit Prosecutor's office declined to press charges.

Prosecution is proceeding in the case of three youths in whose shotgun deaths law enforcement personnel were implicated following a report that snipers were firing from the Algiers Motel. In fact, there is little evidence that anyone fired from inside the building. Two witnesses say that they had seen a man, standing outside of the motel, fire two shots from a rifle. The interrogation of other persons revealed that law enforcement personnel then shot out one or more street lights. Police patrols responded to the shots. An attack was launched on the motel.

The picture is further complicated by the fact that this incident occurred at roughly the same time that the National Guard was directing fire at the apartment house in which Tonya Blanding was killed. The apartment house was only six blocks distant from and in a direct line with the motel.

The killings occurred when officers began on-the-spot questioning of the occupants of the motel in an effort to discover weapons used in the "sniping." Several of those questioned reportedly were beaten. One was a Negro ex-paratrooper who had only recently been honorably discharged, and had gone to Detroit to look for a job.

Although by late Tuesday looting and fire-bombing had virtually ceased, between 7:00 and 11:00 P.M. that night there were 444 reports of incidents. Most were reports of sniper fire.

During the daylight hours of July 26th, there were 534 such reports. Between 8:30 and 11:00 P.M. there were 255. As they proliferated, the pressure on law enforcement officers to uncover the snipers became intense. Homes were broken into. Searches were made on the flimsiest of tips. A Detroit newspaper headline aptly proclaimed: "Everyone's Suspect in No Man's Land."

Before the arrest of a young woman IBM operator in the city assessor's office brought attention to the situation on Friday, July 28th, any person with a gun in his home was liable to be picked up as a suspect.

Of the 27 persons charged with sniping, 22 had charges against them dismissed at preliminary hearings, and the charges against two others were dismissed later. One pleaded guilty to possession of an unregistered gun and was given a suspended sentence. Trials of two are pending.

In all, more than 7,200 persons were arrested. Almost 3,000 of these were picked up on the second day of the riot, and by midnight Monday 4,000 were incarcerated in makeshift jails. Some were kept as long as 30 hours on buses. Others spent days in an underground garage without toilet facilities. An uncounted number were people who had merely been unfortunate enough to be on the wrong street at the wrong time. Included were members of the press whose attempts to show their credentials had been ignored. Released later, they were chided for not having exhibited their identification at the time of their arrests.

The booking system proved incapable of adequately handling the large number of arrestees. People became lost for days in the maze of different detention facilities. Until the later stages, bail was set deliberately high, often at $10,000 or more. When it became apparent that this policy was unrealistic and unworkable, the Prosecutor's office began releasing on low bail or on their own recognizance hundreds of those who had been picked up. Nevertheless, this fact was not publicized for fear of antagonizing those who had demanded a high-bail policy.

Of the 43 persons who were killed during the riot, 33 were Negro and 10 were white. Seventeen were looters, of whom two were white. Fifteen citizens (of whom four were white), one white National Guardsman, one white fireman, and one Negro private guard died as the result of gunshot wounds. Most of these deaths appear to have been accidental, but criminal homicide is suspected in some.

Two persons, including one fireman, died as a result of fallen power lines. Two were burned to death. One was a drunken gunman; one an arson suspect. One white man was killed by a rioter. One police officer was felled by a shotgun blast when his gun, in the hands of another officer, accidentally discharged during a scuffle with a looter.

Action by police officers accounted for 20 and, very likely, 21 of the deaths. Action by the National Guard for seven, and, very likely, nine. Action by the Army for one. Two deaths were the result of action by store owners. Four persons died accidentally. Rioters were responsible for two, and perhaps three of the deaths; a private guard for one. A white man is suspected of murdering a Negro youth. The perpetrator of one of the killings in the Algiers Motel remains unknown.

Damage estimates, originally set as high as $500 million, were quickly scaled down. The city assessor's office placed the loss—excluding business stock, private furnishings, and the buildings of churches and charitable institutions—at approximately $22 million. Insurance payments, according to the State Insurance Bureau, will come to about $32 million, representing an estimated 65 to 75 percent of the total loss.

By Thursday, July 27, most riot activity had ended. The paratroop-. ers were removed from the city on Saturday. On Tuesday, August 1, the curfew was lifted and the National Guard moved out.

12

THE SAN FRANCISCO COMMUNITY RENEWAL PROGRAM: A SUMMARY *

LOUIS K. LOEWENSTEIN
and
CYRIL C. HERRMANN

Six salient characteristics of this summary report should be clear at the outset:

In the first place, it is not about planning, but rather it is a plan, and specifically it is a plan designed for implementation by a city. Because it is structured to fulfill this objective, it may be considered more properly as a program or a set of criteria to achieve a desired end. Therefore, it pays more attention to the diagnosis of the problem and to the means for achieving action than is customary with most plans.

In the second place, this program is restricted to community renewal and hence does not specifically cover such aspects of urban planning as transportation or urban design. It is, however, far broader in scope than are most such studies in the sense that it is concerned with all aspects of the subject: residential, commercial, and industrial renewal and all portions of the city.

In the third place, the implementation is time-phased with a base line of 1966 and the period of time for the action program is twelve years, which is somewhat less than is to be found in most conventional planning efforts. These dozen years are divided into two six-year periods and in this fashion the program is tied into the city's capital budgeting program.

Fourth, this program is policy oriented and, therefore, relates physical renewal to human needs. In this respect it is quite differ-

*Reprinted from *Taming Megalopolis* (Garden City: Doubleday Anchor, 1967), pp. 798-819. By permission of Professor H. Wentworth Eldredge and the authors.

ent from the more orthodox plans and programs which either pay only lip service to the notion that planning is for people or tend to compartmentalize population in one chapter and physical development in another. One reason for this integrative appearance is the fact that a systems analysis approach was used in the preparation of the study and therefore explicit consideration was given to the interdependence of such factors as housing needs, the location of public facilities, and population growth.

Fifth, this section focuses on the problems of one city, San Francisco, and draws in depth from a recent study which was made to suggest solutions to these problems in terms of tools currently available to those who are charged with urban redevelopment.

Finally, this program evolved from the development of a computer model of a residential housing market. This simulation model was designed to achieve the following purposes:

1. To identify and assess the impact of alternative long-range strategies and programs for renewal and development of the city.

2. To serve as an ongoing tool of city government to assist city officials in keeping the program which emerged up to date in the light of changing conditions and changing goals.

3. To have available on a continuing basis a method for testing the consequences of various renewal actions before they actually took place on the ground.

Community renewal is a set of tools and programs designed to eliminate blight, to preserve sound residential and nonresidential areas and to improve others, in accordance with the city's goals and objectives. Thus, how these tools and programs are used depends on the purposes toward which they are directed. Based on our review of various public statements and documents, we have postulated a set of renewal goals and objectives which are both attainable and consistent. These include economic goals and residential goals.

RENEWAL GOALS AND OBJECTIVES

Economic Goals and Objectives

The best opportunities for achieving the largest total income in San Francisco, and ultimately its best distribution, appear to lie in the fields of finance, service, and related activities, and of certain types of specialized manufacturing. Therefore, such activities should be designed to provide the necessary space and facilities for these specific types of activities:

Administrative headquarters for Bay region and Northern California commercial and industrial enterprises.

The port and port-related activities.

Metropolitan distribution and marketing activities.

Metropolitan specialty shopping activities.

Government office and institutional activities.

Cultural, entertainment and convention facilities.

New "incubator"-type firms and enterprises.

Business, industrial, and professional services to support the above-listed functions.

Local services and trades, beyond the categories listed, to serve San Franciscans.

Industrial Goals and Objectives

In view of the benefits to be received from the growth of manufacturing activities which require a high degree of job skill, encouragement should be given to manufacturing activities which need such skills, which can operate in a centralized urban location, and which are compatible with the efforts to expand the finance and service sectors.

To meet the needs of this type of manufacturing activity, efforts should be made to provide the job skills necessary, through job training and re-training programs aimed at upgrading the skills of the resident population. Efforts also should be made to ensure the availability of suitable industrial space by eliminating deficient buildings that cannot be economically adapted to modern manufacturing methods, by upgrading facilities that can be economically adapted, by ensuring that existing industrial facilities and areas are preserved and improved, by reducing congestion, and by providing more open space in industrial areas.

Commercial Goals

Since San Francisco's economic future is closely tied to the proper development of its downtown district as an economic,

social, cultural, and political focal point of the Bay Area, a major
goal is to stimulate such development.

Since the city must provide balanced commercial environments
in keeping with the need of its residents and businesses, another
goal is to develop sound, functional, and attractive neighborhood
community and commercial centers, properly located so that businesses and their clientele are benefited and so that these centers do
not detract from the strength of the downtown district.

Residential Goals and Objectives

Adequate housing in a decent living environment should be
provided for all San Francisco residents.

Certain population groups have preferred and are likely in
the future to prefer to live and work in a central city such as
San Francisco. They are essential to the proper functioning of
those activities believed most appropriate for the city as the Bay
region center. Therefore, the city should be planning and reviewing
its housing and residential areas for these groups: immigrants
from other countries and other parts of the United States including,
but not limited to, minority groups, whose first jobs may be semi-
skilled and/or in service trades; young adults seeking employment or the anonymity of the central city; enterprising persons
with new businesses to develop or new ideas to exploit or sell;
senior citizens for whom a central city has special advantages;
semi-skilled workers and their families; and business executives,
professional men, shopkeepers, and their families.

Each family or household should by 1978 have a safe, sound,
sanitary and adequately sized dwelling unit at a cost it can afford.
When new housing is not available to meet these requirements,
good rehabilitated housing must be provided.

The private market should be encouraged whenever possible
to meet the needs of all the various groups.

Sufficient public housing or rent supplementation should be
provided for those who cannot afford standard private housing.

Present overcrowding and substandard deteriorated housing
(likely to threaten health and safety) should be eliminated and
such possible further conditions forestalled.

The high quality of existing sound dwelling units should be
maintained.

Maximum opportunity for choice of housing and residential location should be ensured for all people.

Adequate community and cultural facilities, as well as adequate housing, should be provided in appropriate areas to meet the needs of people of all ages, single or married.

Low-density, family-oriented areas and a large number of privately owned homes should remain available, to afford middle-income families alternatives within the city to the suburbs.

A variety of higher-density accommodations should be available for young and retired couples, one-parent families and others not needing or wanting single-family dwellings.

Individuals, community organizations, and private groups should be encouraged to participate in the preparation as well as implementation of citywide and neighborhood renewal plans.

It should be possible for those residents wishing to move to other areas of the city to find adequate housing, and for those with strong neighborhood ties to find in their neighborhood the housing and environmental satisfactions they seek.

The City's diversity should be maintained. The loss of middle-income families with children is harmful to the city; the city should seek to retain its present proportion of families with children— approximately 23 percent of the total number of households.

To accommodate the anticipated population growth, the quantity and type of the city's housing supply must be changed considerably over the next twelve years. Part of the need for additional standard housing units can be met by a substantial upgrading of almost all housing units classified as substandard in 1960. There will still be a need for additional units that only can be met by new construction.

All types and sizes of housing units will be needed. Structures suitable for family living will be especially necessary to attract and retain families with children and to accommodate the population expected for this group. Most of these family-type housing units should have more than five rooms and be priced for the middle- to high-income groups. Although rehabilitation and improvement of existing structures will help, the bulk of the demand will have to be met by new construction.

The city lacks sufficient vacant land to build the increased number of new single-family dwellings needed to accommodate families with children. There are several alternatives. Ways and means must be found to divert a large portion of the households without children to other, more economic, higher-density housing, leaving the bulk of the single-family dwellings to families with children. New cooperative or rental quarters, especially the combination high-rise apartment garden and duplex block which has already proved feasible in one project, are possibilities here. New garden apartment developments with open space and other amenities are also possibilities. New building sites might be "created" on reclaimed waterfront land or other publicly owned land. City-owned properties which may be considered surplus for the uses originally intended could be considered for residential development. It would also be possible to renew (redevelop) existing non-residential surplus sites for single-family residential purposes, as well as to renew (redevelop) existing "marginal" single-family areas for higher-density family housing.

Most of the demand for single-family dwellings will be for larger units of five rooms or more. Zoning changes in height and side-yard requirements which would facilitate addition of one or two bedrooms of existing smaller single-family structures would help in meeting the demand for family-type housing.

BARRIERS TO THE LIVING AND WORKING ENVIRONMENT AND WAYS TO OVERCOME THEM

In its efforts to achieve its housing and renewal goals and objectives, the city faces and must overcome a series of barriers which are economic or social in character. Some of the barriers are common to all central cities struggling for environmental improvement. Others, however, are unique to San Francisco, stemming from its history or topography, or special economic or social structure.

Barriers to the Improvement of the Living Environment

These Include:

Low Income. A substantial portion of San Francisco's population has income too low to enable purchase or rental of new or rehabilitated housing.

Age of Structures In 1960, 95 percent of San Francisco's substandard or seriously substandard housing units were more than thirty years old and 99 perent were more than twenty years old. Not all older property is in poor condition, but keeping it in good condition requires more maintenance and repair than is required for newer housing. For this reason, the age of the city's housing units is of serious concern.

HIGH PERCENTAGE OF RENTAL HOUSEHOLDS. In 1960, 65 percent of the housing units were rental units—one of the highest percentages of any major United States city. This situation poses a potential problem, since experience indicates that housing standards in rental structures tend to be lower than in owner-occupied structures. Persons who own the homes in which they live are more likely to maintain their rental properties. The number of renter-occupied structures is likely to increase in the foreseeable future. This will require public policies designed to induce the owners—be they resident in San Francisco or elsewhere—to maintain and when necessary improve their properties.

HIGH COST OF HOUSING. Serious deterrents to the construction of new housing in San Francisco, particularly for the lower- and moderate-income groups, are the high cost of land and the high cost of construction, particularly in hilly areas. The cost of rehabilitating existing dwelling units is also high. If the city's housing and renewal goals are to be met, financial aids will have to be provided to developers of certain types of housing for specially disadvantaged groups, and to landlords of existing housing to allow them to rehabilitate their own property.

RESIDENTIAL SEGREGATION OF RACIAL AND ETHNIC MINORITIES. The tendency to segregate racial and ethnic minorities forces these groups to pay an inordinate proportion of their income for housing. The supply of housing proportion available to minority groups is restricted, causing available structures to become overcrowded and higher-than-normal rents to be established. It also makes it possible and profitable for certain landlords to maintain substandard facilities. Minority groups are disadvantaged in their efforts to find decent housing, and the number of substandard and ultimately seriously substandard housing is significantly increased. Unless the housing market is open to all races and ethnic groups, the limited supply available to them will continue to be of poorer quality.

LIMITED CONCERN FOR HOUSING QUALITY. Census information indicates that many occupants of low-rental housing pay a relatively low proportion of their income for rent. A significant number of these occupants probably could increase their rent to obtain standard housing and still not suffer financial hardship. The reason they do not is indicated by some of the findings of our special study on Renewal Attitudes. This study revealed that many people have limited concern for the quality of the physical environment and hence may pay comparatively little for housing. This limited concern hinders a continued improvement of the housing stock.

TAXATION POLICIES. San Francisco relies heavily on the real property tax for its revenues. The ratio of property taxes to total revenue is one of the highest in the state. Moreover, the burden of taxation is tending to fall more heavily on the improvements on the land itself. With this trend and the threat of the increasing tax rate, owners may be reluctant to improve their property, fearing that the increase in taxes will nullify the benefits of the improvements. This is particularly important in connection with substandard property, since the value of the improvements is low and the value of the land may be increasing.

HIGH COST OF INVESTMENT CAPITAL IN DECLINING AREAS. Owners of property in declining areas find it very difficult to obtain the capital required to rehabilitate or remodel their property. This denies to such owners the opportunity to increase their income by upgrading their property. Consequently, many owners seek additional income by further subdividing or undermaintaining their property, or by overcrowding existing living quarters. The result is aggravation of an already deteriorating situation. If San Francisco is to be successful in maintaining and upgrading its residential environment, means must be found for property owners in these areas to obtain reasonable financing for housing improvement.

RELUCTANCE OF PROPERTY OWNERS TO ACT INDIVIDUALLY. Significant improvements in housing require more than individual action. Many individuals refuse to improve their property because there is no indication that others in the neighborhood will do likewise. The value of any one property depends in great part on the quality of the neighborhood in which it is located. Unless potential investors are convinced that their effort would be part of an active program to upgrade the quality of the entire neighborhood, they are unlikely to invest in any improvements to their properties, and the entire neighborhood will continue to deteriorate.

LACK OF KNOWLEDGE AND EXPERIENCE REGARDING HOME IMPROVEMENTS. Many inexperienced owners need advice on how to make satisfactory and economical improvements and on how to select a reliable rehabilitation contractor. The lack of knowledge may be a sufficient deterrent to turn a general desire and willingness to improve housing into inaction.

ENVIRONMENTAL DEFICIENCIES. Serious environmental and amenity deficiencies detract from the desirability of many areas and inhibit homeowners' willingness to invest in property improvement. The success of efforts to encourage homeowners and owners of rental property to invest more in housing improvements will depend in large part on the city's willingness to do its share by investing in public improvements designed to correct these environmental deficiencies.

Tools and Programs to Overcome Residential Improvement Barriers

Various tools and programs are available to deal with barriers to improvement of housing and the living environment. They will not completely eliminate the barriers, but if they are employed with vigor and imagination they can significantly lessen the harmful effects of such obstacles. Some of these tools and programs—e.g., provision of social services, the antipoverty program, education programs, job training—have not traditionally been viewed as urban renewal measures. However, since they are designed to increase income, and thus eliminate perhaps the most significant barrier to improvement—that of limited financial ability—they must be viewed as integral parts of a renewal program.

Code enforcement is the principal tool which can be used to overcome the barriers of age of structures, high cost of investment capital, and reluctance of property owners to act individually. Housing code enforcement is the process by which city inspectors examine dwellings to determine whether they comply with the code, which sets minimum standards for physical condition, maintenance, and occupancy of all housing and which requires basic equipment and facilities. Housing code enforcement is both a regulatory activity undertaken by the city to protect public health and safety by assuring that all housing is safe and sanitary, and a service to property owners.

Many environmental deficiencies can be corrected through the city's Capital Improvement Program, through spot clearance (using powers derived from a particular urban renewal project called a Conservation and Rehabilitation Project), through amortization provisions in a zoning ordinance, through sign control ordinances and through street tree planting programs.

In some areas of the city, housing cannot be economically brought to a sound condition through code enforcement alone and environmental deficiencies cannot be corrected by the means just described. In these instances the urban renewal tool of clearance and redevelopment is appropriate.

A number of tools and programs are directed toward eliminating the barrier of inadequate earnings' capability, including: housing for low-income individuals, moderate-income private housing constructed under Section 221 (d) 3 of the National Housing Act, and housing for the elderly, constructed under Section 230 of the National Housing Act. Such programs as vocational training, adult education, and retraining programs upgrade earning capability; people can then earn more and thus afford better housing.

Other tools and programs operate directly to increase the amount of income available for housing. For example, rehabilitation grants to low-income homeowners, provided in the Housing Act of 1965, permit them to undertake work which they would otherwise be unable to do.

Barriers to the Improvement of the Working Environment

The major barriers to improving the city's working environment include obsolescent structures, limited room for expansion, high labor cost, high land cost and assembly problems, taxation problems, limited available financing, and environmental deficiency.

Tools and Programs to Overcome Barriers to Commercial and Industrial Renewal

The tools and programs available to overcome these barriers are, briefly: (a) clearance and redevelopment, which provide a means to eliminate obsolete structures, provide limited room for expansion, reduce high land costs, and solve land parcel assembly problems; (b) shifting the ratio of taxes to place more emphasis on land and less on buildings to possibly alleviate property tax problems; and (c) cooperation of the city in zoning, code enforcement, and provision of utilities and transportation access to eliminate environmental deficiencies. Solutions to the problems of financing include the establishment of a public or semi-public development corporation, or of a development credit corporation to increase the supply of loanable funds, and similar forms of financial assistance.

LONG-RANGE POLICIES AND PROGRAM
FOR RENEWAL

The information on changes in population, housing, income, and economic activity developed as part of the CRP indicates that some changes of emphasis of policy guiding San Francisco's renewal programs will be necessary if the city is to meet its goals and objectives. Many of the CRP goals and objectives can be achieved directly through clearance and redevelopment, neighborhood conservation, code enforcement, and public housing, as well as through various financial aids for low-income and moderate-income housing. But these elements should be only part of a broader program for community improvement which includes city services, public works, and socio-economic programs. The policies recommended are designed to provide direction and focus not merely for urban renewal activity, but for such a broad program of community improvement and development.

The proposed over-all policy or strategy to provide an adequate housing supply and attractive physical environment to meet the needs of the projected population may be briefly summarized as follows:

The needs of upper- and middle-income groups are to be met by advancing the quality of existing housing and the physical environment as incomes rise, by encouraging private enterprise to provide new housing where needed (also where necessary, using various special financial aids), and by renewal programs aimed at maintaining and improving the quality of the city's neighborhoods, particularly those deemed uniquely suited for family living.

The needs of lower-income groups are to be met by rent supplements to lower-income persons to permit them to pay for new private housing, by providing standard housing from the existing stock, by direct public investment in new or rehabilitated low-rent housing, and by job-creating and income-improvement programs designed to enhance the earning capacity of lower-income groups so that their incomes will rise and they will thus be able to afford standard housing from their own resources.

To improve the economic base of the entire city, it is recommended that various renewal powers be used to put underutilized commercial and industrial areas to more productive uses.

KEY ELEMENTS OF OVER-ALL POLICY

Within this over-all renewal policy, certain specific policies are considered critical to the achievement of the city's goals and objectives.

Maintaining and Upgrading Existing Housing Stock

Even if new construction is carried on at an increased rate in the years ahead, most San Franciscans in 1978 will be living in housing built before 1939. Some of this existing housing stock is already in poor condition; much of the good housing will need careful maintenance and periodic repairs if it is to remain in good condition. An important element of renewal strategy, therefore, is to make best use of the city's housing stock; to preserve what can be brought to present-day standards, and to retire the obsolete and the irreparable.

To date, the city's residential renewal efforts have been directed primarily at the "bottom" of the housing quality range—the most dilapidated structures in the most seriously blighted areas. We recommend that, while work is continued at the bottom of the housing scale, there should be a major shift in renewal policy to arresting incipient blight. Along with this shift of emphasis to the "middle range" areas, public efforts at the top of the quality scale should be expanded by use of maintenance and surveillance programs.

Renewing Residential Areas for the Present Residents

The primary objective of residential renewal is to provide decent homes and living environments for all citizens of the community. To achieve this objective, it has been necessary or desirable in most cities, including San Francisco, to substantially change the nature and character of the land use in blighted areas. The result has been extensive clearance of houses and other buildings and the relocation of the residents. Neighborhoods programmed for clearance have usually been low-income areas which after redevelopment have generally been repopulated by higher-income groups. Similar results have been seen in many areas designated for rehabilitation; in many instances code enforcement has had similar effects.

This approach to urban renewal admittedly meets the goal of providing decent homes and living environment, though it does so only by relocation. (According to Federal Law, persons displaced by federally assisted renewal projects must be relocated in decent, safe, and sanitary dwellings within their financial means.) However, relocation, no matter how sensitively handled, has a number of disadvantages, and may often result in "pushing the blight around" to other areas of the city.

Until recently, the tools and programs available have left little alternative to heavy relocation than leaving the area completely untouched. Now, however, new urban renewal tools, especially those provided for in the Housing Act of 1965, make it feasible to adopt an alternative policy for carrying out the objectives of residential renewal: namely, rebuilding, rehabilitation, and restoring areas for the use and benefit of people presently living in the neighborhood, if they desire to remain there after renewal.

The principal tools and programs now available are:

Rent supplements for tenancy and ownership to low-income families in 221 (d) 3 housing.

Rehabilitation grants to low-income owners for repair of their homes.

Broadening of authority of local housing authorities to buy or lease existing housing units for low-income families.

Low-interest (3 percent) rehabilitation loans and

Anti-poverty, manpower training and development, vocational education, and other programs designed to improve economic and social well-being of low- and moderate-income households.

With these financial and other programs, it should be possible to provide decent, safe, and sanitary housing that every resident can afford. Therefore, we recommend that San Francisco adopt a policy of renewing residential areas for their present residents if those residents want to remain there after renewal. The city and residents involved would benefit from this policy because it would minimize relocation of those for whom relocation poses the greatest difficulty; help to stabilize neighborhoods and also allow for orderly transition in other neighborhoods; ease the pressure on the limited supply of low-cost housing; minimize the public resources required, not only for clearance but also for direct construction; and permit the maintenance of a viable social structure in a neighborhood.

The use of this policy should be tempered with concern that it does not result in perpetuating ghettos of racial or income classes. Renewal must be of such high quality that some different racial and income groups will be attracted into the areas being renewed.

This recommended policy should be applied to code enforcement and neighborhood conservation efforts, as well as in urban renewal projects.

Linking Physical Renewal with Human Resources Development

Social planning and physical renewal planning must function together if each is to do its job properly. Decisions made in physical planning and renewal have significant social ramifications. On the other hand, decisions about social services and social programs influence where people live and their physical environmental requirements. The quality of social services and facilities available in a neighborhood is crucial to the success or failure of physical renewal programs.

A continuous process of neighborhood improvement concerned as much with human factors as with physical factors must be established. Once a program of neighborhood improvement is initiated, increased individual pride and motivation can well follow.

The formal linking of social and physical planning will not be easy. New administrative mechanisms will have to be devised to achieve it. A formal link in renewal programs, drawing heavily on a community action (anti-poverty) program, is recommended as a central policy and approach in those residential areas requiring extensive treatment and renewal.

Renewal Treatment in Every Area—A Citywide Approach

The various parts of the city have grown, developed, and changed differently and thus have different renewal problems and needs. Some areas have so deteriorated that they no longer serve a significant economic or social purpose; they require extensive renewal treatment and possibly rebuilding. Other areas are basically sound but suffer from the abuses of time and the deterioration of the physical environment; they will require selective renewal treatment to restore them to a sound condition and improve environmental amenities. Other relatively new areas are generally sound and will require only general maintenance. When so defined, every area of the city needs some type of "renewal treatment," ranging from actions designed merely to maintain the present high quality to more extensive actions which involve rebuilding.

The achievement of renewal objectives in every area requires the programming of both private and public actions. Accordingly, the CRP considers "renewal treatment" to mean a combination of private and public actions, taken in sequence, for any given area, to maintain or restore high quality, prevent deterioration, or eliminate deficiencies.

The need for a citywide approach to urban renewal activity has become obvious as more and more communities, including San Francisco, have shown the project-by-project approach to be incapable of dealing with the huge renewal task facing them. Such an approach was not even eliminating blighted areas at the same rate at which blight was occurring in other parts of the city.

At present, legislation and administrative procedures do not reflect this expanding concept of urban renewal. State enabling legislation in California, as in other states, is still project-oriented. Federal financial assistance is largely limited to designated urban renewal projects, although under the Housing Act of 1965 provision is made for the first time for grants to cities to carry out programs of concentrated code enforcement without any specific project orientation. As part of the citywide approach to renewal, we recommend that the city not only designate specific urban renewal projects, but also use its ongoing tools and programs. The key to this approach is programmed code enforcement by means of frequent inspections and careful followups for violations, combined with the investment and reinvestment. Equally essential is a citizenry informed as to the objectives of the renewal program and convinced of its usefulness. Another essential element is the integration of a variety of public services, such as law enforcement, refuse collection, and street tree planting.

Types of Treatment Areas, Policies and Approach

Because all areas require some type of renewal treatment, the city was divided into appropriate "treatment areas." Each treatment area category requires a different approach to renewal, including its own mix of tools and programs, to reflect the different physical, social and economic conditions, the severity of the problems, and the renewal and development opportunities. The categories employed for the long-range renewal program were residential re-building areas, residential improvement areas, residential maintenance areas, industrial-commercial rebuilding areas, and industrial-commercial improvement areas, and industrial-commercial maintenance areas.

Treatment areas, it should be emphasized, are only general categories reflecting broad similarities and conditions, problems, and opportunities; even within each area conditions vary. Their boundaries should not be considered precise or fixed; they are intended to indicate general location and approaches to renewal treatment.

The recommended approaches for the various categories reflect the key elements of the over-all renewal policy described above. For example, the recommended policy for residential rebuilding areas calls for a careful coordination of physical renewal tools and social-economic programs in a time-phased plan of action.

There are five types of renewal treatment "mechanisms" available for each treatment area category. These are:

(a) Clearance and Redevelopment Project. This treatment mechanism is appropriate for many parts of rebuilding areas which cannot otherwise be restored to a sound condition. Federal financial assistance is available for such a project. Where appropriate, this mechanism should be combined and coordinated with the human resources plan.

(b) Conservation and Rehabilitation Project. This treatment mechanism is appropriate for some parts of rebuilding areas and for those improvement-type neighborhoods with a high incidence of housing and environmental deficiencies correctable without substantial clearance. This type of federally assisted urban renewal project is designed to restore the economic and social values of deteriorating residential areas which are basically sound and worth conserving and in which existing buildings, public facilities, and improvement can be economically renewed to a long-term sound condition. Clearance is confined to "spot" clearance to remove blighting influences and buildings unfeasible of rehabilitation, or to provide land for public improvements of facilities. To qualify for this type of treatment under the Federal program, the area must contain such deficiencies that public action is necessary to eliminate and prevent deterioration or blight. The use of this approach makes certain key financial and other aids available, and thus benefits owners and residents. Where appropriate, this treatment mechanism should be combined and coordinated with a human resources plan.

(c) Concentrated Code Enforcement Coupled with Environmental Improvements. This treatment mechanism is appropriate for improvement-type neighborhoods where housing and environmental deficiencies are not so serious as to require a conservation-rehabilitation approach, but are serious enough to require building-by-building compliance and a concentrated environmental upgrading effort. This treatment mechanism has been employed by the city for several years. A new provision of the Housing Act of 1965 established the authority for "programs of concentrated-code enforcement in deteriorated or deteriorating areas in which such enforcement, together with those public improvements to be provided by the locality, may be expected to arrest the decline of the area." Under this provision, the federal government will make grants to a city totalling up to two-thirds of the cost of planning and effecting such programs. These costs may include the provision and repair of necessary streets, curbs, sidewalks, street lights, tree planting, and similar improvements. Homeowners in these areas will be eligible for Section 220 FHA insured rate-market interest loans (which are generally more liberal than conventional loans), for the new three percent interest rehabilitation loans, and for urban renewal relocation aids.

(d) District Housing Inspection and Public Improvements through the City's Capital Improvement Program. This treatment mechanism is appropriate where housing and environmental deficiencies are minor or nonexistent, and therefore is appropriate for certain improvement type of neighborhoods as well as for "maintenance" areas of the city. Under District Housing Inspection, an inspector is assigned to a district on a permanent basis. This type of code enforcement program can prevent the deterioration of existing housing, forestall illegal conversions and overcrowding, and effect a gradual upgrading of the quality of the housing.

This type of code enforcement is best employed where housing conditions are generally good but where the age of buildings or the existence of rental buildings indicates the need for continuing maintenance. It should also be used where urban renewal projects have been completed, to encourage preservation of the values created through renewal and to prolong the usefulness of these areas. Combined with district housing inspection would be the provision of public improvements through the city's Capital Improvement Program.

(e) Reconditioning. This treatment mechanism is appropriate in neighborhoods requiring more extensive treatment but which are not scheduled for redevelopment, conservation, and rehabilitation, or concentrated code enforcement to a standard just short of requiring correction of conditions which necessitate major structural changes or improvements, but do not constitute an immediate health or safety hazard or detract from general livability of the structure. Such reconditioning would be designed to control overcrowding, eliminate hazards, and enforce sound housekeeping and maintenance practices.

THE SIMULATION MODEL

These policies and approaches culminated in a citywide action program which recommended a different type of renewal treatment for each area in San Francisco. The feasibility of this program was tested by means of a simulation model on a computer. The model was in effect a replication of a residential land and building space market in San Francisco. It was purposely designed to be sensitive to public policy decisions and city policy problems. The effects of public action controls on the market were evaluated in the program by introducing into the model alternative hypothetical public actions and goals. An analysis of these effects provided a basis for developing a long-range strategy in the program for renewal. Public actions were introduced in the model as they affected the operation of the real estate market either by interfering with, influencing, or controlling its function. These actions took the form of a zoning code which prohibited certain changes in the use of space from taking place. They also took the form of code enforcement in renewal projects which "artificially" introduced changes in the use and condition of space. Other public actions which were used included:

(1) Financial measures such as tax changes or cost subsidies which affected the price and the quantity and/or quality of the available housing.

(2) Public improvements which altered the relevant attraction of certain neighborhoods in the City.

This in turn affected the demand for space in the neighborhoods and thereby induced spontaneous private investment and rehabilitation construction in such areas. The result and effect of space usage was evaluated in terms of the foregoing City goals and objectives. In this way a time phase program of public actions was able to be selected in order to achieve the objectives of the renewal policy.

Each individual decision-maker was not identified and replicated in the computer. Instead, all those decision-makers who behave in a similar manner were grouped together. Consequently, the City's 1960 population was divided into 114 individual groups. Each group was selected to reflect similar income, family size, race, age, and housing preference. The groups were programmed to be living in 106 neighborhoods, defined through consideration of significant similarities. All dwelling units were grouped into twenty-seven different categories, each of which exists in a variety of physical conditions. These houses were allocated among the 106 neighborhoods indicated by the 1960 census. Investors were postulated as being willing to build new units or rehabilitate existing units whenever it became profitable to do so. The rules that govern this profitability were tied to the yield they will obtain, the price of these buildings, and the cost of such new construction and rehabilitation.

The model was programmed to be dynamic. That is, the computer was instructed so that all the decision-making groups would interact with each other in a manner that replicates their actions in the real world. The model was designed to permit the skilled planner to consider the ramifications of alternate plans before they were executed, but it was not intended to be a highly accurate forecasting tool. It is unique in that the skilled interpreter can use it to investigate all possible combinations of plans and results. It is not tied to a few statistical variables whose usefulness is restricted to specific situations. Neither is it tied to the unrealistic assumption that history will repeat itself and that projections can be made from statistically derived past trends.

Two computer runs were needed for evaluation because the model's primary strength lies in its ability to suggest the *relative* impact of public actions. That is, the most meaningful evaluation involves a comparison between a simulation of the market with the inclusion of public actions and another simulation without these actions. Therefore, one run is needed as a conditional prediction of the housing future of San Francisco under stipulated conditions that *do not* include the plans or programs we desire to evaluate.

The second public action run was identical to the base run, except that it included a simulation of a type of code enforcement, zoning, clearance, and public housing actions that was recommended in the Community Renewal Program. The public actions were simulated to test the efficacy of the recommended program items on the housing market and their ability to push it in the direction of improving the quality of housing available to the residents of San Francisco.

The analysis of these two runs provided the basis for increased confidence in the propriety of the recommended Community Renewal Program and confirmed the usefulness of a model in dealing with a complex system. For example, the public action run indicated that during the six years of the recommended code enforcement program there was a reduction in the number of these substandard and seriously substandard units by approximately nine percent, while the total number of housing units was increasing. On the other hand, the increase in housing units brought with it a three percent *increase* in low-quality units when code enforcement was not simulated. The two runs indicated that code enforcement encouraged the private market to invest in rehabilitation at a rate forty percent higher than in the absence of code enforcement.

13

LEADERSHIP IN A LARGE MANAGER CITY: THE CASE OF KANSAS CITY *

STANLEY T. GABIS

Abstract. Municipal leadership in Kansas City centers on the nonpartisan principle and the council-manager plan. Unlike many other cities with nonpartisan requirements, Kansas City has produced a nonpartisan system that has proved workable over a twenty-year period. But continuance depends on the viability of the Citizens Association, a nonpartisan—or bipartisan—group which has dominated Kansas City politics from its inception in 1941 to the present time, with a four-year break from 1959 to 1963. The Association has experienced some difficulty in keeping its leadership vital and in maintaining a sufficiently broad base to permit participation by the diverse elements of the community. The leadership responsibility of the Association, resumed in 1963, is of major importance in maintaining a stable source of power. Also, relations between the mayor and the manager are crucial, as experiences in the immediate past have shown. Under present arrangements, official and private groups are co-operating in achieving public objectives. A new sophistication is now being demanded of those to whom the manager is accountable.

Any description or assessment of municipal leadership must take into consideration the larger governmental system of which the city is a part and the basic principles which underlie the frame of government. Our treatment moves in both of these directions. Kansas City has enjoyed a special brand of government for the past two decades. It has adhered, with only one major lapse, to a nonpartisan system. Kansas City's nonpolitical character is plausible enough if construed in a narrow sense.

*Reprinted from *The Annals*, 353 (May 1964), 52-63. By permission of the American Academy of Political and Social Science, and the author.

One learns very soon that the city is regarded as a special case among seasoned politicians. It is a "chosen" city, scarcely approximating the "New Jerusalem" but partaking nonetheless of the virtue of a city that has been newly purged. One need only read the remarkable address of Governor Lloyd Stark to the Missouri legislature during the closing-out of the Pendergast system. In recommending that the state regain control of the Kansas City police department, Stark referred to the "arbitrary and despotic power of partisan politics" and "political slavery" and declared that "in the enforcement of law, politics is public enemy number one."[1] Even today the state retains control of the city police through a local board with members appointed by the governor. This is scarcely a negligible factor in city administration, for the charge on the general city budget for police services is slightly over 20 percent and carries very limited budgetary review by the city. The purge some twenty-four years ago had major consequences for municipal leadership, for it created new jurisdictional relationships and a different style of direction. Some might hold that it merely allowed the principles of the charter adopted in 1925 to find expression after lying dormant for fifteen years under the heavy weight of unenlightened despotism.

The county, state, and nation are given over to politics in the full sense of the word. The city, under the dispensation of the early-twentieth-century reformers, can, because of its different nature, operate on a radically different theory. Nonpartisanship and the city-manager idea presuppose a unique quality and blend of rationality, personal detachment, and know-how which can find application in the municipality because its problems are thought to be mainly technical. We have interviewed experienced politicians who are deeply immersed in state and county politics. When the subject of Kansas City was raised, they drew a curtain between the city and the rest of the state. The city, they asserted, can be treated as a technical rather than a political problem. We understood this as a sincere act of faith, will, and intelligence. This is the art of government in the modern sense, for it represents an expression of man's vision and his intention to superimpose on a large human collectivity a set of principles with the full expectation of achieving a desired result.

This radical subordination of political passion and involvement to a dispassionate and technical attitude presupposes certain values

[1]*Kansas City Star*, March 23, 1939, p. 8.

and assumptions about the nature of local government. A consensus is more easily arrived at in the city. Voters can think of issues rather than party labels. The public interest is much more readily discernible in local government, for the voter can readily judge the effect of a proposed program. Local issues can be more readily resolved on their merits than by becoming mixed with questions of party organization, survival, and prestige. An individual's voting behavior can be neatly stratified so that he is encouraged to deal with local issues without getting involved with national or state matters. Individual perspectives derived from socioeconomic status or ethnic background do not seem to have the same relevance in the local setting where men are much closer together and therefore better able to understand each other. Because local government is primarily a technical problem, it is much easier to develop precise, formal criteria for the valid selection of experts to man the highest administrative posts. The professional city manager symbolizes a belief in the great value of technical know-how in solving the city's problems. The mayor can be reduced primarily to a ceremonial figure who propagates the faith and co-ordinates the consensual activities of the council. He should not be intimately involved with the manager's activities.[2]

This is a rough approximation and summary of the axioms which control nonpartisan government. Some of them are reasonable and, when acted on with prudence and understanding, are essential to making the system work. A few of the axioms are simply fictions which are used, as Eric Fromm says, "to catch mice." Several are self-deceptions sometimes believed by clever men who have suspended critical judgment where the "chosen" city is concerned.

Because we seek to describe leadership in Kansas City in relation to the larger governmental system and the underlying principles and axioms of nonpartisan government, we will try to tie the immediate past to the present and delineate actions which suggest both the opportunities and ambiguities which arise as a result of this system or in spite of it.[3] About a decade ago Paul Appleby

[2]For a good discussion of nonpartisanship, see Edward C. Banfield and James Q. Wilson, *City Politics* (Cambridge, Mass.: Harvard University Press and the Massachusetts Institute of Technology Press, 1963), Chap. 12.
[3]Useful material on the recent background of Kansas City government and politics is found in Howard D. Neighbor, *Metamorphosis of Non-Partisan Politics: Kansas City, Missouri* (Kansas City, Mo.: Community Studies, Inc., 1962); and A. Theodore Brown, *The Politics of Reform: Kansas City's Municipal Government—1925-1950* (Kansas City, Mo.: Community Studies, Inc., 1958).

made an interesting observation on leadership which reflects the orientation of this essay:[4]

> Leadership roles . . . are exercised in influencing, identifying and operating within respective areas of discretion. While such areas of discretion widen and contract with particular leaders and with changes in times and circumstances, they are always confined within limits policed by the public and somewhat roughly made clear by history, institutions and custom.

THE PENDERGAST HERITAGE

Nonpartisan government incorporating the idea of a professional city manager was formally adopted in Kansas City in 1925 with the adoption of a new charter. Despite the letter and spirit of the charter, its central provisions did not become really effective until fifteen years later. The proponents of the new charter had not reflected sufficiently on the fact that all frames of government must operate within a political context with power and normative concerns defining the boundaries of possible action. At the time the charter was adopted, Thomas J. Pendergast controlled the Democratic organization in Kansas City. He apparently understood the realities of power infinitely better than the advocates of charter reform. Rather than oppose the new frame of government, he allowed it to pass, and, when it did, he and his organization simply embraced the new system. He controlled the votes and the council. Under the new plan, the council was easier to control because its numbers had been reduced. Because he controlled the council, he could ratify the selection of the manager. The manager served at the pleasure of the council and Pendergast could be assured that the first manager, Henry F. McElroy, would be responsive to the needs of the Democratic organization as well as his personal requirements. This is exactly how the affair turned out. McElroy was recruited shortly after serving a term as one of the three judges (administrators) of Jackson County.[5]

McElroy held the manager post throughout the period of Pendergast dominance, about fifteen years. During this time, his master

---

[4]Paul H. Appleby, *Morality and Administration in Democratic Government* (Baton Rouge, La.: Louisiana State University Press, 1952), p. 102.
[5]Harry S. Truman served on the court with McElroy. Both were protégés of Pendergast. Truman's loyalty to Pendergast lasted until the end.

gained almost total control of the various factions in Kansas City. His sphere of control during the 1930's included Jackson County, and eventually his influence was strongly felt at the state capitol in Jefferson City. His leadership was state-wide, and this in turn gave him an important voice in national party circles. Since the close of the Pendergast system, Kansas City has not been able to produce another leader with state-wide influence. Furthermore, because there is a tendency of a large unbossed city to generate a number of factions, it is fair to say that, with all its deficiencies, Pendergast rule regulated factional activity and made orderly government possible. When the Democratic factions—or Coalition—returned to power in 1959, there was no individual who had the power and authority to unify the activities of factional representatives in the council. During this four-year period, there was, for all practical purposes, no effective government operating in Kansas City.

Pendergast operated with one-party government based on a deliverable vote. He spread the benefits wide enough so that he controlled the vote of the economically and socially depressed and also commanded the allegiance of a sufficient number of well-born and well-to-do to give his system a legitimate basis. His appointments were skillfully made to assure the continuance of his power and to accomplish the minimum requirements of local government. In exceptionally sensitive areas, such as the judiciary and school board, more than normal care was exercised and some good appointments were made. Pendergast operated as a political virtuoso, showing an enormously shrewd understanding in manipulating people and moving the levers of power. He held no official position, but his return was very large. It consisted of despotic power exercised behind the scenes. At a more mundane level, he benefited considerably from his connections. Firms he owned or in which he had an interest virtually monopolized city and county contracts in the construction field, and pressure was frequently brought to bear on private contractors to do business with his concerns. Probably his unofficial status facilitated this arrangement.[6]

Pendergast's great power and facility bred carelessness and perhaps even boredom. Ordinarily, in a competitive political system, sufficient excitement and variety are generated to keep the interests and attention of the participants at a fairly high pitch. The competi-

[6]See Brown, *op. cit.*, pp. 189ff. for results of audit of city records.

tive element was absent from the system. In his later years, Pendergast derived great pleasure from horse-race betting. His wagers were on a very large scale, which suggested a kind of addiction. In a curious way, his interest in horse racing seemed to overshadow his interest in politics. His trial and imprisonment in 1939 on the grounds of receiving large bribes in connection with insurance rebates came rather suddenly. Behind the breaking up of his power was the United States Department of Justice, indirectly the President of the United States, and more directly the governor of Missouri, for the state superintendent of insurance had collaborated with Pendergast in the payoff scheme.[7]

THE CITIZENS ASSOCIATION
(1941 — 1963)

The fall of the Pendergast regime, accompanied as it was by a scandal of national proportions, was a shattering experience for the people of Kansas City and for the entire state. The Pendergast heritage still lingers more as a monument in ruins.

William Reddig suggests that the McElroy (Pendergast) regime was a businessman's government, that the machine was an instrument of the business community during most of its existence in the twenties and thirties. Observing that the reform group which followed Pendergast was a "businessman's government," he raises the question as to whether reform is compatible with the pursuit of private economic interests. Following Lincoln Steffens, he suggests the possibility "that private economic interests by their very nature required corrupt politics."[8] This is surely an oversimplification and distortion of the political and business process. Human power, whether it be found in politics, business, or any other form of human activity, is subject to abuse. Business interests, because they are private, can prosper at the expense of the public interest and with indifference to it until gradually public qualities are destroyed, carrying private interests with them. There are businessmen who can function effectively in their public as well as in their

[7]Extensively discussed in Maurice M. Milligan, *Missouri Waltz* (New York: Charles Scribner's Sons, 1948). Milligan was the United States District Attorney who investigated the vote frauds of the 1930's. At that time, Senator Truman attempted to block Milligan's reappointment. *Ibid.,* p. 160.
[8]William M. Reddig, *Tom's Town* (Philadelphia: J. B. Lippincott Co., 1947, p. 370.

private roles, and a number of them do. But his point carries weight, for a business oligarchy joined with political power might be more dangerous than a political oligarchy, for it can hide behind the cloak of respectability and call on massive economic power to discriminate against those who disagree.

In the Kansas City experience, the opposite happened. Businessmen with reform interests were prominent in organizing the Citizens Association in 1941. This nonpartisan or bipartisan group has dominated Kansas City political life from its inception to the present time, with a four-year break from 1959 to 1963. The Association was an amalgamation or coalition of a variety of different forces and interests. The professions were probably as widely represented as the business interests. Liberal Democrats, conservative and liberal Republicans, and even some members of the hard-core Democratic organization previously associated with Pendergast found their way into Association ranks. Mr. Thomas Gavin, who was well regarded by the administration during the fifties, was endorsed by the Association and is a good example of the latter. Reddig's concern notwithstanding, an important problem which has always faced the Association is keeping capable businessmen interested and involved.

The gradual decline in the Association's effectiveness during the middle and late fifties was caused by two kinds of problems. The first characterizes all organizations—keeping its leadership vital and replenishing sources of supply. The second, which may be even more difficult, involves maintaining a wide enough base to permit broad participation by the diverse elements of the community. The tendency toward exclusiveness, either in the interest of maintaining purity of doctrine or perhaps even encouraging in a subtle way a social class distinction, limited the base. Labor, Negro, and Italian ethnic groups have, in the past, seldom found their way into the Association. This is beginning to change. Two Negroes were elected to the Council in 1963 and are active in the Association. The only holdover in the new Council, Mr. Sal Capra, has roots in the Italian community. He is a young, ambitious lawyer of the new Italian middle class. His sponsor and uncle, Mr. Alex Presta, was until very recently a major Democratic faction leader who controlled the first ward and relied on lower-class ethnic support. After the 1963 election, Presta retired and moved to the suburbs after admitting that his traditional basis for support was disappearing. The upward mobility of his constituents and major urban-renewal activities took their toll.[9]

There are other specific problems in maintaining the coalition. In the 1959 election, which brought the Democratic factions back into power, there was a serious defection in the Citizens Association which reflected a narrowing of the base. Professor Howard D. Neighbor has made a careful analysis of the defector.[10] He defines the defector as one who was in sympathy with the Citizens Association in 1955 but switched to the Democratic Coalition in 1959. In his sample, almost one fourth of these who voted for the Coalition fit the defector pattern. First, the defectors tended to middle or upper-middle income status. Second, the defector identified with the national Democratic party by almost three to one. Neighbor suggests that it is easier for a Democrat to defect than it is for a Republican, who is more likely to sacrifice his national party preference in the interests of the Citizens Association. This is rather ambiguous. It is true that, inasmuch as Missouri voting behavior is normally Democratic, the Association has been reluctant throughout its history to slate a Republican for mayor. Republicans are slated for the city council in a division with Democrats. Republicans usually require some kind of clearance with the Republican county committee. Doubtless, it is a sacrifice for Republicans to take a Democratic mayor each election year. Until 1963 this did not present any real difficulty. At this time, a defection took place among Republicans. Mr. Dutton Brookfield, a prominent businessman and conservative Republican, deserted the Association and formed a separate group known as the Independent Voters Association (IVA) because he failed to receive the endorsement for mayor. If the public had not been so deeply aroused as a result of the poor record of the Democratic Coalition during the previous four years, there could have been serious consequences for the Association. Though the Democratic Coalition gave its support to Brookfield in an effort to defeat the Association, the public was sufficiently aroused to compensate for the Republican

[9]Studying three precincts of the first ward in Kansas City, Richard A. Watson was able to show a definite trend away from the Democrats as a direct result of urban renewal between 1951 and 1959. See his *The Politics of Urban Change* (Public Affairs Monograph Series No. 3; Kansas City, Mo.: Community Studies, Inc., 1963). The trend has been accentuated since 1959.

[10]Neighbor, *op. cit.,* pp. 149 ff.

defection as well as Coalition support. The Democratic defector faces real difficulties. About the only place a Democrat can go locally is back to the Coalition camp. This is very difficult to do because of past associations. The only other possibility is to form a new grouping, which has the effect of adding another faction to the lengthy list. Recently, a new organization has emerged known as the Democratic Council, composed mainly of younger liberal Democrats who are no longer comfortable in the Association and who have little in common with the regular Democratic factions. Some of the 1959 defectors are to be found in this camp.

THE CITY MANAGER

H. F. McElroy's long tenure as manager depended upon a stable base of power. He had this in Pendergast and the boss-controlled council. The same principle applies to L. P. Cookingham, who succeeded McElroy in 1940 and served to 1959. His source of support was the Citizens Association and its representatives on the council. Cookingham took out an extra margin of insurance by establishing a network of Community Councils throughout the city. These are neighborhood organizations which meet periodically and which were originally established to provide a means for stimulating community interest in their neighborhoods. Professional staff was assigned to work with the Councils. There was no explicit political intention, but, over the years, the political implications of the Councils in helping to provide popular support for the manager became clear to anyone with sensitivity to these matters.[11]

After Cookingham resigned in 1959 there was, and continues to be, speculation as to the cause of his departure. The most obvious and probably most valid reason is that, with the defeat of the Citizens Association in that year, a new group took power and simply did not believe in the manager principle. There was additional speculation. Cookingham, it was asserted, had been in office too long; many petty grievances had piled up over the years; he re-

[11]See A. Theodore Brown, "The Politics and Administration of Welfare," in Edward C. Banfield, *Urban Government* (New York: The Free Press of Glencoe, 1961), p. 552.

stricted his activities to middle and upper income groups; he was mainly interested in the physical, and not the human, side of the city. Perhaps there is some degree of plausibility in all of these criticisms. No profession is without its limitations, and some of them are built into the profession. The city manager is no exception. But the complaints seem very minor when compared with Cookingham's outstanding record over nineteen years. We suggest that the crucial factor lay in the leadership of the Citizens Association and the type of men who were slated for the 1955 council. The decline in Cookingham's fortunes began with the 1955 mayor and council. The manager was fortunate in his first two mayors, John B. Gage and William E. Kemp. They understood that the value of the manager principle lay in the expertise the manager could bring to his job and the relative freedom he had in applying this expertise. Also, the profession adheres to rather well-defined standards and ethics which, if seriously violated, lead almost inevitably to the manager's resignation. H. Roe Bartle, who was mayor from 1955 to 1963, paid voluble lip service to the manager principle but never seemed to understand the quality of initiative which had to be left to the manager. If he understood, his personality and inclinations would not let him follow his understanding. He did not hesitate to eclipse the manager and was unable as leader of the council to restrain some of his more ambitious colleagues from upsetting the equilibrium on which the manager depends.

In the face of ambition and aggressiveness, the manager is defenseless and vulnerable, for he can easily be made to appear an authoritarian figure in a very negative sense. It was exactly this approach which was used very effectively in the 1959 election which led to the unseating of Cookingham. Personalities and attitude counted heavily in this unfortunate denouement of a distinguished public official. One must also add the mounting frustration at the intractability of the city's mounting financial problem, which by 1959 had reached the critical stage. There was no effective political leadership willing to grapple with the problem. The Citizens Association had defaulted on its responsibility. It was not until the city experienced four humiliating years of inaction and factionalism under the Democratic Coalition (1959—1963) that it was prepared to restore its mandate to the Citizens Association. By 1963 the Association had become revitalized and was prepared to reassume responsible leadership.

LEADERSHIP — THREE EXAMPLES

Financial crises

From the middle 1950's to the new administration in 1963, the handling of the financial question illustrated the lack of an effective center of leadership and discipline. In 1953 an earnings tax was recommended by consultants as a solution to the growing money problem. The same year the council refused to support state legislation providing for a distribution of a portion of the state income tax to the city. The question of an earnings tax was seriously considered by the council in 1956. A number of the councilmen immersed themselves in detail and, as a result, arrived at a variety of views that scarcely encouraged a unified approach. A positive decision, lacking in enthusiasm, was reached in February 1956, a month before elections. At that time the councilmen agreed that they would *not* carry the question to the voters but would rely on a citizen group. The earnings tax was decisively rejected.

In the 1959 election, the Democratic Coalition candidates pledged that they would not support an earnings tax if elected. They tied their hands very explicitly. Two years after the Coalition victory, one of its leading members on the council admitted he was mistaken and changed his position. In the 1963 campaign, both candidates for mayor advocated the earnings tax. Following the victory of the Citizens Association in the spring of 1963, Carleton F. Sharpe, a city manager of national standing, was hired. With the new mayor, Ilus W. Davis, and the manager working closely together, a systematic campaign for the tax was mounted. Members of the council devoted a large portion of their time over a period of several months addressing groups throughout the community on the question. The mayor and the manager provided strong leadership throughout the campaign. Almost immediately after his election, the new mayor, faced with a deadline, had proceeded to the state capitol and persuaded state leaders of the need for enabling legislation. Influential community leaders also added their voices. The *Kansas City Star* gave unusually strong press support throughout the entire period, including a series of fairly detailed stories on the difficulties a number of departments were experiencing in their programs as a result of financial limitations. The general picture painted was one of a major city falling behind other cities, departments undermanned in crucial categories, city

maintenance behind schedule and equipment in disrepair or increasingly obsolescent, inadequate vermin-control programs, underpaid
personnel, the absence of an adequate pension plan and other
standard fringe benefits. The picture drawn was very convincing.
Powerful community groups which had been hesitant, opposed,
or lukewarm in 1956 supported the mayor and manager with
a new feeling of confidence that had been generated over a period
of several months. Reluctant labor unions—the earnings tax was
a flat half of one per cent with no exemptions—were brought
into line with a frank appeal to self-interest. Without the tax,
the mayor argued, major public construction would be delayed.
Representatives of the construction unions listened, for they needed
jobs for their members. Only a few unions failed to support the
tax. City employees, firemen, and police were mobilized as far
as etiquette would permit and perhaps even more. Again, self-
interest was a key. Department heads went on the stump and
several proved very effective in portraying in graphic detail what
increased revenue would mean to their departments. The Negro
councilmen who joined the government in 1963, after indicating
an initial concern over the fate of pending proposals on public
accommodations and after receiving reassurance that the needs
of the Negro community would receive sympathetic consideration,
supported the tax and devoted themselves energetically to persuading
their constituents to follow suit. The public accommodations bill
was passed prior to the earnings· tax election but, as a result of
a petition initiated by tavernkeepers, has to be submitted to a
referendum as provided by charter. In the November 1963 referendum, the tax received a required two-thirds endorsement, although
of five badly needed bond issues only one received the necessary
two-thirds required under Missouri law.

Personnel crisis

The leadership and community esprit so completely lacking
in 1956 was present in full force in 1963. Widespread public
confidence in the new administration has permitted the mayor
and manager to deal forthrightly with difficult situations. In one
recent case, the firemen's union persuaded a councilwoman to
propose a resolution providing for an increase in salary for firemen
complementing an increase recently given the police, who are
subject to state direction through a local police board and over

whom the city has no direct control. This move in the council was very embarrassing for the manager. After finances, personnel improvements had been given the next highest priority. When Cookingham had left in 1959, department heads and highly trained staff personnel departed or were pressured into resigning by the new council. When Sharpe assumed his duties in June 1963, he found, with few exceptions, that the departments had been stripped of high caliber personnel, and inadequate city pay levels did not allow their replacement. As new department heads were added, salaries were raised for new heads. This could be done by ordinance in each case. But, below the top posts, the entire classification-pay structure was involved, and the need for a survey was strongly indicated. In the fall of 1963, a broad personnel survey was initiated. It was designed to study the entire range of personnel activity — recruiting, training, health and other fringe benefits — as well as classification and pay. The essence of the approach was a systematic and orderly attack on the entire personnel problem. The city's hand had been forced in the case of the police increase, but, if the firemen were given an across-the-board increase several months before pay adjustments for other city employees, any possibility of installing an effective and rational personnel program would be seriously jeopardized. But, perhaps even more important, the demands of the firemen represented a serious challenge to the authority and prestige of the new manager.

In two dramatic confrontations with firemen at their union hall, Sharpe pleaded with them that they await the personnel report due in March 1964. He assured them of his good intentions and pointed to his record in Hartford. The aggressive leader of the union, a city battalion chief, could not be persuaded, and, for several days, firemen demonstrated by circling city hall carrying placards expressing their grievance in terms unflattering to Manager Sharpe. Although the demonstrations were given wide publicity and the wives of firemen bombarded the manager's office with importunate phone calls, public opinion supported the position of the administration. Sharpe had gone on record at one meeting with the firemen declaring that a new manager would have to be found if the city gave in to the pressure. After several days of demonstration and a series of conferences with union leaders and their counsel, a former councilman who had been one of the leaders in bringing about the demise of Cookingham in 1959, the union decided to suspend its demonstration and await the findings of the personnel study and its implementation.

Kansas City Athletics crisis

Another matter, still unresolved at this writing, concerned the future status of the Kansas City Athletics. This major-league ball team had been brought to Kansas City in 1956 and housed in a refurbished municipal stadium amid great fanfare symbolizing a new stage in the development of the city. The previous council, in April 1963, immediately prior to its departure from office, had granted a new stadium lease to the owner, Mr. Charles O. Finley, on terms that were widely regarded as not in the best interests of the city. The new council, on assuming office, decided for reconsideration and negotiations began anew.

The intensity of public attention during various periods of the renegotiation far exceeded anything else of public importance. It is fair to say that the merger of the private University of Kansas City with the University of Missouri in August 1963 created less stir in the community than the prospect that Finley would take his team elsewhere, as he threatened to do repeatedly over the ensuing months. The news media, especially television, gradually developed a most unattractive picture of Finley showing him with a somewhat battered hat, an unshaved profile, and a grim mouth clenching a cigar stub. Finley became a villain in the eyes of the public. Mayor Davis assumed the burden of the negotiations, although Sharpe was deeply involved. Finley followed a procedure of calculated harassment and, as if by design, demanded meetings at odd intervals which insured the maximum disruption of city business. The climax was reached when the matter was appealed by the city to President Cronin of the American League, who in turn called a conference of American League club owners to consider the matter. Before the issue was resolved in favor of the city, two United States Senators from Missouri, Edward V. Long and Stuart F. Symington, became directly involved. Senator Symington, together with city officials, attended the meeting of club owners in January 1964. The noted attorney, Louis Nizer, was retained by Finley, presumably to add to the efforts of regular attorney Mr. Tom Kean, a prominent Chicago politician. The case caused reverberations throughout the sports world and stimulated several members of the United States Senate to think seriously of re-examining the exemptions which organized baseball enjoys under antitrust laws. Throughout this difficult situation, Manager Sharpe received letters of commiseration from fellow city managers around the county.

What is the meaning of these examples? Several ideas are suggested. Each case had the potentiality of destroying the manager. If he had not received affirmative and thoughtful support from the mayor and council, as well as the news media, his situation might have become completely untenable. Provision for a fixed term of office gives some assurance that a strong wind will not endanger the survival of an official. However, the manager serves at the pleasure of the council. His special vulnerability has to be recognized and understood.

The cases also tend to show how it is possible for problems confronting municipal leaders to become deeply involved with larger political and administrative systems far beyond the purview of the city. In an important respect, it is inaccurate to discuss municipal leadership per se if this means disregarding relationships to the larger system, embracing not only the federal, state, and county jurisdictions but important private groups within the city as well.[12]

SUMMARY ANALYSIS

We return to Appleby's statement which provides the unifying thread of this essay. What he is saying suggests an expansive role for leadership contained in the words "influencing," "identifying," and "operating." There is an area of discretion which varies with individuals and situations. There are limits imposed by the public and traditions of society. We believe all of what he says is illustrated in our remarks.

Twenty-three years ago, the Citizens Association was a new creation. Now it has roots and a tradition. Although it can pass as a major local institution, the possibility of collision with longer established political entities is always possible. Recently, a candidate for Democratic nomination for governor of Missouri sought the endorsement of a major leader of the Citizens Association. The Citizens leader has refused to meet with the candidate for governor for fear of jeopardizing a forthcoming bond referendum. This leader is a liberal Democrat with a brilliant political future, but, for the time being, he has accepted the restraints which nonpartisan leadership

[12]Without the support of the *Kansas City Star* and the Kansas City Chamber of Commerce, the earnings tax would not have been passed. Without their continued support on important issues, the manager could not survive. It is instructive to note that both the manager and the executive vice-president of the Chamber of Commerce were recently recruited from Hartford, Connecticut.

place upon him. The former mayor, H. Roe Bartle, has agreed to serve as the candidate's campaign manager in Jackson County. Bartle no longer feels the need for adopting a nonpartisan role. The point is that we have two established systems in incipient conflict, for one refuses to supplement the other in the political sphere. Who can measure the consequences as far as future personal political fortunes are concerned?

The nonpartisan system seems theoretically impossible, yet it has worked with varying degrees of efficiency for more than two decades. It has a direct effect on strategies of publc leadership. In interviews which we conducted to gather material for this essay, we attempted to discover whether the nonpartisan character of Kansas City hampered it in dealing with partisan state officials. The state and city officials thought there was no hindrance on this score. When the city has to deal with the state, its leaders are required to develop specific group support in the community. If this support is impressive, articulate, and united and its case is a good one, the city receives a sympathetic hearing and has good prospects of getting what it wants. There seems to be a basic reasonableness that transcends partisan considerations.

City-county relationships are different. The city and the county seem to operate in two separate worlds, although their headquarters confront one another on the same street. The Democratic factions control the county and are tied in directly to the state and national political system. None of the values which characterize nonpartisanship is in evidence in the county. Yet some of the most crucial problems confronting the city depend on close cooperation between the two jurisdictions. Law enforcement, property assessment, public health, prisons, and metropolitan area planning require a close relationship between the two. It may well be that the conflict in values is a major barrier to co-operation.

The relationship between the mayor and the manager emerges as an important point for consideration. The relationship between Pendergast and McElroy served to bring about an unusually stable balance. But it was a balance that was not effectively policed by the public. Cookingham achieved an excellent balance with his first two mayors and had a misfortune with the third. Davis and Sharpe have developed an excellent relationship in the new administration. Sharpe does not like the word "politics," but he regards "public relations" as being an exceptionally important function. Government for him includes not only the official side but also private groups that can co-operate with the city in achieving public objectives. This requires a dividing line to avoid having the private sphere control the public. Housekeeping responsibilities are important, but secondary to planning and public relationships. The rationale of the manager principle has shifted in emphasis. With this shift, the manager becomes more vulnerable but more valuable. His expertise is not so much technical as prudential in the classic meaning of the term. A new sophistication is now being demanded on the part of those to whom the manager is accountable.

14

THE MAKING OF
THE NEGRO MAYORS 1967*

JEFFREY K. HADDEN, LOUIS H. MASOTTI,
VICTOR THIESSEN

Throughout most of 1967, black power and Vietnam kept this nation in an almost continual state of crisis. The summer months were the longest and hottest in modern U.S. history—many political analysts even felt that the nation was entering its most serious domestic conflict since the Civil War. Over a hundred cities were rocked with violence.

As the summer gave way to autumn, the interest of the nation shifted a little from the summer's riots to the elections on the first Tuesday of November. An unprecedented number of Negroes were running for office, but public attention focused on three elections. In Cleveland, Carl B. Stokes, a lawyer who in 1962 had become the first Democratic Negro legislator in Ohio, was now seeking to become the first Negro mayor of a large American city. In Gary, Ind., another young Negro lawyer, Richard D. Hatcher, was battling the Republican Party's candidate—as well as his own Democratic Party—to become the first Negro mayor of a "medium-sized" city. And in Boston, Louise Day Hicks, a symbol of white backlash, was conducting a "You know where I stand" compaign to capture the mayorality.

Normally, the nation couldn't care less about who would become the next mayors of Cleveland, Gary, and Boston. But the tenseness of the summer months gave these elections enormous significance. If Stokes and Hatcher lost and Hicks won, could Negroes be persuad-

*Reprinted from *Trans-action, 5,* No. 3 (Jan/Feb 1968), 21-30. By permission of *Trans-action* and the authors. Copyright © 1968 by *Trans-action* Magazine, St. Louis, Missouri.

ed to use the power of the ballot box rather than the power of fire bombs?

Fortunately, November 7 proved to be a triumphant day for racial peace. Stokes and Hatcher won squeaker victories, both by margins of only about 1500 votes; in Boston, Kevin H. White defeated Mrs. Hicks by a 12,000 plurality. Labor leader George Meany was exultant—"American voters have rejected racism as a political issue." Negroes in the three cities were also jubilant. In Gary, the most tense of the cities, Richard Hatcher urged the mostly Negro crowd at his headquarters to "cool it." "I urge that the outcome of this election be unmarred by any incident of any kind.... If we spoil this victory with any kind of occurrence here tonight, or anywhere in the city, it will be a hollow victory." The evening *was* cool: Joyous Negroes danced and sang in the streets.

But beyond the exultation of victory remain many hard questions. Now that Cleveland and Gary have Negro mayors, just how much difference will it make in solving the many grave problems that these cities face? Will these victories cool militancy in urban ghettos next summer, or will the momentum of frustration prove too great to put on the brakes? A careful analysis of *how* these candidates won office may help provide the answers.

The focus of this report is on Cleveland because:

As residents of Cleveland, we are more familiar with the campaign and the election.

Cleveland is unique because, in 1965, it had a special census. By matching voting wards with census tracts, we can draw a clearer picture of voting behavior than we could in the other cities, where rapid neighborhood transitions have made 1960 census data quite unreliable in assessing voting patterns. Having examined Cleveland in some detail, we will draw some comparisons with the Gary and Boston elections, then speculate about their significance and implications.

CLEVELAND — CITY IN DECLINE

Cleveland has something less than 2,000,000 residents. Among metropolitan areas in America, it ranks eleventh in size. Like many other American cities, the central city of Cleveland is experiencing an absolute decline in population—residents are fleeing from the decaying core to the surrounding suburbs. The city certainly ranks high both in terms of absolute and proportional decline in the central-city population.

Between 1950 and 1960, the population of the central city declined from 914,808 to 876,050, a loss of almost 39,000. By 1965 the population had sunk to 810,858, an additional loss of 65,000. But these figures are only a partial reflection of the changing composition of the population, since new Negro residents coming into the central city helped offset the white exodus. *Between 1950 and 1960, nearly 142,000 white residents left the central city, and an additonal 94,000 left between 1960 and 1965—nearly a quarter of a million in just 15 years.*

During the same period the numbers of Negro residents of Cleveland rose from 147,847 to 279,352—an increase from 16.1 percent to 34.4 percent of the city's population. There is no evidence that this dramatic population redistribution has changed since the special 1965 census. Some suburbanization of Negroes is beginning on the east and southeast side of the city, but the pace is not nearly so dramatic as for whites. In 1960, approximately 97 percent of the Negroes in the metropolitan area lived in the central city. This percentage has probably declined somewhat since then—16,000 Negro residents have moved to East Cleveland. But the basic pattern of segregation in the metropolitan area remains. The development in East Cleveland is little more than an eastward extension of the ghetto, and the older, decaying residential units the Negroes have moved to are hardly "suburban" in character.

While the population composition of Cleveland is changing rapidly, whites are still a significant majority—about 62 percent. Again like many other central cities, a significant percentage of the white population comprises nationality groups that live in segregated sections, with a strong sense of ethnic identity and a deep fear of Negro encroachment. (In 1964, the bussing of Negro students into Murray Hill, an Italian neighborhood, resulted in rioting).

In 1960, the census classified 43 percent of the central city's white residents as "foreign stock." In that year, five groups—Germans, Poles, Czechs, Hungarians, and Italians—had populations of 25,000 or greater; at least 20 other nationality groups were large enough to have to be contended with in the political arena. But today these ethnic groups—although unwilling to admit it—have become less than the controlling majority they constituted before 1960.

The Cuyahoga River divides Cleveland, physically as well as socially. When Negroes first began to move into the city, during World War I, they occupied the decaying section to the south and east of the central business district. As their numbers grew, they continued pushing in this direction and now occupy the larger part of the eastside (except for some ethnic strongholds). There are no stable, integrated neighborhoods in the central city—only areas in transition from white to black. To the west, the Cuyahoga River constitutes a barrier to Negro penetration.

Ever since 1941, when Frank Lausche was elected, Cleveland has had a succession of basically honest but unimaginative Democratic mayors. These mayors have kept their hold on City Hall by means of a relatively weak coalition of nationality groups. At no point in this 26-year Lausche dynasty did a mayor gather enough power to seriously confront the long-range needs and problems of the city.

By early 1967, the city had seemingly hit rock bottom. A long procession of reporters began arriving to write about its many problems. The racial unrest of the past several years had, during the summer of 1966, culminated in the worst rioting in Cleveland's history. This unrest was continuing to grow as several militant groups were organizing. Urban renewal was a dismal failure; in January, the Department of Housing and Urban Development even cut off the city's urban-renewal funds, the first such action by the Federal Government. The exodus of whites, along with business, shoved the city to the brink of financial disaster. In February, the Moody Bond Survey reduced the city's credit rating. In May, the Federal Government cut off several million dollars of construction funds—because the construction industry had failed to assure equal job opportunities for minority groups. In short, the city was, and remains, in deep trouble. And while most ethnic groups probably continued to believe that Cleveland was the "Best Location in the Nation," the Negro community—and a growing number of whites—were beginning to feel that Cleveland was the "Mistake on the Lake," and that it was time for a change.

Carl Stokes's campaign for mayor was his second try. In 1965, while serving in the state House of Representatives, he came within 2100 votes of defeating Mayor Ralph S. Locher. Stokes had taken advantage of a city-charter provision that lets a candidate file as an independent, and bypass the partisan primaries. Ralph McAllister, then president of the Cleveland School Board, did the same. For his hard line on *de facto* school segregation, however, McAllister had earned the enmity of the Negro community. The Republican candidate was Ralph Perk, the first Republican elected to a county-wide position (auditor) in many years. A second generation Czech-Bohemian, Perk hoped to win by combining his ethnic appeal with his program for the city (Perk's Plan). He had no opposition for his party's nomination. The fourth candidate was Mayor Locher. who had defeated Mark McElroy, county recorder and perennial candidate for something, in the Democratic primary.

It was in the 1965 Democratic primary that the first signs of a "black bloc" vote emerged. The Negroes, who had previously supported incumbent Democratic mayoral candidates, if not enthusiastically at least consistently, made a concerted effort to dump Locher in favor of McElroy. There were two reasons.

Locher had supported his police chief after the latter had made some tactless remarks about Negroes. Incensed Negro leaders demanded an audience with the mayor, and when he refused, his office was the scene of demonstrations, sit-ins, and arrests. At that point, as one of the local reporters put it, "Ralph Locher became a dirty name in the ghetto."

Stokes, as an independent, and his supporters hoped that the Democratic primary would eliminate the *stronger* candidate, Locher. For then a black bloc would have a good chance of deciding the general election because of an even split in the white vote.

Despite the Negro community's efforts, Locher won the primary and went on to narrowly defeat Stokes. Locher received 37 percent of the vote, Stokes 36 percent, Perk 17 percent, and McAllister 9 percent. Some observers reported that a last-minute whispering campaign in Republican precincts—to the effect that "A vote for Perk is a vote for Stokes"—may have given Locher enough Republican votes to win. The evidence: The popular Perk received only a 17 percent vote in a city where a Republican could be expected something closer to 25 percent. Had Perk gotten anything close to 25 percent, Stokes would have probably been elected two years earlier.

Although he made a strong showing in defeat, Carl Stokes's political future looked bleak. No one expected the Democratic leaders to give Stokes another opportunity to win by means of a split vote. Nor were there other desirable elected offices Stokes could seek. Cleveland has no Negro Congressman—largely because the heavy Negro concentration in the city has been "conveniently" gerrymandered. The only district where Stokes might have had a chance has been represented by Charles Vanik, a popular and liberal white, and as long as Vanik remained in Congress Stokes was locked out. Stokes's state Senate district was predominantly white; and a county or state office seemed politically unrealistic because of his race. So, in 1966, Stokes sought re-election to the state House unopposed.

Between 1965 and 1967, Cleveland went from bad to worse, physically, socially, and financially. With no other immediate possibilities, Stokes began to think about running for mayor again. The big question was whether to risk taking on Locher in the primary—or to file as an independent again.

THE PRIMARY RACE

In effect, Stokes's decision was made for him. Seth Taft, slated to be the Republican candidate, told Stokes he would withdraw from the election entirely if Stokes filed as an independent in order to gain the advantage of a three-man general election. Taft had concluded that his best strategy was to face a Negro, *alone,* or a faltering incumbent, *alone,* in the general election. But not both. In a three-man race with Locher and Stokes, Taft correctly assumed that he would be the man in the middle with no chance for victory. (Taft would have preferred to run as an independent—to gain Democratic votes—but the county Republican leader threatened to file *another* Republican candidate unless Taft ran as a Republican.)

Meanwhile, Locher committed blunder after blunder—and Democratic party leaders began to question whether he could actually win another election. In the weeks before filing for the primary, Democratic leaders even pressured Locher to accept a Federal judgeship and clear the way for the president of the city council to run. But the Democratic leaders in Cleveland are not noted for their strength or effectiveness, as is evidenced by the fact that none of the Democratic mayors since 1941 were endorsed by the party when they were first elected. When Locher refused to withdraw the party reluctantly rallied behind him.

Another Democratic candidate was Frank P. Celeste, former mayor of the Republican westside suburb of Lakewood. Celeste established residency in the city, announced his candidacy early, and—despite pressure from the Democratic Party—remained in the primary race.

There was always the possibility that Celeste would withdraw from the primary, which would leave Stokes facing Locher alone. But the threat of Taft's withdrawal from the general election left Stokes with little choice but to face Locher head-on in the primary. A primary race against Locher and a strong Democrat was more appealing than a general election against Locher and a weak Republican.

Now, in 1965 Stokes had received only about 6000 white votes in the city in a 239,000 voter turnout. To win in the primary, he had to enlarge and consolidate the Negro vote—and increase his white support on the westside and in the eastside ethnic wards.

The first part of his strategy was a massive voter-registration drive in the Negro wards—to reinstate the potential Stokes voters dropped from the rolls for failing to vote since the 1964 Presidential election. The Stokes organization—aided by Martin Luther King, Jr., and the Southern Christian Leadership Conference, as well as by grant (in part earmarked for voter registration) from the Ford Foundation to the Cleveland chapter of CORE—did succeed in registering many Negroes. But there was a similar drive mounted by the Democratic Party on behalf of Locher. (Registration figures are not available by race.)

The second part of the Stokes strategy took him across the polluted Cuyahoga River into the white wards that had given him a mere 3 percent of the vote in 1965. He spoke wherever he would be received—to small groups in private homes, in churches, in public and private halls. While he was not always received enthusiastically, he did not confront many hostile crowds. He faced the race issue squarely and encouraged his audience to judge him on his ability.

Stokes's campaign received a big boost when the *Plain Dealer,* the largest daily in Ohio, endorsed him. Next, the *Cleveland Press* called for a change in City Hall, but declined to endorse either Stokes or Celeste. But since the polls indicated that Celeste was doing very badly, this amounted to an endorsement of Stokes.

More people voted in this primary than in any other in Cleveland's history. When the ballots were counted, Stokes had 52.5 per-

TABLE I

	City Totals			Negro Wards			White Wards			Mixed Wards		
	1965 General	1967 Primary	1967 General	1965 General	1967 Primary	1967 General	1965 General	1967 Primary	1967 General	1965 General	1967 Primary	1967 General
Registered Voters	337,803	326,003	326,003	103,123	99,885	99,885	159,419	152,737	152,737	75,261	73,421	73,421
Turnout	239,479	210,926	257,157	74,396	73,360	79,591	111,129	88,525	119,883	53,962	49,105	57,113
% Turnout	70.9	64.7	78.9	72.1	73.4	79.7	69.7	58.0	78.5	71.7	66.9	77.8
Stokes Votes	85,716	110,769	129,829	63,550	70,575	75,586	3,300	13,495	23,158	18,866	26,699	30,872
% Stokes Votes	35.8	52.5	50.5	85.4	96.2	95.0	3.0	15.2	19.3	35.0	54.4	54.1

cent of the votes — he had defeated Locher by a plurality of 18,000 votes. Celeste was the man in the middle, getting only 4 percent of the votes, the lowest of any mayoral candidate in recent Cleveland history.

What produced Stokes's clear victory? Table I (on page 304) reveals the answer. The decisive factor was the size of the Negro turnout. While Negroes constituted only about 40 percent of the voters, 73.4 percent of them turned out, compared with only 58.4 percent of the whites. Predominantly Negro wards cast 96.2 percent of their votes for Stokes. (Actually this figure underrepresents the Negro vote for Stokes, since some of the non-Stokes votes in these wards were cast by whites. Similarly, the 15.4 percent vote for Stokes in the predominantly white wards slightly overestimates the white vote because of the Negro minority.)

Newspaper and magazine reports of the primary election proclaimed that Stokes could not have won without the white vote. Our own estimate — based on matching wards with census tracts, and allowing for only slight shifts in racial composition in some wards since the 1965 special census — is that Stokes received 16,000 white votes. His margin of victory was 18,000. How would the voting have gone if the third man, Celeste, had not been in the race? Many white voters, feeling that Stokes could not win in a two-man race, might not have bothered to vote at all, so perhaps Stokes would have won by an even larger margin. Thus Stokes's inroad into the white vote was not the decisive factor in his primary victory, although it was important.

Stokes emerged from the primary as the odds-on favorite to win — five weeks later — in the general election. And in the first few days of the campaign, it seemed that Stokes had everything going for him.

Stokes was bright, handsome, and articulate. His opponent, Seth Taft, while bright, had never won an election, and his family name, associated with the Taft-Hartley Act, could hardly be an advantage among union members. In addition, he was shy and seemingly uncomfortable in a crowd.

Both the *Plain Dealer* and the *Cleveland Press* endorsed Stokes in the general election.

The wounds of the primary were quickly (if perhaps superficially) healed, and the Democratic candidates was endorsed by both the Democratic Party and Mayor Locher.

Labor — both the A.F.L.-C.I.O. and the Teamsters — also endorsed Stokes.

He had a partisan advantage. Of the 326,003 registered voters, only 34,000 (10 percent) were Republican. The closest any Republican mayoral candidate had come to winning was in 1951, when — in a small turnout — William J. McDermott received 45 percent of the vote.

Stokes had 90,000 or more Negro votes virtually assured, with little possibility that Taft would make more than slight inroads.

Perhaps most important, voting-behavior studies over the years have demonstrated that voters who are confronted by a dilemma react by staying home from the polls. Large numbers of life-long Democrats, faced with voting for a Negro or a Republican by the name of Taft, were likely to stay home.

Had this been a normal election, Democrat Carl Stokes would have won handily. But this was not destined to be a normal election. During the final days of the campaign, Stokes knew he was in a fight for his political life. Those who predicted that the cross-pressures would keep many voters away from the polls forgot that the variable "Negro" had never been involved in an election of this importance.

On Election Day, an estimated 90 percent of those who voted for Locher or Celeste in the Democratic primary shifted to Taft — many pulling a Republican lever for the first time in their life. Was this clearly an unequivocally bigoted backlash? To be sure, bigotry *did* play a major role in the election. But to dismiss the campaign and the election as pure overt bigotry is to miss the significance of what happened in Cleveland and the emerging subtle nature of prejudice in American society.

THE NON-ISSUE OF RACE

A closer look at the personal characteristics and campaign strategy of Seth Taft, the Republican candidate, reveals the complexity and subtlety of the race issue.

In the final days of the Democratic primary campaign, Taft repeatedly told reporters that he would rather run against Locher and his record than against Carl Stokes. On the evening of the primary, Taft appeared at Stokes's headquarters to congratulate him. As far as he was concerned, Taft said, the campaign issue was, who could present the most constructive program for change in Cleveland? Further, he said he didn't want people voting for him simply because he was white. A few days later, Taft even presented a strongly-worded statement to his campaign workers:

> The Cuyahoga Democratic party has issued a number of vicious statements concerning the candidacy of Carl Stokes, and others have conducted whisper campaigns. We cannot tolerate injection of race into this campaign. . . . Many people will vote for Carl Stokes because he is a Negro. Many people will vote for me because I am white. I regret this fact. I will work hard to convince people they should not vote on a racial basis.

Seth Taft's programs to solve racial tensions may have been paternalistic, not really perceptive of emerging moods of the ghetto. But one thing is clear—he was not a bigot. Every indication is that he remained uncomfortable about being in a race in which his chances to win depended, in large part, upon a backlash vote.

Whether Taft's attempt to silence the race issue was a deliberate strategy or a reflection of deep personal feelings, it probably enhanced his chances of winning. He knew that he had the hard-core bigot vote. His task was to convince those in the middle that they could vote for him and *not* be bigots.

Stokes, on the other hand, had another kind of problem. While he had to draw more white votes, he also had to retain and, if possible, increase the 73 percent Negro turnout that had delivered him 96 percent of the Negro votes in the primary. Stokes's campaign leaders feared a fall-off in the voter turnout from Negro wards—with good reason. The entire primary campaign had pushed the October 3 date so hard that some Negroes could not understand why Carl Stokes was not mayor on October 4. Full-page newspaper ads paid for by CORE had stated, *"If you don't vote Oct. 3rd, forget it. The man who wins will be the next mayor of Cleveland!"* So Stokes felt he had to remobilize the Negro vote.

The moment came during the question-and-answer period of the second of four debates with Taft in the all-white westside. Stokes said:

> The personal analysis of Seth Taft—and the analysis of many competent political analysts—is that Seth Taft may win the November 7 election, but for only one reason. That reason is that his skin happens to be white.

The predominantly white crowd booed loudly and angrily for several minutes, and throughout the rest of the evening repeatedly interrupted him. Later, Stokes's campaign manager revealed that his candidate's remark was a calculated risk to arouse Negro interest.

Stokes probably succeeded, but he also gave Taft supporters an
excuse to bring the race issue into the open. And they could claim
that it was *Stokes*, not Taft, who was trying to exploit the race
issue.

To be sure, *both* candidates exploited the race issue. But, for
the most part, it was done rather subtly. Stokes's campaign posters
stated, "Let's do Cleveland Proud"—another way of saying, "Let's
show the world that Cleveland is capable of rising above racial
bigotry." A full-page ad for Stokes stated in bold print, "Vote
for Seth Taft. It Would Be Easy, Wouldn't It?" After the debate,
Taft was free to accuse Stokes of using the race issue—itself a
subtle way of exploiting the issue. Then there was the letter, signed
by the leaders of 22 nationality clubs, that was mailed to 40,000
members in the city. It didn't mention race, but comments such
as "protecting our way of life," "safeguard our liberty," and "false
charges of police brutality" were blatant in their implications. Taft
sidestepped comment on the letter.

No matter how much the candidates may have wanted to keep
race out of the picture, race turned out to be the most important
issue. Both Taft and Stokes could benefit from the issue if they
played it right, and both did use it. And although the Stokes's
remark at the second debate gave white voters an excuse to vote
for Taft without feeling that they were bigots, many whites probably
would have found another excuse.

TAFT AS A STRATEGIST

The fact is that Taft, for all his lackluster qualities, emerged
as a strong candidate. He was able to turn many of his liabilities
into assets.

Taft was able to insulate himself against his Republican identity.
He successfully dissociated himself from his uncle's position on
labor by pointing to his own active role, as a student, against
"right to work" laws. At the same time, he hit hard at Stokes's
record as an off again-on again Democrat. This strategy neutralized,
at least in part, Taft's first political disadvantage—running as a
Republican in a Democratic city.

A second liability was that he came from a wealthy family. Taft
was an Ivy League intellectual, cast in the role of a "do-gooder."
He lived in an exclusive suburb, Pepper Pike, and had bought

a modest home in Cleveland only a few weeks before declaring his candidacy. How, it was frequently asked, could such a man understand the problems of the inner-city and of the poor? Almost invariably the answer was: "Did John F. Kennedy, Franklin D. Roosevelt, and Nelson Rockefeller have to be poor in order to understand and respond to the problems of the poor?" Taft's campaign posters were a side profile that bore a striking resemblance to President Kennedy. Whether he was consciously exploiting the Kennedy image is an open question. But there can be little doubt that when Taft mentioned his Republican heritage, he tried to project an image of the new breed of Republican—John Lindsay and Charles Percy. This image didn't come across very well at first, but as he became a seasoned campaigner it became clearer.

Another liability was that Taft had never held an elected office. His opponent tried to exploit this—unsuccessfully. Taft could point to 20 years of active civic service, including the fact that he was one of the authors of the Ohio fair-housing law. Then too, the charge gave Taft an opportunity to point out that Stokes had the worst absentee record of anyone in the state legislature. Stokes never successfully answered this charge until the last of their four debates, when he produced a pre-campaign letter from Taft commending him on his legislative service. But this came moments *after* the TV cameras had gone off the air.

Still another liability emerged during the campaign. Taft's strategy of discussing programs, not personalities, was seemingly getting him nowhere. He presented specific proposals; Stokes, a skilled debater, succeeded in picking them apart. Stokes himself discussed programs only at a general level and contended that he was best-qualified to "cut the red tape" in Washington. His frequent trips to Washington to confer with top Government officials, before and during the campaign, indicated that he had the inside track.

Taft, realizing at this point that his campaign was not gaining much momentum, suddenly switched gears and began attacking Stokes's record (not Stokes personally). Stokes had claimed he would crack-down on slumlords. Taft discovered that Stokes owned a piece of rental property with several code violations— and that it had not been repaired despite an order from the city. He hit hard at Stokes's absenteeism and his record as a "good" Democrat. He put a "bird-dog" on Stokes and, if Stokes told one group one thing and another group something else, the public heard about it.

TABLE II　Percent Stokes Vote by Ward

WHITE WARDS	% Negro	1965 General	1967 Primary	1967 General
1	.6	3.2	17.2	20.5
2	.3	1.9	12.8	17.4
3	.9	2.5	13.6	22.1
4	.3	3.0	18.2	20.9
5	.6	1.7	11.8	17.8
6	.8	2.3	15.1	16.7
7	.6	3.4	16.5	23.7
8	3.0	6.1	24.7	29.3
9	.2	1.9	12.4	16.4
14	1.4	1.1	12.7	13.0
15	1.4	1.2	9.2	14.1
22	5.7	8.1	22.5	26.3
26	1.1	2.8	16.3	19.9
32	2.4	2.9	10.0	15.3
33	.3	2.5	17.7	21.4
Average		3.0	15.2	19.3

NEGRO WARDS

	% Negro	1965 General	1967 Primary	1967 General
10	91.3	88.7	97.3	96.7
11	91.8	86.3	95.9	96.0
12	82.7	76.9	90.4	90.5
13	75.2	75.8	90.7	88.4
17	99.0	86.6	98.1	97.9
18	89.3	84.0	96.0	95.7
20	91.0	83.0	95.0	92.8
24	92.6	90.6	98.1	98.1
25	90.9	91.3	98.4	98.2
27	85.7	85.2	95.6	94.0
Average		85.4	96.2	95.0

MIXED WARDS

	% Negro	1965 General	1967 Primary	1967 General
16	56.6	50.7	69.9	70.1
19	25.3	29.2	48.0	39.9
21	61.1	55.2	66.3	68.9
23	20.3	9.8	18.2	23.2
28	28.5	26.5	54.8	57.3
29	24.4	26.8	43.2	42.3
30	51.7	51.5	75.3	71.4
31	21.8	16.9	31.8	39.0
Average		35.0	54.4	54.1

The upshot was that in the final days of the campaign Taft captured the momentum. Stokes was easily the more flashy debater and projected a superior image; but Taft emerged as the better strategist.

SHOULD TAFT HAVE WITHDRAWN?

One may ask whether all of this discussion is really relevant, since the final vote was sharply divided along racial lines. In one sense it *is* irrelevant, since it is possible that a weaker candidate than Taft might have run just as well. It is also possible that a white racist might actually have won. Still, this discussion has buttressed two important points.

Taft was not all black, and Stokes was not all white. Taft proved a strong candidate, and—had he been running against Locher instead of Stokes—he might have amassed strong support from Negroes and defeated Locher.

By being a strong candidate, Taft made it much easier for many white Democrats, who might otherwise been cross-pressured into staying home, to come out and vote for him.

Some people felt that Taft should have withdrawn and let Stokes run uncontested. But many of the same people also decried white liberals who, at recent conferences to form coalitions between black-power advocates and the New Left, let black militants castrate them. It is not traditional in American politics that candidates enter a race to lose. Taft was in to win, and he fought a hard and relatively clean campaign—as high a compliment as can be paid to any candidate.

Yet all of this doesn't change the basic nature of the voting. This is clear from the evidence in Table II. Stokes won by holding his black bloc, and increasing his white vote from 15 percent in the primary to almost 20 percent in the general. An enormous amount of the white vote was, whether convert or overt, anti-Negro. It is hard to believe that Catholics, ethnic groups, and laborers who never voted for anyone but a Democrat should suddenly decide to evaluate candidates on their qualifications and programs, and—in overwhelming numbers—decide that the Republican candidate was better qualified. The implication is that they were prejudiced. But to assume that such people perceive themselves as bigots is to oversimplify the nature of prejudice. And to call such people bigots is to make their responses even more rigid—as Carl Stokes discovered after his remark in the second debate with Taft.

This, then, is perhaps an important lesson of the Cleveland election: Bigotry cannot be defeated directly, by telling bigots that they are bigoted. For the most part Stokes learned this lesson well, accumulating as many as 30,000 white votes, nearly five times the number he received in 1965. But another slip like the one in the second debate might have cost him the election.

A few words on the voting for Stokes ward by ward, as shown in the table. Wards 9, 14, and 15—which gave Stokes a comparatively low vote—have the highest concentration of ethnic groups in the city. Not only is there the historical element of prejudice in these areas, but there is the ever-present fear among the residents that Negroes will invade their neighborhoods. (This fear is less a factor in ward 9, which is across the river.)

Wards 26 and 32 also gave Stokes a low percentage of votes, and these wards are also the ones most likely to have Negro migration. They are just to the north of East Cleveland, which is currently undergoing heavy transition, and to the east of ward 27, which in the past few years has changed from white to black. In these two wards, then, high ethnic composition and a fear of Negro migration would seem to account for Stokes's 19.9 and 15.3 percentages.

The highest percentage *for* Stokes in predominantly white areas was in wards 8 and 22. Ward 8 has a growing concentration of Puerto Ricans, and—according to newspaper polls—they voted heavily for Stokes. Ward 22 has a very large automobile-assembly plant that employs many Negroes. Now, in 1965 the ward was 5.7 percent Negro—a large increase from 1960. Since 1965, this percentage has probably grown another 2 or 3 percent. Therefore, if one subtracts the Negro vote that Stokes received in this ward, the size of the white vote is about the same as in other wards.

'IMMINENT DANGER' IN GARY

The race for mayor in Gary, Ind., was not overtly racist. Still, the racial issue was much less subtle than it was in Cleveland. When Democratic chairman John G. Krupa refused to support

Richard D. Hatcher, the Democratic candidate, it was clear that the reason was race. When the Gary newspaper failed to give similar coverage to both candidates and sometimes failed to print news releases from Hatcher headquarters (ostensibly because press deadlines had not been met), it was clear that race was a factor.

Even though race was rarely mentioned openly, the city polarized. While Stokes had the support of the white-owned newspapers and many white campaign workers, many of Hatcher's white supporters preferred to remain in the background—in part, at least, because they feared reprisals from white racists. Hatcher didn't use the black-power slogan, but to the community the election was a contest between black and white. And when the Justice Department supported Hatcher's claim that the election board had illegally removed some 5000 Negro voters from the registration lists and added nonexistent whites, the tension in the city became so great that the Governor, feeling that there was "imminent danger" of violence on election night, called up 4000 National Guardsmen.

Negroes constitute an estimated 55 percent of Gary's 180,000 residents, but white voter registration outnumbers Negroes by 2000 to 3000. Like Stokes, Hatcher—in order to win—had to pull some white votes, or have a singificantly higher Negro turnout.

The voter turnout and voting patterns in Cleveland and Gary were very similar. In both cities, almost 80 percent of the registered voters turned out at the polls. In the Glen Park and Miller areas, predominantly white neighborhoods, Joseph B. Radigan—Hatcher's opponent—received more than 90 percent of the votes. In the predominantly Negro areas, Hatcher received an estimated 93 percent of the votes. In all, Hatcher received about 4000 white votes, while losing probably 1000 Negro votes, at most, to Radigan. This relatively small white vote was enough to give him victory. If Stokes's miscalculation in bringing race into the Cleveland campaign gave prejudiced whites an excuse to vote for Taft, the glaring way the Democratic Party in Gary tried to defeat Hatcher probably tipped the scales and gave Hatcher some white votes he wouldn't have received otherwise.

THE SCHOOL ISSUE IN BOSTON

The Boston election, unlike the Cleveland and Gary elections, didn't pose a Negro against a white, but a lackluster candidate—

Kevin White—against a 48-year-old grandmother who had gained national attention over the past several years for her stand against school integration. On the surface, Mrs. Hicks seems to be an obvious racial bigot. But she herself has repeatedly denied charges that she is a racist, and many who have followed her closely claim that this description is too simple.

Mrs. Hicks, perhaps more than any other public figure to emerge in recent years, reflects the complex and subtle nature of prejudice in America. Her public denial of bigotry is, in all probability, an honest expression of her self-image. But she is basically unaware of, and unwilling to become informed about, the way her views maintain the barriers of segregation and discrimination in American society. In 1963, when the N.A.A.C.P. asked the Boston School Committee to acknowledge the *de facto* segregation in the schools, she refused to review the evidence. Meeting with the N.A.A.C.P., she abruptly ended the discussion by proclaiming: "There is no *de facto* segregation in Boston's schools. Kindly proceed to educational matters." Later, when the State Board of Education presented a 132-page report on racial imbalance in Massachusetts schools, she lashed out at the report's recommendations without bothering to read it.

Mrs. Hicks, like millions of Americans, holds views on race that are born out of and perpetuated by ignorance. John Spiegel, director of Brandeis University's Lemberg Center for the Study of Violence, has summed up the preliminary report of its study of six cities:

> . . . the attitude of whites seems to be based on ignorance of or indifference to the factual basis of Negro resentment and bitterness. . . . If white populations generally had a fuller appreciation of the just grievances and overwhelming problems of Negroes in the ghetto, they would give stronger support to their city governments to promote change and to correct the circumstances which give rise to strong feelings of resentment now characteristic of ghetto populations.

Prejudice is born not only out of ignorance, but also out of fear. There is much about the Negro ghettos of poverty that causes whites, lacking objective knowledge, to be afraid, and their fear in turn reinforces their prejudice and their inability to hear out and understand the plight of the Negro in America.

In Boston, the voter turnout was heavy (71 percent) but below the turnouts in Cleveland and Gary. White accumulated 53 percent of the vote and 12,000 plurality. Compared with Stokes and Hatcher, he had an easy victory. But considering Mrs. Hicks's lack of qualifications and the racial overtones of her campaign, Boston also experienced a massive backlash vote. Had it not been for the final days of the campaign—when she pledged, unrealistically, to raise police and firemen's salaries to $10,000 without raising taxes, and came back from Washington with "positive assurance" that nonexistent Federal monies would cover the raises—she might even have won. But throughout the campaign Mrs. Hicks repeatedly revealed her ignorance of fiscal and political matters. Mrs. Hicks had another handicap: She is a woman. The incredible fact that she ran a close race demonstrated again the hard core of prejudice and ignorance in American society.

Now let us consider the broader implications these elections will have on the racial crisis in America. To be sure, the immediate implications are quite different from what they would have been if Stokes and Hatcher had lost and Mrs. Hicks had won. If the elections had gone the other way, Summer '68 might well have begun November 8. As Thomas Pettigrew of Harvard put it a few days before the election, "If Stokes and Hatcher lose and Mrs. Hicks wins, then I just wonder how a white man in this country could ever look a Negro in the eye and say, 'Why don't you make it the way we did, through the political system, rather than burning us down?'"

THE MEANING OF THE ELECTIONS

But do these victories really alter the basic nature of the racial crisis? There is, true, some reason for hope. But to assume that anything has been fundamentally altered would be disastrous. First of all, it is by no means clear that these elections will pacify militant Negroes—including those in Cleveland, Gary and Boston. In Boston, some militants were even encouraging people to vote for Mrs. Hicks—because they felt that her victory would help unify the Negro community against a well-defined foe. In Cleveland, most militants remained less than enthusiastic about the possibility of a Stokes victory. Of the militant groups, only CORE worked hard for him. In Gary alone did the candidate have the solid support of militants—probably because Hatcher refused to explicitly rebuke Stokely Carmichael and H. Rap Brown, and because his opponents repeatedly claimed that Hatcher was a black-power advocate.

If the Stokes and Hatcher victories are to represent a turning point in the racial crisis, they must deliver results. Unfortunately, Hatcher faces an unsympathetic Democratic Party and city council. Stokes has gone a long way toward healing the wounds of the bitter primary, but it remains to be seen whether he will receive eager support for his programs. Some councilmen from ethnic wards will almost certainly buck his programs for fear of alienating their constituencies.

Stokes and Hatcher themselves face a difficult and delicate situation.

Their margins of victory were so narrow that they, like Kennedy of 1960, must proceed with great caution.

Enthusiasm and promises of change are not the same as the power to implement change. And the two mayors must share power with whites.

They must demonstrate to Negroes that their presence in City Hall has made a difference. But if their programs seem too preferential toward Negroes, they run the risk of massive white resistance.

This delicate situation was clearly seen in the early days of the Stokes administration. Of his first ten appointments, only two were Negroes. Although relations with the police have been one of the most sensitive issues in the Negro ghetto, Stokes's choice for a new police chief was Michael Blackwell, a 67-year-old "hard-liner." This appointment was intended to ease anxieties in the ethnic neighborhoods, but it was not popular in the Negro ghetto. Blackwell, in his first public address after being sworn in, lashed out at the Supreme Court, state laws, and "publicity-seeking clergy and beatniks" for "crippling law enforcement." Cleveland's Negroes are already beginning to wonder whether a Negro in City Hall is going to make any difference.

Some observers believe that Stokes is basically quite conservative, and point to his sponsorship of anti-riot legislation. To be sure, Stokes's position on many issues remains uncertain, but what does seem fairly clear from his early days in office is that his efforts to gain support in white communities is going to lead to disaffection among Negroes. How much and how quickly is a difficult question.

Race relations is only one of many problems that these two

new mayors must face. Stokes has inherited all of the problems that brought national attention to Cleveland last spring—poverty, urban renewal, finance, transportation, air and water pollution, and so on. Hatcher faces similar problems in Gary, and must also cope with one of the nation's worst strongholds of organized crime. If they fail, the responsibility will fall heavier on them than had a white man failed. Some whites will generalize the failures to all Negro politicians, and some Negroes will generalize the failures to the "bankruptcy" of the American political system.

Almost certainly, Washington will be a key factor in determining if these two men succeed. The national Democratic Party has a strong interest in making Stokes and Hatcher look good, for it desperately needs to recapture the disaffected Negro voters before the 1968 national election. But how much can the party deliver? The war in Vietnam is draining enormous national resources and Congress is threatening to slash poverty programs. Even if Federal monies were no problem, there is the question whether *any* of Washington's existing programs are directed at the roots of ghetto unrest. Many informed administrators, scientists, and political analysts feel they are not. And the chances for creative Federal programs seem, at this moment, fairly dim.

Another clear implication of these elections is that white resistance to change remains large and widespread. More than 90 percent of the Democrats in Cleveland who voted for a Democrat in the primary switched, in the general election, to the Republican candidate. Now, not many American cities are currently composed of as many as 35 percent Negroes; the possibility of coalitions to elect other Negro candidates appears, except in a handful of cities, remote. Additional Negro mayoral candidates are almost certain to arise, and many will go down to bitter defeat.

Stokes and Hatcher won because black-voter power coalesced with a relatively small minority of liberal whites. It was not a victory of acceptance or even tolerance of Negroes, but a numerical failure of the powers of discrimination, a failure that resulted in large part because of the massive exodus of whites from the central city. The election of Stokes and Hatcher may break down white resistance to voting for a Negro, but this is, at best, problematical. Also problematical is how bigoted whites will react to the election of a Negro mayor. Their organized efforts to resist change may intensify. As we have already indicated, the pace of white exodus from the central city of Cleveland is already alarming.

And an acceleration of this pace could push the city into financial bankruptcy.

AMERICA HAS BOUGHT A LITTLE TIME

In short, while the implications of the November 7 elections are ambiguous, it does seem that the victories of Stokes and Hatcher, and the defeat of Mrs. Hicks, have kept the door open on the growing racial crisis. America has, at best, bought a little time.

On the other hand, we do not find much cause for optimism in those elections—unlike George Meany, and unlike the *New York Times,* which, five days after the election, published a glowing editorial about "the willingness of most voters today to choose men solely on personal quality and impersonal issues." To us, it would seem that the elections have only accelerated the pace of ever-rising expectations among Negroes. And if results don't follow, and rather rapidly, then we believe that the Negro community's frustration with the American political system will almost certainly heighten.

The hard task of demonstrating that Negroes can actually achieve justice and equality in American still lies ahead.

15

BLACK POWERLESSNESS IN CHICAGO*

HAROLD M. BARON

With Harriet Stulman, Richard Rothstein, and Rennard Davis

THE METHODOLOGY OF THE STUDY

In studying the exclusion of Negroes from the decision-making structure in Chicago, our working assumption was that the men who hold power are those who have been elevated to policy-making positions in powerful institutions, like banks, law firms, and unions. This approach differed from the more popular methodologies of studying community power—thus, we did not try to identify the top decision-makers, and we did not assume that a power élite was at work.

To identify policy-making posts, we relied on these assumptions:

In each major area of metropolitan life, certain enterprises have a disproportionate amount of power—because of their control over human and material resources, or because of their responsibility for making public policy.

Individuals who occupy policy-making posts in these key enterprises have a disproportionate amount of power *within* these institutions.

Policy decisions are made at every level of a bureaucracy. But certain posts within a bureaucracy will structure the range of decision-making for all other posts. Posts that have this responsibility we call "policy-making," and these are the posts we studied.

Under stable conditions, policy-making is the most important way in which power is exercised. In any firm or government

*Reprinted from *Trans-action,* 6, No. 1, (November 1968), 27-33. By permission of *Trans-action* and the authors. Copyright © 1968 by *Trans-action* Magazine, St. Louis, Missouri.

department, policy-makers are relatively few. They are the ones who set the major goals and orientation, while the more numerous *management* is responsible for their implementation. Just as our definition of "policy-making position" was restrictive, so was our definition of "power." In our study, power means the ability to make and enforce decisions for an institution, for a community, or for society at large—and the ability to determine in whose interest these decisions are made.

Our study began with a census of those Negroes occupying public or private policy-making positions. First we identified Cook County's major institutional areas—that is, related types of formally organized activities, such as local government, religious organizations, and business firms. In those areas where we could *not* be exhaustive in our research, we selected one or more representative groups. Corporate law firms, for example, were chosen to represent business-oriented professions and services.

Within each institutional area, we developed criteria to determine how large an individual enterprise or organization had to be before it has significant potential influence and power over other organizations. Next, we determined which positions within these powerful enterprises or organizations had policy-making authority. Finally, we conducted interviews with knowledgeable informants to learn which of the policy-making positions were held by Negroes.

In our study, the chairman of the board of the largest industrial firm was given the same statistical weight as the vice-president of the smallest bank included in the survey. While differentiating between them would have been useful for a study of the total process of decision-making in the Chicago area, our aim was to document only the inclusion or exclusion of Negroes. If there is any methodological bias in our study, then, it operates in favor of employing less strict criteria in determining important positions in order to include at least a few Negroes.

Our census was based on information for the year 1965. Since then, although there have been some shifts in the number and percentage of Negroes in particular organizations, the pattern of power traced remains fundamentally the same.

Until recently, the three principal targets of the civil rights movement in the North were discrimination and inferior conditions in (1) housing for Negroes, (2) jobs for Negroes, and (3) the education of Negroes. But after failing to bring about major changes, many Negroes realized that one reason the status quo in housing, jobs, and education continues is that *the black community lacks control over decision-making*. Negroes remain second-class citizens partly because of the discrimination of individual whites, but mainly because of the way whites control the major institutions of our society. And therefore the fourth major goal of Negro organizations and the civil-rights movement has become the acquisition of power.

It was because of this concern with power for black people that, more than two years ago, the Chicago Urban League—a social-welfare organization dedicated to changing institutions so as to achieve full racial equality—started to study the decision-making apparatus in Cook County, Ill., and particularly how it affects or ignores Negro citizens. (Cook County takes in the city of Chicago, and two-thirds of the population of the surrounding suburban ring included in the Chicago Standard Metropolitan Statistical area.) Among the questions we posed were:

What is the exent of Negro exclusion from policy-making positions in Chicago?

Where Negroes *are* in policy-making positions, what type of positions are these, and where are Negroes in greatest number and authority?

Do Negroes in policy-making positions represent the interests of the Negro community? and

How might an increase in the percentage of Negro policy-makers affect socio-economic conditions for Negroes in general?

What we found was that in 1965 some 20 percent of the people in Cook County were Negro, and 28 percent of the people in Chicago were Negro. Yet the representation of Negroes in policy-making positions was minimal. Of the top 10,997 policy-making positions in the major Cook County institutions included in our study, Negroes occupied only 285—or 2.6 percent.

In government (see Table 1), out of a total of 1088 policy-making positions Negroes held just 58. This 5 percent is about one-fourth of the percentage of Negroes in the total county population. Of the 364 elective posts in the survey, however, Negroes occupied 29, or 8 percent, indicating that the franchise has helped give Negroes representation. Yet Negroes had the most positions, percentagewise, on appointed supervisory boards, such as the Board of Education and the Chicago Housing Authority. There they occupied 10 of the 77 policy-making positions, or about 13 percent.

Negroes were better represented on appointed supervisory boards and in elected (nonjudicial) offices than they were in local administrative positions, or in important federal jobs based in Chicago. Thus, Negroes held 12 percent of the nonjudicial elected posts

TABLE 1

The Exclusion of Negroes from Government
Policy-Making Positions in the
Cook County Public Sector (1965)

	Policy-Making Positions	Positions Held by Negroes	Percent
1. Elected Officials			
U.S. House of Representatives	13	1	8
State Legislature	120	10	8
Cook County — nonjudicial	34	3	9
Chicago — nonjudicial	59	7	12
Cook County — judicial	138	8	6
Total:	364	29	8
2. Appointive Supervisory Boards			
Total:	77	10	13
3. Local Administrative Positions			
City of Chicago	156	2	1
Chicago Board of Education	72	7	9
Metropolitan Sanitary District	7	0	0
Cook County Government	13	1	8
Total:	248	10	4
4. Federal Government			
Civil Service	368	8	2
Presidential Appointments	31	1	3
Total:	399	9	2
Grand Total:	1088	58	5

in Chicago's government, but only a little over 1 percent of the appointive policy-making positions in the city administration. The same anomaly appears at the federal level. There is one Negro out of the 13 U.S. Congressmen from Cook County (8 percent), but Negroes held only one out of 31 Presidential appointments (3 percent), and eight of the 368 top federal civil-service posts (2 percent).

Nonetheless, Negroes have—proportionately—two-and-half-times as many important posts in the public sector as they have in the private sector. As Table 2 indicates, Negroes are virtually barred from policy-making positions in the large organizations that dominate the private institutions in the Chicago area. Out of a total of 9909 positions, Negroes fill a mere 227. This 2 percent representation is only one-tenth of the proportionate Negro population.

TABLE 2
The Exclusion of Negroes from
Private Institutions
Policy-Making Positions in the
Cook County Private Sector (1965)

	Policy-Making Positions	Positions Held by Negroes	Percent
1. Business Corporations			
Banks	2258	7	*
Insurance	533	35	6
Nonfinancial Corporations	4047	0	0
Total:	6838	42	*
2. Legal Profession			
Total:	757	0	0
3. Universities**			
Total:	380	5	1
4. Voluntary Organizations			
Business & Professional	324	3	1
Welfare & Religious	791	69	9
Total	1115	72	6
5. Labor Unions			
Internationals	94	15	16
District Councils	211	20	9
Locals	514	73	14
Total:	819	108	13
Grand Total:	9909	227	2
Grand Total for Public & Private Sectors:	10997	285	2

*Below 1 percent
**Includes the University of Illinois, which is a public body.

The whitest form of policy-making in Chicago is in the control of economic enterprises. Out of 6838 positions identified in business corporations, Negroes held only 42 (six-tenths of 1 percent). Thirty-five of these were in insurance, where Negroes occupy 6 percent of the 533 posts. But all 35 were in two all-Negro insurance firms. The other seven positions were in four smaller banks. In banks in general, Negroes occupied three-tenths of 1 percent of the policy posts. There were no Negro policy-makers at all in manufacturing, communications, transportation, utilities, and trade corporations.

Out of the 372 companies we studied, the Negro-owned insurance companies were the only ones dominated by blacks (see Table 3). And if we had used the same stringent criteria for banks and insurance companies that we used for nonfinancial institutions, there would have been no black policy-makers in the business sector at all.

Now, amazingly enough, Chicago has proportionately more Negro-controlled businesses, larger than neighborhood operations, than any other major city in the North. Therefore, similar surveys in other Northern metropolitan areas would turn up an even smaller percentage of Negro policy-makers in the business world.

The legal profession, represented by corporate law firms, had no Negroes at high policy levels. We are convinced that the same situation would be found in other professions, such as advertising and engineering.

The very prestigious universities—the University of Chicago, Northwestern University, Loyola University, DePaul University, Roosevelt University, the Illinois Institute of Technology, and the University of Illinois (the only public university of the seven)—had a negligible 1 percent Negro representation. Most of these universities had few Negro students, faculty members, or administrators. Five of the seven had no Negro policy-makers. The University of Illinois had one. Roosevelt University, the sole institution that had a number of Negroes at the top, was the newest, and the one with the *least* public support. When this university was founded, its leaders had made a forthright stand on racial questions and a firm commitment to liberal principles.

We included these major universities in our survey because other institutions—public and private—have been placing increasingly greater value on them. Every year hundreds of millions of dollars in endowment and operating funds are given to the Chicago-area schools. After all, their research activities, and their training of skilled personnel, are considered a key to the region's economic

TABLE 3
The Exclusion of Negroes from
Private Establishments
Percentage of Negro Policy-Makers in the
Cook County Private Sector by Establishment (1965)

	Total Estab-lish ments	None	Percentage of Negro Policy-Makers			
			1- 5%	6- 15%	16- 50%	51% +
1. Business Corporations						
Banks	102	98	0	4	0	0
Insurance	30	28	0	0	0	2
Nonfinancial Corporations	240	240	0	0	0	0
2. Legal Professions	54	54	0	0	0	0
3. Universities*	7	5	0	2	0	0
4. Voluntary Organizations						
Business & Professional	5	3	2	0	0	0
Welfare & Religious	14	2	4	7	1	0
5. Labor Unions						
Internationals	4	0	1	1	2	0
District Councils	23	13	0	5	5	0
Locals	33	14	2	8	7	2
Total:	512	457	9	27	15	4

*Includes the University of Illinois, which is a public body.

growth. One indication of the tremendous influence these universities have is that they have determined the nature of urban renewal more than any other institutional group in Chicago (aside from the city government). Without a doubt, the universities have real—not nominal—power. And perhaps it is a reflection of this real power that only five out of 380 policy-making positions in these universities are held by Negroes.

The exclusion of Negroes from the private sector carries over to its voluntary organizations: Negroes are found in only 1 percent of the posts there. It is in the voluntary associations that it is easiest to make symbolic concessions to the black community by giving token representation, yet even here Negroes were underrepresented—which highlights the fundamental norms of the entire sector.

The sectors and individual groups in the Chicago area with the highest Negro representation were those with a Negro constituency—elective offices, supervisory boards, labor unions, and religious and welfare organizations. These four groups accounted for 216 of the posts held by Negroes, or 75 percent, although these four groups have only 19 percent of all the policy-making positions we studied. Labor unions had a larger percentage—13 percent—than any other institution in the private sector. In welfare and religious organizations, whose constituents were often largely Negro, Negroes occupied 8 percent of the positions, the same percentage of the elected public offices they held.

Now, either the black constituency elected the Negroes directly (in the case of elective offices and trade unions); or the Negroes were appointed to posts in an operation whose clients were largely Negro (principal of a Negro school, for example); or Negroes were given token representation on bodies that had a broad public purpose (like religious organizations). By "token representation," we mean—following James Q. Wilson—that "he is a man chosen because a Negro is 'needed' in order to legitimate (but not direct) whatever decisions are made by the agency."

Of the three ways a black consituency had of getting itself represented, the most important was the first. The statistics clearly show the importance of the Negro vote. The elected political offices and the elected trade-union offices account for only 11 percent of all the policy-making positions in Cook County. Yet almost half of all the Negro policy-makers were found in these two areas—137 out of 285.

Nonetheless, even in the major areas where Negro representation was the greatest—labor unions, elective offices, supervisory boards, and religious and welfare organizations—many institutions still excluded Negroes from positions of authority.

There are, of course, few Negroes in the building-trade unions, most of which bar Negroes from membership. Only two out of the 12 building-trade-union organizations we studied had even one Negro in a decisive slot. These two Negroes made up a mere one and a half percent of the policy-making positions in the building-trade unions.

The greatest degree of black representation was found in the former C.I.O. industrial unions. Only one-fourth of these units in the survey totally excluded Negroes from leadership. In almost half, the percentage of Negro policy-makers was over 15 percent—which is above token levels.

The former A.F. of L. unions (not including those in the building trades) had a higher rate of exclusion than those of the C.I.O. Two-fifths of these A.F. of L. unions had no Negroes at all in policy-making posts. But one-third of this group had leaderships that were 15 percent or more Negro. And the only two black-controlled local large enough to be included in this study were in A.F. of L. unions.

In elective offices, the Negro vote certainly does give Negroes some representation—though far below their proportionate number. In public administration, however, where advancement to policy-making offices comes through appointment and influence, Negroes are all but excluded from decisive posts, at both the federal and local levels. Although a very high percentage of all Negro professionals are in public service, they do not reach the top.

The only major governmental operation that had a goodly number of Negroes at the upper level of the bureaucratic hierarchy was the public-school system. Nine percent of the top positions were occupied by Negroes. This unique situation is the result of some fairly recent appointments, made as concessions after an intense civil-rights campaign directed at the Chicago Board of Education. In this instance, one can consider these civil-rights actions as a proxy for Negro votes. Still, this high-level representation in the Chicago school hierarchy did not seem to reflect any uniform policy of including Negroes in management. At the level of principal-ship that was not included as a policy-making position in this study, only 3 percent of the positions were occupied by blacks.

The voluntary welfare and religious associations that were sufficiently important to be included in the study usually had at least a few Negro policy-makers. Only two out of 14 bodies had no Negroes in policy postions (see Table 3), while four organizations had token representation—below 5 percent. None had a Negro majority in the key posts. Only the Chicago Urban League (with 43 percent) had Negroes in more than 15 percent of its policy slots. If individual religious denominations had been among the organizations counted in the survey, there would have been some black-dominated groups. As it was, Negro representation in the United Protestant Federation, which *was* included, came largely from the traditionally Negro denominations. It is of interest to note that, in recent years, Protestant groups have provided

some of the few instances in which Negroes have been elected
to important offices by a constituency that was overwhelmingly
white.

Not only were Negroes grossly underrepresented in Chicago's
policy-making posts, but even where represented they had less
power than white policy-makers. The fact is that *the number
of posts held by Negroes tended to be inversely related to the
power vested in these positions—the more powerful the post,
the fewer the black policy-makers.*

As we have seen, Negroes were virtually excluded from policy-
making in the single most powerful institutional sector—the business
world. In *all* sectors, they were generally placed in positions in
or divided among a board. Rarely were Negroes in positions of
ultimate authority, either as chief executive or as top board officer.

When Negroes ran for a board or for a judicial office on a slate,
their number had been limited by the political parties apportioning
out the nominations. The percentage of Negroes on such boards
or (especially) in judicial offices tended to run lower than the
number of Negroes in legislative posts, for which Negroes run
individually.

It is also true that no Negro has *ever* been elected to one of
the key city-wide or county-wide executive positions, such as
Mayor, City Clerk, or President of the Cook County Board. These
are the positions with the greatest power and patronage.

In welfare agencies, where Negroes have token representation,
they are virtually excluded from the key posts of executive director.
Only five of the 135 directors of medium and of large welfare
agencies were Negro.

Now, it was in the trade-union sector that the highest percentage
of Negroes had policy posts—13 percent. We asked several experts
on the Chicago trade-union movement to list the number of Negroes
among the 100 most powerful trade unionists in the area. Among
the 100 people they named, the number of Negroes ranged from
two to five. This did not surprise us, for it was compatible with
our general knowledge of the number of Negroes with truly powerful
posts in other sectors.

A RULE OF THUMB ON NEGRO POWER

All in all, then, we would suggest the following rule of thumb:
*The actual power vested in Negro policy-makers is about one-
third as great as the percentage of the posts they hold.*

Thus when Negroes elected other Negroes to office, these officers tended to represent small constituencies. For example, the greatest number of Negroes in legislative posts came from relatively small districts that happen to have black majorities. Indeed, according to Cook County tradition, Negroes simply do not hold legislative posts in city, state, or federal government *unless* they represent a district that is mostly black. No district with Negroes in the minority had a Negro representative, even when Negroes constituted the single largest ethnic group. And some districts with a Negro majority had a *white* representative.

Then too, the smaller the district, the more likely it would be homogeneous, and the greater the chances of its having a black majority that could return a Negro to office. In the Chicago area, consequently, Negroes were best represented on the City Council, which is based on 50 relatively small wards, each representing about 70,000 people; Negroes were represented most poorly in the U.S. House of Representatives, for which there are only nine rather large districts in Chicago, each representing about 500,000 people.

Most of the government policy-making posts that Negroes had been appointed to were in operations that had a large Negro clientele, if not a majority—as in the case of the Chicago public schools; or in operations that had largely Negro personnel, as in the case of the post office. On the appointed supervisory boards, in fact, those with as many as two Negro members were the Chicago Board of Education and the Board of Health, both of which serve very large numbers of Negroes.

This limiting of Negro policy-makers to Negro constituencies was quite as evident in the private sector. Three of the four banks with Negroes in policy-making posts were in Negro neighborhoods; and two were the smallest of the 102 banks we studied, and the other two were not much larger. The two insurance firms had mainly Negro clients, and were among the smallest of the 30 studied. In the voluntary organizations, the more they served Negroes, the higher the percentage of Negroes on their boards (although representation was by no means proportionate). Thus, the five Negro executive directors of welfare organizations we studied headed all-Negro constituencies: Three directed moderate-sized neighborhood settlements in the ghetto; one directed a virtually all-Negro hospital; and one directed an interracial agency that has traditionally had a Negro executive.

Still another way of limiting the power of Negro policy-makers, we discovered, was by "processing" them. Public and private institutions, as indicated, tend to have a token representation of Negroes. And many Negroes in these positions have totally identified with the traditional values and goals of the institution, regardless of what they mean to the mass of Negroes. Some of these Negro policy-makers, because of their small numbers and lack of an independent source of power, are neutralized. Others, if they are firm in representing the needs and outlook of the black community, are isolated. The two Negro members of the Chicago Board of Education represented these extremes. Mrs. Wendell Green, a longtime Board member and the elderly widow of a former judge, had been the most diehard supporter of Benjamin Willis, the former Schools Superintendent, through all of his fights against the civil-rights movement. The other Negro—Warren Bacon, a business executive—sympathized with the campaign against inferior, segregated housing and, as a result, has been largely isolated on the Board. He was rarely consulted on critical questions. His vote was usually cast with a small minority, and sometimes alone.

The fact is that the norms and traditions of *any* organization or enterprise limit the amount of power held by black policy-makers. It is no longer bold to assert that the major institutions and organizations of our society have an operational bias that is racist, even though their *official* policies may be the opposite. The Negro policy-maker in one of these institutions (or in a small black-controlled organization dependent upon these institutions, such as the head of a trade-union local) has a certain degree of conflict. If he goes along with the institution, from which he gains power and prestige, he ends up by implementing operations that restrict his minority group. Edward Banfield and James Q. Wilson have neatly pinpointed this dilemma in the political sphere:

> "Not only are few Negroes elected to office, but those who are elected generally find it necessary to be politicians first and Negroes second. If they are to stay in office, they must soft-pedal the racial issues that are of the most concern to Negroes as Negroes."

This pattern is seen in the failure of William Dawson, Cook County's one Negro Congressman, to obtain many Presidential appointments or top federal civil-service posts for Negroes. Theoretically he is in a more strategic position to influence government operations than any other Chicago-based Congressman, since he has 23 years' seniority and holds the important chairmanship of the Government Operations Committee. Yet in 1965 Negroes held only 2 percent of the top federal jobs in Chicago.

Any examination of the real power of Negroes in Chicago requires an examination of the strongest single organization in the Negro community—the Democratic Party. Wilson's study, *Negro Politics*, points out that the strength and cohesiveness of the Negro Democratic organization is largely dependent upon the strength of the total Cook County Democratic organization. The Negro organization is a "sub-machine" within the larger machine that dominates the city. The Negro sub-machine, however, has basically settled for lesser patronage positions and political favors, rather than using its considerable strength to try to make or change policy. Therefore, this Negro organization avoids controversial questions and seeks to avoid differences with the central organization on such vital issues as urban renewal and the schools.

In short, then, not only are Negroes underrepresented in the major policy-making positions in Cook County, but even where represented their actual power is restricted, or their representatives fail to work for the long-term interests of their constituency. It is therefore safe to estimate that Negroes really hold less than 1 percent of the effective power in the Chicago metropolitan area. Realistically, the power structure of Chicago is hardly less white than that of Mississippi.

From these figures it is clear that, at this time, Negroes in the Chicago area lack the power to make changes in the areas of housing, jobs, and education. The basic subjugation of the black community, however, would not end if there were simply more Negroes in policy-making posts. We have seen the prevalence of tokenism, of whites' choosing Negro leaders who are conservative, of their boxing in Negro leaders who are proved to be liberal, of their giving these leaders less actual power than they give themselves.

Our analysis suggests that the best way to increase both the number *and* the power of Negro policy-makers is through unifying the black constituency. Access to policy-making positions could come through both the development of large, black-controlled organizations, and through getting Negroes into white-dominated organizations. If the constituency lacks its own clear set of goals and policies, however, things will surely remain the same. For success depends not just upon formal unity, but upon the nature of the goals set by the black community. In this situation, the overcoming of black powerlessness seems to require the development of a self-conscious community that has the means to determine its own interests, and the cohesiveness to command the loyalty of its representatives. We can safely predict that more and more Negroes will be moved into policy-making positions. The fundamental conflict, therefore, will take place between their cooptation into the established institutions and their accountability to a black constituency.

FURTHER READING SUGGESTED BY THE AUTHOR:

Black Metropolis: A Study of Negro Life in a Northern Metropolis by St. Clair Drake and Horace Cayton, revised edition (New York & Evanston: Harper and Row, 1962). The best study on an urban black community. It contains much relevant material on the exercise of leadership within the community.

Black Power, the Politics of Liberation in America by Stokely Carmichael and Charles V. Hamilton (New York: Random House, 1968). A joint work by an activist and a scholar, and an argument for power through self-determination.

Black Bourgeoisie by E. Franklin Frazier (Glencoe, Ill.: The Free Press, 1957). A short, impressionistic work emphasizing the Negro's lack of significant power or wealth despite pretenses to the contrary by the black middle-class.

Harold M. Baron is a research associate at the Center for Urban Affairs, Northwestern University, and—under a grant from the Russell Sage Foundation—is writing a book on the institutional bases of urban racism. He was formerly the research director of the Chicago Urban League.

16

PUBLIC-REGARDINGNESS AS A
VALUE PREMISE IN VOTING BEHAVIOR*†

JAMES Q. WILSON AND EDWARD C. BANFIELD

Our concern here is with the nature of the individual's attachment
to the body politic and, more particularly, with the value premises
underlying the choices made by certain classes of voters. Our hypothesis is that some classes of voters (provisionally defined as "subcultures" constituted on ethnic and income lines) are more disposed than
others to rest their choices on some conception of "the public interest" or the "welfare of the community." To say the same thing in
another way, the voting behavior of some classes tends to be more
public-regarding and less private—(self- or family-) regarding than
that of others. To test this hypothesis it is necessary to examine
voting behavior in situations where one can say that a certain vote
could not have been private-regarding. Local bond and other expenditure referenda present such situations: it is sometimes possible to
say that a vote in favor of a particular expenditure proposal is incompatible with a certain voter's self-interest narrowly conceived. If
the voter nevertheless casts such a vote and if there is evidence that
his vote was not in some sense irrational or accidental, then it must

*This is a preliminary report of a study supported by the Joint Center for
Urban Studies of M.I.T. and Harvard University and the Rockefeller Founda-
tion. The writers wish to acknowledge assistance from Martha Derthick and
Mark K. Adams and comments from James Beshers, Anthony Downs, Werner
Hirsch, Hendrik Houthakker, H. Douglas Price, and Arthur Stinchcombe.
This paper was originally presented at the Second Conference on Urban Public
Expenditures, New York University, February 21-22, 1964.

†Reprinted from the *American Political Science Review, LVIII,* No. 4
(December 1964), 876-887. By permission of the *American Political Science
Review* and the authors.

be presumed that his action was based on some conception of "the public interest."

Our first step, accordingly, is to show how much of the behavior in question can, and cannot, be explained on grounds of self-interest alone, narrowly conceived. If all of the data were consistent with the hypothesis that the voter acts as if he were trying to maximize his family income, the inquiry would end right there. In fact, it turns out that many of the data cannot be explained in this way. The question arises, therefore, whether the unexplained residue is purposive or "accidental." We suggest that for the most part it is purposive, and that the voters' purposes arise from the conceptions of "the public interest."

I

We start, then, from the simple—and admittedly implausible—hypothesis that the voter tries to maximize his family income or (the same thing) self-interest narrowly conceived. We assume that the voter estimates in dollars both the benefits that will accrue to him and his family if the proposed public expenditure is made and the amount of the tax that will fall on him in consequence of the expenditure; if the estimated benefit is more than the estimated cost, he votes for the expenditure; if it is less, he votes against it. We assume that all proposed expenditures will confer some benefits on all voters. The benefits conferred on a particular voter are "trivial," however, if the expenditure is for something that the particular voter (and his family) is not likely to use or enjoy. For example, improvement of sidewalks confers trivial benefits on those voters who are not likely to walk on them.

Insofar as behavior is consistent with these assumptions—*i.e.,* insofar as the voter seems to act rationally in pursuit of self-interest narrowly conceived—we consider that no further "explanation" is required. It may be that other, entirely different hypothesis would account for the behavior just as well or better. That possibility is not of concern to us here, however.

No doubt, our assumptions lack realism. No doubt, relatively few voters make a conscious calculation of costs and benefits. Very often the voter has no way of knowing whether a public expenditure proposal will benefit him or not. In only one state which we have examined (Florida) do ballots in municipal referenda specify precisely *which* streets are to be paved or *where* a bridge is to be built. Even if a facility is to serve the whole city (*e.g.,* a zoo, civic center, or county hospital), in most cities the ballot proposition is usually so indefinite that the voter cannot accurately judge either the nature or the amount of the benefits that he would derive from the expenditure. Similarly, it is often difficult or impossible for the voter to estimate even the approximate amount of the tax that will fall upon him in consequence of the expenditure. Some states (*e.g.,* Illinois and California) require that the anticipated cost of each undertaking be listed on the ballot (*e.g.,* "$12,800,000 for sewer improvements"). Of course, even when the total cost if given, the voter must depend on the newspapers to tell, or figure out for himself—if he can—how much it would increase the tax rate and how much the increased tax rate would add to his tax bill. Ohio is the only state we have studied where the voter is told on the ballot how the proposed expenditure will affect the tax rate ("17 cents per $100 valuation for each of two years"). Almost everywhere, most of the expenditure proposals are to be financed from the local property tax. Occasionally, however, a different tax (*e.g.,* the sales tax) or a different tax base (*e.g.,* the county or state rather than the city), is used. In these cases, the voter is likely to find it even harder to estimate how much he will have to pay.

We may be unrealistic also both in assuming that the voter takes only *money* costs into account (actually he may think that a proposed civic center would be an eyesore) and in assuming that the only money costs he takes into account are *taxes* levied upon him (actually, if he is a renter he may suppose—whether correctly or incorrectly is beside the point—that his landlord will pass a tax increase on to him in a higher rent).

The realism of the assumptions does not really matter. What does matter is their usefulness in predicting the voters' behavior. It is possible that voters may act *as if* they are well informed and disposed to calculate even when in fact they are neither. If we can predict their behavior without going into the question of how much or how well they calculate, so much the better.

II

On the assumptions we have made, one would expect voters who will have no tax levied upon them in consequence of the passage of

TABLE I.
Relationship Between Percentage of Ward
Voting "Yes" and Percentage of Dwelling
Units Owner Occupied; Various Issues
in Cleveland and Chicago

Issue and Date	Simple Correlation Coefficient (r)
Cleveland (33 wards):	
Administration Building (11/59)	−0.86
County Hospital (11/59)	−0.77
Tuberculosis Hospital (11/59)	−0.79
Court House (11/59)	−0.85
Juvenile Court (11/59)	−0.83
Parks (11/59)	−0.67
Welfare Levy (5/60)	−0.72
Roads and Bridges (11/60)	−0.77
Zoo (11/60)	−0.81
Parks (11/60)	−0.57
Chicago (50 wards):	
County Hospital (1957)	−0.79
Veterans' Bonus (1957)	−0.49
Welfare Building (1958)	−0.67
Street Lights (1959)	−0.83
Municipal Building (1962)	−0.78
Urban Renewal Bonds (1962)	−0.79
Sewers (1962)	−0.79
Street Lights (1962)	−0.81

an expenditure proposal to vote for it even if it will confer only trival benefits on them. Having nothing to lose by the expenditure and something (however small) to gain, they will favor it. In the *very* low-income[1] wards and precincts of the larger cities a high proportion of the voters are in this position since most local public expenditures are financed from the property tax and the lowest-income people do not own property. We find that in these heavily non-home-owning districts the voters almost invariably support all expenditure proposals. We have examined returns on 35 expenditure proposals passed upon in 20 separate elections in seven cities and have not found a single instance in which this group failed to give a majority in favor of a proposal. Frequently the vote is 75 to 80 percent in

[1]Median family income under $3,000 per year. Needless to say, most voters in this category are Negroes.

favor; sometimes it is over 90 percent. The strength of voter support is about the same no matter what the character of the proposed expenditure.[2]

In all of the elections we have examined, non-homeowners show more taste for public expenditures that are to be financed from property taxes than do homeowners. Table I shows by means of product-

TABLE II.
Voting Behavior of Four Major
Economic Groups Compared in Cook County

	Percent "Yes" Vote	
Group	County Hospital (1957)	State Welfare Building (1958)
	(%)	(%)
*High Income Homeowners**		
Winnetka	64	76
Wilmette	55	70
Lincolnwood	47	64
Middle Income Homeowners†		
Lansing	30	54
Bellwood	21	55
Brookfield	22	51
Middle Income Renters‡		
Chicago Ward 44	65	71
Chicago Ward 48	61	72
Chicago Ward 49	64	74
Low Income Renters§		
Chicago Ward 2	88	73
Chicago Ward 3	87	76
Chicago Ward 27	87	78

*Three suburbs with highest median family imcome ($13,200 to $23,200) among all suburbs with 85 percent or more home ownership.
†Three suburbs with lowest median family income ($8,000 to $8,300) among all suburbs with 85 percent or more home ownership.
‡Three wards with highest median family income ($6,200 to $6,800) among all wards with less than 15 percent home ownership (none of the three wards is more than 4 percent Negro).
§Three wards with lowest median family income ($3,100 to $4,100) among all wards with less than 15 percent home ownership (Negro population of wards ranges from 59 to 99 percent).

[2]The cities and elections examined are: Cleveland-Cuyahoga County: Nov., 1956; Nov., 1959; May, 1960; Nov., 1960. Chicago-Cook County: June, 1957; Nov., 1958; Nov., 1959; April, 1962. Detroit-Wayne County: August, 1960; Feb., 1961; April, 1961; April, 1963. Kansas City: Nov., 1960; March, 1962. Los Angeles: Nov., 1962. Miami: Nov., 1956; May, 1960. St. Louis: March, 1962; Nov., 1962; March, 1963.

moment (Pearsonian r) coefficients of correlation the strength and consistency of this relationship over a wide variety of issues in several elections in Cleveland and Chicago.[3] As one would expect, when an expenditure is to be financed from a source other than the property tax the difference between homeowner and non-homeowner behavior is reduced. This is borne out in Table II in which we have compared wards typical of four major economic groups in Cook County (Illinois) in their voting on two issues: first, a proposal to increase county hospital facilities and, second, a proposal to construct a state welfare building. The measures were alike in that they would benefit only indigents; they were different in that their costs would be assessed against different publics: the hospital was to be paid for from the local property tax, the welfare building from state sources, largely a sales tax. Middle-income homeowners showed themselves very sensitive to this difference; the percentage favoring the state-financed measure was twice that favoring the property-tax-financed one. Low-income renters, on the other hand, preferred the property-tax-financed measure to the state-financed one.

Let us turn now to the behavior of voters who do own property and whose taxes will therefore be increased in consequence of a public expenditure. One might suppose that the more property such a voter has, the less likely it is that he will favor public expenditures. To be sure, certain expenditures confer benefits roughly in proportion to the value of property and some may even confer disproportionate benefits on the more valuable properties; in such cases one would expect large property owners to be as much in favor of expenditures as the small, or more so. Most expenditures, however, confer about the same benefits on large properties as on small, whereas of course the taxes to pay for the expenditure are levied (in theory at least) strictly in proportion to the value of property. The owner of a $30,-000 home, for example, probably gets no more benefit from the construction of a new city hall or the expansion of a zoo than does the owner of a $10,000 one; his share of the tax increase is three times as much, however. Very often, indeed, there is an inverse relation between the value of a property and the benefits that accrue to its owner from a public expenditure. The probability is certainly greater that the owner of the $10,000 house will some day use the

[3]The degree of association was also calculated using a nonparametric statistic (Kendall's *tau*). The relationship persists but at low values. Since we are satisfied that the relationship found by r is not spurious, we have relied on it for the balance of the analysis because of its capacity to produce partial correlation coefficients.

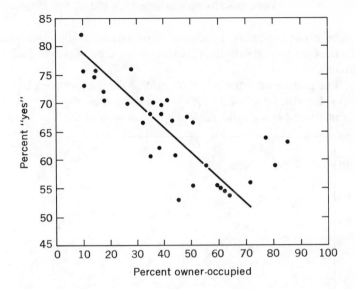

Sources of housing data: U.S. Census of housing, 1960. Figure reprinted from Edward C. Banfield and James Q. Wilson, *City Politics* (Cambridge: Harvard University Press, 1963), p. 238.

FIGURE 1. Relation between percentage voting "yes" on proposition to provide increased county hospital facilities (November 1959) and percentage of dwelling units owner-occupied in the 33 wards of Cleveland.

free county hospital (patronized chiefly by low-income Negroes) than that the owner of the $30,000 house will use it. Since normally the *ratio* of benefits to costs is less favorable the higher the value of the property, one might expect to find a positive correlation between the percentage of "No" votes in a neighborhood and the median value of homes there.

This expectation is not borne out by the facts, however. Table III gives partial correlation coefficients relating the per cent voting "Yes" in the wards of Cleveland and the suburban wards and towns of Cuyahoga County to the median family income in those wards and towns.[4] It shows that the higher the income of a ward or town, the

[4]Only two measures of tax liability can be got from the Census: median home value and median family income. We have used the latter for the most part. The Census classifies all homes valued at over $25,000 together, thereby collapsing distinctions that are important for us. We think, too, that people are more likely to know their incomes than to know the current market value of their homes, and that therefore the Census information on incomes is more reliable. Finally, in neighborhoods populated mostly by renters, median home values are likely to be unrepresentative of the class character of the neighborhood: this is so, for example, where a few owner-occupied slums exist in a district of luxury apartments.

more taste it has for public expenditures of various kinds. That the ratio of benefits to costs declines as income goes up seems to make no difference.[5]

The same pattern appears in a 1960 Flint, Michigan, vote on additional flood control facilities. This is shown graphically in Figure 3. Although there is a considerable dispersion around the line of re-

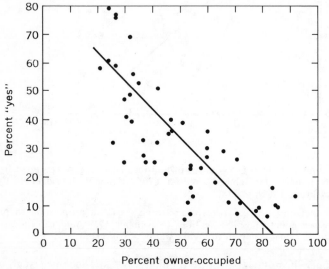

FIGURE 2. Relation between percentage voting "yes" on proposition to provide additional sewer facilities (1962) and percentage of dwelling units owner-occupied in wards of Chicago.

[5]Other studies which suggest that upper-income groups may have a greater preference for public expenditures than middle-income groups include Oliver P. Williams and Charles R. Adrian, *Four Cities: A Study in Policy Making* (Philadelphia: University of Pennsylvania Press, 1963), ch. v; Alvin Boskoff and Harmon Zeigler, *Voting Patterns in a Local Election* (Philadelphia;: J. B. Lippincott Co., 1964), ch. iii; Richard A. Watson, *The Politics of Urban Change* (Kansas City, Mo.: Community Studies, Inc., 1963), ch. iv; and Robert H. Salisbury and Gordon Black, "Class and Party in Non-Partisan Elections: The Case of Des Moines," this REVIEW, Vol. 57 (September, 1963), p. 591. The Williams-Adrian and Salisbury-Black studies use electoral data; the Boskoff-Zeigler and Watson studies use survey data. See also Otto A. Davis, "Empirical Evidence of 'Political' Influences Upon the Expenditure and Taxation Policies of Public Schools," Graduate School of Industrial Administration of the Carnegie Institute of Technology, January, 1964 (mimeo), and William C. Birdsall, "Public Finance Allocation Decisions and the Preferences of Citizens: Some Theoretical and Empirical Considerations," unpublished Ph.D. thesis, Department of Economics, John Hopkins University, 1963. A difficulty with the Davis and Birdsall studies is the size (and thus the heterogeneity) of the units of analysis—entire school districts in one case, entire cities in the other.

gression, in general the higher the home value—and accordingly the more the expected tax—the greater the support for the expenditure.[6]

It may be argued that because of the phenomenon of the diminishing marginal utility of money these findings are not really anomalous. The richer a man is, perhaps, the smaller the sacrifice that an additional dollar of taxation represents to him. Thus, even though the

TABLE III
Partial Correlations Between Median
Family Income of Ward and Percentage "Yes"
Vote on Various Measures, Cleveland and
Suburbs

Area and Issue	Partial Correlation*
Cleveland (33 wards):	
Administration Building	+0.49
County Hospital	+0.64
Tuberculosis Hospital	+0.57
Court House	+0.49
Juvenile Court	+0.66
Parks	+0.48
Welfare Levy	+0.70
Roads and Bridges	+0.61
Zoo	+0.59
Cuyahoga County Suburbs	
(90 wards and towns):	
Administration Building	+0.47
County Hospital	+0.54
Tuberculosis Hospital	+0.43
Court House	+0.60
Juvenile Court	+0.59
Parks	+0.52
Welfare Levy	+0.35
Roads and Bridges	+0.60
Zoo	+0.62

*Controlling for proportion of dwelling units owner-occupied.

[6]Michigan is one of the few states which restricts the right to vote on expenditures to property owners and their spouses. Because the Flint returns were tabulated on a precinct basis, demographic data had to be obtained from block rather than tract statistics; since median family income is given only for tracts, median value of owner-occupied homes had to be used.

Possibly the flood control benefits would be distributed roughly in proportion to the value of properties; about this we cannot say. However, it is worth noting that the vote in Flint on other expenditures which presumably would *not* distribute benefits in proportion to the value of properties (*e.g.,* parks) followed the same pattern.

well-to-do voter may get no more benefit than the poor one gets and may have to pay a great deal more in taxes, an expenditure proposal may nevertheless be more attractive to him. He may be more willing

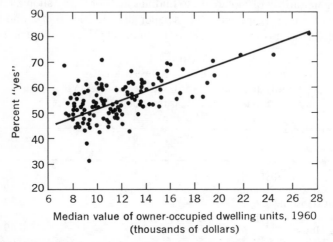

Median value of owner-occupied dwelling units, 1960
(thousands of dollars)

Note: Only property owners and their spouses could vote.
Source of housing data: U.S. Census of Housing, 1960.
Figure reprinted from Banfield and Wilson, *City Politics*, p. 239.

FIGURE 3. Relation between percentage voting "yes" on proposition to provide additional flood control facilities (November 1960) and median value of owner-occupied dwelling units in the precincts of Flint, Michigan.

to pay a dollar for certain benefits than his neighbor is to pay fifty cents because, having much more money than his neighbor, a dollar is worth only a quarter as much to him.

Differences in the value of the dollar to voters at different income levels account in part for the well-to-do voter's relatively strong taste for public expenditures. They can hardly account for it entirely, however. For one thing, they do not rationalize the behavior of those voters who support measures that would give them only trivial benefits while imposing substantial costs upon them. The suburbanite who favors a county hospital for the indigent which he and his family will certainly never use and for which he will be heavily taxed is not acting according to self-interest narrowly conceived no matter how little a dollar is worth to him.

Moreover, if the well-to-do voter places a low value on the dollar when evaluating some expenditure proposals, one would expect him to place the same low value on it when evaluating all others. In fact, he does not seem to do so; indeed, he sometimes appears to place a *higher* value on it than does his less-well-off neighbor. Compare, for example, the behavior of the Cook County (Illinois) suburbanites who voted on a proposal to build a county hospital (an expenditure which would confer only trivial benefits on them and for which they would be taxed in proportion to the value of their property) with the behavior of the same suburbanites who voted on a proposal to give a bonus of $300 to Korean War veterans (an expenditure from which the well-to-do would benefit about as much as the less-well-to-do and for which they would not be taxed disproportionately, since the bonus was to be financed from state, not local, revenues, and the state had neither an income tax nor a corporate profits tax). As Figures 4 and 5 show, the higher the median family income of a voting district, the larger the percentage voting "Yes" on the welfare building (the rank-order correlation was +0.57), but the *smaller* the percentage voting "Yes" on the veterans' bonus (the rank-order correlation was −0.71).

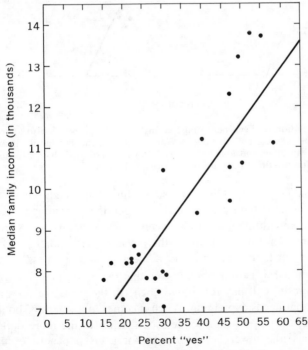

FIGURE 4. Relation between percentage voting "yes" on proposition to provide increased county hospital facilities (1957) and median family income in the suburban cities and towns of Cook County, Illinois, in which two-thirds or more of the dwelling units are owner-occupied.

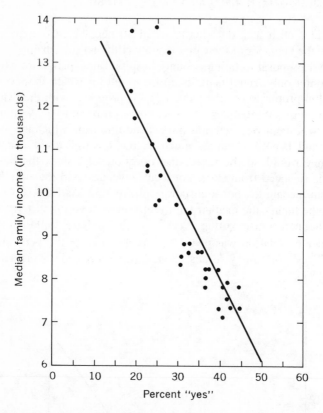

FIGURE 5. Relation between percentage voting "yes" on proposition to approve a $300 bonus for veterans of Korean War (1958) and median family income in the suburban cities and towns of Cook County, Illinois, in which two-thirds or more of the dwelling units are owner-occupied.

In Cuyahoga County, Ohio, the same thing happened. There the higher the median family income, the larger the percentage voting for all the expenditure proposals except one—a bonus for Korean War veterans. On this one measure there was a correlation of −0.65 between median family income and percentage voting "Yes."

Thus, although it is undoubtedly true that the more dollars a voter has, the more he will pay for a given benefit, the principle does not explain all that needs explaining. When it comes to a veterans' bonus, for example, the opposite principle seems to work: the more dollars the voter has, the fewer he will spend for a given benefit of that sort.

That there is a positive correlation between amount of property owned (or income) and tendency to vote "Yes" does not, of course,

imply that a majority of property owners at *any* income level favors
expenditures: the correlation would exist even if the highest income
voters opposed them, provided that at each lower level of income voters opposed them by ever-larger majorities. In fact, middle-income
homeowners often vote against proposals that are approved by both
the very poor (renters) and the very well-to-do (owners). Table IV
gives a rather typical picture of the proposals that are to be financed from the property tax in Cuyahoga County (Ohio).

Not infrequently the highest-income districts support expenditure
proposals by very large majorities—indeed, sometimes by majorities
approaching those given in the property-less slums. Table V compares
the percentage voting "Yes" in the high-income, high-homeownership
precincts of three city-county areas with the percentage of all voters

TABLE IV
Voting Behavior of Four Major
Economic Groups Compared in
Cuyahoga County

Group	Percent "Yes" Vote	
	County Hospital (1959)	County Court House (1959)
	(%)	(%)
*High-Income Homeowners**		
Pepper Pike	69	47
Beachwood	72	47
Middle-Income Homeowners†		
Olmstead Township	51	28
Garfield Heights (Ward 4)	48	29
Lower-Middle-Income Renters‡		
Cleveland Ward 31	76	66
Low Income Renters§		
Cleveland Ward 11	73	63
Cleveland Ward 17	74	62

*Two suburbs with highest median family income ($15,700 and $19,000) of
all suburbs with 85 percent or more home ownership.
†Two suburbs with lowest median family income ($6,800 and $7,000) of
all suburbs with 85 percent or more home ownership.
‡The one ward with less than 15 percent home ownership and which is less
than 10 percent Negro (median income: $4,700).
§Two wards with lowest median family incomes ($3,400 and $3,600) of
all wards with less than 15 percent home ownership (Negro population of
wards was 90 and 97 percent).

in these areas who voted "Yes."[7] Except for Detroit and Dade County, where only property owners and their spouses may vote on expenditures, the city-county totals include large numbers of renters. Even so, the high-income precincts are comparatively strong in their support of all expenditures.

III

When we hold constant the precentage of home ownership, percentage of nonwhites, and median family income, a negative correlation appears between the percentage of voters in the wards of Cleveland who are of foreign stock and the percentage of the total vote in those wards that is "Yes." This is shown in Column 1 of Table VI.[8] Of the many foreign stocks in Cleveland, the Poles and Czechs have the strongest distaste for expenditures. Colume 2 of Table VI shows how markedly the presence of Poles and Czechs in a voting district affects the "Yes" vote.[9] In the suburbs the correlation is only slightly weaker, but significant at the .001 level in all but two cases and in

[7]We isolated all precincts in Census tracts having median family incomes of at least $10,000 a year, with at least 70 percent home ownership (the central city of Chicago was excepted here), and at least 70 percent of the population third- (or more) generation native born.

[8]A person is of "foreign stock" if he was born abroad or if one or both of his parents was born abroad. We believe that the reason why a significant relationship does not appear for the suburbs is that there is a considerable number of Jews among the foreign stock of the suburbs. In the central city, there are practically no Jews. Like other Jews, Jews of Eastern European origin tend to favor expenditures proposals of all kinds. Their presence in the suburbs, therefore, offsets the "No" vote of the non-Jews of foreign stock.

[9]Since no home-owning ward or town in Cuyahoga County is more than 25 percent Polish-Czech according to the 1960 Census, it may be that no inferences can be drawn from the voting data about Polish-Czech behavior. Three considerations increase our confidence in the possibility of drawing inferences, however. (1) Only first- and second-generation Poles and Czechs are counted as such by the Census, but third- and fourth-generation Poles and Czechs tend to live in the same wards and towns; thus the proportion of the electorate sharing Polish-Czech cultural values (the relevant thing from our standpoint) is considerably larger than the Census figures suggest. (2) When other factors are held constant, even small increases in the number of Poles and Czechs are accompanied by increases in the "No" vote; nothing "explains" this except the hypothesis that the Poles and Czechs make the difference. (3) When we take as the unit for analysis not wards but precincts of a few hundred persons that are known to contain very high proportions of Poles and Czechs, we get the same results. Because we are using ecological, not individual, data, we are perforce analyzing the behavior of ethnic "ghettos" where ethnic identification and attitudes are probably reinforced. Poles in non-Polish wards, for example, may behave quite differently.

TABLE V
Percentage Voting "Yes" on Expenditures in Home-Owning, Upper-Income "Old-Stock" Precincts in Various Counties

County, Issue, and Date	Percent "Yes" Vote in Upper-Income Precincts	Percent "Yes" Vote in County As a Whole
	(%)	(%)
Detroit-Wayne County		
Sewers (8/60)	83.6	64.3
Increase School tax limit	52.0	39.0
Build Schools (4/63)	52.0	33.4
Increase sales tax (11/60)	78.6	47.8
Kansas City — Jefferson County		
Increase school taxes (11/60)	68.6	54.9
Build jails (3/62)	86.3	78.0
Sewage treatment plant (11/60)	93.2	81.6
Miami-Dade County		
Highways (5/60)	71.2	53.0
Schools (1955)	90.8	92.1

TABLE VI
Partial Correlations Between Selected "Ethnic" Variables and Percentage Voting "Yes" on Expenditures in Cleveland and Cuyahoga County Wards and Towns*

Issue	Foreign Stock		Polish-Czech		Negro	
	City	Suburbs	City	Suburbs	City	Suburbs
Admin. Building	−0.40	ns†	−0.54	−0.17	ns	ns
County Hospital	ns	ns	−0.79	−0.40	ns	ns
TB Hospital	ns	−0.22	−0.74	−0.46	ns	ns
Court House	−0.47	ns	−0.58	−0.28	ns	ns
Juvenile Court	−0.46	ns	−0.74	−0.40	ns	ns
Parks (1959)	−0.41	ns	−0.62	−0.31	−0.49	ns
Welfare Levy	−0.58	ns	−0.71	−0.49	ns	ns
Roads and Bridges	−0.48	ns	−0.66	−0.40	ns	ns
Zoo	−0.62	ns	−0.71	−0.40	ns	ns
Parks (1960)	ns	ns	ns	−0.50	ns	ns

*These are partial correlation coefficients derived from a regression analysis in which home ownership, median family income, and two "ethnic" variables have been held constant.

†If the correlations were not significant at the .05 level (Student's t), "ns" is entered in the table. The critical values were based on 27 degrees of freedom for the city data and 84 degrees of freedom for the suburban data.

these at the .01 level. The complete correlation table shows that in all but three cases the percentage of Poles and Czechs is a more important influence on voting than median family income, and is second in influence only to home ownership. In two of the three exceptional cases, indeed, it was *more* important than home ownership.

TABLE VII
Percentage of Various "Ethnic" Precincts
Voting "Yes" on Selected Expenditures
in Chicago

Ethnic Group and Number of Precincts	Percent Voting "Yes" On:				
	Co. Hosp. (6/57)	Vet's Bonus (11/58)	Urban Renewal (4/62)	City Hall (5/62)	School (4/59)
	(%)	(%)	(%)	(%)	(%)
*Low Income Renters**					
Negro (22)	84.9	80.2	88.6	82.3	97.8
Irish (6)	61.3	55.3	45.7	46.3	79.4
Polish (26)	60.1	54.6	57.1	53.8	81.8
Middle Income Home- Owners†					
Negro (13)	66.8	54.9	69.6	49.8	88.9
Irish (6)	54.6	44.1	22.0	27.2	64.2
Polish (38)	47.4	40.0	14.6	15.2	58.3

*Average median family income under $6,000 per year; at least two-thirds of all dwelling units renter-occupied.
†Average median family income between $7,500 and $10,000 a year for whites; over $6,000 a year for Negroes. At least 80 percent of all dwelling units owner-occupied.

The findings in Column 3 of Table VI are surprising. We expected a positive correlation between percentage of Negroes and the strength of the "Yes" vote. Deficiencies in the data may possibly account for the absence of any correlation: there are not enough home-owning Negroes or enough very low-income whites in Cleveland to make a really satisfactory matching of wards possible.

In order to get a closer view of ethnic voting it is necessary to forego general correlations and instead to examine individual precincts known to be predominantly of a single ethnic group. In Tables VII and VIII we show how selected "ethnic" precincts belonging to two income and home-ownership classes voted in several elections

in the Chicago and Cleveland areas.[10] There is a remarkable degree
of consistency in the influence of both ethnicity and income or home-
ownership, whether viewed on an intra- or inter-city basis. In Chicago, for example, the low-income renters in *every* case voted more
favorably for expenditures than did the middle-income home-owners
of the same ethnic group. Within the same economic class, however,
ethnicity makes a striking difference. Low-income Negro renters are
in *every* case more enthusiastic by a wide margin about public expenditures than low-income Irish or Polish renters. Middle-income Negro

TABLE VIII

Percentage of Various "Ethnic" Precincts
Voting "Yes" on Selected Expenditures in
Cleveland and Cuyahoga County

Ethnic Group and Number of Precincts	Percent Voting "Yes" on:				
	Co. Hosp. (11/59)	Court House (11/59)	Parks (11/59)	Welfare Levy (5/60)	Vet's Bonus (11/56)
	(%)	(%)	(%)	(%)	(%)
*Low-Income Renters**					
Negro (16)	78.6	67.3	52.6	85.9	89.9
Italian (10)	68.8	53.3	43.5	49.9	74.8
Polish (6)	54.9	39.9	28.1	33.7	71.6
Middle-Income Home-Owners†					
Negro (8)	68.1	54.0	39.6	73.2	79.2
Italian (7)	59.3	49.7	41.1	56.8	66.8
Polish (12)	52.9	35.8	34.3	46.4	61.7
Upper-Income Home-Owners‡					
Anglo-Saxon (11)	70.6	51.4	57.2	64.8	53.7
Jewish (7)	71.7	47.1	48.4	64.5	56.8

*Average median family income less than $6,000 per year; at least two-thirds
of all dwelling units renter-occupied.
†Average median family income between $7,000 and $9,000 a year for
whites; over $6,000 a year for Negroes. At least 75 percent of all dwelling
units owner-occupied.
‡Average median family income over $10,000 per year; over 85 percent of
all dwelling units owner-occupied.

[10]The method by which these precincts were selected is given in the Appendix.
Unfortunately, it proved impossible to identify relatively homogeneous precincts
typical of other ethnic groups at various income levels and degrees of home-
ownership. For example, middle-income Jews tend to be renters, not home
owners, and there are practically no low-income Jewish precincts in either
city. A complete list of these precincts is available from the authors.

home-owners are in *every* case more enthusiastic about the same proposals than middle-income Irish or Polish home-owners. (In passing it is worth noting that Negroes are two or three times more favorable toward urban renewal—despite the fact that they are commonly the chief victims of land clearance programs—than Irish or Polish voters.)

Essentially the same relationships appear in Table VIII for Cleveland-Cuyahoga County. With one exception (Italians voting on the welfare levy), low-income renters in an ethnic group are more favorable to expenditures than middle-income home-owners in the same ethnic group. Low-income Negro renters are the most favorable to all proposals and middle-income Negro home-owners are more favorable to them than are the other middle-income ethnic groups. Aside from the veterans' bonus (a special case), both the "Anglo-Saxon" and the Jewish upper-income home-owners are more favorable to expenditures than any middle-income groups except the Negro.

IV

We have shown both that a considerable proportion of voters, especially in the upper income groups, vote against their self-interest narrowly conceived and that a marked ethnic influence appears in the vote. Now we would like to bring these two findings together under a single explanatory principle.

One such principle—but one we reject—is that the voters in question have acted irrationally (either in not calculating benefits and costs at all or else by making mistakes in their calculations) and that their irrationality is a function of their ethnic status. According to this theory, the low-income Polish renter who votes against expenditures proposals that would cost him nothing and would confer benefits upon him and the high-income Anglo-Saxon or Jewish home-owner who favors expenditures proposals that will cost him heavily without benefitting him would both behave differently if they thought about the matter more or if their information were better.

A more tenable hypothesis, we think, is that voters in some income and ethnic groups are more likely than voters in others to take a public-regarding rather than a narrowly self-interested view of things—*i.e.,* to take the welfare of others, especially that of "the community" into account as an aspect of their own welfare.[11] We offer the additional hypothesis that both the tendency of a voter to take a public-regarding view and the content of that view (*e.g.,* whether or not he thinks a Korean war veterans' bonus is in the public interest) are largely functions of his participation in a subculture that is definable in ethnic and income terms. Each subcultural group, we think, has a more or less distinctive notion of how much a citizen ought to sacrifice for the sake of the community as well as of what the welfare of the community is constituted; in a word, each has its own idea of what justice requires and of the importance of acting justly. According to this hypothesis, the voter is presumed to act rationally; the ends he seeks are not always narrowly self-interested ones, however. On the contrary, depending upon his income and ethnic status they are more or less public-regarding.[12]

That his income status does not by itself determine how public-regarding he is, or what content he gives to the public interest, can be shown from the voting data. As we explained above, generally the higher a home-owner's income the more likely he is to favor expenditures. This is partly—but only partly—because the value of the dollar is usually less to people who have many of them than to people who have few of them. We suggest that it is also because upper-income people tend to be more public-regarding than lower-income people. We do not think that income *per se* has this effect; rather it is the ethnic attributes, or culture, empirically associated with it. It happens that most upper-income voters belong, if not by inheritance then by adoption, to an ethnic group (especially the Anglo-Saxon and the Jewish) that is relatively public-regarding in its outlook; hence ethnic influence on voting is hard to distinguish from income influence.

In the three scatter diagrams which comprise Figure 6 we have tried to distinguish the two kinds of influence. For this figure, we divided all wards and towns of Cleveland and Cuyahoga County in which 85 or more percent of the dwelling units were owner-occupied into three classes according to median home value. Diagram 6a shows the voting where that value was more than $27,000; diagram 6b shows it where it was $19,000-27,000, and diagram 6c shows it where it was less

---

[11]*Cf.* Anthony Downs, "The Public Interest: Its Meaning in a Democracy," *Social Research,* Vol. 29 (Spring 1962), pp. 28-29.

[12]The proposition that "subculture" can be defined in ethnic and income terms is highly provisional. We are looking for other and better criteria and we think we may find some. But so far as the present data are concerned, ethnic and income status are all we have.

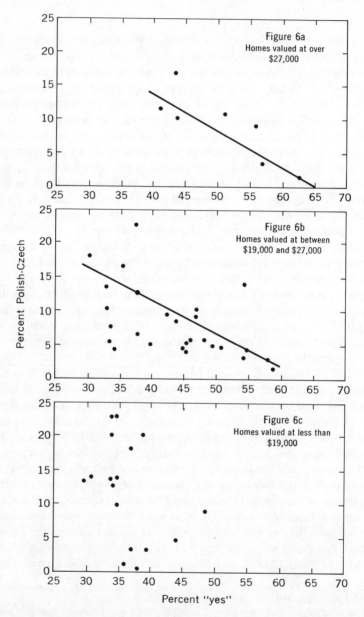

FIGURE 6. Relation between percentage voting "yes" on proposition to provide additional zoo facilities (1960) and proportion of ward or town population which is of Polish or Czech foreign stock in Cuyahoga County, Ohio; at three median home value levels (only wards and towns with 85 percent or more owner-occupied dwellings used).

than $19,000. The horizontal and vertical axes are the same for all diagrams; each diagram shows the relationship between the percentage of voters in the ward or town who are Polish-Czech (vertical axis) and the percentage of "Yes" vote on a proposal to expand the zoo (horizontal axis). In the group of wards and towns having the lowest median home value (diagram 6c) the presence of Polish-Czech voters made little difference; these wards and towns were about 65 percent against the proposal no matter how many Poles and Czechs lived in them. In both groups of higher home-value wards and towns, however, Poles and Czechs were conspicuously less favorable to the proposal than were the rest of the voters. Among the non-Polish-Czech voters in these higher home-value wards and towns, Anglo-Saxons and Jews were heavily represented; therefore it seems plausible to conclude that, as compared to Poles and Czechs in these two income groups, the Anglo-Saxons and Jews were decidedly public-regarding.

Another interpretation of the behavior of the Poles and Czechs is possible, however. It may be that they had the welfare of the community in view also but defined it differently than did the Anglo-Saxons and the Jews. They may have thought that the particular expenditure proposed, or for that matter all public expenditures, would do the community more harm than good. (This would rationalize the behavior of those low-income renters—see Table VIII—who voted against proposals giving them benefits without any costs.)[13] Whatever may be true of the Poles and Czechs, it seems clear that upper-income Anglo-Saxons, and to a somewhat lesser degree Jews, tend to vote on public-regarding grounds *against* some proposals (notable those, like veterans' bonuses and city employees' pension benefits and pay increases) that they regard as serving "special interests" rather than "the community as a whole."

When we know more about each of the various subcultures—especially about the nature of the individual's attachment to the

---

[13]Two other explanations are possible and, in our opinion, plausible. One is that the low-income renters may have taken into account costs to them other than taxes—*e.g.,* the cost, (perhaps monetary) of changes in the neighborhood that would ensue from expenditures. (Irish objections to urban renewal in Chicago may have been due, not to a fear of higher taxes, but to fear of neighborhood "invasion" by Negroes displaced from land clearance projects.) The other is that in these precincts a much higher proportion of renters than of home-owners may have stayed away from the polls. In Cleveland (though not, interestingly, in Chicago) voter turnout is highly correlated with home ownership and almost all white renter precincts have at least a few home-owners in them. Conceivably—we think it unlikely—all those who voted in some "renter" precincts were actually owners.

society, his conception of what is just, and the extent of the obligation he feels to subordinate his interest to that of various others (*e.g.,* the community)—we should doubtless be able to make and test more refined hypotheses about voting behavior.

APPENDIX

We chose the "ethnic" precincts for Tables VII and VIII by inspecting census tract data and then visiting the precincts that appeared to be predominantly of one ethnic group to get confirmatory evidence from well-informed persons and from a view of the neighborhoods. We could have used a less impressionistic method (*e.g.,* counting the proportion of ethnic names on voter registration lists), but since we wanted only to identify precincts that are predominantly of one ethnic group, not to place them on a scale of ethnicity, this did not appear necessary.

Having identified the "ethnic" precincts, we divided them into two (sometimes three) income groups on the basis of census data. As we indicate on the tables, with one exception we used the same cutting points to separate the income levels of all ethnic groups. The exception was the Negro. The income distribution among Negroes is so skewed to the low end of the scale that "middle-income" has to be defined differently for Negroes than for whites. We identified "middle-income Negro" precincts by selecting from among all precincts that were at least 85 percent Negro and had an owner-occupancy rate of at least 80 percent those few with the highest median family incomes. Some of these precincts turned out to have median incomes as low as $6,000 a year, which is about $1,000 less than any of the "middle-income white" precincts had. If we had made the cutting point higher, however, we would not have had enough middle-income Negro precincts to work with. In our opinion, Negroes with incomes of $6,000 are about as likely to "feel" middle-income as are whites with incomes of $7,000.

PART III

MACRO-STUDIES —

THE OVERALL COMPARATIVE PICTURE

INTRODUCTION

One way to test the validity of the ideas presented in the theory section of this reader is to match them against the studies of specific people, problems, and city politics of the micro-studies of the second section. Another way is to consider them against the findings of this section, or "macro-studies," the overall comparative picture. By "macro-studies," we mean research efforts which consider the totality of cities or some aspect of them—all attitudes, all expenditures, all characteristics. By comparative, we have in mind and have selected studies which utilize a large number of cities as the setting for the testing of hypotheses, as many as several hundred in some instances. Micro-studies give the flavor of urban political life. Macro-studies provide the broad data base from which we can add generalizations about behavior to specific and impressionistic knowledge. Everyone wants to be able to know something about cities that is, more or less, true for all cities, or at least specified *types* of cities under predictable conditions. For this form of knowledge, one must turn to studies such as those which follow.

Thomas R. Dye in "City-Suburban Social Distance and Public Policy" tests a number of hypotheses about what the real differences between cities and suburbs are. He starts with the interesting premise that for such postulated differences to be meaningful, they must be reflected in the actual policy choices which communities make. He used as his research base expenditure decisions made by five Wisconsin core cities and 38 of their surrounding suburbs. While Dye found important city-suburban differences in educational expenditures, these tended to decline as one moved into the smaller core city areas. This finding suggests that city-suburban differences are magnified by urban specialization. Aside from the education differences, however, Dye found that cities spend more per capita than suburbs. The reader should ask himself which of the articles in the theory section Dye's data can be held against for evaluation? Agger, Goldrich and Swanson surely. What about the Ostrom, Tiebout, and Warren piece?

357

The following article, "Differentiation and Cooperation in the Metropolitan Area," by Dye, Liebman, Williams, and Herman can also be read as tests of the ideas put forth in the earlier theory efforts, especially those by Agger *et al,* Ostrom *et al,* and also Holden. The authors here examine the interrelationships of 238 separate municipalities in the Philadelphia metropolitan area. They compare the actual level of cooperation among contiguous municipalities in the service areas of schools, sewerage, and police radios with the potential levels if everyone cooperated in all cases with everyone else. Finding important differences they try to analyze these in terms of the communities themselves. What types of communities are most likely to cooperate? Which least likely to do so? What are the key variables which underlie the patterns? Some fascinating answers emerge from this difficult to construct but easily readable research.

In "A Comparison of Political Attitude and Activity Patterns in Central Cities and Suburbs," Joseph Zikmund considers the question of city-suburban similarities and differences from the data based on survey research. Using the Michigan Survey Research Center's national sample, he looks at attitudes and reported activity of individuals living in the different types of communities. His method, which he explains quite clearly for the layman, is an ingenious type of correlation procedure called "components analysis"; it allows one to assess the various "weight" each variable contributes to the differences one finds. His findings in the *national* sample are equally intriguing: the key to differences appear to be across metropolitan areas, or within individual ones. The idea of a *national* set of city behaviors contrasted to a *national* set of suburban ones does not seem to hold much water. The reader might keep these findings in mind when he reads selections Seven and Eight in this same section.

The Alford and Scoble article, "Political and Socioeconomic Characteristics of Cities," shifts the focus. It concentrates on what might be called a sub-aspect of the hypothesis that differences in city politics are connected to group conflicts or at least to group differences in the populations of urban communities. Using a very broad data base—all American cities with populations over 25,000—the authors test the proposition that social characteristics of a community are associated with the structural form of city government it utilizes. Although the data base and the research method are different, the Massotti and Bowen study, "Communities and Budgets. The Sociology of Municipal Expenditures," pursues a different aspect of the same question. The issue in this study is whether differences in the socioeconomic characteristics of cities underlie the policy choices which cities make. The data are 38 socioeconomic characteristics of 18 Ohio cities with more than 50,000 people and the actual records of per capita and total budgetary spending of 12 types in those cities. The method is a somewhat complicated one called "factor analysis," which shows, in effect, whether there is an underlying common dimension in spending behavior. Both the findings and the conclusions are highly suggestive. The reader might ask: do these findings confirm the hypotheses advanced in the Wood article of the theory section?

Woo Sik Kee's article, "Central City Expenditures and Metropolitan Areas," considers still another aspect of the relationship between city socioeconomic characteristics and policy. Kee does two things. He discusses the differences between central cities and their surrounding areas for 36 metropolitan areas in the United States. Then he analyzes the relationships among a selected set of variables and spending for each type of community. Some of his findings, while interesting, are probably not unexpected—for example, that property owners in cities do not like to be taxed for municipal spending. But Kee has one finding of considerable interest to those who want to help core cities out of their financial dilemma. He finds that one key indicator has an enormous impact on what cities do, and this indicator is manipulable as a matter of public political choice. That indicator is the assignment of fiscal responsibilities among the units of government plus the chosen arrangement of state aid. Kee's article should be read with the theoretical concepts from the Holden and Ostrow, Warren, and Tiebout articles held firmly in mind.

"Political Ethos and the Structure of City Government" by Raymond E. Wolfinger and John O. Field examines a very broad series of questions about city politics, particularly such issues as the relationship of ethnicity to governmental form and policy making, and also the connections between size and region and other political variables. The authors consider data from 309 American cities with over 50,000 population in 1960. Much of their argument is a test of the propositions about "public-regardingness" and "private-regardingness" set forth in the selection by Banfield and Wilson in Section Two of this reader. Thus Wolfinger and Field operationalize into a series of testable hypotheses the idea that differences in "ethos" held by quite identifiable elements in cities shape both the choice of form of government and the style of politics to be pursued.

The findings of the Wolfinger and Field article are exceptionally numerous. The Banfield and Wilson theory does not appear to survive their tests. While a public-regarding syndrome of governmental characteristics is uncovered, there is no pure private-regarding syndrome. On policy issues, no pattern at all seems to occur in the direction Banfield and Wilson would predict between ethnicity and the areas of urban renewal, city planning and expenditures, and civil service. This is not to say that Wolfinger and Field uncover no patterns in their study. Quite the contrary is the case: they seem to find that one can specify rather precisely what kind of governmental structures a community will choose if he knows what *region* of the country the city is in. This and other assertions make this one of the most provocative articles ever written in the study of American cities, and also a model of the kind of comparative proposition testing research which is possible.

"Reformism and Public Policies in American Cities" by Robert L. Lineberry and Edmund P. Fowler continues the arguments about the role of the reform movement and effects of structure and socioeconomic characteristics on American city politics. In a sense, Lineberry and Fowler are trying to test all at once three sets of variables that we have encountered up to this point in two by two sequences. They analyze structure, characteristics, and policy outputs and the interrelationships among them, using correlation and multiple correlation on a data base of 200 cities with over 50,000 population. In contrast to the Alford and Scoble findings, Lineberry and Fowler do not find reformed cities to be "the natural habitat of the upper-middle class." In other words, in their sample of cities income differences are not the major differences between cities with council-manager as opposed to mayorality systems. But reformed cities are more homogeneous on other indicators.

The basic hypothesis of the Lineberry and Fowler piece is that the reform movement, as embodied in certain governmental structures, does have the effect of reducing political responsiveness to certain kinds of demands. The test is levels of taxation and expenditure policies in the different cities. In finding some confirmation for this hypothesis, the authors conclude that Banfield and Wilson may have been right about the "ethos" theory. The reader should ask himself if he agrees. Another interesting finding is that the more structural reformed characteristics a city possesses, the less responsive it seems to become. Given the widespread public interest today in "participatory democracy" and the demands for full rights of citizenship by students, the poor, the black and other long deprived groups, evidence such as this calls into question whether the city reform movement is not fundamentally undemocratic. It maximizes efficiency perhaps but, as its creators intended, dilutes political responsiveness. It is a point worth considering since hundreds of American cities rely upon the council-manager format.

"Policy Maps of City Councils and Policy Outcomes: A Developmental Analysis" by Heinz Eulau and Robert Eyestone is the last article in the reader, but in some ways the most important. It is a report on an extensive study of city councilmen and city councils in the San Francisco Bay Area, the most extensive interview project ever done in urban political studies. Further, in an intellectually revolutionary way it transforms urban studies from a type of isolated position by applying sophisticated concepts of development. On top of this, it attempts to use survey data, coming from interviews with individuals, to characterize institutions which govern—*i.e.,* city councils.

The conceptual apparatus of the article is very thorough. The authors seek to test the relationships among city environment (age, size, resources), political leadership (city councilmen), and public policies (expenditures for services and also for "control"—planning for example). They posit that the cities they start with are actually in five "stages of development" in terms of the policies they are pursuing at the time of the study—retarded, emergent, transitional, maturing, and advanced. Two of these stages, emergent and transitional, are seen as exceptionally volatile "phases" of development. The authors think that the development process is a straight line *mediated through* the attitudes of the city council. And what choices the city council will make as it responds to the community's environment in turn is broken down into three variables.

Thus Eulau and Eyestone see city councilmen as possessing three-part "policy maps." They have perceptions of the problems of their communities, preferences among alternatives, and policy "images" or ideas about the future. Through this set of intervening variables contained in the council, the authors posit, the actual policy choices are filtered. The authors test twelve hypotheses emerging from their theoretical model, using the data from the Bay Study. All of their findings are interesting; one, about the relationship of resources to policy is especially intriguing. It seems as if the politicians—and the way they see their "roles"—are very important in determining what a city will do. They may be more important than the physical and material resources a community starts with. Such a finding is not inconsistent with the Long or Salisbury theoretical articles at the beginning of the reader. One other aspect of the Eulau-Eyestone article is worth noting: in its conceptual scope, elaborate presentation of propositions, and far-reaching use of field-gathered data, work of this kind is likely to be a prototype of future urban studies.

Urban studies as a field, and the study of urban politics within political science, have a long way to go before all the major important questions have been considered to any degree. In fact, it is no doubt true that many of the most important questions have not even been asked. Prescriptive wisdom, the kind of knowledge that leads to successful problem solving, seems to the editor to be even further away in the future. Still, looking back on the twenty-five articles in this reader one realizes how much knowledge about urban processes is available today as compared to just ten years ago. In an intellectual sense there is cause for optimism that the cities may at some near point be well understood. In a political sense, needless to say, the present state of the cities leads to no such easy conclusion. Yet understanding must always undergird and precede constructive change and, in an environment where many indicators are less than propitious, it is worthwhile to note that first-rate scholars and a whole generation of students are homing in on the urban scene. Everyone can hope that these efforts lead to some good ends.

17

CITY-SUBURBAN SOCIAL DISTANCE AND PUBLIC POLICY*†

THOMAS R. DYE

Abstract This study describes certain policy differences between
city and suburban governments and attempts to link these to city-
suburban differences in status and life style which have been described by urban sociologists. Differences in the social character
of city and suburbs appear to result in identifiable contrasts in
educational and municipal expenditure levels, and in levels and
purposes of taxation and indebtedness. In larger urbanized areas,
where status and life style differences between city and suburb
are more pronounced, differences in the policy choices of city and
suburban governments are great. But in smaller urbanized areas,
where city-suburban social differences are small, there is less differential in the policy choices of city and suburban governments.

At least since the elaboration of the Burgess zonal hypothesis in
1924, urban sociology has been concerned with the social correlates
of increasing distance from the center of the metropolis.[1] City-
suburban differences in status, life style, education, wealth, leisure,
ethnicity, familism, and culture have been extensively documented.[2]

*Reprinted from *Social Forces,* Vol. 43, No. 1 (September 1965). By permis-
sion of *Social Forces.*
†This research was supported in part by the University of Wisconsin Urban
Program under the terms of a grant by the Ford Foundation.
[1]See Ernest W. Burgess, "The Growth of the City," in Robert E. Park, Ernest W.
Burgess, and Roderick D. McKenzie, *The City* (Chicago: University of Chi-
cago Press, 1925), pp. 47-62.
[2]See William M. Dobriner, *Class in Suburbia* (Englewood Cliffs, New Jersey:
Prentice-Hall, 1963); William M. Dobriner (ed.), *The Suburban Community*
(New York: G. P. Putnam's Sons, 1958); George A. Lundberg, Mirra Ko-
marovsky, and Mary McInerny, *Leisure: A Suburban Study* (New York:
Columbia University Press, 1934); William H. Whyte, Jr., *The Organization*

Recently political scientists, Robert Wood and Scott Greer among others, have pictured contrasting styles of city and suburban policies.[3] But if these observations of social distance between city and suburb are to be politically meaningful, they must eventually be related to differences in the public policy choices of city and suburban governments. If cities and suburbs are differentiated along important social indices, we can expect real and persistent contrasts in the policy choices of their local governments. Persons with different occupations, educations, and incomes are likely to demand different types and emphases in government services. Families with children have different ideas about school systems than have those without children. Persons well-equipped to compete for jobs and income in a free market often view government welfare activities differently from those not so well-equipped. Persons who have a large investment in property view taxation in a different light from those who do not. And so on.

The social patterns of suburban living help to determine the policies suburbanites choose for their governments to follow, and the same is true for the city. Differences in the social character of city and suburb can be expected to produce differences in public policy. The object of the research reported here is to describe in a systematic fashion contrasts in the policy choices of city and suburban governments which can be attributed to their separate social character. But before we examine contrasts in city and suburban policy choices, let us describe city-suburban social distance more precisely.

First of all, a suburb is defined here to mean a densely settled non-agricultural community adjacent to and dependent upon a large cen-

---

Man (New York: Doubleday & Co., 1956); Sylvia Fava, "Suburbanism as a Way of Life," *American Sociological Review,* 21 (February 1956), pp. 34-37; Herbert T. Gans, "Urbanism and Suburbanism as a Way of Life," in Arnold Rose (ed.), *Human Behavior and Social Processes* (New York: Houghton Mifflin Co., 1961); Esref Shevky and Wendell Bell, *Social Area Analysis* (Stanford: Stanford University Press, 1955).

[3]Robert C. Wood, *Suburbia Its People and Their Politics* (New York: Houghton Mifflin Co., 1958); Scott Greer, "The Social Structure and Political Process of Suburbia," *American Sociological Review,* 24 (October 1959), pp. 514-526; Scott Greer, *Governing the Metropolis* (New York: John Wiley & Sons, 1962); Scott Greer, *The Emerging City* (New York: The Free Press of Glencoe, 1962); G. Edward Janosik, "The New Suburbia," *Current History,* 31 (August 1956), pp. 91-95; Fred Greenstein and Raymond Wolfinger, "The Suburbs and Shifting Party Loyalties," *Public Opinion Quarterly,* 22 (Winter 1958), pp. 473-493; Jerome Manis and Leo Stine, "Suburban Residence and Political Behavior," *Public Opinion Quarterly,* 23 (Winter 1959), pp. 483-489; Edward C. Banfield, "The Politics of Metropolitan Area Organization," *Midwest Journal of Political Science,* 1 (May 1957), pp. 77-91.

tral city.[4] By "dependent" it is meant that suburban communities represent sources and destinations of the internal circulation of goods and people that make up the daily rhythm and activity of the large metropolis. A suburb may either supply manpower and consumers for the metropolis or it may use the manpower and produce the goods of the metropolis. Typically, perhaps, people who live in the suburbs work in the central city, but there are many examples of the reverse situation. And in larger urbanized areas people may live in one suburb and work in another. But the distinguishing feature of a suburb remains its economic dependency upon, and extensive intercourse with, the larger metropolis.

Following U.S. Census Bureau usage, a suburb can be operationally defined as that part of an "urbanized area" lying outside of the central city. The Census Bureau identified 213 urbanized areas in the 1960 census. An urbanized area consists of a city of 50,000 or more plus its surrounding ring of contiguous high density suburban area. This ring follows census enumeration districts and is not always coterminous with the boundaries of political units. This ring is the best operational approximation of the sociological concept of a suburb.[5]

The locus of this study was the five urbanized areas of Wisconsin—Milwaukee, Madison, Green Bay, Racine, and Kenosha. In addition to the five central cities of these urbanized areas, 38 units of local government were selected to represent suburbia. These were the 38 local governments in Wisconsin which lay wholly within urbanized areas and, of course, outside of central cities.

Generalizing about suburbs involves certain risks. While this study attempts to identify characteristics of suburbs and suburban governments, readers are cautioned that individual suburbs may be very different from one another.[6] Differences between some suburbs may

[4]See William T. Martin, "The Structuring of Social Relationships Engendered by Suburban Residence," *American Sociological Review,* 21 (August 1956), pp. 446-453.

[5]The alternative approach is to define suburbia as that part of the "metropolitan area" lying outside of the central city. However, a "metropolitan area," in contrast to an "urbanized area," is defined by county boundaries rather than population density, and includes rural territory with few social linkages with the metropolis. See U.S. Bureau of Census, *U.S. Census of Population 1960,* "Number of Inhabitants," PC(1)-1A (Washington, D.C.: U.S. Government Printing Office, 1961); and Richard A. Kurtz and Joanne B. Eicher, "Fringe and Suburb: A Confusion of Concepts," *Social Forces,* 37 (October 1958), pp. 32-37.

[6]See for example, Bennett M. Berger, *Working Class Suburb* (Berkeley: University of California Press, 1960).

TABLE 1.

Status Characteristics of Cities and Suburbs
in Wisconsin and 213 Urbanized Areas in the U.S.

	Persons Over 25			Family Income	
	Median School Years	Percent High School Graduates	Percent Employed "White Collar"	Median	Percent Over $10,000
U.S. Urbanized Areas					
213 Cities	10.7	40.9	45.1	5945	16.6
All Suburbs	12.0	50.9	50.3	7114	24.1
Difference	1.3	10.0	5.2	1169	7.5
Milwaukee Area					
City	10.4	39.7	40.1	6664	16.7
Suburbs	12.1	54.4	51.6	7785	28.7
Difference	1.7	14.7	11.5	1121	12.0
Madison Area					
City	12.5	65.3	58.7	6799	20.6
Suburbs	12.6	70.1	59.0	7376	24.7
Difference	0.1	4.8	0.3	577	4.1
Green Bay Area					
City	11.2	46.3	43.9	5981	11.7
Suburbs	12.0	50.1	43.3	6483	17.2
Difference	0.8	3.9	−0.6	502	5.5
Racine Area					
City	10.5	40.6	41.0	6758	18.2
Suburbs	10.5	40.8	37.4	7237	25.8
Difference	0	0.2	−3.6	479	7.6
Kenosha Area					
City	10.3	36.8	34.5	7035	21.5
Suburbs	10.5	38.2	27.2	7192	20.0
Difference	0.2	1.4	−7.3	157	−1.5

be as great or greater than differences between suburbs and the central city. For example, River Hills and West Milwaukee, both suburbs of Milwaukee, represent prototypes of the middle class residential suburb and working class industrial suburb respectively. In West Milwaukee 83 percent of the tax base is in industrial or commercial property; the male labor force is 73 percent blue collar; only five percent of the population over 25 is college educated; and the median family income was $6,846 in 1959. In River Hills the entire tax base is in residential property; the male labor force is 58 percent white collar; 32 percent of the population over 25 is college educated; and the median family income is $12,622. Yet for purposes of analysis we have chosen to talk about *all* suburbs. For in aggregate terms the social character of suburbia can be clearly distinguished from that of the central city.

CITY AND SUBURB: STATUS DIFFERENCES

America's suburbs house greater proportions of white collar employees, college graduates, and middle income families than its central cities. Table 1 shows several common measures of status for the central city and surrounding ring of Wisconsin's five urbanized areas, together with comparable figures for all 213 urbanized areas in the nation. Absolute differences between city and suburb for each of these measures are also shown. Status differentials in favor of the suburbs are very pronounced in larger urbanized areas and averages for all 213 urbanized areas are heavily weighted by these larger areas. However, Leo Schnore reports that status differentials in smaller urbanized areas are not as great as in larger areas and often favor the city rather than the suburbs.[7] The relationship between size or urbanized area and city-suburban social distance can be observed among Wisconsin's five urbanized areas, which are arranged in Table 1 according to size. The most pronounced status differences favoring the suburbs are found in Milwaukee, the state's largest urbanized area. Status differences are much smaller in the smaller urbanized areas—Green Bay, Racine, and Kenosha. A minus sign in Table 1 indicates that status differences favor the city rather than the suburbs.

CITY AND SUBURB: LIFE STYLE DIFFERENCES

A familistic or child-centered life style can be identified in certain social statistics.[8] One measure is the "fertility ratio" or the number

[7]Leo Schnore, "The Socio-Economic Status of Cities and Suburbs," *American Sociological Review,* 28 (February 1963), pp. 76-85.
[8]Social statistics measuring a familistic life style are discussed at length in Esref Shevky and Wendell Bell, *Social Area Analysis* (Stanford: Stanford University Press, 1956).

of children born per 1,000 women 15 to 44 years of age. Another measure is the percent of women age 14 or over who are in the work force. A large number of children per 1,000 married females of child-bearing age, together with a small proportion of women who work, suggests a family-centered culture. In addition, the single-family free-standing house is the *sine qua non* of familistic living in an affluent society. Cumulatively these three life style measures are said to identify a familistic or child-centered way of life.

The city is hardly the place for most child-centered amenities. Evidence indicates that parents in contemporary America seek to maximize family life in the suburbs. Table 2 shows that (1) there are proportionately more children in the suburbs than in central cities, (2) a larger proportion of suburban mothers stay home to take care of these children, and (3) a larger proportion of suburban families are housed in single-family units. The non-familistic life style is characteristic of central cities where there are proportionately fewer children, more apartment living, and greater numbers of employed mothers. Wisconsin's cities and suburbs are representative of the national pattern in this regard. A familistic life style in suburbia suggests the importance of the most fundamental of child amenities —the school. Not only are there more children in the suburbs, but suburban parents manage to keep larger proportions of them in school. The differences between city and suburban public school enrollment percentages are particularly apparent in the 14 to 17 year old age category.

There is some tendency for the suburbs of smaller urbanized areas to be less differentiated from their central cities in terms of life style than the suburbs of larger urbanized areas. Smaller cities seem to be able to support a familistic life style as well as their suburbs. This national pattern is apparent in Wisconsin. Note that the cities in Wisconsin's smaller urbanized areas keep more of their 14 to 17 year olds in school than their suburbs; this is in direct contrast to the pattern in larger urbanized areas.

CITY AND SUBURB: DIFFERENCES IN POLICY CHOICES

What are some of the consequences of city-suburban social and life style differences for the policy choices of local governments?[9]

[9]The data on government expenditures and taxation in this study were derived from the public records of the Wisconsin Department of Audit, Department

TABLE 2.
Life Style Characteristics of Cities and Suburbs
in Wisconsin and 213 Urbanized Areas in the U.S.

	Fertility Ratio	Percent Females In Labor Force	Percent Single Family Dwelling Units	Percent 14-17 Years Old In School
U.S. Urbanized Areas				
213 Cities	1541	39.6	43.0	86.5
All Suburbs	1715	34.1	77.6	91.0
Difference	174	5.5	34.6	4.5
Milwaukee Area				
City	1598	40.2	39.0	91.1
Suburbs	1752	32.2	75.1	95.0
Difference	154	8.0	36.1	3.9
Madison Area				
City	1256	45.0	53.0	91.6
Suburbs	1930	38.3	76.6	96.0
Difference	774	6.7	23.6	4.4
Green Bay Area				
City	1851	33.3	64.3	93.7
Suburbs	2162	28.9	85.6	91.8
Difference	211	4.4	21.3	− 1.9
Racine Area				
City	1770	37.6	58.9	90.7
Suburbs	2133	32.5	84.0	86.4
Difference	363	5.1	25.1	− 4.3
Kenosha Area				
City	1771	34.3	58.7	92.1
Suburbs	1706	33.6	75.6	82.2
Difference	− 65	.7	16.9	− 9.9

of Taxation, and Superintendent of Public Instruction. These records are
drawn from the fiscal reports of local governments. Because of the many
problems created by differences in methods of accounting and reporting,
and differences in degrees of accuracy and completeness, in these reports,
inferences from such data are warranted only where clear and consistent
trends are apparent.

First of all, Table 3 indicates that the child-centered life style of suburbia is reflected in the education policies of suburbs in Wisconsin's two largest urbanized areas. More dollars were spent on educating the average school child in the suburbs of Milwaukee and Madison than were spent on the average child in these central cities. Sixteen of the 18 suburbs in Milwaukee County spent more per pupil for operating their public schools than the City of Milwaukee. Four of Madison's seven suburbs spent more per pupil than Madison. These suburbs house residents of higher than average social status. This condition together with the child-centered character of suburban living tends to produce high educational aspiration levels. Suburban parents with high hopes and plans for their children's occupational success focus concern upon the school system, and this concern is reflected in higher per pupil educational expenditures.

On the other hand, in the smaller urbanized areas of Green Bay, Racine, and Kenosha, a different pattern of school expenditures emerged. The cities spent more per pupil than the suburbs. Thus, it would appear that in larger urban areas, where social and life style differences between city and suburb are more pronounced, public expenditures reflect these differences; but in smaller urbanized areas, where social and life style differences between city and suburb are slight, differences between city and suburb in educational expenditures are slight or run opposite to the expected direction.

Central cities show substantially higher operating expenditures per capita than suburbs. This is true in both large and small urbanized areas. The central city provides the essential physical plant for the entire urbanized area. The maintenance of this physical plant requires city residents to make higher per capita operating expenditures than those required of suburbanites. In addition, many expenditures in suburban communities are shifted from public to private spending (private septic tanks instead of public sewers, private instead of public recreation, etc.). In general, suburbanites demand and get less in the way of public services than city residents; but in the larger urbanized areas the demand for public services in the suburbs more closely corresponds to city services. Differences in the service demands upon city and suburban governments are greatest in the areas of police protection, recreation, and health. This again reflects a concentration in the city of people who are likely to require these services, in contrast to the suburbs.

Local government is never more visible to the taxpayer than when he receives his yearly tax bill. Taxes had much to do with the migra-

TABLE 3.
Differential in Tax and Expenditure Policies
of City and Suburban Governments in Wisconsin
by Urbanized Area, 1960

	Total Operating School Expenditures $ Per Pupil	Total Operating Municipal Expenditures $ Per Capita	Full Value Property Tax Rate (in Mills)				Indebtedness	
			Total	Municipal	School	County	$ Per Capita	$ Per $1000 Full Value
Milwaukee Area								
City	438	87	31.0	11.3	12.4	8.9	163	32
18 Suburbs	590	67	26.7	4.0	13.2	9.1	189	28
Madison Area								
City	441	75	25.9	9.9	11.7	4.4	223	40
7 Suburbs	467	31	25.2	2.8	17.3	4.8	79	22
Green Bay Area								
City	455	69	22.5	6.6	10.3	5.3	178	32
6 Suburbs	405	34	20.0	4.4	9.8	5.8	55	11
Racine Area								
City	401	62	24.9	7.5	13.4	3.8	204	40
5 Suburbs	394	24	18.0	1.4	15.0	3.9	4	1
Kenosha Area								
City	435	62	26.5	5.7	15.0	5.6	201	40
2 Suburbs	365	12	22.2	.9	14.8	6.0	0	0

tion of the "pioneer suburbanites," those who moved to the suburbs in the 1930's and 1940's. At that time, suburban living offered a significant savings in property taxation over what were thought to be heavy city taxes. But the tax advantage of the suburbs turned out partly to be a "self-denying prophecy": the more people who fled to suburbs to avoid heavy taxes, the greater the demand for public services in these new communities and the higher suburban taxes became to meet these new demands. Table 3 indicates the tax burden in Wisconsin's suburbs continues to remain somewhat lighter than the tax burden in the cities. (Tax burden is measured here by the effective tax rate on full value of property, thus taking into account differentials in assessment ratios.)

The differential between city and suburb in tax burden is a product of differences in *municipal* taxes rather than school taxes. If we look only at *municipal* taxes, the differential in tax burden between city and suburb is very great; not one suburb in the entire sample even approached its central city in terms of *municipal* tax burden. School taxes make up a far larger proportion of the tax burden of the suburbs than the central cities. The child-centered concerns of suburbia are directly reflected in tax policy. School taxes are apparently less objectionable to suburbanites than municipal taxes. Thus even if the total tax burden in the suburbs was *not* lighter than the city, suburbanites might still see an advantage in a tax structure with a heavy emphasis on support for public education.

With regard to indebtedness, most suburbs were able to steer a fiscally more conservative course than the central cities. Only in the Milwaukee area was the per capita debt of all suburbs higher than the central city. Yet even here the debt load upon property in the suburbs—debt load per $1,000 of market value—was lighter than in the city. About one-third of the debt compiled by central cities was for school purposes, while over three-quarters of all suburban debt was incurred for school purposes.

SUMMARY

City and suburb in Wisconsin differ in their emphasis on family living, in their educational levels, in the nature of their work force, and in their degree of affluence. The larger the urbanized area, the greater the social differences between city and suburb. Previously, political participation, voting behavior, and other measures of political style had been established as correlates of city-suburban social differences.[10] The research reported here suggests that differences in the social character of city and suburb also produce identifiable contrasts in the public policy choices of city and suburban governments. Suburbanites chose to spend more on public education than city dwellers, but less on municipal services. Suburbanites chose to do without many municipal services, or shift the costs of these services into the area of private spending, or get away without providing these services because the central city provided them for the entire urbanized area.

The result is a lower overall tax bill in the suburbs. The difference in tax burden between city and suburb would be even greater if suburbanites did not chose to spend more per pupil on education than city residents. This produces higher school taxes in the suburbs than in the city. The suburbs also manage to limit their indebtedness more than cities, and most of the indebtedness incurred by suburbs is for school rather than municipal purposes. City-suburban policy contrasts in smaller urbanized areas do not parallel contrasts in larger urbanized areas. In larger urbanized areas, where status differences between city and suburb are more pronounced, the suburbs spend considerably more per pupil for education than the city. But in smaller urbanized areas, where status differences between city and suburb are not as great, there is less differential in school expenditures and this differential favors the city rather than the suburbs. The suburbs of larger urbanized areas more closely approach the city in the provision of municipal services and in overall tax burden than the suburbs of smaller urbanized areas.

[10]See footnote 3.

18

DIFFERENTIATION AND COOPERATION
IN A METROPOLITAN AREA* †

THOMAS R. DYE
CHARLES S. LIEBMAN
OLIVER P. WILLIAMS
HAROLD HERMAN

A distinguishing characteristic of metropolitan areas is a real specialization, or differentiation among spatially defined subpopulations with respect to class or status, life style, and economic function. To sociologists the relationship between specialization and urbanization is a commonplace. Their analysis has commonly centered on isolating the types of specialization and their discrete effects. Ecologists have described functionally differentiated zones and sectors and have even identified specific behavioral patterns associated with the residents of particular areas. To the political scientist, one of the most interesting attributes of metropolitan areas is the fact that urban specialization very often coincides with political boundaries. Not only has the familiar bedroom community become incorporated as a political entity, but within metropolitan regions one can also find industrial enclaves, recreational resorts, commercial centers,

*Reprinted from the *Midwest Journal of Political Science, VII,* No. 2 (May 1963) 145-155. By permission of the Wayne State University Press and the authors.
†Revised version of a paper presented at the 1962 annual meetings of the American Political Science Association. This paper is from a larger study by the authors on urban differentiation and political choice in a metropolitan area. The technique of comparing agreeing and non-agreeing pairs of municipalities was developed in the Seminar on Interdisciplinary Research in Political Integration, University of Pennsylvania, under the leadership of Professor Karl Deutsch. We wish to express our appreciation to James Toscano for his helpful cooperation in sharing his data and findings for his study approaching cooperative arrangements from a different perspective. See his "Transaction Flow Analysis in Metropolitan Areas," Memorandum No. 4, University of Pennsylvania Studies of Social Values and Public Policy.

374

intellectual retreats, racial and ethnic ghettoes, company towns, and religious colonies which correspond roughly with local political units.

A central hypothesis of this paper and of the large study upon which it is based is that social and economic differentiation among communities in a metropolitan area is associated with differing local governmental policies. Local governmental decisions in a metropolitan area are made at hundreds of decision centers, each set in a separate social and economic environment, each responding to different types of interests, and each struggling to maintain a separate existence. As a result of these differing conditions, local governments can be expected to select differing policy alternatives designed to cope with specific interests within their constituencies.

Yet because of the interdependency of urban communities, some interests express themselves through demands for integrative or cooperative actions among local governments. Frequently it is suggested that certain services can be administered more economically and planned more intelligently when handled on an area-wide basis, or at least on a multi-jurisdictional basis. These arguments are often encountered with regard to schools, water supply, police protection, waste disposal, libraries, and street maintenance. Cooperative responses of local communities to jointly felt pressures of urbanization are not uncommon. The popular forms of cooperative responses among urban communities include the interjurisdictional agreement and joint authorities.

Students of political integration at the international level have suggested that policy concensus is the basis of viable political integration. If this same proposition is operative at the intermunicipal level and if the pattern of local policy choices is associated with social and economic differences among municipalities, then one should be able to observe the effect of urban differentiation on integrative arrangements in a metropolitan area. In short, it is our hypothesis that intermunicipal cooperation in a metropolitan area is a function of social and economic distance. Intermunicipal cooperation will tend to occur more frequently among communities which are similar in character and less frequently among highly differentiated communities. In this paper we shall attempt to set forth this hypothesis about the effect of urban differentiation on patterns of intermunicipal cooperation in an operational manner and to test it with reference to characteristics of local governments within the Philadelphia metropolitan area.

There are 238 municipalities covering the Pennsylvania sector of the Philadelphia metropolitan area. Although they range in size and density from the core city of Philadelphia with nearly two million persons to sparsely populated rural townships with less than 300 inhabitants, each of these local governments has substantially the same legal powers with which to structure its internal life and to cope with social and economic diversity. Recognizing that specialization and differentiation increases with urbanization, a distinction was made between the urban and semi-rural portions of the metropolitan area. The definition of urban as opposed to semi-rural was established at 500 persons per square mile, a figure chosen to approximate the state of urbanization of an area when urban services are generally initiated by the local government. According to this classification there were 90 urban and 135 semi-rural municipalities composing the study's sample; 12 communities were dropped from analysis because of large institutional populations which interfered with social and economic measurement.

In addition to the development of satisfactory measures of social, life style, and economic diversities, several other conditions were required for the hypothesis to be tested: (1) To have a cooperative arrangement, the potential cooperators must have or want to have the same service. (If one community has a police force and another neither has nor wants one, there is no basis for a cooperative operation of a police radio transmitter); (2) For a particular service, some municipalities must have selected a cooperative approach and others rejected it. (There must be a basis for comparing cooperating and non-cooperating communities); (3) While not absolutely essential, local governments must generally be contiguous for cooperation to be feasible. Thus in the analysis which follows, only the relationships between contiguous municipalities are subject to examination.

For the purposes of this paper, urban differentiation was operationally defined by three indices; these indices were selected for their relevance to decisions involving one or more of the most common types of interjurisdictional agreements. They are "social rank," market value per capita, and party voting.

1. *"Social rank."* This is an adaptation of an objective measure of community social status developed by sociologists Eshref Shevky and Wendell Bell which gives equivalent weight to occupational and educational attributes of a community's population. The occupational factor is the percent of employed males in professional, managerial and sales occupations. The educational factor is the percent of persons over 25 years old with one or more years of college education. The percentages for each factor are first standardized

in a range from 0 to 100 which assigns a zero score to the community with the lowest percent in the college age or status occupational class and 100 to the highest community. Once the two standard scores are computed, they can be averaged. Thus every local unit is assigned a social rank score.

2. *Market value per capita*. A measure of community wealth which indicates the kind of financial resources which a municipality would bring to a cooperative enterprise.

3. *Party vote*. Partisan officials are the negotiators of cooperative arrangements. The percent Republican of the total vote for Governor in 1950 was used to identify the general partisan orientation of each community.

Cooperation is defined here as the joint financing of a service facility which is operated administratively as a single system. A cooperative arrangement may take the form of a contract, a joint authority, or a joint board. Non-cooperation is defined as the lack of any cooperative arrangement between contiguous municipalities which provide similar services. In the study area there are numerous cooperative arrangements for particular services. These arrangements represent local choices and are not imposed by higher legal authorities. The principal functional areas of cooperation are schools, sewers, police radio, libraries, water and solid waste disposal. Only in the first three areas is there a large enough number of cases to accommodate statistical analysis. Fortunately, these three functional areas represent three distinctly different kinds of local policies. Schools are an expression of the life style of a community but sewers and police radio systems are not. Both schools and sewers represent large financial commitments but police radio systems do not.

With 238 municipalities in the study area, there are 28,203 possible pairs of municipalities and therefore that same number of possible intermunicipal relationships. But if our analysis of intermunicipal relationships is limited to geographically contiguous municipalities, this figure is reduced to 534, the total number of pairs of contiguous municipalities.[1] This reduction was accomplished by inspecting a map of the area. Using the density classification, there were 198 pairs in the urban area, 294 in the rural and 42 pairs comprised of one urban and one rural municipality.

[1]There were 66 pairs of contiguous municipalities which were eliminated because each involved at least one of the 12 municipalities with high institutional populations.

Since each of the 534 pairs consists of two municipalities and each municipality is described by three measures of urban differentiation, it was possible to identify quantitatively the social and economic distance involved in each pair of municipalities along three separate indices. The absolute difference in index scores between paired municipalities constituted the measures of social and economic distance; three measures of social and economic distance were available for each pair, namely, social rank, per capita market value, and party voting. The smaller the difference in any index for a pair of communities, the more similar the communities in that pair are to each other, and the less social and economic distance exists between them. The larger the differences in the index scores between two municipalities in a pair, the more dissimilar these municipalities are said to be. The central hypothesis of this paper can now be stated in operational terms. *If intermunicipal cooperation in a metropolitan area is a function of social and economic distance between communities, the mean of the differences in index values will be smaller for cooperating than for non-cooperating pairs of municipalities.*

Table I presents the data on school arrangements. For the hypothesis to be borne out, the mean of the differences for cooperating pairs must always be less than for non-cooperating ones. Table I indicates that this is the case to the greatest extent in the urban area, is barely corroborated in the semi-rural one, and only partially so in the rural-urban—the area comprised of those mixed pairs of rural and urban municipalities.

The major incentive for cooperative school arrangements is the pooling of resources in constructing high schools. Both from a capital financing and a curricular standpoint, small municipalities have greater difficulty building high schools independently. As the number of pairs in the various categories of Table I indicate, the total incidence of agreement is greater in the semi-rural than the urban areas (urban 26 and semi-rural 162). This difference however, cannot be explained merely by the differences in size of urban and semi-rural municipalities. According to current Pennsylvania state policy, school districts should have at least 5,000 pupils. This means that ideally most municipalities with under 25,000 persons should be parties to joint arrangements. According to this standard only 12 urban and one semi-rural municipality are large enough to have independent systems. In fact there are many more than twelve urban municipalities with independent systems, but none in the semi-rural area. Indeed many

TABLE I. SCHOOLS
Mean Differences Among Pairs of Cooperating and Non-Cooperating Municipalities

	Urban			Rural-Urban			Semi-Rural		
	Cooperating	Non-Cooperating	Total	Cooperating	Non-Cooperating	Total	Cooperating	Non-Cooperating	Total
Social Rank	10.4	16.9	16.0‡	8.6	14.1	12.8†	7.3	7.8	7.5
Market Value Per Capita	$1,131	$1,467	$1,424	$1,685	$1,437	$1,515	$957	$994	$974
Percent Republican	9.0	11.5	11.2*	7.1	10.2	9.2*	8.0	8.8	8.4
Number of Pairs	26	172	198	13	29	42	162	132	294

*Differences between cooperating and non-cooperating pairs of municipalities are significant at the .10 level of significance.
†Differences between cooperating and non-cooperating pairs of municipalities are significant at the .05 level of significance.
‡Differences between cooperating and non-cooperating pairs of municipalities are significant at the .01 level of significance.

379

urban municipalities which are quite small maintain their independence through *ad hoc* tuition arrangements with various neighboring governmental units.

Our hypothesis suggests that the more extensive use of cooperative school arrangements in the semi-rural area is a function, in part, of the lesser social distance among pairs there than is found in the urban area. Note that in the "Total" column the mean of the differences is larger for each index value for the urban area. Urban specialization tends to create sharp social breaks which follow municipal boundaries. Thus the intermunicipal social distances influence not only the pattern of cooperation, but also its extent. Only 26 out of 198 urban pairs had agreements, while, 162 out of 294 rural ones did. The urban-rural pairs lie in between with 13 out of 29 cooperating. The 26 urban pairs which did cooperate were atypical for the sample area. The mean differences in social rank for the entire urban area is 16.0, but only 10.4 for the cooperating communities. A similar pattern holds for the other three variables although not always at a high level of significance.

In the urban-rural area the mean differences in market value-per-capita between cooperating and non-cooperating pairs is in the opposite direction of that expected. Since none of the differences in market value-per-capita in any of the three sample areas are at a .10 level of significance, the difference in the urban-rural area might have arisen solely due to chance. It may also be a function of the market value index which does not always coincide with the year in which an agreement took place; variances of as much as ten years between index and agreement year are included.[2] Most communities do not experience rapid demographic changes. However, along the fringes of the urban area the most rapid shifts take place. Fringe area industrialization and large housing developments are the most common form which these changes take. It is likely that some disparities in market value per capita have taken place subsequent to the development of joint school systems. The hypothesis is supported even in this changing area with regard to social rank and the related variable, party voting. Either populations channeling into fringe areas are not upsetting the social balance of agreeing pairs, or changes in social composition occur at a slower rate than any of our other indexes. Our observation is that both these propositions are true.

[2]Methodologically, data for indices of agreeing pairs should be gathered at the time agreements occur. Aside from nonavailability of data in all years, there is a problem of selecting the proper year for an index of non-cooperating pairs.

In the semi-rural area the differences in means are all in the expected direction but at less than a .10 level of significance. Additional applications of the social rank concept to the Philadelphia metropolitan area suggest an explanation for this apparent difference between urban and semi-rural behavior. We suspect that social rank is not as determinative an influence in the public policies of semi-rural areas as in urban areas, where the closeness, size and more frequent interactions of populations evoke greater consciousness of differences in community social status.

Education is one of the more vital policy areas through which local communities may express particular cultural and social styles of living. Another service, which is essential for urban living, but which has very little to do with life style, is the disposal of sewage. The analysis was repeated for sewage disposal agreements. One of the conditions for analysis was that both potential parties to an agreement must provide the service in question; thus only sewered communities are included in the sample. The condition confined the sample to the contiguously urbanized area around the core city. A review of the first portion of Table II under the heading "TOTAL" indicates that there is little difference between agreeing and non-agreeing pairs with respect to social rank and party vote. There are significant differences with respect to community wealth. The conclusion might be drawn that municipalities do not mind negotiating with neighbors of differing social rank and party over matters of as little social significance as sewage, but are concerned about their neighbors' wealth because the maintenance and future expansion of the joint system will be influenced by the tax situation of the members. However, as the remaining portions of the Table show, this is only partially true.

The municipalities along the Delaware River are old industrial locations. They frequently have substantial tax bases, but low social ranking populations. As one goes up the tributary streams from the River, the social rank rises. Since sewage "runs down hill," the low status communities have had a monopoly of the access points for sewer trunks to the river. For the higher status upstream communities to solve their problems, they must deal with the lower status downstream communities. Table II lists all sewered communities with systems emptying directly into the Delaware River from the Delaware-Pennsylvania state boundary to Bensalem Township, which represents the strip of prewar river front development. These are labeled "DELAWARE RIVER OUTLET."

TABLE II. SEWER AGREEMENTS
Mean Differences Among Pairs of Cooperation and Non-Cooperating Municipalities

	Total			Delaware River Outlet			Other Outlets		
	Cooperating	Non-Cooperating	Total	Cooperating	Non-Cooperating	Total	Cooperating	Non-Cooperating	Total
1 Social Rank	15.9	15.3	15.6	17.4	11.9	16.1	11.2	18.0	15.0*
2 Market Value Per Capita	$1,223	$1,829	$1,440†	$1,278	$2,194	$1,506†	$1,057	$1,537	$1,324
3 Percent Republican	10.5	11.4	10.8	11.2	10.3	10.8	8.5	12.3	10.6
Number of Pairs	113	63	176	85	28	113	28	35	63

*Differences between cooperating and non-cooperating pairs of municipalities are significant at the .01 level of significance.
†Differences between cooperating and non-cooperating pairs of municipalities are significant at the .05 level of significance.

These pairs of municipalities with sewer agreements have higher mean social rank difference (though not significantly higher) than the pairs of municipalities without sewer agreements. However, with regard to taxable wealth (market value per capita) the agreeing municipalities in the Delaware River Outlet sample have a significantly smaller mean difference than the pairs of municipalities without sewer agreements. Joint sewer systems are rarely financed by uniform tax rates applying to all participating municipalities. Rather the shares to be paid by each municipality are worked out at the time of the agreement. Nevertheless, as was indicated above, the economic well-being of cooperating municipalities is a matter of vital concern to the partners. High status municipalities in the Delaware River Outlet sample had no choice but to negotiate agreements with low status communities, but it would appear that they sought to cooperate with those low status communities that were high in taxable resources.

The differences in party voting between agreeing and non-agreeing pairs in the Delaware River Outlet sample is similar to the social rank pattern. This is not surprising since there is a .703 coefficient of correlation between social rank of each municipality and the percent Republican in the election used for the party affiliation index.

The remainder of the sewered communities not in the Delaware River Outlet sample are shown in Table II under the heading "OTHER OUTLETS." These municipalities are located further up the streams from the Delaware River and along the Schuylkill and its tributaries. In these areas, municipalities frequently have a range of choice in deciding which other communities, if any, they will join in building sewerage systems. Here there is no solidly built-up riparian industrial strip monopolizing river access.

Agreements among these communities occur between those of similar status (social rank). It is interesting that although the agreeing communities also resemble each other more closely than do the non-agreeing communities with respect to taxable wealth. The difference between agreeing and non-agreeing communities is not statistically significant, even at the .10 level. It would appear that where a range of choice does exist, status is a more important determinant of agreement than is taxable resources.

Party voting again shows the same pattern as social rank. The question may be raised whether it is social rank or the party affiliation of the negotiators which influences the pattern of cooperative arrangements. The data indicates that social rank is the more important variable. In both school and sewer agreements, whenever there are

significant differences between agreeing and non-agreeing municipalities with respect to social rank, there are also significant differences (up to the .10 level) with respect to party voting. But in
each instance, differences in social rank are greater (they are at a
higher level of statistical significance) than are differences in party
voting.

School and sewerage systems have entirely differing social and cultural connotations, but both involve expensive capital facilities.
Thus in each case the formation of cooperative systems means at least
protracted negotiations among the leadership representing the communities, though perhaps little general public involvement in the case
of sewer systems. The formation of a cooperative police radio network
involves very modest financial contributions from participating municipalities, is of concern primarily to police technicians, and is a
subject which generally should involve the general public very little.
Here the pattern of cooperation indicates no preference for similar
municipalities among cooperating pairs. Table III gives the results
for all pairs which have police radios. Only pairs from the urban area

TABLE III. POLICE RADIO AGREEMENTS
Mean Differences Among Cooperating and
Cooperating Municipalities*

	Cooperating	Non-Cooperating	Total
1 Social Rank	14.2	17.1	15.9
2 Market Value Per Capita	$1,645	$1,304	$1,445
3 Percent Republican	11.3	11.5.	11.4
Number of Pairs	80	114	194

*None of the differences were significant at the .10 level.

are thereby included. For this rather minor service, social and economic distances apparently do not control the pattern of cooperation.

The interjurisdictional agreement and the joint authority are the
most popular forms of metropolitan political integration at the present time. Operations performed with data on these forms of integration in the Philadelphia Metropolitan Area tend to support the hypothesis that intermunicipal cooperation is a function of social and
economic distance. A real specialization appears to be an important
obstacle to cooperative relations among urban communities. It was
observed that cooperative arrangements are more frequent in the rela-

tively undifferentiated semirural sectors of the metropolitan area and less frequent in the highly differentiated urban sectors. It was also observed that what cooperation did occur among the urbanized communities of the metropolitan area tended to occur among communities which were socially and economically similar rather than dissimilar. In addition, our findings indicate that social distance is a more important determinant of cooperation than is economic distance.[3]

These findings suggest that social and economic differentiation among urban communities may be fundamental to the whole question of metropolitan government. The highly differentiated character of metropolitan communities may operate to maintain our present "fragmented" structure of local government and to inhibit the growth of intergovernmental cooperation. Of course social science at least since Durkheim has been acutely aware that interdependence is a concomitant of specialization and that our interdependent system must be organized in some manner. The demand for effective organization of metropolitan areas is likely to continue. But because of the highly differentiated character of urban communities, integrative demands are likely to be accommodated through patterns of cooperation which least conflict with the divisive effects of differentiation.

---

[3]For a discussion of changes in social and economic variables affecting interjurisdictional cooperation, see the authors' "Social Status, Tax Resources and Metropolitan Cooperation," *National Tax Journal,* XVI (March 1963) 56-62.

19

A COMPARISON OF POLITICAL ATTITUDE AND ACTIVITY PATTERNS IN CENTRAL CITIES AND SUBURBS*†

JOSEPH ZIKMUND

This study indicates that urban and suburban attitude and activity patterns may not be as different as previously suspected and that there may be greater differences among people from separate metropolitan areas than among people from the central city and suburbs of the same metropolitan area.

It is now common practice in social science research to use the convenient, three-way urban-suburban-rural classification to distinguish among the several geographic areas and kinds of people in the United States.[1] These three categories seem to describe roughly our intuitive understanding of the political and social forces in this country. Certainly, urban-rural (or urban-frontier) differences go back to the earliest colonial years and have been emphasized continuously in historical and social science literature since that time. The urban-suburban division, by contrast, is new, and it undoubtedly reflects the desire on the part of social scientists to bring the twentieth-century suburban phenomenon into an established urban-rural frame of reference.

Despite the wide acceptance of this theoretical distinction between central cities and suburbs as geographic entities and between urban

*Reprinted from *Public Opinion Quarterly, XXXI,* No. 1 (Spring 1967), 69-75. By permission of *Public Opinion Quarterly* and the author.
†The author wishes to express his appreciation to the Inter-University Consortium for Political Research, Survey Research Center, Ann Arbor, Michigan, which provided the data and financial support for the project, and to Miss Caroline Wolf and Mrs. Milda Hedblom of the University of Minnesota, who helped with the research for this study.
[1]Bernard Lazerwitz, "Suburban Voting Trends: 1948 to 1956," *Social Forces,* Vol. 39, No. 1, 1960, pp. 29-36.

and suburban residents as individuals, very little empirical research has been done to test the validity of this idea. In actual fact, we do not know how different or how similar urbanites and suburbanites really are. The purpose of this study is to begin to explore this problem with regard to urban and suburban patterns of political attitudes and political action.

THE STUDY

The data for this study come from a pyramided sample of urban and suburban interviews taken in seven, self-representing, major metropolitan areas as part of the Survey Research Center's 1952, 1958, 1962, and 1964 national election polls. In total, 729 urban interviews and 731 suburban interviews are included.[2]

Four kinds of political data are used for each respondent: first, the person's general attitudes toward government and politicians; second, his (or her) party identification; third, his level of political interest; and, fourth, his level of political activity, his party loyalty in past presidential elections, and his record of split-ticket voting.[3]

[2]The interviews are distributed into fourteen city and suburban subsamples, as follows:

Metropolitan Area	Central-city Interviews	Suburban Interviews
Boston	31	73
Chicago	123	106
Detroit	60	82
Los Angeles	108	152
New York	280	186
Philadelphia	69	65
San Francisco	58	67

[2]The metropolitan area samples taken by the Survey Research Center are subdivided into three categories—central city, suburban, and rural fringe. The "suburban" portion of these samples is designed to represent the full range of "suburbs" in each particular metropolitan area. The author has checked the places used by the Center for its "suburban" samples in the metropolitan areas involved in this study and is confident that they meet his own standards for differentiating suburbs from central cities, satellite cities, and rural fringe. Readers who wish to make a similar check for themselves may consult the Center's Codebooks for each of the elections used in this study. These are readily available on request through the Inter-University Consortium for Political Research.

[3]Because the questions related to the respondent's general attitude toward government and politicians were included in only two of the four polls, the samples for these questions are about half the size of the samples for the other questions.

Two distinct types of statistical procedure are used to analyze these data. First, the proportions of interviewees giving similar responses to particular questions are compared between the total, nationwide (seven metropolitan areas) central-city sample and the total, nation-wide suburban sample. Accompanying these comparisons are the re-sults from difference-of-proportions tests run on each of the compar-isons to determine its level of statistical significance.[4] From this we can begin to determine, generally, just how different or similar urbanites and suburbanites across the nation really are.

Second, the results from an analysis-of-variance test are presented to show the relative importance of three distinct kinds of forces that affect urban-suburban attitude and activity patterns. These forces are (1) the nationwide urban-suburban division implied in the urban-suburban-rural classification scheme; (2) the *inter*-metropolitan-area differences appearing when we disregard the urban-suburban division within each particular metropolitan area and treat the entire metro-politan area (central city and suburbs together) as a single analytical unit; and (3) the urban-suburban differences within each of the seven individual metropolitan areas. By working with each of the fourteen urban and suburban subsamples as if it were an independent, coequal unit, it is possible to break down the total variance of these four-teen subsamples around their group mean into its component parts— that is, the part attributable to a nationwide city-suburb division, the part attributable to differences among metropolitan areas, and the part attributable to city-suburb differences within each indivi-dual metropolitan area.[5] In this way we can measure the relative importance of a nationwide urban-suburban division as compared with other relevant forces that may affect political attitude and activity patterns among urban and suburban residents.

DATA AND ANALYSIS

Table 1 compares the proportion of urban and suburban inter-viewees across the nation making similar responses to particular atti-

[4]Hubert M. Blalock, *Social Statistics,* New York, McGraw-Hill, 1960, pp. 176-178.
[5]For more technical explanations, see Donald E. Stokes, "A Variance Components Model of Political Effects," in J. M. Claunch, ed., *Mathematical Applications in Political Science: Arnold Foundation Monograph XII,* Dallas, Arnold Foundation of Southern Methodist University, 1965; E. A. Haggard, *Intraclass Correlation and the Analysis of Variance,* New York, Dryden, 1958; and Blalock, *op. cit.,* pp. 242-271.

TABLE 1

Comparisons of Attitude and Activity Patterns
between the Total Urban Sample and the
Total Suburban Sample

Political Attitude or Activity	Per Cent of Urban Sample [a]	Per Cent of Suburban Sample [a]	Statistical Significance at .05 [b]
Attitude:			
Believe "hardly any" people running the government are crooked	22	27	NS
Believe "quite a lot" of people running the government are crooked	27	25	NS
Believe that people in government waste "not very much" tax money	11	8	NS
Believe that people in government waste "a lot" of tax money	49	43	S
Believe one can "always" trust the government in Washington	15	14	NS
Believe one can trust the government in Washington "only some of the time"	26	24	NS
Party identification:			
Generally identify as "independents"	14	23	S
Generally identify as "Democrats"	62	42	S
Generally identify as "Republicans"	24	35	S
Interest:			
Have "high" interest in election campaign	35	38	NS
Party loyalty:			
Talked to people during recent campaign in partisan way	31	27	NS
Voted for candidates of "different" parties in past presidential elections	33	39	S
Voted a split ticket at state or local level in most recent general election	17	28	S

[a] Figure in each cell is the per cent of the particular sample giving the response indicated.
[b] NS = not significant; S = significant.

tude and activity questions. From this table it is evident that clear-cut, average differences do not always exist between urban and suburban respondents. Statistically significant differences appear, as expected, with regard to party identification, party loyalty in past presidential elections, split-ticket voting, and one of the basic attitude questions. All of the other comparisons show no significant difference between urban and suburban attitude and activity patterns.[6]

Table 2 indicates the proportion of variance among the fourteen subsamples attributable to nationwide urban-suburban differences, to inter-metropolitan area differences, and to intra-metropolitan city-suburban differences. Once again, the data are somewhat irregular; however, a few general patterns are discernible. First, the nationwide city-suburban division is the *least* influential of the three kinds of forces studied. In only 1 of the 13 comparisons presented does the national city-suburban distinction account for more than 50 per cent of the total variance among the fourteen subsamples, and in 10 instances out of 13 it accounts for less than 20 per cent of the total variance. By contrast, inter-metropolitan area differences account for more than 50 per cent of the variance in 8 of the 13 cases. Averaging together the data for all 13 comparisons, 51 per cent of the total variance is attributable to inter-metropolitan differences, 35 per cent to intra-metropolitan urban-suburban differences, and only 14 per cent to a nationwide urban-suburban division.

CONCLUSIONS

The idea that one can make a meaningful city-suburban distinction at the national level involves a number of empirically testable assumptions. Among the most important of these is that, on the average, there are meaningful differences between the political attitude and political activity patterns of a nationwide sample of urban residents and the political attitude and political activity patterns of a nationwide sample of suburban residents. In addition, this idea as-

[6]Similar comparisons to those found in Table 1 were also made with the education level of the respondents held constant. This, of course, divided the sample into even smaller groups and reduced statistical significance to an unacceptable range. However, the general trends from this analysis indicate that education differences alone do not account for the urban and suburban political differences noted in Table 1.

The difference-of-porportions test used in this analysis assumes a random sample. The data come from clustered samples. The effect of this is to increase the variability of the actual results. As a consequence, statistics based on the normal curve are likely to overestimate the probability of differences between the two samples and to underestimate the similarities. Thus, the use of clustered samples in no way affects those findings that show similar response patterns between urban and suburban samples (Leslie Kish, *Survey Sampling,* New York, Wiley, 1965, p. 161).

TABLE 2

Proportion of Total Variance among Fourteen
Urban and Suburban Subsamples Attributable to
Nationwide Urban-Suburban, Inter-metropolitan-area,
and Intra-metropolitan-area (Urban-Suburban)
Differences [a]

	Per Cent of Total Variance Attributed to		
Political Attitude or Activity	Nationwide Urban-Suburban Difference	Inter-metropolitan Area Differences	Intra-metropolitan Area Difference [b]
Attitude:			
Believe "hardly any" people running the government are crooked	0	65	35
Believe "quite a lot" of people running the government are crooked	0	37	63
Believe that people in government waste "not very much" tax money	4	62	34
Believe that people in government waste "a lot" of tax money	12	57	31
Believe one can "always" trust the government in Washington	6	37	57
Believe one can trust the government in Washington "only some of the time"	6	82	12
Party identification:			
Generally identify as "independents"	54	16	30
Generally identify as "Democrats"	46	7	47
Generally identify as "Republicans"	14	26	60
Interest:			
Have "high" interest in election campaign	3	84	13
Party loyalty:			
Talked to people during recent campaign in partisan way	4	82	14
Voted for candidates of "different" parties in past presidential elections	4	65	31
Voted a split ticket at state or local level in most recent general election	31	60	9
Mean average for columns	14	52	34

[a] The figure in each cell is the per cent of the total variance among the 14 subsamples with regard to the particular response that can be attributed to the urban-suburban or metropolitan-area factor in question. Each row adds to 100 per cent.
[b] The figures in this column are the combined influence of intra-metropolitan area differences and of a small residue of other factors not included in the three major kinds of differences being studied.

sumes that the importance of other forces (other than a nationwide urban-suburban difference) influencing urban and suburban attitude and activity patterns is small and that the effects of these other forces are random or unidentifiable by current research techniques. The data presented above cast serious doubts on the validity of both these assumptions, for we find that there is little or no difference between some urban and suburban attitude and activity patterns and that the nationwide urban-suburban division is the *least* rather than the most influential of the forces used to explain these urban and suburban data patterns.

If some kind of nationwide urban-suburban distinction does not prove to be very useful in explaining the attitude and activity patterns of urban and suburban residents in the United States, then what tack should social scientists take to try to solve this problem? The analysis of variance presented above clearly points to the individual metropolitan area as the most fruitful focus of attention for this kind of research.

Recent evidence indicates that the rapid growth of suburbia during the 1940's and 1950's can best be explained as a somewhat haphazard overflow of urban people into the surrounding suburbs and rural areas.[7] In addition, we are coming to realize that all parts of a particular metropolitan area share common problems and a common political, social, and economic environment. The political experiences and attitudes of all the people in a metropolitan area are necessarily different from those of people outside the vague metropolitan boundaries. The metropolis has its own newspapers and its own radio and television stations. Economic integration brings together similar people from all parts of the metropolitan areas. The urban stockbroker and the suburban stockbroker are likely to differ politically only on intra-metropolitan issues, and the same holds for the urban blue-collar worker and his suburban counterpart. From this perspective, the key to an accurate understanding of the suburban phenomenon rests with theories and research that concentrate on each particular metropolitan area and on the unique environment it provides for suburbs and suburban residents.

[7]Fred W. Wirt, "The Political Sociology of American Suburbia," *The Journal of Politics,* Vol. 27, No. 3, 1965, pp. 664-666.

20

POLITICAL AND SOCIOECONOMIC
CHARACTERISTICS
OF AMERICAN CITIES*†

ROBERT R. ALFORD AND HARRY M. SCOBLE‡

Why should political and socioeconomic characteristics of a city be related to its form of government? For several reasons, we cannot assume that any set of factors will correlate with the form of government: (1) Changing the constitutional framework of local government is difficult, especially if it has been changed quite recently. Although there is little evidence on this score, it seems a fair assumption that neither activists nor voters will be prepared to make frequent changes. (2) State laws prescribe one or another form or make change difficult. (3) Such change is difficult to translate into successful political action, even if the city contains a majority of social groups likely to favor a certain form. (4) As a consequence of the above, a city is likely to possess a given form for many years, through periods of considerable social and economic change.

Nevertheless, as will be shown, such relationships exist, and this paper attempts a partial explanation. This article extends to all U.S. cities over 25,000 population (in 1960) the findings and implications of several previous studies concerning the relationship between forms of government and socioeconomic characteristics of American cities. Liebman analyzed the economic functions of 21 Cook

*Reprinted from *Municipal Yearbook 1965*, pp. 82-98. By permission of the International City Managers' Association.
†Professor Alford is with the Department of Sociology, University of Wisconsin. Professor Scoble is with the Department of Political Science, University of California, Los Angeles.
‡We are indebted to Leo Schnore, Herbert Jacob, and Jane Hood for critical comments, and to the National Science Foundation, through the Computing Center at the University of Wisconsin, for assistance with the data.

County (Illinois) suburbs, Kessel examined growth rates, economic base, and foreign-born population of cities between 25,000 and 250,000 population, and Schnore and Alford studied the relation between a number of population and economic characteristics of suburbs and their forms of government. For reasons of space no direct citations will be made, but a number of ideas come from these previous publications.[1]

FORMS OF CITY GOVERNMENT

We must make certain initial assumptions about the character of these forms of government, assumptions which cannot here be defended in detail. The council-manager form is assumed to be more "business-like" and less "politicized" than either the commission or the mayor-council form, in the sense that the manager form implies agreement upon the major goals of city government by dominant social groups. By "politicized" we mean that the form encourages or allows interest group representation, by "professionalized" that it encourages efficient implementation of specified goals. We have no evidence concerning the actual differences in performance of city services, or whether certain groups actually have less potential influence over city decisions under the council-manager form than in the other forms. The fact that manager cities are less likely to have partisan elections, and more likely to have at-large rather than ward elections, means that other features of the governmental framework are consistent with an assumption of consensus on an "anti-political" governmental structure by dominant groups.

The commission form is essentially nonpolitical, but of a different character than the council-manager form, stressing "nonprofessional" implementation of agreed-upon goals. This type of government is probably less likely to be able to handle new goals or new problems than the manager form, since its commissioners head administrative departments. The commission form is usually regarded as obsolete, and its declining incidence is consistent with this view. Only 15

[1]See Charles Liebman, "Functional Differentiation and Political Characteristics of Suburbs," *American Journal of Sociology,* LXVI (March, 1961), 485-491; John H. Kessel, Governmental Structure and Political Environment," *American Political Science Review,* LV (September, 1962), 615-620; Leo F. Schnore and Robert R. Alford, "Forms of Government and Socioeconomic Characteristics of Suburbs," *Administrative Science Quarterly,* VII (June, 1963), 1-17.

per cent of American cities have the commission form, and it will be treated here, for the most part, as a residual category.

The mayor-council form may be regarded as an intermediate type, less centralized than the council-manager form, more centralized than the commission form, and allowing for a variety of forms of political representation and levels of administrative efficiency. When combined with the other aspects of the most professionalized, non-political form—nonpartisanship and at-large elections—it may be quite similar to a manager form.

Three major variables may be related to one or another form of government: (1) the *social heterogeneity* of the population (along such lines as religion, race, or ethnicity), (2) its *class composition* (the proportion of persons in white-collar occupations, or with college education), and (3) its population *growth and mobility*. Social heterogeneity—the existence of sizable groups with diverse political cultures and demands—favors a more "politicized," less centralized, less professionalized form because there is not as great a consensus among politically active groups upon the proper goals of city government and a greater need for access and representation from diverse groups. A relatively high proportion of middle-class persons favors a less politicized form because such groups are less likely to have political demands inconsistent with the centralized, efficient form. Population growth and mobility favor a less politicized form because cities are facing new problems requiring administrative and managerial skills, at the same time that a low proportion of the population is settled into stable social and political groups.

These hypotheses do not imply that the council-manager form is only possible where all major social groups agree upon the proper goals for party government. Certainly most city managers must deal with many social and political cleavages. Also, the very existence of the manager form may represent a victory for one social group over another. The fact (to be shown) that the manager form is *less* likely rather than more likely in heavily working-class cities indicates that the simple presence of a majority of one social class does not create a consensus favoring the manager form (assuming, of course, that our hypotheses about the nature of the forms are correct). The social class composition of a city may be regarded as an element of social heterogeneity, if there is a large enough working class to provide a political base of opposition for the "natural" leaders of a community: the educated professional and business groups.[2]

[2]See Edward Banfield and James Q. Wilson, *City Politics* (Cambridge: Harvard University Press, 1963), Chapter 13, for a summary of the relevant literature,

Our basic assumption is that the more cleavage in a city—regardless of the source—the more highly politicized a government it is likely to have, if the sources of social and political diversity have channels of political expression. Unfortunately, we have no independent measure of whether the mayor-council form allows more interest-group representation and influence than the council-manager form.

This paper sorts out the relative importance of some of these factors for the form of government of American cities. Some factors, such as statutory control by the states, serve to confound the relations here discussed, but we have not been able to take them into account. All of the characteristics dealt with can be plausibly interpreted as fitting some theory about the relation of political forms to their economic and social "environment." The problem, of course, is that in some instances the characteristics of cities are so highly correlated that it is impossible to separate them after the fact (so to speak) by comparing the effects of certain characteristics while simultaneously holding other characteristics "constant." If almost all eastern cities are heavily industrialized, with a high proportion of foreign-born persons, a low proportion of migrant persons, and a fairly low average level of education, and almost all western cities are just the opposite, then clearly the effect of one factor cannot be distinguished from another. But it would be significant if we should discover that it is the occupational composition of the population, rather than its mobility, which is related to the adoption of the council-manager plan. Only a few such interrelations can be discussed in this paper.

EMPIRICAL INDICATORS

The indicators used can be summarized as follows:

Occupation and Education.

The existence of a high proportion of white-collar persons or of persons with at least a high school education suggests that a politi-

---

and a discussion of how the white, Anglo-Saxon, Protestant middle-class ethos favors the "good government," council-manager form. See also Eugene Lee, *The Politics of Nonpartisanship* (Berkeley: University of California Press, 1960); Gladys Kammerer *et at., City Managers in Politics: An Analysis of Manager Tenure and Termination* (University of Florida Monographs: Social Sciences, No. 13, Winter, 1962); and Charles R. Adrian, *Governing Urban America* (New York: McGraw-Hill, 1961).

cally important segment of the electorate will favor a professional manager, since the ideals and goals of the manager are not inconsistent with their view of city government. The manager form is consistent with an antipolitical and efficient running of the business of government typical of a white-collar, business political point of view.

Growth.

Growing cities have a smaller proportion of the population with stable roots in the community and connections with groups with political demands. Therefore, the population is likely to have a more instrumental approach to city government and is more likely to accept or want professional administration of city services.

Size.

The larger the city, the more socially heterogeneous it is likely to be, and therefore the more likely to have competing interest groups demanding political access, and the more likely to have a "politicized" form.

Mobility.

Cities with highly mobile populations, like cities which are growing, are less likely to have stable political groupings, and more likely to have populations which demand efficient, business-like government rather than a government responsive to traditional groups' desires for representation and access. Growth is associated with mobility, but there can be high mobility without high growth. We have no data on the type of mobility, nor on which groups are mobile, and these may be more important than the sheer quantity of movement.

Ethnic Diversity.

Cities with higher proportions of persons of recent foreign origin are more likely to be politically and culturally heterogeneous, and they require "political" rather than "administrative" forms.

Religious Diversity.

Cities with higher proportions of children going to private schools —a crude measure of religious diversity—are, again, more likely to be politically and culturally heterogeneous.

Racial Diversity.

Cities with higher proportions of nonwhites are certainly, at this stage of American history, likely to be politically and culturally heterogeneous.

The last three are measures of social heterogeneity. The first is a good indication of the degree of ethnic diversity in the city, and the second represents as good a measure of religious diversity as we have from census data. Probably most of the children in private schools are Catholic, except in the Midwest where many are Lutheran. Regardless of which religious group (or any other private group) has its own schools, this is an indication of local cleavage along lines which might well be politically relevant and require a more politicized form of government. Nonwhites as recorded by the census are not all Negroes, but this generally is a good index of the Negro composition of a city.

It must be emphasized that we are not arguing that any of these characteristics of cities "cause," in any direct sense, the adoption of a particular form of government. The social and political *processes* involved must be inferred from the crude cross-sectional indicators that are available.

Different forms of government are not evenly distributed in the major regions of the United States. As expected, the Far West, the newest and most rapidly growing region of the nation, has a far higher proportion of manager cities than any other region; the East has the lowest (see Table 6). Whether the associations of certain other factors with governmental forms are merely due to their regional character will be seen later.

INITIAL FINDINGS

All of the suggested relations between social and economic characteristics of cities and their forms of government are borne out by the tables that follow, which were selected from a range of possible measures of the major factors: social heterogeneity, class composition, and population growth and mobility. Because of space limitations, certain two-variable tables have been omitted if they are repeated in later three-variable tables. Thus form of government by region is given in the totals column of Table 6, by mobility in Table

8, by occupational composition in Table 7, by foreign parentage in Table 11, and by nonwhite composition in Table 12.[3]

Table 1 shows the relation of forms of government to the metropolitan status and employing character of cities. No clear relationship is shown, and, although other tables will not be given, there seems to be no independent influence of these two factors upon the adoption of a form of government when other characteristics are examined simultaneously.

Consistent with the hypothesis that social heterogeneity increases with the size of cities, and therefore the incidence of professionalized government should drop, Table 2 shows that fewer large cities have the council-manager plan. There are no striking differences of form among the middle-sized cities.

Growth is clearly related to form of government, as seen in Table 3. Growing cities are more likely to have the council-manager form, less likely to have commission and mayor-council forms. Similarly, cities with highly mobile populations are considerably more likely to have managers than cities with stable populations. (See Table 8. The association of mobility and form remains exactly the same when size of city is controlled).

Turning to the economic and social class character of cities, we see in Tables 7 and 4 that both indicators used—white-collar proportion and educational attainment—are consistent with the generalizations advanced.[4] Cities with a high proportion of white-collar persons, or of high-school educated persons, are considerably more likely to have manager forms than cities with low proportions.

Tables 11 and 5 show that only two measures of social heterogeneity are clearly related to form of government: the proportion of

[3]One methodological qualification must be kept in mind. The cities have been divided into three approximately equal groups on most variables. A comparison of the association of a variable with form of government can be made by simply adding up percentage differences, but a different set of cutting points would result in different percentages and possibly different relative weights of the variables. There is little reason to assume that any relationships found here would reverse or disappear with a rearrangement of the data, but it is possible that some of the internal comparisons would shift slightly. Before these divisions into three groups and the three-variable tables were made, the two-variable associations of each factor with form of government were examined with a more detailed breakdown into eight or nine classifications, and no serious internal reversals were noted. There is reason to believe, therefore, that the arbitrary cutting points do not affect the relationships presented and discussed.

[4]From data not given on relation of form of government to the economic base of cities, as defined in the 1959 *Municipal Year Book,* industrial and manufacturing cities are much less likely to have the council-manager form than are retail and diversified cities.

TABLE 1
Form of Government by Metropolitan Status[1]

Form of Government	Central City			Suburb			Independent City	
	Employing	Balanced	Dormitory	Employing	Balanced	Dormitory	Employing	Balanced
Manager	45%	31%	58%	42%	38%	53%	53%	55%
Commission	16	21	15	21	10	12	15	13
Mayor-council ...	39	48	27	37	52	35	32	32
100%[2] = ...	(103)	(86)	(26)	(57)	(50)	(107)	(96)	(100)

[1]Information on metropolitan status was not available for 49 cities. The categories are those presented in the *1959 Municipal Year Book*. An INDEPENDENT city (I) is not located in a Standard Metropolitan Statistical Area., as designated by the Bureau of the Budget; a CENTRAL city (C) and a SUBURB (S) are likewise designated by the Bureau of the Budget according to certain criteria. DORMITORY (D), BALANCED (B), and EMPLOYING (E) cities are classified according to the number of persons who work in a city as compared with the number of working people who live there. An independent city, by definition, cannot be a dormitory city.

[2]In this and subsequent tables, "100%" indicates that percentage add up to 100 and that the total number of cities, by categories, is shown in parentheses.

TABLE 2
Form of Government by Size of City

Form of Government	Size (thousands)			
	25-50	50-100	100-200	200 +
Manager	51%	48%	45%	37%
Commission	14	16	17	12
Mayor-council	35	36	38	51
100% = ...	(338)	(174)	(69)	(59)

TABLE 3
Form of Government and Population Change

Form of Government	Population Decline			Population Growth		
	High (7-29%)	Medium (4-6%)	Low (0-3%)	Low (0-15%)	Medium (16-44%)	High (45% +)
Manager	26%	30%	30%	39%	48%	70%
Commission	36	27	14	17	12	8
Mayor-council	38	43	56	44	40	22
100% = ...	(50)	(40)	(37)	(152)	(181)	(178)

Percentages refer to population loss or gain in the city from 1950 to 1960. These changes may reflect alterations in city boundaries, which were not taken into account in this study.

the native-born population which has one or both foreign-born parents, and the proportion of elementary school children which is attending private school.

Cities with a high proportion of nonwhite population (more than 15 per cent) are somewhat more likely to have the commission form, and cities with a low proportion of nonwhites are slightly more likely to have a mayor-council form, but the differences are neither great nor consistent. (See Table 12.)

Up to this point, we have shown that nearly all of the characteristics of cities considered are related to their forms of government. High mobility, low private school population, high white-collar population, low proportion of native-born persons of foreign parentage, high level of population growth, high level of education, and smaller size are all associated with the council-manager rather than the mayor-council form, and in roughly that order of association, judging from the percentage-point differences shown in the tables.

The three major factors—social heterogeneity, class composition, and growth or mobility—are all important, regardless of which indicator is used. The only exception is nonwhite composition.

TABLE 4
Form of Government and Education

Form of Government	Per Cent Completing High School		
	Low (18-40%)	Medium (41-49%)	High (50-89%)
Manager	33%	49%	67%
Commission	21	12	10
Mayor-council	46	39	23
100% =	(247)	(203)	(190)

Percentages refer to the proportion of the population ages 25 and over with four years of high school or more.

TABLE 5
Form of Government and Private School
Population

Form of Government	Private School Population		
	Low (0-9%)	Medium (10-24%)	High (25-69%)
Manager	67%	50%	24%
Commission	15	15	16
Mayor-council	18	35	60
100% =	(185)	(282)	(173)

Percentages refer to the proportion of the elementary school population which is in a private school.

INTERRELATIONSHIPS OF THE FACTORS

It is the task of this section to consider which of these factors are independently related to form of government, and which are related only because they are correlated with others.

Is the apparent association of mobility with forms of government due simply to the fact that Far West cities have more mobile populations and are also more likely to have the council-manager form? Regions differ greatly in the mobility of their cities' populations, as Table 6 shows, but the effect of mobility does not disappear. The manager form is generally more likely in more mobile cities, and both commission and mayor-council forms are less likely, regardless of the region.

In eastern cities higher mobility reduces the incidence of commission and increases the likelihood of manager forms, but it is not associated with the mayor-council form. In the Midwest, the commission form is not related to mobility. In the Far West, where most cities have managers, the manager form is only slightly more likely in high mobility cities. It may be noted that no cities at all in the Far West have the lowest level of mobility in the tripartite division used here.

Thus, mobility remains important, even within regions, although there is a strong association of both mobility and form of government with the region in which a city is located.

Table 7, showing the interrelations of occupational composition, population mobility, and form of government, may clarify the connections of these variables further. The table shows that mobility is closely related to occupational composition: heavily white-collar cities have far more mobile populations than heavily blue-collar cities. As we have already shown, both mobility and occupational composition are closely related to the form of government. The question is: what is the nature of the relation of these two factors to form of government? Are white-collar populations more likely to have manager forms simply because they are more mobile, and therefore have less stake in local government policies and will relinquish control to a professional manager? This table may help specify the conditions under which a white-collar population is related to a particular form of government, or explain why there is such a connection.

The table shows that among high mobility cities, the proportion of white-collar persons in the city makes little or no difference in the form of government, but that a small difference does remain in the less mobile cities. The association of mobility with form, however, is hardly reduced at all. The average percentage-point difference for the manager form attributable to mobility, controlling for occupational composition, is $+45$, for mayor-council $+36$, while the average percentage-point difference attributable to occupational composition, controlling for mobility, is $+11$ for the manager form, $+6$ for the mayor-council form. Thus, mobility is more significantly related to forms of government than is occupational composition.

The interrelations of population change (both growth and decline) and mobility as they relate to forms of government must now be examined. Mobility is certainly related to growth, as Table 8 shows,

TABLE 6
Form of Government[1] by Region[2] and Mobility

Region	Mobility [3]			Total
	Low (2-11%)	Medium (12-20%)	High (21-58%)	
East				
Manager	16%	29%	42%	21%
Commission	30	13	0	24
Mayor-council	54	58	58	55
100% =	(111)	(38)	(12)	(161)
Total	69%	24	7	100%
Midwest				
Manager	33%	32%	64%	37%
Commission	7	11	11	10
Mayor-council	60	57	25	53
100% =	(63)	(88)	(28)	(179)
Total	35%	49	16	100%
Far-West				
Manager	(1)	76%	84%	81
Commission	(0)	10	3	5
Mayor-council	(1)	14	13	14
100% =	(2)	(42)	(71)	(115)
Total	2%	36	62	100%
South				
Manager	31%	57%	71%	61%
Commission	31	20	15	19
Mayor-council	38	23	14	20
100% =	(16)	(83)	(86)	(185)
Total	9%	45	46	100%

[1]Information on form of government was not available for 3 Eastern cities, 11 Midwest cities, 16 Far West cities and 6 Southern cities.

[2]All 676 cities over 25,000 population are included in the regions: "East" (Maine, New Hampshire, Vermont, Massachusetts, Connecticut, Rhode Island, New York, New Jersey, Pennsylvania, Maryland, Delaware, District of Columbia); "Midwest" (Ohio, Indiana, Illinois, Michigan, Wisconsin, Minnesota, Iowa, North Dakota, South Dakota, Nebraska); "Far West" (Montana, Idaho, Colorado, Utah, Wyoming, Arizona, New Mexico, California, Oregon, Washington, Nevada, Alaska, Hawaii); "South" (Texas, Oklahoma, Kansas, Missouri,

but the two characteristics of a city may be somewhat independent (particularly in these data, because the growth data do not take account of annexations, and the measure of mobility is migration from different counties in the United States between 1955 and 1960). No cities have both high mobility and a decline in population, as Table 8 shows, although such a combination is possible if many more persons leave than enter. Considering both of these indicators of growth and mobility simultaneously allows some control for the lack of information on annexations.

Table 8 shows that mobility is far more important than population change as a factor in forms of government. When mobility is controlled, the effect of population change is reduced. On the other hand, the association with mobility remains high, even when population change is controlled. We infer that the association of population change with form of government depends upon mobility. Growth or decline without much mobility, by annexations or by out-migration without in-migration, is not strongly related to the form of government.

Now let us bring together the two major factors—mobility and religious diversity—which have been found to be most closely related to forms of government. Again, they are related, because the more mobile cities have fewer children in private school. There is probably more reliance in such cities upon government to provide essential services than on traditional institutions based upon religious and ethnic subcommunities. Many of these cities are in the Far West, of course. While it may seem to fly in the face of common sense, such an association may be a sign of less cultural and political heterogeneity in mobile cities. Stable populations may be more likely to

---

Arkansas, Alabama, Louisiana, Mississippi, Florida, Georgia, North Carolina, South Carolina, Virginia, West Virginia, Kentucky, Tennessee).

[3]Mobility refers to the residents five years old and older who were living in a different county on April 1, 1955.

The average (for all regions) percentage-point difference for mobility is +26 for the manager form, +14 for the mayor-council form. The figure 26 was reached by subtracting 16 per cent from 42 per cent in the first row of the table, then 33 from 64, 76 from 84, 31 from 71. The resulting numbers, 26, 31, 8, and 40, were added together, and divided by four to produce +26. This is a crude quantitative measure of the association of mobility with the manager form, controlling for region. The figure +14 was produced by a similar procedure for the mayor-council rows. This procedure was used in tables to follow, and the "average percentage-point difference" is given at the foot of each table. The same procedure for columns instead of rows produces the association of the other variable with form of government. A plus indicates that the association is in the direction of the hypothesis.

TABLE 7

Form of Government by Proportion in White-Collar
Occupations and Mobility

Proportion in White Collar Occupations[1]	Mobility			Total
	Low (2-11%)	Medium (12-20%)	High (21-58%)	
Low (15-35%)				
Manager	17%	37%	79%	32%
Commission	25	16	14	20
Mayor-council	58	47	7	48
100% = ...	(127)	(77)	(28)	(232)
Total	55%	33	12	100%
Medium (36-42%)				
Manager	32%	46%	69%	51%
Commission	18	12	9	12
Mayor-council	50	42	22	37
100% = ...	(38)	(96)	(67)	(201)
Total	19%	48	33	100%
High (43-85%)				
Manager	36%	57%	73%	62%
Commission	16	16	9	13
Mayor-council	48	27	18	25
100% = ...	(25)	(74)	(94)	(193)
Total	13%	38	49	100%

[1]White collar refers to persons employed in professional, technical, managerial, clerical, and sales occupations.

Average percentage-point difference for mobility: council-manager form, +45; mayor-council, +36. Average percentage-point difference for occupational composition: manager, +11; mayor-council, +6.

develop institutions based upon whatever religious and ethnic sub-cultures exist.

Table 9 shows the relations of mobility and religious diversity, as measured by the proportion of elementary school children in private school, to form of government. Both factors are independently and strongly related to forms of government. The average percentage-

TABLE 8
Form of Government by Mobility and
Population Change

Mobility	Population Decline			Population Growth			Total
	High (7-29%)	Medium (4-6%)	Low (0-3%)	Low (0-15%)	Medium (16-44%)	High (45%+)	
Low (2-11%)							
Manager	19%	25%	26%	25%	19%	28%	23%
Commission	40	31	16	16	11	5	22
Mayor-council ...	41	44	58	59	71	67	55
100% = ...	(42)	(32)	(19)	(51)	(27)	(21)	(192)
Total	22%	17	11	27	14	11	100%
Medium (12-20%)							
Manager	—%	—%	27%	40%	47%	63%	47%
Commission	—	—	13	20	12	9	14
Mayor-council ...	—	—	60	40	41	28	39
100% = ...	(8)	(8)	(15)	(83)	(93)	(43)	(250)
Total	3%	4	6	33	37	17	100%
High (21-58%)							
Manager	—%	—%	—%	72%	61%	81%	73%
Commission	—	—	—	6	15	7	9
Mayor-council ...	—	—	—	22	24	12	18
100% = ...	(0)	(0)	(3)	(18)	(61)	(114)	(196)
Total	—%	—	2	9	31	58	100%

Average percentage-point difference for population change: manager, +18;
mayor-council, +23. Average percentage-point difference for mobility: manager,
+47; mayor-council, +46.

point difference for mobility, controlling for private school population, is +35 and +18 per cent for manager and mayor-council
forms, respectively, and +27 and +35 per cent for private school
population, controlling for mobility. What is perhaps more important
is the fact that they are additive in their effects. Taking both factors
into account provides a high level of predictability of the form of
government of a city. Of cities with the lowest mobility and the

highest proportion of children in private school, 18 per cent have a manager form, 16 a commission form, 66 per cent a mayor-council form, as contrasted with 78, 9, and 13 per cent, respectively, in cities with the highest mobility and the lowest proportion of children in private schools. Fully 55 per cent of the few cities with low mobility and few children in private schools have the commission form.

TABLE 9

Form of Government by Mobility and
Proportion of Children in Private Schools

| Mobility | Private School Population | | | |
	Low (0-9%)	Medium (10-24%)	High (25-69%)	Total
Low (2-11%)				
Manager	27%	30%	18%	23%
Commission	55	25	16	22
Mayor-council	18	45	66	55
100% = ...	(11)	(77)	(104)	(192)
Total	6%	40	54	100%
Medium (12-20%)				
Manager	56%	47%	35%	47%
Commission	18	14	11	14
Mayor-council	26	39	54	39
100% = ...	(73)	(123)	(55)	(251)
Total	29%	49	22	100%
High (21-58%)				
Manager	78%	74%	28%	73%
Commission	9	6	29	9
Mayor-council	13	20	43	18
100% = ...	(101)	(82)	(14)	(197)
Total	51%	42	7	100%

Average percentage-point difference for private school population: manager, +27; mayor-council, +35. Average percentage-point difference for mobility: manager, +35; mayor-council, +18.

TABLE 10

Form of Government by Region and Proportion
of Children in Private Schools

| Region | Private School Population | | | Total |
	Low (0-9%)	Medium (10-24%)	High (25-69%)	
East[1]				
Manager	...%	26%	17%	21%
Commission	...	26	22	24
Mayor-council	...	48	61	55
100% =	(1)	(77)	(83)	(161)
Total	...%	48	52	100%
Midwest[1]				
Manager	42%	43%	30%	37%
Commission	17	9	9	10
Mayor-council	41	48	61	53
100% =	(12)	(90)	(77)	(179)
Total	7%	50	43	100%
Far West[1]				
Manager	89%	78%	...%	81%
Commission	4	6	...	5
Mayor-council	7	16	...	14
100% =	(44)	(68)	(3)	(115)
Total	38%	59	3	100%
South[1]				
Manager	62%	64%	40%	61%
Commission	19	19	20	19
Mayor-council	19	17	40	20
100% =	(128)	(47)	(10)	(185)
Total	69%	25	6	100%

[1]See Table 6 for listing of states in each region.

Average percentage-point difference for private school population: manager, +10; mayor-council, +14.

Although the proportion of children in private school in a city is closely related to its form of government, this association is reduced when the same relationship is examined within regions (see Table 10). Such a finding is difficult to interpret. Does this mean that the original association of religious diversity with form of government is spurious? Or merely that the region in which a city is located is correlated highly with both the religious composition of the com-

TABLE 11

Form of Government by Mobility and Foreign
Parentage

Foreign Parentage [1]	Mobility			Total
	Low (2-11%)	Medium (12-20%)	High (21-58%)	
Low (0-9%)				
Manager	27%	47%	72%	54%
Commission	46	17	15	20
Mayor-council	27	36	13	26
100% = ...	(26)	(108)	(79)	(213)
Total.............................	12%	51	37	100%
Medium (10-19%)				
Manager	31%	54%	75%	59%
Commission	26	14	3	11
Mayor-council	43	32	22	30
100% = ...	(35)	(81)	(88)	(204)
Total.............................	17%	40	43	100%
High (20-40%)				
Manager	21%	37%	70%	32%
Commission	16	11	10	14
Mayor-council	63	52	20	54
100% = ...	(131)	(62)	(30)	(223)
Total.............................	59%	28	13	100%

[1] Persons native-born of foreign or mixed parentage.

Average percentage-point difference for mobility: manager, +46; mayor-council, +26. Average percentage-point difference for foreign parentage: manager, +6; mayor-council, +20.

munity, its mobility, and its form of government? We do not really know what it means for a city to be located in a given region, aside from historical patterns of growth and development, and possibly the diffusion of political forms from adjacent and older cities.

Table 11 shows the relations of the ethnic diversity of cities (as measured by the proportion of persons who are native-born of either foreign or mixed parentage) to mobility and form of government. Here, as in Table 9, we see a difference in the social characteristics of commission and mayor-council forms. Unlike the mayor-council form, commission forms are considerably less likely to be found in cities with high ethnic diversity, and taking the mobility of the population into account increases this difference considerably. Fully 46 per cent of the 26 least mobile, least ethnically diverse cities have the commission form. This is consistent with the findings of Table 9.

Although cities with a lower proportion of persons of foreign ancestry have more mobile populations, both factors independently correlate with forms of government. Mobility however, is far more closely related to governmental form than is foreign parentage.

Table 12 shows that foreign parentage is related to form of government, even when the proportion of nonwhites in the cities is controlled, for both mayor-council and council-manager forms. The average percentage-point difference for foreign parentage is $+28$ for the manager form, $+22$ for the mayor-council form. When, in contrast, foreign parentage is controlled, and the association of non-white composition with forms is examined, differences are small or even reversed from the expected direction. (Also, when region is controlled, there is no relation between governmental form and non-white composition.) A high proportion of nonwhites does not, therefore, lead to a greater likelihood of a mayor-council form of government. It is possible that this is because nonwhites have not hitherto had an effective political voice. Ethnic groups of European origin and Catholics seem to be the sources of social heterogeneity related to form of government.

CONCLUSION

To summarize: white, Anglo-Saxon, Protestant, growing, and mobile cities are highly likely to be manager cities; ethnically and religiously diverse but nonmobile industrial cities are highly likely to be mayor-council cities. The commission form is associated with declining population, low mobility, a low white-collar composition

TABLE 12

Form of Government by Foreign Parentage
and Nonwhite Composition

Nonwhite	Foreign Parentage			Total
	Low (0-9%)	Medium (10-19%)	High (28-40%)	
Low (less than 1.0%)				
Manager	...%	56%	32%	39%
Commission	...	6	10	10
Mayor-council	...	38	58	51
100% = ...	(7)	(50)	(89)	(146)
Total.............................	5%	34	61	100%
Medium Low (1.0-4.9%)				
Manager	61%	59%	42%	53%
Commission	14	15	16	15
Mayor-council	25	26	42	32
100% =...........................	(36)	(72)	(64)	(172)
Total.............................	21%	42	37	100%
Medium High (5.0-14.9%)				
Manager	57%	63%	27%	50%
Commission	12	6	17	11
Mayor-council	31	31	56	39
100% =...........................	(58)	(52)	(48)	(158)
Total.............................	37%	33	30	100%
High (15.0-79.0%)				
Manager	53%	60%	14%	49%
Commission	25	20	18	23
Mayor-council	22	20	68	28
100% = ...	(112)	(30)	(22)	(164)
Total.............................	68%	18	14	100%

Average percentage-point difference for foreign parentage: manager, +28; mayor-council, +22. Average percentage-point difference for nonwhite composition: manager, +7; mayor-council, −4.

and a low educational level, and low ethnic and religious diversity. Native, probably Protestant declining industrial cities are thus highly likely to be commission cities.

Some possible causal connections of these factors with governmental form may be suggested, subject to the qualifications already given. Mobility appears to explain the association of economic and class composition with form. It is apparently through mobility that a political base is changed, because mobile blue-collar cities are as likely to have managers as mobile white-collar cities. Similarly mobility seems to explain how population growth and decline affect form of government. It is not just growth, but primarily the fact of a sizable mobility on the part of a city's population which destroys the potential political opposition to a professional city manager. Mobility does not explain, however, why the religious composition of a city is related to forms of government.

We may conceive of both population growth and mobility as intervening variables, serving to loosen the social and political ties of persons to their community and rendering ineffective those characteristics of the population which would otherwise bring forth political demands. Class composition and social heterogeneity or homogeneity are stable long-term characteristics of a city's population. Growth and mobility are more likely to be temporary characteristics, although it is obvious that they may ultimately change the class composition and heterogeneity of a city. For purposes of our present investigation, all of these variables can be regarded as snapshots of processes of social and political change.

Unfortunately we have no data on changes in form of government, but we may venture a concluding speculation. We would expect more change in forms of government in certain types of cities, where the political influence of different social groups varies over time and the city "vacillates" between a concern for efficiency and a concern for representation of group interests. Thus, we would expect that highly mobile and heterogeneous cities would experience considerable pressure for change in form of government. Growing but heavily blue-collar cities should exhibit similar conflicts since they face the "cross-pressures" of (1) need for an efficient, professionalized administration to solve their problems of growth, and (2) need for a political form well adapted to providing representation for diverse subcultures and subcommunities. Such cities have no stable set of "predispositions" toward a given form of government but are pushed in several different directions, much like the "cross-pressured" voters in the classic voting studies.

21

COMMUNITIES AND BUDGETS:
THE SOCIOLOGY OF MUNICIPAL
EXPENDITURES*

LOUIS H. MASOTTI and DON R. BOWEN

This paper reports the findings of a preliminary investigation of the
extent to which municipal budget expenditures reflect various measures of the socioeconomic environment within which budgetary decisions are made. The study was undertaken on the premise that the
community budget can be viewed as public policy spelled out in dollars and cents, and that budget decisions represent the allocation of
certain kinds of values. The initial hypothesis was that these allocations are made, not in a vacuum, but in response to the characteristics of the community involved. More specifically it was hypothesized
that the budget of a community would vary with the socioeconomic
characteristics of the population.[1]

Since the hypothesis was fairly straightforward, but the factors
which might influence budget allocations were not known it was
decided to employ a factor analysis—a research technique which
demanded the minimum prior commitment to specific relationships.[2]

*Reprinted from *Urban Affairs Quarterly,* 1, No. 2 (December 1965), 39-58.
By permission of Urban Affairs Quarterly.

[1]This hypothesis has been investigated by others using various data, samples and
techniques. See, for example, Harvey E. Brazer, *City Expenditures in the United
States* (New York: National Bureau of Economic Research, 1959); Seymour
Sacks and William F. Hellmuth, *Financing Government in a Metropolitan Area*
(New York: The Free Press of Glencoe, 1961); Robert C. Wood, *1400 Governments* (Garden City, New York: Doubleday and Co., 1964). References to
similarities and differences in methodology and findings between this study and
those preceding it will be alluded to where relevant.

[2]Factor analysis is a method designed to facilitate the uncovering of basic
underlying variables. It involves a series of operations based on mathematical
theory to solve systems of equations. For an introduction to the technique and

Following this decision, a "sample" of cities was selected. The sample was composed of all cities in Ohio with a population of over 50,000 in 1960 (N = 18). The sample was limited to Ohio in an effort to minimize differences in the reporting of expenditures which might vary with state statutory regulations.[3] Cities over 50,000 population were selected because the sources of data yielded considerably more information on the socioeconomic characteristics of these cities than it did for those under 50,000. Since the sample was in no sense random, it is impossible to speak of generalizing in any rigorous sense, from the findings presented below to comparable cities. Hence the research must be seen as merely exploratory, but hopefully provocative.

METHODOLOGY

There were eighteen cities in Ohio which fitted into the initial definition. For these cities twelve categories of expenditure were adapted from data found in the *Compendium of City Government Finance in 1961.*[4] Education was omitted because the problem of overlapping and/or independent jurisdictions precludes comparable data. The eighteen cities were then ranked according to the amount they spent on each of the twelve budgetary items measured by (a) per capita expenditure, and (b) the percent of their total budget expended on each item. Two different measures of expenditures were used to ascertain what, if any, differences might be found using differing ways of ranking expenditures.

Following the selection of the categories of budgetary expenditures, thirty-eight items were chosen as socioeconomic characteris-

---

its mathematical theory see L. L. Thurstone, *Multi-Factor Analysis* (Chicago: University of Chicago Press, 1947); K. J. Holzinger and H. H. Harman, *Factor Analysis: A Synthesis of Factorial Methods* (Chicago: University of Chicago Press, 1941). Less technical presentations will be found in Benjamin Fruchter, *Introduction to Factor Analysis* (New York: D. Van Nostrand Co., Inc., 1954); H. H. Harman, *Modern Factor Analysis* (Chicago: University of Chicago Press, 1960); R. B. Cattell, *Factor Analysis* (New York: Harper & Bros., 1956).

[3]Specifically, because some states distribute governmental functions in slightly different ways; in addition there are differences in accounting for and reporting expenditures within the various functional categories. Cf. Brazer, *op. cit.,* p. 16.

[4]U.S. Department of Commerce, Bureau of the Census (G-CF61—No. 2) (Washington, D.C.: GPO, 1962). Separate categories in this publication were combined in two instances (health and hospitals, sewers and sanitation) for purposes of the present analysis.

tics of the eighteen communities.[5] The cities then were ranked for each of these thirty-eight characteristics (Table 1). Thus each of the eighteen cities in the sample were described by fifty items of information—thirty-eight socioeconomic characteristics and twelve items of budgetary expenditure. However, because of the two different ways of measuring expenditures there were actually two lists of fifty items each which described the cities. One consisted of thirty-eight socioeconomic characteristics and twelve budgetary items measured by per capita expenditure; the other was made up of thirty-eight socioeconomic characteristics plus twelve budgetary items measured by the percent of the total city budget devoted to each item. At this point the two lists were coded, punched and reduced to two 50 by 50 matrices on which separate factor analyses were run.[6]

The factor analysis technique was employed for several reasons. First it was suspected that all or some of the fifty different items of information were actually measures of the same underlying factors. If these basic factors could be discovered, the project could be conceptually simplified by reducing fifty items to a few factors. Second, as previously indicated, the technique did not require an advance preduction or commitment to a set of hypotheses about the kinds of factors which would be uncovered. Third, since the project was conceived with a particular interest in expenditures, it was hoped that the budgetary items would exhibit strong associations with the factors uncovered.

GENERAL FINDINGS

Three underlying factors were uncovered which account for approximately sixty-five percent of the variance in each of the two factor analyses. Additional factors could be adduced but they were

[5]Originally, sixty-six socioeconomic characteristics selected from the 1960 population census and the 1958 Census of Business were used. These represented all the items thought to be at all relevant. The original sixty-six were reduced to thirty-eight on the basis of a simple correlation analysis. Items which did not yield a correlation of ±.5 or better with at least one of the twelve expenditure categories were omitted.

[6]Calculations were made on a Univac 1107. Our thanks are due to Mr. Gerry McNichols of Case Institute of Technology who rendered invaluable assistance in programming and interpreting the results. The authors would also like to thank the Graduate Council of Western Reserve University for making funds available to process the data used in this study.

TABLE 1

Eighteen Ohio Cities Ranked (High to Low) for Thirty-Eight
Selected Socioeconomic Characteristics Used in Per Capita
Expenditure and Percent of Budget Factor Analyses

	CHARACTERISTICSa INCLUDED IN BOTH PER CAPITA AND PERCENT ANALYSES	Akron	Canton	Cincinnati	Cleveland	Cleveland Hts	Columbus	Dayton	Euclid	Hamilton	Kettering	Lakewood	Lima	Lorain	Parma	Springfield	Toledo	Warren	Youngstown
1	Population	5	8	2	1	15	3	6	14	11	17	13	18	12	9	10	4	16	7
2	Area	4	12	3	2	17	1	6	15	13	9	18	16	10	8	11	5	14	7
3	Density	12	3	7	2	5	13	4	8	10	18	1	9	17	16	14	6	11	15
4	% Pop. growth, 1950-60	8	13	17	—	11	4	7	2	5	—	—	12	3	3	9	10	11	—
5	Pop. change, 1950-60 (±)	8	11	3	1	14	5	7	17	16	18	18	15	12	1	9	10	6	16
6	% Pop. non-white	7	7	3	14	2	11	2	13	14	16	1	10	16	15	6	6	9	4
7	% Pop. over 21 yrs.	10	3	4	3	2	9	9	16	13	18	1	14	15	17	12	8	8	5
8	% Pop. over 65 yrs.	11	3	8	4	13	13	2	14	15	18	1	16	15	17	6	6	12	8
9	% Deaths/1000	12	3	8	9	15	13	2	16	17	18	5	14	15	18	5	6	11	7
10	Median family income	7	5	16	6	2	11	9	4	18	2	3	18	13	3	17	5	9	14
11	% Pop./fam. income under $3000	12	15	1	12	3	8	6	16	1	18	—	2	13	17	3	4	14	7
12	Median years schlg./pop. 25 yrs. +	8	5	17	4	2	6	12	13	14	2	2	7	7	18	10	8	1	14
13	% Pop. 25+/w/5 yrs. schl. or less	10	5	4	18	2	6	9	10	15	1	7	7	13	3	12	9	6	15
14	% Pop. 25 +/compld. HS	9	3	9	1	12	11	5	12	15	3	1	18	4	3	16	11	7	1
15	% total labor force unemployed	7	2	9	9	17	10	11	5	12	1	3	10	16	15	14	11	1	16
16	% civ. lab. force emplyd. mfg. dur. gds.	1	14	6	9	11	12	12	3	6	—	16	13	13	4	5	5	8	7
17	% tot. labr. force using pub. trans.	11	10	3	1	4	15	1	3	6	2	7	8	4	1	16	4	18	5
18	% Pop. in single fam. d.u.'s	10	9	18	17	16	5	11	16	2	2	2	9	4	6	8	14	15	9
19	% Pop. living in strctrs. blt. 1950-60	8	16	15	14	17	10	5	13	6	16	18	12	3	3	11	13	7	9
20	% h.u.s. w/2+ persons/rm.	12	11	1	18	18	6	4	13	2	—	17	10	3	15	8	14	9	7

TABLE 1 (continued)

#		Characteristic																			
21	%	h.u.s. newly occupd., 1950-60	11	13	2	6	18	1	4	16	3	5	9	8	12	13	7	11	10	17
22	%	h.u.s. owner occupd.	6	12	18	17	4	15	14	3	9	2	16	11	5	1	13	10	8	7
23	%	Pop. in sound strctrs.	9	14	18	12	2	15	10	4	11	3	5	17	6	1	16	7	8	13
24	%	occd. units w/wash. mach.	7	10	18	14	11	17	15	6	9	2	16	12	5	1	8	13	4	3
25	%	occd. units w/food freezr.	11	12	17	18	13	7	4	5	1	14	8	9	3	6	10	15	16	
26	%	occd. units w/TV	7	15	17	16	6	14	8	3	12	2	4	18	5	1	10	9	11	13
27	%	occd. units w/phones	6	9	18	17	1	16	13	4	11	3	5	15	14	2	12	8	10	7
28	%	occd. units w/1 auto	9	10	18	17	16	12	14	2	3	7	6	4	8	1	5	13	15	11
29	%	occd. units w/2 autos or more	7	14	17	18	2	11	16	4	12	1	8	13	6	3	15	9	5	10
30	%	RTE-b service stas.	4	6	18	17	12	8	5	16	10	1	14	12	15	2	3	7	9	11
31	%	RTE-b apparel, assessories	16	10	9	6	1	14	15	4	12	17	13	3	5	18	8	11	2	7
32	%	RTE-b furn., furnishgs.	16	8	18	14	11	10	7	3	9	1	17	5	6	15	4	13	2	12
33	%	RTE-b eating, drinkg.	5	4	8	2	17	6	3	11	7	16	15	13	14	18	9	1	10	12

CHARACTERISTICSa INCLUDED IN PER CAPITA ANALYSIS ONLY

#		Characteristic																			
34	%	Pop. decrease, 1950-60	—	2	5	1	—	—	—	3	—	3	18	13	—	5	17	8	6	15	4
35	%	Fams. w/income over $10,000	7	16	10	14	1	12	9	4	11	2	3	2	8	5	10	7	8	6	15
36	%	employed persons/white col. jobs	11	14	9	17	6	12	4	13	3	3	2	8	18	5	10	7	15	16	1
37	%	RTE-b lumber, hdwr., bldg. matls.	12	7	18	13	17	11	9	16	6	2	3	4	5	10	8	14	15	1
38	%	RTE-b general merchandise	14	15	7	7	9	5	18	1	9	16	3	4	2	5	17	13	11	12

CHARACTERISTICSa INCLUDED IN PERCENT ANALYSIS ONLY

#		Characteristic																			
34	%	Median age	9	5	6	7	1	17	12	7	16	18	2	14	15	13	11	3	10	4
35	%	Pop. w/for. or mixed parentage	11	10	12	7	3	14	15	2	16	13	4	17	6	1	18	9	8	5
36	%	labr. force empd. wholesl./ret'l trade	12	6	10	15	2	5	14	17	16	13	8	3	1	9	11	4	18	7
37	%	serve estmts. — personal services	11	7	14	13	1	10	8	4	16	2	15	3	17	12	9	5	6
38	%	serve estmts. — hotels, motels	4	5	14	10	13	9	12	8	—	15	2	3	—	7	6	1	10

a. Data adapted from U.S. Bureau of the Census, *County and City Data Book, 1962* (Washington: GPO, 1962) TABLE 6.
b. "Retail Trade Establishments."

not judged to be as significant as the first three.[7] Most of the fifty items of information in each of the two analyses turned out to be measures of at least the first three factors. In both analyses there is little doubt that the first and most explanatory underlying factor (approximately 40 per cent of the total variance) is socioeconomic status (SES).[8] The second most important factor (i.e., percentage of variance explained) appears to be the age of the residents, and the third seems to be population mobility, whether budget items are analyzed in terms of the percent of total budget or per capita expenditure. A more detailed comparison of the per capita and percent of budget analyses will be made below, but the specific findings for each will be reported first.

FINDINGS: PER CAPITA EXPENDITURE ANALYSIS

As noted above, when budgets are compared by per capita expenditure the single most important underlying factor was socioeconomic status (41.7% of the variance). The best measures of high SES for the eighteen Ohio cities are measures of consumption, e.g., the possession of more than one car, home food freezers or television sets. Direct measures of higher income and education are also strong indicators of this factor. Conversely, such items as low incomes and a

---

[7]The analyses isolated seven additional factors which together accounted for only about 20% of the variance. Hence we concentrated on the three most significant factors and, for the present at least, dismissed the others.

[8]Although his analysis employs a different sample and technique, this finding gains some support from Brazer's conclusion, *op. cit.*, pp. 29, 56, that income is the single most important variable for explaining variance in city expenditures both for his national sample of 432 cities and the subsample of thirty-two Ohio cities. Sacks and Hellmuth, *op. cit.*, p. 125, note that per capita wealth is important to the explanation of variance in such functional categories as police, fire and general control for all cities in the Cleveland Metropolitan Area. This latter finding, however, should be set alongside the general conclusion that two other independent characteristics, size and assessed valuation, are generally as important as wealth in explaining variations in per capita city expenditures. Wood, *op. cit.*, pp. 40-42, using the same analytic technique employed in the present study (factor analysis), found that several items, such as residential affluence and prevalence of low income families, are related to expenditures in all functional categories on a per capita basis for a subsample of 64 Northern New Jersey communities in the New York Metropolitan Area. Both of these items appear to us to be included within the factor we have called socioeconomic class. Wood has also observed that the names affixed to factors should be recognized for what they are—identification tags, not complete descriptions of the contents. *Op. cit.*, p. 35.

high proportion of non-whites in the community indicate a lower socioeconomic level in the city. Table 2 summarizes and compares the
per capita and percent of budget factor loadings for the expenditure
categories and selected socioeconomic variables used in this study.

Among the budgetary items included with the first factor, Table
2 indicates relatively high positive factor loadings for the expenditure categories and selected socioeconomic variables used in this
study.

Among the budgetary items included with the first factor, Table
2 indicates relatively high positive factor loadings for high expenditures on police, fire protection, general control, water, housing
and urban renewal, parks and recreation, and employee retirement.
The positive factor loadings in this case are indications that lower
SES communities spend a relatively greater amount of money on these
items. Hence, in treating other community budgets we would expect
that greater than average expenditures on the above items would be
a reflection of a community ranked low in socioeconomic status. While
this "expectation" cannot be taken as a reliable prediction because
of the non-random character of the sample in both space and time,
it does constitute a guideline for further inquiry.

On the other hand, such items of expenditure as highways, health
and hospitals, sewers and sanitation, and interest do not appear to
be related in any significant way to the socioeconomic class factor
although, as will be seen, they are indicators of other factors.

Finally, what is perhaps one of the most interesting findings relates
to per capita expenditures on welfare. The factor loading is positive
indicating that higher expenditures on welfare are a measure of lower
SES, as might be expected. However, it is not as high as some of the
other items related to this factor. Welfare expenditures are commonly
thought to be the most obvious fiscal consequence of a lower socio-
economic class city. However the analysis argues that it is not as responsive to variations in socioeconomic status among these cities nor
is it as good an indicator of low socioeconomic status as are such
items as police, fire or any of five other expenditure categories.[9]

The second most important factor, when budgets are compared
on the basis of per capita expenditure, was judged to be the age of
the residents of the community.[10] This factor explains 15.2 per cent
of the total variance which when added to factor one (socioeconomic

[9]Cf. Sacks and Hellmuth, *op. cit.*, p. 125.
[10]Wood, *op. cit.*, pp. 41-43, finds that age is generally more important in
accounting for differing rates of per capita expenditures in all functional
categories than are such items as low income prevalence, residential affluence

TABLE 2

Variable Loadings of Percent of Budget and Per Capita Factor Analyses Compared

Variable	Factor I "SES" Percent	Per Capita	Factor II "AGE" Percent	Per Capita	Factor III "Mobility" Percent	Per Capita
1 % families w/income under $3000	.917	.909				
2 % housing units owner occpd.	−.896	−.891				
3 % occpd. units w/TV	−.893	−.867				
4 % occpd. units w/2 autos or more	−.876	−.887				
5 % pop. in structures built 1950-60	−.868	−.810	.387			.414
6 % occpd. units w/telephone	−.857	−.859	−.414	−.368		
7 % pop. in sound structures	−.843	−.840	−.441	−.423		
8 % occpd. units w/food freezers	−.836	−.870				
9 Median family income	−.802	−.804	−.470	−.503		
10 % pop.non-white	.800	.867	.309			
11 % RTEa — eating, drinking	.778	.784				
12 Median yrs. schling./pop. 25 yrs. +	−.778	−.800	−.473	−.497		
13 % total labor force — unemployed	.764	.770	.308	.469		
14 % occpd. units w/washing machine	−.757	−.740	.445			−.392
15 % pop. in sngl. fam. dwelling units	−.747	−.746	.371	.536		−.425
16 % pop. 25 yrs. +/completed high school	−.737	−.780	−.505	−.524		
17 EMPLOYEE RETIREMENT EXPENDITURE	.711	.756	−.616	−.477		−.465
18 Deaths/1000	.705	.647	−.493	−.425		
19 % occpd. units w/1 auto	−.698	−.700				
20 % RTEa — service stations	−.686	−.687	.302			
21 GENERAL CONTROL EXPENDITURE	.661	.686			−.316	
22 HOUSING/URBAN RENEWAL EXPENDITURE	.648	.705			.493	.529
23 % pop. 25 yrs. +/w/5 yrs. or less schling.	.641	.684			−.359	
24 Population	.615	.695			.497	.512
25 Population growth, 1950-60	−.608	−.539			.421	.565

TABLE 2 (continued)

#	Variable						
26	Population change (+ or −), 1950-60	−.593	−.529	−.725	−.642		.568
27	% pop. over 65 yrs. old	.589	.511				−.440
28	% service establhmts.— hotels, motels	.580				−.600	
29	SEWER/SANITATION EXPENDITURE	−.573				−.311	
30	% housing units w/2+ persons per room	.553	.599	.697	.624		
31	Area	.541	.616			.500	.552
32	HIGHWAY EXPENDITURE	−.523		.409			
33	WATER UTILITY EXPENDITURE	.522	.725			−.595	−.323
34	INTEREST EXPENDITURE	−.495					.750
35	Density	.486	.471	−.636	−.712	.310	
36	% RTE[a] — furniture, home furnishings	−.440	−.441		.346	−.446	−.357
37	% pop. w/foreign or mixed parentage	−.430		−.484			
38	% total labor force using public transport'n	.379	.426	−.516	−.658	.534	.415
39	POLICE EXPENDITURE	−.359	.817			−.342	
40	% housing units newly occpd, 1958-60	.358	.355	.426		.507	
41	% pop. over 21 yrs. old	.356	.310	−.905	.881		
42	% service establhmts.— personal services			−.560		−.350	
43	WELFARE EXPENDITURE		.440			−.325	−.494
44	% RTE[a] — apparel, accessories			−.418		−.665	
45	HEALTH/HOSPITAL EXPENDITURE			−.471	−.531		
46	Median age			−.946			
47	PARKS & RECREATION EXPENDITURE		.604	−.437	−.465		
48	% total labor force empld. mfg. non-durables					.508	.342
49	% total labor force empld. wholesale/retail					−.481	
50	FIRE EXPENDITURE		.794			−.691	
51	% families w/income over $10,000		−.698		−.618		
52	% RTE[a] — general merchandise						
53	% employed persons/white collar jobs		−.597		−.720		
54	Population decrease, 1950-60				.353		
55	% RTE[a] — lumber, hrdwr, building matr'ls		−.407				−.426

a. "Retail Trade Establishments."

status) accounts for 56.9 per cent. The best single measures of this factor are direct measures of age (percent of the population over twenty-one, and over sixty-five) and the mortality rate. All three of these have high negative factor loadings indicating that they are measures of an older community; positive factor loadings in this factor are related to a younger community. Here the measures indicate that such items as population in single family dwelling units (a characteristic strongly associated with new suburbs, whose population is generally younger), houses built since 1950, and unemployment (which tends to be disproportionately concentrated among younger persons) are all indications or measures of a relatively younger population.

In terms of the specific items of expenditure, allocations for health and hospitals, employee retirement, and parks and recreation have high negative factor loadings. This simply means that increasing expenditures on these items reflects an increasingly older community. The other nine categories of expenditure do not appear to be significantly related to this factor.

An examination of the loadings for the third underlying factor led to the conclusion that it was population mobility.[11] This factor by itself accounts for nine per cent of the total variance, making the cumulative variance explained by factors one, two, and three 65.9 per cent. Relatively high factor loadings for such items as population change, population growth, and percentage of the 1960 population living in structures built between 1950-1960 indicate that a community is experiencing high mobility. On the negative side, certain businesses appear to be peculiarly associated with low mobility which suggests the conclusion that only in relatively settled communities are businesses such as apparel stores or furniture stores likely to account for a relatively high percentage of the total num-

---

or housing density. The contrast appears to us to be due to the fact, as noted above, that these three latter characteristics are all included within the factor we have called socioeconomic class.

[11]Brazer, *op. cit.*, pp. 29, 46, 53, notes that rate of population growth is of little significance in explaining variation in per capita city expenditures for both his national sample and the subsample of Ohio cities. He does, however, note that it is important for his subsample of California cities where growth is an important characteristic. Insofar as the differences in findings are not due to differences in analytic techniques and samples, it appears that our sample of 18 Ohio cities in 1960 is comparable to Brazer's sample of California cities in 1950 in that the cities used here include a number of rapidly growing suburbs, hence we would suspect that the factor we have called mobility would now loom larger than it did when Brazer's study was made. In addition, of course, the factor we have called mobility includes other measures besides rate of population growth.

ber of retail firms. In addition, items such as population over 65 and the mortality rate also appear to be negative indicators of mobility (i.e., relative immobility) in the community. These are, of course, also measures of the factor we have called age, but there is an obvious relationship between communities with older residents and communities with a relatively less mobile population.

Of the expenditure items, three appear to be measures of the mobility factor.[12] Interest and housing-urban renewal have high positive loadings on this factor, i.e., they are measures of relatively greater mobility in the community. High expenditure on interest is characteristic of newer communities which experience mobility. Greater expenditure on public housing and urban renewal is associated with larger cities with relatively poor neighborhoods where mobility is also likely to be high. In the direction of less mobility, the only budgetary item with a significant factor loading is water utility expenditure. This suggests that relatively greater expenditures on a water utility would indicate an older, more settled community.

To summarize the findings for the twelve categories of budgetary expenditure: when measured by the per capita amount spent by the eighteen communities, such things as police, fire protection, general control, and welfare are measures of lower socioeconomic status.[13] Generally speaking, we would expect that relatively higher expenditures on these items, discovered in other cities, would reflect this underlying factor. Moreover, these items do not appear to be measures of other factors; the loadings for these expenditures on the remaining two factors were not statistically significant.

One expenditure item, health and hospitals, is related only to the age factor. The direction of the loading indicates that rising expenditures for this function in comparison to other communities is a reflection of an older community. Similarly in the mobility factor, interest expenditure is the one item unambiguously related to this factor alone. The sign of the loading shows that higher expenditures on interest is an indicator of relatively higher mobility.

Four of the twelve expenditure categories, housing and urban renewal, water supply, parks and recreation and employee retirement, are significant measures of more than one factor. However, in two cases, employee retirement and water supply, it appears that they are

---

[12]Sacks and Hellmuth, *op. cit.,* p. 105, note that a static population is associated with increasing total operating expenditures but since they do not break this down into functional expenditure categories the finding cannot be compared to the results obtained here.

[13]Cf. Wood, *op. cit.,* pp. 42-43, for comparable findings.

better measures of SES than of any other factor. Employee retirement is a measure of both lower SES (.756) and old age (.477). Water supply is related to lower SES (.725) and greater stability (−.323). In both cases the loading for SES is considerably higher than for the competing factor and leads to the conclusion that higher city expenditures on these items are primarily a reflection of a less affluent community.

The remaining two cases, parks and recreation and housing and urban renewal, are not so clear. Parks and recreation is related to lower SES (.604) and to old age (− .465). Housing and urban renewal is related to lower SES (.705) and to greater mobility (.579). Although in both cases the loading for SES is higher than those for other factors they are not enough higher to justify assigning these expenditures to the first factor alone. Hence, comparatively greater allocations of funds for both of these latter functions must be interpreted as a reflection of either underlying factor.

Finally, the factor analysis of per capita expenditures revealed no discernible significant relation between two of the twelve functions, highways and sewers and sanitation, and any of the three underlying factors.

FINDINGS: PERCENT OF BUDGET ANALYSIS

For comparative purposes, a second factor analysis was made using municipal budget expenditures as a percentage of the total budget. As in the first analysis, socioeconomic status, age, and mobility (in that order) emerge as the three most significant underlying factors (Table 2). Together they account for 65.3 percent of the variance.

When budgets are compared on the basis of the proportion spent on each of the budgetary categories, the single most important factor is again SES, which accounts for 38.0 percent of the variance. However, despite this general similarity, there are some striking differences which need to be explained.

As in the case of the per capita analysis, the best indicators of high socioeconomic status communities are measures of consumption (e.g., possession of cars, food freezers and televisions) and direct measures of income (median family income). Conversely, the best measures of lower socioeconomic status are income, unemployment, and the percentage of the population which is non-white. However, for two budget items the direction of the factor loadings is the reverse of that found in the per capita analysis. Expenditures on police and general control have negative factor loadings, i.e., they are associated with high socioeconomic class rather than low as was the case when budgets were compared on a per capita expenditure basis.

To explain this reversal it is necessary to introduce an additional consideration about the size of the cities. Most of the cities which were ranked high on the various measures of socioeconomic class were among the smaller cities in the sample.[14] Expenditures on police and general control are a necessary item in any city's budget and are likely to appear as a greater percentage of a small city's budget, which often does not include the range of expenditure found in the budgets of the larger cities.[15] While per capita expenditures on police are less for the smaller and generally more wealthy cities, what they do spend on this item assumes a large proportion of a relatively limited budget. Thus in the per capita factor analysis both police expenditure and· general control are a reflection of lower socioeconomic status and in the per cent of budget analysis they indicate higher status. This apparent contradiction is explained by the fact that per capita expenditure controls for the differences in the size of the cities, while per cent of budget expenditure does not.[16]

A comparison of the two analyses also reveals that on a percent of budget basis expenditures for highways, interest, and sewers and sanitation are indicators of relatively more affluent communities while on a per capita basis these categories are unrelated to socioeconomic standing. Again the explanation seems to lie in the fact that these are major expenditures which will almost certainly loom large in a smaller city budget as a percent of allocations. Since the smaller cities tend to be disproportionately more affluent, these expenditure items are related to high SES.

The second most important percent of budget factor, as in the per capita expenditure analysis, is age (16.3 percent of the variance explained). The community characteristics which measure this factor

[14]The 1960 population of the eighteen cities used in this analysis (smallest to largest) are as follows: (See Table 1 for the ranking of specific socioeconomic characteristics): Lima (51,037); Kettering (54,462); Warren (59,648); Cleveland Heights (61,813); Lakewood (66,154); Lorain (68,932); Euclid (69,998); Hamilton (72,354); Springfield (82,723); Parma (82,845); Canton (113,631); Youngstown (166,689); Dayton (262,332); Akron (290,351); Toledo (318,003); Columbus (471,316); Cincinnati (502,550); Cleveland (876,050).

[15]All eighteen cities spent some of their funds on these two items whereas a few did not allocate funds for some of the other budget items. e.g., housing and urban renewal, public welfare, water. See Table 1.

[16]On this point, see Glenn W. Fisher, "Revenue and Expenditure Patterns in Five Large Cities," ECONOMICS AND BUSINESS 3 (Autumn, 1963), pp. 61-72.

are comparable to the same factor in the first analysis. Such variables as the percentage of the population over sixty-five, the percentage over twenty-one, and median age have high negative factor loadings meaning that they reflect an older community. High positive loadings on items such as persons living in houses built since 1950, newly occupied houses, single family dwelling units, and the proportion of unemployed reflect a younger community.

As for specific expenditure items, significant negative factor loadings for employee retirement and health and hospitals indicate that these two items are measures of greater age. They also appear as measures of an older community in the per capita analysis. One additional expenditure item—highways—emerges as a reflection of age variations among the communities studied, which did not appear in the per capita analysis. Younger and newer cities will spend a greater percentage of their budgets on roads but the per capita expenditure analysis indicates that the amount spent does not vary significantly ($> \pm .300$). The younger communities also happen to be the smaller ones and expenditure on highways will appear as a greater proportion of a more limited budget.

The third percent of budget factor, which explains eleven percent of the variance, was again labeled mobility. Although there is some similarity between the items which appear as good indices in this and the per capita analysis, they were somewhat stronger in the latter. Housing units newly occupied and population growth both reflect a relatively high rate of population turnover. Although the age indicators (e.g., population over 65, mortality rate) of relative immobility disappeared in this analysis, retail and service establishments (e.g., furniture, apparel, hotels-motels) again emerged as significant indices of community stability.

Among the budgetary items, two show up here which also appeared in the per capita factor analysis. These are expenditures on housing and urban renewal, associated with higher mobility, and expenditures on water supply, associated with lower mobility. Precisely the same relations were noted in the per capita analysis. Two additional items which appear only in the percent of budget analysis are welfare and fire expenditure. The first emerges as a weak and the second as a strong measure of low mobility. The later finding can be explained by the interrelationship of the age and mobility factors. The less mobile communities also tend to be the older ones where the older buildings require a considerable amount of money to be spent on fire protection. However, the fact that fire expenditures are not associated with stability in the per capita analysis, where the size of the community and the budget are controlled, argues that the relationship between them in the percent of budget analysis is perhaps deceptive.

To summarize the twelve categories of budget expenditure for the percent of budget analysis: relatively high expenditures on employee retirement, housing and urban renewal and water supply indicate a lower socioeconomic status city. All three of these items are measures of lower SES whether budgets are ranked on a per capita expenditure basis or on the percent of budget basis.

Expenditures on general control, police, sewers and sanitation and interest, when relatively high, indicate an upper socioeconomic status community when budgets are compared on the percent of total base. For two of these items, police and general control, the percent of budget analysis contradicts the per capita analysis, i.e., on a per capita basis they measure lesser affluence, and on a percent of budget basis they reflect a relatively greater affluence. This was judged to be due to the fact that these items are necessary expenditures for any city, and hence would loom larger as a percent of comparatively limited small city budgets, which also happen to be associated with the richer communities in the sample. The same explanation was offered for the other two items, which appear in this analysis as measures of higher socioeconomic status (higher expenditures on interest and sewers and sanitation), but which do not appear at all related to this factor in the per capita analysis.

In the case of the second factor (age), higher expenditures on health and hospitals, employee retirement, and parks and recreation indicate an older community, and higher expenditures on highways appear to be a measure of a relatively younger city. The first three are also measures of an older community when budgets are compared on the per capita basis. Highways does not appear to be related to age when the size of the community is controlled in the per capita analysis.

The last factor, mobility, is best measured by higher budgetary allocations for fire protection, housing/urban renewal and water supply. Increasing expenditures on fire and water supply indicate a more stable community and, for housing/urban renewal, greater population mobility. Two of these, water supply and housing/urban renewal measure the same thing in the same direction in the per capita expenditure analysis. The third, higher expenditures on fire protection, is not significantly related to the mobility factor when expenditures are compared on a per capita basis.

Among the twelve categories of budgetary items in the percent of budget analysis there are three which are measures of more than one factor. Employee retirement is a measure of both lower socio-economic class communities (.711) and older communities (.616). These do not differ enough to justify a conclusion that high employee retirement expenditures are an indication of either factor alone and, for the time being, such a finding must be accepted as indicating either lower socioeconomic class cities or older cities. A second item which overlapped was water supply. Higher expenditures on water appear to be a reflection of both a more stable community (− .595) and a lower socioeconomic class community (.522). Again the factor loadings are ambiguous and high expenditures on this item must be taken to indicate the presence of either factor. The third ambiguous case was expenditure on housing and urban renewal which indicated both lower class (.648) and higher mobility (.483). In this case it would seem that greater expenditures on housing and urban renewal are a better indicator of socio-economic class than of mobility. However, such a conclusion can only be tentative at best.

CONCLUSION

This study began with the assumption that at least a certain degree of variation in city expenditure patterns was a reflection of the environment of the city. Budget-makers, like other decision-makers, do not operate in a social vacuum. They respond to those pressures and opportunities which they perceive, and when these forces are large and gross, such as the characteristics we have been discussing in this paper, the responses of different decision-makers to similar stimuli are likely to be similar. That assumption seems borne out by the results reported above for eighteen Ohio cities. Variations among the cities in the levels of expenditure for twelve functional categories are associated with variations in three underlying factors—socioeconomic status, age and mobility.

In large part these results are comparable to other investigations. The exact similarities and differences are pinpointed above and need not be repeated here. Suffice it to say that we do not consider our results significantly enough at variance with other reported findings to conclude that either they or we are mistaken. The positive way of putting this is that, despite differences of sample and analytic technique, the results here by and large confirm other investigations of the relations between socioeconomic characteristics and levels of expenditure. We have included a larger number of socioeconomic characteristics than other studies but the number of cities used is smaller.[17] The gains and losses of this procedure have not made any significant difference between the outcomes here and those of other studies.

There is one significant independent variable which other investigations have included that is omitted here; namely, the size of the community. Both of our ways of measuring expenditures, per capita expenditure and percent of total budget expenditure, were designed to control for the size of the community. There is disagreement in the existing literature about the relation of size to total expenditures.[18] However, there seems to be general agreement (confirmed here) that size is unrelated to variations in per capita expenditure rates.[19] We did, of course, include total population as one of the socioeconomic characteristics in the analysis. It turned out to be significantly associated with lower SES and higher mobility as a single item measuring those two underlying factors,[20] but it was not one of the identifiable factors by itself.

As a side comment on the various ways of measuring city expenditures, it developed that the percent of budget measure is an imperfect instrument for controlling for the size of the community when compared with per capita expenditure. This is so because there are certain functions, e.g. police, which all cities undertake and which demand a certain fixed level of initial expenditure. If

---

[17]*Brazer, op. cit.,* p. 25, uses six independent variables in analyzing variations in expenditures for a national sample of 432 cities and subsamples of 35 California cities, 30 Massachusetts cities and 32 Ohio cities. Sacks and Hellmuth, *op. cit.,* p. 89, use three independent variables to explain variation for subsample of 20 cities and 42 villages in the Cleveland Metropolitan Area. Wood, *op. cit.,* pp. 39-40, included seven socioeconomic characteristics in his factor analysis for a sample of 64 New Jersey cities in the New York Metropolitan Area. In a sense, of course, we have used only three variables—SES, age and mobility— to explain variations in expenditures. The difference is that we began with a total of 38 socioeconomic characteristics and reduced these to three underlying factors as a result of the factor analysis rather than committing ourselves to a single measure of such a factor as SES beforehand.

[18]Sacks and Hellmuth, *op. cit.,* p. 93 and Wood, *op. cit.,* p. 39 both argue that community size is the single most important variable bearing on total operating expenditures. Brazer concludes that for his national sample size is not significantly related to total operating expenses. *Op. cit.,* p. 25.

[19]Brazer, *op. cit.,* p. 28; Sacks and Hellmuth, *op. cit.,* p. 119; Wood, *op. cit.,* pp. 39-40.

[20]See Table 2.

the total community budget is relatively small, as it tends to be for the smaller cities, then this expenditure appears as a larger percentage of the total budget for the smaller city than it does for a larger city. This distortion, while possible for per capita expenditures, is not nearly so important for this latter way of measuring money spent. Another point influencing this relation is that the larger cities undertake to furnish a greater range of functions, hence the percent of their total budgets devoted to any one is smaller than for the smaller cities which do not undertake so many activities.

In general we conclude that we would expect that variations in city expenditures, however measured, would be in part accounted for by differences in the three factors discussed here. This expectation is in no sense a rigorous prediction. The limitations of the sample in both space and time preclude that degree of methodological sophistication. However, the comparability between our results and those of other investigations (also suffering from similar sample limitations) encourage us in the belief that there is a sociology of municipal budget-making, i.e., that expenditure rates do respond to differences in the socioeconomic environment. Hopefully the direction and degree of this relation has been in part delineated by the above findings.

22

CENTRAL CITY EXPENDITURES AND METROPOLITAN AREAS*†

WOO SIK KEE

Recent empirical studies of expenditure behavior of central cities, although very extensive, have not been too satisfactory, partly because they had been limited to the analysis only within given areas, classes of government, or functions; and partly because they failed to recognize the fiscal interdependence between state and local governments on the one hand, and among local governments on the other.[1]

The purpose of this paper is to discuss critical differences of socioeconomic and governmental characteristics between the city and areas outside the central city in 36 selected Standard Metropolitan Statistical areas (SMSA's).[2] Secondly, by incorporating the effects

*Reprinted from *The National Tax Journal, XVIII,* No. 4 (December 1965), 337-353. By permission of *The National Tax Journal* and the author.
†This study was originally undertaken as a part of the Maxwell Graduate School Research Project Metropolitan Area Finance Studies," sponsored by the Brookings Institution. The Methodology of the analysis and "sample" of the central cities employed in this paper are based on the author's doctoral dissertation submitted to the Maxwell Graduate School of Syracuse University in 1964.

[1]Among these recent studies are Amos H. Hawley, "Metropolitan Population and Municipal Government Expenditures in Central Cities," *Journal of Social Issues,* Vol. VII, 1951; Stanley Scott and Edward L. Feder, *Factors Associated with Variations in Municipal Expenditures Levels,* University of California at Berkeley, 1957; and Harvey E. Brazer, *City Expenditures in the United States,* National Bureau of Economic Research, 1959.
[2]The term "central city" follows the definition established by United States Bureau of the Census. According to that definition, a central city generally contains 50,000 inhabitants or more. If, however, two or more adjacent

on city expenditures of intergovernmental fiscal responsibilities into multiple regression analysis, the results (i.e., the relationships between the level of per capita city expenditures and selected explanatory variables) are shown. The final section of this paper will summarize the major findings of the study and conclude with some policy implications.

I. DIFFERENTIALS IN METROPOLITAN AREAS: CENTRAL CITIES VERSUS SUBURBS

A. *Variations in general characteristics*

In order to account for the differences in public finance characteristics found to exist between "central cities" and the remainder of the metropolitan areas examined, 36 SMSA were selected for the following reasons. This group exhibited variations in geographic location, population size, and also in patterns of state and local governmental system in which these cities were found. In 1957 (the only year for which comprehensive data were available) the areas so selected had an estimated population of 35.2 million persons, of which 20.2 million were in the core cities.[3]

Total populations of central cities varied from 60,000 in Atlantic City to 7,782,000 in New York City, whereas the areas outside the 36 SMSAs ranged in population from 29,000 in Norwalk to 2,913,-000 in New York City. It is also noted that the ratio of central city population to the metropolitan area population varied from 24% in the Newark and Paterson-Clifton-Passaic SMSAs to 75.5% in the Houston SMSA.

Public services of the 36 metropolitan areas in 1957 were provided by a total of 4,482 various local units of government, while the core

---

counties each have a city of 50,000 inhabitants or more (or twin cities with a combined population of at least 50,000) and the cities are within 20 miles of each other (city limits to city limits), they are included in the same "central city" unless there is definite evidence that the two cities are not economically and socially integrated. For example, of all the central cities of 36 SMSAs, Albany-Schenectady-Troy, Patterson-Clifton-Passaic, Tampa-St. Petersburg, and Utica-Rome are integrated as four separate "central cities." The rest of the 36 selected cities are: Atlanta, Atlanta City, Baltimore, Binghamton, Bridgeport, Buffalo, Cleveland, Hartford, Houston, Jacksonville, Jersey City, Kansas City, Madison, Memphis, Miami, Milwaukee, Nashville, Newark, New York, Norwalk, Rochester, Sacramento, St. Louis, San Antonio, San Diego, San Jose, Savannah, Seattle, Spokane, Stamford, Syracuse and Toledo.
[3] Populations in 1957 were estimated by the linear interpolation as used by the Census Bureau and also by taking into account city annexations.

areas were served by only 172 local governments. Total units of local governments for both central cities and their respective SMSAs are distributed as follows:

TABLE I

Distribution of Local Governments in the
36 Selected Standard Metropolitan Statistical
Areas and their Central Cities, by Types, 1957[4]

Units of Local Government	SMSAs	Central Cities
Total local government	4,482	172
School districts	1,734	30
Other local governments, total	2,748	142
Counties	64	34
Municipalities	1,022	42
Townships	526	0
Special districts	1,136	66

As shown in Table I, the local government pattern in metropolitan areas is unbelievably complex. At the time of the 1957 Census of Governments, there was an average of approximately 125 local governments per standard metropolitan statistical area—the latter as defined by the 1960 census. But there was a wide range of variations starting from a few units in some instances, to several hundred in others. In contrast with the 36 metropolitan areas as a whole, the central cities of these selected areas had a relatively smaller number of local governments, an average of about 3 units per city. The range of variations among these central cities was from 2 units in some cities such as Baltimore, Bridgeport, and Buffalo, to 14 in the case of the central city of San Antonio.

The relative complexity of governmental patterns within metropolitan areas—central city versus its suburbs—is presented not only by the comparative numbers of those patterns but also by their frequent territorial overlapping. Furthermore, heterogeneity of fiscal characteristics in the metropolitan areas is very acute in the areas surrounding the central cities as compared to the cities themselves. For example, per capita personal income of the central cities varied from $1,281 in Nashville to $2,800 in Stamford. But in the remaining

[4]Source: U.S. Bureau of Census, *U.S. Census of Governments: 1957, Local Government Finances in Standard Metropolitan Areas*, Vol. III, No. 6 and *Local Government in Standard Metropolitan Areas*, Vol. I, No. 2.

parts of the metropolitan areas, the range of income variation was $1,357 in Memphis to $5,527 in Stamford.[5]

In addition to differences in the number of local governments and per capita personal income between the central cities and the remaining parts of the 36 SMSAs, there is a great variation in density of population. The Population Census of 1960 reports that central cities in our sample areas varied in density from 1,616 persons per square mile in Utica-Rome to 24,697 persons in New York City. In the rest of the 36 metropolitan areas, the population density ranged from 56 persons per square mile in Spokane SMSA to 1,588 persons in New York SMSA. It is of interest to find that there was a relatively normal distribution of population density among the central cities of the selected metropolitan areas. There was, however, a strong tendency of bi-modal distribution among areas outside these cities taken as units. This tendency was indicated by the fact that not a single area outside the city had a population density of between 730 to 1,218 persons, while their median density was 356 persons per square mile. It seems to indicate that there are apparently two different types of areas which together are classified as "outside central cities"; one is an aggregate of urban communities with a population density of 1,218 or more persons per square mile and the other is a group of rural areas with a population density of 730 or less persons.

As has been noted so far, extreme variations in government, income and population characteristics among the areas outside the central cities covered indicate difficulties involved in a systematic approach to the suburban communities around the central city as a unit. Since our major concern here is to compare the level of public expenditure in central cities to those of the remaining portions of the metropolitan areas as a whole, the problems are somewhat less difficult.

B. *Variations in Public Spending*

Table II shows that there are substantial differences between the central cities and the remainder of metropolitan areas as regards to per capita total expenditure and other major expenditure categories. Part of such differences undoubtedly stems from the differences in population characteristics, degree of urbanization, the level of income, and social and economic preferences in the covered

[5]High per capita incomes shown for the three separate areas outside of Hartford, Norwalk and Stamford central cities are mainly due to the inclusion of exceptionally rich suburban communities such as West Hartford town, Westport town, and Greenwich town.

areas. However, the hypothesis suggested here is that a large part of the differences in per capita local expenditures within metropolitan areas is attributable to the differences in the distribution of governmental responsibilities between the state and its political subdivisions. Factors accounting for such differences are state aid, the local portion of state and local service responsibilities, and other variables which indicate differences in state and local fiscal systems.

Hawley, and particularly Brazer, using 1953 fiscal data, have proved that total per capita expenditure of the central cities examined was closely related to the ratio of the central city to the total population of its metropolitan area. Their hypothesis was based on two considerations. First, suburban residents who work, play or shop in the central city add to the need for streets, parking, and other facilities. Second, the suburbanites also add to the demand on the city's public services such as police and fire protection, recreation, sanitation, and others. In his multiple regression analysis for 40 large cities, Brazer found the coefficient of simple correlation between the metropolitan population ratio and total per capita expenditure to be −.582.[6]

More recently Brazer has demonstrated that consistently higher expenditures are being incurred in the central cities than in the rest of the metropolitan areas.[7] But as shown in Table II for 36 SMSAs, there is no clear-cut indication that the level of total per capita expenditures in the central cities is higher than those for the remaining parts of the metropolitan areas. While it is true that in many instances the central city spends relatively more than the areas outside the city, such differences do not, in themselves, establish the evidence that the residents of the suburban area impose a net expenditure burden on the central city. On the other hand, in cases where the suburban communities as a whole spend more than their central city, it is often because of relatively greater state aid to the areas outside the city.

The problems of expenditure burdens concerned with the central city vs. suburbs are much more difficult than can be explained by a simple comparison of their per capita expenditure levels. For instance, in many cases where a central city has a higher level of per capita expenditure compared with the rest of the metropolitan

[6]Brazer, op. cit., Table c-5, pp. 80-81.
[7]Harvey E. Brazer, "Some Fiscal Implications of Metropolitanism" in Guthrie S. Birkhead (ed.), Metropolitan Issues: Social, Governmental, Fiscal, Maxwell Graduate School, Syracuse University, February, 1962.

TABLE II

Per Capita General Expenditures of Local Governments in Central Cities and Outside of Central Cities, 36 Selected Standard Metropolitan Statistical Areas: 1957

(Amounts in Dollars)

Central Cities in 36 SMSAs	Total General Expenditure		Total Education		Education Excluding Capital Outlays		Highways		Health and Hospitals		Public Welfare	
	Central Cities	Outside Central Cities	Central Cities	Outside Central Cities	Central Cities	Outside Central Cities	Central Cities	Outside Central Cities	Central Cities	Outside Central Cities	Central Cities	Outside Central Cities
Albany-Schenectady-Troy, N.Y.	$172.03	$188.09	$62.66	$104.54	$52.14	$76.81	$15.65	$22.48	$ 6.91	$ 5.82	$16.15	$15.03
Atlanta, Ga.	157.72	100.29	54.68	52.74	50.54	39.15	21.65	8.78	13.98	11.99	3.37	1.74
Atlantic City, N.J.	232.39	140.12	46.92	51.87	46.07	48.72	17.77	17.88	15.04	9.17	14.51	12.47
Baltimore, Md.	199.41	141.77	59.09	70.62	47.09	47.23	19.46	18.64	11.30	1.35	17.89	3.20
Binghamton, N.Y.	227.74	185.44	69.33	107.66	67.11	88.36	11.49	20.26	41.86	10.40	26.86	9.85
Bridgeport, Conn.	145.47	148.71	40.52	89.87	40.21	63.90	5.54	10.43	10.58	5.52	2.16	.55
Buffalo, N.Y.	193.38	210.19	51.91	98.81	45.35	73.26	16.65	20.62	11.62	11.86	18.50	16.38
Cleveland, Ohio	179.99	186.38	49.56	85.36	44.03	60.36	19.10	21.55	11.15	6.15	11.80	10.68
Hartford, Conn.	186.37	154.35	51.15	102.77	46.85	64.66	7.57	11.62	12.22	.57	5.28	.62
Houston, Texas	155.35	186.97	64.71	125.69	46.53	85.92	17.66	14.10	7.51	.65	1.48	1.46
Jacksonville, Fla.	175.28	91.29	55.82	55.82	42.80	42.80	15.58	3.37	10.03	6.30	.87	.75
Jersey City, N.J.	237.04	194.14	50.44	52.25	49.18	50.90	6.33	8.12	47.30	17.78	11.65	11.12
Kansas City, Mo.-Kans.	186.38	111.68	63.37	55.40	54.99	34.40	25.11	12.96	18.69	5.25	.99	6.23
Madison, Wis.	241.37	177.19	70.94	81.27	57.27	58.74	37.62	33.04	11.28	7.00	17.83	16.75
Memphis, Tenn.	124.86	79.39	36.62	58.76	29.19	43.25	14.23	4.93	14.26	3.17	1.04	.57
Miami, Fla.	225.82	168.52	70.03	70.03	46.86	46.86	10.02	11.09	13.16	13.22	2.83	2.99
Milwaukee, Wis.	229.30	209.84	50.98	88.51	39.54	53.23	31.94	26.26	25.45	17.41	16.58	13.29
Nashville, Tenn.	151.85	75.33	42.99	54.83	42.25	43.08	12.82	6.15	16.48	4.82	1.25	.58
Newark, N.J.	242.68	181.06	75.79	88.06	63.96	62.81	6.48	11.50	36.33	11.09	12.68	7.05
New York, N.Y.	256.63	259.38	63.24	140.17	50.41	89.11	18.22	22.39	27.75	8.40	28.37	10.68
Norwalk, Conn.	145.34	195.41	80.78	139.35	53.15	107.51	5.56	10.43	1.84	.83	1.33	.79

TABLE II (Continued)

Per Capita General Expenditures of Local Governments in Central Cities and Outside of Central Cities, 36 Selected Standard Metropolitan Statistical Areas: 1957

(Amounts in Dollars)

Central Cities in 36 SMSAs	Total General Expenditure		Total Education		Education Excluding Capital Outlays		Highways		Health and Hospitals		Public Welfare	
	Central Cities	Outside Central Cities	Central Cities	Outside Central Cities	Central Cities	Outside Central Cities	Central Cities	Outside Central Cities	Central Cities	Outside Central Cities	Central Cities	Outside Central Cities
Paterson-Clifton-Passaic, N.J.	$154.96	$156.76	$55.61	$ 81.20	$51.20	$56.13	$ 6.55	$11.38	$ 9.22	$ 6.42	$ 8.64	$ 5.09
Rochester, N.Y.	200.24	195.90	52.99	91.94	47.94	62.53	17.45	17.61	15.83	9.67	22.74	22.95
Sacramento, Calif.	255.77	189.10	82.94	104.23	66.27	69.50	16.55	7.73	16.88	15.13	29.76	29.76
St. Louis, Mo.-Ill.	148.96	123.69	45.73	71.16	41.10	52.00	10.08	15.20	20.62	4.56	.85	2.56
San Antonio, Texas	113.17	104.26	48.32	87.45	34.68	59.57	16.55	3.00	5.80	.09	.20	.98
San Diego, Calif.	191.25	188.68	71.52	90.13	57.43	67.33	17.28	9.14	6.73	11.91	20.84	20.73
San Jose, Calif.	226.16	203.36	73.64	107.94	61.05	66.82	19.18	12.00	15.80	11.45	23.83	23.83
Savannah, Ga.	112.26	61.22	35.79	33.31	35.53	33.06	6.45	2.13	9.68	8.86	2.02	1.62
Seattle, Wash.	173.90	141.78	57.17	87.31	47.71	65.96	26.35	10.87	4.50	6.30	.15	.16
Spokane, Wash.	164.58	139.19	66.69	99.47	50.02	67.95	26.73	14.91	4.24	2.93	.38	.28
Stamford, Conn.	151.12	205.46	64.13	114.77	61.79	81.38	9.89	16.37	2.07	6.22	3.50	2.90
Syracuse, N.Y.	198.17	201.25	53.96	89.54	50.53	74.64	27.90	32.03	8.15	6.53	20.03	20.94
Tampa, St. Petersburg, Fla.	159.21	88.82	48.46	45.33	41.86	38.90	15.31	7.05	24.28	1.72	.79	1.13
Toledo, Ohio	171.64	154.92	58.49	87.84	54.18	59.00	15.39	11.11	11.15	7.76	9.27	9.23
Utica-Rome, N.Y.	191.79	215.96	62.04	125.68	53.08	87.26	27.58	31.56	14.59	7.66	17.72	15.42
Mean of 36 cities	185.54	159.83	58.02	85.84	49.16	61.72	16.55	14.41	14.84	7.09	10.39	8.34
Standard deviation	39.44	46.53	11.77	25.95	8.67	17.06	7.87	7.90	10.29	4.58	9.50	8.13

Source: Derived from U.S. Bureau of the Census, *U.S. Census of Governments, 1957*, Vol. III, No. 6, *Local Government Finances in Standard Metropolitan Areas* (Washington: U.S. Government Printing Office, 1959), Table 4; county expenditures in total and individual functions were allocated by the ratio of central city to county population, based on 1957 estimates of county population and central city population including annexation up to 1957.

area, the total usually includes expenditures incurred for additional functions such as public housing and urban renewal, all characteristics of cities, but excludes expenditures of voluntary fire fighting and privately operated sanitation services, the latter being characteristic of outlying areas.

A more adequate comparison between expenditure levels of central cities and areas outside those cities is made by individual functions. Table II shows the relatively higher education expenditures in the suburbs, which reflect the fact that rapid population growth in these areas requires large capital outlays for new school construction. In 1957, in 30 out of 36 selected SMSAs, the suburban communities surrounding central cities as units spent more than their core cities for education, including capital outlays. Of these 30 areas, 23 were more than $20 per capita higher, and in the cases of the Jacksonville and Miami SMSA, the level of expenditure for education outside the central city was the same as inside the city.[8]

If, however we subtract sums spent for capital outlay from the total educational expenditure, there is no uniformity as to the relative level of expenditures between areas outside the central cities and the central cities themselves. We may expect highway expenditures to be higher outside central cities because they tend to be inversely related to population density, but there is no clear indication of this trend. With respect to health and hospitals, central cities, being a center for urban services, tend to have consistently higher expenditures than the surrounding suburban communities.

Furthermore, Table II presents startling variations in the level of per capita expenditures being incurred for highways, health and hospitals, and public welfare, whether they be of those central cities or of areas outside the cities. To compare the relative dispersions of the various classes of expenditure, the coefficient of variation was computed for each function inside as well as outside the selected central cities.

As indicated in Table III, the coefficients of variation inside and outside selected central cities were 21.3 per cent and 29.1 per cent, respectively, in the case of total per capita expenditures. But in the case of public welfare, the ratios were many times higher in both central cities and areas outside the cities. It should be noted that there is no great difference in the relative dispersions of the total and indi-

[8]It is due to the fact that public education for both the central city and the area outside the city of each SMSA (Jacksonville and Miami) is provided entirely by the county-wide school district—Duval School District and Dade County School District respectively.

vidual functional groups of expenditures between the central city and
the rest of the metropolitan area.

TABLE III

Coefficients of Variation for Per Capita Expenditures
of the 36 Selected Central Cities and Areas Outside
the Cities, by Major Functions, 1957

Per Capita Expenditure	Central Cities	Outside the Cities
Total general expenditure	21.3	29.1
Total education	20.3	30.2
Education excluding capital outlays	17.6	27.6
Highways	47.6	54.8
Health and hospitals	69.3	64.6
Public welfare	91.4	97.5

Note: The coefficient of variation provides a measure of variation independent
of the size of the units of measurement involved, and hence permits inter-
functional and inter-jurisdictional comparisons. The formula used here is
$V = s/\bar{x}$, where s is standard deviation and $\bar{x}$ is arithmetic mean of the
sample.
Source: Derived from Table II.

The resulting variation of per capita expenditures of each individual
category once again indicates the fact that there is a great difference in the allocation of functional responsibilities between state
and local governments. It seems to be most important for the analysis
of fiscal behavior of central cities to treat adequately the fiscal
interdependence of state and local governments within metropolitan
areas. State governments and practices are also responsible for the
allocation of revenue sources of state and local governments within
metropolitan areas. At this point, though it is not directly related
with this study, we would like to suggest that an empirical examination of revenue behavior of central cities be made by using the same
approach adopted in the expenditure study.

II. FACTORS ASSOCIATED WITH VARIATIONS IN THE LEVEL OF PER CAPITA EXPENDITURES

A. *Total general, non-educational and non-aided expenditures*

The results of the multiple regression analysis are presented in
Table IV and Table V for both the total expenditure and each of the
major expenditure categories of 36 central cities including the over-

lapping units of local government. The regression model is formulated by using six alternative independent variables for each of the selected dependent variables. For example six independent variables used for the total expenditure analysis are:

(1) per capita income;
(2) owner-occupied housing units as per cent of total occupied units;
(3) population density;
(4) ratio of central city population to total SMSA population;
(5) ratio of state and local functional responsibility;
(6) per capita state aid.[9]

The coefficient of multiple correlation for the total general expenditure of 36 central cities was .840. In other words, six independent variables together explain 70.6 per cent of the variability of total general expenditure. Thus the predicting power of the regression equation for the 36 central cities is about two percentage points less than the regression computed by Brazer for the nation's 40 largest cities in 1953. The difference between the two multiple correlation coefficients could possibly be due to the inclusion of irregular amounts of capital spending in our equation.

In addition to the analysis of total general expenditure, the multiple regression equations are estimated for the total non-educational and non-aided expenditures separately. The coefficients of multiple correlation for these two expenditure categories are respectively .852 and .753. The latter correlation coefficient is the smallest among all of the above three expenditure categories. The apparent reason for the failure to explain total non-aided expenditures is that there is far less influence of state aid on this category of expenditures than on all other expenditure categories. The relative importance of the independent variables, however, can be understood more clearly by the beta coefficient.

As shown in Table IV per capita state aid has the highest positive beta coefficient of .401 and .433 respectively for total general and total non-educational expenditures. For total non-aided expenditures it has the second highest beta coefficient of .352. State aid remains

[9]The amount of local state aid was broken down into two categories, educational and non-educational aid. Total per capita aid was employed only in the regression model of total expenditures, whereas educational aid was used in the analysis of educational expenditures; the difference between the two was employed in the analysis of all the non-educational expenditure categories. A further breakdown of the non-educational category of state aid for each central city would undoubtedly contribute to the explanation of variation in each of the non-educational categories, although the necessary data were not available for the purpose.

TABLE IV

Simple and Partial Correlations and Standardized
Regression Coefficients: Per Capita Expenditures of
36 Central Cities in Relation to
Selected Variables, 1957

Dependent Variables	Independent Variables				
	Per Capita Income	Ratio of Owner-occupied Housing Units	Population Density	Ratio of Central City Population	Pupils in ADA per 1,000 Population
	Simple Correlation Coefficients				
Total general expenditure	.277	−.373	.436	−.440	——
Education, total	.618	.201	——	−.204	.129
Education, excluding capital outlays	.623	.008	——	−.447	−.056
Highways	.147	.350	−.271	——	——
Health and hospitals	−.153	−.486	.561	−.273	——
Public welfare	.285	——	.301	−.247	——
Total non-aided expenditure	.062	−.594	.536	−.506	——
Total non-educational expenditure	.105	−.489	.525	−.429	——
	Last Order Partial Correlation Coefficients				
Total general expenditure	.392	−.277	.131	−.309	n.c.
Education, total	.690	.073	n.c.	−.309	.352
Education, excluding capital outlays	.750	−.015	n.c.	−.549	.320
Highways	.310	.144	−.154	n.c.	n.c.
Health and hospitals	.038	−.090	.352	−.077	n.c.
Public welfare	−.016	n.c.	.215	−.064	n.c.
Total non-aided expenditure	.068	−.325	.149	−.353	n.c.
Total non-educational expenditure	.144	−.324	.156	−.316	n.c.
	Standardized Regression Coefficients				
Total general expenditure	.257	−.272	.115	−.206	n.c.
Education, total	.646	.060	n.c.	−.250	.317
Education, excluding capital outlays	.651	−.010	n.c.	−.429	.211
Highways	.203	.119	−.132	n.c.	n.c.
Health and hospitals	.034	−.112	.420	−.066	n.c.
Public welfare	−.010	n.c.	.122	−.038	n.c.
Total non-aided expenditure	.050	−.387	.158	−.291	n.c.
Total non-educational expenditure	.085	−.306	.131	−.204	n.c.

as the most important variable, even when all other remaining independent variables are held constant. These relationships are shown by the highest partial correlation coefficient of .442 for total general expenditure, .512 for total non-educational expenditure, and .360 for total non-aided expenditure.

One of the most striking findings of this study is the consistently negative associations between the ratio of owner-occupied dwellings and each of the expenditure categories considered here. This variable exhibits the second highest negative beta coefficient of −.272 and −.306 respectively for total general and non-educational expenditures. The same variable has the highest beta coefficient of −.387 for total non-aided expenditures. These relationships consistently support the hypothesis that communities with a relatively large num-

TABLE IV (continued)

Ratio of Employed Persons in Manufacturing Industries	Ratio of Nonwhite Population	Ratio of Total Local Expenditures	Ratio of Local Expenditure for Highways	Ratio of Local Expenditure for Health and Hospitals	Dummy Variable for Public Welfare (State vs. Local)	Per Capita State Aid, Total	Per Capita State Aid, Education	Per Capita State Aid, Other than Education
			Independent Variables					
			Simple Correlation Coefficients					
—	—	.612	—	—	—	.587	—	—
—	—	.175	—	—	—	—	.379	—
—	—	.278	—	—	—	—	.356	—
−.273	—	—	.673	—	—	—	—	.622
—	—	—	—	.438	—	—	—	.150
—	−.363	—	—	—	.713	—	—	.746
—	—	.341	—	—	—	—	—	.331
—	—	.633	—	—	—	—	—	.597
			Last Order Partial Correlation Coefficients					
n.c.	n.c.	.295	nc.	n.c.	n.c.	.442	n.c.	n.c.
n.c.	n.c.	.343	n.c.	n.c.	n.c.	n.c.	.162	n.c.
n.c.	n.c.	.440	n.c.	n.c.	n.c.	n.c.	.177	n.c.
−.435	n.c.	n.c.	.581	n.c.	n.c.	n.c.	n.c.	.336
n.c.	n.c.	n.c.	n.c.	.400	n.c.	n.c.	n.c.	.017
n.c.	−.209	n.c.	n.c.	n.c.	.451	n.c.	n.c.	.657
n.c.	n.c.	−.044	n.c.	n.c.	n.c.	n.c.	n.c.	.360
n.c.	n.c.	.305	n.c.	n.c.	n.c.	n.c.	n.c.	.512
			Standardized Regression Coefficients					
n.c.	n.c.	.256	n.c.	n.c.	n.c.	.401	n.c.	n.c.
n.c.	n.c.	.270	n.c.	n.c.	n.c.	n.c.	.127	n.c.
n.c.	n.c.	.307	n.c.	n.c.	n.c.	n.c.	.118	n.c.
−.299	n.c.	n.c.	.532	n.c.	n.c.	n.c.	n.c.	.273
n.c.	n.c.	n.c.	n.c.	.379	n.c.	n.c.	n.c.	.014
n.c.	−.140	n.c.	n.c.	n.c.	.368	n.c.	n.c.	.522
n.c.	n.c.	−.041	n.c.	n.c.	n.c.	n.c.	n.c.	.352
n.c.	n.c.	.241	n.c.	n.c.	n.c.	n.c.	n.c.	.433

n.c. = not computed

ber of owner-occupied homes are much more reluctant to pay property tax and hence tend to spend less on the provision of public services than those with relatively more tenant-occupied homes.

The ratio of central city population to its SMSA population also contributes substantially more toward the explanation of the variability of the three expenditure categories. The central city population ratio has the third highest beta coefficient of −.291 and the second highest partial correlation coefficient of −.353 for total non-aided expenditures. These results are consistent with the Hawley-Brazer hypothesis that the central city tends to provide some important municipal and non-aided public services—especially police and fire protection, recreation, sanitation, and sewerage for the non-resident suburban population. However, our results fall far short of answering the question of who is bearing a net burden, because the suburbanite, through his contracts with the city, contributes in part to the city expenditures. The central city population ratio has also substantially

TABLE V

Multiple Correlation and Net Regression Coefficients:
Per Capita Expenditures of 36 Central Cities in Relation to Selected Variables, 1957

Dependent Variables	Constant	Independent Variables					
		Per Capita Income	Ratio of Owner-occupied Housing Units	Population Density	Ratio of Central City Population	Pupils in ADA per 1,000 Population	Ratio of Employed Persons in Manufacturing Industries
Total general expenditure	88.07	.031** (.014) ***	−.887 (.571)	.859 (1.205)	−.506* (.290) *	n.c.	n.c.
Education, total	−27.35	.024 (.005) ***	.058 (.148)	n.c.	−.183 (.105) ***	.140 (.069) *	n.c.
Education, excluding capital outlays	−4.98	.017 (.003)	−.007 (.092)	n.c.	−.231 (.065) ***	.079 (.043)	n.c.
Highways	−2.61	.005 (.003)	.077 (.098)	−.197 (.234)	n.c.	n.c.	.224 (.086) **
Health and hospitals	.79	.001 (.005)	−.095 (.195)	.819* (.405)	−.042 (.101)	n.c.	n.c.
Public welfare	1.55	−.0003 (.0035)	n.c. *	.220 (.186)	−.023 (.006)	n.c.	n.c.
Total non-aided expenditure	125.31	.003 (.009)	−.704 (.380) *	.662 (.814)	−.399* (.197) *	n.c.	n.c.
Total non-educational expenditure	94.03	.009 (.012)	−.880 (.477)	.869 (1.020)	−.444 (.247)	n.c.	n.c.

444

TABLE V (continued)

| | Independent Variables | | | | | | | | |
Dependent Variables	Ratio of Non-white Population	Ratio of Total Local Expenditures	Ratio of Local Expenditure for Highways	Ratio of Local Expenditure for Health and Hospitals	Dummy Variable for Public Welfare (State vs. Local)	Per Capita State Aid, Total	Per Capita State Aid, Education	Per Capita State Aid, Other than Education	Coefficient of Multiple Correlation
Total general expenditure	n.c.	.999 (.602) *	n.c.	n.c.	n.c.	.859** (.324)	n.c.	n.c.	.840
Education, total	n.c.	.314 (.160) **	n.c.	n.c.	n.c.	n.c.	.188 (.213)	n.c.	.773
Education, excluding capital outlays	n.c.	.263 (.100) ***	n.c.	n.c.	n.c.	n.c.	.128 (.133)	*	.843
Highways	n.c.	n.c.	.276 (.072) ***	n.c.	n.c.	n.c.	n.c.	.133 (.069)	.846
Health and hospitals	n.c.	n.c.	n.c.	.231 (.098) **	n.c.	n.c.	n.c.	.009 (.097) ****	.686
Public welfare	.105 (.091)	n.c.	n.c.	n.c.	7.311 (2.685) **	n.c.	n.c.	.308 (.066) ****	.864
Total non-aided expenditure	n.c.	−.090 (.384) *	n.c.	n.c.	n.c.	n.c.	n.c.	.482** (.232) ****	.753
Total non-educational expenditure	n.c.	.832 (.448)	n.c.	n.c.	n.c.	n.c.	n.c.	.937 (.292)	.852

n.c. = not computed.
Figures in parentheses are the standard errors of the regression coefficients.
*Significant at .90 level of confidence under the assumptions of normality of the underlying distributions of simple random sampling, and of independence between observations.
**Significant at .95 level of confidence (under same conditions as above).
***Significant at .99 level of confidence (under same conditions as above).

445

significant beta and partial correlation coefficients in relation to the two remaining expenditure categories.

The income variable has the fourth highest positive beta coefficient of .257 and the second highest partial correlation coefficient of .392 for total general expenditure but it has little influence on the remaining two expenditure categories.

The expenditure allocation variable makes a significant contribution to the multiple relationship of both total general and non-educational expenditure. It has beta and partial correlation coefficients of .256 and .241 for total general expenditure and .295 and .305 for total noneducational expenditure. Local fiscal patterns are more clearly understood when the allocation of state and local functional responsibilities are taken into account. Aside from using this allocation variable as an explanatory variable in the multiple regression analysis, important relationships can be revealed between per capita expenditure and independent variables by holding differences of state-local governmental structures constant. The relationships are explicitly shown by the coefficients of multiple-partial correlation; they are .728, .737 and .714 separately for total general, non-educational, and non-aided expenditures. In other words, the five remaining variables account for 53.0 per cent, 54.3 per cent and 51.0 per cent of total variability that is not explained by the differences in the allocation of state and local responsibilities. These percentages indicate once again the relative importance of the traditional socio-economic factors including state aid in explaining the variability of central city expenditures.

B. *Individual expenditures.*

In this section of the paper findings of multivariate analysis are presented by individual functions—education, highways, health and hospitals, and public welfare. While public education is predominantly a local governmental function, the other three individual functions are provided by both state and local governments. Thus a large part of the variation in these three expenditures is due to the extent to which state governments are directly engaged in these fiscal activities. Per capita educational spending is also included in this section of the study, not so much because of the variations in allocation of functional responsibilities between states and local units of government, but because it is the most important single local government function.

The availability of fiscal data makes it possible to formulate separate regression models for current and total spending on education but not for the other three expenditure categories. As shown in Table V, the multiple correlation coefficients are .773 for total education, .843 for current education, .846 for highways, .686 for health and hospitals, and .864 for public welfare expenditures.[10] The regression models computed respectively for current education and highway expenditures explain the variations of expenditures more than twice as much as did the model made by Brazer in 1953. The striking difference in the predicting power of the two regression equations is partly due to the application of new variables and partly due to the refinements of the same variables used by Brazer.

New variables employed in these multiple regression analyses are: local proportion of state and local expenditure responsibility, the ratio of owner-occupied dwellings, the ratio of nonwhite population, and dummy variable for public welfare (state vs. local).[11] The expenditure allocation variable exhibits the highest beta coefficient of .532 for highway expenditures. It has also the second highest beta coefficient of .379 for health and hospitals and .307 for current educational expenditure. Instead of the allocation variable, a dummy variable is used for public welfare and it has the second highest beta coefficient of .368. Although the last-order partial correlation coefficients are, in general, smaller than the simple correlation coefficients, the allocation variable has the most important partial correlation coefficients with respect to expenditure on highways and health and hospitals, and the second and the third most important coefficients regarding public welfare and current educational spending: they are .581 for highways, .400 for health and hospitals, .451 for public welfare, and .440 for education. The high partial correlation coefficient for education is rather surprising because public education, unlike the other three expenditure categories, is mainly a local function. On second thought, however, it is explicable, since practically all the central cities with low per capita expenditures are found in Southern states in which state governments are engaged proportionately more in direct expenditures for education. The range of variation among the 15 selected states varies from 28.7 per cent in Georgia

[10]Brazer, *City Expenditures in the United States,* pp. 54-55, found multiple correlation coefficients of .590 for current education, .512 for current highways, and .895 for public welfare expenditures by using six independent variables. Brazer's 40 large city analysis, which is the only one comparable to the present study, excludes expenditures on health and hospitals. The category of public welfare included in his study is state direct expenditure, and hence is not relevant here.

[11]See Daniel B. Suits, "Use of Dummy Variables in Regression Equations," *Journal of the American Statistical Association* (December 1957) pp. 548-551.

to 5.8 per cent in New York. Thus the close association between the allocation variable and per capita educational spending seems to be a reflection of some uncertain socio-economic characteristics of the region where the cities are found. For example, central cities with a proportionately low ratio of state and local responsibilities are found mostly in Southern states, and these cities tend to spend less per capita on education, not only because the Southern cities are poor but also because the need to spend in relation to ability to pay is very high, measured by either the percentage of school children attending private schools or by the number of students in ADA in relation to the size of the communities. This relationship is clearly indicated by multiple-partial correlation coefficients of .829 and .765 respectively for current and total spending on education as compared with the multiple correlation coefficients of .843 and .773.

As stated earlier, the use of the property tax in financing local governmental responsibilities suggests another variable for explaining differences in expenditure levels. In the belief that central cities with relatively large numbers of owner-occupied homes have some tendency to spend less because residents of these cities perceive a relatively heavy property tax burden, the ratio of owner-occupied dwellings is employed for the regression models. Contrary to expectation, this variable emerges in most cases as the least significant factor in determining the variability of individual expenditures. It has the lowest beta coefficients and the lowest partial correlation coefficients in cases of education and highway expenditures and somewhat higher coefficients for health and hospitals. The implications to be drawn from these findings are not altogether clear. The fact that the variations in total expenditure are much better accounted for by this variable than those of individual functions may be indicative of a minimum feature of total expenditures. What the results seem to indicate is that individual expenditures are internally competitive with each other, and that there is a much more limited range of discretion in spending for all functions than in the determination of the sub-components of the total.

Of all six independent variables used in the regression analysis, per capita income is the most crucial factor determining the level of educational expenditure of the central city. Differences in the level of income also exert some influence on highway expenditures but almost no influence on the remaining two expenditure categories. The income variable employed in this study is the sum of money received by 1960 population in 1959. This income measure defined by the Census is somewhat similar to "personal income" reported in the National Income Accounts of the Department of Commerce. But the difference between the two income concepts is mainly due to the inclusion of imputed income. The results show that the per capita money income defined by the Census has the highest beta coefficient of .651 and the highest partial correlation coefficient of .750 for current education spending. It is also significant beyond the 0.01 level of confidence for both total and current educational expenditure. These relationships clearly demonstrate that per capita income is a much more adequate measure of the willingness to pay for public education than other alternatives available. Findings of our analysis, therefore, confirm the hypothesis that educational spending is mostly determined by income. Per capita income shows a relatively high beta coefficient of .203 and a partial correlation coefficient of .310 for highways, but the coefficients are of negligible magnitude for both health and hospitals and public welfare. The lack of income influences on these expenditures may be due to the fact that these individual functions are greatly determined by need factors rather than by the community's willingness to pay.

Next to income, the ratio of central city population to its SMSA population emerges as the most influential variable on the level of educational spending. In comparison with previous findings by Brazer, the distribution of metropolitan area population has a much stronger influence on educational spending. It has the second highest negative beta coefficient of −.429 and also the second highest partial correlation coefficient of −.549 for current expenditure on education, but the same coefficients are of little significance for other remaining expenditure categories.[12] The close association between the two variables is, as has been the case with the expenditure allocation variable, a reflection of some regional characteristics, especially South vs. non-South. Central cities selected from Southern states are, in general, surrounded by a relatively smaller proportion of SMSA populations in comparison with their Northern conterparts. For example, if the 36 central cities are ranked according to the size of the central city population ratio, the three highest ratios are found in the Southern cities of San Antonio 85.6%, Memphis 79.4%, Savannah 79.3% and the three lowest ratios in the non-Southern cities of Paterson-Clifton-Passaic 23.6%, Hartford 30.8%, San Jose 31.8%. Southern cities in comparison with their Northern counterparts seem to have some uncertain socio-economic characteristics that affect un-

---

[12]Brazer, *City Expenditures in the United States,* p. 56, found the beta coefficient of −.284 in his multiple regression analysis of 40 city expenditures on education.

favorably the level of per capita expenditures for public education.

For education two more variables—state aid for education and the number of pupils in ADA per 1,000 population—are employed in this regression analysis to explain the variations in the level of per capita education spending. State aid shows a much smaller influence on educational spending than expected. In fact, state aid has a slightly higher beta coefficient and partial correlation coefficient than the least significant variable (the ratio of owner-occupied homes in this case). What these findings suggest is that state aid for specific purposes, including educational aid, is first to stimulate new activities and secondly to take care of unusual needs in certain areas. It seems feasible to consider the second type of state aid as permanent and those types intended to stimulate some new activities as temporary. In view of the traditional practices of states of granting aids to their local units of government for public education, it is not surprising to find that the major portion of educational aids are regarded as permanent and hence the state aid has relatively smaller stimulating effects on educational spending. On the contrary, state aids for non-educational purposes are considered less permanent and hence have a stronger influence on the level of expenditures on highways and public welfare. Table IV and Table V indicate that state aids are statistically significant at the 0.01 level for public welfare and the 0.10 level of confidence for highway expenditures. State aids have the highest beta coefficient of .522 and the highest partial correlation coefficient of .657 for public welfare expenditure. This is the third most important variable in explaining the variation in highway expenditures.

The number of students in ADA per 1,000 population is used for the regression analysis of educational expenditure as an approximate index of needs for public education. Findings of the analysis show that this variable is statistically significant at the 0.10 level of confidence for both total and current educational expenditures. The same variable has the beta coefficient of .317 and partial correlation coefficient of .352 for total expenditure, and the respective coefficients for current expenditure on education are .241 and .320. The results are consistent with the hypothesis that expenditures for public schools are determined to a considerable extent by the ratio of students to the population.

The population density is not of great significance in an explanation of variations in the total and individual category of expenditures, with one exception. It is the most important factor in determining the level of expenditure on health and hospitals, as shown in Table

IV and Table V. It has the highest beta coefficient of .420 and also the highest partial correlation coefficient of .352. This variable is statistically significant at the 0.10 level of confidence.

It is also noted that other variables such as the proportion of employed persons in manufacturing industries to total employment and the ratio of non-white to total population show considerable importance in explaining the variability of expenditures respectively for highways and public welfare. Surprisingly enough the results seem to contradict the hypotheses that per capita expenditures on highways are smaller in those cities in which a smaller percentage of persons is employed in manufacturing industries, and that per capita expenditures for public welfare are larger in those cities in which a larger percentage of population is non-white.

III. SUMMARY AND CONCLUSIONS

A. *Summary*

The most consistent contributions toward the explanation of total general expenditures are state aid, the ratio of central city population to its SMSA population, per capita income and, to a somewhat lesser extent, the local proportion of state and local expenditure responsibility and the ratio of owner-occupied dwellings to total residences. Educational expenditure, although it is mainly income determined, is significantly influenced by the number of students in ADA per 1,000 population in addition to the ratio of central city population to its SMSA population and the local proportion of state and local expenditure responsibility. On the other hand, determinants of per capita total non-educational expenditure are state aid, the ratio of owner-occupied dwellings to total residences, the ratio of central city population to its SMSA population and the allocation of expenditure responsibility between state and its local units of government. For highways, only three factors—state aid, the employment ratio in manufacturing industries to total employment, and the expenditure allocation variable for highways—account for the major part of explained variance. Differences in the population density and the allocation variable are major factors in determining the level of expenditures for health and hospitals. As noted earlier, the variability of this expenditure category is most difficult to explain by factors reflecting public spending. Apparent reasons for this are that some of the city hospitals are charging fees for hospital care and treatment, and extend their services to the wide range of population surrounding the central cities. Unlike the other expenditure categories, state aid contributes almost nothing to the explanation of per capita expenditure on health and hospitals. On the contrary, state aid is the single most important determinant of public welfare expenditure. To some important degree per capita expenditure on public welfare is influenced also by the allocation of this service responsibility between state and its local units of government.

Finally, the analysis of deviant cities made in Appendix B indicates some possibilities for further explanation of central city expenditure variations, if adequate data become available. Per capita property valuation, for example, might show a significant relationship to total per capita expenditures as well as to certain individual expenditure categories. Moreover, the level of services provided and the efficiency with which local government services are performed will undoubtedly have an influence on the level of central city expenditures—a city with an inefficient government will have to spend more money than an efficiently run city to get the same level and quality of services. Some of these factors can be measured but data are not available, and others are beyond quantitative measurements. For these reasons it was not possible to take some important factors into account in the analyses and thereby to determine the extent to which the unexplained variance is due to their exclusions.

B. *Implications*

From the basic findings of the empirical studies described in this paper some significant implications can be drawn concerning future changes in local government expenditures as well as the orientation of public policies in metropolitan area finance.

While it is hazardous to venture prognoses on the basis of a cross-section analysis for any one year, certain key variables employed in the multiple regression analysis indicate the future trends of local government expenditures in central cities. Changes in the socio-economic and demographic environments measured by such variables as per capita income, the distribution of metropolitan population between a central city and its outlying areas, the ratio of owner-occupied dwelling units, the number of students in proportion to the city's population, etc., may account for future changes in the level of public spending in the central cities. The values of these factors, however, cannot be manipulated by public policy because they are determined by forces outside the realm of choice. On the other hand, the major factors that are greatly associated with variation in central city expenditure levels are those whose values can be influenced by policy measures. These policy instrument variables are the assignment of functional responsibilities between a state and its local units of government as well as between the local governments, and also various arrangements of state aid systems.

The results of the analyses suggest that the key to understanding the expenditure variations of the nation's central cities is the role of the states in delegating specific functional responsibility or responsibilities to its local units of government. Regardless of whether central city expenditures include those of overlapping local governments, the influence of state aid on local government expenditure is expected to be strong and positive in the future. The empirical findings of impacts for both state aid and the allocation of functional responsibilities on local government spending provide city planners, administrators, and others concerned with the metropolitan area finance with a useful guideline for the formulation of new objectives and for fiscal planning. Moreover, they suggest some potential avenues for change in patterns of fiscal activities by altering such "policy parameters" as the relative roles of states in their direct participation and state aid. From the analytical point of view, the findings of this study clearly demonstrate that the traditional approach to local government finance studies in a governmental vacuum has been faulty, and it misleads the policy-makers into conceptual difficulties, if not operational ones.

23

POLITICAL ETHOS AND THE STRUCTURE OF CITY GOVERNMENT* †

RAYMOND E. WOLFINGER
and JOHN OSGOOD FIELD

For years specialists in local politics have deplored the anecdotal quality of literature in the field and have called for theoretically-based comparative research. One of the most stimulating and ambitious attempts in this direction is Edward C. Banfield and James Q. Wilson's theory of "public-regardingness" and "private-regardingness," which states that much of what Americans think about the political world can be subsumed under one or the other of these conflicting orientations and that the prevalence of one ethos over the other influences the style, structure, and outcome of local politics.[1] Banfield and Wilson attribute these two ethics to different elements in the population and hypothesize that a number of political forms and policies are manifestations of each ethos. We intend to examine the associations between these hypothesized consequences and the demographic characteristics that are said to be the bases of the two ethics.

*Reprinted from *The American Political Science Review, LX,* No. 2 (June 1966), 306-326. By permission of *The American Political Science Review* and the authors.

†We are grateful to Kuan Lee for writing programs and supervising computer runs for the data analysis, to Richard A. Brody, Jay Kadane, and Morris Zelditch, Jr. for advice on statistical matters, to James D. Barber, Martha Derthick, Heinz Eulau, Genevieve Knupfer, Sheilah R. Koeppen, Nelson W. Polsby, Alan Rosenthal, Gilbert Y. Steiner, Aaron B. Wildavsky, James Q. Wilson, and Barbara Kaye Wolfinger for their advice and comments at various stages of our research, and to the Graduate Division of Stanford University and the Stanford Computation Center for financial assistance.

[1]This is one of the major themes of their *City Politics* (Cambridge: Harvard University Press and the M.I.T. Press, 1963); see also James Q. Wilson and Edward C. Banfield, "Public-Regardingness as a Value Premise in Voting Behavior," this Review, 58 (December, 1964), 876-887.

I. THE THEORY OF THE TWO ETHICS

Banfield and Wilson take their cue from a famous passage in Richard Hofstadter's *The Age of Reform* contrasting native and immigrant political values in the early twentieth century:

> Out of the clash between the needs of the immigrants and the sentiments of the natives there emerged two thoroughly different systems of political ethics. . . . One, founded upon the indigenous Yankee-Protestant political traditions, and upon middle-class life, assumed and demanded the constant, disinterested activity of the citizen in public affairs, argued that political life ought to be run . . . in accordance with general principles and abstract laws apart from and superior to personal needs . . . The other system, founded upon the European backgrounds of the immigrants, upon their unfamiliarity with independent political action, their familiarity with hierarchy and authority, and upon the urgent needs that so often grew out of their migration, took for granted that the political life of the individual would arise out of family needs, interpreted political and civic relations chiefly in terms of personal obligations, and placed strong personal loyalties above allegiance to abstract codes of law or morals. It was chiefly upon this system of values that the political life of the immigrant, the boss, and the urban machine was based.[2]

Many specialists in local politics have referred to this passage in one context or another, but it remained for Banfield and Wilson to develop from it a comprehensive and persuasive theory to explain many aspects of American municipal politics. They introduce their argument as follows:

> There is a tendency for (urban cleavages) to coalesce into two opposite patterns. These patterns reflect two conceptions of the public interest that are widely held. The first, which derives from the middle class ethos, favors what the municipal reform movement has always defined as "good government"—namely efficiency, impartiality, honesty, planning, strong executives, no favoritism, model legal codes . . . The other conception of the public interest (one never explicitly formulated as such, but one all the same) derives from the "immigrant ethos." This is the conception of those people who identify with the ward or neighborhood rather than the city "as a whole," who look to politicians for "help" and "favors," . . . and who are far less interested in the efficiency, impartiality, and honesty of local government than in its readiness to confer material benefits of one sort or another upon them.[3]

[2](New York: Knopf, 1955), pp. 8-9.
[3]Banfield and Wilson, p. 46.

At first reading there are troublesome points in this passage, as in Hofstadter's. Is a strong executive part of the old American political ideal? Are these "public-regarding" old settlers the same people who are usually considered devotees of Adam Smith's very private-regarding doctrine that the individual should pursue his own interests and that the public good would be achieved from the sum of individual interests? Did the peasants who came here from the monarchies of 19th century Europe introduce graft and the spoils system to America, or did they learn their bad habits from the Yankees? Did the Yankees withdraw from local politics because they could not stomach the newcomers' sordid political customs or because, outnumbered by the immigrants whom they had rebuffed and exploited, they wanted to avoid the consequences of the resulting hostility? Have Yankees led fights for municipal reform because they are more upstanding or because they find corruption a handy club with which to beat their opponents?[4]

It is well known, however, that many cities with large foreign-stock populations tend to have political orders in which good government is subordinated to favoritism and machine politics. Tammany Hall, the formidable Democratic organization in Chicago, and the confused, crooked Boston scene come immediately to mind. Furthermore, reform campaigns in these cities tend to be led by upper-middle-class Yankees and Jews whose life styles and political perspectives are a world apart from the outlook of ward heelers and clubhouse politicians.

But then one can easily think of an equal number of cases on the other side of the argument. Until its recent reformation, was Kansas City (11 per cent foreign stock) any less tainted than Boston (46 per cent)?[5] The South and the border states have notoriously corrupt politics and are just as notoriously Anglo-Saxon. Farther north, in Indiana, only 8 per cent of the residents are of foreign stock, but state employees are "maced" 2 per cent of their pay for the benefit of the ruling political party. In Pennsylvania, dominated until a dozen years ago by a Republican party based on small-town, native-

---

[4]Here, with Banfield and Wilson, we refer not to the stylish young liberal club members of California and Manhattan, but to the more conservative "good government" forces in many cities.

[5]Throughout this article the "percent foreign stock" or "percent ethnic" refers to the proportion of a city's 1960 population that is foreign born or native born with at least one parent born abroad. Nineteen per cent of the total U.S. population is of foreign stock. Data on nativity and parentage are from U.S. Bureau of the Census, *County and City Data Book, 1962* (Washington: U.S. Government Printing Office, 1962).

born Americans, at least 40,000 state jobs are at the disposal of the party that wins control of the state government.[6]

The most obvious fact that emerges from this recital is that such comparisons are idle. Attempts to verify the existence of the two ethics and analyze their political consequences will have to proceed beyond discussion of simple honesty and dishonesty. Fortunately Banfield and Wilson have elaborated their basic hypothesis by drawing from the general theory of conflicting ethics a number of propositions about specific manifestations of one ethos or the other. "The logic of the middle class ideal implies also certain institutional arrangements" conducive to government by experts in the interests of the city as a whole: the city manager plan, nonpartisan ballots, election of the city council at large, or, if wards are used, from large districts.[7] On the other hand, the private-regarding ethos favors mayors, partisan ballots, and election of councilmen from wards, preferably small ones. The differences between the two ethics are said to be reflected as well in various municipal policies. The public-regarding ethos favors complete civil service coverage of city employees in order to maximize the professional and impartial conduct of public business. On the other hand, the private-regarding ethos emphasizes favoritism and patronage and therefore opposes civil service. Because the public-regarding ethos is concerned with the city as a whole and with long-range attempts to manage and improve the local environment, it favors city planning and urban renewal. The private-regarding ethos opposes such policies because they interrupt neighborhood patterns and impose unwelcome restraints on the city's residents.

Other writers have seen much of this conflict as a clash between middle-class admiration of efficiency and the working-class' desires for representation of their interests.[8] Some critics of Banfield and Wilson say that the labels for the two ethics are much too value-laden and that preferences described as selfish or unselfish could more properly be interpreted in terms of the different interests of

[6]Perhaps because so much of the best scholarly research on local politics has been conducted close to the great universities of the Northeast and perhaps also because most serious nonacademic writers live in a few northeastern cities, political organizations in these cities have been described at great length, while very little is known about existing machines in other parts of the country.

[7]Banfield and Wilson, p. 330; see also *ibid.,* pp. 92, 95, 154, 170.

[8]See, e.g., Leo F. Schnore and Robert F. Alford, "Forms of Government and Socioeconomic Characteristics of Suburbs," *Administrative Science Quarterly,* 8 (June, 1963), 1-17.

different social classes.[9] For example, the fact that poor people protest urban renewal projects may be due not so much to private-regardingness as to the fact that the houses demolished in such projects usually are the homes of the poor.

These caveats are not germane to this study. We are not concerned for the moment with either the morality or the consequences of any particular governmental form or policy, nor are we concerned with how and where particular legal forms can be subverted by local political styles. We are examining the relationship between various forms and policies and the social properties of the relevant cities. It is sufficient for this purpose only to assume that the differences between the alternative forms are worth talking about.

A more important question remains: is the independent variable ethnicity or occupational status? Some parts of the country have scarcely any foreign-stock population, while the distribution of social classes is, of course, fairly even not only from one region to another, but also among most cities. Moreover, cities with large ethnic populations do not necessarily have small middle classes. The correlation coefficient between per cent ethnic and per cent in white collar occupations for all New England cities of over 50,000 population is $-.04$; it is faintly positive for other regions with appreciable ethnic populations: .29 in the Middle Atlantic states, .20 in the Midwest, and .24 in the West.[10]

Banfield and Wilson seem to consider the two dimensions interchangeable. Sometimes they attribute the two ethics to ethnicity, sometimes to social class, and sometimes they mingle both explanations. The weight of evidence suggests that ethnicity is meant to be the controlling independent variable. The theme of the two ethics is introduced in a discussion of cleavages between old settlers and immigrants.[11] In a more recent work they remark, "We do not think that income *per se* has this effect [making people private- or public-regarding]; rather it is the ethnic attributes, or culture, empirically associated with it."[12] But this interpretation is confounded by state-

---

[9]See especially Herbert Kaufman's review of *City Politics* in this Review, 58 (June, 1964), 422-423. Kaufman asks, "are those measures designated 'public-regarding' by Banfield and Wilson *really* manifestations of selfless fellow feeling or are they the self-serving policies of a particular group in society that is trying to hold on to what it has?" (p. 423).

[10]In these computations the Midwest includes Ohio, Indiana, Illinois, Iowa, Michigan, Minnesota, and Wisconsin.

[11]Banfield and Wilson, pp. 38-46.

[12]Wilson and Banfield, p. 885.

ments like this: "This assimilation of lower-class people into the middle class has, of course, entailed their assimilation to the political ethos of the Anglo-Saxon-Protestant elite . . ."[13]

Is a combination of ethnicity and working-class status the origin of the private-regarding ethos? If so, why would upward mobility produce a change? It might be argued that private-regardingness is a consequence of ethnic consciousness, which disappears when middle-class status is attained. But the available data indicate that social mobility often has little effect on ethnic consciousness.[14] Nor is it plausible that upward-mobile ethnics will readily abandon their political perspectives in favor of views more characteristic of the middle class.[15]

Some of these difficulties may be resolved if "middle class" is interpreted, for present purposes, as "upper middle class." Indeed, in some passages Banfield and Wilson indicate that the important line of demarcation is between professional and business people on the one hand and lower status groups on the other. But the bulk of their treatment of the two ethics contradicts this. In particular, their discussion of the likelihood that "the middle class will in the very long run assimilate the lower class entirely"[16] suggests that they include everyone in a white collar occupation in the "middle class" as far as the two ethics are concerned.

Banfield and Wilson do not explain why immigrants should be private-regarding. Their silence on this point is a source of numerous complications. Did the immigrants bring the private-regarding ethos with them from their former countries or was it a product of interaction between their predispositions and the conditions of life they found in the United States? Hofstadter seems to favor the latter interpretation, but Banfield and Wilson speak of the ethos that "the new immigrants brought with them."[17] If the immigrants came with the private-regarding ethos, one would expect to find it distributed around the country in proportion to the number of persons of foreign stock. (This assumes, of course, that immigrants from different countries have similar inclinations to private-regardingness. Banfield and Wilson do not consider this point, except to single

[13]Banfield and Wilson, p. 123; see also *ibid.*, p. 329.
[14]Raymond E. Wolfinger, "The Development and Persistence of Ethnic Voting," this Review, 59 (December, 1965), 896-908.
[15]In other areas of political behavior the upward mobile tend to have characteristics midway between their old and new classes; see James A. Barber, Jr., *Social Mobility and Political Behavior* (Chicago: Rand McNally, forthcoming).
[16]Banfield and Wilson, p. 123.
[17]*Ibid.*, p. 40.

out Polish-Americans as particularly likely to be private-regarding, for reasons that are not explained.)[18]

On the other hand, if the ethos is a response to American life, one would expect that its distribution would be related not only to the proportion of immigrants in the population, but also to the character of their experience in America. Typical immigrant experiences differed considerably from one region to another. This was notably true of the West, where non-Anglo-Saxon immigrants arrived with or on the heels of the earliest settlers. All shared the rigors of pioneering and the profits and instabilities of boom economies.[19] Compared to those in the settled Eastern cities, immigrants to the West were better off and better educated; labor was scarcer, wages were higher, and class distinctions were weaker and more unstable.[20] Status and income were neither so fixed nor so strongly stratified. If private-regardingness is an acquired characteristic, it seems likely that different regional immigrant histories might produce different levels of attachment to the ethos or perhaps different manifestations of it.

These observations do not invalidate the ethos theory, but they do suggest some necessary modifications. In particular, since the quality of the immigrant experience differed from region to region, it appears that a given level of foreign-stock population in, say, California and New York might produce very different levels of private-regardingness in the two places.[21] Our findings support this inference.

Several pieces of published research bear on the ethos theory. John H. Kessel found that the mayor form was more common in cities with large ethnic populations.[22] Schnore and Alford report the same findings in their study of 300 suburbs, but the difference here is slight: 9.3 per cent foreign-born population in mayor cities compared to 8 per cent in manager cities.[23] Both studies also found that manager cities had larger proportions of residents in white-collar

[18]*Ibid.*, p. 235.

[19]See, e.g., Louis Berg, "Peddlers in Eldorado," *Commentary*, July, 1965, pp. 64-66.

[20]Earl Pomeroy, *The Pacific Slope* (New York: Alfred A. Knopf, 1965).

[21]Similarly, an analysis of local voting returns in the 1960 presidential election showed considerable regional variation in the responses of similar Protestant voting groups to President Kennedy's candidacy; see Lucy S. Davidowicz and Leon J. Goldstein, *Politics in a Pluralist Democracy* (New York: Institute of Human Relations Press, 1963).

[22]John H. Kessel, "Governmental Structure and Political Environment: A Statistical Note about American Cities," this Review, 56 (September, 1962), 615-620.

[23]Schnore and Alford, *op. cit.*, p. 12.

occupations.[24] Phillips Cutright suggests that partisan elections are more likely to be found where "community cleavages" are intense, because such divisions provide "political parties with the social basis necessary for effective organization and sufficient activity necessary for survival as a community force."[25] He used two measures of "high cleavage": more than 50 per cent of the population employed in manufacturing indicates economic cleavage; while more than 20 per cent Catholics indicates religious cleavage. By either measure, high-cleavage cities were more likely to use the partisan ballot.[26]

These studies have severe limitations as sources of evidence for the ethos theory. They are concerned with only two of its dependent variables. More important, they do not include controls for third variables, particularly region. Since some parts of the country are almost devoid of foreign-stock residents (and Catholics), it is reasonable to try to separate the influence of region from that of local population characteristics. Furthermore, western and southwestern cities, whatever their economic bases, tend to have larger white-collar populations than cities in the Northeast and Midwest. Because of the historical development of land-use patterns, these cities usually have more extensive residential neighborhoods with suburban characteristics, and thus have suffered less from the postwar flight to the suburbs that has reduced middle class populations in core cities elsewhere.

II. RESEARCH DESIGN

The ethos theory states that the city manager form of government, the nonpartisan ballot, at-large election of city legislators, big wards, civil service coverage of municipal employees, city planning, and

[24]Edgar L. Sherbenou found that Chicago suburbs with higher priced homes are very likely to use the manager form, while more modest towns all have mayors; see his "Class, Participation, and the Council-Manager Plan," *Public Administration Review*, 21 (Summer, 1961), 131-135.

[25]Phillips Cutright, "Nonpartisan Electoral Systems in American Cities," *Comparative Studies in Society and History*, 5 (January, 1963), p. 218.

[26]One proposition of the ethos theory states that public-regardingness is manifested in support for expansion of many government services that do not benefit the individual, but that will increase his tax payments. In their own work Banfield and Wilson have found that, among homeowners subject to property taxes, support for such measures to be financed by property taxation rises with the median income and home value of the voting unit. They also found that voting units with large foreign-stock populations were less likely to support

urban renewal are favored by the public-regarding ethos, which is a prominent aspect of the political perspectives of white Anglo-Saxon Protestants. The opposing private-regarding ethos, rooted in the immigrant experience, favors the mayor form, the partisan ballot, ward election of city legislators, and small wards; it is opposed to civil service, city planning, and urban renewal.[27] We have treated all these features as dependent variables and examined their relationship to the key independent variable, the proportion of a city's population that is of foreign stock. Other independent variables include social class (measured by the percentage of the labor force employed in white collar occupations), median family income, and educational level (measured by the median school years completed by residents aged 25 or over). We examined the relationship between each independent and dependent variable within each major region of the United States. We also measured the degree of association between ethnicity and each dependent variable while controlling for social class, income, and education. The dependent variables and their hypothesized relationships to the two ethics are summarized in Figure 1.

FIGURE 1
The Dependent Variables

	Private-Regarding	Public-Regarding
Form of Government	Mayor	Manager
Type of Ballot	Partisan	Nonpartisan
Method of Electing Councilmen	Wards	At Large
Size of Council Districts	Small	Large
Civil Service Coverage	Less	More
City Planning Expenditures	Low	High
Urban Renewal	Low	High

This study includes all 309 incorporated cities with 1960 populations in excess of 50,000 persons, excluding Washington, D.C. Data on all dependent variables except urban renewal were taken

such measures. They believe that the controlling element in these relationships is ethnicity, and attribute the findings to the prevalence of the private-regarding ethos among ethnic group members; see Banfield and Wilson, pp. 237-240; and Wilson and Banfield.

[27]A number of other political forms, styles, and policies are said to be favored by one or the other of the two ethics. Data permitting inter-city comparisons are not available on these other variables.

from *The Municipal Year Book 1963*.[28] The magnitude of urban renewal programs was measured by capital grants per capita for each city. Raw data on capital grants were obtained from the *Urban Renewal Directory* for December 31, 1963.[29] A variety of demographic data for each city was obtained from the *County and City Data Book, 1962*.

Cities are not always free to make their own decisions on what governmental forms they will adopt and what policies they will follow. State constitutions and legislatures often interfere with home rule by requiring cities to conform to particular forms or preventing them from adopting others. We have investigated this problem at some length and consulted scholars and officials of several professional organizations in the field of municipal goverment.[30] Whenever state law imposes constraints on cities' free choice with respect to any dependent variable we have omitted such cities from the relevant analyses.

It might be argued that our index of ethnicity is both too exclusive and too inclusive. Foreign-stock population percentages exclude Negroes, who might be considered inclined to the private-regarding ethos.[31] But 1960 levels of Negro population in northern cities reflect recent migration. In most such cities Negroes were scarce and politically unimportant until the postwar years; as with all newcomers, they still have not mobilized themselves so as to exert political strength commensurate with their numbers. In the South, of course, Negroes have been disfranchised until recently. Most southern cities have now gone a long way toward removing impediments to Negro voting, but the recency and unevenness of this development makes it difficult to use numbers as an index of Negro political influence.

[28]Orin F. Nolting and David S. Arnold (eds.), *The Municipal Year Book 1963* (Chicago: The International City Managers' Association, 1963).

[29]Urban Renewal Administration, *Urban Renewal Directory, December 31, 1963* (Washington: Urban Renewal Administration, 1964).

[30]For information on state restrictions on home rule we are grateful to, among others, David S. Arnold of the International City Managers' Association, William N. Cassella, Jr. of the National Municipal League, Eugene C. Lee of the Institute of Governmental Studies of the University of California (Berkeley), and Keith Ocheltree of the Public Personnel Association.

[31]Banfield and Wilson do not include Negroes in those groups they consider disposed to private-regardingness, although some political goals they attribute to Negroes, such as desires for representation and "recognition," might be thought to incline them in that direction (Banfield and Wilson, pp. 158-159, 293-294, 307-308). On the other hand, Negroes are described as disproportionately public-regarding in their voting on bond issues (*ibid.*, pp. 237-239).

The criterion might be considered too inclusive in that most Jews are first- or second-generation Americans, and Banfield and Wilson say that at least upper-middle-class Jews are public regarding.[32] Jews amount to three or four per cent of the total American population. Almost all of them live in northern cities; more than a quarter live in New York City, where they comprise almost 30 per cent of the population. Aside from New York and a few other places, Jews have not been sizable parts of most cities' populations. Since only some Jews are exempted from the charge of private-regardingness and since we exclude the very large cities where most of them live from many of our computations, this problem is not so great.

In recent years many Jews have moved to the cities of southern Florida, some of which now have foreign-stock populations as large as any northern community. (In fact, Miami Beach, 53 per cent of whose population is ethnic, leads the nation in this category.) Since most Jewish Floridians have lived in the state only a few years, they are unlikely to have political influence in proportion to their numbers, and so one would not expect that the political practices of Florida cities would fully reflect their preferences. These cities are the exceptions to the general rule that 1960 levels of ethnic populations are a fairly reliable index of each city's relative ethnicity over the past fifty years.*

The ethos theory does not refer to the actual incidence of its various dependent variables, but to attitudes toward the variables.[33] Therefore, propositions specifying relationships between cities' population characteristics and their political forms and policies are infer-

---

[32]See, e.g., *ibid.,* pp. 42, 123, 330. While upper-middle-class Jews are often classified with Yankees as adherents of the public-regarding ethos, Banfield and Wilson do not say if they are any more likely to be public-regarding than Catholics of similar social status.

*This statement was based on inspection of the relevant census reports. It can now be put in a more precise form as a result of a recent study of 268 American cities with populations in 1930 of 30,000 or more (all such cities except a few constrained by state law from changing their form of government): "The percentage of foreign-born persons in 1930 correlates (Pearsonian r) .96, .95, and .89 with the percentages of foreign born in 1940, 1950, and 1960 respectively." See Daniel N. Gordon "Immigrants and Urban Governmental Form in American Cities, 1933-1960," *American Journal of Sociology,* Vol. 73 (September 1968).

[33]We think it unlikely that most individuals' political knowledge has developed to the point of having opinions about, say, the relative merits of ward and at-large elections. Thus the ethics may exist at two levels: as general value systems for most people and as a set of specific political preferences for their leaders.

ences from the ethos theory, not parts of the theory itself. These inferences are based on the assumptions that the strength of the public- and private-regarding ethics is related to the magnitude of the population groupings that supposedly give rise to one ethos or the other, *and* that the two ethics are important causal factors in city politics. Banfield and Wilson seem to have made the same assumption: "Obviously the social and ecological structure of a city largely determines which view as to the proper role of government will prevail in it."[34]

How valid are these inferences? Obviously it would be unwise to assert that there is a simple causal relationship between public attitudes toward a particular governmental feature and the likelihood that that feature will be adopted. Many other considerations affect the nature of local political institutions. Some of these other factors, such as state law, can be identified. Others, such as the interrelationship of other demographic variables, can be controlled by statistical manipulation. The effect of city size and region can also be controlled. Other factors, such as different national origins of immigrants, can be partially and indirectly isolated by analyzing the data by region.

When all these other variables have been taken into account, we do not think it untenable to assume that if the two ethics: a) exist, b) have the properties attributed to them, and c) are associated with the ethnic composition of urban populations, then this will be reflected in statistical associations between a specific hypothesized dependent variable and levels of ethnicity, when such associations are examined in large groups of cities. This assumption does not deny the existence of other independent variables, but it does require that the ethos be of sufficient importance so that, *in the aggregate,* its influence will be discernible. If the hypothesized relationship between ethnicity and a given political form is not found, three conclusions can be considered: a) a preference for that form is not part

---

[34]Banfield and Wilson, p. 55. Our interpretation of this statement is based on its context, Banfield and Wilson's citation of the Sherbenou and Schnore— Alford correlational studies in support of their proposition about public-regardingness and the city manager plan (*ibid.,* p. 169n), and passages like this:
"Many council-manager cities are upper-class or middle-class in character; few if any are predominantly lower-class. In the Chicago area, for example, . . . eighteen of the twenty cities with the highest home values had the (manager) plan, whereas none of the thirty-one cities with the lowest home values had it. Its popularity with people of the upper and middle classes explains its popularity in small communities, which are more likely to consist predominantly of those classes than are large ones" (*ibid.,* p. 169).

of the ethos; b) the ethos is not related to ethnicity; c) the two ethics are not translated into political reality.

We will explore three general questions in the following sections. First, to what extent do the structural dependent variables—form of government, type of ballot, and method of electing councilmen—go together? For example, do cities with mayors also use the partisan ballot and elect their councilmen from wards? Second, how do cities differ by size and region with respect both to ethnicity and to the structural dependent variables? Third, and most important, what are the relationships between ethnicity and the dependent variables?

III. THE CONSISTENCY OF POLITICAL FORMS

All the structural manifestations of public-regardingness were elements in the municipal reform movement that began with the 20th century. Civil service, nonpartisanship, at-large elections, and big districts were principal features of the National Municipal League's "municipal program," issued in 1900. Together with the manager plan and city planning, these measures were incorporated in the League's "Model City Charter," promulgated in 1916 and reissued several times subsequently.[35] Since these various features have all been part of a package, jointly promoted and presumably reflecting the same spirit, one might expect that they would be found together in practice.[36] This conclusion follows both from the logic of Banfield and Wilson's argument and from their statement that "people who are decidedly public-regarding or decidedly private-regarding on one matter tend to be so on all matters."[37]

Of the 309 cities, 146 use the manager form, 126 have elected mayors, and 37 have commission government. We will omit the commission cities from consideration because this form does not figure in the ethos theory. Of the cities with mayors or managers, 85 use the partisan and 186 use the nonpartisan ballot (information on one city is missing); 153 cities elect their councilmen at large, 67

[35]*Ibid.*, p. 141. The International City Managers' Association considers non-partisanship and at-large election "main features" of the manager system (*ibid.*, p. 172).

[36]Cf. Banfield and Wilson, "The connection between the partisan and district systems, as between the nonpartisan and at-large systems, is of considerable significance, for, as we shall see later, the connected elements tend in both cases to produce the same style of politics and to reinforce one another" (p. 90).

[37]*Ibid.*, p. 235.

elect them from wards, and 49 cities use a combination of the two methods (data on two cities are missing).[38] How do these features go together? If a city follows one ethos in one structural feature, will it be consistent with the same ethos in the other two features? It is clear that there will be less than a perfect fit in this respect, since the number of cities with a particular private-regarding feature ranges from 126 (with mayors) to 67 (electing councilmen from wards).

Manager cities are fairly consistent in their adoption of the other two structural variables: 85 per cent of them use the nonpartisan ballot, 81 per cent elect their councilmen at large, and 70 per cent use both the nonpartisan ballot and at-large elections. Mayor cities are much less consistent: half of them have partisan elections, 41 per cent elect their councilmen from wards, and only 23 per cent follow both of these private-regarding practices. As Table 1 shows, cities with mayors seem to be very eclectic in their choice of governmental institutions. Less than a quarter of them are "pure" private-

TABLE 1

Type of Ballot and Method of Electing
Councilmen in Manager and Mayor Cities

Form of Government and Type of Ballot	Method of Electing Councilmen			
	Ward	At-Large	Combination	Totals
Manager:				
Partisan	3% (4)	11% (16)	1% (2)	15% (22)
Nonpartisan	9 (13)	70 (101)	6 (9)	85 (123)
	12% (17)	81% (117)	7% (11)	100% (145)[a]
Mayor:				
Partisan	23% (28)	11% (14)	17% (21)	51% (63)
Nonpartisan	18 (22)	18 (22)	14 (17)	49 (61)
	41% (50)	29% (36)	31% (38)	100% (124)[b]

a Data on method of electing councilmen missing for one city.
b Data on method of electing councilmen or type of ballot missing for two cities.

[38]Cities that elect at least three-quarters of their municipal legislators from wards are classified as using the ward system; the same criterion is used with the at-large system. Cities that elect more even proportions by the two methods are classified as "'combination" cities. Since all cities using the commission form elect the commission at large, they are omitted from these tabulations.

regarding types and almost as many cities have each of the five other possible combinations of type of ballot and method of electing councilmen.

Three out of four cities with partisan local elections have mayors, but less than half of these partisan mayor cities also elect councilmen from wards. Partisan manager cities overwhelmingly prefer at-large elections. Where local elections are nonpartisan, two out of three communities are on the manager plan; and most of these cities also elect their councilmen at large. These data are presented in Table 2.

Cities electing councilmen from wards are very likely to have mayors, as are cities with a combination of ward and at-large elections. Both of these groups of cities are rather evenly split between partisan and nonpartisan ballots. By a similar three-to-one ratio, at-large cities have managers, and most of these communities also have nonpartisan elections.

In short, there is a recognizable "public-regarding" structural syndrome in American cities. Most of the manager cities have followed the advice of the National Municipal League and adopted nonpartisan ballots and at-large elections. But the opposite is not

TABLE 2

Form of Government and Method of Electing
Councilmen in Cities Using the Partisan and
Nonpartisan Ballot [a]

Type of Ballot and Form of Government	Method of Electing Councilmen			
	Ward	At-Large	Combination	Totals
Partisan:				
Mayor	33% (28)	16% (14)	25% (21)	74% (63)
Manager	5 (4)	19 (16)	2 (2)	26 (22)
	38% (32)	35% (30)	27% (23)	100% (85)
Nonpartisan:				
Mayor	12% (22)	12% (22)	9% (17)	33% (61)
Manager	7 (13)	55 (101)	5 (9)	67 (123)
	19% (35)	67% (123)	14% (26)	100% (184)[b]

a Cities with the commission form of government have been excluded from this table.
b Data on method of electing councilmen are not reported for two cities.

true; there is no "private-regarding" syndrome. Instead, cities with mayors have, in fairly equal proportions, every conceivable combination of the other two structural variables. Forty-eight per cent of all cities with mayors or managers are "pure types"; the others are hybrids of one sort or another.

TABLE 3

Type of Ballot and Form of Government in
Cities Electing Councilmen from Wards,
At Large, and by a Combination of Methods [a]

Method of Election and Type of Ballot	Form of Government		
	Mayor	Manager	Totals
By Wards:			
Partisan	42% (28)	6% (4)	48% (32)
Nonpartisan	33 (22)	19 (13)	52 (35)
	75% (50)	25% (17)	100% (67)
At Large:			
Partisan	9% (14)	10% (16)	20%[b](30)
Nonpartisan	14 (22)	66 (101)	80 (123)
	23% (36)	76% (117)	100% (153)
By a Combination:			
Partisan	43% (21)	4% (2)	47% (23)
Nonpartisan	35 (17)	18 (9)	53 (26)
	78% (38)	22% (11)	100% (49)

[a] Cities with the commission form of government have been excluded from this table.
[b] Does not sum to 19% because of rounding.

Civil service coverage of municipal employees is another element in the "good government" package and in the public-regarding ethos. *The Municipal Year Book* reports civil service coverage of various classes of municipal employees. These data refer only to the formal regulations. Undoubtedly the prevailing political style in many cities subverts the personnel laws. In Chicago, for example, all municipal workers except those in public utilities are "covered" by civil service. In fact, of course, a great many jobs in the Chicago government can be used for patronage purposes with little difficulty. Nevertheless we assume that in the aggregate the extent of official civil service coverage gives some indication of the reality of public personnel policies.[39] We have used *The Municipal Year Book* reports to develop four levels of civil service coverage that apply to almost all cities:

Level 1. All employees covered; 106 cities.
Level 2. All employees except manual workers covered; 13 cities.
Level 3. Only firemen and policemen covered; 57 cities.
Level 4. No civil service coverage; 33 cities.

Iowa, New York, and Ohio require their cities to use merit systems; in Massachusetts all local employees come under the jurisdiction of the state civil service commission. Since cities in these four states are not free to make their own personnel policies, we have excluded them from all tabulations involving civil service coverage.

We have compared the civil service coverage of municipal employees in mayor and manager cities.[40] Table 4 shows the proportion of each type of city that has each of the four levels of coverage. A slightly larger share of manager cities has complete coverage and somewhat more mayor cities are at level 2. These differences are small, however, and equal proportions of both groups are at levels 3 and 4. There is little more than a random chance that the two

TABLE 4
Form of Government and Level of
Civil Service Coverage [a]

Level of Civil Service Coverage	Mayor	Manager
1. All employees covered	49%	56%
2. All but manual workers covered	10	2
3. Only policemen and firemen covered	25	25
4. No civil service coverage	16	17
Total	100%	100%
N	(61)	(110)

a Excludes cities in Indiana, Iowa, Massachusetts, New York and Ohio.

[39]"However important may be the evasions of the civil service system in particular cases, it is clear that in general the effect of the system everywhere has been to make it increasingly difficult for the parties to maintain effective discipline over their workers by giving and with-holding jobs" (*ibid.*, p. 209).

[40]State law in Anglo-Saxon Indiana makes it almost impossible for cities there to deviate from the mayor form of government. Since form of municipal government is not subject to local choice, we have excluded the nine Indiana cities from the tabulation presented in Table 4. Several other states interfere with home rule in this respect, but their cities all use the commission form and on this ground are excluded from our tabulations.

alleged manifestations of the public-regarding ethos, city manager government and civil service protection, will be found together.

The various hypothesized manifestations of the two ethics are often found in "inconsistent" combinations. This suggests that the two ethics may be somewhat less differentiated from each other than Banfield and Wilson say. The forces influencing a city's choice of any one of these variables probably differ considerably in strength and composition from the factors influencing choices of other variables. These data indicate the unevenness of the wave of structural reform that swept over American cities in the twentieth century. They also suggest that the pressures for and against different items in the catalogue of reform were not as similar as has been assumed.

IV. CITY SIZE AND REGION AS INDEPENDENT VARIABLES

The second general question is how cities of different size and in different regions vary in their formal governmental characteristics and in the ethnic level of their populations.

TABLE 5
Governmental Forms and City Size

Size	Form of Government [a]		Type of Ballot [b]	Method of Election [c]		Number in Each Size Category
	Mayor	Manager	Partisan	Ward	At-Large	
Over 1 million	100%	—	40%	60%	20	5
500,000 to 1 million	73%	27	33%	27%	53	15
250,000 to 500,000	43%	40	23%	17%	73	30
100,000 to 250,000	39%	48	40%	20%	67	79
50,000 to 100,000	37%	51	29%	22%	60	180
Mean for all cities over 50,000	41%	47	32%	22%	62	
N	(126)	(146)	(98)	(67)	(190)	(309)

a Cities with the commission form of government have been excluded from these columns but not from the base on which the percentages were computed.
b All other cities use the nonpartisan ballot, except for one city for which data on type of ballot are missing.
c Cities using a combination of the ward and at-large method have been excluded from these columns but not from the base on which the percentages were computed. Data on the method used in three cities are missing.

TABLE 6
Foreign-Stock Population and City Size

Proportion of Population of Foreign Stock	Population Size		
	Over 250,000	100,000 to 250,000	50,000 to 100,000
0% to 9.9%	30%	32%	26%
10% to 19.9%	16	15	21
20% to 29.9%	18	28	21
30% to 39.9%	28	10	14
40% to 49.9%	6	14	13
50% and over	2	1	6
	100%	100%	100% [a]
Per cent of cities with 20% or more foreign stock	54%	53%	53%

[a] Sums to more than 100% because of rounding.

Size turns out to make surprisingly little difference with respect either to ethnicity or structural characteristics. Cities with more than half a million residents are much more likely to have mayors, but below this point there is only a slight trend toward use of the manager form as size declines further.[41] (Mayors become more popular again in cities below 50,000 population.) Only cities with more than a million inhabitants are much more likely to elect their council members from wards; below this level the trend is slightly and irregularly toward the at-large system. The pattern is more uneven with respect to type of ballot. Cities with populations of more than a million and those in the 100,000 to 250,000 category are most likely to have partisan elections (although the nonpartisan ballot is still preferred by 60 per cent of the cities in each category), and cities in the quarter to half million group are least likely to hold partisan elections. But these differences are not, by and large, very great, and there is no consistent relationship between size and use of one ballot or the other. These data are presented in Table 5.

Similar findings hold with respect to the relationship between size and ethnicity. As Table 6 shows, small and medium-sized cities are

[41]Cf. Banfield and Wilson, "The larger the city, generally speaking, the more is at stake politically, and consequently the greater the effort that professional politicians will put forth to avoid being displaced. This is certainly a factor that generally tends to prevent adoption of the (city manager) plan in a large city" (pp. 182-183).

just as likely as the country's biggest cities to have large foreign stock populations. Whatever its importance in other areas, a city's size is an unimportant variable either for ethnicity or (with the exceptions noted) governmental structure.

The major operational conclusion to be drawn from these findings is that size need not be controlled in examining relationships between ethnicity and the structural dependent variables, except to exclude cities of over half a million population when form of government is a variable, and cities of over a million when analyzing the method of electing councilmen. Controlling for size turned out to be unnecessary for another reason: when we did it, there was no change in the results that are presented later in this paper.

Tables 7 and 8 show the distribution of alternative forms of government, types of ballot, and methods of electing councilmen in different parts of the country. These tables demonstrate the striking regional variations in each of these characteristics. The mayor form is the predominant one in the Northeast, is somewhat favored in the Midwest, unpopular in the South, and even less popular in the West.[42] The distribution is similar for the type of ballot; partisan elections are preferred only in the Northeast. There are, however, two quite different patterns in the two sub-regions of the Northeast.

TABLE 7
Form of Government and Type of Ballot—
by Region

Region	Form of Government			Type of Ballot		Number of Cities in Region
	Mayor	Manager	Commission	Partisan	Nonpartisan	
Northeast	65%	18	17	61%	39	76
Midwest	55%	37	8	33%	67	84
West	15%	81	3	5%	95	59
South	22%	59	19	19%	81	74
Border	38%	56	6	44%	56	16
All cities over 50,000	41%	47%	12%	32%	68%	
N	(126)	(146)	(37)	(98)	(210)	(309)

[42]The western cities are those in the conventionally defined eleven western states, plus Honolulu. The Northeast includes the six New England states plus New York, New Jersey, and Pennsylvania. The Midwest includes Ohio, Indiana, Illinois, Iowa, Michigan, Minnesota, Wisconsin, North Dakota, South Dakota, Nebraska, and Kansas. The South includes the eleven ex-Confederate states.

TABLE 8
Method of Electing Councilmen by Region,
Excluding Commission Cities

Region	Ward	At-Large	Combina-tion	Total	
				%	N
Northeast	31%	38	31	100	61
Midwest	33%	46	21	100	76
West	18%	75	7	100	57
South	13%	73	13	99[a]	60
Border	33%	53	13	99[a]	15
(All cities) over 50,000	25%	57%	18%	100%	
N	(67)	(153)	(49)		(269)

a Does not sum to 100 because of rounding.

Mid-Atlantic cities (in New York, New Jersey, and Pennsylvania) use the partisan ballot by a ratio of more than four to one, while almost two-thirds of the New England cities have nonpartisan local elections. Elsewhere in the country the nonpartisan system is heavily favored; in the West only three cities have partisan elections.[43] Regional variations in methods of electing councilmen are much milder as Table 8 shows. Midwestern and northeastern cities are most addicted to the "private-regarding" alternative; almost one third of each group elect legislators from wards. Three quarters of the cities in the West and South use the at-large system.

Just as regional variations in structure are immense, so are they in levels of ethnicity. As Table 9 demonstrates, the Northeast is the most ethnic part of the country, with 94 per cent of its cities having more than the national average (19 per cent) of first- and second-generation Americans, and more than half being over 40 per cent foreign stock. The New England sub-region has the heaviest concentration of immigrants and their children; 27 of the 33 New England cities in our sample are at least 40 per cent ethnic. The distribution is somewhat less skewed in the Midwest. Just under half

[43]Most western cities examined here are in California, where all cities use the nonpartisan ballot. California law does *not* require nonpartisan local elections, however. In 1913 the legislature required "general-law" cities (those without charters) to use the nonpartisan ballot. This did not apply to charter cities, of which there were 70 in 1960, including the communities in our sample. Any California municipality of more than 3500 persons may adopt its own charter. See Eugene C. Lee, *The Politics of Nonpartisanship* (Berkeley and Los Angeles: University of California Press, 1960), pp. 13-15, 23.

TABLE 9
Foreign-Stock Population of
Cities—by Region

Proportion of Population of Foreign Stock	North-east	Mid-west	West	South	Border
0% to 9.9%	3%	16%	2%	80%	69%
10% to 19.9%	4	31	31	11	19
20% to 29.9%	17	24	53	4	6
30% to 39.9%	24	24	12	3	6
40% to 49.9%	40	6	3	—	—
50% and over	13	—	—	3a	—
Totals	101%b	101%b	101%b	101%b	100%
Per cent of cities with 20% or more foreign stock	94%	54%	68%	10%	12%

a Miami Beach and Laredo.
b Does not sum to 100 because of rounding.

of the cities there are less than 20 per cent ethnic, with almost all the rest in the 20 to 40 per cent range. The western cities show a different pattern; 84 per cent of them fall between 10 and 30 per cent foreign stock. Almost all the southern and border cities are homogeneously native, except for a few towns on the Mexican border and in the Florida resort belt. The foreign-stock residents in the former cases are, of course, largely Mexicans who have not participated heavily in local politics.[44] In the latter case the ethnics are mostly Jews who have moved to Florida in recent years.

V. ETHNICITY AND POLITICAL STRUCTURES

We come now to the central question, the relationship between cities' ethnic populations and political forms. It might be assumed that the preceding section has already answered the question with a resounding affirmation of the ethos theory, for those regions with

[44]For a description of Mexican-American political apathy in one Texas border city see Edward C. Banfield, *Big City Politics* (New York: Random House, 1965), pp. 76-78.

the largest foreign stock populations have the highest proportion of cities with elements of the private-regarding ethic. There are some exceptions to this, notably in the popularity of nonpartisanship in New England and in the consistent deviation of the West, but by and large the pattern is as predicted by the ethos theory.

More precise measures produce the same result. Excluding cities with a commission form of government and comparing the mean foreign stock populations of cities with mayors and with managers, we find that mayor cities have a much higher mean ethnic population. All mayor cities have a mean foreign-stock population of 29 per cent; those with a manager form are 18 per cent foreign stock. This difference is significant at the .001 level of confidence.[45]

But since both ethnicity and types of governmental structure vary markedly from one part of the country to another, it is necessary to control for region when examining the relationships between these variables. The South, for example, has few foreign-stock residents and few institutional manifestations of the private-regarding ethos. Indeed, the relationship in the South is so strong that it probably accounts in large part for the nationwide findings described in the preceding paragraph. But it would be rash to attribute southern political patterns to the scarcity of immigrants there. (Southern and border cities are excluded from the following intra-region comparisons because there is so little variation in the level of their foreign-stock populations.)

When the relationship between ethnicity and form of government is examined *within* regions, this control eliminates most of the apparent relationship. (We have also controlled for size by eliminating all cities of more than 500,000 population.) Northeastern cities with mayors have a mean ethnic population of 39 per cent; those with managers are 40 per cent foreign stock. The predicted relationship is found in the Midwest,[46] where cities with mayors average 6 per cent more ethnic than cities with managers. This difference is significant at the .05 level. There is a similar finding in the West, although its importance is diminished by the fact that only six western cities have mayors.[47] It is noteworthy that the northeastern

[45]The significance of differences between means was measured with a two-tailed t test.

[46]In this and all other analyses of relationships between form of government and socioeconomic variables, the nine Indiana cities have been omitted.

[47]Controlling for social class by means of analysis of covariance did not produce greater differences in ethnicity between the two types of city. Whenever relationships between a dependent variable and a demographic independent variable are described in this paper, we have also controlled for the possible influence

TABLE 10
Form of Municipal Government and Selected Population Characteristics of Cities Under 500,000 Population—by Region

Population Characteristic	Northeast			Midwest			West		
	Mayor	Manager	Sig.[a]	Mayor	Manager	Sig.	Mayor	Manager	Sig.
% foreign stock	39%	40%	n.s.	26%	20%	.05	26%	22%	n.s.
% white collar	42%	46%	n.s.	45%	49%	n.s.	51%	50%	n.s.
Median family income in 1959	$6200	$6395	n.s.	$6755	$6883	n.s.	$6481	$6975	n.s.
Median school years[b]	10.3	11.0	.05	11.2	11.4	n.s.	12.1	12.0	n.s.
Number of cities	(44)	(14)		(32)	(30)		(6)	(47)	

[a] The difference between mayor and manager cities for the relevant demographic variable, in a given region, is measured with a two-tailed t test.
[b] For adults 25 and older.

477

manager cities are much more ethnic than cities in other parts of
the country that use the mayor form.[48] This suggests that there is
no nationally relevant level of ethnicity above which one form of
government is likely to predominate, i.e., there is no threshold
level of ethnicity. These data are summarized in Table 10.

The only discernible variable distinguishing mayor and manager
cities in the Northeast is the proportion of their populations in white-
collar occupations, and even here the difference is neither large nor
statistically significant. The residents of northeastern mayor cities
average 42 per cent in white-collar jobs, compared to 46 per cent
in manager cities. The same difference is true in the Midwest. No
such relationship is found in western cities. The levels of median
income in manager cities are somewhat higher in all three regions.
The differences range from $128 in the Midwest to $494 in the
West. In the West this probably reflects nothing more than variations
in the cost of labor, since there is no difference in the mean size of
the working-class populations of the two types of cities there. Northeastern manager cities tend to have somewhat higher levels of education: 11.0 median school years completed as opposed to 10.3 in
the mayor cities. There are no such differences in the Midwest and
West.

The *nationwide* pattern of distribution of partisan and nonpartisan
ballots is quite similar to that of form of government. All cities
using the partisan ballot have a mean ethnic population of 25 per
cent; those using nonpartisan ballots have a mean ethnic population
of 21 per cent. While this difference is considerably smaller than
that for forms of government, it is still significant at the .01 level.

This faint relationship breaks down or even reverses when examined within regions. As Table 11 shows, northeastern cities using a
nonpartisan ballot have considerably *larger* ethnic populations than
those which use the partisan ballot: 43 per cent v. 34 per cent; this
difference is significant at the .001 level. This striking negative
finding is due largely to New England, which is the most ethnic
part of the country and where 64 per cent of the cities use the nonpartisan ballot. There is no difference between those midwestern
cities using the nonpartisan ballot and those that do not. There is a

---

of other demographic variables by analysis of covariance. Except where noted,
this procedure did not increase or diminish the explanatory power of the
independent variable being examined.

[48]The same is true for the other structural dependent variables; the "public-
regarding" northeastern cities are more ethnic than "private-regarding" cities
in other parts of the country (see Tables 11 and 12).

TABLE 11

Type of Ballot and Selected Population
Characteristics—by Region

Population Characteristic	Northeast			Midwest			West		
	Partisan	Nonpartisan	Sig.[a]	Partisan	Nonpartisan	Sig.[a]	Partisan	Nonpartisan	Sig.[a]
% foreign stock	34%	43%	.001	23%	22%	n.s.	28%	23%	n.s.
% white collar	42%	41%	n.s.	45%	46%	n.s.	49%	50%	n.s.
Median family income in 1959	$6099	$6058	n.s.	$6689	$6607	n.s.	$6330	$6917	n.s.
Median school years[b]	10.3	10.4	n.s.	11.0	11.2	n.s.	12.1	12.0	n.s.
Number of cities	(46)	(29)		(28)	(56)		(3)	(56)	

a A two-tailed t test was used to measure the significance of the difference between partisan and nonpartisan cities with respect to the relevant demographic variable in a given region.

b For adults 25 years of age and older.

difference among western cities in the predicted direction. It is not statistically significant, perhaps because only three western cities have partisan elections.

Examination of other demographic indices reveals no consistent patterns. Neither class, income, nor education is related to use of one type of ballot or the other. Controlling for third variables such as occupation and income did not produce greater relationships between any demographic variable and the presence of party labels in municipal elections.

The method of electing city councilmen is also unrelated to the level of foreign-stock population. As Table 12 indicates, there are no differences in foreign-stock population between northeastern cities electing their legislators from wards and at large, nor are there differences with respect to any other demographic measure.[49] In the Midwest at-large cities are 4 per cent less ethnic and also have slightly more middle class residents (2 per cent) and a higher median income ($115). While all these differences are in the predicted direction, none is statistically significant, much less of any substantive consequence. Western cities electing councilmen from wards have *fewer* ethnic residents and slightly larger middle-class populations, but these differences are even smaller than those in the Midwest.

The salient conclusion to be drawn from these data is that one can do a much better job of predicting a city's political forms by knowing what part of the country it is in than by knowing anything about the composition of its population. The reasons for this may lie in certain regional historical experiences related to the influx of immigrants and the responses to their needs reflected in municipal political systems. We will discuss the importance of regional differences in the concluding section of this paper. For the present, it is sufficient to note that only in the Midwest can we detect relationships in the direction predicted by the ethos theory with respect to two of the three dependent variables we have examined.

In addition to analyzing each of these dependent variables singly, we have combined them. There are eight possible combinations of form of government (we limit ourselves to mayor and manager), type of ballot, and method of electing councilmen (here limited to ward or at-large, omitting combinations), as shown in Table 13. Within each region we have computed the mean foreign stock popu-

---

[49]The five cities with populations of more than a million persons have been excluded from these tabulations involving methods of electing councilmen.

TABLE 12

Method of Electing City Councilmen and Selected Population Characteristics of Cities With Less Than One Million Population—by Region

Population Characteristic	Northeast			Midwest			West		
	Ward	At-Large	Sig.[a]	Ward	At-Large	Sig.	Ward	At-Large	Sig.
% foreign stock	38%	38%	n.s.	25%	21%	n.s.	21%	23%	n.s.
% white collar	43%	43%	n.s.	45%	47%	n.s.	52%	50%	n.s.
Median family income in 1959	$6211	$6157	n.s.	$6643	$6758	n.s.	$6713	$6926	n.s.
Median school years[b]	10.4	10.5	n.s.	10.9	11.2	n.s.	12.3	12.0	n.s.
Number of cities	(18)	(25)		(24)	(35)		(9)	(43)	

[a] Significance measured with a two-tailed t test.
[b] For adults 25 and older.

lations of those cities with each combination of characteristics. Conceivably the "pure type" cities would be more likely to display the ethnic characteristics said to be related to one ethos or the other. We can also evaluate Banfield and Wilson's suggestion that:

> Among the modifications that might make the (city manager) plan more acceptable and more workable in cities (whether large or small) having a politically significant lower class are the following: partisan rather than nonpartisan elections, election of some councilmen on a ward rather than an at-large basis . . .[50]

As Table 13 shows, there is no consequential difference in the ethnic populations of any of the groups of cities, in any region, except for "pure" public-regarding cities in the Midwest; these 18 cities have, on the average, fewer ethnic residents than do cities with any of the other seven combinations. In the Northeast the "pure" public-regarding cities have, in the aggregate, slightly larger foreign-stock populations than the "pure" private-regarding cities. Combining the manager form with partisan voting and ward-elected councilmen does not seem to have had the appeal suggested by Banfield and Wilson.

The difference between the two ethics is also said to be reflected in the size of the districts represented by members of the municipal legislature where wards, in fact, exist. Small districts are thought to be a consequence of the dominance of the private-regarding ethos, while large districts, which force each councilman to respond to a more heterogeneous constituency, reflect the public-regarding ethic. This proposition can be tested by examining relationships between the size of cities' ethnic populations and the number of persons represented by their ward-elected councilmen. If the proposition were valid, one would find negative correlations—that is, the larger the districts, the fewer the ethnic residents in the city.

As usual, the proposition is confirmed on a nationwide basis. For all cities with at least some ward-elected councilmen the correlation coefficient (Pearson's r) between the foreign-stock population and the number of persons represented by each ward-elected councilman is $-.23$. This is significant at the .05 level.[51] The coefficient remains at about the same level when a partial correlation is computed to control for social class; similar results are found when other variables are controlled.

[50]Banfield and Wilson, pp. 183-184.
[51]Significance of correlations is measured by the F value.

TABLE 13

Mean Foreign Stock Population of Cities with Each Combination of Form of Government, Type of Ballot, and Method of Electing Councilmen—by Region [a]

Governmental Combination	Northeast per cent ethnic	Northeast N	Midwest per cent ethnic	Midwest N	West per cent ethnic	West N
Mayor-Partisan-Ward	40	16	26	7	23	1
Mayor-Partisan-At-Large	33	9	33	2	—	0
Mayor-Nonpartisan-Ward	37	2	27	12	25	5
Manager-Partisan-Ward	26	1	19	2	—	0
Manager-Nonpartisan-Ward	—	0	27	4	19	4
Manager-Partisan-At-Large	40	4	25	5	22	1
Mayor-Nonpartisan-At-Large	44	3	24	9	37	2
Manager-Nonpartisan-At-Large	43	7	18	18	22	40

a Cities using the commission form or a combination of ward and at-large election have been excluded from this table.

The relationship persists when size is controlled. For cities with populations between 100,000 and 250,000 the coefficient is $-.30$; it falls only to $-.26$ when social class is partialled. Both of these values fall just short of the .05 level of confidence. In the smaller cities the coefficient is $-.28$ whether or not other variables are controlled; this is significant at the .05 level.

Once again, however, examining the data on a regional basis alters the picture drastically. In the Northeast the coefficient for all cities is .02; this vanishes entirely when class is controlled. In the Midwest the relationship is slightly in the predicted direction ($-.16$), and persists when other variables are controlled, but falls short of statistical significance. In the West the 14 cities with some ward-elected councilmen present a strikingly different pattern; the relationship is opposite to that predicted by the ethos theory. The simple correlation coefficient is .30, which falls to .24 when class is controlled. Neither of these values is significant at the .05 level. It appears that the confirmation of the proposition obtained by examining cities on a nationwide basis is primarily an artifact of regional differences.

VI. ETHNICITY AND PUBLIC POLICY

The ethos theory states that the private-regarding ethic is hostile to civil service, city planning, and urban renewal. In this section we will test this proposition by examining the relationships between ethnicity and indices of these policies.

There is a strong relationship between a city's size and the likelihood that its municipal employees will be under civil service. As Table 14 shows, cities with more than 250,000 residents are very likely to have complete coverage; only one of the 28 cities in this group for which we have data does not have any coverage at all. A bare majority of cities with populations from 100,000 to 250,000 have total coverage, while more than 40 per cent either have none or protect only firemen and policemen. The trend continues for smaller cities.

Table 15 shows the foreign-stock populations of cities with different levels of civil service coverage, with size controlled. The data seem to contradict the ethos theory powerfully. Those cities with complete coverage have the highest foreign-stock populations in

TABLE 14
Civil Service Coverage and Size of City [a]

Level of Civil Service Coverage	Over 250,000	100,000 to 250,000	50,000 to 100,000
1. All employees covered	75%	51%	45%
2. All but manual workers covered	14	6	5
3. Only policemen and firemen covered	7	25	32
4. No civil service coverage	4	18	18
Total	100%	100%	100%
N	(28)	(51)	(130)

[a] Cities in Indiana, Iowa, Massachusetts, New York, and Ohio are excluded from all tables concerning civil service coverage.

every size category except the largest, and even there the cities with minimal coverage are by far the least ethnic.

As with all our other nationwide findings, these striking relationships are an artifact of regional differences. Controlling for region makes it clear that the very low ethnic population of the cities with scanty coverage is due to the contribution of southern and border cities, which characteristically have neither extensive civil service coverage nor large foreign-stock populations. Unfortunately for the ethos theory, however, data for the rest of the country do not support the hypothesis. The ethnic populations of western and mid-

TABLE 15
Civil Service Coverage and Foreign-Stock
Population—by Size

Level of Civil Service Coverage	Mean per cent foreign-stock in population:		
	Over 250,000	100,000 to 250,000	50,000 to 100,000
1. All employees covered	21%	23%	24%
2. All but manual workers covered	24	15	16
3. Only policemen and firemen covered	6	10	18
4. No civil service coverage	4	16	14

TABLE 16
Civil Service Coverage and Foreign-Stock Population—by Region

Level of Civil Service Coverage	Mean per cent foreign-stock in population:							
	Northeast		Midwest		West		South	
	%	N	%	N	%	N	%	N
1. All employees covered	40	18	23	25	23	38	13	20
2. All but manual workers covered	38	3	22	3	—	—	7	6
3. Only policemen and firemen covered	23	11	23	16	21	4	7	23
4. No civil service coverage	45	2	21	6	21	8	4	13

TABLE 17

Correlations Between Per Cent Foreign-Stock
and City Planning Expenditures Per Capita —
by Size and Region [a]

Size of City	North-east	Mid-west	West
Over 250,000	−.11	.22	−.10
	(8)[b]	(15)	(10)
100,000 to 250,000	−.22	−.25	.21
	(21)	(19)	(14)
50,000 to 100,000	−.04	.23	.09
	(47)	(50)	(35)

[a] The value in each cell is the Pearsonian r of the relationship between per cent ethnic population and city planning expenditures per capita, for the given group of cities. A negative correlation is in the direction predicted by the ethos theory.
[b] Numbers in parentheses are the number of cases in each cell.

western cities do not differ appreciably from one level of coverage to the next. There are considerable differences among northeastern cities, but their impact is, if anything, contradictory to the theory. The eleven northeastern cities in which only policemen and firemen are protected have the fewest ethnic residents. The two cities with the least coverage have the highest mean ethnic populations, but this exceeds the mean for the 18 cities with complete coverage by only 5 per cent. In short, ethnicity does not make any difference in any region so far as civil service coverage is concerned. Relationships with other demographic variables are no more evident.

City planning supposedly comes close to being anathema to the private-regarding ethos. We have correlated per capita city planning expenditures with foreign-stock percentages for cities of different sizes and in different regions. These data are summarized in Table 17. If the ethos theory were correct in this respect, we would find negative correlations, presumably at some level of statistical significance. No such pattern can be discerned in Table 17. Five of the nine cells show negative correlations, ranging from −.04 to −.25. Positive correlation coefficients range from .09 to .23. It is difficult to regard these results as due to anything but chance. These relationships do not change when partial correlations are computed to control for social class.

For somewhat the same reasons that they are believed to oppose city planning members of ethnic groups are said to be hostile to urban renewal. The amount of the federal capital grants reserved for a city is an accurate index of the extent of its commitment to urban renewal. We have used capital grants per capita as a comparative measure.[52]

While probably every city with more than 50,000 residents "needs" at least some urban renewal, it would be unsafe to assume that the need is equally important or recognized everywhere. The compact, aging cities of the industrial East and Midwest are losing residents and businesses to the suburbs, while most southern and western cities are growing more prosperous and populous. Quasi-ideological opposition to urban renewal is stronger in the latter areas.[53]

Renewal activity is also a function of a city's size. While 86 per cent of cities with populations over 250,000 have at least one renewal project in the action phase, this is true of 71 per cent of cities with populations between 100,000 and 250,000, and only 47 per cent of cities in the 50,000 to 100,000 category.

For these reasons we have controlled for size and region when correlating ethnicity and urban renewal grants per capita. The findings, summarized in Table 18, resemble those for city planning. There is no consistent relationship, either in one region or in the country as a whole. Partial correlations to control for social class do not materially change this picture.[54]

The conventional wisdom holds that city governments headed by mayors are more responsive to the political preferences of ethnic groups. If this were the case and if ethnics were opposed to city planning and urban renewal, we would expect to find that while

[52]We counted all projects classified in the execution stage, or where a loan and grant contract was approved but not yet formally executed, in the December 31, 1963 directory. A renewal project in the execution stage at the end of 1963 is the product of prior decisions extending at least two or three years into the past.

[53]Several western and southern states were very slow to pass enabling legislation to permit their cities to undertake urban renewal projects; one or two states still impose severe restraints in this regard. We excluded southern states from our analysis; the western states that followed this policy do not, with one exception, contain cities with populations over 50,000.

[54]Amos H. Hawley has found an inverse relationship between the proportion of businessmen and professionals in a city's population and the likelihood that it has begun to carry out a renewal project. See his "Community Power and Urban Renewal Success, " *American Journal of Sociology,* 68 (January, 1963), 422-431. Hawley's study does not take account of the magnitude of a city's program. It has been criticized on other grounds by Bruce C. Straits, "Community Action and Implementation of Urban Renewal," *ibid.,* 71 (July, 1965), 77-82. See also Hawley's rejoinder, *ibid.,* pp. 82-84.

TABLE 18

Correlations Between Percent Foreign-Stock
and Urban Renewal Capital Grants Per
Capita—by Size and Region [a]

Size of City	North-east	Mid-west	West
Over 250,000	−.54	.12	.72[b]
	(8)	(15)	(10)
100,000 to 250,000	.05	−.16	.34
	(21)	(19)	(14)
50,000 to 100,000	−.10	.02	.17
	(47)	(50)	(35)

a The value in each cell is the Pearsonian *r* of the relationship between per cent ethnic population and urban renewal capital grants per capita for all federally-aided urban renewal projects in the execution stage. A negative correlation is in the direction predicted by the ethos theory.
b Significant at the .05 level. This is the only value to attain this level of confidence.

there was no relationship between ethnicity and the extent of these policies in all cities, such a relationship might appear in mayor cities. That is, in political systems where members of ethnic groups supposedly have more influence, this influence might be manifested in lower expenditures on city planning and urban renewal.[55] We can test this proposition by further subdividing the classes of cities in Tables 17 and 18 into mayor cities and manager cities (discarding those with the commission form). These tabulations are summarized in Tables 19 and 20.

This manipulation of the data does not yield any greater relationships between ethnicity and city planning, as Table 19 demonstrates. There are no consistent tendencies in any part of the country for the correlation coefficients in mayor cities to be in the negative direction. Table 20, on urban renewal, provides one ray of hope for the ethos theory in the cell for small midwestern cities. Those cities with mayors have a correlation coefficient of −.43 between foreign-stock population and urban renewal capital grants per capita. This value is just short of significance at the .05 level. The coefficient for small western cities is almost as high, but there are only four cities in this group with mayors. Interpretation of Table 20 is, by and large, a

[55] An earlier study found no relationship between form of local government and magnitude of urban renewal. See George S. Duggar, "The Relation of Local Government Structure to Urban Renewal," *Law and Contemporary Problems*, 26 (1961), 49-69.

TABLE 19

Correlations Between Percent Foreign-Stock and City Planning Expenditures Per Capita in Mayor and Manager Cities— by Size and Regions [a]

Size of City	Northeast		Midwest		West	
Over 250,000	mayor −.11	manager [b]	mayor .21	manager −.44	mayor .75	manager −.16
100,000 to 250,000	mayor −.39	manager .08	mayor −.37	manager −.65	mayor [c]	manager .23
50,000 to 100,000	mayor .11	manager −.12	mayor .23	manager .12	mayor .32	manager .13

a The value in each cell is the product moment correlation coefficient of the relationship between per cent ethnic population and city planning expenditures per capita, for those cities with the indicated form of government and size and region. A negative correlation is in the direction predicted by the ethos theory, which also predicts larger negative correlations for the mayor cities.

b One manager city in group.

c No mayor cities in group.

TABLE 20

Correlations Between Percent Foreign-Stock and Urban Renewal Capital Grants per Capita in Mayor and Manager Cities — by Size and Region [a]

Size of City	Northeast		Midwest		West	
	mayor	manager	mayor	manager	mayor	manager
Over 250,000 population	−.55	[b]	.15	−.08	.60	.90
100,000 to 250,000	.06	.24	.21	.41	[c]	.34
50,000 to 100,000	−.05	−.14	−.43[d]	−.14	−.41[e]	.21

a The value in each cell is the product moment correlation coefficient of the relationship between per cent ethnic population and urban renewal capital grants per capita, for those cities with the indicated form of government and size and region. The ethos theory predicts negative correlations, greater in mayor cities than in manager ones.

b One manager city in group.

c No mayor cities in group.

d Almost significant at the .05 level; the only value in either Table 19 or 20 that comes this close.

e Four cities in this sub-group.

491

matter of temperament. This one weak finding, in a mass of negative evidence, does not impress us as very important.

VII. CONCLUSIONS

Several conclusions can be drawn from the foregoing findings: (1) Contrary to specific propositions in the ethos theory, some of the political forms and policies are not manifestations of either ethos. (2) The two ethics are not as ethnically differentiated as has been suggested. (3) The ethics, as described, do not exist. (4) The propositions about manifestations of the ethics and their ethnic roots are all correct, but there are so many other factors bearing on political outcomes that the prevailing ethos in a city is not very important. The data at hand do not permit us to evaluate these conclusions, but we can be fairly confident of one other assertion: the propositions of the ethos theory need to be modified to account for special circumstances that limit their validity. Regional variations are the most obvious examples of such circumstances; they are a good starting point for this discussion.

The ethos theory is irrelevant to the South, where most municipal institutions seem to be corollaries of the region's traditional preoccupation with excluding Negroes from political power. A one-party system removes temptations to appeal to Negro voters, as does the city manager plan. With only one party, the partisan ballot is not meaningful. At-large elections minimize Negro voting strength. In view of these considerations, the scarcity of immigrants in the South appears to be a superfluous explanation for its local governmental practices.[56]

---

[56]This southern concern with unity may also explain why Mexican-Americans in Texas have been so apolitical, in contrast to the political involvement of immigrants in the North. Perhaps the political participation of newly arrived minority groups is enhanced when the political environment is competitive. European immigrants to northern cities typically arrived in political arenas where partisan competition motivated both sets of contenders to appeal for their votes. As the immigrants acquired political skill, their prices rose until they had attained political influence at least somewhat in proportion to their numbers. But if immigrants come to a political system where the elites shun conflict with each other, they are likely to find that the interest of those elites is to exclude them from politics rather than appeal for their support. The impact of immigrant political values obviously would be far greater in the former case.

For other special reasons the theory is also inapplicable to the West, where cities do have a considerable range of foreign-stock populations. We suggested one cause earlier: the immigrant experience in the West was different, hence the conditions that allegedly produce private-regardingness did not develop there. This different history also probably accounts for the relatively low levels of ethnic consciousness in the West. Inhabitants of the West have never been as fascinated as Easterners with national origins (except where Orientals and Mexicans are concerned), and therefore the region has not displayed the ethnic politics characteristic of the East.[57] Some manifestations of the private-regarding ethos are conducive to ethnic politics. The election of councilmen from wards, for instance, makes it much easier to bestow "recognition" on nationality groups. In the absence of civil service regulations it is easier to give every ethnic group its "fair share" of public jobs without having to worry about qualifications. Where politics is viewed as conflict among nationality groups for jobs, nominations, and spoils, institutional forms consistent with these aspirations are likely to flourish, *quite apart from any other prevailing view of the political world.* Obviously, ethnic salience is a prerequisite of ethnic politics. A strategy of "recognizing" nationality groups is meaningless if most group members do not see politics in ethnic perspectives. To the extent that ethnic salience contributes to the strength of private-regardingness, one would expect that the ethos would be less evident in those places where ethnicity is not as prominent a feature of political life as it is in the Northeast.

Yet the theory also fares badly in the Northeast. It might be argued that this reflects a different kind of historical circumstance. Perhaps the Yankees there, anticipating their submergence in the rising tide of immigrants, took steps to minimize this trend by changing the political structure accordingly. This might, for instance, explain why northeastern cities that use the nonpartisan ballot are so much more ethnic than the region's cities that adhere to the partisan ballot. But this explanation presents several difficulties. Even those cities with, say, partisan elections, are highly ethnic. A generation ago ethnics must have been even more numerous in them. Why, then, did the Yankees in those cities not take steps to protect their interests? Why were the Yankees apparently most successful in those cities where

[57]Regional differences in ethnic politics and salience are discussed at greater length in Wolfinger, *op. cit.,* p. 898.

the ethnics were most numerous? Why did the ethnics not change the system back when they took over?

When Yankees are as outnumbered as they are in the Northeast, they may prefer a system that gives them some minority representation. Perhaps any self-conscious minority prefers institutions that guarantee it representation and a chance to maximize its political resources, and there is no doubt that Yankees are a self-conscious minority in urban New England. When Boston city councilmen were elected from wards some Yankees and Jews won seats. But when Boston adopted the public-regarding at-large system only Italians and Irishmen could get elected.[58]

Possibly the politics of the Northeast, with its virulent ethnic tensions, produces in the Yankees the same orientations that the ethnics are said to have. They develop the same interests in recognition, representation of their parochial interests, favors from city hall, and so on. When the choice is between doing business with a private-regarding regime and political isolation, perhaps all but the stiffest Brahmins adapt to the private-regarding style. This would explain why ethnicity appears to be worthless as an independent variable in the Northeast: everyone there except possibly the cosmopolitan upper-middle-class has succumbed to private-regardingness.[59] The triumph of the immigrants is complete. The out-numbered, affronted, overpowered Yankees go along with the immigrant political style both because they have to and because its values have replaced their own in the community.

The Midwest provides the best evidence for the ethos theory, but even there the differences between "public-regarding" and "private-regarding" cities are small and uneven.

---

[58]Banfield and Wilson, p. 95.

[59]As we noted earlier, the scanty scholarly knowledge of nonmetropolitan political machines may be due to the fact that most of the best research on local politics has been done at schools like Harvard, Columbia, and Chicago. These universities are located in cities where politics is conducted almost entirely by members of ethnic groups. From the vantage point of Hyde Park or Harvard Square, almost everyone not connected with the university is an ethnic. Political practices in such cities typically are "private-regarding." Much of the opposition to these practices comes from people connected with or attracted to universities, that is, mostly from Jews and Protestants. College faculties and their social satellites are scarcely typical of the Protestant middle class. Banfield and Wilson may be overgenerous to the bulk of the Anglo-Saxon population. While professors and account executives are not particularly interested in patronage, ticket fixing, and the like, these and other elements of the private-regarding style may be quite congenial to people who have little in common with college faculties but nonmembership in the Catholic Church.

Whatever the utility of these assorted speculations about the ethos theory, we still have not explained our striking positive finding, the great variations in each of the structural variables from one region to the next. Outside the South regional variations may reflect to some extent interaction between cities' natural histories and prevailing political enthusiasms at crucial periods in those histories. Most eastern and midwestern cities were important communities in the 19th century, before the National Municipal League's various structural reforms were seriously proposed. Their political institutions were well established and had seen hard service in the first generation of industrialization. Politicians generally had vested interests in maintaining the existing forms and most political actors had at least developed means of dealing with those forms. These attachments and accommodations were weaker and less developed in newer cities or cities undergoing tremendous growth. They were even more irrelevant when it came to deciding on governmental institutions for brand new communities. In such cases there was no presumption in favor of the status quo, and the writers of municipal constitutions were responsive to contemporary political fashions.

Most southwestern and western cities were villages, at best, until the early twentieth century, when the new municipal governmental forms were all the rage. We think that regional differences in the age of cities may explain a good deal of the striking regional variations in form of government, type of ballot, and method of electing councilmen.

While sudden growth is the most common occasion on which constitutions are written *de novo,* other conditions may present similar opportunities. This seems most likely to happen after a major political upheaval. For example, California's wholesale conversion to local nonpartisanship was a result of the Progressives' great victory over the Southern Pacific Railroad in the election of 1910. Anxious to capitalize on their triumph, the Progressives were extraordinarily receptive to the prevailing nostrums of reform. Twenty years before, these measures were not yet plausible alternatives. Twenty years later, sophisticated reformers would have placed far less faith in such changes.

In short, the ethos theory clearly needs a good deal of modification. Whether a revised version will have much explanatory power remains to be seen.

24

REFORMISM AND PUBLIC POLICIES
IN AMERICAN CITIES*†

ROBERT L. LINEBERRY
AND
EDMUND P. FOWLER

A decade ago, political scientists were deploring the "lost world of municipal government" and calling for systematic studies of municipal life which emphasized the political, rather than the administrative, side of urban political life.[1] In recent years, this demand has been generously answered and urban politics is becoming one of the most richly plowed fields of political research. In terms originally introduced by David Easton,[2] political scientists have long been concerned with inputs, but more recently they have focused their attention on other system variables, particularly the political culture[3] and policy outputs of municipal governments.[4]

*Reprinted from The American Political Science Review, *LXI,* No. 3 (September 1967), 701-716. By permission of *The American Political Science Review* and the authors.

†The authors are indebted to Professors Robert T. Daland, James W. Prothro, William R. Keech and James Q. Wilson for comments on an earlier draft of this paper. For assistance in statistical and methodological questions, the advice of Professor Hubert Blalock and Mr. Peter B. Harkins has been invaluable. The authors, of course, assume responsibility for all interpretation and misinterpretation.

[1]Lawrence J. R. Herson, "The Lost World of Municipal Government," this REVIEW, 51 (June, 1957), 330-345; Robert T. Daland, "Political Science and the Study of Urbanism," *ibid.,* 491-509.

[2]David Easton, "An Approach to the Analysis of Political Systems," *World Politics,* 9 (April, 1957), 383-400.

[3]Edward C. Banfield and James Q. Wilson, *City Politics* (Cambridge: Harvard University Press and the MIT Press, 1963); see also James Q. Wilson and Edward C. Banfield, "Public-Regardingness as a Value Premise in Voting Behavior," this REVIEW, 58 (December, 1964), 876-887.

[4]See, for example, Thomas R. Dye, "City-Suburban Social Distance and Public Policy," *Social Forces,* 4 (1965), 100-106; Raymond Wolfinger and

The present paper will treat two policy out-puts, taxation and expenditure levels of cities, as dependent variables. We will relate these policy choices to socio-economic characteristics of cities and to structural characteristics of their governments. Our central research concern is to examine the impact of political structures, reformed and unreformed, on policy-making in American cities.

I. POLITICAL CULTURE, REFORMISM AND POLITICAL INSTITUTIONS

The leaders of the Progressive movement in the United States left an enduring mark on the American political system, particularly at the state and municipal level. In the states, the primary election, the referendum, initiative and recall survive today. The residues of this *Age of Reform,*[5] as Richard Hofstadter called it, persist in municipal politics principally in the form of manager government and at-large and nonpartisan elections. The reformers were, to borrow Banfield and Wilson's phrase, the original embodiment of the "middle class ethos" in American politics. They were, by and large, White Anglo-Saxon Protestants reacting to the politics of the party machine, which operated by exchanging favors for votes.[6]

It is important that we understand the ideology of these reformers if we hope to be able to analyze the institutions which they created and their impact on political decisions. The reformers' goal was to "rationalize" and "democratize" city government by the substitution of "community oriented" leadership. To the reformers, the most pernicious characteristic of the machine was that it capitalized on socio-economic cleavages in the population, playing on class antagonisms and on racial and religious differences. Ernest S. Bradford, an early advocate of commission government with at-large elections, defended his plans for at-large representation on grounds that

. . . under the ward system of governmental representation, the ward receives the attention, not in proportion to its needs but to

---

John Osgood Field, "Political Ethos and the Structure of City Goverment," this REVIEW, 60 (June, 1966), 306-326; Edgar L. Sherbenou, "Class, Participation, and the Council-Manager Plan," *Public Administration Review,* 21 (Summer, 1961), 131-135; Lewis A. Froman, Jr., "An Analysis of Public Policies in Cities," *Journal of Politics,* 29 (February, 1967), 94-108.

[5](New York: Alfred A. Knopf, 1955).

[6]John Porter East, *Council Manager Government: The Political Thought of Its Founder, Richard S. Childs* (Chapel Hill: University of North Carolina Press, 1965), p. 18.

the ability of its representatives to 'trade' and arrange 'deals' with
fellow members. . . . Nearly every city under the aldermanic system offers flagrant examples of this vicious method of 'part representation.' The commission form changes this to representation of
the city as a whole.[7]

The principal tools which the reformers picked to maximize this
"representation of the city as a whole" were the commission, and
later the manager, form of government, the nonpartisan election and
the election at-large. City manager government, it was argued,
produced a no-nonsense, efficient and business-like regime, where
decisions could be implemented by professional administrators rather
than by victors in the battle over spoils. Nonpartisan elections
meant to the reformer that state and national parties, whose issues
were irrelevant to local politics anyway, would keep their divisive
influences out of municipal decision-making. Nonpartisan elections,
especially when combined with elections at-large, would also serve
to reduce the impact of socio-economic cleavages and minority
voting blocs in local politics. Once established, these institutions
would serve as bastions against particularistic interests.

Banfield and Wilson have argued that the "middle class ethos" of
the reformers has become a prevalent attitude in much of political
life. The middle class stands for "public regarding" virtues rather
than for "private regarding" values of the ethnic politics of machines
and bosses. The middle class searches for the good of the "community
as a whole" rather than for the benefit of particularistic interests.[8]
Agger, Goldrich and Swanson, in their study of two western and two
southern communities have documented the rise of a group they call
the "community conservationists," who "see the values of community life maximized when political leadership is exercised by men
representing the public at large, rather than 'special interests'."[9]
Robert Wood has taken up a similar theme in his penetrating
analysis of American suburbia. The "no-party politics of suburbia"
is characterized by "an outright reaction against partisan activity,
a refusal to recognize that there may be persistent cleavages in the
electorate and an ethical disapproval of permanent group collaboration as an appropriate means of settling disputes."[10] This ideo-

---

[7]Ernest S. Bradford, *Commission Government in American Cities* (New
York: Macmillan, 1911), p. 165.
[8]Banfield and Wilson, *op. cit.*, p. 41.
[9]Robert Agger, Daniel Goldrich, and Bert E. Swanson, *The Rulers and the
Ruled* (New York: John Wiley and Sons, 1964), p. 21.
[10]Robert C. Wood, *Suburbia: Its People and Their Politics* (Boston: Houghton Mifflin Co., 1959), p. 155.

logical opposition to partisanship is a product of a tightly-knit and homogeneous community, for "nonpartisanship reflects a highly integrated community life with a powerful capacity to induce conformity."[11]

Considerable debate has ensued over both the existence and the consequences of these two political ethics in urban communities. Some evidence has supported the view that reformed governments[12] are indeed found in cities with higher incomes, higher levels of education, greater proportions of Protestants and more white-collar job-holders. Schnore and Alford, for example, found that "the popular image of the manager city was verified; it does tend to be the natural habitat of the upper middle class." In addition, manager cities were "inhabited by a younger, more mobile population that is growing rapidly."[13]

More recently Wolfinger and Field correlated socio-economic variables—particularly ethnicity and region—to political structures. They concluded that "the ethos theory is irrelevant to the South . . . inapplicable to the West . . . fares badly in the Northeast . . . " and that support for the theory in the Midwest was "small and uneven."[14]

TABLE 1.
Independent Variables

1. Population, 1960
2. Per cent population increase or decrease, 1950-60
3. Per cent non-white
4. Per cent of native population with foreign born or mixed parentage
5. Median income
6. Per cent of population with incomes below $3000
7. Per cent of population with incomes above $10,000
8. Median school years completed by adult population
9. Per cent high school graduates among adult population
10. Per cent of population in white collar occupations
11. Per cent of elementary school children in private schools
12. Per cent of population in owner-occupied dwelling units

---

[11]*Ibid.,* p. 154.

[12]We refer to cities characterized by commission or manager government, nonpartisan elections, and at-large constituencies as "reformed." Our use of the term is historical and no value position on reformism's merits is intended. To refer to reformed cities as "public regarding" or "middle class" is, it seems, to assume what needs to be proved.

[13]Leo Schnore and Robert Alford, "Forms of Government and Socio-Economic Characteristics of Suburbs," *Administrative Science Quarterly,* 8 (June, 1963), 1-17. See also the literature cited in Froman, *op. cit.*

[14]Wolfinger and Field, *op. cit.,* pp. 325-326.

Region proved to be a more important predictor of both government forms and of policy outputs like urban renewal expenditures than did the socio-economic composition of the population.

In our view, it is premature to carve a headstone for the ethos theory. It is our thesis that governments which are products of the reform movement behave differently from those which have un-reformed institutions, even if the socio-economic composition of their population may be similar. Our central purpose is to determine the impact of both socio-economic variables and political institutions (structural variables) on outputs of city governments. By doing this, we hope to shed some additional illumination on the ethos theory.

II. RESEARCH DESIGN

Variables.

The independent variables used in this analysis, listed in Table 1, consist of relatively "hard" data, mostly drawn from the U.S. census.[15] These variables were selected because they represent a variety of possible social cleavages which divide urban populations—rich vs. poor, Negro vs. White, ethnic vs. native, newcomers vs. old-timers, etc. We assume that such social and economic characteristics are important determinants of individual and group variations in political preferences. Data on each of these independent variables were gathered for each of the two hundred cities in the sample.[16]

Our principal theoretical concern is with the consequences of variations in the structural characteristics of form of government, type of constituency and partisanship of elections. The variable of government form is unambiguous. Except for a few small New England towns, all American cities have council-manager, mayor-council or commission government. There is, however, somewhat more ambiguity in the classification of election type. By definition, a "nonpartisan election is one in which no candidate is identified on the ballot by party affiliation."[17] The legal definition of non-

[15]The source for the first nine variables is *The City and County Data Book* (Washington: United States Bureau of the Census, 1962). For the last three variables, the source is Orin F. Nolting and David S. Arnold (eds.), *The Municipal Yearbook 1965* (Chicago: International City Managers' Association, 1965), pp. 98 ff.

[16]We used a random sample of 200 of the 309 American cities with populations of 50,000 or more in 1960. All information on the forms of government and forms of election are drawn from *The Municipal Yearbook, 1965, op. cit.*

[17]Banfield and Wilson, *op cit.,* p. 151.

partisanship conceals the wide variation between Chicago's and Boston's nominal nonpartisanship and the more genuine variety in Minneapolis, Winnetka and Los Angeles.[18] We will quickly see, though, that formal nonpartisanship is not merely an empty legal nicety, but that there are very real differences in the political behavior of partisan and nonpartisan cities, even though we are defining them in legal terms only.[19]

Our classification of constituency types into only two groups also conceals some variation in the general pattern. While most cities use either the at-large or the ward pattern of constituencies exclusively, a handful use a combination of the two electoral methods. For our purposes, we classified these with district cities.

The dependent variables in this study are two measures of public policy outputs. A growing body of research on local politics has utilized policy measures as dependent variables.[20] The present research is intended to further this study of political outputs by relating socio-economic variables to expenditure and taxation patterns in cities with varying political structures.

The dependent variables are computed by a simple formula. The measure for taxation was computed by dividing the total personal income of the city into the total tax of the city, giving us a tax/income ratio. Similarly, dividing expenditures by the city's aggregate personal income gave us an expenditure/income ratio as the measure for our second dependent variable. These measures, while admittedly imperfect,[21] permit us to ask how much of a city's income it is willing to commit for public taxation and expenditures.

[18]For Minneapolis, see Robert Morlan, "City Politics: Free Style," *National Municipal Review,* 48 (November, 1949), pp. 485-490; Winnetka, Banfield and Wilson, *op. cit.,* p. 140; Los Angeles, Charles G. Mayo, "The 1961 Mayoralty Election in Los Angeles: The Political Party in a Non-partisan Election," *Western Political Quarterly,* 17 (1964), 325-339.

[19]At least one other variable may produce a given institutional form in a city—the legal requirements of a state government, which vary from state to state and may even vary for different kinds of cities within the same state. We have not taken account of this variable because systematic information on comparative state requirements in this area was unavailable to us. However, Wolfinger and Field consulted several experts and eliminated cities which are not given free choice over their institutions. Nevertheless, a comparison of our figures with theirs revealed no important differences.

[20]See footnote 4, *supra.*

[21]We recognize that these are only rough indicators of city finance policies. Definitions of taxation vary from city to city and what may be financed from taxes in one city may be financed from fees in another. Expenditures present a more complex problem because the types and amounts of state transfer payments vary from state to state according to state laws, the division of governmental labor in a state, the incomes and sizes of cities, not to mention

Hypothesis.

Much of the research on city politics has treated reformed institutions as dependent variables. Although we shall briefly examine the social and economic differences between reformed and unreformed cities, our principal concern will be to explore the *consequences* for public policy of political institutions. From our earlier discussion of the political culture of cities we hypothesized that:

1. The relationship between socio-economic cleavages and policy outputs is stronger in unreformed than in reformed cities.

This hypothesis focuses on the intention of the reformers to minimize the role of particularistic interests in policy making.

III. REFORMED AND UNREFORMED CITIES: A COMPARISON

The economic and social contrasts between reformed and unreformed cities have been the subject of much research,[22] and for our purposes we may be brief in our treatment. We divided the independent variables into three groups, one measuring population size and growth, a second containing social class indicators and a third including three measures of social homogeneity. The means and standard deviations for each variable by institutional category are found in Table 2.

It should initially be noted that population size and growth rate fairly clearly separate the reformed from the unreformed cities. As Alford and Scoble have amply documented.[23] the larger the city, the greater the likelihood of its being unreformed; the faster its growth rate, the more likely a city is to possess manager government,

political factors at the state level. We think it important, however, that our independent variables explain a large proportion of the variation in municipal outputs as we measured them. No doubt one could explain an even larger proportion of the variation in measures which specify different functional reponsibilities of cities. At least these measures constitute a starting point, and we hope others will improve on them.
The source of our output measures was the *County and City Data Book, op. cit.*
[22]See, for example, Robert Alford and Harry Scoble, "Political and Socio-Economic Characteristics of American Cities," *The Municipal Yearbook 1965, op. cit.,* pp. 82-97; Sherbenou, *op. cit.;* John H. Kessel, "Governmental Structure and Political Environment," this REVIEW, 56 (September, 1962), 615-620.
[23]Alford and Scoble, *op. cit.* The particularly large differences found between the populations of reformed and unreformed cities reflect the fact that New York City and several other urban giants are included in the sample.

TABLE 2.
Comparison of the Means (and Standard Deviations) of Socio-Economic Characteristics of Reformed and Unreformed Cities

Independent Variable	Government Type		
	Mayor-Council	Manager	Commission
Population:			
Population (10³)	282.5 (858.6)	115.7 (108.0)	128.6 (115.2)
% Change, 1950-60	36.4% (118.8)	64.1% (130.4)	18.5% (36.7)
Class:			
Median Income	$6199. (1005.0)	$6131. (999.6)	$5425. (804.4)
% under $3000	15.3% (7.0)	17.3% (6.9)	21.5% (7.9)
% over $10,000	16.9% (7.2)	17.5% (6.7)	12.5% (3.7)
% high school graduates	40.7% (10.8)	48.1% (8.9)	41.6% (10.4)
Median Education (yrs.)	10.7 (1.1)	11.4 (.89)	11.0 (2.1)
% Owner-Occupied Dwelling Units	54.9% (15.1)	57.3% (13.6)	54.6% (13.7)
% White collar	44.1% (9.0)	48.1% (7.1)	44.2% (7.6)
Homogeneity:			
% Nonwhite	10.6% (11.5)	11.6% (10.8)	16.5% (14.9)
% Native with Foreign Born or Mixed Parentage	19.7% (9.9)	12.4% (8.3)	11.7% (10.7)
% Private School Attendance	23.5% (11.9)	15.3% (11.8)	16.6% (11.8)
	N=85	N=90	N=25

Independent Variable	Election Type	
	Partisan	Nonpartisan
Population:		
Population (10³)	270.8 (1022.1)	155.8 (198.7)
% Population Increase 1950-1960	17.1 (40.1)	58.3% (136.1)

TABLE 2 (continued)

Class:		
Median Income	$5996 (904.5)	$6074 (1045.5)
% under $3000	16.8% (7.1)	17.2% (7.2)
% over $10,000	16.1% (6.1)	16.7% (7.0)
% High School Graduates	40.5% (9.2)	45.3% (10.6)
Median Education (yrs.)	10.6 (1.1)	11.2 (1.2)
% Owner-Occupied Dwelling Units	51.5% (14.4)	57.7% (13.8)
% White Collar	43.5% (7.5)	46.7% (8.3)
Homogeneity:		
% Nonwhite	13.0% (11.9)	11.5% (11.8)
% Native with Foreign Born or Mixed Parentage	17.5% (10.7)	14.7% (9.6)
% Private School Attendance	24.1% (13.6)	16.9% (11.3)
	N = 57	N = 143

	Constituency Type	
Independent Variable	District	At-Large
Population:		
Population (10³)	246.9 (909.8)	153.6 (191.2)
% Population Increase 1950-1960	23.1% (36.4)	59.1% (143.7)
Class:		
Median Income	$6297 (965.2)	$5942 (1031.9)
% under $3000	14.7% (6.5)	18.2% (7.6)
% over $10,000	17.7% (7.1)	16.0% (6.6)
% High School Graduates	43.6% (10.9)	44.4% (10.4)
Median Education (yrs.)	10.9 (1.1)	11.2 (1.2)
% Owner-Occupied Dwelling Units	55.1% (14.4)	56.9% (14.5)
% White Collar	45.2% (9.4)	46.3% (7.5)
Homogeneity:		
% Non-white	9.8% (10.6)	13.0% (12.3)
% Native with Foreign Born or Mixed Parentage	18.9% (9.4)	13.4% (9.7)
% Private School Attendance	23.2% (12.5)	16.6% (11.7)
	N = 73	N = 127

nonpartisan and at-large elections. These differences are largely accounted for by the fact that very large cities are most likely to (1) have unreformed institutions and (2) be stable or declining in population. Since neither of these variables emerged as particularly important predictors of our output variables, we relegated them to secondary importance in the rest of the analysis.

The data in Table 2 indicate that reformed cities (at least those over 50,000) do not appear to be "the natural habitat of the upper middle class." While reformed cities have slightly more educated populations and slightly high proportions of white collar workers and home ownership, unreformed cities have generally high incomes. In any case, whatever their direction, the differences are not large. What is striking is not the differences between the cities but the similarities of their class composition.

Homogeneity is easily one of the most ambiguous terms in the ambiguous language of the social sciences. We have followed Alford and Scoble who used three measures of homogeneity: for ethnicity, the per cent of population native born of foreign born or mixed parentage; for race, the per cent non-white; and for religious homogeneity, the per cent of elementary school children in private schools. The last measure, while indirect, was the only one available, since data on religious affiliation are not collected by the Census Bureau.

With the exception of race, reformed cities appear somewhat more homogeneous than unreformed cities. While the differences in homogeneity are more clear-cut than class differences, this hardly indicates that reformed cities are the havens of a socially homogeneous population. Although the average nonpartisan city has 16.9 per cent of its children in private schools, this mean conceals a wide range— from 2 to 47 per cent.

Our findings about the insignificance of class differences between reformed and unreformed cities are at some variance with Alford and Scoble's conclusions. There is, however, some support for the argument that reformed cities are more homogeneous. While we used cities with populations of over 50,000, their sample included all cities over 25,000; and varying samples may produce varying conclusions. The only other study to analyze cities over 50,000 was Wolfinger and Field's and our conclusions are generally consistent with theirs. We differ with them, however, on two important questions.

First, Wolfinger and Field argued that what differences there are between unreformed and reformed cities disappear when controls for region are introduced: "The salient conclusion to be drawn from these data is that one can do a much better job of predicting a city's political form by knowing what part of the country it is in than by knowing anything about the composition of its population."[24] Since regions have had different historical experiences, controls for region are essentially controls for history, and more specifically, historical variation in settlement patterns. The problem with this reasoning, however, is that to "control" for "region" is to control not only for history, but for demography as well: to know what region a city is in *is* to know something about the composition of its population. Geographical subdivisions are relevant subjects of political inquiry only because they are differentiated on the basis of attitudinal or socio-economic variables. The South is not a distinctive political region because two surveyors named Mason and Dixon drew a famous line, but because the "composition of its population" differs from the rest of the country.

It is therefore difficult to unravel the meaning of "controlling" for "region" since regions are differentiated on precisely the kinds of demographic variables which we (and Wolfinger and Field) related to reformism. Cities in the Midwest, for example, have a much higher proportion of home ownership (64%) than cities in the Northeast (44%), while northeastern cities have more foreign stock in their population (27%) than the Midwest (16%). Hence, to relate ethnicity to political reformism and then to "control" for "region" is in part to relate ethnicity to reformism and then to control for ethnicity. Consequently, we have grave reservations that the substitution of the gross and unrefined variable of "region" for more refined demographic data adds much to our knowledge of American cities. "Controlling" for "region" is much more than controlling for historical experiences, because region as a variable is an undifferentiated *potpourri* of socio-economic, additudinal, historical and cultural variations.[25]

We also differ with Wolfinger and Field in their assertion that their analysis constituted a test of the ethos theory. As we understand it, Banfield and Wilson's theory posits that particular attitudes are

---

[24]*Op. cit.,* p. 320.

[25]In statistical parlance, the problem with "region" as an independent variable might be described as treating a complicated background variable as the first variable in a specific developmental sequence. But, as Blalock argues, ". . . *one should avoid complex indicators that are related in unknown ways to a given underlying variable.* Geographical region and certain background variables appear to have such undesirable properties": Hubert M. Blalock, *Causal Inferences in Nonexperimental Research* (Chapel Hill: University of North Carolina Press, 1964), p. 164 (italics in original).

held by persons with varying sociological characteristics (ethnic groups and middle class persons, in particular) and that these attitudes include preferences for one or another kind of political institution. But relating the proportion of middle class persons in a city's population to its form of government says nothing one way or another about middle class preferences. An important part of understanding, of course, is describing and it is certainly useful to know how reformed cities differ from unreformed cities.

In our view, however, such tests as Wolfinger and Field used cannot logically be called explanations, in any causal sense. The most obvious reason is that they violate some important assumptions about time-order: independent variables are measured with contemporary census data, while the dependent variables are results of decisions made ten to fifty years ago. Moreover, this problem is multiplied by the difficulty of inferring configurations of political power from demographic data. Presumably, their assumption is that there is a simple linear relationship between sheer numbers (or proportions) of, say, middle class persons and their political power: the larger the size of a group in the city's population, the easier it can enforce its choice of political forms. At least one prominent urban sociologist, however, has found empirical support for precisely the opposite proportion. Hawley concluded that the smaller the proportion of middle class persons in a city, the greater their power over urban renewal policies.[26] Similarly, it may also be dubious to assume that the size of an ethnic population is an accurate indicator of influence of ethnic groups. Although we recognize the importance of describing the socio-economic correlates of political forms, the logical problems involved suggest the need for a good deal of caution in interpreting these differences as explanations.[27]

In any case, the question of why the city adopts particular structures is of less interest to us than their consequences for public policy. It is to this analysis that we now turn.

IV. POLICY OUTPUTS AND THE RESPONSIVENESS OF CITIES

We are now in a position to take three additional steps. First, we can compare the differences in policy outputs between reformed

[26]Amos Hawley, "Community Power and Urban Renewal Success," *American Journal of Sociology,* 68 (January, 1963), 422-431.
[27]See also the exchange between Banfield and Wilson and Wolfinger and Field in "Communications," this REVIEW, 60 (December, 1966), 998-1000.

and unreformed cities. Second, we can assess the cumulative impact of socio-economic variables on these policy choices. Finally, we can specify what variables are related in what ways to these output variables. In essence, we can now treat political institutions, not as dependent variables, but as factors which influence the *level* of expenditures and taxation and the *relationship* between cleavage variables and these outputs.

Differences between reformed and unreformed cities' outputs. Contrary to Sherbenou's conclusions about Chicago suburbs,[28] our data indicate that reformed cities both spend and tax less than unreformed cities, with the exception of expenditures in partisan and nonpartisan cities. It appears that partisan, mayor-council and ward cities are less willing to commit their resources to public purposes than their reformed counterparts. What is of more importance than the difference in outputs, however, is the relative responsiveness of the two kinds of cities to social cleavages in their population.

TABLE 3.

Mean Values of Tax/Income and
Expenditure/Income Ratios, by
Structural Characteristics

Structural Variables	Taxes /Income	Expenditures /Income
Election type:		
Partisan	.032	.050
Nonpartisan	.030	.053
Government type:		
Mayor-Council	.037	.058
Manager	.024	.045
Commission	.031	.057
Constituency type:		
Ward	.036	.057
At-large	.027	.049

The responsiveness of cities. We have argued that one principal goal of the reform movement was to reduce the impact of partisan, socio-economic cleavages on governmental decision making, to immunize city governments from "artificial" social cleavages—race, religion, ethnicity, and so on. As Banfield and Wilson put their argument, the reformers "assumed that there existed an interest

[28]Sherbenou, *op. cit.,* pp. 133-134.

('the public interest') that pertained to the city 'as a whole' and that should always prevail over competing, partial (and usually private) interests."[29] The structural reforms of manager government, at-large, and nonpartisan elections would so insulate the business of governing from social cleavages that "private regarding" interests would count for little in making up the mind of the body politic. But amid the calls of the reformers for structural reforms to muffle the impact of socio-economic cleavages, a few hardy souls predicted precisely the opposite consequence of reform: instead of eliminating cleavages from political decision-making, the reforms, particularly the elimination of parties, would enhance the conflict. Nathan Matthews, Jr., a turn-of-the-century mayor of Boston, issued just such a warning:

> As a city is a political institution, the people in the end will divide into parties, and it would seem extremely doubtful whether the present system, however illogical its foundation be, does not in fact produce better results, at least in large cities, than if the voters divided into groups, separated by property, social or religious grounds.[30]

Matthews recognized implicitly what political scientists would now call the "interest aggregation" function of political parties.[31] Parties in a democracy manage conflict, structure it, and encapsulate social cleavages under the rubric of two or more broad social cleavages, the parties themselves. "Parties tend to crystallize opinion, they give skeletal articulation to a shapeless and jelly-like mass . . . they cause similar opinions to coagulate . . . "[32] The parties "reduce effectively the number of political opinions to manageable numbers, bring order and focus to the political struggle, simplify issues and frame alternatives, and compromise conflicting interests."[33] Since parties are the agencies of interest aggregation, so the argument goes, their elimination makes for greater, not lesser, impact of social cleavages on political decisions.

Political scientists have recently confirmed Matthews' fears, at least with regard to electoral behavior in partisan and nonpartisan elections.

[29]*Op. cit.,* p. 139.

[30]Quoted in Banfield and Wilson, *op. cit.,* p. 154.

[31]For a discussion of the concept of interest aggregation, see Gabriel Almond, "Introduction: A Functional Approach to Comparative Politics," in Gabriel Almond and James S. Coleman (eds.), *The Politics of Developing Areas* (Princeton: Princeton University Press, 1960), pp. 38-45.

[32]Maurice Duverger, *Political Parties* (New York: Science Editions, 1963), p. 378.

[33]Frank J. Sorauf, *Political Parties in the American System* (Boston: Little, Brown and Co., 1964), pp. 165-166.

DIAGRAM 1

Proportion of variation explained (R^2) in
Taxation policy with twelve socio-economic
variables, by institutional characteristics.[a]

Independent Variables	Structural Variables	Dependent Variable
	Reformed Institution:	
	Government: Commission 62%	
	Government: Council-Manager 42%	
	Election: Nonpartisan 49%	
Twelve Socio-	Constituency: At-Large 49%	
Economic Variables		Tax/Income Ratio
	Unreformed Institution:	
	Government: Mayor-Council 52%	
	Election: Partisan 71%	
	Constituency: Ward/Mixed 59%	

[a] In the total sample, the twelve independent variables explained 52% of the
variation in taxes.

DIAGRAM 2

Proportion of variation explained (R^2) in expenditure
policy with twelve socio-economic variables,
by institutional characteristics.[b]

Independent Variables	Structural Variables	Dependent Variable
	Reformed Institution:	
	Government: Commission 59%	
	Government: Council-Manager 30%	
	Constituency: At-Large 36%	
Twelve Socio-	Elections: Nonpartisan 41%	
Economic Variables		Expenditure/Income Ratio
	Unreformed Institution:	
	Government: Mayor-Council 42%	
	Constituency: Ward/Mixed 49%	
	Elections: Partisan 59%	

[b] In the total sample, the twelve independent variables explained 36% of the
variation in expenditures.

Evidence points to the increased impact of socio-economic cleavages
on voting when a nonpartisan ballot is used than when the election
is formally partisan. Gerald Pomper studied nonpartisan municipal
elections and compared them with partisan elections for the New
Jersey State Assembly in Newark. He concluded that the "goal of

nonpartisanship is fulfilled, as party identification does not determine the outcome. In place of party, ethnic affiliation is emphasized and the result is 'to enhance the effect of basic social cleavages'."[34] If (1) this is typical of other American cities and if (2) electoral cleavages can be translated effectively into demands on the government in the absence of aggregative parties, then we might assume that the reformed institutions would reflect cleavages more, rather than less, closely than unreformed ones.

Essentially, then, there are two contrasting views about the consequences of municipal reform. One, the reformers' ideal, holds that institutional reforms will mitigate the impact of social cleavages on public policy. The other argues that the elimination of political parties and the introduction of other reforms will make social cleavages more, rather than less, important in political decision-making.

The measurement of responsiveness.

We have hypothesized that socio-economic cleavages will have less impact on the policy choices of reformed than unreformed governments. Thus, one could do a better job of predicting a city's taxation and expenditure policy using socio-economic variables in partisan, mayor and ward cities than in nonpartisan, manager and at-large cities. Operationally, we will test this hypothesis by using multiple correlation co-efficients. Squaring these coefficients, called "multiple R's," will give us a summary measure of the total amount of variation in our dependent variables explained by our twelve independent variables.[35] The results of the correlation analysis are summarized in Diagrams 1 and 2.

On the whole, the results of the correlation analysis strikingly support the hypothesis, with the exception of commission cities. Thus, we can say, for example, that our twelve socio-economic variables explain 71 per cent of the variations in taxation policy in partisan cities, and 49 per cent of the variation in nonpartisan cities. In commission cities, however, socio-economic variables predict substantially more variation in both taxes and expenditures

[34]Gerald Pomper, "Ethnic and Group Voting in Nonpartisan Municipal Elections," *Public Opinion Quarterly*, 30 (Spring, 1966), p. 90; see also, J. Leiper Freeman, "Local Party Systems: Theoretical Considerations and a Case Analysis," *American Journal of Sociology*, 64 (1958), 282-289.
[35]It is possible that the difference between any two correlations may be a function of very different standard deviations of the independent variables. A quick look at Table 2, however, suggests that this is not likely to affect the relationships we find.

than in the unreformed mayor-council cities.[36] The anomaly of commission governments is interesting, for they present, as we will see, marked exceptions to virtually every pattern of relationships we found. The substantial explanatory power of these socio-economic variables is not altered, but confirmed, by examining the variables independently. The rest of the correlations show a consistent pattern: reformed cities are less responsive to cleavages in their population than unreformed cities.

If one of the premises of the "political ethos" argument is that reformed institutions give less weight to the "private regarding" and "artificial" cleavages in the population, that premise receives striking support from our analysis. Our data suggest that when a city adopts reformed structures, it comes to be governed less on the basis of conflict and more on the basis of the rationalistic theory of administration. The making of public policy takes less count of the enduring differences between White and Negro, business and labor, Pole and WASP. The logic of the bureaucratic ethic demands an impersonal, apolitical settlement of issues, rather than the settlement of conflict in the arena of political battle.

V. TO SPEND OR NOT TO SPEND

If efforts to expand or contract the scope of government stand at the core of municipal political life,[37] they are nowhere better reflected than in the taxation and expenditure patterns of cities. A generation ago, Charles Beard wrote, "In the purposes of which appropriations are made the policies of the city government are given concrete form—the culture of the city is reflected. Indeed, the history of urban civilization could be written in terms of appropriations, for they show what the citizens think is worth doing and worth paying for."[38] Pressures to expand and contract government regula-

---

[36]Wolfinger and Field, *op. cit.*, p. 312, " . . . omit the commission cities from consideration since this form does not figure in the ethos theory." Historically, however, commission government was the earliest of the structures advocated by the Progressives and is quite clearly a product of the reform era. While history tells us that commission cities can not legitimately be excluded from the fold of reformism, they appear to be its black sheep, characterized by low incomes, low population growth and large proportions of non-whites. In fact, they present a marked contrast to both mayor-council and manager cities.

[37]Agger *et al.*, *op. cit.*, pp. 4-14.

[38]Charles A. Beard, *American Government and Politics* (New York: Macmillan, 1924, 4th edition), p. 727.

tions and services are almost always reflected one way or another in the municipal budget. Labor, ethnic groups, the poor and the liberal community may press for additional services and these must be paid for; the business community may demand municipal efforts to obtain new industry by paring city costs to create a "favorable business climate"; or businessmen may themselves demand municipal services for new or old business. In any case, few political conflicts arise which do not involve some conflict over the budget structure.

Class variables and public policies.

Part of the political rhetoric associated with the demand for a decrease in the scope of the national government is the argument that the initiative for policy-making should rest more with the state and local governments. Opposition to high federal spending levels, as V. O. Key has demonstrated, is found more often among persons with middle class occupations than among blue-collar workers.[39] It is not inconceivable that the middle class argument about state and local responsibility might be more than political rhetoric, and that at the local level, middle class voters are willing to undertake major programs of municipal services, requiring large outlays of public capital. Wilson and Banfield have argued that the "public regarding" upper-middle class voters in metropolitan areas are often found voting for public policies at variance with their "self-interest narrowly conceived," and that "the higher the income of a ward or town, the more taste it has for public expenditures of various kinds."[40] Similarly a longitudinal study of voting patterns in metropolitan Cleveland found that an index of social rank was positively correlated with favorable votes on welfare referenda.[41] If these data reflect middle class willingness to spend on a local level, they might indicate that the "states' rights" argument was more than ideological camouflage: middle class voters stand four-square behind public expenditures at the local level even when they oppose those expenditures from the national government. Therefore, we hypothesized that:

[39]V. O. Key, *Public Opinion and American Democracy* (New York: Alfred A. Knopf, 1961), p. 124.
[40]Wilson and Banfield, *op. cit.,* p. 876. Footnote 5 in the same article conveniently summarized research supporting this proposition.
[41]Eugene S. Uyeki, "Patterns of Voting in a Metropolitan Ares: 1938-1962," *Urban Affairs Quarterly,* 1 (June, 1966), 65-77.

2a. The more middle class the city, measured by income, education and occupation, the higher the municipal taxes and expenditures.

In line with our general concern of testing the impact of political structures on municipal policies, we also hypothesized that:

2b. Unreformed cities reflect this relationship more strongly than reformed cities.

With respect to hypothesis 2a, the data in Table 4 on three middle class indicators are unambiguous and indicate a strong rejection of the hypothesis. However, we measure social class, whether by income, education or occupation, class measures are negatively related to public taxes and expenditures.

It is possible, however, that income does not have a linear, but rather a curvilinear relationship with municipal outputs. Banfield and Wilson argue that "In the city, it is useful to think in terms of three income groups—low, middle, and high. Surprising as it may seem to Marxists, the conflict is generally between an alliance of low-income and high-income groups on one side and the middle-income groups on the other."[42] If the relationship between income and expenditure is curvilinear, then we should expect to find that proportions of both low and high income groups were positively correlated with outputs. Our data, however, lend no support to this notion of a "pro-expenditure" alliance. Rather, the proportion of the population with incomes below $3,000 is positively correlated with expenditures in all city types (although the relationships are small) and the proportion of the population in the above $10,000 bracket is negatively correlated with expenditures. Summing the two measures and correlating the combined measure with outputs produced no correlation greater than .15 and the relationships were as likely to be negative as positive. Tests for non-linearity also suggested that no such coalition exists in the cities in our analysis.

To be sure, aggregate data analysis using whole cities as units of analysis is no substitute for systematic survey data on middle class attitudes, but it is apparent that cities with larger middle class population have lower, not higher expenditures. As we emphasized earlier, the "ethos theory" deals with attitudes and the behavior of individuals, while our data deal with cities and their behavior. The coalition suggested by Banfield and Wilson, however, is not discernible at this level of aggregation in these cities.

[42] Banfield and Wilson, *op. cit.*, p. 35.

TABLE 4
Correlations Between Middle Class Characteristics and Outputs in Reformed and Unreformed Cities

Correlations of	Government Type			Election Type		Constituency Type	
	Mayor-Council	Manager	Com-mission	Partisan	Non-Partisan	Ward	At-large
Taxes with:							
Median income	−.13	−.24	−.19	.03	−.19	−.17	−.22
White collar	−.23	−.12	−.62	−.21	−.33	−.30	−.32
Median education	−.36	−.22	−.08	−.45	−.24	−.48	−.18
Expenditures with:							
Median income	−.19	−.32	−.43	−.04	−.32	−.23	−.34
White collar	−.24	−.23	−.58	−.18	−.39	−.32	−.35
Median education	−.32	−.36	−.26	−.36	−.38	−.44	−.32

TABLE 5
Correlations Between Owner Occupancy and Government Outputs in Reformed and Unreformed Cities

Correlations of Owner Occupancy with:	Government Type			Election Type		Constituency Type	
	Mayor-Council	Manager	Commission	Partisan	Non-Partisan	Ward	At-large
Taxes	−.57	−.31	−.73	−.64	−.45	−.56	−.48
Expenditures	−.51	−.23	−.62	−.62	−.40	−.50	−.40

Hypothesis 2b is not consistently borne out by the data. In fact, the relationships between middle class variables and outputs are, if anything, stronger in the reformed cities than in their unreformed counterparts. One would not want to make too much of the data, but a large body of literature on city politics, which we discuss below, suggests that reformed institutions maximize the power of the middle class.

We originally assumed that the proportion of owner-occupied dwelling units constituted another measure of middle class composition, but it soon became apparent that it was only weakly related to income, occupation and education measures. Nevertheless, it emerged as the strongest single predictor of both expenditure and taxation policy in our cities. We hypothesized that:

3a. Owner-occupancy and outputs are negatively correlated, and

3b. Unreformed cities reflect this relationship more strongly than reformed cities.

Hypothesis 3a is consistently borne out in the data presented in Table 5. These relationships were only slightly attenuated when we controlled for income, education and occupation. No doubt self-interest (perhaps "private regardingness") on the part of the home owner, whose property is intimately related to the tax structure of most local governments, may account for part of this relationship. Moreover, home ownership is correlated (almost by definition) with lower urban population density. High density, bringing together all manner of men into the classic urban mosaic, may be itself correlated with factors which produce demands for higher expenditures—slums, increased needs for fire and police protection, and so on.

In confirmation of hypothesis 3b, the unmistakable pattern is for unreformed cities to reflect these negative relationships more strongly than the manager, nonpartisan and at-large cities, although commission cities show their usual remarkably high correlations.

Homogeneity variables and public policies.

Dawson and Robinson, in their analysis of state welfare expenditures, found strong positive relationships between the ethnicity of a states's population and the level of its welfare expenditures.[43] If

---

[43]Richard E. Dawson and James A. Robinson, "The Politics of Welfare," in Herbert Jacob and Kenneth Vines (eds.), *Politics in the American States* (Boston: Little, Brown and Co., 1965), pp. 398-401.

this is symptomatic of a generalized association of ethnic and religious minorities with higher expenditures, we might find support for the hypothesis that:

4a.   The larger the proportion of religious and ethnic minorities in the population, the higher the city's taxes and expenditures.

And, if our general hypothesis about the impact of political institutions is correct, then:

4b.   Unreformed cities reflect this relationship more strongly than reformed cities.

The correlations between ethnicity, religious heterogeneity and outputs (see Table 6) are, with one exception, positive, as predicted by hypothesis 4a. These associations may reflect the substantial participation by ethnic groups in municipal politics long after the tide of immigration has been reduced to a trickle.[44] The relatively intense politicization of ethnic groups at the local level,[45] the appeals to nationality groups through "ticket balancing" and other means, and the resultant higher turnout of ethnic groups than other lower status groups,[46] may produce an influence on city government far out of proportion to their number.

We found when we related all twelve of our independent variables to outputs in various city types that the associations were much weaker in cities we have labeled reformed. The correlations for ethnicity and religious homogeneity show a generally similar pattern, with commission cities exhibiting their usual erratic behavior. The data, then, show fairly clear support for hypothesis 4b.

The third variable of our homogeneity indicators—per cent of population non-white—had almost no relationship to variation in outputs, regardless of city type. We found the same weak correlations for the poverty income variable, which was, of course, strongly related to the racial variable. An easy explanation suggests that this is a consequence of the political impotence of Negroes and the poor, but one should be cautious in inferring a lack of power from the lack of a statistical association.

We have dealt in this section with factors which are positively and negatively related to spending patterns in American cities. While social class variables are associated negatively with outputs, two

[44]Raymond Wolfinger, "The Development and Persistence of Ethnic Voting," this Review, 59 (December, 1965), 896-908.
[46]Robert E. Lane, Political Life (Glencoe, Ill.: The Free Press, 1959), pp. 236-243.
[46]Ibid.

TABLE 6
Correlations Between Ethnicity and Religious Heterogeneity and Outputs in Reformed and Unreformed Cities

Correlations of:	Government Type			Election Type			Constituency Type	
	Mayor-Council	Manager	Commission	Partisan	Non-Partisan	Ward	At-large
Taxes with:							
Ethnicity	.49	.26	.57	.61	.43	.56	.40
Private School Attendance	.38	.15	.37	.33	.37	.41	.25
Expenditures with:							
Ethnicity	.36	.02	.21	.48	.21	.44	.13
Private School Attendance	.34	−.01	.07	.25	.24	.40	.05

measures of homogeneity, private school attendance and ethnicity are related to higher taxes and spending. Examining the strengths of these correlations in cities with differing forms, we found some support for our general hypothesis about the political consequences of institutions, especially for the homogeneity variables and the home ownership variable. Interestingly, however, this was not the case with class variables.

VI. REFORMISM AS A CONTINUOUS VARIABLE

The central thrust of our argument has been that reformed governments differ from their unreformed counterparts in their responsiveness to socio-economic cleavages in the population. Logically, if the presence of one feature of the "good government" syndrome had the impact of reducing responsiveness, the introduction of additional reformed institutions should have an additive effect and further reduce the impact of cleavages on decision-making. We therefore decided to treat "reformism" as a continuous variable for analytic purposes and hypothesized that:

5. The higher the level of reformism in a city, the lower its responsiveness to socio-economic cleavages in the population.

We utilized a simple four-point index to test this hypothesis, ranging from the "least reformed" to the "most reformed." The sample cities were categorized as follows:

1. Cities with none of the reformed institutions (i.e., the government is mayor-council, elections are partisan and constituencies are wards).
2. Cities with any one of the reformed institutions.
3. Cities with two of the reformed institutions.
4. Cities with three reformed institutions (i.e., the government is either manager or commission, elections are nonpartisan and constituencies are at-large).

We can not overemphasize the crudity of this index as an operationalization of the complex and abstract concept of "reformism." Nonetheless, we think some of the relationships we found are strongly suggestive that reformism may in reality be a continuous variable.

To test this hypothesis, we took four variables which had moderate-to-strong correlations with our dependent variables and computed simple correlations in each reform category. If our hypothesis is correct, the strength of the correlations in Table 7 should decrease

TABLE 7
Correlations Between Selected Independent
Variables and Output Variables by Four
Categories of Reformism

Correlations of:	Reform Scores			
	1 (least reformed)	2	3	4 (most reformed)
Taxes with:				
Ethnicity	.62	.41	.50	.34
Private School Attendance	.40	.32	.28	.25
Owner-Occupancy	−.70	−.39	−.54	−.44
Median Education	−.55	−.27	−.32	−.13
Expenditures with:				
Ethnicity	.51	.27	.41	.05
Private School Attendance	.46	.23	.16	.08
Owner-Occupancy	−.67	−.30	−.54	−.38
Median Education	−.49	−.19	−.38	−.37

regularly with an increase in reform scores. While there are some clear exceptions to the predicted pattern of relationships, there is some fairly consistent support for the hypothesis. Even when the decreases in the strengths of the correlations is irregular, there is a clear difference between cities which we have labeled "most reformed" and "least reformed."

Again, we would not want to attach too much importance to the results of this rough-and-ready index. But, the patterns support our previous argument about the impact of reformism: the more reformed the city, the less responsive it is to socio-economic cleavages in its political decision-making.

VII. A CAUSAL MODEL AND AN INTERPRETATION

A causal model.

The implicit, or at times explicit, causal model in much of the research on municipal reformism has been a simple one: socio-economic cleavages cause the adoption of particular political forms. A more sophisticated model would include political institutions as one of the factors which produce a given output structure in city politics. We hypothesize that a causal model would

DIAGRAM 3
A hypothesized causal model.

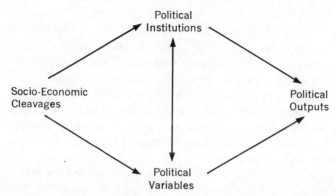

include four classes of variables: socio-economic cleavages, political variables (including party registration, structure of party systems, patterns of aggregation, strength of interest groups, voter turnout, etc.), political institutions (form of government, type of elections and types of constituencies), and political outputs. Diagram 3 depicts one possible causal model.

This study has of necessity been limited to exploring the linkages between socio-economic cleavages, political institutions and political outputs. We found that political institutions "filter" the process of converting inputs into outputs. Some structures, particularly partisan elections, ward constituencies, mayor-council governments and commission governments, operate to maximize the impact of cleavage indicators on public policies. We conclude by discussing some of the reasons why different structures have varying impacts on the conversion process.

An interpretation.

Three principal conclusions may be derived from this analysis.

1. Cities with reformed and unreformed institutions are not markedly different in terms of demographic variables. Indeed, some variables, like income, ran counter to the popular hypothesis that reformed cities are havens of the middle class. Our data lent some support to the notion that reformed cities are more homogeneous in their ethnic and religious populations. Still, it is apparent that reformed cities are by no means free from the impact of these cleavages.

2. The more important difference between the two kinds of cities is in their behavior, rather than their demography. Using multiple correlation coefficients, we were able to predict municipal outputs more exactly in unreformed than in reformed cities. The translation of social conflicts into public policy and the responsiveness of political systems to class, racial, and religious cleavages differ markedly with the kind of political structure. Thus, political institutions seem to play an important role in the political process—a role substantially independent of a city's demography.

3. Our analysis has also demonstrated that reformism may be viewed as a continuous variable and that the political structures of the reform syndrome have an additive effect: the greater the reformism, the lower the responsiveness.

Through these political institutions, the goal of the reformers has been substantially fulfilled, for nonpartisan elections, at-large constituencies and manager governments are associated with a lessened responsiveness of cities to the enduring conflicts of political life. Or, as Stone, Price and Stone argued in their study of changes produced by the adoption of manager governments, the council after the reform "tended to think more of the community as a whole and less of factional interests in making their decisions."[47]

The responsiveness of a political institution to political conflicts should not be confused with the "responsibility" of a political system as the latter term is used in the great debate over the relative "responsibility" of party systems.[48] In fact, the responsiveness of political forms to social cleavages may stand in sharp contrast to "responsible government" on the British model. Presumably, in American cities, partisan elections, ward constituencies, and mayor-council governments maximize minority rather than majority representation, assuring greater access to decision-makers than the reformed, bureaucratized and "de-politicized" administrations.

Partisan electoral systems, when combined with ward representation, increase the access of two kinds of minority groups: those which are residentially segregated, and which may as a consequence

[47]Harold Stone, Don K. Price and Kathryn Stone, *City Manager Government in the United States* (Chicago: Public Administration Service, 1940), p. 238.
[48]The standard argument for party responsibility is found in the works of E. E. Schattschneider, esp., *Party Government* (New York: Farrar and Rinehart, 1942) and in the report of the Committee on Political Parties of the American Political Science Association, *Toward a More Responsible Two-Party System* (New York: Rinehart, 1950).

of the electoral system demand and obtain preferential consideration from their councilmen; and groups which constitute identifiable voting blocs to which parties and politicians may be beholden in the next election. The introduction of at-large, nonpartisan elections has at least five consequences for these groups. First, they remove an important cue-giving agency—the party—from the electoral scene, leaving the voter to make decisions less on the policy commitments (however vague) of the party, and more on irrelevancies such as ethnic identification and name familiarity.[49] Second, by removing the party from the ballot, the reforms eliminate the principal agency of interest aggregation from the political system. Hence, interests are articulated less clearly and are aggregated either by some other agency or not at all. Moreover, nonpartisanship has the effect of reducing the turnout in local elections by working class groups,[50] leaving office holders freer from retaliation by these groups at the polls. Fourth, nonpartisanship may also serve to decrease the salience of "private regarding" demands by increasing the relative political power of "public regarding" agencies like the local press.[51] And when nonpartisanship is combined with election at-large, the impact of residentially segregated groups or groups which obtain their strength from voting as blocs in municipal elections is further reduced.[52] For these reasons, it is clear that political reforms may have a significant impact in minimizing the role which social conflicts play in decision-making. By muting the demands of private-regarding groups, the electoral institutions of reformed governments make public policy less responsive to the demands arising out of social conflicts in the population.

The structure of the government may serve further to modify the strength of minority groups over public policy. It is significant in this respect to note that commission governments, where social cleavages have the greatest impact on policy choices, are the most decentralized of the three governmental types and that manager governments are relatively the most centralized.[53] From the point

[49]See Pomper, *op, cit.*; and Freeman, *op. cit.*

[50]Robert Salisbury and Gordon Black, "Class and Party in Partisan and Nonpartisan Elections: The Case of Des Moines," this Review, 57 (September, 1963), 584-592.

[51]One newspaperman said on nonpartisan politics that "You can't tell the players without a scorecard, and we sell the scorecards": Banfield and Wilson, *op. cit.*, p. 157.

[52]Oliver P. Williams and Charles Adrian, *Four Cities* (Philadelphia: University of Pennsylvania Press, 1963), pp. 56-57.

[53]Alford and Scoble, *op. cit.*, p. 84.

of view of the reformer, commission government is a failure and their number has declined markedly in recent years.[54] This greater decentralization of commission and of mayor-council governments permits a multiplicity of access points for groups wishing to influence decision-makers.[55] It may also increase the possibilities of collaboration between groups and a bureaucratic agency, a relationship which has characterized administrative patterns in the federal government. As a result of this decentralization, group strength in local governments may be maximized.

It is important in any analysis of reformism to distinguish between the factors which produce the *adoption* of reformed institutions and the *impact* of the new political forms once they have been established. We can offer from our data no conclusions about the origins of reformed structures, for it is obviously impossible to impute causation, using contemporary census data, to events which occurred decades ago. Once a city has institutionalized the reformers' ideals, however, a diffused attitude structure may be less helpful in explaining the city's public policy than the characteristics of the institutions themselves. With the introduction of these reforms, a new political pattern may emerge in which disputes are settled outside the political system, or in which they may be settled by the crowd at the civic club at the periphery of the system.[56] If they do enter the political process, an impersonal, "non-political" bureaucracy may take less account of the conflicting interests and pay more attention to the "correct" decision from the point of view of the municipal planner.

These conclusions are generally consistent with the ethos theory developed by Banfield and Wilson. If one of the components of the middle class reformer's ideal was "to seek the good of the community as a whole" and to minimize the impact of social cleavages on political decision-making, then their institutional reforms have served, by and large, to advance that goal.

---

[54]In our view, the failure of the commission government to achieve the intended reforms is more plausible as an explanation of its demise than its administrative unwieldiness—the conventional explanation.

[55]Williams and Adrian, *op. cit.,* pp. 30-31.

[56]Carol E. Thometz discusses the role of the "Civic Committee" in decision-making in Dallas: see *The Decision-Makers* (Dallas: Southern Methodist University Press, 1963).

25

POLICY MAPS OF CITY COUNCILS AND POLICY OUTCOMES: A DEVELOPMENTAL ANALYSIS* †

HEINZ EULAU
ROBERT EYESTONE

THE PROBLEM

In spite of common challenges stemming from the common environment shared by all cities in a metropolitan region, continued and even increasing social and economic differentiation among and within cities rather than homogenization and integration are the most significant features of the contemporary metropolitan scene.[1] Cities within the same metropolitan region are not only maintaining but also developing distinct and unique "public life styles."[2] Urban sociology and urban geography have raised a multitude of questions

*Reprinted from *The American Political Science Review*, LXII, No. 2 (March 1968) 124-143. By permission of *The American Political Science Review* and the authors.

†The larger project of which this analysis is a part, the City Council Research Project, is sponsored by the Institute of Political Studies, Stanford University, and is supported by the National Science Foundation under contract GS 496.

[1]See, for instance, the recent work by Oliver P. Williams et al., *Suburban Differences and Metropolitan Policies: A Philadelphia Story* (Philadelphia: University of Pennsylvania Press, 1965).

[2]Oliver P. Williams in a recent paper has argued that metropolitan regions are collections of small groups of residents and the economic superstructures necessary to sustain them. Each group is characterized by the choice of a distinctive life style, and because members of the various groups wish to live in congenial environments they tend to be found in similar locations throughout the region. Precisely where they are located is a matter of economics and the remnants of past land uses in the region, but the fact of congeniality is a major cause of similarity in location choice. See "A Framework for Metropolitan Political Analysis," prepared for the Conference on Comparative Research in Community Politics, held at Athens, Georgia, November 16-19, 1966.

and given a multitude of answers in seeking to account for the fact that cities facing basically similar challenges from the environment react so differently to these challenges. Most relevant research deals with the problem of differentiation and its effects on the development of cities in terms of historical settlement patterns, economic location and growth, or geographical space distribution.[3]

But differences in municipal life styles may also be the result of differences in public policies deliberately pursued by local governments in the metropolitan area. If this is so, the common pressures from the environment are evidently interpreted differently in the process of public decision-making that seeks to cope with them. It would seem, then, that metropolitan cities are in different stages of policy development. Leaving aside momentarily the meaning of "stages of policy development," we can ask a number of questions that may shed light on the relationship between environmental pressures and public policies designed to meet these pressures. If cities are in different stages of policy development, how can the stages be identified? Is policy development linear and "progressive," or is it reversible? Do the stages of policy development in fact correspond to relevant conditions of the environment? But if there are no differences in environmental challenges, what makes for arrested development in one city, while a similarly challenged city takes off or another is highly developed? On the other hand, if cities are in different stages of development, is it due to their possessing uneven resource capabilities by which environmental problems can be solved? But how can one explain why cities with equal resources adopt quite different public policies? What is the character of the policies designed to meet environmental challenges? Are they attempts to adjust the city to the changing environment, or are they attempts to control the environment, or both?

Questions like these in turn direct our attention to the need for exploring the policy perspectives of urban decision-makers. How do municipal policy-makers perceive their community's environment and problems stemming from environmental conditions? What are their short-term policy positions, and what are their long-range policy images of the future? Are their perceptions of problems, policy orientations and expectations related to the city's stage of

---

[3]See, for instance, F. Stuart Chapin, Jr. and Shirley F. Weiss (eds.), *Urban Growth Dynamics* (New York: John Wiley & Sons, 1962); Wilbur R. Thompson, *A Preface to Urban Economics* (Baltimore: Johns Hopkins University Press, 1965); the relevant literature is legion.

policy development? And if this is the case, what are we to make of the relationship from a theoretical point of view? Although we do not propose to deal with all of these questions, it seems to us that they provide the cutting edge of an empirical theory of urban public policy.

THE PROJECT

This study of the policy maps of city councils in relationship to city policy development is part of a much larger project on municipal legislative bodies conducted in the ninety-odd cities of the San Francisco Bay metropolitan region since 1964.

The data used in this report come from the following sources: (a) city size, density and growth data from the 1960 and 1965 Censuses of Population; (b) city per capita assessed valuation data and expenditure data for planning and amenities from the *Annual Report of Financial Transactions concerning Cities of California,* for the fiscal years 1958-1959 to 1965-1966, published by the State Controller; and (c) data concerning council policy maps from interviews with city councilmen conducted in 1966 and 1967.

The interviews, using both open-ended and closed questions, averaged about three hours in length. In addition, councilmen were asked, at the end of each interview, to fill out a written questionnaire. Interviews were held, as the tabulation below shows, in 89 cities located in eight counties around the San Francisco Bay. Two

	Number of Councils	Number of Councilmen
Interview targets	89	488
Access refused	− 2	− 10
	87	478
Deficient council data	− 4	− 12
	83 (93%)	466
Interview refusals		− 31
		435 (89%)
No budget data available for analysis	− 6	
	77 (87%)	

councils refused to cooperate altogether, and in four others not enough councilmen were interviewed to permit analysis at the council level. Inadequate budget data in the case of six cities incorporated after 1959 further reduced the number of councils available for this analysis to 77. One city, incorporated after interviewing had begun, has been excluded from the study as has been the city-county of San Francisco because its Board of Supervisors is a much more professionalized legislative body than the other councils of the region.

THE MODEL

The model guiding the analysis is a partial one, and we shall not be dealing in the analysis with all of its relevant empirical components.[4] The model predicts city policy development as a response to external and internal features of the urban environment. The external features include, but are not exhausted by, city size, density and growth as the most immediate symptoms of common challenges from the environment, as well as city resources as environmental constraints on policy outcomes. The internal features include, but are not exhausted by, the demands for certain policies made by individuals and groups as well as the policy orientations which local decision-makers themselves bring to or formulate in the course of the policy-making process. The model seeks to order these component variables and relate them to each other in a theoretically meaningful manner.

The model assumes that city size, density and growth as well as resources are antecedent variables; that individual or group demands and decision-makers' policy orientations are intervening variables; and that policy outcomes and resultant stages of policy development are consequent variables. Of course, in empirical reality neither city size, density or growth nor city resources are truly independent precisely because public policies may be designed to control the city's environment or increase its resources. But for the purpose of short-term analysis we can assume these variables to be independent.

[4]More complete studies, using multiple correlation and regression analyses, will appear in forthcoming publications of the City Council Research Project. But see also our earlier report: Robert Eyestone and Heinz Eulau, "City Councils and Policy Outcomes: Development Profiles," in James Q. Wilson (ed.), *City Politics and Public Policy* (New York: John Wiley & Sons, 1968).

Although we shall not deal with individual or group demands in this paper, they are likely to be related to the city's demographic features. For instance, the larger a city's population, the more and more diverse demands are likely to be made on policy-makers (and, moreover, the more and more diverse demands for policies coping with problems stemming from environmental challenges are likely to be made). On the other hand, decision-makers' policy orientations should be independent of environmental variables, though they are likely to be related to the policy preferences of individuals or groups that are not independent of pressures from the environment.

Policy outcomes are assumed to follow each other in a characteristic sequence that constitutes the city's policy development. These outcomes are responses to environmental challenges, such as those occasioned by high population density or a high growth rate. Moreover, they are indicative of policy-makers' willingness to utilize city resources. Changes in city size or density due to growth as well as in resource capability bring about changes in policy outcomes that move the city along from one stage to another in the developmental process. The process of policy development need not be unidirectional; at least temporary reversals are possible.

Environmental challenges may or may not be perceived by policy-makers as "problems" requiring action. Even if problems are not perceived and no action is taken, there is a policy that is reflected in policy outcomes. Policy-makers' sensitivity to environmental challenges is influenced by the demands that are made on them as well as by their own policy preferences and policy images. Therefore, city policy development is not only due to changes in the environment but is mediated by policy-makers' orientations to action. For instance, whether or not resources are mobilized for development depends to a large extent on demands made on government as well as on the policy preferences of policy-makers.

However, policy-makers' perceptions of problems, policy positions and policy images—their "policy maps," so to speak—are themselves not independent of policy development. Because policy development is cumulative in that past policy outcomes constrain current policy proposals—what is feasible and what is not—policy maps are likely to be formulated, consciously or unconsciously, within the restrictive context of the stage of development in which a city is momentarily located. In other words, policy-makers cannot do as they please. The model assumes, therefore, that decision-makers' policy maps reflect as well as shape policy development.

Not all the propositions that can be derived from the model will be tested in this study. We present the model to give direction to the analysis. Particular hypotheses derived from the model will be introduced as we proceed. Our major objective is to demonstrate the utility of the typology of policy development that we construct from city budget data as indicators of policy outcomes and, indirectly, of public policy.

THE CONCEPTS AND MEASURES

1. *Policy and policy outcomes.*

"Policy" is defined as the relationship of a governmental unit to its environment. It finds expression in general programs and specific decisions, or in policy declarations of decision-makers. But because a policy need not be declared to be a policy, analysis cannot rely on manifest statements or overt decisions alone but must concern itself with policy outcomes. By policy outcomes we mean the concrete manifestations of policy—revenues, expenditures, regulations, court decisions, the exertion of police power, and so on. Policy outcomes, then, reflect the orientations of policy-makers, regardless of whether or not a conscious decision has been made. On the other hand, because policy outcomes may at times represent unanticipated results not intended by policy-makers, policy analysis cannot altogether ignore policy declarations. In fact, the relationship between policy intentions and policy outcomes challenges the analyst of public policy.

To develop our concept of policy further, we conceive of public policy as a response of government to challenges or pressures from the physical and social environment. Changes in public policy either adjust or adapt the political system to environmental changes, or they bring about changes in the environment. Which course of action is chosen depends on a multitude of factors—the structure of the political system, its human and physical capabilities, the degree of mass or elite involvement in the political process, the vitality of private associations making public demands; and, last but not least, the perceptions, preferences and orientations of policy-makers.

The problematics of policy-making arise out of the relationship between changes in the environment that require some response, the ways in which these changes are experienced as challenges by decision-makers, and the values that decision-makers may seek in formulating policy. Policy, then, is a response to environmental pressures, both physical and social, as well as anticipation of a future state of affairs. If this is the case, a change in policy is both causal and purposive: it is "caused" by environmental challenges, but it is also directed toward a goal and shaped by a purpose. The tension arising out of the simultaneous impact of causal and purposive "forcings" is a basic dilemma in the scientific study of politics.

Analysis of policy outcomes through time requires a classification of policies.[5] We distinguish between "adaptive" and "control" policies. The measure used as an indicator of an adaptive policy is the percentage of *total* government expenses spent for health, libraries, parks, and recreation.[6] These major accounting categories used to report expenditures presumably include the major amenities offered by cities. A "high amenities" city differs from a city with a traditional services orientation in that it spends less of city income for fire and police services or public works.[7]

The measure used to indicate a city's control policy is the percentage of all *general* government expenses spent by the planning commission. *General* government expenses include essentially all administrative expenses and salaries *not* included under fire, police or recreation categories, and so on.[8]

[5]Much classificatory activity, in the field of public policy analysis as elsewhere, is a game. Either the inventors of classifications and typologies do not make it clear just what analytical purpose the classification is to serve, or they may even imply that by having a classification they have explained something. We make this point to have it understood that we are not interested in justifying or defending the particular typology of policy development that we have constructed, but in examining its utility in the analysis at hand.

[6]Since education and public welfare policies are not made at the city level in California, we cannot use expenditures in these areas as measures of policy outcomes.

[7]The amenities measure is an attempt to tap Williams' and Adrian's concept of amenities. See Oliver P. Williams and Charles R. Adrian, *Four Cities: A Study in Comparative Policy Making* (Philadelphia: University of Pennsylvania Press, 1963), pp. 198-225.

[8]Expenses by the planning commission include both expenses and outlays, therefore encompassing the range of items from paper supplies to salaries of full-time city planners to special outside studies commissioned by the city planning commission. California State law requires every city to have a planning commission, but this body may be, and frequently is, a standing committee of citizens appointed by the city council and incurring no expenses charged against the city. Therefore, the actual dollar amount spent by the planning commission would seem to be a good indicator of the extent of a city's commitment to the idea of planning as a way to control the environment. General government expenses are used as the percentage base rather than total government expenses in order to make planning definitionally independent of amenity expenditures.

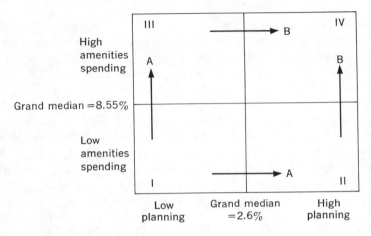

Fig. 1. Categories of policy outcomes over eight-year period.

2.   *Policy development and its measurement.*

Policy outcomes are responses to changes and challenges in the environment. Policy development refers to a set of policy outcomes that follow each other sequentially through time. If the annual outcomes are similar, we speak of the resulting profile as a *stage* of policy development. Three stages will be identified: *retarded, transitional,* and *advanced.*[9] The median of medians for all cities with respect to planning and amenities expenditures over a period of eight years serves as the criterion of similar or dissimilar outcomes.

The definition of a set of sequential and similar outcomes as a stage presupposes continuity and stability. But the conception of development implies that one stage may, sooner or later, be followed by a new stage. It is unlikely that one stage will suddenly yield to another. Not only may development revert; even if development is "progressive," the transformation from one stage to the next may involve a series of dissimilar outcomes—some outcomes characteristic of an earlier stage, others characteristic of a later stage. If this

[9]It is important to keep in mind that while we are using categories reminiscent of such concepts as "traditional," "transitional" and "modern" used in the literature of comparative politics, our observations cover only a small segment of that part of the historical developmental process usually called "modern." It is all the more significant that, even within this small part, we can locate cities in clearly different stages of policy development. This suggests that a concept like "modern" disguises a great deal of the variance that more microscopic analysis can reveal. The point is that our stages "correspond" only analytically to similarly conceived stages used in the long-term analysis of national development.

occurs, an eight-year profile cannot easily be assigned to one stage or another. Put differently, we cannot easily predict whether the system will remain in the earlier stage or move into a later stage.

To cope with this possibility, we define a set of sequential but dissimilar policy outcomes as a *phase* of development. The notion of phase suggests that the sequence is less clearly bounded and, perhaps, of shorter duration than a stage. As we are constructing three stages of development, we must provide for two phases—an *emergent* phase that indicates movement from the retarded to the transitional stage, and a *maturing* phase that is located between the transitional and advanced stages.

Figure 1 illustrates how annual policy outcomes are assigned to a stage or phase of policy development. If planning and amenities expenditures fall below the grand medians in every year of the eight-year sequence, the profile is classified as *retarded* (cell I); if one or the other type of expenditures falls above the grand medians, the profile is designated as transitional (cells II and III); and if both planning and amenities expenditures are above the medians in all eight years, the profile is being assigned to the *advanced* stage of development (cell IV). If during the eight-year sequence expenditures move across the median lines, the profiles represent phases of development: outcomes moving from cell I to cells II or III (arrows A) are classified as *emergent;* those moving from cells I, II or III into cell IV (arrows B) are designated as *maturing.*

Cases of "reversals" for which the model does not provide are being assigned to stages or phases of development in such a way that "reversal errors" are reduced as much as possible. This involves informed but hopefully not arbitrary assignment decisions.[10] We are satisfied that the reversals are not sufficient to invalidate the typology of policy development. As Table 1 shows, for the 82 cities whose policy profiles can be identified over an eight-year period, there were 572 opportunities for change in annual outcomes.[11] Of these opportunities eighty, or fourteen per cent, represented reversals from one year to the next. In the other 86 per cent of opportunities, there either was no change, that is, all outcomes remained in the same

[10]For a more detailed discussion of how the development typology was constructed and cities assigned to a stage or phase of policy development, see Eyestone and Eulau in Wilson, *op. cit.*

[11]This calculation is made as follows: over eight years, each city's annual outcomes could change seven times. This would make for 82 × 7, or 574 opportunities for all cities. However, as we missed data for the first fiscal year in two cities, we must deduct two opportunities, giving us the 572 figure.

TABLE 1.
Developmental Typology of City Policy Profiles
with Opportunities for Change and Reversals

Development Type	Cities N =	Opportunities N =	Number of Reversals				Reversals	
			(1)	(2)	(3)	(4)	N =	% =
Retarded	11	76	7	2			11	14
Emergent	14	98	5	5	1		18	18
Transitional	26	182	9	6		1	25	14
Maturing	15	104	5	6	1		20	19
Advanced	16	112	4	1			6	5
	82	572	30	20	2	1	80	14

stage over all eight years; or change occurred in the hypothesized ("progressive") direction. Reversals in stable stage cities are due, of course, to the assignment of some "impure" cases where reversals seem to be only temporary deviations from the regular pattern.

A validity test. In order to test the validity of the typological constructs and the underlying assumptions, we can divide the eight-year period into two four-year periods and assign each period's profile to either a stage or phase of policy development. Cross-tabulation permits us to inspect the internal movement of the policy profiles from one period to the next. If our assumptions and assignments are reasonably valid, we should be able to predict, from knowledge of a profile's location on the development scale in the first four-year period, where it will be located in the second four-year period. We predict that cities in a stage of development are less likely to move than cities in a phase of development. We also predict that when there is movement, it is more likely to be in the hypothesized "progressive" direction than in a reversed direction. Table 2 presents the results.

It is readily evident that, with some exceptions, both predictions are supported by the data. Of the 50 cities in stages of development during the 1958-1961 period, thirty or 60 per cent remained in the same stage during the following 1962-1965 period; but of the 32 cities in a phase of development during the earlier period, only nine or 28 per cent remained there in the later period. If we consider the direction of movements, it appears that of the 20 cities in stages during the earlier period that did move, sixteen or 80 per cent advanced in the expected direction. But this result is, of course, largely a function of the boundaries set to the typology: retarded cities can only move forward and advanced cities can only move backward. More significant, therefore, is the fact that none of the advanced cities reverted, suggesting that once this plateau is reached, institutionalization of policies makes reversal unlikely; and the further fact that of the ten transitional cities that did move, six moved forward and four backward. Similarly, of the 14 emergent cities that moved, ten or 71 per cent moved forward as expected and only four returned to the retarded stage in the later period; but of the nine moving maturing cities, a bare majority of five reverted to the transitional stage. Of course, these results, whether "favorable" or not from the developmental standpoint, may be influenced by the original data. Some policy outcomes as measured are in some cases very close to the median of medians cutting point that serves as the criterion for assignment, so that we may be dealing here with errors over which we have no control. Nevertheless, we believe that the weight of the evidence is sufficient to warrant our interpretation of Table 2. It is also noteworthy that few of the movements, either forward or backward, exceed one step at a time. Of the 26 cities moving forward and having an opportunity to do so by *more* than one step (i.e., those retarded, emergent and transitional in the first period), twenty-one or 81 per cent moved one step only; and of the nine cities moving backward and having an opportunity for more moves (i.e., those transitional and maturing in the first period), all but one reverted only one step.

Reversed development is an empirical fact of life. While stages of development as conceived by historians are inevitably consecutive and irreversible, policy development is in fact reversible. Although we assume that in general stages and phases follow each other in "progressive" order, an assumption that the results of Table 2 certainly do not falsify, no rigid assumptions need or should be made about the direction of change. Policy is the creation of men and can be changed by men, within certain contraints imposed by environmental necessities, in whatever direction they prefer. Otherwise the concept of policy would make little sense.

3. *Resource capability.*

A city's resource capabilities can be measured in a variety of ways. Ideally, we would like to think of resource capability as the maximum amount of income a city can expect annually when serious efforts are made to tap all possible income sources, including current revenues from taxes, borrowed funds, grants in aid, or income

TABLE 2

Policy Development of Cities in Developmental
Sequence from 1958-61 to 1962-65

State of Development in 1958-61	State of Development in 1962-65				
	Retarded $N = 11$	Emergent $N = 14$	Transitional $N = 26$	Maturing $N = 15$	Advanced $N = 16$
Retarded $N = 16$	6	9			1
Emergent $N = 16$	4	2	7	3	
Transitional $N = 24$	1	3	14	5	1
Maturing $N = 16$			5	7	4
Advanced $N = 10$					10

from utilities, and so on. However, we have no way to determine whether such efforts have been made. Moreover, were we to use the readily available city income figures as a measure of resource capability, the measure would contravene our assumption that some cities are more pressed for revenue than others. Nor can we use a measure equivalent to per capita gross national product that is used in the comparative study of nations.[12] For a high proportion of the production of any city crosses city boundaries and is not available to support local government expenditures. Needed is a measure of the wealth remaining wholly within city limits and available to local taxation or such state taxation as is refundable to the city.

The measure we are using is, therefore, total assessed valuation per capita subject to local taxation for fiscal 1965-1966, as determined by the California State Board of Equalization. In using this measure we assume that wealth in the form of private, commercial and industrial property will be a potential source of revenue, and that per capita assessed valuation is a rough indicator of a city's resource capability.[13] A city will hesitate to institute new programs or expand old ones if it has a low level of assessed valuation per capita, but may be more inclined to do so if it has a high level of valuation.

[12]For a discussion of system capabilities, see Gabriel A. Almond, "A Developmental Approach to Political Systems," *World Politics,* 17 (January, 1965), 195-203.
[13]Assessed valuation includes private houses and property, commercial property and industrial property. From private property a city derives personal property revenues and a portion of state income tax revenues; from commercial property it receives property and sales tax revenues; and from industrial property it gets property tax revenues.

4. *Policy maps.*

Policy, we must remember, is a theoretical concept imposed on observed reality. Regardless of whether specific decisions have been deliberately made or not, what we observe are policy outcomes from which city policy is inferred. If, as we shall suggest, policy outcomes as summarized in the typology of policy development are positively related to indicators of what we may consider environmental challenges, the presumption that the policy was intended to meet the pressures of the environment is strong, but it is only a presumption. And because it is only a presumption, the investigation of policy-makers' "policy maps" becomes an important component of policy analysis.

What do we mean by "policy map"? In the first place, we assume that if policy is a response to environmental challenges, these challenges will have been perceived by policy-makers. They may choose, consciously or unconsciously, not to act, but such non-action is also a response that will be reflected in policy outcomes. By being perceived the environmental challenges become "problems" or "policy issues." In order to tap this facet of the policy map, we asked this question:

> Mr. Councilman, before talking about your work as a councilman and the work of the council itself, we would like to ask you about some of the problems facing this community. In your opinion, what are the two most pressing problems here in (city)?

The policy map consists, secondly, of the policy-maker's recommendations for action or "policy positions"—those preferences that he either brings into the policy-making situation or evolves in the course of decision-making. Again, his not consciously entertaining a policy position on an issue is yet to be considered a policy orientation and a component of his policy map. We therefore asked this question:[14]

> Now, looking toward the future, what one community-wide improvement, in your opinion, does this city "need most" to be attractive to its citizens?

Finally, we assume that the policy map includes the policy-maker's "ends-in-view" or values—those hopes and expectations concerning

---

[14]This is not the only question we asked in this connection. For instance, we also asked a great many closed "agree-disagree" questions some of which we used in the earlier analysis, in Wilson, *op. cit.*

the future which policy decisions are to bring about. The following question was designed to yield what one may think of as the "policy image":

> Now, taking the broadest view possible, how do you see (city) in the future? I mean, what kind of a city would you personally like (city) to be in the next twenty-five years?

Whether these three components of the policy map constitute a consistent whole, a "perspective" as Harold Lasswell would call it,[15] is an empirical question not central to the present study, but one we shall speculate about in the conclusion. Needless to say, perhaps, knowledge of the policy map does not permit prediction about the outcome of decision-making on any particular policy issue. But we proceed on the assumption that policy maps represent important linkages between environmental challenges and public policies.

5.   *Units of analysis and interpretation.*

Although the data on policy maps come from interviews with individuals, our analysis uses councils as the units of analysis. Decision-making by legislative bodies is a collective act. Not the individual councilman but the council, as a whole or under the majority rule, is the effective policy-maker. Past research on legislatures, following in the wake of voting studies, has analyzed the behavior of individuals *in* the legislature in order to make statements about the behavior *of* legislatures. This procedure presents serious problems of inference. Because policy outcomes as measured by budget data are due to collective decisions (or non-decisions), the legislative group rather than the individual legislator is the more viable unit of analysis. Council perceptions, positions or images are therefore constructed or reconstructed from data about individuals or provided by individuals, permitting us to make statements about city councils and not about city councilmen. We shall report the rules followed in this procedure in the text or footnotes.[16] This type of analysis is of course made possible by the relatively large (though for satisfactory statistical purposes still all too small) number of

---

[15]See Harold D. Lasswell and Abraham Kaplan, *Power and Society: A Framework for Political Inquiry* (New Haven: Yale University Press, 1950), p. 25.

[16]This is not the place to discuss the methodological problems and procedures involved in "stepping up" the data from the level of the individual (micro-analysis) to the level of the group (macro-analysis). Suffice it to say that our empirical results justify the viability of the procedures, although we would be the first to admit that many technical problems remain to be solved.

legislative groups being investigated. As far as we know, no similar type of analysis using as many as eighty or so units has ever been undertaken in the comparative study of legislative bodies.

In reading and interpreting the tables, a number of methodological considerations must be kept in mind. In the first place, we are dealing with data that come from truly independent sources—the federal Census reporting population characteristics, city budgets reporting financial allocations, and interviews with city councilmen. These different kinds of data are used to construct quite different properties of the units—city councils—that we are observing. The Census yields data that are best interpreted as representing the council's "contextual" properties; the budget data are representative, in a very direct sense, of the council's "emergent" properties; and the interview data provide the basis for "aggregate" properties.[17] To relate properties as diverse as these is extraordinarily difficult. But for this reason one cannot simply write off even modest relationships between variables as not significant.

Second, the typology of policy development that serves as our major device for ordering the data is not a simple continuum. While the five types constitute an ordinal ranking on a scale from "more developed" to "less developed," they also represent qualitative differences associated with different levels of development. In other words, a city's movement from one stage into another may be due to structural changes in causal factors rather than simple gradual increases. This means that variables related to city policy development may well exhibit sharp changes at certain points in the developmental sequence rather than incremental changes from one stage to another. For instance, a council's orientation to action may change radically after it has left the retarded stage and entered the emergent phase and then not change at all. Also, variables need not change monotonically across the five developmental types. Development may be related, for instance, to city growth in the early stages or phases but may decline in the advanced cities. Or cities at the three intermediate levels of policy development may show char-

---

[17]Paul F. Lazarsfeld has written in many places about the variety of "group properties" that need to be distinguished in analysis lest errors of inference be made. See, for instance, Paul F. Lazarsfeld, "Evidence and Inference in Social Research," in Daniel Lerner (ed.), *Evidence and Inference* (New York: The Free Press, 1959), pp. 117-125; or Paul F. Lazarsfeld and Herbert Menzel, "On the Relation between Individual and Collective Properties," in Amitai Etzioni, *Complex Organizations* (New York: Holt, Rinehart and Winston, 1961), pp. 422-440. We are not dealing with the global, structural or relational properties of councils in this analysis.

TABLE 3.
Relationships between City Size, Density and
Growth and Policy Development*

		Policy Development				
		Retarded $N=11$	Emergent $N=14$	Transitional $N=26$	Maturing $N=15$	Advanced $N=16$
Population Size						
	< 10,000	82%	79%	35%	13%	0%
	10-50,000	18	21	46	67	44
	> 50,000	0	0	19	20	56
		100%	100%	100%	100%	100%
Density						
	< 2,000	73%	58%	19%	41%	0%
	2-4,000	18	28	50	26	44
	> 4,000	9	14	31	33	56
		100%	100%	100%	100%	100%
Growth Rate						
	< 10%	54%	36%	43%	13%	19%
	10-50%	46	49	39	47	62
	> 50%	0	14	19	40	19
		100%	100%	100%	100%	100%

*Size and density data for 1965; growth rate for 1960-65.

acteristics not shared by the least and mos˙ developed cities. Or cities in the two phases of development may be more similar to each other than to cities in the immediate neighboring stages.

Finally, we are less impressed by "significant differences" in a statistical sense that we might find than by patterns in the distribution of the data that make theoretical sense. The small number of cases also makes difficult the controlling of one variable by another that is so necessary if spurious relationships and false interpretations are to be avoided. We have used the control technique in relating resource capability to policy development, but we have not done so with the interview data, largely because the frequencies of cases in particular cells of the tables would be greatly strained by the procedure. This makes it all the more necessary to view each table not as an isolated entity unrelated to any other table. Rather, it is the weight of all the tables inspected simultaneously that must be considered in making inferences or drawing conclusions.

THE ANALYSIS

1. *Environmental challenges and policy development.*

City size, density and growth rate are direct indicators of challenges from the environment that every city faces. They bring in their wake problems that the city council may seek to solve through policies that adapt the city to the environment or that control environmental pressures. As the typology of city policy development is built on outcomes that reflect such policies, it follows:

> *Hypothesis 1a:* The larger a city's size, the more developed is city policy likely to be.
> *Hypothesis 1b:* The greater a city's density, the more developed is city policy likely to be.
> *Hypothesis 1c:* The greater a city's growth, the more developed is city policy likely to be.

Table 3 shows that the three hypotheses are not falsified by the data. Moreover, the data show a pattern of policy development that, with two exceptions, is highly linear. We have no explanation for the deviation from the pattern of the transitional cities in the low density category. With regard to growth we note, as we perhaps might have expected, a levelling-off of the effect of growth in the advanced stage, the terminus of development. Apparently, once policy development has reached the advanced stage, growth is likely to be marginal in its effect on city policy.

The data suggest that city councils adopt policies which are congruent with needs rooted in pressures from the environment. Whatever the declared policy objectives of city fathers, they tend to follow policies that either adapt the city to or seek to control the environment.

2. *Resource capability and policy development.*

The resources available to a city government are an important constraint on the expenditures it can make and the policies it can follow. Resource capability is largely an objectively limiting factor, but it is also subjective in that its limiting effect is interpreted by the city council before it becomes a factor in the policy-making process. For instance, the council estimates how high a tax rate city residents are willing to approve. High resource capability is necessary for policy development, but it is not sufficient. Nevertheless, we hypothesize:

> *Hypothesis 2:* The higher a city's resource capability, the more developed is city policy likely to be.

Table 4, Part A, shows that there is no support for the hypothesis. In fact, more of the retarded cities seem to have high resource capability than any of the other cities in various stages or phases of development. However, the distributions may be misleading. As we suggested, policy development is dependent on policy-makers' willingness to mobilize resources, and their willingness to do so may depend on the intensity of pressures from the environment *regardless* of available resources. Therefore, one must control the relationship between resource capability and policy development by such indicators of environmental challenges as size, density or growth rate. Table 4, B, reports the findings.

In the smaller cities, presumably less subject to environmental challenges, fewer of the more developed than of the less developed cities are low in resource capability, just as hypothesized; but development also declines in cities of the same size with high capability, counter to the hypothesis. In the larger cities, on the other hand, resource capability is highly related to policy development in the advanced stage.

Controls for density reveal the same pattern even more distinctly. In the low density, high capability cities policy development declines, counter to the hypothesis; but in the densely populated cities high resource capability is related to policy development across the continuum in linear order.

Finally, if resource capability is controlled by growth rate, the developmental process clearly follows the hypothesized pattern only in the high growth cities with high assessed valuation (and again in linear fashion except for levelling off in the advanced stage). The data do not permit us to say anything about the slow-growing, low capability cities; but in the slow-growth, high capability and the high growth, low capability cities Hypothesis 2 is clearly falsified.

Policy-makers evidently respond to environmental pressures less in terms of the resources that are available than in terms of their willingness to mobilize these resources. It is for this reason that inquiry into policy-makers' perceptions of city problems, policy positions and policy images becomes an important part of policy analysis.

3. *Problem perceptions and policy development.*

Environmental challenges are not self-evident. They become evident only if and when they give rise to "problems" that come to the attention of policy-makers. The perception of a problem means

TABLE 4.
Relationship between City Resource
Capability and Policy Development

Assessed Valuation Per Capita	Policy Development				
	Retarded $N = 11$	Emergent $N = 14$	Transitional $N = 26$	Maturing $N = 15$	Advanced $N = 16$
Part A					
>$2,600	54%	28%	38%	33%	44%
$1,700-2,600	18	44	24	47	25
<1,700	27	28	38	20	31
	100%	100%	100%	100%	100%
Part B					
Size <25,000					
<$1,700	27%	28%	24%	13%	6%
>$1,700	73	72	39	54	6
Size >25,000					
<$1,700	—	—	15	7	25
>$1,700	—	—	23	27	62
	100%	100%	100%	100%	100%
Density <2,000					
<$1,700	9%	14%	0%	7%	0%
>$1,700	63	44	19	33	0
>2,000					
<$1,700	19	14	38	13	32
>$1,700	9	28	43	47	68
	100%	100%	100%	100%	100%
Growth <10%					
<$1,700	9%	0%	19%	0%	6%
>$1,700	46	36	23	13	13
>10%					
<$1,700	18	28	19	20	25
>$1,700	27	36	39	67	56
	100%	100%	100%	100%	100%

that traditional ways of doing things—policies—are inadequate or at the very least that their adequacy is in question. It is through the perception of problems, then, that the policy process is set in mo-

TABLE 5.
Relationship between Problem Diversity
and Policy Development

Diversity Score Quartile	Policy Development				
	Retarded $N = 9$	Emergent $N = 12$	Transitional $N = 25$	Maturing $N = 15$	Advanced $N = 16$
I. (Most)	45%	33%	20%	27%	6%
II.	22	17	28	20	44
III.	22	33	28	13	31
IV. (Least)	11	17	24	40	19
	100%	100%	100%	100%	100%
Index	+34	+16	−4	−13	−13

tion. But, if policy-makers do not respond to problems generated by environmental challenges, either by not perceiving them or not acting upon them, this does not mean that there is no policy. It simply means that prevailing policy continues.

In collegial bodies like legislatures or councils a problem is a problem if the members *between them* are aware of the problem, but it is not necessary for all or even most of the members to perceive it. Different members have access to different aspects of the environment. Because of varied membership elected collegial bodies can be more sensitive to the environment than administrative hierarchical organizations. "Problem diversity" therefore refers to the absolute number of different problems articulated by a council,

TABLE 6.
Relationship between Problem Visibility
and Policy Development

Visibility Score Quartile	Policy Development				
	Retarded $N = 9$	Emergent $N = 12$	Transitional $N = 25$	Maturing $N = 15$	Advanced $N = 16$
I. (High)	22%	17%	28%	40%	12%
II.	11	33	24	13	45
III.	0	25	36	20	31
IV. (Low)	67	25	12	27	12
	100%	100%	100%	100%	100%
Index	−45	−8	+16	+13	0

adjusted for comparison across councils by the total number of mentions in each council.[18] Because as we have seen, the more developed cities face more severe environmental challenges, we formulate:

Hypothesis 3: The more diverse the problems perceived by a council, the more developed is city policy likely to be.

Table 5 shows that this hypothesis is falsified by the data. In fact, problem diversity is greatest among the councils of the retarded cities where one might least expect it and declines almost linearly in the following stages and phases, though there is some levelling off at the more developed end of the development continuum.

How can one interpret this finding? One plausible answer is that policy develops in response to few but intensively felt problems, while a multitude of minor problems that are not critical do not stimulate the policy process. If this is so, we should expect that problems are more "visible" to the council as a whole in the more developed than in the less developed cities. A measure of "problem visibility" must take account not only of the absolute number of problems that are articulated, but also of the number of councilmen who articulate any one problem.[19] We postulate:

Hypothesis 4: The more visible problems are to the council, the more developed is city policy likely to be.

Table 6 tends to support the hypothesis, although there is some dropping-off at the advanced stage. One might expect this because, as the very concept "advanced" suggests, a council in this stage of policy development is likely to have the challenges stemming from the environment well in hand. As a result, not only are fewer problems perceived in this stage, but the few problems are so self-evident that, though of great urgency, they fail to stand out as particularly visible.

Problem visibility may be thought of as setting the council's legislative agenda. The more visible a problem, the more likely it is to be considered by the council. But the visibility is at most a

[18]That is, the absolute number of individual problems named was divided by all problem responses made in a council. The resulting scores, that could range from zero to one, were rank-ordered and divided into the quartile ranges used in the analysis.

[19]That is, the number of problems named was multiplied by the number of respondents and divided by all responses squared. The resulting score was subtracted from one to rank-order the councils from high to low. The formula then is: $1 - NP \times NR/r^2$, where NP = number of problems, NR = number of respondents, and r = number of total responses.

TABLE 7.

Relationship between Agreement on Specific
Problem and General Problem Area and
Policy Development

Single Problem Agreement	Policy Development				
	Retarded N = 9	Emergent N = 12	Transitional N = 25	Maturing N = 15	Advanced N = 16
67-100%	22%	50%	36%	47%	46%
51-66%	45	25	32	20	43
50-50%	33	25	32	33	13
	100%	100%	100%	100%	100%
Index	−11	+25	+4	+14	+33
Problem Area Agreement					
67-100%	33%	17%	32%	13%	37%
51-66%	0	8	16	54	13
0-50%	67	75	52	33	50
	100%	100%	100%	100%	100%
Index	−34	−58	−20	−20	−13

necessary and not a sufficient condition for legislative action. In order to act, the council must in fact be agreed that the problem is a problem. We therefore measure the degree of council agreement on the single most visible problem as well as council agreement on the general policy area that seems most problematic.[20] We propose:

Hypothesis 5: The more agreement on the single most visible problem, the more developed is city policy likely to be.

Hypothesis 6: The more agreement on the most visible problem area, the more developed is city policy likely to be.

Table 7 tends to support these hypotheses, but we note an interesting deviation from the expected patterns in the cities of the emer-

[20]The measure of agreement on a single problem is simply the proportion of councilmen among all respondents who mentioned the most frequent problem. For the measure of problem area agreement, the number of responses in the area receiving the most responses was divided by the number of responses in all areas. Five "problem areas" were provided for classification of individual problems: Services and Utilities, Amenities, Promotion and Development, Social and Remedial Problems, and Governmental and Intergovernmental Problems.

TABLE 8.
Problems and Problem Areas Perceived As Pressing by City Councils

Types of Problems Perceived	Policy Development						Total N = 77
	Retarded N = 9	Emergent N = 12	Transitional N = 25	Maturing N = 15	Advanced N = 16		
Services & Utilities							
Sewerage & drainage	1	1	5	2	—		9
Sanitation & disposal	—	1	—	—	—		1
Water sources	1	—	1	—	1		3
Financing services	—	1	2	4	3		10
Total in Area	2	3	8	6	4		23
Per Cent in Area	22%	25%	32%	40%	25%		30%
Amenities							
Total in Area	—	—	—	—	—		—
Promotion & Development							
Planning, master plan	—	1	—	—	3		4
Zoning & maintenance	2	1	4	—	—		7
Transportation & traffic	—	1	5	2	3		11
Attract business & industry	—	1	2	—	—		3
Urban renewal & development	—	1	—	—	3		4
Assessment and taxes	—	—	—	2	—		2
Total in Area	2	5	11	4	9		31
Per cent in Area	22%	42%	44%	27%	57%		40%

TABLE 8. (continued)

Types of Problems Perceived	Policy Development					
	Retarded N=9	Emergent N=12	Transitional N=25	Maturing N=15	Advanced N=16	Total N=77
Social & Remedial						
Water pollution	—	—	—	—	1	1
Race & ethnic problems	—	—	—	—	1	1
Educational problems	—	—	—	1	—	1
Housing	1	—	—	—	—	1
Total in Area	1	—	—	1	2	4
Per cent in Area	11%	0%	0%	7%	12%	5%
Governmental & Intergovernmental						
Annexation	1	—	—	—	—	1
Local government personnel	—	1	—	—	—	1
Citizen participation	—	—	—	—	1	1
Total in Area	1	1	—	—	1	3
Per cent in Area	11%	8%	0%	0%	6%	4%
Not Classifiable	3	3	6	4	0	16
	34%	25%	24%	26%	0%	21%
Grand total	100%	100%	100%	100%	100%	100%

gent phase. While on the single problem measure more councils in the emergent phase reveal high agreement, these councils are least agreed on the general area of problems facing their cities. We can only speculate on these results. It may be that being in the emergent phase is, on the one hand, a disorienting condition that makes it difficult to achieve agreement on the general area of problems that require action; but that, precisely because of this condition, high agreement can be reached on the single most urgent problem. However, we also note that all councils, regardless of level of policy development, can evidently reach agreement more readily on a specific problem than on a general area of related problems.

What kinds of problems or problem areas are most salient to city councils? And is such salience related to policy development? Although we do not propose to introduce a formal hypothesis, we are altogether unprepared for the results obtained. Taking all those councils where at least three councilmen had named the same problem, we obtain the findings reported in Table 8.

As Table 8 shows, no three councilmen in any council, whatever the city's stage or phase of development, articulated problems relating to amenities; and only a few councils on various levels of development mustered enough members who considered planning or zoning as especially pressing problems. We shall leave it to another occasion to interpret the full implications of the results reported in Table 8. Suffice it to say here that problems involving provisions for amenities clearly do not rank high on the agenda of problems considered pressing. Put differently, amenities appear to be luxuries that councils are willing to indulge in only after other urban prob-

TABLE 9.
Reasons Given for Problems and
Policy Development

Type of Reasons	Policy Development [*]				
	Retarded $N=9$	Emergent $N=12$	Transitional $N=25$	Maturing $N=15$	Advanced $N=16$
Operational-financial	22%	8%	36%	20%	25%
Inevitable-uncontrollable	78	92	84	73	62
Political	11	17	12	27	38

*Percentages total more than 100 since any one council could give sets of reasons that are numerically tied.

lems, notably sewerage and drainage, financing of services and transportation, have been solved. But planning and zoning also do not stand out as pressing problems. Either these matters are being satisfactorily handled already, so that they are perceived as problems by only a few councils, or they are not recognized as viable means for coping with environmental challenges.[21]

When asked why they considered a problem to be a problem, a variety of reasons were given by councilmen that could be coded into three categories—operational and financial, political, and inevitable or uncontrollable. Councils were characterized in terms of the dominant set of reasons that were given.[22] We do not entertain any particular hypothesis about how councils on various levels of development are likely to rationalize their city's problems. But we note two results in Table 9. First, great majorities of councils in all cities, regardless of level of policy development, attribute community problems to circumstances beyond their control. This is to say that a substantial number of problems, as we have speculated all along, have their roots in environmental conditions. But we also note that "political" reasons are given by more councils as we move from the retarded to the advanced stage of development. The linearity of the data suggests that politicization of the decision-making milieu in these cities may well be related to policy development. The more politicized the social environment, the more likely it seems to be that policy development takes place.

4. *Policy positions and policy development.*

Once problems have been identified and agreed upon as agenda items, the legislature or council will seek to evolve a policy position.

[21]Our measure of salience, as mentioned in the text, was whether a problem or problem area was mentioned by at least three respondents. We shall not try to interpret the proportions obtained for the services and utilities as well as promotion and development areas across the developmental continuum because the results may be an artifact of council size. As five councils in the transitional stage, three in the maturing phase and seven in the advanced stage had more than five members (usually seven), and as no retarded or emergent council had more than five members, clearly any one problem had more of a chance to be named by at least three respondents in the more developed cities. But as, for instance, nine of the advanced councils had only five members, yet all advanced councils are accounted for in naming at least one problem, the council size factor does not seem to have too much of a distorting effect. But we note it as interesting that the more developed a city's policy, the more councils tend to mention problems related to utilities and services and to promotion and development.

[22]The dominant set of reasons was simply defined as that set which included the most responses among all sets, regardless of absolute number.

TABLE 10.
Relationship between Improvement Diversity
and Policy Development

Improvement Score Quartile	Policy Development				
	Retarded $N=9$	Emergent $N=12$	Transitional $N=25$	Maturing $N=15$	Advanced $N=16$
I. (Most)	33%	50%	20%	13%	31%
II.	33	17	36	33	0
III.	11	8	16	27	57
IV. (Least)	22	25	28	27	12
	100%	100%	100%	100%	100%
Index	+11	+25	−8	−14	+19

A policy position by the council, whether held by all members or only a majority, is of course an emergent property of the council following upon interaction, deliberation and possibly compromise, and it is not simply the addition of individual members' policy preferences. What we are tapping, then, when we ask individual councilmen to suggest the "most needed" community-wide improvement and then aggregate these recommendations, is not the council's policy as it emerges in the voting situation, but rather the initial state of a council position before the legislative process has had an opportunity to affect the decisional outcome.[23] But as actual council

TABLE 11.
Relationship between Improvement Visibility
and Policy Development

Improvement Score Quartile	Policy Development				
	Retarded $N=9$	Emergent $N=12$	Transitional $N=25$	Maturing $N=15$	Advanced $N=16$
I. (High)	11%	25%	28%	7%	31%
II.	22	17	16	46	31
III.	33	25	24	40	13
IV. (Low)	33	33	32	7	25
	100%	100%	100%	100%	100%
Index	−22	−8	−4	0	+6

[23]We could argue our case more liberally on statistical ground and possibly test it if we had more and numerically more diverse legislative bodies available for analysis: the larger a legislative body, the more likely it is that averaged individual preferences will approximate, if not correspond to, the preference of the collectivity.

policy is reflected in the policy outcomes out of which the typology of policy development is constructed, inquiry into the hypothetical initial state of the policy process can shed light on the dynamics of policy-making. We shall first explore the diversity and visibility of improvement recommendations made by councils in varying stages and phases of policy development. Again we stipulate:

Hypothesis 7: The more diverse improvements recommended in a council, the more developed is city policy likely to be.

And again, as with problem perceptions, we find the diversity hypothesis falsified by the data.[24] As Table 10 shows, highly diverse improvement proposals are just as likely to be made in the less developed councils. However, though problem and improvement proposal diversity is low in the more developed cities, and perhaps be-

TABLE 12.
Relationship between Agreement on Specific
Improvement and General Improvement Area
and Policy Development

Single Improvement Agreement	Policy Development				
	Retarded $N=9$	Emergent $N=11*$	Transitional $N=25$	Maturing $N=15$	Advanced $N=16$
67-100%	11%	0%	12%	7%	6%
51- 66%	0	36	20	33	19
0- 50%	89	64	68	60	75
	100%	100%	100%	100%	100%
Index	−78	−64	−56	−53	−69
Improvement Area Agreement					
67-100%	22%	45%	40%	60%	37%
51- 66%	45	45	28	33	44
0- 50%	33	10	32	7	19
	100%	100%	100%	100%	100%
Index	−11	+35	+8	+53	+18

*One council in this type could not be properly measured and had to be dropped from the tabulation.

[24]The improvement diversity measure was constructed in the same way as the problem diversity measure. See fn. 18, above.

cause of it, we expect that the improvement recommendations that are made are highly visible in these cities. Hence:

Hypothesis 8: The more visible the improvements recommended in a council, the more developed is city policy likely to be.

Table 11 supports the hypothesis.[25] Recommendations for improvements are more visible in the developed than the less developed cities, and only in maturing and advanced cities do a majority of councils fall into the two upper visibility quartiles.

We expect on the basis of this finding that councils in the more developed cities are more agreed on what specific improvements or what general improvement areas are needed than councils in the less developed cities:

Hypothesis 9: The more agreement there is in a council on the single most needed improvement, the more developed is city policy likely to be.

Hypothesis 10: The more agreement there is in a council on a general improvement area, the more developed is city policy likely to be.

Table 12 presents the data.[26] They represent some interesting findings. In the first place, with respect to agreement on the single most visible improvement proposal made, there is a very low level of agreement regardless of a city's location on the policy development continuum. Only few councils are highly agreed, and only a few more manage to achieve better than simple majority agreement. In all types of city policy development, majorities of the councils fall below the majority criterion needed for agreement. Interestingly, and though the percentage differences are small, fewer councils in both types of "phase" cities are in the non-agreement category than councils in the "stage" cities. But, in general, we must consider Hypothesis 9 as being falsified by the data.

If we turn to the less demanding Hypothesis 10—less demanding because agreement is needed only on a general area rather than on a specific case of improvement—the data give only weak support to the hypothesis. Although few of the retarded councils are high on improvement area agreement and the more developed councils tend in the expected direction, the significant aspect of the table is that only one council in each of the two types of "phase" cities is unable to achieve a minimal level of agreement. The tendency already noted

[25]The improvement visibility measure was constructed in the same manner as the problem visibility measure. See fn. 19, above.

[26]The improvement agreement measures are the same as those used in connection with problem agreement. See fn. 20, above.

TABLE 13.

Relationship between Needed Improvement Areas
and Policy Development

Improvement Area	Policy Development				
	Retarded $N=9$	Emergent $N=11$	Transitional $N=25$	Maturing $N=15$	Advanced $N=16$
Services and utilities	0%	0%	0%	7%	0%
Promotion and development	0	8	4	14	25
Amenities	11	25	28	26	25
Less than 3 informants	89	67	68	53	50
	100%	100%	100%	100%	100%

in connection with single improvement agreement is exaggerated under the less demanding condition of general improvement area agreement.

What are we to make of these unexpected findings? Are they merely due to random fluctuations in the data, or are they of theoretical significance? We must seek an explanation in the nature of the emergent and maturing phases of policy development as these were defined. Cities in these phases undergo sudden bursts of activity, reflected in policy outcomes, that move them from one stage into another. It would seem that this unfolding of policy-making "energy" is greatly aided by *pre-decisional* agreement or at least by relatively little disagreement in councils as to what improvements or areas of improvement are most needed. This finding and our interpretation suggest that we are tapping a very real component of the policy process by aggregating individual responses into a group response.[27]

What types of improvement were recommended by the councils that are agreed? Because of the dispersion of single improvement recommendations, we shall present only the data on improvement areas.[28] What is of interest in the data presented in Table 13 is, first of all, that the improvement areas are quite different from the comparable problem areas of Table 8. Only one council in a maturing city suggested services and utilities as an area needing im-

[27]We would like to point out here that we had very similar results in the earlier study in which we used a *closed* agree-disagree scale measuring attitudes concerning the scope of government activity and in which we used *individual* councilmen as our units of analysis: see Eyestone and Eulau, in Wilson, (ed.), *op. cit.*

[28]An improvement area was assumed to be salient in council preferences if at least three respondents articulated problems in the area.

provements. But while no council had perceived amenities as a *problem,* a fourth of the councils in each of the developmental types, except the retarded, reported that amenities constitute an area where improvements are needed.

This discontinuity in council policy maps from problem perceptions to policy positions requires explanation. Does it mean that councils do not behave rationally? One might be inclined to think so, but discontinuity is not necessarily the same thing as inconsistency. Because amenities are not recognized as "problems," it does not follow that councils may not wish to pursue policies to obtain amenities for their cities. For policies, we argued, are not simple conditioned responses to environmental challenges; they are also the products of those ends-in-view, values or images of the future that policy-makers carry with them into the policy-making situation. While the policy positions articulated in response to the question about needed improvements may not be relevant to the problems that councils perceived and articulated, they are certainly not inconsistent with them. The results suggest that policy images are important components of the council's policy map as a whole.

5. *Policy images and policy development.*

What kind of future a legislative body envisages is likely to color its perceptions of environmental challenges and its current policy preferences. But images of the future are also likely to be projections of current trends in a city's policy development. They tend to orient the council toward the future and may influence future development, but they are not independent of present tendencies. Moreover, the more limited the legislature's jurisdiction, the better-defined its image is likely to be. In the case of municipal councils whose tasks are well set by statutory requirements and limitations we can expect that long-range goals are well-defined.

Because we know that policy development varies with demographic indicators of environmental challenges such as size, density and growth, and because we also can assume that these indicators are highly related to ecological factors such as residential patterns or level of industrialization, we hypothesize:

Hypothesis 11a: The more developed a city's policy, the more will councils tend to envisage the city's future as "balanced" or industrial.

Hypothesis 11b: The less developed a city's policy, the more will councils tend to envisage the city's future as residential and/or recreational.

TABLE 14.
Relationship between Policy Image
and Policy Development

Content of Image	Policy Development				
	Retarded N=9	Emergent N=12	Transitional N=25	Maturing N=15	Advanced N=16
Residential-recreational	56%	50%	52%	27%	13%
Split or non-classifiable	22	8	12	7	19
Balanced and/or industrial	22	42	36	66	68
	100%	100%	100%	100%	100%

The ease with which it was possible to classify responses into the categories of "residential" or "recreational," on the one hand, and of "balanced" or "industrial," on the other hand, supports our speculation that long-range images or goals are likely to be well-defined in legislative bodies with limited scopes of action.[29] As Table 14 shows, the reciprocal Hypotheses 11a and 11b are well supported by the data.

Because policy images are well-defined, we hypothesize that there is a great deal of agreement within the councils on policy goals. But as, by definition, the less developed cities are engaged in a more limited range of activities than the more developed ones, we can expect the difference to be reflected in the level of agreement:

Hypothesis 12: The less developed a city's policy, the greater the proportion of councils reaching high agreement on the image of city future.

Table 15 supports the hypothesis. It not only supports it but reveals an extraordinarily high level of agreement, especially in the retarded and emergent cities where two-thirds and more of the councils are unanimously agreed on the policy image. But in the transitional maturing and advanced cities, too, most councils agree on long-range goals by overwhelming majorities. We are dealing here, it seems, with that substantive consensus on values that facilitates the democratic process of bargaining, compromise and adjustment. It is within this consensus that disagreements over particular policies can be resolved and lasting community conflicts be reduced to man-

[29]Because an "industrial" future was envisaged in only a handful of councils, we combined this category with the "balanced" category which implies that the council envisages a balance in residential, commercial and industrial development.

TABLE 15.

Relationship between Agreement on Policy Image
and Policy Development

Policy Image Agreement	Policy Development				
	Retarded $N=9$	Emergent $N=12$	Transitional $N=25$	Maturing $N=15$	Advanced $N=16$
100%	78%	67%	52%	53%	50%
67-99%	0	25	32	27	31
51-66%	0	0	4	13	0
Split or non-classifiable	22	8	12	7	19
	100%	100%	100%	100%	100%

ageable format. However, the fact that agreement on future goals is inversely related to policy development represents a profound dilemma for democratic theory.

CONCLUSION

A metropolitan city's development toward distinct and differentiated styles of social life is powerfully shaped by policies that are responses to challenges from the metropolitan environment. Whether a city stands still, moves forward to reach a new level of development or reverts to an earlier state depends on the strength of such challenges as can be measured by city size, density or growth rate. In general, development involves the adoption of policies that either adapt the city to the changing environment or control the environment. In this process of adjustment and control through appropriate policies the city's resource capabilities seem to play only a limited part. It appears that policy-makers' willingness to tap city resources in order to adopt appropriate policies is a critical component of the policy development process.

Policy-makers' willingness to set their city on a course of development depends on the content of their policy maps—how they perceive the problems facing the city, what preferences they entertain with regard to policy alternatives, and how they envisage the city's future. In general, it seems that municipal decision-makers' policy maps constitute a consistent whole, although there may be discontinuities and deviations. It also appears, in general, that the various components of the policy map are meaningfully related to the stage or phase of city policy development. There is in the councils of a metropolitan region such as that around the San Francisco Bay a satisfactory level of agreement on what the problems are that cities in different stages of development face, and there is very high agreement on what the city's future should be like. There is less agreement, as one might expect, on the specific policies that should be adopted to obtain the goals that are envisaged, but there is sufficient agreement on the general area of issues that needs attention.

It has been the burden of our argument that the systematic study of public policy cannot be content with correlating indicators of environmental challenges or indicators of resource capability to policy outcomes. Rather, it was our assumption that policy development is greatly influenced by the predilections, preferences, orientations and expectations of policy-makers—in short, by the political process itself. The data presented in the analysis, though limited, confirm the validity of this assumption. Yet, as we noted, the fact that level of agreement on policy goals seems to be inversely related to policy development raises many problems for the policy-maker. Not the least important is the question of how a developed community can maintain a sufficient consensus on public goals. In the city councils of the San Francisco Bay metropolitan region a high level of agreement on policy goals still exists. Whether it will continue to exist in the face of increasing differentiation of areas within the city challenges the urban political process.